# International Documents on Corporate Responsibility

*To those individuals and organisations who have and will contribute to the topic of corporate responsibility under international law:*

*If you have an apple and I have an apple and we exchange these apples then you and I will still each have one apple. But if you have an idea and I have an idea and we exchange these ideas, then each of us will have two ideas.*

*George Bernard Shaw*

Published by
Edward Elgar Publishing Limited
Glensanda House
Montpellier Parade
Cheltenham
Glos GL50 1UA
UK

Edward Elgar Publishing, Inc.
136 West Street
Suite 202
Northampton
Massachusetts 01060
USA

A catalogue record for this book
is available from the British Library

**Library of Congress Cataloguing in Publication Data**

International documents on corporate responsibility / edited by Stephen Tully.
p. cm.
Includes bibliographical references and index.
1. Corporate governance—Law and legislation. 2. International law. 3. Social responsibility of business. I. Tully, Stephen.

K1327.I58 2005
346′.0664—dc22 2005047805

ISBN 1 84376 819 4 (cased)

Typeset by Cambrian Typesetters, Camberley, Surrey
Printed and bound in Great Britain by MPG Books Ltd, Bodmin, Cornwall

# International Documents on Corporate Responsibility

*Edited by*

Stephen Tully

*Law Department, London School of Economics and Political Science, UK*



**Edward Elgar**
Cheltenham, UK • Northampton, MA, USA

# Contents

# Abbreviations

| | |
|---|---|
| AAPMN | Australian–Asian Pacific Mining Network |
| ACC | American Chemistry Council |
| ACF | Australian Conservation Foundation |
| AGM | annual general meeting |
| AI | Amnesty International |
| AIA | advance informed agreement |
| AIP | Apparel Industry Partnership |
| AMD | acid mine drainage |
| AML | Anti-Money Laundering |
| APEC | Asian Pacific Economic Cooperation |
| APELL | Awareness and Preparedness for Emergencies at the Local Level |
| ASEAN | Association of South East Asian Nations |
| ATCA | Alien Tort Claims Act |
| *ATS* | *Australian Treaty Series* |
| BASD | Business Action for Sustainable Development |
| BAT | best available techniques |
| BCSE | Business Council for Sustainable Energy |
| BEP | best environmental practice |
| BHF | Business Humanitarian Forum |
| BIAC | Business and Industry Advisory Committee (OECD) |
| BIFU | Banking Insurance and Finance Union |
| BINGO | business and industry non-governmental organisation |
| BISNIS | Business Information Service for the Newly Independent States |
| BRT | Business Roundtable |
| BSN | Boussois-Souchon-Neuvesel (now part of the Danone Group) |
| BSR | Business for Social Responsibility |
| CAA | Community Aid Abroad |
| CAT | Committee against Torture |
| CBD | Convention on Biological Diversity |
| CBSR | Canadian Business for Social Responsibility |
| CCC | Clean Clothes Campaign |
| CCW | Certain Conventional Weapons |
| CEDAW | Convention on the Elimination of All Forms of Discrimination Against Women |
| CEFIC | European Chemical Industry Council |
| CEO | chief executive officer |
| CEPPA | Council on Economic Priorities Accreditation Agency |
| CER | corporate environmental reporting |
| CERD | Committee on the Elimination of Racial Discrimination |
| CFCs | chlorofluorocarbons |
| CIME | Committee on International Investment and Multinational Enterprises (OECD) |

| | |
|---|---|
| CIP | Corporate Involvement Program |
| CJM | Christian Jail Ministry |
| CLNI | Convention on Limitation of Liability in Inland Navigation |
| CMA | Chemical Manufacturers Association |
| CMT | cut-make-and-trim |
| CMW | Committee on the Protection of the Rights of All Migrant Workers and Members of their Families |
| COFI | Committee on Fisheries (FAO) |
| *Consol TS* | *Consolidated Treaty Series* |
| COP | Conference of the Parties |
| CORE | Corporate Responsibility Coalition |
| CRC | Committee on the Rights of the Child |
| CROC | Convention on the Rights of the Child |
| CRT | Caux Round Table |
| CSD | Commission on Sustainable Development (UN) |
| CSR | corporate social responsibility |
| CTR | Claims Tribunal Reports (Iran–US) |
| DNA | deoxyribonucleic acid |
| Doc | Document Reference |
| DTCI | Division on Transnational Corporations and Investment (UNCTAD) |
| EC | European Community |
| ECOSOC | Economic and Social Council (UN) |
| EEC | European Economic Community |
| EEZ | exclusive economic zone |
| EHS | environment, health and safety |
| EIA | environmental impact assessment |
| EITI | Extractive Industries Transparency Initiative |
| EMAS | Eco-Management and Audit Scheme |
| EMP | European Monitoring Platform |
| EMS | environmental management system |
| ERT | European Roundtable of Industrialists |
| ESCR | economic, social and cultural rights |
| ESD | ecologically sustainable development |
| ETI | Ethical Trading Initiative |
| *ETS* | *European Treaty Series* |
| EU | European Union |
| FAO | Food and Agriculture Organisation |
| FCTC | Framework Convention on Tobacco Control |
| FIDIC | International Federation of Consulting Engineers |
| FoEI | Friends of the Earth International |
| FSC | Forest Stewardship Council |
| GAP | good agricultural practice |
| GATT | General Agreement on Tariffs and Trade |
| GB | governing body |
| GC | governing council |
| GE | Global Exchange |
| GhG | greenhouse gas |
| GMI | Global Mining Initiative |

| | |
|---|---|
| GPA | Global Programme of Action |
| GPAT | Global Programme against Trafficking in Human Beings (UN) |
| GRI | Global Reporting Initiative |
| HC | House of Commons (UK) |
| HCFCs | Hydrochlorofluorocarbons |
| HFC | Hydrofluorocarbons |
| HIV/AIDS | human immunodeficiency virus/acquired immune deficiency syndrome |
| HNS | hazardous and noxious substances |
| HRW | Human Rights Watch |
| IAEA | International Atomic Energy Agency |
| IATA | International Air Transport Association |
| IBFAN | Infant Baby Food Action Network |
| IBLF | International Business Leaders Forum |
| IBRD | International Bank for Reconstruction and Development |
| ICAO | International Civil Aviation Organization |
| ICC | International Chamber of Commerce |
| ICCA | International Council of Chemical Associations |
| ICCPR | International Covenant on Civil and Political Rights |
| ICEF | International Federation of Chemical, Energy and General Workers' Unions |
| ICESCR | International Covenant on Economic, Social and Cultural Rights |
| ICFTU | International Confederation of Free Trade Unions |
| ICIFI | International Council of Infant Formula Industries |
| ICJ | International Court of Justice |
| ICME | International Council on Mining and the Environment |
| ICMM | International Council on Mining and Metals |
| ICRC | International Committee of the Red Cross |
| ICSID | International Centre for the Settlement of Investment Disputes |
| ICTR | International Criminal Tribunal for Rwanda |
| ICTY | International Criminal Tribunal for the former Yugoslavia |
| IDP | internally displaced person |
| IFCS | Intergovernmental Forum on Chemical Safety |
| IFPMA | International Federation of Pharmaceutical Manufacturers' Association |
| IGU | International Gas Union |
| IHL | International Humanitarian Law |
| ILC | International Law Commission |
| *ILM* | *International Legal Materials* |
| ILO | International Labour Organisation |
| *ILR* | *International Law Reports* |
| ILRF | International Labour Rights Fund |
| IMF | International Monetary Fund |
| IMM | integrated materials management |
| IMO | International Maritime Organisation |
| IMT | International Military Tribunal |
| INN | international non-proprietary names |
| IOE | International Organisation of Employers |
| IPCC | Intergovernmental Panel on Climate Change |
| IPCS | International Programme on Chemical Safety |
| IPIECA | International Petroleum Industry Environmental Conservation Association |

| | |
|---|---|
| IPM | integrated pest management |
| IPP | independent power producer |
| IPPC | integrated pollution prevention and control |
| IRPTC | International Register of Potentially Toxic Chemicals |
| ISBA | International Seabed Authority |
| ISO | International Organisation for Standardisation |
| ITS | International Trade Secretariat |
| IUF | International Union of Food, Agricultural, Hotel, Restaurant, Catering, Tobacco and Allied Workers' Associations |
| Keidanren | Japan Federation of Economic Organisations |
| LLMC | Limitation of Liability for Maritime Claims |
| LMO | living modified organism |
| *LNTS* | *League of Nations Treaty Series* |
| MaLAM | Medical Lobby for Appropriate Marketing |
| MARPOL | International Convention for the Prevention of Marine Pollution from Ships |
| MCA | Minerals Council of Australia |
| MIE | Multinational Industrial Enterprise |
| MMSD | Mining Minerals and Sustainable Development |
| MNC | multinational corporation |
| MNE | multinational enterprise |
| MOP | Meeting of the Parties |
| MRL | maximum residue limit |
| MSC | Marine Stewardship Council |
| NACE | National Association of Corrosion Engineers |
| NAFTA | North American Free Trade Agreement |
| NGO | non-governmental organisation |
| NHO | Confederation of Norwegian Business and Industry |
| NIEO | New International Economic Order |
| OAS | Organisation of American States |
| *OASTS* | *Organisation of American States Treaty Series* |
| OAU | Organisation of African Unity |
| *OB* | *Official Bulletin* |
| OCA | Oceans and Coastal Areas (UNEP) |
| ODA | Official Development Assistance |
| OECD | Organisation for Economic Cooperation and Development |
| OFII | Organisation for International Investment |
| OFR | operating and financial review |
| OHCHR | Office of the High Commissioner for Human Rights |
| OHS | occupational health services/occupational health and safety |
| *OJEC* | *Official Journal of the European Community* |
| OPRC | Oil Pollution Preparedness, Response and Co-operation |
| PCBs | polychlorinated biphenyls |
| PIC | prior informed consent |
| PMC | private military company |
| POPs | persistent organic pollutants |
| PVI | private voluntary initiative |
| PWBLF | Prince of Wales Business Leaders Forum |
| R&D | research and development |

| | |
|---|---|
| SAI | Social Accountability International |
| SD | sustainable development |
| SDRs | special drawing rights |
| SIA | social impact assessment |
| SME | small and medium-sized enterprise |
| SVN | Social Venture Network |
| TNC | transnational corporation |
| TOT | transfer of technology |
| TRIPS | Agreement on Trade-Related Aspects of Intellectual Property Rights |
| UDHR | Universal Declaration on Human Rights |
| UK | United Kingdom |
| *UKTS* | *UK Treaty Series* |
| UN | United Nations |
| UNCED | UN Conference on Environment and Development |
| UNCLOS | UN Convention on the Law of the Sea |
| UNCTAD | UN Conference on Trade and Development |
| UNCTC | UN Centre on Transnational Corporations |
| UNDP | UN Development Programme |
| UNDPI | UN Department of Public Information |
| UNDTCI | UN Division on Transnational Corporations and Investment (UNCTAD) |
| UNECE | UN Economic Commission for Europe |
| UNEP | UN Environment Programme |
| UNESCO | UN Educational, Scientific and Cultural Organisation |
| UNFCCC | UN Framework Convention on Climate Change |
| UNGA | UN General Assembly |
| UNGASS | UN General Assembly Special Session |
| UNHCHR | UN High Commissioner for Human Rights |
| UNHCR | UN High Commissioner for Refugees |
| UNHRC | UN Human Rights Committee |
| UNICEF | UN International Children's Fund |
| UNIDO | UN International Development Organisation |
| UNODC | UN Office on Drugs and Crime |
| UNRISD | UN Research Institute for Social Development |
| UNTCMD | UN Transnational Corporations and Management Division |
| *UNTS* | *UN Treaty Series* |
| US BRT | US Business Roundtable |
| USA | United States of America |
| USCIB | US Council for International Business |
| USSR | Union of Soviet Socialist Republics |
| UV-B | ultra-violet solar radiation having biological effects |
| WBCSD | World Business Council for Sustainable Development |
| WEF | World Economic Forum |
| WFSGI | World Federation of the Sporting Goods Industry |
| WHA | World Health Assembly (WHO) |
| WHO | World Health Organisation |
| WRI | World Resources Institute |
| WSSD | World Summit on Sustainable Development |
| WTO | World Trade Organisation |

# Preface

Multiple indictments have been listed against international law, classically understood to only describe interactions between states. This legal system risks obsolescence as the 'guardian of a museum which only a few will enter while the mainstream of life flows past outside its windows' (Lachs, 1986: 110). The proposal to substitute it with a novel 'transnational law' (Jessup, 1956: 106) linguistically preserves the global community as a state-centric domain and is another form of 'self-protecting myopia' which keeps other entities at the periphery (Alston, 1997). An all-embracing perspective would apply to and govern relationships between those entities operating both within and beyond the artificial construct of national boundaries. Constitutional considerations, for example, could be appended to an ever-expanding 'cosmopolitan law' (Held, 2003). Neo-positivists counter that international law is sufficiently resilient and adaptable to new developments (Simma and Paulus, 1999: 307). Contemporary international relations is noteworthy for the inclusion of intergovernmental organisations, non-governmental organisations (NGOs), trade unions, individuals and – the concern of this volume – corporations (Hofmann and Geissler, 1999).

Corporations participate on the basis of their functional capacity rather than antiquated sovereign attributes. Although they make many positive contributions to economic development, full employment and technology transfer, they may also be associated with several negative effects including undermining labour rights, environmental pollution, interfering within local political affairs, extenuating wealth inequalities and anti-competitive behaviour. Corporations are accordingly independently powerful actors if not authoritative decision makers (Higgins, 1994: 4, 50). Their demands upon the disaggregated or fragmented state at least have an 'explanatory relevance' (Slaughter et al., 1998: 383) for global outcomes which can grow to become a legally influential role (Reisman, 1997).

As a working formula, transnational corporations can be defined as decision-making centres located within one state and conducting commercial operations within one or more others (Annuaire de L'Institut de Droit International, 1978: 339). The corporate form is a legal fiction as a result of which several general principles are ordinarily assumed. First, juridical persons enjoy their own separate existence distinct from that of their members or organisers. Second, the corporate capacity for acquiring rights and obligations and questions of operation, merger and dissolution are governed by the law of the place of its organisation. As affirmed, for example, by Article 1(1) of the European Convention on the Establishment of Companies (1966 *ETS* No 57), incorporation is largely limited to national law. A 'de-nationalised' corporation is not merely a theoretical possibility: consider, for example, EC Regulation No 2137/85 (1985) on European Economic Interest Groupings and EC Regulation No 2157/2001 on the Statute for a European Company (*OJEC* (2000) L291/1). None the less, national commercial law, environmental regulation and labour law among others remain highly influential (and are typically determinative) in circumscribing permissible commercial conduct. Corporations are relatively 'invisible' under international law (Johns, 1994: 922). Third, the existence of a body corporate and the effectiveness of its legal acts are dependent on recognition through the operation of law. Indeed, corporations may enjoy legal personality even when that of their place of incorporation is questionable

(Section 1, Foreign Corporations Act 1991 (UK)). Finally, in executing the purposes for which juridical persons are organised, the national law of the place where commercial acts are performed typically applies.

The proposition that national law enjoys pre-eminent authority as indicia for appropriate corporate behaviour is affirmed by international law. United Nations (UN) General Assembly Resolution 3281 of 1974, otherwise known as the Charter of Economic Rights and Duties of States, recognises that each government enjoys the right 'to regulate and supervise the activities of transnational corporations within its national jurisdiction and take measures to ensure that such activities comply with its laws, rules and regulations and conform with its economic and social policies'. This statement does not imply that international law has no role to play in regulating commercial activity (see, for example, Kamminga and Zia-Zarifi, 2000; Abrahams, 2004). Indeed, the Charter of Economic Rights and Duties of States itself acknowledges that governments should cooperate in exercising their right to regulate at national levels. For example, although governments enjoy the right to exploit their own natural resources pursuant to their own environmental policies, they are also expected to further develop international law with respect to liability and compensation for activities under their jurisdiction or control.

International cooperation is also identified under the Charter of the UN as the means by which governments solve 'international problems of an economic, social, cultural, or humanitarian character, and in promoting and encouraging respect for human rights' (Article 1(3)). Cross-border business activity creates a series of very particular legal problems (Angelo, 1968) such that it cannot be comprehensively regulated by national law. Unilateral attempts by governments to do so give rise to competing jurisdictional claims between the place of establishment, incorporation or seat of management (the 'home' state) and the location of commercial operations (the 'host' state). The extraterritorial extension of national law in any given instance may prove controversial. As a consequence, 'the global reach of transnational corporations is not matched by a coherent global system of accountability' (UN Secretary-General, 1996: para 72).

Several additional trends raise the question of corporate responsibility. These include an increasingly integrated global economy; the perception that corporations enjoy rights through trade liberalisation and investment protection agreements outweighing other interests; the prominence of corporations as social actors; the rapid growth in communications technology; the transfer of hitherto public responsibilities (such as providing essential services, security forces, jail administration and immigration controls) to the private sector through privatisation; frequent expressions of public concern for the detrimental impacts of commercial behaviour, including greater consumer awareness as a result of NGO activism; shareholder demands for more effective corporate governance techniques including decision-making transparency; greater pressures to address the interests of so-called 'stakeholder' groups; increasingly detailed (and occasionally intrusive) intergovernmental regulation at the regional and international levels; and finally, continuing reliance upon voluntary compliance measures as a complement to strict 'command and control' regulatory approaches.

Notwithstanding that their juridical personality derives from national law, existing treatises on the subject (Wagner, 1986; Seidl-Hohenveldern, 1987) accept that within transnational space, corporations are independently influential actors in their own right. Globalisation, however defined, has positioned corporations at the very heart of national economic development (UN Secretary-General, 1992: paras 4, 15–17). Their incorporeal nature or commercial purposes do not preclude them from concluding contracts or enjoying standing before international courts or tribunals on an equal footing with governments (Ijalaye, 1978: Ch. 5). Legal dogma retorts that corporate personality under international law is limited and derivative, that is, only enjoyed to the extent provided by governments (*Texaco v Libya* (1977) 53 *ILR* 389: para 47). Hence, any norms generated within investment agreements between corporations and governments are not opposable against other actors (see *Award in the Matter of an Arbitration Between Kuwait and the American Independent Oil Company* (*AMINOIL*) (1982) 21 *ILM* 976: para 157).

These propositions fail to consider the extent to which commercial relations with international standard-setting institutions have evolved (Dell, 1990). During the 1970s, these relationships were characterised by mutual mistrust and ineffective communication (Boarman and Schollhammer, 1975). The 'triangular diplomacy' model reasoned that corporations competed with governments for control over limited resources (Stopford and Strange, 1991: 19–23). That corporations no longer occupy the political periphery is clear, inasmuch as contemporary interaction contemplates the notion of partnership (Tesner and Kell, 2000). Cooperation with the private sector through continuous dialogue is one means of averting the possibility that corporations will simply shift their activities to areas beyond public supervision (in other words, regulatory avoidance). Such a rationale justifies corporate input into public policy formation wherever available (see, for example, UNECE: the Aarhus Convention, 1998) and channelling regulatory responsibilities upwards to institutions at the intergovernmental level (Zito, 1998). Corporations currently enjoy consultative status within international organisations and are regularly invited to participate in or observe intergovernmental conferences whose products appear within this volume.

The upshot is to acknowledge commercial contributions to the formation, implementation and enforcement of international law. It could be argued that fluid and erratic economic activity is too malleable for containment within a static legal order (Vagts, 1970: 743–4). However, continuing to exclude corporations could equally weaken the international legal structure (Charney, 1983: 749). Without resolving this question, it is sufficient for present purposes to recognise that non-state actors contribute to the social construction of legal norms (Mertus, 2000: 544–5).

The natural corollary of expansive rights and privileges of participation are obligations and duties (in short, responsibility) for the faithful implementation of negotiated outcomes. For example, when outlining her 'vision of ethical business' in 1998, Mary Robinson, the-then UN High Commissioner for Human Rights, noted that every corporation 'has a legitimate right to be concerned and the responsibility to promote human rights'. It is axiomatic that rights and privileges must be exercised responsibly. Furthermore, rights-bearers must be subject to accountability mechanisms commensurate with their degree of influence. In a similar vein, Georg Kell, the overall coordinator of the UN Global Compact, commented in 2003 that 'ultimately, power and responsibility cannot be separated'.

'Responsibility' is the state or fact of being responsible. When used as an adjective, 'responsible' means answerable to another or liable to be called to account. However, the concept of 'responsibility' employed in this text goes well beyond the substantive grounds for prospective liability to encompass its functional sense. 'Responsible' as a noun also means undertaking to play a particular role. The business case for embedding a culture of responsibility within commercial practice springs from enlightened economic self-interest. For individual firms, accountability enhances reputations, facilitates risk management, provides competitive advantages and improves productivity. Maintaining the so-called 'social licence to operate' contributes to sustainable business growth and market stability. That said, unlike business ethics or 'good corporate citizenship' there may be little if any opportunity for management to voluntarily opt out of legal compliance. Corporations are not averse to enhanced accountability provided that certain conditions are met: for example, the non-discriminatory application of regulatory controls or freedom to choose the manner of implementing regulatory objectives. Several corporations have also accepted that they carry an 'extended responsibility' for the operational behaviour of affiliates and suppliers, notwithstanding the concepts of separate corporate personality and limited liability.

In what ways is international law relevant for business? Classical international legal theory doggedly adheres to the notion that international law is only ever indirectly binding upon corporations. This occurs when either conventions or state practice rising to the level of customary international law have been duly implemented or incorporated under national law. The direct application of international law to non-state actors or the horizontal application thereof between them and without the prism of national law unreservedly diminishes the governmental role at national levels just as international law ordinarily curtails the right of states to regulate. However, the responsibility of governments to monitor and regulate private behaviour to protect the public interest employs the same means as effecting discrimination against non-nationals. Alternatively, where the exercise of regulatory authority by governments is weak and ineffective or a failure of good governance occurs, attention naturally turns to the inherent capacity of other actors. Corporations have been famously cautioned against assuming unanticipated (and unprofitable) roles which divert attention from the economic responsibilities incumbent upon business (Friedman, 1970: 33). However, exploiting the particularity of national law justifiably attracts condemnation where it qualifies, for example, as apartheid or slave labour. Resort to the guidance offered by international standards is accordingly the most defensible position. International norms enjoy the authority of universal consensus by the international community including persuasive moral weight free from parochial national law. Reputable companies cannot fail to observe the origins of international agreements even where voluntary (Weisglas, 1982: 18). More pertinently, affirming these instruments is a relatively costless technique for reinforcing governmental commitments (Kline, 1980: 11–12).

The purpose of this volume, as suggested by its title, is to define the parameters of corporate responsibility from existing and emergent international principles. Effort is necessary for the assembly and not the translation. UN Secretary-General Kofi Annan, when he first proposed a Global Compact to the international business community at the World Economic Forum (WEF) during 1999, astutely observed that the universal values applicable to corporations have already been defined by existing international agreements. For example, strict environmental liability emerged for corporations at the international level during the early 1990s (UNTCMD, 1993). International law is not as underdeveloped, overly rigid or lacking in specificity as may be imagined. Firms are addressees of international instruments in so far as they euphemistically qualify as a 'non-governmental organisation' (typical of the older conventions), are independently identified as 'transnational corporations' or 'multinational enterprises' (the predominant terminology of the 1970s), are generically referred to as 'the private sector' (popular during the 1980s) or are known (more recently) as simply 'business and industry'. UN parlance may moreover embrace politically organised business groups, ad hoc corporate coalitions, national manufacturing associations and industry bodies as business and industry NGOs (BINGOs). Irrespective of their structure or role, all constituents within a state are 'members of the international community'.

International law is directly applicable to corporations, irrespective of size, in such diverse fields as human rights, international criminal and environmental law, labour standards, international trade, armed conflict, sustainable development, corruption, consumer protection, restrictive business practices and corporate governance. *International Documents on Corporate Responsibility* identifies the international position both generally and in respect of specific economic sectors (such as the nuclear or fishing industries).

Can the universal values embodied within international norms be wholly and uncritically transplanted into rules of corporate liability? The conclusion from even a rudimentary comparison of the documents within this volume is that appropriate private sector roles and responsibilities have already been identified within existing law. For example, environmental treaties self-evidently facilitate trade in chemicals, defer to best commercial practice with respect to technological development, extol continuous improvement for environmental management or are amended in view of insurance market capacity. Corporations need not assume those roles and responsibilities ordinarily expected of and discharged by other entities. Corporate functions are dictated by economic considerations and commercial roles need not replicate governmental ones. Similarly, the degree of responsibility within the commercial sphere of influence on any given question requires *inter alia* an appreciation of the obligations imposed upon government. Corporate responsibility is not to be equated with subtracting 'public' sector accountability from the entire field of 'private' responsibility, however permeable the public/private divide proves to be. For example, private conduct which can be attributed to governments under international law entails state responsibility (Article 2, Articles on Responsibility of States for Internationally Wrongful Acts, 2001). Corporations are by implication responsible for 'private' acts or omissions independently imputable to them. Finally, private actors cannot undertake activities when governments are prohibited from doing so. Corporate officers and employees as individuals are obligated to respect generally recognised international norms such as those encapsulated within UN conventions and other international instruments. That international law establishes minimum standards for all is reflected in the fact that conventions typically permit governments to implement more stringent measures.

It could be suggested that several instruments, even if applicable to corporations, do not constitute law *per se*. However, it is characteristic of the incremental lawmaking process that formally non-legally binding materials (so-called 'soft law') subsequently undergoes a process of 'hardening'. Political declarations, General Assembly resolutions and programmes of action may lead to intergovernmentally agreed guidelines, principles or codes of conduct of an experimental nature which are subsequently reviewed in the light of the experience gained. These instruments are in turn frequently precursors to multilateral agreements ultimately facilitating the formulation, adoption and implementation of national policies, laws and regulations. The constancy of regulatory refinement, either through interlocking instruments of cascading legal quality and variable specificity or cross-cutting initiatives in response to the political imperatives of the day occupies players in a veritable game of jenga at the global level.

Although intergovernmental codes may be formally superseded by instruments of relatively greater authority, they are not simply relegated to inconsequentiality. Such instruments continue to occupy an ancillary role in identifying appropriate roles and responsibilities. Their voluntary nature does not 'exclude the possibility of the emergence of customary international law on any issue of multinational enterprise conduct on which there is State practice, including such practice in the context of follow-up proceedings' (Baade, 1980, p. 9). It is moreover instructive to recall the deliberations of the UN Centre on Transnational Corporations whose observations in relation to the UN Code of Conduct on Transnational Corporations carry a generalisable resonance:

> A code of Conduct on transnational corporations, whether in legally binding or non-binding form, represents an effort to formulate expectations which Governments collectively feel justified to hold with regard to the conduct of transnational corporations. It becomes thereby a 'source' of law for

> national authorities as well as for the transnational enterprises themselves, since both can rely on and utilize the Code to fill gaps in relevant laws and practices. In this manner, the Code may become a springboard for legally-creative action by national courts and other authorities, and even by transnational corporations themselves, to the extent that the latter may help to shape pertinent legal principles through their continuous practice. (UNCTC, 1978, p. 8)

Intergovernmental codes of conduct can delineate commercial roles and responsibilities in explicit detail, thereby facilitating the transition to a conventional instrument and enhancing the prospects for subsequent implementation. Within an orthodox understanding of the contemporary international system conventions are only strictly binding upon governments, notwithstanding that private sector roles are also envisaged. The standards of appropriate commercial practice by way of a complement to the agreed conduct by governments remain located within the code. By this reasoning conventions and codes both serve as basic reference points for all actors until such time as adequate and effective regulatory frameworks have been instituted at national levels. The claim to authority enjoyed by intergovernmental codes of conduct is more than merely persuasive for corporations, particularly where they have participated in processes of formulation, implementation and review. As prospective models for legislative or administrative measures, these instruments are open to adoption by governments and have been referred to by national courts when evaluating the propriety of corporate conduct.

It could similarly be argued that private voluntary initiatives (PVIs) drafted by corporations and other entities are not ostensibly binding. Indeed, the US Council for International Business, for example, resists efforts to render codes *de facto* binding through consumer labelling, and rejects input by external groups who lack responsibility for commercial performance (USCIB, 1997; 1998: 3–4). Corporate codes of conduct may be defined as written policies or statements voluntarily expressing the commitment of management to specific courses of conduct. Mention could also be made of so-called 'multi-stakeholder initiatives' which include other actors in the processes of standard-setting, reporting, auditing and certification in relation to social, labour or environmental issues. Operating alongside orthodox (governmental) sources of regulation, therefore, are global framework agreements between international trade union secretariats and transnational corporations as well as tools formulated by NGOs purporting to control commercial operations (on so-called 'civil' regulation, see Bendell, 2000). Corporations adopt these instruments to implement management values, enhance reputations, counter adverse criticism and improve economic performance (through employee recruitment, retention and performance, better supply chain management, product differentiation and brand recognition). PVIs frequently address fair business practices, the rule of law, fair employment, labour rights, environmental stewardship and corporate citizenship (BSR, 2000; USCIB, 2001).

PVIs do not possess formal legal authority since they have not been formulated by governments, classically the principal lawmakers (Braithwaite and Drahos, 2000). Notwithstanding claims to universal credibility through the invocation of international standards, many PVIs affirm the relatively greater authority and detail of the legislative membranes afforded by national governments. However, their status in no way preconditions their practical effectiveness. Corporate adherence to peer-based norms could constitute a prerequisite for market participation through the identification and application of 'best-of-sector' techniques. Self-enunciated behavioural standards also give rise to expectations of future conduct upon which others are entitled to rely. The failure to do so tempts accusations of misleading advertising or deceptive conduct (Lu, 2000). For example, the Californian Supreme Court in *Kasky v Nike, Inc.* (27 *Cal.* 4th 939) observed that 'when a business enterprise, to promote and defend its sales and profits, makes factual representations about its own products or its own operations, it must speak truthfully'.

The theory of self-regulation also supports the assertion that corporations may create standards applicable unto themselves (Jenkins, 2001; UNCTAD, 2003). Merchants have long codified best commercial practice with a view to facilitating exchange and incidentally fill regulatory vacuums. Corporate codes of conduct could simply be a contemporary manifestation of *lex mercatoria* (Horn, 1980: 45), whose private origins do not prevent subsequent adoption by governments as law. Voluntarily pursuing environmentally sound practices may lead regulatory development to commercial advantage and minimise regulatory adaptation costs (EC, 1993; UNCTAD, 1993). Reciprocally, principles of international environmental law – for example, intergenerational equity, the precautionary principle, the polluter-pays principle and the non-transferability or non-transformation of waste – are affirmed and strengthened by private initiatives. Interestingly, the International Organisation of Employers (IOE), for example, espouses the view that Conventions of the International Labour Organisation (ILO) are drafted as legislative guidance for governments and are not conceived for direct practical implementation by firms through inclusion in individual codes of conduct.

PVIs have signalled renewed interest in corporate social responsibility (CSR) by both intergovernmental organisations (see, for example, UNCTAD, 1999; ILO, 2003) and corporate proponents (WBCSD, 1999). Frequently accompanied by greater stakeholder interaction, CSR can be defined as the voluntary integration of social, environmental and other non-economic concerns into commercial operations (EC, 2002: 5). The WEF, for example, has called upon corporations to provide leadership, define key issues, maintain transparency and effect positive change so that CSR becomes a central component of modern business strategy (WEF, 2002). Politically organised business groups have also attempted to formulate commercial criteria which measure social performance (see, for example, CBSR, 2001). However eminently laudable these efforts may be, they do not detract from the obligations applicable to business.

Criticisms have been made that corporate codes are vaguely defined public relations tools, possess an incomplete scope, pose undesirable anticompetitive implications, deter effective regulation and undermine the position of organised labour. The IOE agrees that the limits of such tools must be realistically appreciated (IOE, 1999a: 12; 1999b). It is apparent from the content of intergovernmental and NGO codes that corporations are not expected to implement universal values in a manner identical to governments and others. Corporate and NGO codes are distinctive for their non-legal enforcement and verification techniques such as independent monitoring, auditing, certification, ongoing external review and internal complaints procedures. Penalties for non-compliance include fines, declarations, expulsion from membership and refusal to trade. Codes may also be accompanied by stakeholder consultation, full disclosure and commitments to continuous improvement. Hence, PVIs which promote higher standards for market leaders are useful complements to regulatory measures instituted by governments which ensure adherence by commercial laggards to minimum requirements.

### Editorial Note on the Selection and Treatment of Materials

*International Documents on Corporate Responsibility* reflects recognition from a multiplicity of actors to the reality of corporate responsibility in various fields (economic, social, environmental or more particularly legal) and to varying degrees of specificity. Whatever the particular institutional vision may be, the agreed policy objectives, obligations and PVIs contained within the present volume are symptomatic of a broader corporate accountability agenda at the international level (Calder and Culverwell, 2004; UNRISD, 2004). The need to rationalise existing conventions, guidelines, principles and standards and avoid 'code fatigue' within the private sector is self-evident. This text could constitute a starting point towards the eventual codification of international norms within a convention on corporate accountability, possibly emanating from the Organisation for Economic Cooperation and Development (OECD). That such a process has commenced is heralded by the emergence in 2003 of the UN Norms on the Responsibilities of Transnational Corporations and other Business Enterprises with regard to Human Rights. Whereas human rights and labour standards apply to all corporations irrespective of the size and nature of economic activity, corporate environmental responsibilities appear to be relatively more sector and subject specific. Attempts at codification beyond a level of generality (for example, simply affirming the precautionary, polluter pays and non-transformation of waste principles) will prove more challenging. By way of an alternative to replicating the human rights model through, say, the UN Environment Programme, the UN Code of Conduct for Transnational Corporations abandoned during the early 1990s could be revived and updated. Creating institutional mechanisms at the international level for enforcing corporate responsibility would be a necessary procedural accompaniment.

The objective of this collection is to provide decision-makers from the commercial, governmental, activist or scholastic communities with a convenient collection of texts essential to an appreciation of corporate responsibility. Regrettable omissions from this volume are inevitable and the following is offered by way of explanation, apology and justification. The commercial capacity for both positive and negative contributions first calls for an implicit distinction between mere corporate camouflage for illegal activities and legitimate businesses. The principal beneficiary of this volume will be that particular risk-bearing individual who competitively pursues personal reward and exemplifies the qualities of managerial flair and entrepreneurial spirit: the businessperson. The relevant yardstick for inclusion was therefore as follows: what elementary information would the ordinary businessperson lacking specialist knowledge require to gain an understanding of the relevant issues? *International Documents on Corporate Responsibility* will have fulfilled its mandate if commercially minded actors become acquainted with the international consensus in various fields, possess an informed awareness of their existing responsibilities and can effectively participate in governmental and/or non-governmental debates which define their future role as well as that of others.

Identifying the substantive international provisions directly pertinent to corporate responsibility demands difficult decisions. This objective inevitably entails the partial exclusion of state responsibility, which is regrettable since as noted above the public–private distinction is neither static nor clear-cut. Intergovernmental obligations crafted for the benefit of non-state actors constitute the basis for multiple interactions with and between private entities. For example, the voluminous materials with respect to international trade, capital movements and investment protection could have been expected to have been included. Without diminishing their significance, commercial roles and responsibilities arising from the World Trade Organisation (WTO), Codex Alimentarius and the International Organisation for Standardisation (ISO) have reluctantly been omitted on account of their length and specificity.

With a view to succinctness, the editor has selectively distilled the most important features of any given instrument without intending to eviscerate it of meaningful content. In addition to the substantive grounds for and scope of operator liability, it is implicitly assumed that the treaty provisions of particular commercial interest relate to property rights, labour relationships, environmental protection, technology transfer, financial arrangements and the protections afforded to confidential commercial information. Provisions contemplating participation in decision-making, opportunities to provide input and access to information whether as an NGO, commercial entity or member of the public are also extracted since they are relevant to prospective corporate roles.

The editor acknowledges that several conventional obligations (including territorial application, compliance measures, jurisdiction and extradition) are relevant to national implementation and/or subsequent enforcement and will therefore have a determinative impact upon corporations. This is particularly true of ILO conventions, recommendations and declarations. However, many of the prominent instruments have been reproduced elsewhere in the literature and, rather than repeat what is available, readers are encouraged to refer to full text versions for specific items of interest. For these reasons, declarations, reservations and technical annexes to conventions have not been extracted. The relevant intergovernmental agreement will require a careful case-specific assessment for the prospect of a commercially satisfactory solution.

Additionally relevant for businesses but nevertheless omitted in this volume are provisions establishing institutional machinery or monitoring mechanisms (namely, meetings of state parties, subsidiary or technical bodies, oversight committees and international secretariats). For example, procedural rules commonly contemplate the representation of and participation by appropriately qualified national or international NGOs (including business groups) as observers to Conferences of the Parties (COPs) unless one-third of governments object. It is also frequently envisaged that governments will utilise where appropriate the services and cooperation of competent non-governmental bodies, thereby establishing the foundations for close working relationships during subsequent implementation.

The preference for substance over procedure on the question of corporate responsibility under international law renders superfluous the mechanical paraphernalia defining the relationship between international and national law. Common treaty provisions which have been excluded from this volume include voting rights, national reporting obligations, formulating programmes of action, identifying national focal points or competent authorities, concluding further bilateral or multilateral arrangements and negotiating additional annexes or protocols. Also omitted are final clauses including provisions with respect to reservations, revision or amendment, inter-state dispute settlement mechanisms, means of expressing consent to be bound (ratification, acceptance, approval, accession or signature), entry into force, denunciation or withdrawal, notification, registration, publication, authentic languages and designated depositories.

As observed above, corporations also take into account to varying degrees the expectations of other actors. The unique perspectives of industry associations, trade unions and NGOs may be reflected in codified form. One could also distinguish between principles (non-specific overarching values which underpin commercial behaviour) and standards (specific benchmarks for achievement). The latter may consist of specific procedures, identifiable performance outcomes, best-of-sector approaches or certification requirements. These documents have been included on the basis that they may not be readily available, are frequently referred to during intergovernmental negotiations and are directly relevant to commercial operations. It was also desirable to illustrate the flavour and complexity of different perspectives rather than be overly comprehensive. Although informative, codes of conduct formulated by individual companies have been omitted since they reflect the particular specialisation and unique circumstances confronting that firm, typically emanate from market leaders and may not be generally representative of industry.

Given the dynamism inherent in corporate responsibility and the proliferation of privately formulated instruments, the content of this volume has been deliberately restricted to the most important precedents established in each field. Among the many challenges as editor is keeping abreast of contemporary developments: novel initiatives constantly emerge and existing ones are revised and updated. There were numerous candidates for inclusion, and where this was not possible a reference is made to a readily ascertainable source. Internet references for prominent institutions are provided so that readers may follow subsequent developments.

The breakdown into parts is occasionally artificial, given overlapping content. However, the order of presentation is first and foremost binding conventions or policy documents outlining global political agenda collected by subject matter, then intergovernmental codes of conduct, corporate codes and finally instruments from other non-state actors. Each document is formatted to 'house style' and accompanied by a brief explanatory commentary which sketches its significance for corporations and briefly outlines its origins, negotiating history and principal participants. The practical orientation to this volume is served by identifying further reference material of historical and contemporary interest for additional reading (including relevant decisions of national courts and international tribunals). Editorial notes for intergovernmental documents also identify their date of adoption, entry into force and official reference. Since in most cases only extracts of official documents are offered, these commentaries also summarise significant omissions such as additional provisions, technical annexes or implementation procedures.

Extrapolating corporate roles and responsibilities from those of other actors – for example, the entitlements and constraints arising under international humanitarian law – requires a judicious mix of interpretation and creativity. Irrespective of their status, readers are reminded that conventions, statutes and codes of conduct are subject to similar rules of interpretation. Such documents are to be interpreted in good faith in accordance with their ordinary meaning in the light of their context (including preambular paragraphs) and purpose. Supplementary means of interpretation such as the circumstances of adoption or preparatory work are permissible where meanings are left ambiguous, obscure or absurd.

Any shortcomings including errors or omissions committed during reproduction, formatting or editing are entirely those of the editor for which he offers his sincere apologies. Suggestions for inclusion or improvement are always welcome. Finally, I wish to thank Luke Adams, Nep Athwal, Caroline McLin, Kate Emmins and all their colleagues at Edward Elgar for their immeasurable assistance and encouragement.

## References

Abrahams, D. (2004), *Regulating Corporations: A Resource Guide*, Geneva: United Nations Research Institute for Social Development.

Alston, P. (1997), 'The myopia of the handmaidens: international lawyers and globalisation', *European Journal of International Law*, 8, 435–48.

Angelo, H.G. (1968), 'Multinational corporate enterprises: some legal and policy aspects of a modern socio-economic phenomenon', *Recueil des Cours*, **125** (3), 443–606.

Annuaire de L'Institut de Droit International (1978), 'Resolution 3: MNEs', *Annuaire de L'Institut de Droit International Session d'Oslo, 2nd Sess, 30 Aug–8 Sept 1977*, **57** (2), Basel: Basler Zeitung.

Articles on Responsibility of States for Internationally Wrongful Acts, UN General Assembly Resolution 56/83 (2001).

Baade, H.W. (1980), 'The legal effects of codes of conduct for MNEs', in Norbert Horn (ed.), *Legal Problems of Codes of Conduct for MNEs*, Deventer: Kluwer, pp. 3–38.

Bendell, J. (ed.) (2000), *Terms for Endearment: Business, NGOs and Sustainable Development*, Sheffield: Greenleaf.

Boarman, P.M and H. Schollhammer (eds) (1975), *MNCs and Governments: Business–Government Relations in an International Context*, New York: Praeger.

Braithwaite, J. and P. Drahos (2000), *Global Business Regulation*, Cambridge: Cambridge University Press.

BSR (2000), 'Comparison of Selected Social Responsibility-related Standards', San Francisco.

Calder, F. and M. Culverwell (2004), 'Following-up the World Summit on Sustainable Development Commitments on Corporate Social Responsibility', Interim Report, London: Royal Institute of International Affairs (RIIA).

Canadian Business for Social Responsibility (CBSR) (2001), 'The CBSR Guidelines for Corporate Social Performance', Ottawa.

Charney, J.I. (1983), 'TNCs and developing public international law', *Duke Law Journal*, **32**, 748–88.

Dell, S. (1990), *The UN and International Business*, Durham, NC: Duke University Press.

EC (1993), Council Regulation No. 1936/93 allowing voluntary participation by companies in the industrial sector in a Community eco-management and audit scheme (EMAS) (1993) *OJEC* L168 Vol 36.

EC (2002), Communication on Corporate Social Responsibility: A Business Contribution to Sustainable Development, COM/2002/347/FINAL.

Friedman, M. (1970), 'The social responsibility of business is to increase its profits', *NY Times Magazine*, 13 September, 32–125.

Held, D. (2003), 'The changing structure of international law: sovereignty transformed?', in D. Held and A. McGrew (eds), *The Global Transformation Reader*, Cambridge: Polity Press, pp. 162–76.

Higgins, R. (1994), *Problems and Process: International Law and How We Use It*, Oxford: Clarendon Press.

Hofmann, R. and N. Geissler (eds) (1999), *Non-State Actors as New Subjects of International Law*, Berlin: Duncker & Humblot.

Horn, N. (1980), 'Codes of conduct for MNEs and transnational *lex mercatoria*: an international process of learning and law making', in N. Horn (ed.), *Legal Problems of Codes of Conduct for MNEs*, Deventer: Kluwer, pp. 39–81.

Ijalaye, D.A. (1978), *The Extension of Corporate Personality in International Law*, New York: Oceana Publications.

International Labour Office (2003), 'Corporate social responsibility: myth or reality?', Labour Education Paper No. 130, Geneva: ILO.

IOE (1999a), 'Codes of Conduct, Position Paper', Geneva.

IOE (1999b), 'Resolution on Codes of Conduct', Geneva.

Jenkins, R. (2001), 'Corporate Codes of Conduct: Self-Regulation in a Global Economy', Programme on Technology, Business and Society, Paper No. 2, Geneva: United Nations Research Institute for Social Development.

Jessup, P.C. (1956), *Transnational Law*, New Haven, CT: Yale University Press.

Johns, F. (1994), 'The invisibility of the TNC: an analysis of international law and legal theory', *Melbourne University Law Review*, **19**, 893–923.

Kamminga, M. and S. Zia-Zarifi (2000), *Liability of Multinational Corporations under International Law*, The Hague: Kluwer Law International.

Kline, J.M. (1980), 'Entrapment or opportunity: structuring a corporate response to international codes of conduct', *Columbia Journal of World Business*, **15** (2), 6–13.

Lachs, M. (1986), 'Law in the world of today' in A. Bos and H. Siblesz (eds), *Realism in law-making: Essays on International Law in Honour of Willem Riphagen*, Dordrecht: Martinus Nijhoff, p. 101.

Lu, S.-P. (2000), 'Corporate codes of conduct and the FTC: advancing human rights through deceptive advertising law', *Columbia Journal of Transnational Law*, **38**, 603–29.

Mertus, J. (2000), 'Considering non-state actors in the new millennium: toward expanded participation in norm generation and norm application', *New York University Journal of International Law and Politics*, **32** (2), 537–66.

Reisman, M. (1997), 'Designing and managing the future of the state', *European Journal of International Law*, **8**, 409–20.

Seidl-Hohenveldern, I. (1987), *Corporations in and under International Law*, Cambridge: Grotius.

Simma, B. and A.L. Paulus (1999), 'The responsibility of individuals for human rights abuses in internal conflicts: a positivist view', *American Journal of International Law*, **93** (2), 302–16.

Slaughter, A.-M., A.S. Tulumello and S. Wood (1998), 'International law and international relations theory: a new generation of interdisciplinary scholarship', *American Journal of International Law*, **92** (3), 367–97.

Stopford, J.M. and S. Strange (1991), *Rival States, Rival Firms: Competition for World Market Shares*, Cambridge: Cambridge University Press.

Tesner, S. and G. Kell (2000), *The UN and Business: A Partnership Recovered*, New York: St Martin's Press.

UN Research Institute for Social Development (UNRISD) (2004), 'Corporate Social Responsibility and Business Regulation', Research and Policy Brief No. 1, Geneva.

UN Secretary-General (1992), 'TNCs in the New World Economy: Issues and Policy Implications', UN Doc E/C.10/1992/5.

UN Secretary-General (1996), 'Report on the Impact of the Activities and Working Methods of TNCs', UN Doc E/CN.4/Sub.2/1996/12.

UNCTAD (1993), 'Environmental Management in TNCs: Report on the Benchmark Corporate Environmental Survey', UN Doc ST/CTC/149.

UNCTAD (1999), 'The Social Responsibility of TNCs', UN Doc UNCTAD/ITE/IIT/Misc.21.

UNCTAD (2003), *Self-Regulation of Environmental Management: Guidelines Set by World Industry Associations for Their Members' Firms: An Update 1996–2003*, New York: UN.

UNCTC (1978), 'Certain Modalities for Implementation of a Code of Conduct in Relation to its Possible Legal Nature', UN Doc E/C.10/AC.2/9.

UNECE (1998), Convention on Access to Information, Public Participation in Decision-making and Access to Justice in Environmental Matters (the Aarhus Convention) 38 *ILM* 517.

UNTCMD (1993), 'International Environmental Law: Emerging Trends and Implications for TNCs', UN Doc ST/CTC/137.

USCIB (1997), 'Statement on Codes of Conduct: Old Solutions to New Problems', Policy Paper, New York.

USCIB (1998), 'USCIB Position Paper on Codes of Conduct', New York.

USCIB (2001), 'USCIB Compendium of Corporate Responsibility Initiatives', Washington, DC.

Vagts, D.F. (1970), 'The MNE: a new challenge for transnational law', *Harvard Law Review*, **83**, 739–92.

Wagner, G.A. (1986), 'Likes and dislikes in international law: the company', *Netherlands International Law Review*, **33**, 227.

WBCSD (1999), *Corporate Social Responsibility: Meeting Changing Expectations*, Geneva.

WEF (2002), 'The Global Corporate Leadership Challenge for CEOs and Boards', Davos.

Weisglas, M. (1982), 'International business and the UN Code', in UNCTC, *The CTC Reporter*, **12**, 16–18.

Zito, A.R. (1998), 'Comparing environmental policy-making in transnational institutions', *Journal of European Public Policy*, **5** (4), 671–90.

# Acknowledgements

The conventions, PVIs and other documents collected within the present volume are the visible products of considerable planning and effort, difficult negotiations, laborious attention to detail, a willingness to compromise and an awareness of practicalities. Their common characteristic is a perception by all participants that corporate responsibility is an opportunity, not a threat. This compilation would not have arisen without the participants' commitment to the task, dedicated enthusiasm in questioning preconceived boundaries and concerted efforts at refining our understanding of the nature and propriety of commercial roles and responsibilities. This volume is without exception a tribute to their achievements and I hope they find it provocatively useful in pursuing their own particular agendas and activities.

The editor gratefully acknowledges the generous permission of the following organisations to reproduce the material, documents and conventions compiled within the present volume:

Caux Round Table.
Ceres.
Clean Clothes Campaign.
Ethical Trading Initiative.
Friends of the Earth International.
Her Majesty's Stationery Office (UK).
International Chamber of Commerce.
International Labour Rights Fund.
International Union of Food, Agricultural, Hotel, Restaurant, Catering, Tobacco and Allied Workers' Associations (IUF).
Irish National Caucus.
Leon H. Sullivan Foundation.
Marine Stewardship Council International Ltd.
Mineral Policy Institute.
Minerals Council of Australia.
Office of the High Commissioner for Human Rights (UN).
Oxfam–Community Aid Abroad.
Secretariat of the Basel Convention on the Control of Transboundary Movements of Hazardous Wastes and Their Disposal.
Secretariat of the Convention on Biological Diversity.
Secretariat of the European Communities.
Secretariat of the International Gas Union.
Secretariat of the International Labour Organisation.
Secretariat of the International Maritime Organisation.
Secretariat of the International Seabed Authority.
Secretariat of the Organisation for Economic Cooperation and Development.
Secretariat of the UN Economic Commission for Europe.
Secretariat of the UN Environment Programme.

Secretariat of the UN Framework Convention on Climate Change.
Secretariat of the World Health Organisation.
World Federation of the Sporting Goods Industry.

Please note that only European Community legislation printed in the paper edition of the *Official Journal of the European Community* (*OJEC*) is deemed authentic. Also note that the PVIs and other documents contained herein, particularly the older ones, may no longer accurately reflect the current views, policy or approach of either the organisation concerned or its current membership in the light of developments occurring since the instrument was first formulated.

Every effort has been made to secure and acknowledge copyright permission in advance by contacting copyright owners. The editor wishes to tender his apologies for any accidental infringement. He would be pleased to come to a suitable arrangement in conjunction with the publisher and the rightful owners in each case.

The editor has used his best endeavours to ensure that the URLs (uniform resource locators) for external websites referred to in this book are correct and active at the time of going to press. However, since the editor has no responsibility for these websites, he can make no guarantee that a site will remain live or that the content is or will remain appropriate.

Finally, although the most recent developments were incorporated during the preparation of this volume, the documents and commentary contained herein in no way constitute legal advice, and professional assistance should be sought if desired.

# PART I

# International Instruments

# 1. UN: the Global Compact, 2004

**Commentary**: UN Secretary-General Kofi Annan first proposed the Global Compact (source: www.unglobalcompact.org/Portal) in an address to the World Economic Forum during 1999, and Principle 10 was added in 2004. The Compact is derived from leading intergovernmental instruments and therefore enjoys universal consensus. Each principle is accompanied by a useful explanatory commentary which suggests practical implementation measures. The Compact is administered by a network of organisations: the Global Compact Office, six UN agencies (OHCHR, UNEP, ILO, UNDP, UNIDO and UNODC) and approximately 2000 companies and other stakeholders. Companies commit in writing to publicly promoting the Compact and completing a 'Communication on Progress' which describes how the principles are reflected in commercial operations. This process is not intended to enforce corporate adherence. The initiative has given rise to a series of multi-stakeholder fora and global policy dialogues concerning conflict prevention, sustainable development, HIV/AIDS in the workplace, corporate roles and responsibilities, supply chain management, partnerships, transparency, anti-corruption and sustainable consumption. Outcomes include a 'Business Guide to Conflict Impact Assessment and Risk Management', 2002 and Global Compact/OHCHR (2004), *Embedding Human Rights in Business Practice*, Geneva. See further, UN Secretary-General (2004), 'Final Report of the Global Compact Leaders Summit'; UN Global Compact (2003), 'The Global Compact Resource Package'.

The Global Compact asks companies to embrace, support and enact, within their sphere of influence, a set of core values in the areas of human rights, labour standards, the environment, and anti-corruption:

**Human Rights**

Principle 1: Businesses should support and respect the protection of internationally proclaimed human rights.

Principle 2: make sure that they are not complicit in human rights abuses.

**Labour Standards**

Principle 3: Businesses should uphold the freedom of association and the effective recognition of the right to collective bargaining.

Principle 4: the elimination of all forms of forced and compulsory labour.

Principle 5: the effective abolition of child labour.

Principle 6: the elimination of discrimination in respect of employment and occupation.

**The Environment**

Principle 7: Businesses should support a precautionary approach to environmental challenges.

Principle 8: undertake initiatives to promote greater environmental responsibility.

Principle 9: encourage the development and diffusion of environmentally friendly technologies.

**Anti-corruption**

Principle 10: Businesses should work against all forms of corruption, including extortion and bribery.

# 2. UN: Draft Code of Conduct on Transnational Corporations, 1990

**Commentary**: One feature of the assertion by newly independent developing States for a New International Economic Order in 1974 (UNGA Resolution 3201) was exercising greater regulatory control over foreign direct investment. A Group of Eminent Persons was appointed to study the impact of corporations upon development and international relations: UN Doc E/5500/Rev.1 (1974). ECOSOC Resolutions 1908 (1974) and 1913 (1974) established a Commission on TNCs with the Centre on TNCs acting as secretariat. Their 'highest priority' of work was a code of conduct: for previous drafts see UNCTC, TNCs: 'Codes of Conduct, Formulations by the Chairman', UN Doc E/C.10 2/8 (1978) & UNCTC, 'Draft Code of Conduct on TNCs', UN Docs E/1983/17/Rev1 and E/1988/39/Add1.

Political disagreements between governments were reduced to several key issues by the mid-1980s: ECOSOC, 'TNCs: Issues Involved in the Formulation of a Code of Conduct', UN Doc E/C.10/17 (1976); UNCTC, 'Secretariat Report on the Outstanding Issues in the Draft Code of Conduct on TNCs', UN Doc E/C.10/1984/S/5 (1984); ECOSOC, 'Work on the Formulation of the UN Code of Conduct on TNCs', UN Doc E/C.10/1985/S/2; UNCTC, 'The UN Code of Conduct on TNCs', UN Doc ST/CTC/Ser.A/4 (1986). This included the standard of compensation for expropriated property under international law: Robinson P. (1986), 'The Question of a Reference to International Law in the UN Code of Conduct on TNCs', UN Doc ST/CTC/Ser.A/1 (1986); Vagts D.F. (1986), 'The Question of a Reference to International Obligations on the UN Code of Conduct on TNCs: A Different View', UN Doc ST/CTC/Ser.A/2 (1986). Negotiators were also mindful of developments elsewhere: UNCTC, 'TNCs: Aspects of Possible Relationships between the Work on a Code of Conduct and Related Work in UNCTAD and ILO', UN Doc E/C.10/AC.2/5 (1978).

The Chairman of the Negotiating Committee observed that since 'the vast majority of its provisions have already been accepted', the Code 'will receive the support of the overwhelming majority of countries from all regional groups' (Letter accompanying the final version of the Code, UN Doc E/1990/94, extracted below). Consideration was given to its final form: UNCTC, 'TNCs: Certain Modalities for Implementation of a Code of Conduct in Relation to its Possible Legal Nature', UN Doc E/C.10/AC.2/9 (1978). One proposal was as an UNGA Resolution: Bergman M.S. (1987), 'The norm-creating effect of a UNGA Resolution on TNCs', in Snyder F.E. and Surakiart S. (eds), *Third World Attitudes Toward International Law: An Introduction*, Dordrecht: Martinus Nijhoff. However, the Code was ultimately abandoned in the early 1990s on account of dissipating governmental interest, the desirability of attracting foreign direct investment, codes formulated in other fora, loss of business support and reliance upon self-regulation: UNCTC, 'The New Code Environment', UN Doc ST/CTC/Ser.A/16 (1990). In 1992 the UNCTC was renamed the Division on TNCs and Investment (DTCI) and relocated to UNCTAD: UNGA Resolution 47/212B (1993). For CTC reporters issued between 1976 and 1990, see http://unctc.unctad.org/aspx/ctcTitle.aspx.

Intergovernmental cooperation contemplated by the Code (and not extracted below) includes information exchange, consultation and concluding further agreements (paras 59–63). National implementation measures include publication, promotion, consideration in regulatory decision-making and reporting the experience gained (para 66). International machinery (paras 67–70) envisages *inter alia* the UNCTC periodically assessing implementation every two years based on information derived from governments or NGOs and 'providing clarifications on provisions of the Code'. Additional functions include information collection or dissemination and annual reporting. Representatives from trade unions, business, consumer and other groups may express their views. Paragraph 71 anticipated a review of the Code after six years. See further, Feld W.J. (1976), 'UN supervision over MNCs: realistic expectation or exercise in futility', *Orbis Journal of World Affairs*, **19** (4), 1499; Feld W.J. (1980), *MNCs and UN Politics: The Quest for Codes of Conduct*, New York: Pergamon; Lansing P. and Rosaria A. (1991), 'An analysis of the UN Proposed Code of Conduct for TNCs', *World Competition*, **14**, 35–7.

**Definitions and Scope of Application**

1. (a) This Code is universally applicable to enterprises, irrespective of their country of origin and their ownership, including private, public or mixed, comprising entities in two or more countries, regardless of the legal form and fields of activity of these entities, which operate under a system of decision-making, permitting coherent policies and a common strategy through one or more decision-making centres, in which the entities are so linked, by ownership or otherwise, that one or more of them may be able to exercise a significant influence over the activities of others and, in particular, to share knowledge, resources and responsibilities with the others. Such enterprises are referred to in this Code as TNCs.
   (b) The term 'entities' in the Code refers to both parent entities – that is, entities which are the main source of influence over others – and other entities, unless otherwise specified in the Code.
   (c) The term 'transnational corporation' in the Code refers to the enterprise as a whole or its various entities.
   (d) The term 'home country' means the country in which the parent entity is located. The term 'host country' means a country other than the home country in which an entity other than the parent entity is located.
   (e) The term 'country in which a TNC operates' refers to a home or host country in which an entity of a TNC conducts operations.

2. For the application of this Code, it is irrelevant whether or not enterprises described in paragraph 1 (a) above are referred to in any country as TNCs.
4. The provisions of the Code addressed to TNC reflect good practice for all enterprises. Subject to the provisions of paragraph 52, wherever the provisions of the Code are relevant to both, TNCs and domestic enterprises shall be subject to the same expectations with regard to their conduct.

## Activities of Transnational Corporations

### *A. General*

RESPECT FOR NATIONAL SOVEREIGNTY AND OBSERVANCE OF DOMESTIC LAWS, REGULATIONS AND ADMINISTRATIVE PRACTICES

7. TNCs shall respect the national sovereignty of the countries in which they operate and the right of each State to exercise its permanent sovereignty over its natural wealth and resources.
8. An entity of a TNC is subject to the laws, regulations and established administrative practices of the country in which it operates.
9. TNCs shall respect the right of each State to regulate and monitor accordingly the activities of their entities operating within its territory.

ADHERENCE TO ECONOMIC GOALS AND DEVELOPMENT OBJECTIVES, POLICIES AND PRIORITIES

10. TNCs should carry out their activities in conformity with the development policies, objectives and priorities set out by the Governments of the countries in which they operate and work seriously towards making a positive contribution to the achievement of such goals at the national and, as appropriate, the regional level, within the framework of regional integration programmes. TNCs should co-operate with the Governments of the countries in which they operate with a view to contributing to the development process and should be responsive to requests for consultation in this respect, thereby establishing mutually beneficial relations with these countries.
11. TNCs should carry out their operations in conformity with applicable intergovernmental co-operative arrangements concluded by the countries in which they operate.

REVIEW AND RENEGOTIATION OF CONTRACTS AND AGREEMENTS

12. (a) Contracts or agreements between Governments and TNCs should be negotiated and implemented in good faith. In such contracts or agreements, especially long-term ones, review or renegotiation clauses should normally be included.
    (b) In the absence of such clauses and where there has been a fundamental change of the circumstances on which the contract or agreement was based, TNCs, acting in good faith, should co-operate with Governments for the review or renegotiation of such contract or agreement.

ADHERENCE TO SOCIO-CULTURAL OBJECTIVES AND VALUES

13. TNCs should respect the social and cultural objectives, values and traditions of the countries in which they operate. While economic and technological development is normally accompanied by social change, TNCs should avoid practices, products or services which cause detrimental effects on cultural patterns and socio-cultural objectives as determined by Governments. For this purpose, TNCs should respond positively to requests for consultations from Governments concerned.

RESPECT FOR HUMAN RIGHTS AND FUNDAMENTAL FREEDOMS

14. TNCs shall respect human rights and fundamental freedoms in the countries in which they operate. In their social and industrial relations, TNCs shall not discriminate on the basis of race, colour, sex, religion, language, social, national and ethnic origin or

political or other opinion. TNCs shall conform to government policies designed to extend equality of opportunity and treatment.

NON-COLLABORATION BY TRANSNATIONAL CORPORATIONS WITH THE RACIST MINORITY REGIME IN SOUTH AFRICA

15. In accordance with the efforts of the international community towards the elimination of apartheid in South Africa,

(a) TNCs shall refrain from operations and activities supporting and sustaining the racist minority regime of South Africa in maintaining the system of apartheid;
(b) TNCs shall engage in appropriate activities within their competence with a view to eliminating racial discrimination and all other aspects of the system of apartheid;
(c) TNCs shall comply strictly with obligations resulting from Security Council decisions and shall fully respect those resulting from all relevant UN resolutions.

NON-INTERFERENCE IN INTERNAL AFFAIRS OF HOST COUNTRIES

16. Without prejudice to the participation of TNCs in activities that are permissible under the laws, regulations or established administrative practices of host countries, and without prejudice to paragraph 8 of the Code, TNCs shall not interfere in the internal affairs of host countries.

NON-INTERFERENCE IN INTERGOVERNMENTAL RELATIONS

17. TNCs shall not interfere in intergovernmental relations provided that this provision shall not preclude such activities as are sanctioned within the framework of bilateral or multilateral co-operation.
18. TNCs should not request Governments acting on their behalf to take the measures referred to in the second sentence of paragraph 65.
19. With respect to the exhaustion of local remedies, TNCs should not request Governments to act on their behalf in any manner inconsistent with paragraph 65.

ABSTENTION FROM CORRUPT PRACTICES

20. (a) TNCs shall refrain, in their transactions, from the offering, promising or giving of any payment, gift or other advantage to or for the benefit of a public official as consideration for performing or refraining from the performance of his duties in connection with those transactions.
(b) TNCs shall maintain accurate records of any payments made by them to any public official or intermediary. They shall make available these records to the competent authorities of the countries in which they operate, upon request, for investigations and proceedings concerning those payments.

## *B. Economic, Financial and Social*

OWNERSHIP AND CONTROL

21. TNCs should make every effort so to allocate their decision making powers among their entities as to enable them to contribute to the economic and social development of the countries in which they operate.
22. To the extent permitted by national laws, policies and established administrative practices of the country in which it operates, each entity of a TNC should co-operate with

the other entities, in accordance with the actual distribution of responsibilities among them and consistent with paragraph 22 [*sic*], so as to enable each entity to meet effectively the requirements established by the laws, policies and regulations of the country in which it operates.

23. TNCs should carry out their personnel policies in accordance with the national policies of each of the countries in which they operate which give priority to the employment and promotion of its nationals at all levels of management and direction of the affairs of each entity so as to enhance the effective participation of its nationals in the decision-making process.
24. TNCs should contribute to the managerial and technical training of nationals of the countries in which they operate and facilitate their employment at all levels of management of the entities and enterprises as a whole.

EMPLOYMENT CONDITIONS AND INDUSTRIAL RELATIONS

25. For the purposes of this Code, the principles set out in the Tripartite Declaration of Principles concerning MNEs and Social Policy, adopted by the Governing Body of the ILO, should apply in the field of employment, training, conditions of work and life and industrial relations.

BALANCE OF PAYMENTS AND FINANCING

26. TNCs shall carry out their operations in conformity with laws and regulations and with full regard to the policy objectives set out by the countries in which they operate, particularly developing countries, relating to balance of payments, financial transactions and other issues dealt with in the subsequent paragraphs of this section. These obligations are without prejudice to multilaterally agreed trade rules and sound commercial practices.
27. TNCs should respond positively to requests for consultation on their activities from the Governments of the countries in which they operate, with a view to contributing to the alleviation of pressing problems of balance of payments and finance of such countries.
28. TNCs should, where appropriate, contribute to the promotion and diversification of exports in the countries in which they operate and to an increased utilization of goods, services and other resources which are available in these countries.
29. TNCs should be responsive to requests by Governments of the countries in which they operate, particularly developing countries, concerning the phasing over a limited period of time of the repatriation of capital in case of disinvestment or remittances of accumulated profits, when the size and timing of such transfers would cause serious balance-of-payments difficulties for such countries.
30. TNCs should not, contrary to generally accepted financial practices prevailing in the countries in which they operate, engage in short-term financial operations or transfers or defer or advance foreign exchange payments, including intra-corporate payments, in a manner which would increase currency instability and thereby cause serious balance-of-payments difficulties for the countries concerned.
31. TNCs should not impose restrictions on their entities, beyond generally accepted commercial practices prevailing in the countries in which they operate, regarding the transfer of goods, services and funds which would cause serious balance-of-payments difficulties for the countries in which they operate.
32. When having recourse to the money and capital markets of the countries in which they operate, TNCs should not, beyond generally accepted financial practices prevailing in

such countries, engage in activities which would have a significant adverse impact on the working of local markets, particularly by restricting the availability of funds to other enterprises. When issuing shares with the objective of increasing local equity participation in an entity operating in such a country, or engaging in long-term borrowing in the local market, TNCs should consult with the Government of the country concerned upon its request on the effects of such transactions on the local money and capital markets.

TRANSFER PRICING

33. In respect of their intra-corporate transactions, TNCs should not use pricing policies that are not based on relevant market prices, or, in the absence of such prices, the arm's length principle, which have the effect of adversely affecting the tax revenues, the foreign exchange resources or other aspects of the economy of the countries in which they operate.

TAXATION

34. TNCs shall not, contrary to the laws and regulations of the countries in which they operate, use their corporate structure and modes of operation, such as the use of intra-corporate pricing which is not based on the arm's length principle, or other means, to modify the tax base on which their entities are assessed.

COMPETITION AND RESTRICTIVE BUSINESS PRACTICES

35. For the purposes of this Code, the relevant provisions of the Set of Multilaterally Agreed Equitable Principles and Rules for the Control of Restrictive Business Practices adopted by the UNGA in its resolution 35/63 of 5 December 1980 apply in the field of restrictive business practices.

TRANSFER OF TECHNOLOGY

36. (a) TNCs shall conform to the transfer of technology laws and regulations of the country in which they operate. They shall co-operate with the competent authorities of those countries in assessing the impact of international transfers of technology in their economies and consult with them regarding the various technological options which might help those countries, particularly developing countries, to attain their economic and social development.

(b) TNCs in their transfer of technology transactions should, in accordance with the criteria set forth in the Set of Multilaterally Agreed Equitable Principles and Rules for the Control of Restrictive Business Practices, avoid restrictive practices which adversely affect the international flow of technology, or otherwise hinder the economic and technological development of countries, particularly developing countries.

(c) TNCs should contribute to the strengthening of the scientific and technological capacities of developing countries, in accordance with the science and technology established policies and priorities of those countries. TNCs should undertake substantial research and development activities in developing countries and should make full use of local resources and personnel in this process.

CONSUMER PROTECTION

37. TNCs shall carry out their operations, in particular production and marketing, in accordance with national laws, regulations, administrative practices and policies concerning

consumer protection of the countries in which they operate. TNCs shall also perform their activities with due regard to relevant international standards, so that they do not cause injury to the health or endanger the safety of consumers or bring about variations in the quality of products in each market which would have detrimental effects on consumers.

38. TNCs shall, in respect of the products and services which they produce or market or propose to produce or market in any country, supply to the competent authorities of that country on request or on a regular basis, as specified by these authorities, all relevant information concerning:
    (a) Characteristics of these products or services which may be injurious to the health and safety of consumers including experimental uses and related aspects;
    (b) Prohibitions, restrictions, warnings and other public regulatory measures imposed in other countries on grounds of health and safety protection on these products or services.

39. TNCs should disclose to the public in the countries in which they operate all appropriate information on the contents and, to the extent known, on possible hazardous effects of the products they produce or market in the countries concerned by means of proper labelling, informative and accurate advertising or other appropriate methods. Packaging of their products should be safe and the contents of the product should not be misrepresented.

40. TNCs should be responsive to requests from Governments of the countries in which they operate and be prepared to co-operate with international organizations in their efforts to develop and promote national and international standards for the protection of the health and safety of consumers to meet the basic needs of consumers.

ENVIRONMENTAL PROTECTION

41. TNCs shall carry out their activities in accordance with national laws, regulations, established administrative practices and policies relating to the preservation of the environment of the countries in which they operate and with due regard to relevant international standards. TNCs should, in performing their activities, take steps to protect the environment and where damaged to rehabilitate it and should make efforts to [develop/apply] adequate technologies for this purpose.

42. TNCs shall, in respect of the products, processes and services they have introduced or propose to introduce in any country, supply to the competent authorities of that country on request or on a regular basis, as specified by these authorities, all relevant information concerning:
    (a) Characteristics of these products, processes and other activities including experimental uses and related aspects which may harm the environment and the measures and costs necessary to avoid or at least to mitigate their harmful effects;
    (b) Prohibitions, restrictions, warnings and other public regulatory measures imposed in other countries on grounds of protection of the environment on these products, processes and services.

43. TNCs should be responsive to requests from Governments of the countries in which they operate and be prepared where appropriate to co-operate with international organizations in their efforts to develop and promote national and international standards for the protection of the environment.

*C. Disclosure of Information*

44. TNCs should disclose to the public in the countries in which they operate, by appropriate means of communication, clear, full and comprehensible information on the structure, policies, activities and operations of the TNC as a whole. The information should include financial as well as non financial items and should be made available on a regular annual basis, normally within six months and in any case not later than 12 months from the end of the financial year of the corporation. In addition, during the financial year, TNCs should wherever appropriate make available a semi-annual summary of financial information.

The financial information to be disclosed annually should be provided where appropriate on a consolidated basis, together with suitable explanatory notes and should include, *inter alia*, the following:

(a) A balance sheet;
(b) An income statement, including operating results and sales;
(c) A statement of allocation of net profits or net income;
(d) A statement of the sources and uses of funds;
(e) Significant new long-term capital investment;
(f) Research and development expenditure.

The non-financial information referred to in the first subparagraph should include, *inter alia*:

(a) The structure of the TNC, showing the name and location of the parent company, its main entities, its percentage ownership, direct and indirect, in these entities, including shareholdings between them;
(b) The main activity of its entities;
(c) Employment information including average number of employees;
(d) Accounting policies used in compiling and consolidating the information published;
(e) Policies applied in respect of transfer pricing.

The information provided for the TNC as a whole should as far as practicable be broken down:

(i) By geographical area or country, as appropriate, with regard to the activities of its main entities, sales, operating results, significant new investments and number of employees;
(ii) By major line of business as regards sales and significant new investment.

The method of breakdown as well as details of information provided should be determined by the nature, scale and interrelationships of the TNC's operations, with due regard to their significance for the areas or countries concerned.

The extent, detail and frequency of the information provided should take into account the nature and size of the TNC as a whole, the requirements of confidentiality and effects on the TNC's competitive position as well as the cost involved in producing the information.

The information herein required should, as necessary, be in addition to information required by national laws, regulations and established administrative practices of the countries in which TNCs operate.

45. (a) TNCs shall supply to the competent authorities in each of the countries in which they operate, upon request or on a regular basis as specified by those authorities, and in accordance with national legislation, all information required for legislative and administrative purposes relevant to the activities and policies of their entities in the country concerned.

(b) TNCs shall, to the extent permitted by the provisions of the relevant national laws, regulations, established administrative practices and policies of the countries concerned, supply to competent authorities in the countries in which they operate information held in other countries needed to enable them to obtain a true and fair view of the operations of the TNC concerned as a whole in so far as the information requested relates to the activities of the entities in the countries seeking such information.

(c) The provisions of paragraph 52 concerning confidentiality shall apply to information supplied under the provisions of this paragraph.

46. (a) With due regard to the relevant provisions of the ILO Tripartite Declaration of Principles concerning MNEs and Social Policy and in accordance with national laws, regulations and practices in the field of labour relations, TNCs shall provide to trade unions or other representatives of employees in their entities in each of the countries in which they operate, by appropriate means of communication, the necessary information on the activities dealt with in this Code to enable them to obtain a true and fair view of the performance of the local entity and, where appropriate, the corporation as a whole. Such information shall include, where provided for by national law and practices, *inter alia*, prospects or plans for future development having major economic and social effects on the employees concerned.

(b) Procedures for consultation on matters of mutual concern should be worked out by mutual agreement between entities of TNCs and trade unions or other representatives of employees in accordance with national law and practice.

(c) Information made available pursuant to the provisions of this paragraph should be subject to appropriate safeguards for confidentiality so that no damage is caused to the parties concerned.

TREATMENT OF TRANSNATIONAL CORPORATIONS

47. In all matters relating to the Code, States shall fulfil, in good faith, their obligations under international law.

48. States have the right to regulate the entry and establishment of TNCs including determining the role that such corporations may play in economic and social development and prohibiting or limiting the extent of their presence in specific sectors.

49. TNCs shall receive fair and equitable treatment in the countries in which they operate.

50. Subject to national requirements for maintaining public order and protecting national security and consistent with national constitutions and basic laws, and without prejudice to measures specified in legislation relating to the declared development objectives of the developing countries, entities of TNCs should be entitled to treatment no less favourable than that accorded to domestic enterprises in similar circumstances.

51. The importance of endeavouring to assure the clarity and stability of national policies, laws, regulations and established administrative practices is acknowledged. Laws and

regulations affecting TNCs should be publicly and readily available. To the extent appropriate, relevant information regarding decisions of competent administrative bodies relating to TNCs should be disseminated.

52. Information furnished by TNCs to the authorities in each of the countries in which they operate containing confidential business information shall be accorded reasonable safeguards normally applicable in the area in which the information is provided, particularly to protect its confidentiality.

53. In order to achieve the purposes of paragraph 24 relating to managerial and technical training and employment of nationals of the countries in which TNCs operate, the transfer of those nationals between the entities of a TNC should, subject to the laws and regulations of the countries concerned, be facilitated.

54. TNCs are entitled to transfer all payments legally due. Such transfers are subject to the procedures laid down in the relevant legislation of host countries, such as foreign exchange laws, and to restrictions for a limited period of time emanating from exceptional balance of payment difficulties.

55. It is acknowledged that States have the right to nationalize or expropriate the assets of a TNC operating in their territories, and that adequate compensation is to be paid by the State concerned, in accordance with the applicable legal rules and principles.

56. An entity of a TNC is subject to the jurisdiction of the country in which it operates.

57. Disputes between States and entities of TNCs, which are not amicably settled between the parties, shall be submitted to competent national courts or authorities. Where the parties so agree, or have agreed, such disputes shall be referred to other mutually acceptable or accepted dispute settlement procedures.

58. Where the exercise of jurisdiction over TNCs and their entities by more than one State may lead to conflicts of jurisdiction, States concerned should endeavour to avoid or minimize such conflicts, and the problems to which they give rise by following an approach of moderation and restraint, respecting and accommodating the interests of Other States.

INTERGOVERNMENTAL CO-OPERATION

64. States should not use TNCs as instruments to intervene in the internal or external affairs of other States and should take appropriate action within their jurisdiction to prevent TNCs from engaging in activities referred to in paragraphs 16 and 17 of this Code.

65. Government action on behalf of a TNC operating in another country shall be subject to the principle of exhaustion of local remedies provided in such a country and, when agreed among the Governments concerned, to procedures for dealing with international legal claims. Such action should not in any event amount to the use of any type of coercive measures not consistent with the Charter of the United Nations and the Declaration on Principles of International Law concerning Friendly Relations and Co-operation among States in accordance with the Charter of the United Nations.

# 3. UN: Charter of Economic Rights and Duties of States, 1974

**Commentary**: UNGA Resolution 3281 (1974) emerged in the context of the assertion by newly independent developing States for an NIEO: see also, UNGA Resolutions 3201 & 3202 (1974). On corporations and the NIEO, see UNCTC, 'Progress Made Towards the Establishment of the NIEO: the Role of TNCs', UN Docs E/C.10/74 & E/1980/40. Concomitant with permanent sovereignty over natural resources, governments enjoy the inalienable right to expropriate: *Sedco Inc v NIOC (Second Interlocutory Award)* (1986) 10 *Iran–US CTR* 180: 198. Expropriation must result from the bona fide exercise of law in a non-discriminatory manner for a public purpose and upon the payment of compensation: see, for example, *Amoco International Finance Corp v Iran* (1987) 15 *Iran–US CTR* 189: paras 140–42. As regards the quantum of compensation, developing States, concerned by capacity to pay, espoused the view that governments were entitled to determine an 'appropriate' amount in accordance with national law whereas developed States, concerned by unjust enrichment, argued that customary law required compensation to be prompt, adequate and effective. Article 2(2)(c), which reflects the Calvo doctrine – that foreign investors ought to settle their disputes in the national courts of host States – was accordingly rejected by the developed States. Expropriatory measures will be scrutinised for their substance and effect rather than their form and governmental intent: *Tippetts v TAMS-ATTA* (1985) 6 *Iran-US CTR* 219: 225. On the phenomena of 'creeping' expropriation, see *Starrett Housing Corp v Iran (Interlocutory Award)* (1983) 4 *Iran–US CTR* 122. On environmental regulation amounting to expropriation, see ICSID, *Southern Pacific Properties (Middle East) Ltd v Egypt*, Case No ARB/84/3 (1993): para 154; ICSID, *Metalclad Corp v United Mexican States*, Case No ARB(AF)/97/1 (2000): para 111; ICSID, *Compania del Desarrollo de Santa Elena SA v Republic of Costa Rica*, Case No ARB/96/1 (2000): para 71. See also ICSID, *Marvin Ray Feldman Karpa (CEMSA) v United Mexican States*, Case No ARB(AF)/99/1 (2002): 59.

**Article 2**

1. Every State has and shall freely exercise full permanent sovereignty, including possession, use and disposal, over all its wealth, natural resources and economic activities.
2. Each State has the right:

   (a) To regulate and exercise authority over foreign investment within its national jurisdiction in accordance with its laws and regulations and in conformity with its national objectives and priorities. No State shall be compelled to grant preferential treatment to foreign investment;
   (b) To regulate and supervise the activities of TNCs within its national jurisdiction and take measures to ensure that such activities comply with its laws, rules and

regulations and conform with its economic and social policies. TNCs shall not intervene in the internal affairs of a host State. Every State should, with full regard for its sovereign rights, cooperate with other States in the exercise of the right set forth in this subparagraph;

(c) To nationalize, expropriate or transfer ownership of foreign property, in which case appropriate compensation should be paid by the State adopting such measures, taking into account its relevant laws and regulations and all circumstances that the State considers pertinent. In any case where the question of compensation gives rise to a controversy, it shall be settled under the domestic law of the nationalizing State and by its tribunals, unless it is freely and mutually agreed by all States concerned that other peaceful means be sought on the basis of the sovereign equality of States and in accordance with the principle of free choice of means.

# 4. UN: Declaration on Permanent Sovereignty over Natural Resources, 1962

**Commentary**: As a corollary to territorial sovereignty, UNGA Resolution 1803 (1962) expresses the right of self-determination of peoples and has since been affirmed *inter alia* by the ICCPR and ICESCR (below). The Declaration reflects customary international law: *Texaco v Libya* (1978) 17 *ILM* 1: paras 87–8; *Kuwait v AMINOIL* (1982) 21 *ILM* 976: para 143. However, the scope and implications of the principle of permanent sovereignty over natural resources are still debatable: see further ICJ, the *East Timor Case (Portugal v Australia)* (1995) *ICJ Rep* 90; *Case Concerning Certain Phosphate Lands in Nauru (Nauru v Australia)* (1992) *ICJ Rep* 240.

See further, Schrijver N. (1997), *Sovereignty over Natural Resources: Balancing Rights and Duties*, Cambridge: Cambridge University Press.

2. The exploration, development and disposition of such resources, as well as the import of the foreign capital required for these purposes, should be in conformity with the rules and conditions which the peoples and nations freely consider to be necessary or desirable with regard to the authorization, restriction or prohibition of such activities.
3. In cases where authorization is granted, the capital imported and the earnings on that capital shall be governed by the terms thereof, by the national legislation in force, and by international law. The profits derived must be shared in the proportions freely agreed upon, in each case, between the investors and the recipient State, due care being taken to ensure that there is no impairment, for any reason, of that State's sovereignty over its natural wealth and resources.
4. Nationalization, expropriation or requisitioning shall be based on grounds or reasons of public utility, security or the national interest which are recognized as overriding purely individual or private interests, both domestic and foreign. In such cases the owner shall be paid appropriate compensation, in accordance with the rules in force in the State taking such measures in the exercise of its sovereignty and in accordance with international law. In any case where the question of compensation gives rise to a controversy, the national jurisdiction of the State taking such measures shall be exhausted. However, upon agreement by sovereign States and other parties concerned, settlement of the dispute should be made through arbitration or international adjudication.
6. International co-operation for the economic development of developing countries, whether in the form of public or private capital investments, exchange of goods and services, technical assistance, or exchange of scientific information, shall be such as to further their independent national development and shall be based upon respect for their sovereignty over their natural wealth and resources.

8. Foreign investment agreements freely entered into by or between sovereign States shall be observed in good faith. States and international organizations shall strictly and conscientiously respect the sovereignty of peoples and nations over their natural wealth and resources in accordance with the Charter and the principles set forth in the present resolution.

# 5. Friends of the Earth International: Proposed International Convention on Corporate Accountability, 2002

**Commentary**: Friends of the Earth International (FoEI) is an international network of environmental NGOs spanning some 70 countries. It proposed an international convention at the Johannesburg World Summit on Sustainable Development in 2002: see FoEI (2002), 'Towards Binding Corporate Accountability: A FoEI Position Paper for the WSSD', www.foe.co.uk/resource/briefings/corporate_accountability.pdf). The Convention imposes additional directors' duties with respect to reporting and prior consultation; extends corporate liability; establishes mechanisms for adversely affected stakeholders to obtain redress and secure access to justice; establishes community rights to natural resources; establishes minimum environmental, social, labour and human rights behavioural standards; introduces sanctions; extends the role of the International Criminal Court; improves monopoly controls; and establishes implementation mechanisms.

**Elements of Binding Corporate Accountability**

A framework for binding corporate accountability would (directly or indirectly):

1. Introduce Duties on Corporations
   Impose duties on publicly traded companies, their directors and board-level officers to:

   (i) report fully on their environmental and social impacts, on material risks and on breaches of environmental or social standards (such reports to be independently verified);
   (ii) ensure effective prior consultation with affected communities, including the preparation of Environmental Impact Assessments (EIA) for significant activities and full public access to all relevant documentation; and
   (iii) take the negative environmental and social impacts of their activities fully into account in their corporate decision making.

2. Extend Liability of Corporations
   Extend legal liability to directors for corporate breaches of national environmental and social laws and to directors and corporations for breaches of international laws or agreements.
3. Introduce Rights of Redress for Citizens
   Guarantee legal rights of redress for citizens and communities adversely affected by corporate activities, including:

(i) access for affected people anywhere in the world to pursue litigation where parent corporations claim a 'home' are domiciled or listed;
(ii) provision for legal challenge to company decisions by those with an interest; and
(iii) a legal aid mechanism to provide public funds to support such challenges.

4. Establish Community Rights to Resources
Establish human and community rights of access to and control over the resources needed to enjoy a healthy and sustainable life, including rights:

(i) over common property resources and global commons such as forests, water, fisheries, genetic resources and minerals for indigenous peoples and local communities;
(ii) to prior consultation and veto over corporate projects, against displacement; and
(iii) to compensation or reparation for resources expropriated by or for corporations.

5. Establish Consistently High Standards of Behaviour
Establish (and enforce) high minimum environmental, social, labour and human rights standards for corporate activities – based for example on existing international agreements and reflecting the desirability of social and differential treatment for developing countries.
6. Introduce Sanctions
Establish national legal provision for suitable sanctions for companies in breach of these new duties, rights and liabilities (wherever the breaches occur) such as:

(i) suspending national stock exchange listing;
(ii) withholding access for such companies to public subsidies, guarantees or loans;
(iii) fines; and
(iv) in extreme cases the withdrawal of limited liability status.

7. Extend Role of International Criminal Court
Extend the jurisdiction of the International Criminal Court to try directors and corporations for environmental, social and human rights crimes.
8. Improve Monopoly Controls
Establish international controls over mergers and monopolistic behaviour by corporations.
9. Establish an Implementation Mechanism
Establish a continuing structure and process to monitor and review the implementation and effectiveness of the convention.

# 6. Additional initiatives

## i. OECD: Guidelines for Multinational Enterprises, 2000

**Commentary**: The OECD (www.oecd.org) promotes policies for achieving the highest sustainable economic growth and employment, rising living standards, financial stability and the expansion of multilateral trade (Art 1, OECD Convention, 1960; entry into force 1961). Member States are largely industrialised countries.

The Guidelines for MNEs form part of the 1976 Declaration on International Investment and MNEs, a political commitment to facilitate investment within the OECD. The Declaration additionally included legally binding decisions with respect to national treatment, conflicting requirements and international investment incentives and disincentives (see OECD, 'Declaration and Decisions on International Investment and MNEs: Basic Texts'). The Guidelines are recommendations addressed to MNEs operating in or from adhering countries (the 33 OECD Member States plus Argentina, Brazil and Chile) and constitute voluntary principles and standards for responsible business conduct. The content includes concepts and principles, general policies, disclosure, employment and industrial relations, environmental protection, combating bribery, consumer interests, science and technology, competition and taxation. They have been reviewed on five occasions (1979, 1982, 1984, 1991 and 2000).

Promotion and implementation occurs through National Contact Points, the OECD Committee on International Investment and Multinational Enterprises (CIME) which periodically or at the request of Member States holds exchanges of view, the two OECD advisory committees (the Business and Industry Advisory Committee (BIAC) and the Trade Union Advisory Committee) and NGOs: see Decision of the OECD Council and Procedural Guidance, 2000. The clarifications procedure elucidates how the Guidelines apply to particular business situations and is not intended to assess the propriety of an individual firm's conduct. This has given rise to a form of jurisprudence which guides the interpretation and application of the Guidelines: see OECD CIME, 'The OECD Guidelines for MNEs: Text, Commentary and Clarifications', OECD Doc DAFFE/IME/WPG(2000)15/FINAL (2001). See further, OECD, 'Annual Report on the Guidelines for MNEs', 2003; 'OECD Guidelines for MNEs: A Key Corporate Responsibility Instrument', Policy Brief, 2003; and the roundtables concerning corruption and environmental protection. Additionally noteworthy are the OECD 'Principles of Corporate Governance', 2004.

### ii. UN General Assembly: Millennium Declaration, 2000

**Commentary**: The Millennium Declaration (UN Doc A/55/L2; www.un.org/millennium) establishes many political commitments of varying specificity. International policy objectives relevant to commercial activity include transnational crime (particularly people trafficking, the sale of children, child prostitution and child pornography), the arms trade, foreign direct investment, technology transfer, political participation at the national and international levels, the media role, essential drugs, public–private partnerships for sustainable development and multilateral trade: see paragraphs 9, 25, 26 & 28. In particular:

20. We also resolve:

- To encourage the pharmaceutical industry to make essential drugs more widely available and affordable by all who need them in developing countries.
- To develop strong partnerships with the private sector, and with civil society organizations, in pursuit of development and poverty eradication.

30. We resolve, therefore:

- To give greater opportunities to the private sector, NGOs and civil society in general, to contribute to the realization of the Organization's goals and programmes.

# PART II

# Regional Instruments

# 7. European Parliament: Resolution on EU Standards for European Enterprises operating in Developing Countries: towards a European Code of Conduct, 1999

**Commentary**: The extracts below are derived from the 'Report on European Union standards for European Enterprises operating in developing countries: towards a European Code of Conduct' by Rapporteur Richard Howitt on behalf of the European Parliament's Committee on Development and Cooperation, 17 December 1998, European Parliament Document Reference PE 228.198/DEF. The Explanatory Statement to the Resolution (A4-0508/98 (1999), *OJEC* C104/180) observes that the European Parliament 'has consistently supported the need to develop and monitor codes of conduct for the corporate sector', particularly in the context of human rights (1996), foreign direct investment within third States (1997) and fair trade (1998). It supports PVIs provided that they reflect internationally agreed minimum standards and are accompanied by appropriate monitoring systems. The Parliament has assumed 'a more active role in standard-setting' in the light of the number of European corporations lacking codes relative to their US counterparts, to strengthen its development assistance programme and to assist small businesses to respond to proliferating but inconsistent initiatives. An EU Code 'could create a level playing field, reward best practice and drive up standards in underperforming companies': Report of the EU Committee on Development and Cooperation, A4-0508/98 (1998).

Consultations occurred with industry, trade unions, NGOs, indigenous groups, international organisations, academics and parliamentarians: see the Hearing on EU standards for European Enterprises operating in developing countries, Committee on Development and Cooperation, 1998. The Development Committee also held parliamentary hearings during 2000.

A European Monitoring Platform provides for a complaints procedure and remedial action. It would receive and consider business reports describing compliance with international standards. However, the Platform would not determine working conditions or wages subsisting within developing States which are a matter for negotiation between relevant parties. The Resolution also contemplates *inter alia* ensuring corporate compliance through the European Development Fund (paras 18–21), resort to the European Social Dialogue (22) and strengthening international institutions (27–9). To standardise voluntary codes within Europe and spread their impact beyond market leaders, the Model European Code would apply to any company registered within the EU as well as their contractors, suppliers and licensees, irrespective of the industrial sector. However, the Committee on External Economic Relations considered in 1998 that any code must be strictly voluntary. In its view, 'extraterritorial action ... to arrive at implementing mechanisms and punitive measures against European firms on the basis of individual complaints by their employees in developing countries also appear to be legally doubtful'. Rapporteur Howitt proposed interim resort to Parliamentary auditing mechanisms so that European companies could highlight their positive contributions and make their activities within developing States more transparent. The Code remains under consideration by the EC on the basis that voluntary initiatives do not preclude mandatory regulation: Howitt, Update on progress towards EU standards for European enterprises operating in developing countries, 2000 & 2001; Howitt, 'European Parliament votes to regulate Multinational Companies', Press Release, 31 May 2002.

The European Council has recently reaffirmed 'the EU's commitment to actively promoting corporate responsibility and accountability including through the full development and effective implementation of intergovernmental agreements and measures, international initiatives and public–private partnerships, and appropriate national regulations': EU General Affairs Council (2002), 'Council Conclusions on Development: Follow-up of the WSSD', Press Release No 12067/02: para 14. See further, EC, Green Paper on Promoting a European Framework for Corporate Social Responsibility, COM/2001/366/FINAL & European Council Resolution C39/3 (2003) on Corporate Social Responsibility.

## The European Parliament

*Voluntary Codes of Conduct*

1. Welcomes and encourages voluntary initiatives by business and industry, trade unions and coalitions of NGOs to promote codes of conduct, with effective and independent monitoring and verification, and stakeholder participation in the development, implementation and monitoring of Codes of Conduct; emphasises, however, that codes of conduct cannot replace or set aside national or international rules or the jurisdiction of governments; considers that codes of conduct must not be used as instruments for putting MNEs beyond the scope of governmental and judicial scrutiny;
2. Stresses that the content of a code, the process by which it is determined and implemented, must involve those in developing countries who are covered by it;
3. Believes that special attention must be paid to implementing codes in respect of workers in the informal sector, sub-contractors and in free trade zones, notably concerning recognition of the right to form independent trade unions; and against corporate collusion in violations of human rights;
4. Believes that a code should recognise the responsibilities of companies operating in conflict situations by ensuring that a Code covers the Amnesty International Human Rights Principles for Companies, Human Rights Watch recommendations to companies, and the UN Code of Conduct for Law Enforcement Officials;
5. Stresses that Indigenous peoples and their communities should benefit from such codes of conduct recognising their important role for sustainable development;
6. Welcomes the fact that in the present context of globalisation of trade flows and communications as well as of increased vigilance of NGOs and consumer associations, it seems to be increasingly in the own interest of multinational undertakings to adopt

and implement voluntary codes of conduct, if they want to avoid negative publicity campaigns, sometimes leading to boycotts, public relation costs and consumer complaints;

7. Considers that enterprises should contribute economically to the development process in the affected areas, but they should not be allowed to implement social or economic projects, which should be the responsibility of the state;
8. Recommends that an 'evolutionary approach' be weighted towards a continuous and gradual improvement of standards; takes the view that this must reflect the enterprises' own obligations to make improvements;

*European Enforcement Mechanism*

9. Reiterates its request to the Commission and the Council to make proposals, as a matter of urgency, to develop the right legal basis for establishing a European multilateral framework governing companies' operations worldwide and organise for this purpose consultations with those groups of society who would be covered by the code;
10. Recommends, that a model Code of Conduct for European Businesses should comprise existing Minimum Applicable international standards:

    (i) the ILO Tripartite Declaration of Principles concerning MNEs and Social Policy and
    (ii) the OECD Guidelines for MNEs;
    (iii) in the field of labour rights: the ILO core Conventions;
    (iv) in the field of human rights: the UN Declaration and different Covenants on Human Rights;
    (v) in the field of minority and indigenous peoples' rights: ILO Convention no. 169, Chapter 26 of Agenda 21, 1994 Draft UN Declaration on the Rights of Indigenous Peoples, UN Declaration on the Elimination of All Forms of Racial Discrimination;
    (vi) in the field of environmental standards: UN Convention on Biological Diversity, the Rio Declaration and the European Commission proposal for the development of a code of conduct for European logging companies (COM(89)0410);
    (vii) in the field of security services: Common Article 3 of the Geneva Conventions and Protocol II, and the UN Code of Conduct for Law Enforcement Officials;
    (viii) in the field of corruption: the OECD anti-bribery convention and the European Commission communication on legislative measures against corruption (COM(97) 0192/FIN);

    but should also include consideration of new international standards which are currently developed;
11. Calls on the Commission to study the possibility of setting up a European Monitoring Platform (EMP), ( already proposed by some trade associations) in close collaboration with the social partners, NGOs from North and South and representatives of indigenous and local communities; with the purpose of granting workers and the local population in host countries anywhere in the world some form of protection from oppression, abuse and exploitation and aim for socially and environmentally sustainable operations in countries where national laws are inadequate or not enforced and international laws and conventions not ratified;

12. Recommends that an EMP would consist of independent experts and a board of representatives from European business, international trade unions, and international environmental and human rights organisations; believes that an independent monitoring and verification body could only prove useful if it is highly skilled, if it has appropriate procedures and, above all, if it is widely accepted as being objective and impartial;
13. Recommends that business and industry provide dissemination of information of their voluntary initiatives and conduct to the EMP so that their compliance with a European Code of conduct, international standards and private voluntary codes of practice (if adopted) could be properly assessed;
14. Recommends that the EMP promote dialogue on standards met by European enterprises, the identification of best practice, together with being open to receive complaints about corporate conduct from community and/or workers' representatives and the private sector in the host country, NGOs or consumer organisations, from individual victims or from any other source;

*Other Actions at the European Level*

24. Request the European Council confirm the interpretation in the 1968 Brussels Convention that, for cases of basic duty of care, legal action may be taken against a company in the EU country where its registered office is, in respect of any third country throughout the world, and calls on the Commission to study the possibility of enacting legislation, which open European courts to lawsuits involving damage done by MNEs, thus creating a precedence for developing customary international law in the field of corporate abuse;
25. Calls on the Commission to ensure that consideration is given, with an appropriate legal base, to incorporating core labour, environmental and human rights international standards when reviewing European company law including the new EU Directive on a European-incorporated company, together with reporting requirements on social and environmental performance; further calls for an appropriate consultation process with the social partners and NGOs on such a process;
26. Calls on the Commission to bring forward proposals for a system of incentives for companies complying with international standards developed in close consultation and cooperation with consumer groups and human rights and environmental NGOs – such as in procurement, fiscal incentives, access to EU financial assistance and publication in the *Official Journal*;

*Actions within International Institutions*

28. Strongly recommends that in connection with negotiations on investment agreements which could be concluded in either the OECD or the WTO, the European Union not only contributes to establishing the legitimate rights of European enterprises, but also their duties in the field of environment, labour and human rights; strongly supports a mechanism for systematic monitoring of MNEs and for individual complaint against them to be incorporated in such an agreement . . .

# 8. Additional initiatives

## i. Organisation of American States: Permanent Council Resolution 154 on the Behaviour of Transnational Enterprises Operating in the Region and the Need for a Code of Conduct to be Observed by Such Enterprises, 1975

**Commentary**: Established in 1948, the OAS promotes inter-American cooperation between its member States with respect to democracy, governance, human rights, peace and security, trade, economic development and corruption. Resolution 154 (167/75) was unanimously approved (OAS Document OEA/Ser G, CP/RES 154) and arose in response to improper commercial interference in political affairs, bribery and other illegal activity. The Resolution condemned such acts, initiated information exchange and called for 'a study of the principles that should govern the activities of transnational enterprises for the purpose of preparing a draft code of conduct which such enterprises should observe' (para 2).

## ii. Eastern and Southern African States Preferential Trade Area: Charter on a Regime of Multinational Industrial Enterprises, 1990

**Commentary**: Article 4, Annex VIII of the Treaty for the Establishment of the Preferential Trade Area (PTA) for Eastern and Southern African States (21 *ILM* 479 (1982)) provides *inter alia* that Member States will encourage the establishment of multinational industrial enterprises (MIEs). Formulated over seven years, the Charter seeks to generate investment capital and closer economic integration between Eastern and Southern African States through regional companies. Key provisions include establishment (Article 5), incentives and guarantees (Articles 15 & 16) and uniquely a special development tax (Article 19).

## iii. Andean Group: Commission: Decisions 220 (1987), 226 (1989) and 292 (1991) on a Uniform Code on Andean Multinational Enterprises

**Commentary**: This series of decisions was intended to encourage the formation of bi- or multinational enterprises through the provision of appropriate incentives, particularly with respect to double taxation and employment.

# PART III

# National Instruments

# 9. USA: Alien Tort Claims Act, 1789

**Commentary**: Initial cases under the ATCA (28 *USC* s1350 (1994)) established the civil liability of individuals, principally former or serving government officials: *Filartiga v Pena-Irala* 630 *F.2d* 876 (2d Cir 1980); *In re Estate of Ferdinand E. Marcos Human Rights Litigation* 32 *ILM* 106 (1993) (CA 9th Cir). *Kadic v Karadzic* 70 *F.3d* 232 (2d Cir 1995) established the liability of private actors. The blossoming jurisprudence contemplates US and foreign corporations possibly being held civilly liable for human rights violations and environmental damage committed by overseas subsidiaries: see *Abdullahi v Pfizer Inc* 2002 US Dist LEXIS 17436 (SDNY 2002) vacated and remanded by 77 *Fed App* 48 (2d Cir 2003); *Aldana Villeda v Fresh Del Monte Produce Inc* 305 *F. Supp 2d* 1285 (SD Fla 2003); *Alomang v Freeport McMoRan Inc* No 96-2139 LEXIS 15908 (ED La 1996); *Amlon Metals Inc v FMC Corp* 775 *F. Supp* 668 (SDNY 1991); *Aquinda v Texaco Inc* 850 *F. Supp* 282 (SDNY 1994), 945 *F. Supp* 625 (SDNY 1996) & 303 *F.3d* 470 (2d Cir 2002); *Bano v Union Carbide Corp* 273 *F.3d* 120 (2d Cir 2001) & 2003 US Dist LEXIS 4097; *Beanal v Freeport-McMoRan Inc* 969 *F. Supp* 362 (ED La 1997) & 197 *F.3d* 161 (5th Cir 1999); *Bigio v Coca-Cola Co* 239 *F.3d* 440 (2d Cir 2000); *Bowoto v Chevron* 2004 US Dist LEXIS 4603 (ND Cal 2004); *Dow Chemical Co v Castro Alfaro* 786 *SW 2d* 674 (Tex SC 1990); *Eastman Kodak Company v Kavlin* 978 *F. Supp* 1078 (SD Fla 1997); *Estate of Rodriguez v Drummond Co* 256 *F. Supp 2d* 1250 (ND Ala 2003); *Flores v Southern Peru Copper Corporation* 253 *F. Supp 2d* 510 (SDNY 2002) & 343 *F.3d* 140 (2d Cir 2003); *John Doe & Ors v Exxon Mobil Corp & Ors* Civ No 01-1357 (DC DC 2001); *Jota v Texaco Inc* 157 *F.3d* 153 (2d Cir 1998); *Khulumani v Barclays* (Case No 02-CV5952 (SDNY 2002); *Maugein v Newmont Mining Corp* 298 *F. Supp 2d* 1124 (D.Colo 2004); *Mendonca v Tidewater Inc* 159 *F. Supp 2d* 299 (ED La 2001) rehearing and writ denied in 862 *So. 2d* 505 (La App 4th Cir 2004); *Ntsebeza et al v Citigroup et al* (SDNY DC 2004); *Presbyterian Church of Sudan et al v Talisman Energy Inc & the Republic of Sudan* 244 *F. Supp 2d* 289 (SDNY 2003); *Sarei v Rio Tinto PLC* 221 *F. Supp 2d* 1116 (CD Cal 2002); *Sequihua v Texaco Inc* 847 *F. Supp* 61 (SD Tex 1994); *Sinaltrainal v Coca-Cola Co* 256 *F. Supp 2d* 1345 (SD Fla 2003) & 16 *Fla L Weekly Fed D* 388 (SD Fla 2003); *Wiwa v Royal Dutch Petroleum Company* 226 *F.3d* 88 (2nd Cir 2000) cert den 532 *US* 941 (2001). See as a result of *Sosa v Alvarez-Machain et al* 331 *F.3d* 604 (9th Cir 2003) & 542 *US* (2004) (US): *In re Agent Orange Product Liability Litigation*, No. 04-CV-400, 2005 WL 555582 (EDNY 10 Mar 2005).

**Sec. 1350 – Alien's Action for Tort**

The district courts shall have original jurisdiction of any civil action by an alien for a tort only, committed in violation of the law of nations or a treaty of the United States.

# 10. USA: Massachusetts State Act Regulating State Contracts with Companies doing Business with or in Burma (Myanmar), 1996

**Commentary**: The Massachusetts Act (Massachusetts General Laws Chapter 7, s22G-22M) illustrates the leverage exerted by government procurement over commercial behaviour. The technique was also used against US corporations to address South African apartheid. The Act contemplated a restricted purchase list (section 22J) and annual reporting (22M). Under section 22L, contracts violating these provisions would become void. However, the Act only applied to those entered into after its entry into force, thereby leaving existing contracts unaffected until renewal. The National Foreign Trade Council successfully challenged the constitutionality of this Act for infringing the federal foreign affairs power, violating the foreign commerce clause and subverting federal legislation: *National Foreign Trade Council v Baker* 26 *F. Supp 2d* 287 (D Mass 1998); *National Foreign Trade Council v Natsios* 181 *F.3d* 38 (1st Cir 1999); *Crosby v National Foreign Trade Council* 2000 US LEXIS 4153 (US Sup Ct). Additionally noteworthy is that this Act was challenged by the EC and Japan in 1997 as inconsistent with the WTO's Agreement on Government Procurement. Although the WTO's dispute settlement mechanism was invoked during 1998, the panel was suspended in 1999 on account of the Supreme Court's decision.

**Section 1**

*Section 22G*

For the purposes of sections twenty-two H to twenty-two M, inclusive, the following words shall, unless the context indicates otherwise, have the following meanings:

'Comparable low bid or offer': a responsive and responsible bid or offer which is no more than ten percent greater than the lowest bid or offer submitted for goods or a service.

'Distribution agreement': an agreement to guarantee a contract for the supply of goods or a service.

'Doing business with Burma (Myanmar)':

(a) having a principal place of business, place of incorporation or its corporate headquarters in Burma (Myanmar) or having any operations, leases, franchises, majority-owned subsidiaries, distribution agreements, or any other similar agreements in Burma (Myanmar), or being the majority-owned subsidiary, licensee or franchise of such a person;

(b) providing financial services to the government of Burma (Myanmar), including providing direct loans, underwriting government securities, providing any consulting advice or assistance, providing brokerage services, acting as a trustee or escrow agent, or otherwise acting as an agent pursuant to a contractual agreement;
(c) promoting the importation or sale of gems, timber, oil, gas or other related products, commerce in which is largely controlled by the government of Burma (Myanmar), from Burma (Myanmar);
(d) providing any goods or services to the government of Burma (Myanmar).

'Essential': necessary in order that an agency or authority may perform its mission, there being no substitute, to avoid irreparable harm to agency or authority programs.

'Franchise': authorization by a person to sell his products.

'License': permission granted by a person to another, or to the government of Burma (Myanmar), to exercise a certain privilege or to carry on a particular business.

'Person': any individual and any partnership, firm, association, corporation, or other entity, or their subsidiaries.

*Section 22H*

(a) Except as otherwise provided in this section, a state agency, a state authority, the house of representatives or the state senate may not procure goods or services from any person listed on the restricted purchase list maintained by the secretary, or who is determined through affidavit or through other reliable methods to meet the criteria for so being listed.
(b) A state agency, a state authority, the house of representatives or the state senate may procure goods or services from a person who is on or who is so determined to meet the criteria of the restricted purchase list only after certifying in writing to the secretary or, in the case of a state authority, to the chief operating officer that:

    (1) the procurement is essential; and
    (2) compliance with paragraph (a) would eliminate the only bid or offer, or would result in inadequate competition.

(c) In any solicitation, a state agency, a state authority, the house of representatives or the senate shall provide ample notice of the requirements of this section. Prior to reviewing responses to bid documents for any procurements, or, if there are none, prior to entering into any contractual arrangement, the awarding authority shall obtain from such person seeking a contract a statement, under the pains and penalties of perjury, from an authorized representative of such person seeking a contract, on a form to be provided by the awarding authority, declaring the nature and extent to which said person is engaging in activities which would subject said person to inclusion on the restricted purchase list.
(d) In any procurement that includes bidders or offerors who are on or meet the criteria of the restricted purchase list, the awarding authority may award the contract to a person who is on or who meets the criteria of the restricted purchase list only if there is no comparable low bid or offer by a person who is not on the restricted purchase list.

(e) A person with operations in Burma (Myanmar) for the sole purpose of reporting the news, or solely for the purpose of providing goods or services for the provision of international telecommunications shall not be subject to the provisions of sections twenty-two G to twenty-two M, inclusive.

*Section 22I*
Notwithstanding the provisions of section twenty-two H, a state agency may purchase medical supplies intended to preserve or prolong life or to cure, prevent, or ameliorate diseases, including hospital, nutritional, diagnostic, pharmaceutical and non-prescription products specifically manufactured to satisfy identified health care needs, or for which there is no medical substitute. The determination of whether no medical substitute exists shall be made by the state agency requiring the supply, pursuant to general standards of good medical and professional practice. That state agency shall give notice to the state purchasing agent in writing, certifying compliance with this exemption, said notice and certification being sufficient to allow the purchase of medical supplies under this exemption . . .

*Section 22J*
(a) The secretary shall establish and maintain a restricted purchase list. The restricted purchase list shall contain the names of all persons currently doing business with Burma (Myanmar).
(b) In establishing the restricted purchase list, the secretary shall consult United Nations reports, resources of the Investor Responsibility Research Center and the Associates to Develop Democratic Burma, and other reliable sources. The secretary shall also place the name of any person who, in the statement described in section twenty-two H, declared that he meets the criteria for being so listed.
(c) The restricted purchase list shall be updated at least once every three months.
(d) The secretary shall provide the lists to all state agencies and state authorities and to the house of representatives and to the senate.

*Section 22K*
The secretary is hereby authorized and directed to promulgate regulations to assure the timely and effective implementation of sections twenty-two G to twenty-two M, inclusive.

*Section 22L*
Any contract entered into in violation of sections twenty-two G to twenty-two M, inclusive, shall be void.

*Section 22M*
Annually on or before January first, the secretary shall file a report with the clerks of the senate and the house of representatives detailing compliance with sections twenty-two G to twenty-two M, inclusive.

**Section 2**
Subsection (a) of section 40F of said chapter 7, as appearing in the 1994 Official Edition, is hereby amended by adding the following paragraph: It shall be the policy of the commonwealth that the commissioner shall not sell, rent, or dispose of any real property including but not limited to granting the right to lay, construct, maintain, or operate pipelines through,

over, across, or under land, water, park, reservation or highway of the commonwealth, its agencies or its political subdivisions, to any person doing business in or with Burma (Myanmar). The commissioner may sell, rent, or dispose of said property or grant said rights to said person only after certifying in writing to the speaker of the house of representatives and president of the senate that such action is essential to protect the health and safety of the public.

**Section 3**

The provisions of this act shall apply to contracts entered into after the effective date of this act. Any existing contract shall remain in full force and effect and not be subject to the provisions of this act until such time as the renewal of the contractual agreement.

# 11. UK: Performance of Companies and Government Departments (Reporting) Bill, 2004

**Commentary**: Coinciding with the UK government's proposals for large companies to annually publish an operating and financial review (OFR), Amnesty International (UK) and the Corporate Responsibility Coalition (CORE) introduced the document below as a private member's bill. Although it enjoyed a second reading in 2004 and has been debated several times by the House of Commons, the Bill has not yet passed into law. The Bill is an illustration of producing annual reports and expanding directors' duties with respect to the social, environmental and economic impacts of commercial operations. Section 5 identified those companies required to publish operating and financial reviews and section 4 required approval from the board of directors.

**1. Operating and Financial Review**

1. The directors of a company must, for each financial year of the company in which it is a major company, prepare an operating and financial review.
2. The directors must secure that the information contained in the operating and financial review is such that the review will, in their opinion, achieve the review objective.
3. The review objective is: providing such information as will permit the members of the company, as of the approval date, to make an informed assessment of:

   (a) the company's operations;
   (b) its financial position;
   (c) its future strategies and prospects; and
   (d) its impacts on the environment and on any communities in which the company operates . . .

**2. Compulsory Content of Operating and Financial Review**

1. In order to achieve the review objective, an operating and financial review must contain at least the core elements.
2. The core elements are:

   (a) a statement of the company's business in the financial year to which the operating and financial review relates;
   (b) a fair review of the performance during the financial year and of the position of the company at the end of that year; and

(c) a fair projection of the prospects for the company's business and of events which will, or are likely to, substantially affect that business.

**3. Duty to Consider Including Other Matters in Operating and Financial Review**

1. If the directors of a company are required to form an opinion for the purposes of section 1(2), they must consider whether the inclusion of information about any matter mentioned in subsection (2) is necessary in order to achieve the review objective.

2. The matters are:

(a) the management structure of the company;
(b) receipts from, and returns to, members of the company in the financial year to which the operating and financial review relates in relation to shares held by them;
(c) the impact of the company's operations, policies, products and procurement practices in relation to employment;
(d) the impact of the company's operations, policies, products and procurement practices on the environment;
(e) the impact of the company's operations, policies, products and procurement practices on social and community issues;
(f) the company's performance, in the financial year to which the operating and financial review relates, in carrying out the policies mentioned in paragraphs (c) to (e); and
(g) matters not falling within the preceding paragraphs which affect, or may affect, the company's reputation . . .

**8. Directors' Duties**

A director of a company must act in accordance with:

(a) the company's constitution, and
(b) decisions taken under the constitution (or by the company, or any class of members, under any enactment or rule of law as to means of taking company or class decisions), and must exercise his powers for their proper purpose.

**9. Promotion of Company's Objectives**

1. A director of a company must in any given case:

(a) act in the way he decides, in good faith, would be most likely to promote the success of the company for the benefit of its members as a whole (excluding anything which would breach his duty under section 8);
(b) in deciding what would be most likely to promote that success, take account in good faith of all the material factors that it is practicable in the circumstances for him to identify; and
(c) take all reasonable steps to minimise the impact of the company's impact on the communities it affects and on the environment.

2. In this section 'the material factors' means:

   (a) the likely consequences (short and long term) of the actions open to the director, so far as a person of care and skill would consider relevant; and
   (b) all such other factors as a person of care and skill would consider relevant, including such of the matters in subsection (3) below as he would consider so.

3. Those matters are:

   (a) the company's need to foster its business relationships, including those with its employees and suppliers and the customers for its products or services;
   (b) its need to have regard to the impact of its operations on the communities affected and on the environment;
   (c) its need to maintain a reputation for high standards of business conduct; and
   (d) its need to achieve outcomes that are fair as between its members . . .

# 12. Australia: Corporate Code of Conduct Bill, 2000

**Commentary**: This private member's bill arose in response to the *Baia Mare* spill by an Australian company in Papua New Guinea. Some 43 organisations lodged submissions with the Australian Parliamentary Joint Statutory Committee on Corporations and Securities. Although 'drafted with the best of intentions', the Committee considered this Bill to be 'impracticable and unwarranted' and recommended abandoning such an 'unnecessary and unworkable' initiative: 'Report of the Corporate Code of Conduct Bill 2000', Canberra, 2001: para 4.5. Several members of that Committee concluded that 'its time has not yet come': Comments by Labour Members on the Corporate Code of Conduct Bill, 2000. Others concluded that 'while the current Bill needs amendment, there is a demonstrated need for it': Australian Democrats, 'Minority Report on the Corporate Code of Conduct Bill 2000': para 89. The non-adoption of this Code mirrors the fate of the Corporate Code of Conduct Bill 2000 (US) brought before the US House of Representatives by Congresswoman McKinney. This draft contemplated preferential government procurement, withdrawing financial assistance and prospective corporate liability within US courts.

## Part 1 Preliminary

*3. Objects of Act*

1. The objects of this Act are:

   (a) to impose environmental, employment, health and safety and human rights standards on the conduct of Australian corporations or related corporations which employ more than 100 persons in a foreign country; and
   (b) to require such corporations to report on their compliance with the standards imposed by this Act; and
   (c) to provide for the enforcement of those standards.

2. To avoid doubt, a body corporate to which this Act applies is not required to take any action to meet the requirements of this Act in respect of its operations in a foreign country that it would not be required to take in respect of its operations in Australia.

*4. Extraterritorial Operation*

This Act applies outside Australia but does not apply in relation to any corporation outside Australia unless that corporation employs or engages the services of 100 or more persons in a country other than Australia and is:

(a) a trading or financial corporation formed within the limits of the Commonwealth; or
(b) a holding company of such a corporation; or
(c) a subsidiary of such a corporation; or
(d) a subsidiary of a holding company of such a corporation.

6. *Interpretation*
In this Act, unless the contrary intention appears:

basic needs means nutritious food, clothing, health care, education, potable water, child care, transportation, housing and energy.

ecosystem means a dynamic complex of plant, animal and micro-organism communities and their non-living environment interacting as a functional unit.

environment includes:

(a) ecosystems and their constituent parts, including people and communities; and
(b) natural and physical resources; and
(c) the qualities and characteristics of locations, places and areas; and
(d) the social, economic and cultural aspects of a thing mentioned in paragraph (a), (b) or (c).

forced or compulsory labour means all work or service which is exacted from any person under the threat of any penalty, and for which that person has not offered himself or herself voluntarily, but does not include any work or service:

(a) of a purely military character exacted by virtue of a law providing for compulsory military service; or
(b) which forms part of the normal civic obligations of the citizens of a self-governing country; or
(c) required to be performed as a consequence of a conviction in a court of law, provided that the work or service is to be performed only under the control of a public authority; or
(d) required in cases of emergency, famine, war or serious threat.

industrial undertaking means:

(a) mines, quarries and other works for the extraction of minerals, including oil and gas, from the earth or seabed; or
(b) industries in which articles are manufactured, altered, cleaned, repaired, finished, adapted for sale, broken up or demolished, or in which materials are transformed; or
(c) the generation or transmission of electricity; or
(d) the distribution of gas or water; or
(e) the construction, reconstruction, maintenance, repair, alteration or demolition of any building or structure; or
(f) the transport of passengers or goods by road, rail, air, sea or inland waterway, including the handling of goods at docks, quays, wharves and warehouses.

living wage means a wage sufficient to meet the basic needs of a family of two adults and three children in the country or region they are resident in.

minimum international labour standards means standards contained in the following International Labor Organization Conventions as agreed under Australian law:

(a) Freedom of Association and Protection of the Right to Organize Convention (No. 87);
(b) Right to Organize and Collective Bargaining Convention (No. 98);
(c) Forced Labour Convention (No. 29);
(d) Abolition of Forced Labour Convention (No. 105)
(e) Discrimination (Employment and Occupation) Convention (No. 111);
(f) Equal Remuneration Convention (No. 100);
(g) Minimum Age Convention (No. 138);
(h) Occupational Safety and Health (No. 155).

precautionary principle means that lack of full scientific certainty should not be used as a reason for postponing a measure to prevent degradation of the environment where there are threats of serious or irreversible environmental damage.

## Part 2 Corporate Codes of Conduct

7. *Environmental standards*
1. An overseas corporation which undertakes any activity in a place must take all reasonable measures to prevent any material adverse effect on the environment in and around that place from that activity.
2. Without limiting subsection (1), an overseas corporation must:

   (a) at least once in every period of 12 months, collect and evaluate information regarding the environmental impacts of its activities; and
   (b) establish objectives for the measurement of its environmental performance; and
   (c) monitor and assess its compliance with those objectives; and
   (d) provide timely information to its employees and to members of the public in any place in which it undertakes activities on the actual and potential environmental impacts of the activities of the corporation; and
   (e) have appropriate policies on matters of environmental safety, including (where applicable) the handling of hazardous materials and the prevention and control of environmental accidents; and
   (f) undertake environmental impact assessments of all new developments, including providing an opportunity for public comment on the assessment; and
   (g) have regard to the precautionary principle in carrying out the actions mentioned in paragraphs (a) to (f).

8. *Health and Safety Standards*
1. An overseas corporation must take all reasonable measures to promote the health and safety of its workers.
2. Without limiting subsection (1), an overseas corporation must:

(a) provide a safe and healthy workplace for its employees; and
(b) provide satisfactory sanitary conditions at a workplace; and
(c) not require its employees to work for more than 5 consecutive hours without a break of at least 20 minutes; and
(d) not require its employees to work for more than 12 hours each day; and
(e) not require its employees to work more than 48 hours each week without the agreement of the employees; and
(f) have appropriate policies for responding to an accident or medical emergency at a workplace; and
(g) provide adequate education and training to employees in health and safety matters, including the prevention of accidents.

*9. Employment Standards*

1. An overseas corporation must not use or obtain the benefit of any forced or compulsory labour.
2. An overseas corporation must not use or obtain the benefit of the labour of any child under the age of fourteen years in any public or private industrial undertaking.
3. An overseas corporation must:

(a) as a minimum, pay all its workers a living wage; and
(b) not dismiss a worker for reasons of illness or accident; and
(c) respect the freedom of its workers to associate; and
(d) respect the right of its workers to organise independently and bargain collectively; and
(e) enable any complaints about conditions of labour to be forwarded to independent authorities; and
(f) comply with minimum international labour standards.

*10. Human Rights Standards*

1. Subject to subsection (2), in any matter which relates to the employment or occupation of a person, an overseas corporation must not distinguish, exclude or prefer a person on the basis of race, colour, sex, sexuality, religion, political opinion, national extraction or social origin if this has the effect of nullifying or impairing equality of opportunity or treatment in that employment or occupation.
2. Subsection (1) does not apply to any distinction, exclusion or preference:

(a) in respect of a particular job based on the inherent requirements of the job; or
(b) in connection with employment as a member of the staff of an institution that is conducted in accordance with the doctrines, tenets, beliefs or teachings of a particular religion or creed, where that distinction, exclusion or preference is made in good faith in order to avoid injury to the religious susceptibilities of adherents of that religion or creed; or
(c) in connection with established governmental policies which specifically promote greater equality of employment opportunity.

*12. Duty to Observe Consumer Health and Safety Standards*

1. An overseas corporation must ensure that any goods or services which it provides satisfy the required standards for consumer health and safety for those goods or services in Australia and in any country in which it undertakes activities.

2. An overseas corporation must take all reasonable measures to prevent any serious threat to public health in any country in which it undertakes activities which might occur from the consumption or use of products made by that corporation.
3. An overseas corporation must take all reasonable measures to remove any serious threat to public health in any country in which it undertakes activities which has occurred from the consumption or use of products made by that corporation.

*13. Consumer Protection and Trade Practices Standards*

1. An overseas corporation must not, in any country in which it undertakes activities, engage in any conduct that is misleading or deceptive or which is likely to mislead or deceive.
2. An overseas corporation must not, in any country in which it undertakes activities, enter into or carry out or give effect to any anti-competitive agreement with another person.

## Part 3 Reporting

*14. Reports to Australian Securities and Investments Commission*

1. Before 31 August each year, an overseas corporation (the corporation) must lodge with the Australian Securities and Investments Commission a Code of Conduct Compliance Report in accordance with subsection (2).
2. Subject to subsection (3), a Code of Conduct Compliance Report must include:

    (g) a statement of the environmental impact, prepared by an independent auditor, of the activities of the corporation in each country (other than Australia) in which the corporation undertakes activities; and
    (h) a statement of any foreseeable risk factors that might arise as a result of the activities of the corporation in each country in which it operates (other than Australia); and
    (i) a statement of any contraventions of standards or laws relating to the environment, employment, health and safety and human rights by the corporation in each country in which it operates (other than Australia); and
    (j) a statement of the social, ethical and environmental policies of the corporation; and
    (k) any other matter relevant to the environmental, employment, health and safety and human rights standards observed by the corporation.

3. If a corporation is required to lodge reports with the Australian Securities and Investments Commission apart from under this section, the corporation is not required to include in a report under subsection (2) any information that it has provided to the Commission in another report.
4. A corporation which, without reasonable excuse, fails to lodge a Code of Conduct Compliance Report is guilty of an offence punishable on conviction by a fine not exceeding 2000 penalty units.
5. If a corporation contravenes subsection (4) and:

    (a) an executive officer of the corporation knew that, or was reckless or negligent as to whether, the contravention would occur; and

(b) the officer was in a position to influence the conduct of the corporation in relation to the contravention; and
(c) the officer failed to take all reasonable steps to prevent the contravention; the officer contravenes this subsection.

6. An executive officer who is guilty of an offence under subsection (5) is liable, on conviction, to pay a fine not exceeding 1000 penalty units.

*15. Reports to the Parliament*

1. The Australian Securities and Investments Commission must prepare an annual report on compliance with the provisions of this Act.
2. The Australian Securities and Investments Commission must forward a copy of the annual report prepared under subsection (1) to the Treasurer before 31 December in each year.
3. The Treasurer must cause a copy of the annual report forwarded under subsection (2) to be laid before each House of the Parliament within 14 sitting days of that House after receiving the report.

## Part 4 Enforcement

*16. Civil penalties*

1. Conduct which contravenes a provision in Part 2 renders an overseas corporation liable to proceedings for the recovery of a civil penalty.
2. If an overseas corporation contravenes a provision in Part 2 and:

(a) an executive officer of the corporation knew that, or was reckless or negligent as to whether, the contravention would occur; and
(b) the officer was in a position to influence the conduct of the corporation in relation to the contravention; and
(c) the officer failed to take all reasonable steps to prevent the contravention; the executive officer also contravenes that provision . . .

*17. Civil actions*

1. Where an overseas corporation contravenes a provision of Part 2, any person who suffers loss or damage as a result may bring an action in the Federal Court of Australia.
2. Where an overseas corporation contravenes a provision of Part 2, any person who is reasonably likely to suffer loss or damage as a result may bring an action in the Federal Court of Australia.
3. If the Federal Court of Australia is satisfied that a person has suffered loss or damage as a result of a contravention of a provision of Part 2, the Court may:

(a) grant an injunction to prevent any further loss or damage; and
(b) make an order for compensation.

4. If the Federal Court is satisfied that a person is reasonably likely to suffer loss or damage as a result of a contravention of a provision of Part 2, the Court may grant an injunction to prevent any further loss or damage.

5. In this section, person means any person, whether resident in Australia or elsewhere, and includes any body corporate or association of persons.
6. An action may be taken under subsection (1) or (2), on behalf of a person to whom either subsection applies, by a body corporate or association of persons whose principal objects include protection of the public interest.

# PART IV

# Instruments for the International Protection of Human Rights

# 13. UN: Norms on the Responsibilities of Transnational Corporations and Other Business Enterprises with Regard to Human Rights, 2003

**Commentary**: In 1998 the UN Sub-Commission on the Promotion and Protection of Human Rights began assessing commercial impacts upon human rights through a Working Group on the Working Methods and Activities of TNCs: Sub-Commission Resolution 1998/8. Since it was considered 'appropriate to examine all these questions in a broader framework' (UN Doc E/CN.4/Sub.2/1998/6: para 28), consideration was given to formulating a 'new comprehensive set of rules' representing expected standards of corporate behaviour (UN Doc E/CN.4/Sub.2/1996/12: para 74). All interested constituencies including business were invited to participate: UN Doc E/CN.4/Sub.2/1999/9: paras 5, 37. Individual firms and corporate coalitions were prepared to contribute to an authoritative set of principles if this would 'establish a level playing field for business competition' (UN Doc E/CN.4/Sub.2/2002/WG.2/WP.1/Add.1: paras 16, 60). Differences of view arose with respect to the scope of application, legal nature, title, purpose and manner of implementation: UN Docs E/CN.4/Sub.2/2001/WG.2/WP.1/Add.3 (2001) and E/CN.4/Sub.2/2002/13.

The resulting Norms (UN Doc E/CN.4/Sub.2/2003/12/Rev.2 (2003)) draw upon ILO Conventions, human rights treaties and intergovernmental guidelines as well as industry or commodity group initiatives, framework agreements between multinationals and workers' organisations, self-imposed corporate codes and model guidelines from both NGOs and trade unions: UN Doc E/CN.4/Sub.2/2001/WG.2/WP.1/Add.2 (2001). They were approved by the Sub-Commission through Resolution 2003/16: UN Doc E/CN.4/Sub.2/2003/L.11; see further, www.ohchr.org). The Norms seek to identify contemporary expectations, rationalise existing standards and enable the integration of human rights principles into commercial decision-making: see further, Commentary, UN Doc E/CN.4/Sub.2/2003/38/Rev.2. The UN Human Rights Commission affirmed that the Norms have no legal standing and observed that the Sub-Commission does not perform any monitoring function in relation to them: UN Doc E/CN.4/2004/L.11/Add.7 and Decision 2004/116. The norm-generating effect of this instrument therefore remains to be seen in the light of further consultation with all interested parties. See further, UNHCHR (2005), Report on the responsibilities of transnational corporations and related business enterprises with regard to human rights, UN Doc E/CN.4/2005/91. In 2005 the UN Commission on Human Rights appointed a special representative to clarify standards of corporate responsibility, elaborate upon the regulatory role of states, explore the concepts of complicity and sphere of influence, develop methodologies for undertaking human rights impact assessments and to compile a compendium of best commercial and governmental practices: see UN Doc E/CN.4/2005/L.87. For industry comments, see the Joint Written Statement submitted by the ICC and IOE, UN Doc E/CN.4/Sub.2/2003/NGO/44; ICC/IOE, 'Joint views on the draft Norms', Paris, 2004. For NGO comments, see, for example, Amnesty International, 'The UN Human Rights Norms for Business', 2004. See further, the Working Group's background document (UN Doc E/CN.4/Sub.2/1995/11), the UN Secretary-General Report (UN Doc E/CN.4/Sub.2/1996/12 & Corr.1) and the background document prepared by Mr El-Hadji Guissé (UN Doc E/CN.4/Sub.2/1998/6). For academic commentary, see Vagts D.F. (2003), 'The UN Norms for transnational corporations', *Leiden Journal of International Law*, **16**, 795–802.

## A. General Obligations

1. States have the primary responsibility to promote, secure the fulfilment of, respect, ensure respect of and protect human rights recognized in international as well as national law, including ensuring that TNCs and other business enterprises respect human rights. Within their respective spheres of activity and influence, TNCs and other business enterprises have the obligation to promote, secure the fulfilment of, respect, ensure respect of and protect human rights recognized in international as well as national law, including the rights and interests of indigenous peoples and other vulnerable groups.

## B. Right to Equal Opportunity and Non-Discriminatory Treatment

2. TNCs and other business enterprises shall ensure equality of opportunity and treatment, as provided in the relevant international instruments and national legislation as well as international human rights law, for the purpose of eliminating discrimination based on race, colour, sex, language, religion, political opinion, national or social origin, social status, indigenous status, disability, age – except for children, who may be given greater protection – or other status of the individual unrelated to the inherent requirements to perform the job, or of complying with special measures designed to overcome past discrimination against certain groups.

## C. Right to Security of Persons

3. TNCs and other business enterprises shall not engage in nor benefit from war crimes, crimes against humanity, genocide, torture, forced disappearance, forced or compulsory labour, hostage-taking, extrajudicial, summary or arbitrary executions, other violations of humanitarian law and other international crimes against the human person as defined by international law, in particular human rights and humanitarian law.
4. Security arrangements for TNCs and other business enterprises shall observe international human rights norms as well as the laws and professional standards of the country or countries in which they operate.

## D. Rights of Workers

5. TNCs and other business enterprises shall not use forced or compulsory labour as forbidden by the relevant international instruments and national legislation as well as international human rights and humanitarian law.

6. TNCs and other business enterprises shall respect the rights of children to be protected from economic exploitation as forbidden by the relevant international instruments and national legislation as well as international human rights and humanitarian law.
7. TNCs and other business enterprises shall provide a safe and healthy working environment as set forth in relevant international instruments and national legislation as well as international human rights and humanitarian law.
8. TNCs and other business enterprises shall provide workers with remuneration that ensures an adequate standard of living for them and their families. Such remuneration shall take due account of their needs for adequate living conditions with a view towards progressive improvement.
9. TNCs and other business enterprises shall ensure freedom of association and effective recognition of the right to collective bargaining by protecting the right to establish and, subject only to the rules of the organization concerned, to join organizations of their own choosing without distinction, previous authorization, or interference, for the protection of their employment interests and for other collective bargaining purposes as provided in national legislation and the relevant conventions of the ILO.

**E. Respect for National Sovereignty and Human Rights**

10. TNCs and other business enterprises shall recognize and respect applicable norms of international law, national laws and regulations, as well as administrative practices, the rule of law, the public interest, development objectives, social, economic and cultural policies including transparency, accountability and prohibition of corruption, and authority of the countries in which the enterprises operate.
11. TNCs and other business enterprises shall not offer, promise, give, accept, condone, knowingly benefit from, or demand a bribe or other improper advantage, nor shall they be solicited or expected to give a bribe or other improper advantage to any Government, public official, candidate for elective post, any member of the armed forces or security forces, or any other individual or organization. TNCs and other business enterprises shall refrain from any activity which supports, solicits, or encourages States or any other entities to abuse human rights. They shall further seek to ensure that the goods and services they provide will not be used to abuse human rights.
12. TNCs and other business enterprises shall respect economic, social and cultural rights as well as civil and political rights and contribute to their realization, in particular the rights to development, adequate food and drinking water, the highest attainable standard of physical and mental health, adequate housing, privacy, education, freedom of thought, conscience, and religion and freedom of opinion and expression, and shall refrain from actions which obstruct or impede the realization of those rights.

**F. Obligations with Regard to Consumer Protection**

13. TNCs and other business enterprises shall act in accordance with fair business, marketing and advertising practices and shall take all necessary steps to ensure the safety and quality of the goods and services they provide, including observance of the precautionary principle. Nor shall they produce, distribute, market, or advertise harmful or potentially harmful products for use by consumers.

## G. Obligations with Regard to Environmental Protection

14. TNCs and other business enterprises shall carry out their activities in accordance with national laws, regulations, administrative practices and policies relating to the preservation of the environment of the countries in which they operate, as well as in accordance with relevant international agreements, principles, objectives, responsibilities and standards with regard to the environment as well as human rights, public health and safety, bioethics and the precautionary principle, and shall generally conduct their activities in a manner contributing to the wider goal of sustainable development.

## H. General Provisions of Implementation

15. As an initial step towards implementing these Norms, each TNC or other business enterprise shall adopt, disseminate and implement internal rules of operation in compliance with the Norms. Further, they shall periodically report on and take other measures fully to implement the Norms and to provide at least for the prompt implementation of the protections set forth in the Norms. Each TNC or other business enterprise shall apply and incorporate these Norms in their contracts or other arrangements and dealings with contractors, subcontractors, suppliers, licensees, distributors, or natural or other legal persons that enter into any agreement with the TNC or business enterprise in order to ensure respect for and implementation of the Norms.
16. TNCs and other businesses enterprises shall be subject to periodic monitoring and verification by UN, other international and national mechanisms already in existence or yet to be created, regarding the application of the Norms. This monitoring shall be transparent and independent and take into account input from stakeholders (including non governmental organizations) and as a result of complaints of violations of these Norms. Further, TNCs and other businesses enterprises shall conduct periodic evaluations concerning the impact of their own activities on human rights under these Norms.
17. States should establish and reinforce the necessary legal and administrative framework for ensuring that the Norms and other relevant national and international laws are implemented by TNCs and other business enterprises.
18. TNCs and other business enterprises shall provide prompt, effective and adequate reparation to those persons, entities and communities that have been adversely affected by failures to comply with these Norms through, *inter alia*, reparations, restitution, compensation and rehabilitation for any damage done or property taken. In connection with determining damages in regard to criminal sanctions, and in all other respects, these Norms shall be applied by national courts and/or international tribunals, pursuant to national and international law.
19. Nothing in these Norms shall be construed as diminishing, restricting, or adversely affecting the human rights obligations of States under national and international law, nor shall they be construed as diminishing, restricting, or adversely affecting more protective human rights norms, nor shall they be construed as diminishing, restricting, or adversely affecting other obligations or responsibilities of TNCs and other business enterprises in fields other than human rights.

## I. Definitions

20. The term 'transnational corporation' refers to an economic entity operating in more than one country or a cluster of economic entities operating in two or more countries

whatever their legal form, whether in their home country or country of activity, and whether taken individually or collectively.

21. The phrase 'other business enterprise' includes any business entity, regardless of the international or domestic nature of its activities, including a TNC, contractor, subcontractor, supplier, licensee or distributor; the corporate, partnership, or other legal form used to establish the business entity; and the nature of the ownership of the entity. These Norms shall be presumed to apply, as a matter of practice, if the business enterprise has any relation with a TNC, the impact of its activities is not entirely local, or the activities involve violations of the right to security as indicated in paragraphs 3 and 4.
22. The term 'stakeholder' includes stockholders, other owners, workers and their representatives, as well as any other individual or group that is affected by the activities of TNCs or other business enterprises. The term 'stakeholder' shall be interpreted functionally in the light of the objectives of these Norms and include indirect stakeholders when their interests are or will be substantially affected by the activities of the TNC or business enterprise. In addition to parties directly affected by the activities of business enterprises, stakeholders can include parties which are indirectly affected by the activities of TNCs or other business enterprises such as consumer groups, customers, Governments, neighbouring communities, indigenous peoples and communities, non governmental organizations, public and private lending institutions, suppliers, trade associations, and others.
23. The phrases 'human rights' and 'international human rights' include civil, cultural, economic, political and social rights, as set forth in the International Bill of Human Rights and other human rights treaties, as well as the right to development and rights recognized by international humanitarian law, international refugee law, international labour law, and other relevant instruments adopted within the UN system.

# 14. UN: The Universal Declaration of Human Rights, 1948

**Commentary**: As stated in its preamble, UNGA Resolution 217A (1948) is a 'common standard of achievement for all'. See further UN, Fiftieth Anniversary of the UDHR, Basic Information Kit No 1, 1998. Regional human rights instruments include the European Convention for the Protection of Human Rights and Fundamental Freedoms 213 *UNTS* 222 (1950); the European Social Charter 529 *UNTS* 89 (1961); the American Convention on Human Rights (1969) 1144 *UNTS* 123; the Additional Protocol to the American Convention on Human Rights in the Area of Economic, Social and Cultural Rights (1988) *OASTS* 69; the African (Banjul) Charter on Human and People's Rights 21 *ILM* 58 (1982); the Arab Charter on Human Rights 18 *Human Rights Law Journal* 151 (1997).

From the OHCHR (2000), see, for example, 'Business and Human Rights: A Progress Report', Geneva. For business perspectives, see the Business Leaders Initiative on Human Rights, www.blihr.org. For joint business–NGO perspectives, see Confederation of Danish Industries/Danish Centre for Human Rights/Industrialization Fund for Developing Countries, *Defining the Scope of Business Responsibility for Human Rights Abuses Abroad*, Copenhagen, c1999; AI/PWBLF, *Human Rights: Is It Any of Your Business?* London, 2000. For NGO perspectives, see, for example, International Council on Human Rights Policy (2002), *Beyond Voluntarism: Human Rights and the Developing International Legal Obligations of Companies*, Versoix.

For academic commentary, see, for example, D'Amato A. (1979), 'Are human rights good for international business?', *Northwestern Journal of International Law and Business*, **1**, 22–32; Cassel D. (1996), 'Corporate initiatives: a second human rights revolution?', *Fordham International Law Journal*, **19**, 1963–84; Meyer W.H. (1996), 'Human rights and MNCs: theory versus quantitative analysis', *Human Rights Quarterly*, **18** (2), 368–97; Frey B.A. (1997), 'The legal and ethical responsibilities of TNCs in the protection of international human rights', *Minnesota Journal of Global Trade*, **6**, 152–88; Addo M. (ed.) (1999), *Human Rights Standards and the Responsibility of Transnational Corporations*, The Hague: Kluwer Law International; Dubin L. (1999), 'The direct application of human rights standards to, and by, TNCs', *International Commission of Jurists – The Review*, **61**, 35–66; Clapham A. and Jerbi S. (2001), 'Categories of corporate complicity in human rights abuses', *Hastings International and Comparative Law Review*, **24**, 339–49; Muchlinski P. (2001), 'Human rights and multinationals: is there a problem?', *International Affairs*, **77** (1), 31–47; Greathead S. (2002), 'The multinational and the "new stakeholder": examining the business case for human rights', *Vanderbilt Journal of Transnational Law*, **35** (2), 719–27; Paust J.J. (2002), 'Human rights responsibilities of private corporations', *Vanderbilt Journal of Transnational Law*, **35**, 801–25.

**Preamble**
... Now, therefore the General Assembly proclaims this Universal Declaration of Human Rights as a common standard of achievement for all peoples and all nations, to the end that every individual and every organ of society, keeping this Declaration constantly in mind, shall strive by teaching and education to promote respect for these rights and freedoms and by progressive measures, national and international, to secure their universal and effective recognition and observance ...

**Article 1**
All human beings are born free and equal in dignity and rights ...

**Article 2**
Everyone is entitled to all the rights and freedoms set forth in this Declaration, without distinction of any kind, such as race, colour, sex, language, religion, political or other opinion, national or social origin, property, birth or other status ...

**Article 3**
Everyone has the right to life, liberty and security of person.

**Article 4**
No one shall be held in slavery or servitude; slavery and the slave trade shall be prohibited in all their forms.

**Article 5**
No one shall be subjected to torture or to cruel, inhuman or degrading treatment or punishment.

**Article 6**
Everyone has the right to recognition everywhere as a person before the law.

**Article 7**
All are equal before the law and are entitled without any discrimination to equal protection of the law ...

**Article 8**
Everyone has the right to an effective remedy by the competent national tribunals for acts violating the fundamental rights granted him by the constitution or by law.

**Article 9**
No one shall be subjected to arbitrary arrest, detention or exile.

**Article 10**
Everyone is entitled in full equality to a fair and public hearing by an independent and impartial tribunal, in the determination of his rights and obligations and of any criminal charge against him.

**Article 11**
1. Everyone charged with a penal offence has the right to be presumed innocent until proved guilty according to law in a public trial at which he has had all the guarantees necessary for his defence . . .

**Article 12**
No one shall be subjected to arbitrary interference with his privacy, family, home or correspondence, nor to attacks upon his honour and reputation . . .

**Article 13**
1. Everyone has the right to freedom of movement and residence within the borders of each state.
2. Everyone has the right to leave any country, including his own, and to return to his country.

**Article 14**
1. Everyone has the right to seek and to enjoy in other countries asylum from persecution . . .

**Article 15**
1. Everyone has the right to a nationality . . .

**Article 16**
1. Men and women of full age, without any limitation due to race, nationality or religion, have the right to marry and to found a family. They are entitled to equal rights as to marriage, during marriage and at its dissolution . . .

**Article 17**
1. Everyone has the right to own property alone as well as in association with others.
2. No one shall be arbitrarily deprived of his property.

**Article 18**
Everyone has the right to freedom of thought, conscience and religion . . .

**Article 19**

Everyone has the right to freedom of opinion and expression . . .

**Article 20**

1. Everyone has the right to freedom of peaceful assembly and association.
2. No one may be compelled to belong to an association.

**Article 21**

1. Everyone has the right to take part in the government of his country, directly or through freely chosen representatives . . .

**Article 22**

Everyone, as a member of society, has the right to social security and is entitled to realization, through national effort and international co-operation and in accordance with the organization and resources of each State, of the economic, social and cultural rights indispensable for his dignity and the free development of his personality.

**Article 23**

1. Everyone has the right to work, to free choice of employment, to just and favourable conditions of work and to protection against unemployment.
2. Everyone, without any discrimination, has the right to equal pay for equal work.
3. Everyone who works has the right to just and favourable remuneration ensuring for himself and his family an existence worthy of human dignity, and supplemented, if necessary, by other means of social protection.
4. Everyone has the right to form and to join trade unions for the protection of his interests.

**Article 24**

Everyone has the right to rest and leisure, including reasonable limitation of working hours and periodic holidays with pay.

**Article 25**

1. Everyone has the right to a standard of living adequate for the health and well-being of himself and of his family, including food, clothing, housing and medical care and necessary social services, and the right to security in the event of unemployment, sickness, disability, widowhood, old age or other lack of livelihood in circumstances beyond his control . . .

**Article 26**

1. Everyone has the right to education . . .

**Article 27**

1. Everyone has the right freely to participate in the cultural life of the community, to enjoy the arts and to share in scientific advancement and its benefits.
2. Everyone has the right to the protection of the moral and material interests resulting from any scientific, literary or artistic production of which he is the author.

**Article 28**

Everyone is entitled to a social and international order in which the rights and freedoms set forth in this Declaration can be fully realized.

**Article 29**

1. Everyone has duties to the community in which alone the free and full development of his personality is possible.
2. In the exercise of his rights and freedoms, everyone shall be subject only to such limitations as are determined by law solely for the purpose of securing due recognition and respect for the rights and freedoms of others and of meeting the just requirements of morality, public order and the general welfare in a democratic society . . .

**Article 30**

Nothing in this Declaration may be interpreted as implying for any State, group or person any right to engage in any activity or to perform any act aimed at the destruction of any of the rights and freedoms set forth herein.

# 15. UN: International Covenant on Civil and Political Rights, 1966

**Commentary**: The ICCPR (1966) 999 *UNTS* 171 (entry into force 1976) is administered by the Committee on Human Rights, an independent body of experts which evaluates government reports on the implementation of the Covenant and issues general comments on thematic issues. The First Optional Protocol gives the Committee competence to examine individual complaints with regard to alleged violations by State Parties and the Second Optional Protocol concerns the abolition of the death penalty. See further, www.ohchr.org.

**Article 1**

1. All peoples have the right of self-determination. By virtue of that right they freely determine their political status and freely pursue their economic, social and cultural development.
2. All peoples may, for their own ends, freely dispose of their natural wealth and resources without prejudice to any obligations arising out of international economic co-operation, based upon the principle of mutual benefit, and international law. In no case may a people be deprived of its own means of subsistence.

**Article 2**

1. Each State Party to the present Covenant undertakes to respect and to ensure to all individuals within its territory and subject to its jurisdiction the rights recognized in the present Covenant, without distinction of any kind, such as race, colour, sex, language, religion, political or other opinion, national or social origin, property, birth or other status.
3. Each State Party to the present Covenant undertakes:

   (a) To ensure that any person whose rights or freedoms as herein recognized are violated shall have an effective remedy . . .

**Article 3**

The States Parties to the present Covenant undertake to ensure the equal right of men and women to the enjoyment of all civil and political rights set forth in the present Covenant.

**Article 5**

1. Nothing in the present Covenant may be interpreted as implying for any State, group or person any right to engage in any activity or perform any act aimed at the destruction of

any of the rights and freedoms recognized herein or at their limitation to a greater extent than is provided for in the present Covenant . . .

**Article 6**

1. Every human being has the inherent right to life . . .

**Article 7**

No one shall be subjected to torture or to cruel, inhuman or degrading treatment or punishment. In particular, no one shall be subjected without his free consent to medical or scientific experimentation.

**Article 8**

1. No one shall be held in slavery; slavery and the slave-trade in all their forms shall be prohibited.
2. No one shall be held in servitude.
3. (a) No one shall be required to perform forced or compulsory labour;
   (b) Paragraph 3 (a) shall not be held to preclude, in countries where imprisonment with hard labour may be imposed as a punishment for a crime, the performance of hard labour in pursuance of a sentence to such punishment by a competent court;
   (c) For the purpose of this paragraph the term 'forced or compulsory labour' shall not include:

      (i) Any work or service, not referred to in subparagraph (b), normally required of a person who is under detention in consequence of a lawful order of a court, or of a person during conditional release from such detention;
      (ii) Any service of a military character and, in countries where conscientious objection is recognized, any national service required by law of conscientious objectors;
      (iii) Any service exacted in cases of emergency or calamity threatening the life or well-being of the community;
      (iv) Any work or service which forms part of normal civil obligations.

**Article 9**

1. Everyone has the right to liberty and security of person . . .

**Article 10**

1. All persons deprived of their liberty shall be treated with humanity and with respect for the inherent dignity of the human person . . .

**Article 11**

No one shall be imprisoned merely on the ground of inability to fulfil a contractual obligation.

**Article 12**

1. Everyone lawfully within the territory of a State shall, within that territory, have the right to liberty of movement and freedom to choose his residence.
2. Everyone shall be free to leave any country, including his own . . .

**Article 14**

1. All persons shall be equal before the courts and tribunals. In the determination of any criminal charge against him, or of his rights and obligations in a suit at law, everyone shall be entitled to a fair and public hearing by a competent, independent and impartial tribunal established by law . . .

**Article 16**

Everyone shall have the right to recognition everywhere as a person before the law.

**Article 17**

1. No one shall be subjected to arbitrary or unlawful interference with his privacy, family, home or correspondence, nor to unlawful attacks on his honour and reputation . . .

**Article 18**

1. Everyone shall have the right to freedom of thought, conscience and religion. This right shall include freedom to have or to adopt a religion or belief of his choice, and freedom, either individually or in community with others and in public or private, to manifest his religion or belief in worship, observance, practice and teaching . . .

**Article 19**

1. Everyone shall have the right to hold opinions without interference.
2. Everyone shall have the right to freedom of expression . . .

**Article 20**

1. Any propaganda for war shall be prohibited by law.
2. Any advocacy of national, racial or religious hatred that constitutes incitement to discrimination, hostility or violence shall be prohibited by law.

**Article 21**

The right of peaceful assembly shall be recognized . . .

**Article 22**

1. Everyone shall have the right to freedom of association with others, including the right to form and join trade unions for the protection of his interests.
2. No restrictions may be placed on the exercise of this right other than those which are prescribed by law and which are necessary in a democratic society in the interests of

national security or public safety, public order (*ordre public*), the protection of public health or morals or the protection of the rights and freedoms of others. This article shall not prevent the imposition of lawful restrictions on members of the armed forces and of the police in their exercise of this right . . .

**Article 23**

1. The family is the natural and fundamental group unit of society and is entitled to protection by society and the State . . .

**Article 24**

1. Every child shall have, without any discrimination as to race, colour, sex, language, religion, national or social origin, property or birth, the right to such measures of protection as are required by his status as a minor, on the part of his family, society and the State . . .

**Article 25**

Every citizen shall have the right and the opportunity, without any of the distinctions mentioned in article 2 and without unreasonable restrictions:

(a) To take part in the conduct of public affairs, directly or through freely chosen representatives . . .

**Article 26**

All persons are equal before the law and are entitled without any discrimination to the equal protection of the law . . .

**Article 27**

In those States in which ethnic, religious or linguistic minorities exist, persons belonging to such minorities shall not be denied the right, in community with the other members of their group, to enjoy their own culture, to profess and practise their own religion, or to use their own language.

**Article 47**

Nothing in the present Covenant shall be interpreted as impairing the inherent right of all peoples to enjoy and utilize fully and freely their natural wealth and resources.

# 16. UN: International Covenant on Economic, Social and Cultural Rights, 1966

**Commentary**: The ICESCR (1966) 993 *UNTS* 3 (entry into force 1976) is administered by the Committee on Economic, Social and Cultural Rights, a body of independent experts which evaluates government reports concerning progressive implementation and issues general comments interpreting particular provisions. The Committee cannot consider individual complaints, although a draft Optional Protocol has been under consideration for a lengthy period. See further, www.ohchr.org. For the application of economic, social and cultural rights to corporations under the African Charter on Human and Peoples' Rights, see *African Commission on Human and Peoples' Rights, Social and Economic Rights Action Centre & the Centre for Economic and Social Rights v Nigeria*, Communication No 55 (1996). On violations, see the 1997 Maastricht Guidelines on Violations of Economic, Social and Cultural Rights (1998) 20 *Human Rights Quarterly* 691. For academic commentary, see Scott C. (2001), 'MNEs and emergent jurisprudence on violations of economic, social and cultural rights', in Eide A., C. Krause and A. Rosas (eds), *Economic, Social and Cultural Rights: A Textbook*, Kluwer: The Hague (2nd edn) pp. 563–95.

**Article 1**

1. All peoples have the right of self-determination. By virtue of that right they freely determine their political status and freely pursue their economic, social and cultural development.
2. All peoples may, for their own ends, freely dispose of their natural wealth and resources without prejudice to any obligations arising out of international economic co-operation, based upon the principle of mutual benefit, and international law. In no case may a people be deprived of its own means of subsistence . . .

**Article 2**

1. Each State Party to the present Covenant undertakes to take steps, individually and through international assistance and co-operation, especially economic and technical, to the maximum of its available resources, with a view to achieving progressively the full realization of the rights recognized in the present Covenant by all appropriate means, including particularly the adoption of legislative measures.
2. The States Parties to the present Covenant undertake to guarantee that the rights enunciated in the present Covenant will be exercised without discrimination of any kind as to race, colour, sex, language, religion, political or other opinion, national or social origin, property, birth or other status . . .

**Article 3**

The States Parties to the present Covenant undertake to ensure the equal right of men and women to the enjoyment of all economic, social and cultural rights set forth in the present Covenant.

**Article 4**

The States Parties to the present Covenant recognize that, in the enjoyment of those rights provided by the State in conformity with the present Covenant, the State may subject such rights only to such limitations as are determined by law only in so far as this may be compatible with the nature of these rights and solely for the purpose of promoting the general welfare in a democratic society.

**Article 5**

1. Nothing in the present Covenant may be interpreted as implying for any State, group or person any right to engage in any activity or to perform any act aimed at the destruction of any of the rights or freedoms recognized herein, or at their limitation to a greater extent than is provided for in the present Covenant . . .

**Article 6**

1. The States Parties to the present Covenant recognize the right to work, which includes the right of everyone to the opportunity to gain his living by work which he freely chooses or accepts, and will take appropriate steps to safeguard this right.
2. The steps to be taken by a State Party to the present Covenant to achieve the full realization of this right shall include technical and vocational guidance and training programmes, policies and techniques to achieve steady economic, social and cultural development and full and productive employment under conditions safeguarding fundamental political and economic freedoms to the individual.

**Article 7**

The States Parties to the present Covenant recognize the right of everyone to the enjoyment of just and favourable conditions of work which ensure, in particular:

(a) Remuneration which provides all workers, as a minimum, with:

  (i) Fair wages and equal remuneration for work of equal value without distinction of any kind, in particular women being guaranteed conditions of work not inferior to those enjoyed by men, with equal pay for equal work;
  (ii) A decent living for themselves and their families in accordance with the provisions of the present Covenant;

(b) Safe and healthy working conditions;
(c) Equal opportunity for everyone to be promoted in his employment to an appropriate higher level, subject to no considerations other than those of seniority and competence;

(d) Rest, leisure and reasonable limitation of working hours and periodic holidays with pay, as well as remuneration for public holidays.

**Article 8**

1. The States Parties to the present Covenant undertake to ensure:

   (a) The right of everyone to form trade unions and join the trade union of his choice, subject only to the rules of the organization concerned, for the promotion and protection of his economic and social interests. No restrictions may be placed on the exercise of this right other than those prescribed by law and which are necessary in a democratic society in the interests of national security or public order or for the protection of the rights and freedoms of others;
   (b) The right of trade unions to establish national federations or confederations and the right of the latter to form or join international trade-union organizations;
   (c) The right of trade unions to function freely subject to no limitations other than those prescribed by law and which are necessary in a democratic society in the interests of national security or public order or for the protection of the rights and freedoms of others;
   (d) The right to strike, provided that it is exercised in conformity with the laws of the particular country.

2. This article shall not prevent the imposition of lawful restrictions on the exercise of these rights by members of the armed forces or of the police or of the administration of the State.
3. Nothing in this article shall authorize States Parties to the ILO Convention of 1948 concerning Freedom of Association and Protection of the Right to Organize to take legislative measures which would prejudice, or apply the law in such a manner as would prejudice, the guarantees provided for in that Convention.

**Article 9**

The States Parties to the present Covenant recognize the right of everyone to social security, including social insurance.

**Article 10**

The States Parties to the present Covenant recognize that:

1. The widest possible protection and assistance should be accorded to the family, which is the natural and fundamental group unit of society . . .
2. Special protection should be accorded to mothers during a reasonable period before and after childbirth. During such period working mothers should be accorded paid leave or leave with adequate social security benefits.
3. Special measures of protection and assistance should be taken on behalf of all children and young persons without any discrimination for reasons of parentage or other conditions. Children and young persons should be protected from economic and social exploitation. Their employment in work harmful to their morals or health or dangerous to life or likely to hamper their normal development should be punishable by law. States

should also set age limits below which the paid employment of child labour should be prohibited and punishable by law.

**Article 11**

1. The States Parties to the present Covenant recognize the right of everyone to an adequate standard of living for himself and his family, including adequate food, clothing and housing, and to the continuous improvement of living conditions. The States Parties will take appropriate steps to ensure the realization of this right, recognizing to this effect the essential importance of international co-operation based on free consent.
2. The States Parties to the present Covenant, recognizing the fundamental right of everyone to be free from hunger, shall take, individually and through international co-operation, the measures, including specific programmes, which are needed:

   (a) To improve methods of production, conservation and distribution of food by making full use of technical and scientific knowledge, by disseminating knowledge of the principles of nutrition and by developing or reforming agrarian systems in such a way as to achieve the most efficient development and utilization of natural resources . . .

**Article 12**

1. The States Parties to the present Covenant recognize the right of everyone to the enjoyment of the highest attainable standard of physical and mental health.
2. The steps to be taken by the States Parties to the present Covenant to achieve the full realization of this right shall include those necessary for:

   (b) The improvement of all aspects of environmental and industrial hygiene . . .

**Article 13**

1. The States Parties to the present Covenant recognize the right of everyone to education . . .

**Article 15**

1. The States Parties to the present Covenant recognize the right of everyone:

   (a) To take part in cultural life;
   (b) To enjoy the benefits of scientific progress and its applications;
   (c) To benefit from the protection of the moral and material interests resulting from any scientific, literary or artistic production of which he is the author.

3. The States Parties to the present Covenant undertake to respect the freedom indispensable for scientific research and creative activity . . .

**Article 25**

Nothing in the present Covenant shall be interpreted as impairing the inherent right of all peoples to enjoy and utilize fully and freely their natural wealth and resources.

# 17. UN: International Convention on the Elimination of All Forms of Racial Discrimination, 1965

**Commentary**: The Convention (1966) 660 *UNTS* 195 (entry into force 1969) is administered by the Committee on the Elimination of Racial Discrimination which assesses reports by States Parties, issues general recommendations on thematic issues and examines inter-State complaints. CERD may also consider communications from individuals or groups of individuals alleging violations by State Parties and an early-warning procedure facilitates further monitoring. See further, www.ohchr.org. See also, UNESCO 1978 Declaration on Race and Racial Prejudice, UN Doc E/CN.4/Sub.2/1982/2/Add.1, Annex V; UNGA Resolution 36/55 (1981) on the Declaration on the Elimination of All Forms of Intolerance and of Discrimination Based on Religion or Belief; Durban Declaration and Programme of Action, 'Report of the World Conference against Racism, Racial Discrimination, Xenophobia and Related Intolerance', UN Doc A/CONF.189/12 (2001). On bilateral investment treaties and anti-discrimination legislation, see *Wickes v Olympic Airways* 745 *F.2d* 363 (CA 1984).

**Article 1**

1. In this Convention, the term 'racial discrimination' shall mean any distinction, exclusion, restriction or preference based on race, colour, descent, or national or ethnic origin which has the purpose or effect of nullifying or impairing the recognition, enjoyment or exercise, on an equal footing, of human rights and fundamental freedoms in the political, economic, social, cultural or any other field of public life.
2. This Convention shall not apply to distinctions, exclusions, restrictions or preferences made by a State Party to this Convention between citizens and non citizens.
3. Nothing in this Convention may be interpreted as affecting in any way the legal provisions of States Parties concerning nationality, citizenship or naturalization, provided that such provisions do not discriminate against any particular nationality.
4. Special measures taken for the sole purpose of securing adequate advancement of certain racial or ethnic groups or individuals requiring such protection as may be necessary in order to ensure such groups or individuals equal enjoyment or exercise of human rights and fundamental freedoms shall not be deemed racial discrimination, provided, however, that such measures do not, as a consequence, lead to the maintenance of separate rights for different racial groups and that they shall not be continued after the objectives for which they were taken have been achieved.

**Article 2**

1. States Parties condemn racial discrimination and undertake to pursue by all appropriate means and without delay a policy of eliminating racial discrimination in all its forms and promoting understanding among all races, and, to this end:

   (b) Each State Party undertakes not to sponsor, defend or support racial discrimination by any persons or organizations;
   (d) Each State Party shall prohibit and bring to an end, by all appropriate means, including legislation as required by circumstances, racial discrimination by any persons, group or organization . . .

**Article 4**

States Parties condemn all propaganda and all organizations which are based on ideas or theories of superiority of one race or group of persons of one colour or ethnic origin, or which attempt to justify or promote racial hatred and discrimination in any form, and undertake to adopt immediate and positive measures designed to eradicate all incitement to, or acts of, such discrimination and, to this end, with due regard to the principles embodied in the Universal Declaration of Human Rights and the rights expressly set forth in article 5 of this Convention, *inter alia*:

(a) Shall declare an offence punishable by law all dissemination of ideas based on racial superiority or hatred, incitement to racial discrimination, as well as all acts of violence or incitement to such acts against any race or group of persons of another colour or ethnic origin, and also the provision of any assistance to racist activities, including the financing thereof;
(b) Shall declare illegal and prohibit organizations, and also organized and all other propaganda activities, which promote and incite racial discrimination, and shall recognize participation in such organizations or activities as an offence punishable by law . . .

**Article 5**

In compliance with the fundamental obligations laid down in article 2 of this Convention, States Parties undertake to prohibit and to eliminate racial discrimination in all its forms and to guarantee the right of everyone, without distinction as to race, colour, or national or ethnic origin, to equality before the law, notably in the enjoyment of the following rights:

(a) The right to equal treatment before the tribunals and all other organs administering justice;
(b) The right to security of person and protection by the State against violence or bodily harm, whether inflicted by government officials or by any individual group or institution;
(d) Other civil rights, in particular:
(e) Economic, social and cultural rights, in particular:

   (i) The rights to work, to free choice of employment, to just and favourable conditions of work, to protection against unemployment, to equal pay for equal work, to just and favourable remuneration;
   (ii) The right to form and join trade unions . . .

(f) The right of access to any place or service intended for use by the general public, such as transport, hotels, restaurants, cafés, theatres and parks.

# 18. UN: Convention on the Elimination of All Forms of Discrimination against Women, 1979

**Commentary**: CEDAW (UN Doc A/34/46, entry into force 1981) is administered by the Committee on the Elimination of Discrimination against Women which assesses national reports. An Optional Protocol (UN Doc A/54/49 (2000), entry into force 2000) provides for it to consider communications by individuals or groups of individuals alleging violations by State Parties. See further, www.ohchr.org. See also, Convention on the Political Rights of Women 193 *UNTS* 135 (entry into force 1954); UNGA Resolution 3318 (1974) concerning the Declaration on the Protection of Women and Children in Emergency and Armed Conflict; UNGA Resolution 48/104 (1993) concerning the Declaration on the Elimination of Violence against Women; UNCTC/ILO (1985), 'Women Workers in MNEs in Developing Countries', Geneva.

**Article 1**

For the purposes of the present Convention, the term 'discrimination against women' shall mean any distinction, exclusion or restriction made on the basis of sex which has the effect or purpose of impairing or nullifying the recognition, enjoyment or exercise by women, irrespective of their marital status, on a basis of equality of men and women, of human rights and fundamental freedoms in the political, economic, social, cultural, civil or any other field.

**Article 2**

States Parties condemn discrimination against women in all its forms, agree to pursue by all appropriate means and without delay a policy of eliminating discrimination against women and, to this end, undertake:

(b) To adopt appropriate legislative and other measures, including sanctions where appropriate, prohibiting all discrimination against women;

(e) To take all appropriate measures to eliminate discrimination against women by any person, organization or enterprise . . .

**Article 6**

States Parties shall take all appropriate measures, including legislation, to suppress all forms of traffic in women and exploitation of prostitution of women.

**Article 11**

1. States Parties shall take all appropriate measures to eliminate discrimination against women in the field of employment in order to ensure, on a basis of equality of men and women, the same rights, in particular:

   (a) The right to work as an inalienable right of all human beings;
   (b) The right to the same employment opportunities, including the application of the same criteria for selection in matters of employment;
   (c) The right to free choice of profession and employment, the right to promotion, job security and all benefits and conditions of service and the right to receive vocational training and retraining, including apprenticeships, advanced vocational training and recurrent training;
   (d) The right to equal remuneration, including benefits, and to equal treatment in respect of work of equal value, as well as equality of treatment in the evaluation of the quality of work;
   (e) The right to social security, particularly in cases of retirement, unemployment, sickness, invalidity and old age and other incapacity to work, as well as the right to paid leave;
   (f) The right to protection of health and to safety in working conditions, including the safeguarding of the function of reproduction.

2. In order to prevent discrimination against women on the grounds of marriage or maternity and to ensure their effective right to work, States Parties shall take appropriate measures:

   (a) To prohibit, subject to the imposition of sanctions, dismissal on the grounds of pregnancy or of maternity leave and discrimination in dismissals on the basis of marital status;
   (b) To introduce maternity leave with pay or with comparable social benefits without loss of former employment, seniority or social allowances;
   (c) To encourage the provision of the necessary supporting social services to enable parents to combine family obligations with work responsibilities and participation in public life, in particular through promoting the establishment and development of a network of child-care facilities;
   (d) To provide special protection to women during pregnancy in types of work proved to be harmful to them.

3. Protective legislation relating to matters covered in this article shall be reviewed periodically in the light of scientific and technological knowledge and shall be revised, repealed or extended as necessary.

**Article 13**

States Parties shall take all appropriate measures to eliminate discrimination against women in other areas of economic and social life in order to ensure, on a basis of equality of men and women, the same rights, in particular:

(b) The right to bank loans, mortgages and other forms of financial credit;

**Article 14**

1. States Parties shall take into account the particular problems faced by rural women and the significant roles which rural women play in the economic survival of their families, including their work in the non-monetized sectors of the economy, and shall take all appropriate measures to ensure the application of the provisions of the present Convention to women in rural areas.
2. States Parties shall take all appropriate measures to eliminate discrimination against women in rural areas in order to ensure, on a basis of equality of men and women, that they participate in and benefit from rural development and, in particular, shall ensure to such women the right:

   (d) To obtain all types of training and education, formal and non-formal, including that relating to functional literacy, as well as, *inter alia*, the benefit of all community and extension services, in order to increase their technical proficiency;
   (e) To organize self-help groups and co-operatives in order to obtain equal access to economic opportunities through employment or self employment;
   (g) To have access to agricultural credit and loans, marketing facilities, appropriate technology and equal treatment in land and agrarian reform as well as in land resettlement schemes;
   (h) To enjoy adequate living conditions, particularly in relation to housing, sanitation, electricity and water supply, transport and communications.

**Article 15**

2. States Parties shall accord to women, in civil matters, a legal capacity identical to that of men and the same opportunities to exercise that capacity. In particular, they shall give women equal rights to conclude contracts and to administer property and shall treat them equally in all stages of procedure in courts and tribunals.
3. States Parties agree that all contracts and all other private instruments of any kind with a legal effect which is directed at restricting the legal capacity of women shall be deemed null and void . . .

**Article 16**

1. States Parties shall take all appropriate measures to eliminate discrimination against women in all matters relating to marriage and family relations and in particular shall ensure, on a basis of equality of men and women:

   (h) The same rights for both spouses in respect of the ownership, acquisition, management, administration, enjoyment and disposition of property, whether free of charge or for a valuable consideration.

# 19. UN: Convention on the Rights of the Child, 1989

**Commentary**: The Convention (UN Doc A/44/49(1989), entry into force 1990) is administered by the Committee on the Rights of the Child (CRC), a body of independent experts which assesses national reports on implementation and issues general comments on thematic issues. Although it cannot consider individual complaints, the CRC also monitors implementation of the Optional Protocols on the Involvement of Children in Armed Conflicts (UN Doc A/54/49, Vol III (2000), entry into force 2002) and on the Sale of Children, Child Prostitution and Child Pornography (extracted below). In addition to the provisions extracted below, State Parties have also recognised for every child the rights to non-discriminatory treatment (Article 2), life (6), a name, nationality and identity (7 & 8), freedom of expression (13 & 14), freedom of association and peaceful assembly (15), the highest attainable standard of health (24), social security (26), an adequate standard of living (27), education (28 & 29), culture (30) and rest and leisure (31). Under Article 18, parents have the primary responsibility for the upbringing and development of children. However, special provisions apply to adopted (Articles 20 & 21) and disabled children (23). See further, www.ohchr.org.

**Article 1**

For the purposes of the present Convention, a child means every human being below the age of eighteen years unless under the law applicable to the child, majority is attained earlier.

**Article 3**

1. In all actions concerning children, whether undertaken by public or private social welfare institutions, courts of law, administrative authorities or legislative bodies, the best interests of the child shall be a primary consideration.
3. States Parties shall ensure that the institutions, services and facilities responsible for the care or protection of children shall conform with the standards established by competent authorities, particularly in the areas of safety, health, in the number and suitability of their staff, as well as competent supervision.

**Article 11**

1. States Parties shall take measures to combat the illicit transfer and non-return of children abroad . . .

**Article 13**

1. The child shall have the right to freedom of expression; this right shall include freedom to seek, receive and impart information and ideas of all kinds, regardless of frontiers, either orally, in writing or in print, in the form of art, or through any other media of the child's choice.
2. The exercise of this right may be subject to certain restrictions, but these shall only be such as are provided by law and are necessary:

   (a) For respect of the rights or reputations of others; or
   (b) For the protection of national security or of public order (*ordre public*), or of public health or morals.

**Article 17**

States Parties recognize the important function performed by the mass media and shall ensure that the child has access to information and material from a diversity of national and international sources, especially those aimed at the promotion of his or her social, spiritual and moral well-being and physical and mental health. To this end, States Parties shall:

(a) Encourage the mass media to disseminate information and material of social and cultural benefit to the child and in accordance with the spirit of article 29;
(b) Encourage international co-operation in the production, exchange and dissemination of such information and material from a diversity of cultural, national and international sources;
(c) Encourage the production and dissemination of children's books;
(d) Encourage the mass media to have particular regard to the linguistic needs of the child who belongs to a minority group or who is indigenous;
(e) Encourage the development of appropriate guidelines for the protection of the child from information and material injurious to his or her well-being, bearing in mind the provisions of articles 13 and 18.

**Article 18**

1. States Parties shall use their best efforts to ensure recognition of the principle that both parents have common responsibilities for the upbringing and development of the child. Parents or, as the case may be, legal guardians, have the primary responsibility for the upbringing and development of the child. The best interests of the child will be their basic concern.
2. For the purpose of guaranteeing and promoting the rights set forth in the present Convention, States Parties shall render appropriate assistance to parents and legal guardians in the performance of their child-rearing responsibilities and shall ensure the development of institutions, facilities and services for the care of children.
3. State Parties shall take all appropriate measures to ensure that children of working parents have the right to benefit from child-care services and facilities for which they are eligible.

**Article 28**

1. States Parties recognize the right of the child to education, and with a view to achieving this right progressively and on the basis of equal opportunity, they shall, in particular:

   (a) Make primary education compulsory and available free to all;
   (b) Encourage the development of different forms of secondary education, including general and vocational education, make them available and accessible to every child, and take appropriate measures such as the introduction of free education and offering financial assistance in case of need;
   (c) Make higher education accessible to all on the basis of capacity by every appropriate means;
   (d) Make educational and vocational information and guidance available and accessible to all children . . .

**Article 29**

1. States Parties agree that the education of the child shall be directed to:

   (a) The development of the child's personality, talents and mental and physical abilities to their fullest potential;
   (b) The development of respect for human rights and fundamental freedoms, and for the principles enshrined in the Charter of the United Nations;
   (c) The development of respect for the child's parents, his or her own cultural identity, language and values, for the national values of the country in which the child is living, the country from which he or she may originate, and for civilizations different from his or her own;
   (d) The preparation of the child for responsible life in a free society, in the spirit of understanding, peace, tolerance, equality of sexes, and friendship among all peoples, ethnic, national and religious groups and persons of indigenous origin;
   (e) The development of respect for the natural environment.

2. No part of the present article or article 28 shall be construed so as to interfere with the liberty of individuals and bodies to establish and direct educational institutions, subject always to the observance of the principle set forth in paragraph 1 of the present article and to the requirements that the education given in such institutions shall conform to such minimum standards as may be laid down by the State.

**Article 32**

1. States Parties recognize the right of the child to be protected from economic exploitation and from performing any work that is likely to be hazardous or to interfere with the child's education, or to be harmful to the child's health or physical, mental, spiritual, moral or social development.
2. States Parties shall take legislative, administrative, social and educational measures to ensure the implementation of the present article. To this end, and having regard to the relevant provisions of other international instruments, States Parties shall in particular:

(a) Provide for a minimum age or minimum ages for admission to employment;
(b) Provide for appropriate regulation of the hours and conditions of employment;
(c) Provide for appropriate penalties or other sanctions to ensure the effective enforcement of the present article.

**Article 33**
States Parties shall take all appropriate measures, including legislative, administrative, social and educational measures, to protect children from the illicit use of narcotic drugs and psychotropic substances as defined in the relevant international treaties, and to prevent the use of children in the illicit production and trafficking of such substances.

**Article 34**
States Parties undertake to protect the child from all forms of sexual exploitation and sexual abuse. For these purposes, States Parties shall in particular take all appropriate national, bilateral and multilateral measures to prevent:

(a) The inducement or coercion of a child to engage in any unlawful sexual activity;
(b) The exploitative use of children in prostitution or other unlawful sexual practices;
(c) The exploitative use of children in pornographic performances and materials.

**Article 35**
States Parties shall take all appropriate national, bilateral and multilateral measures to prevent the abduction of, the sale of or traffic in children for any purpose or in any form.

**Article 36**
States Parties shall protect the child against all other forms of exploitation prejudicial to any aspects of the child's welfare.

**Article 37**
States Parties shall ensure that:

(a) No child shall be subjected to torture or other cruel, inhuman or degrading treatment or punishment . . .
(b) No child shall be deprived of his or her liberty unlawfully or arbitrarily . . .

# 20. UN: Optional Protocol to the Convention on the Rights of the Child on the Sale of Children, Child Prostitution and Child Pornography, 2000

**Commentary**: The Optional Protocol (UN Doc A/54/49 Vol III (2000), entry into force 2002) furthers Articles 1, 11, 21 and 32–7 of the Convention on the Rights of the Child. The 1999 International Conference on Combating Child Pornography on the Internet emphasised closer cooperation between governments and the internet industry and called for the global criminalisation of producing, distributing, exporting, transmitting, importing, intentionally possessing or advertising child pornography. See further, World Congress against the Commercial Sexual Exploitation of Children: 1996 Stockholm Declaration and Agenda for Action for the Prevention of the Sale of Children, Child Prostitution and Child Pornography (First Congress) and the 2001 Yokohama Global Commitment (Second Congress) (www.csecworldcongress.org).

**Article 1**

States Parties shall prohibit the sale of children, child prostitution and child pornography as provided for by the present Protocol.

**Article 2**

For the purposes of the present Protocol:

(a) Sale of children means any act or transaction whereby a child is transferred by any person or group of persons to another for remuneration or any other consideration;
(b) Child prostitution means the use of a child in sexual activities for remuneration or any other form of consideration;
(c) Child pornography means any representation, by whatever means, of a child engaged in real or simulated explicit sexual activities or any representation of the sexual parts of a child for primarily sexual purposes.

**Article 3**

1. Each State Party shall ensure that, as a minimum, the following acts and activities are fully covered under its criminal or penal law, whether such offences are committed domestically or transnationally or on an individual or organized basis:

(a) In the context of sale of children as defined in article 2:

(i) Offering, delivering or accepting, by whatever means, a child for the purpose of:

a. Sexual exploitation of the child;
b. Transfer of organs of the child for profit;
c. Engagement of the child in forced labour;

(ii) Improperly inducing consent, as an intermediary, for the adoption of a child in violation of applicable international legal instruments on adoption;

(b) Offering, obtaining, procuring or providing a child for child prostitution, as defined in article 2;
(c) Producing, distributing, disseminating, importing, exporting, offering, selling or possessing for the above purposes child pornography as defined in article 2.

2. Subject to the provisions of the national law of a State Party, the same shall apply to an attempt to commit any of the said acts and to complicity or participation in any of the said acts.
3. Each State Party shall make such offences punishable by appropriate penalties that take into account their grave nature.
4. Subject to the provisions of its national law, each State Party shall take measures, where appropriate, to establish the liability of legal persons for offences established in paragraph 1 of the present article. Subject to the legal principles of the State Party, such liability of legal persons may be criminal, civil or administrative . . .

**Article 7**
States Parties shall, subject to the provisions of their national law:

(a) Take measures to provide for the seizure and confiscation, as appropriate, of:

(i) Goods, such as materials, assets and other instrumentalities used to commit or facilitate offences under the present protocol;
(ii) Proceeds derived from such offences . . .

**Article 9**
4. States Parties shall ensure that all child victims of the offences described in the present Protocol have access to adequate procedures to seek, without discrimination, compensation for damages from those legally responsible.
5. States Parties shall take appropriate measures aimed at effectively prohibiting the production and dissemination of material advertising the offences described in the present Protocol.

**Article 10**
1. . . . States Parties shall also promote international cooperation and coordination between their authorities, national and international NGOs and international organizations . . .

# 21. UN: Convention relating to the Status of Refugees, 1951

**Commentary**: The Convention (189 *UNTS* 150, entry into force 1954) is supervised by the UN High Commissioner for Refugees (UNHCR, www.unhcr.ch). The Protocol Relating to the Status of Refugees (606 *UNTS* 267 (1967), entry into force 1967) amends the principal Convention as if the words 'as a result of events occurring before 1 January 1951' and 'as a result of such events' were omitted. See further, Convention Governing the Specific Aspects of Refugee Problems in Africa 1001 *UNTS* 45 (entry into force 1974); the Declaration on the Human Rights of Individuals Who are not Nationals of the Country in which They Live, UNGA Resolution 40/144 (1985); UNHCR, 'Handbook on Procedures and Criteria for Determining Refugee Status under the 1951 Convention and the 1967 Protocol relating to the Status of Refugees', UN Doc HCR/IP/4/Eng/REV.1 (1992). Corporate acts coupled with either the inability of governments to protect refugees or commercial encouragement to that effect constitutes complicity sufficient to qualify as persecution under the Convention: *Re Attorney-General of Canada and Ward; UNHCR et al* (1993) 103 *DLR* (4th) 1; *Dankha* (1998) 111 *ILR* 503.

**Article 1. Definition of the Term 'Refugee'**

A. For the purposes of the present Convention, the term 'refugee' shall apply to any person who:

(2) As a result of events occurring before 1 January 1951 and owing to well-founded fear of being persecuted for reasons of race, religion, nationality, membership of a particular social group or political opinion, is outside the country of his nationality and is unable or, owing to such fear, is unwilling to avail himself of the protection of that country; or who, not having a nationality and being outside the country of his former habitual residence as a result of such events, is unable or, owing to such fear, is unwilling to return to it . . .

**Article 13. Movable and Immovable Property**

The Contracting States shall accord to a refugee treatment as favourable as possible and, in any event, not less favourable than that accorded to aliens generally in the same circumstances, as regards the acquisition of movable and immovable property and other rights pertaining thereto, and to leases and other contracts relating to movable and immovable property.

**Article 14. Artistic Rights and Industrial Property**

In respect of the protection of industrial property, such as inventions, designs or models, trade marks, trade names, and of rights in literary, artistic and scientific works, a refugee shall be accorded in the country in which he has his habitual residence the same protection as is accorded to nationals of that country. In the territory of any other Contracting States, he shall be accorded the same protection as is accorded in that territory to nationals of the country in which he has his habitual residence.

**Article 17. Wage-earning Employment**

1. The Contracting States shall accord to refugees lawfully staying in their territory the most favourable treatment accorded to nationals of a foreign country in the same circumstances, as regards the right to engage in wage-earning employment.
2. In any case, restrictive measures imposed on aliens or the employment of aliens for the protection of the national labour market shall not be applied to a refugee who was already exempt from them at the date of entry into force of this Convention for the Contracting State concerned, or who fulfils one of the following conditions:

    (a) He has completed three years' residence in the country;
    (b) He has a spouse possessing the nationality of the country of residence. A refugee may not invoke the benefit of this provision if he has abandoned his spouse;
    (c) He has one or more children possessing the nationality of the country of residence.

3. The Contracting States shall give sympathetic consideration to assimilating the rights of all refugees with regard to wage-earning employment to those of nationals, and in particular of those refugees who have entered their territory pursuant to programmes of labour recruitment or under immigration schemes.

**Article 18. Self-Employment**

The Contracting States shall accord to a refugee lawfully in their territory treatment as favourable as possible and, in any event, not less favourable than that accorded to aliens generally in the same circumstances, as regards the right to engage on his own account in agriculture, industry, handicrafts and commerce and to establish commercial and industrial companies.

**Article 24. Labour Legislation and Social Security**

1. The Contracting States shall accord to refugees lawfully staying in their territory the same treatment as is accorded to nationals in respect of the following matters;

    (a) In so far as such matters are governed by laws or regulations or are subject to the control of administrative authorities: remuneration, including family allowances where these form part of remuneration, hours of work, overtime arrangements, holidays with pay, restrictions on home work, minimum age of employment, apprenticeship and training, women's work and the work of young persons, and the enjoyment of the benefits of collective bargaining;

(b) Social security (legal provisions in respect of employment injury, occupational diseases, maternity, sickness, disability, old age, death, unemployment, family responsibilities and any other contingency which, according to national laws or regulations, is covered by a social security scheme) . . .

2. The right to compensation for the death of a refugee resulting from employment injury or from occupational disease shall not be affected by the fact that the residence of the beneficiary is outside the territory of the Contracting State.

**Article 30. Transfer of Assets**

1. A Contracting State shall, in conformity with its laws and regulations, permit refugees to transfer assets which they have brought into its territory, to another country where they have been admitted for the purposes of resettlement.
2. A Contracting State shall give sympathetic consideration to the application of refugees for permission to transfer assets wherever they may be and which are necessary for their resettlement in another country to which they have been admitted.

# 22. UN: Guiding Principles on Internal Displacement, 1998

**Commentary**: Formulated by the UN Human Rights Commission, the Principles (UN Doc E/CN.4/1998/53/Add.2, Annex) define a normative framework for internally displaced persons (IDPs). The Introductory Note states that the Principles 'restate existing norms and seek to clarify grey areas and fill in the gaps' within international humanitarian law, human rights law and refugee law: see further, 'Compilation and Analysis of Legal Norms', UN Doc E/CN.4/1996/52/Add.2. The foreword observes that these Principles 'provide valuable practical guidance to Governments, other competent authorities, intergovernmental organizations and NGOs'. Commercial interests are engaged with respect to large-scale development projects (Principles 5 & 6), employment (22), offering humanitarian assistance (25) and property (21 & 29). Natural resource extraction can exacerbate local armed conflict and contribute to human rights violations: Canadian Department of Foreign Affairs and International Trade (2000), *Human Security in Sudan: The Report of a Canadian Assessment Mission*, Ottawa. See further, World Bank, Operational Directive 4.30 (1990) on Involuntary Resettlement, Washington, DC.

**Introduction: Scope and Purpose**

2. For the purposes of these Principles, internally displaced persons are persons or groups of persons who have been forced or obliged to flee or to leave their homes or places of habitual residence, in particular as a result of or in order to avoid the effects of armed conflict, situations of generalized violence, violations of human rights or natural or human-made disasters, and who have not crossed an internationally recognized State border.
3. These Principles reflect and are consistent with international human rights law and international humanitarian law. They provide guidance to:

   (d) Intergovernmental and non-governmental organizations when addressing internal displacement.

**Principle 2**

1. These Principles shall be observed by all authorities, groups and persons irrespective of their legal status and applied without any adverse distinction . . .

**Principle 5**

All authorities and international actors shall respect and ensure respect for their obligations under international law, including human rights and humanitarian law, in all circumstances, so as to prevent and avoid conditions that might lead to displacement of persons.

**Principle 6**

1. Every human being shall have the right to be protected against being arbitrarily displaced from his or her home or place of habitual residence.
2. The prohibition of arbitrary displacement includes displacement:

   (c) In cases of large-scale development projects, which are not justified by compelling and overriding public interests;

3. Displacement shall last no longer than required by the circumstances.

**Principle 11**

2. Internally displaced persons, whether or not their liberty has been restricted, shall be protected in particular against:

   (a) Rape, mutilation, torture, cruel, inhuman or degrading treatment or punishment, and other outrages upon personal dignity, such as acts of gender-specific violence, forced prostitution and any form of indecent assault;
   (b) Slavery or any contemporary form of slavery, such as sale into marriage, sexual exploitation, or forced labour of children; and
   (c) Acts of violence intended to spread terror among internally displaced persons. Threats and incitement to commit any of the foregoing acts shall be prohibited.

**Principle 21**

1. No one shall be arbitrarily deprived of property and possessions.
2. The property and possessions of internally displaced persons shall in all circumstances be protected, in particular, against the following acts:

   (a) Pillage;
   (b) Direct or indiscriminate attacks or other acts of violence;
   (c) Being used to shield military operations or objectives;
   (d) Being made the object of reprisal; and
   (e) Being destroyed or appropriated as a form of collective punishment.

3. Property and possessions left behind by internally displaced persons should be protected against destruction and arbitrary and illegal appropriation, occupation or use.

**Principle 22**

1. Internally displaced persons, whether or not they are living in camps, shall not be discriminated against as a result of their displacement in the enjoyment of the following rights:

   (b) The right to seek freely opportunities for employment and to participate in economic activities . . .

**Principle 25**

1. The primary duty and responsibility for providing humanitarian assistance to internally displaced persons lies with national authorities.
2. International humanitarian organizations and other appropriate actors have the right to offer their services in support of the internally displaced. Such an offer shall not be regarded as an unfriendly act or an interference in a State's internal affairs and shall be considered in good faith . . .

**Principle 27**

1. International humanitarian organizations and other appropriate actors when providing assistance should give due regard to the protection needs and human rights of internally displaced persons and take appropriate measures in this regard. In so doing, these organizations and actors should respect relevant international standards and codes of conduct.

**Principle 29**

2. Competent authorities have the duty and responsibility to assist returned and/or resettled internally displaced persons to recover, to the extent possible, their property and possessions which they left behind or were dispossessed of upon their displacement. When recovery of such property and possessions is not possible, competent authorities shall provide or assist these persons in obtaining appropriate compensation or another form of just reparation.

# 23. Additional initiatives

## i. UN: Vienna Declaration and Programme of Action, 1993

**Commentary**: The principal outcomes of the World Conference on Human Rights (UN Doc A/CONF.157/24 (Part I), 1993) apply to business and industry as 'groups', 'organs of society', 'institutions', 'non-governmental organisations', actors within 'the development field' or 'private' sphere and 'members of the international community'. Paragraphs of relevance include the right to development, illicitly dumping toxic or dangerous substances (paragraph 11), racism (15), sexual harassment, exploiting or trafficking in women (18 & 38), and economically or sexually exploiting children including child pornography, child prostitution and the sale of organs (21 & 48). Additionally noteworthy is respecting the exercise of minority rights in private (paragraph 19) and eliminating violence against women in their private life (38). The Declaration and Programme of Action recognises the important contributions of NGOs in promoting and implementing human rights (paragraphs 38 & 52) including the media (39). Governments with NGO assistance should promote increased human rights awareness and mutual tolerance (paragraph 82). Finally, governments are urged to 'incorporate standards as contained in international human rights instruments in domestic legislation and to strengthen national structures, institutions and organs of society which play a role in promoting and safeguarding human rights' (paragraph 83).

## ii. UN: Declaration on the Right and Responsibility of Individuals, Groups and Organs of Society to Promote and Protect Universally Recognised Human Rights and Fundamental Freedoms, 1999

**Commentary**: UNGA Resolution 53/144 (1999) marks the fiftieth anniversary of the UDHR. For the draft text, see Commission on Human Rights Resolution 1998/7; ECOSOC Official Records, UN Doc E/1998/23, Chapter II, Section A. NGOs (which can include corporations in UN parlance) were invited 'to intensify their efforts to disseminate the Declaration and to promote universal respect and understanding thereof'. Governments have the prime responsibility and duty to protect, promote and implement human rights (Articles 2 & 14) through national law consistent with their international obligations (3). The Declaration *inter alia* recognises the rights to access information (Article 6), propose new ideas (7), participate in public affairs (8), participate in peaceful activities (12) and promote awareness (16). It also identifies the roles and responsibilities applicable to corporations as a 'group' of individuals or 'institution'. In particular, everyone possesses the right, individually and in association with others, to promote human rights and strive for their realisation at national and international levels (Article 1). Since everyone owes duties to the community, individuals, groups, institutions and NGOs play an important role in safeguarding and advancing democratic societies, institutions and processes (Article 18). Finally, nothing permits governments to support or promote the activities of individuals, groups of individuals, institutions or NGOs contrary to the provisions of the UN Charter (Article 20).

### iii. Confederation of Norwegian Business and Industry (NHO): Human Rights from the Perspective of Business and Industry – A Checklist, 1998

**Commentary**: Prepared in collaboration with Amnesty International (Norway), the Checklist (www.nho.no/files/5095checklist_human_rights.pdf) 'is intended to clarify the obligations that business and industry will face in the field of human rights, and to learn more about the questions and dilemmas such obligations may entail for a company'. Observing that 'Norwegian enterprises must take a stand on human rights issues today to a far greater extent than ever before', the Preface notes that 'Norwegian enterprises bear a clear responsibility for following the same business principles and devoting the same attention to human rights abroad as they do at home'. The Checklist identifies a series of management considerations pertaining to the rights to freedom from discrimination, personal safety and security, freedom of opinion and expression, freedom of peaceful assembly and association, participation in political life, work, rest and leisure, adequate living standards, education, minority rights and prohibiting slavery and torture. Primary responsibility for implementation rests with corporate managers and owners. See further, NHO (2003), 'Corporate Social Responsibility', Oslo; NHO/Oslo Peace Research Institute (2003), 'Corporate Actors in Zones of Conflict: Responsible Engagement', Oslo; NHO (2000), 'Standpoint Corruption', Oslo.

### iv. Norwegian Forum for Development and Environment: Guidelines concerning Human Rights and Environment for Norwegian Companies Abroad, 1999

**Commentary**: The Forum is a network serving approximately 60 Norwegian NGOs in the environmental and development field. The Guidelines (www.milli.no/~forum/dokumenter/guidelines.rtf) were formulated by the TaskForce on the Internationalisation of Norwegian Trade and Industry. It 'encourages the view that Norwegian companies with interests abroad are accountable for the social and environmental aspects of their own and related activities and thus also have an obligation to avoid activities which have significant negative consequences for humans and the environment'. The Guidelines consist of 21 principles relating to labour and human rights, environmental protection, prior consultation, legal compliance, access to information, establishing ethical guidelines and demonstrating care in zones of conflict.

### v. Amnesty International UK Business Group: Human Rights Guidelines for Companies, 1998

**Commentary**: Amnesty International is a human rights NGO. The Guidelines (www.amnesty.org.uk/business/pubs/hrgc.shtml) are an introductory checklist of human rights principles. They contemplate establishing corporate policies on human rights, ensuring that security arrangements are consistent with international standards on law enforcement, community engagement, ensuring freedom from discrimination, prohibiting slavery and implementing safe and healthy working conditions. The strategic planning and policy framework provides further recommendations for achieving these objectives. Although primary responsibility for implementation and monitoring rests with individual companies, including a role for other stakeholders such as NGOs and local communities affords greater transparency and credibility to commercial operations. Although they no longer accurately represent its current policy, approach or analysis of corporate responsibility within this field, see also Human Rights Watch, 'Working Guidelines on Business and Human Rights', New York, 1997.

### vi. Various NGOs: The Quito Declaration on the Enforcement and Realization of Economic, Social and Cultural Rights in Latin America and the Caribbean, 1998

**Commentary**: The South American Platform for Democracy, Human Rights and Development, the Latin American Association of Promoter Organizations, the Latin American League of the International Federation of Human Rights and the Centre for Economic and Social Rights organised a convention in Ecuador during 1998 for the promotion of economic, social and cultural rights (ESCR). Formulated over three days by NGOs from the fields of development, human rights, labour, women's rights and indigenous rights, the Declaration (available through www.cesr.org) provides a frame of reference for realising ESCR within Latin America. Although governments have the primary obligation to respect, protect and promote ESCR, other actors such as MNCs also have the duty to respect these rights and may be held accountable for violations (paragraph 17). Corporations are called upon to adopt social ethics guidelines and codes of conduct, respect ILO standards, assume legal responsibility for the impact of their activities and permit independent oversight and/or regular monitoring by civil society organisations (paragraphs 88–91).

## vii. UNESCO: Declaration on Fundamental Principles concerning the Contribution of the Mass Media to Strengthening Peace and International Understanding, to the Promotion of Human Rights and to Countering Racialism, Apartheid and Incitement to War, 1978

**Commentary**: UNGA Resolution 59 (1946) observed that 'freedom of information requires as an indispensable element the willingness and capacity to employ its privileges without abuse'. UNGA Resolution 110 (1947) condemned all forms of propaganda and Resolution 127 (1947) invited governments to combat the diffusion of false or distorted reports. UNESCO General Conference Resolution 4.301 (1970) noted the fundamental contribution to be made by the information media to furthering international understanding and cooperation in the interests of peace and human welfare. The Declaration was adopted by UNESCO's General Conference at its twentieth session: see UNESCO's Standard-Setting Instruments, *Volume IV C*, Paris (1994); www.unesco.org. It promotes *inter alia* access to information, education and protecting journalistic freedom.

# PART V

# International Labour Standards

# 24. ILO: Declaration on Fundamental Principles and Rights at Work, 1998

**Commentary**: The ILO is the constitutionally mandated organisation for establishing international labour standards (www.ilo.org). These take the form of Conventions and Recommendations (available through www.ilo.org/ilolex/english/index.htm). Conventions create legally binding obligations upon ratification by Member States whereas Recommendations are non-binding instruments providing guidance on policy, legislation and practice. The former may contemplate Members completing annual reports on the implementation measures adopted. The ILO's distinctive tripartite nature means that national delegations are composed of two government representatives and one delegate each from national employer and worker organisations. Employers are represented by the International Organisation of Employers (IOE): see IOE (2000), 'ILO Standards', Position Paper, Geneva. See generally, UNCTAD–DTCI (1994), 'World Investment Report 1994: TNCs, Employment and the Workplace', UN Doc UNCTAD/DTCI/10.

Employers' and workers' organisations may be consulted by governments at national levels on measures to give effect to ILO Conventions: see ILO Convention No 144 (1976) Concerning Tripartite Consultation to Promote the Implementation of International Labour Standards (entry into force 1978); ILO Recommendation No 113 (1960) concerning Consultation (Industrial and National Levels); ILO Recommendation No 152 (1976) concerning Tripartite Consultation (Activities of the ILO). See also, ILO Convention No 81 (1947) and Recommendation No 81 (1947) concerning Labour Inspection; Convention No 129 (1969) concerning Labour Inspection (Agriculture); and Convention No 135 (1971) concerning Workers' Representatives. For academic commentary, see Johnson J.L. (1998), 'Public–private–public convergence: how the private actor can shape public international labour standards', *Brooklyn Journal of International Law*, **24** (1), 291–334.

The Declaration on Fundamental Principles and Rights at Work commits governments to respect and promote labour rights and principles from four categories whether or not they have ratified the relevant Conventions. The follow-up procedure envisages the completion of annual reports for review by a Committee of Independent Expert Advisers and the ILO's Governing Body: see Introduction by the ILO Declaration Expert-Advisers to the Compilation of Annual Reports, ILO Doc GB.289/4 (2004). Technical cooperation also builds local capacity. The ILO Director-General completes an annual Global Report identifying relevant trends: see 'Organizing for Social Justice' (2004), 'Time for Equality at Work' (2003), 'A Future without Child Labour' (2002),.'Stopping Forced Labour' (2001) and 'Your Voice at Work' (2000). See generally, ILO (2003), *Fundamental Rights at Work and International Labour Standards*, Geneva. The IOE will encourage implementation of the Declaration: IOE (1998), 'The ILO Declaration on Fundamental Principles and Rights at Work: A Guide for Employers', Geneva. See further, USCIB (1998), 'ILO Declaration on

Fundamental Principles and Rights at Work', New York. For an implementation agreement between European employers and workers, see EuroCommerce/Euro-Fiet (1999), 'Agreement on Fundamental Rights and Principles at Work', Brussels. See further, Luz Vega Ruiz M. and Martinez D. (2002), *Fundamental Principles and Rights at Work: Value, Viability, Incidence and Importance as Elements for Economic Progress and Social Justice*, Geneva: ILO.

**The International Labour Conference,**
Recalls:

(a) that in freely joining the ILO, all Members have endorsed the principles and rights set out in its Constitution and in the Declaration of Philadelphia, and have undertaken to work towards attaining the overall objectives of the Organization to the best of their resources and fully in line with their specific circumstances;
(b) that these principles and rights have been expressed and developed in the form of specific rights and obligations in Conventions recognized as fundamental both inside and outside the Organization.

Declares that all Members, even if they have not ratified the Conventions in question, have an obligation arising from the very fact of membership in the Organization to respect, to promote and to realize, in good faith and in accordance with the Constitution, the principles concerning the fundamental rights which are the subject of those Conventions, namely:

(a) freedom of association and the effective recognition of the right to collective bargaining;
(b) the elimination of all forms of forced or compulsory labour;
(c) the effective abolition of child labour; and
(d) the elimination of discrimination in respect of employment and occupation . . .

Stresses that labour standards should not be used for protectionist trade purposes, and that nothing in this Declaration and its follow-up shall be invoked or otherwise used for such purposes; in addition, the comparative advantage of any country should in no way be called into question by this Declaration and its follow-up.

# 25. ILO: Convention No 87 (1948) Concerning Freedom of Association and Protection of the Right to Organise (entry into force 1950)

**Commentary**: The right to organise trade unions has been recognised by the ILO as a fundamental right for workers, irrespective of the level of development of member states. For ILO perspectives, see ILO (1985), *Freedom of Association: Digest of Decisions and Principles of the Freedom of Association Committee of the Governing Body of the ILO*, 3rd edn, Geneva. For academic commentary, see Swepston L. (1998), 'Human Rights Law and Freedom of Association: Development through ILO Supervision', *International Labour Review*, **137**, 169–94. For a historical perspective, see Dunning H. (1998), 'The Origins of Convention No. 87 on Freedom of Association and the Right to Organize', *International Labour Review*, **137**, 149–67. See further, ILO (1998), 'An Annotated Bibliography: International Protection of Freedom of Association', *International Labour Review*, **137**, 259–93.

**Article 2**
Workers and employers, without distinction whatsoever, shall have the right to establish and, subject only to the rules of the organisation concerned, to join organisations of their own choosing without previous authorisation.

**Article 3**
1. Workers' and employers' organisations shall have the right to draw up their constitutions and rules, to elect their representatives in full freedom, to organise their administration and activities and to formulate their programmes.
2. The public authorities shall refrain from any interference which would restrict this right or impede the lawful exercise thereof.

**Article 4**
Workers' and employers' organisations shall not be liable to be dissolved or suspended by administrative authority.

**Article 5**
Workers' and employers' organisations shall have the right to establish and join federations and confederations and any such organisation, federation or confederation shall have the right to affiliate with international organisations of workers and employers.

**Article 7**
The acquisition of legal personality by workers' and employers' organisations, federations and confederations shall not be made subject to conditions of such a character as to restrict the application of the provisions of Articles 2, 3 and 4 hereof.

**Article 8**
1. In exercising the rights provided for in this Convention workers and employers and their respective organisations, like other persons or organised collectivities, shall respect the law of the land.
2. The law of the land shall not be such as to impair, nor shall it be so applied as to impair, the guarantees provided for in this Convention.

**Article 10**
In this Convention the term organisation means any organisation of workers or of employers for furthering and defending the interests of workers or of employers.

# 26. ILO: Convention No 98 (1949) Concerning the Application of the Principles of the Right to Organise and Bargain Collectively (entry into force 1951)

**Commentary**: See further, Recommendation No 163 (1981) concerning Collective Bargaining.

**Article 1**

1. Workers shall enjoy adequate protection against acts of anti-union discrimination in respect of their employment.
2. Such protection shall apply more particularly in respect of acts calculated to:
   (a) make the employment of a worker subject to the condition that he shall not join a union or shall relinquish trade union membership;
   (b) cause the dismissal of or otherwise prejudice a worker by reason of union membership or because of participation in union activities outside working hours or, with the consent of the employer, within working hours.

**Article 2**

1. Workers' and employers' organisations shall enjoy adequate protection against any acts of interference by each other or each other's agents or members in their establishment, functioning or administration.
2. In particular, acts which are designed to promote the establishment of workers' organisations under the domination of employers or employers' organisations, or to support workers' organisations by financial or other means, with the object of placing such organisations under the control of employers or employers' organisations, shall be deemed to constitute acts of interference within the meaning of this Article.

**Article 3**

Machinery appropriate to national conditions shall be established, where necessary, for the purpose of ensuring respect for the right to organise as defined in the preceding Articles.

**Article 4**

Measures appropriate to national conditions shall be taken, where necessary, to encourage and promote the full development and utilisation of machinery for voluntary negotiation between employers or employers' organisations and workers' organisations, with a view to the regulation of terms and conditions of employment by means of collective agreements.

# 27. ILO: Convention No 29 (1930) Concerning Forced or Compulsory Labour (entry into force 1932)

**Commentary**: For the failure of a government to effectively observe this Convention, see ILO, 'Report of the Commission of Inquiry appointed under Article 26 of the ILO Constitution to examine the observance by Myanmar of the Forced Labour Convention', ILO Doc GB.273 (1998); ILO, 'Second Report of the Director-General to the members of the Governing Body on measures taken by Myanmar following the recommendations of the Commission of Inquiry established to examine its observance of the Forced Labour Convention', ILO Doc GB.277/6 (2000). For the responses of the IOE and national employer organisations in this instance, see ILO, 'Developments concerning the question of the observance by Myanmar of the Forced Labour Convention', ILO Doc GB.280/6 (2001): paras 22–31. See also, *John Doe I v Unocal Corp* 963 *F. Supp* 880 (DC Cal 1997) & 248 *F.3d* 915 (9th Cir 2001) & vacated and rehearing granted en banc 2003 WL 359787 (9th Cir 2003); *National Coalition Gov't of the Union of Burma v Unocal Inc* 176 *FRD* 329 (DC Cal 1997). For academic commentary, see Ramasastry A. (2002), 'Corporate complicity: from Nuremberg to Rangoon: an examination of forced labor cases and their impact on the liability of MNCs', *Berkeley Journal of International Law*, **20** (1), 91–151. See further, Recommendation No 35 (1930) concerning Forced Labour (Indirect Compulsion).

**Article 1**

1. Each Member of the ILO which ratifies this Convention undertakes to suppress the use of forced or compulsory labour in all its forms within the shortest possible period.

**Article 2**

1. For the purposes of this Convention the term forced or compulsory labour shall mean all work or service which is exacted from any person under the menace of any penalty and for which the said person has not offered himself voluntarily.
2. Nevertheless, for the purposes of this Convention, the term forced or compulsory labour shall not include:

   (a) any work or service exacted in virtue of compulsory military service laws for work of a purely military character;
   (b) any work or service which forms part of the normal civic obligations of the citizens of a fully self-governing country;

(c) any work or service exacted from any person as a consequence of a conviction in a court of law, provided that the said work or service is carried out under the supervision and control of a public authority and that the said person is not hired to or placed at the disposal of private individuals, companies or associations;
(d) any work or service exacted in cases of emergency, that is to say, in the event of war or of a calamity or threatened calamity, such as fire, flood, famine, earthquake, violent epidemic or epizootic diseases, invasion by animal, insect or vegetable pests, and in general any circumstance that would endanger the existence or the well-being of the whole or part of the population;
(e) minor communal services of a kind which, being performed by the members of the community in the direct interest of the said community, can therefore be considered as normal civic obligations incumbent upon the members of the community, provided that the members of the community or their direct representatives shall have the right to be consulted in regard to the need for such services.

**Article 4**

1. The competent authority shall not impose or permit the imposition of forced or compulsory labour for the benefit of private individuals, companies or associations . . .

**Article 5**

1. No concession granted to private individuals, companies or associations shall involve any form of forced or compulsory labour for the production or the collection of products which such private individuals, companies or associations utilise or in which they trade.
2. Where concessions exist containing provisions involving such forced or compulsory labour, such provisions shall be rescinded as soon as possible, in order to comply with Article 1 of this Convention.

**Article 6**

Officials of the administration, even when they have the duty of encouraging the populations under their charge to engage in some form of labour, shall not put constraint upon the said populations or upon any individual members thereof to work for private individuals, companies or associations.

**Article 8**

1. The responsibility for every decision to have recourse to forced or compulsory labour shall rest with the highest civil authority in the territory concerned.
2. Nevertheless, that authority may delegate powers to the highest local authorities to exact forced or compulsory labour which does not involve the removal of the workers from their place of habitual residence . . .

**Article 9**

Except as otherwise provided for in Article 10 of this Convention, any authority competent to exact forced or compulsory labour shall, before deciding to have recourse to such labour, satisfy itself:

(a) that the work to be done or the service to be rendered is of important direct interest for the community called upon to do work or render the service;
(b) that the work or service is of present or imminent necessity;
(c) that it has been impossible to obtain voluntary labour for carrying out the work or rendering the service by the offer of rates of wages and conditions of labour not less favourable than those prevailing in the area concerned for similar work or service; and
(d) that the work or service will not lay too heavy a burden upon the present population, having regard to the labour available and its capacity to undertake the work.

**Article 10**

1. Forced or compulsory labour exacted as a tax and forced or compulsory labour to which recourse is had for the execution of public works by chiefs who exercise administrative functions shall be progressively abolished.
2. Meanwhile, where forced or compulsory labour is exacted as a tax, and where recourse is had to forced or compulsory labour for the execution of public works by chiefs who exercise administrative functions, the authority concerned shall first satisfy itself:

   (a) that the work to be done or the service to be rendered is of important direct interest for the community called upon to do the work or render the service;
   (b) that the work or the service is of present or imminent necessity;
   (c) that the work or service will not lay too heavy a burden upon the present population, having regard to the labour available and its capacity to undertake the work;
   (d) that the work or service will not entail the removal of the workers from their place of habitual residence;
   (e) that the execution of the work or the rendering of the service will be directed in accordance with the exigencies of religion, social life and agriculture.

**Article 11**

1. Only adult able-bodied males who are of an apparent age of not less than 18 and not more than 45 years may be called upon for forced or compulsory labour. Except in respect of the kinds of labour provided for in Article 10 of this Convention, the following limitations and conditions shall apply:

   (a) whenever possible prior determination by a medical officer appointed by the administration that the persons concerned are not suffering from any infectious or contagious disease and that they are physically fit for the work required and for the conditions under which it is to be carried out;
   (b) exemption of school teachers and pupils and officials of the administration in general;
   (c) the maintenance in each community of the number of adult able-bodied men indispensable for family and social life;
   (d) respect for conjugal and family ties.

2. For the purposes of subparagraph (c) of the preceding paragraph, the regulations provided for in Article 23 of this Convention shall fix the proportion of the resident adult able-bodied males who may be taken at any one time for forced or compulsory labour, provided always that this proportion shall in no case exceed 25 per cent. In fixing this proportion

the competent authority shall take account of the density of the population, of its social and physical development, of the seasons, and of the work which must be done by the persons concerned on their own behalf in their locality, and, generally, shall have regard to the economic and social necessities of the normal life of the community concerned.

**Article 12**

1. The maximum period for which any person may be taken for forced or compulsory labour of all kinds in any one period of twelve months shall not exceed sixty days, including the time spent in going to and from the place of work.
2. Every person from whom forced or compulsory labour is exacted shall be furnished with a certificate indicating the periods of such labour which he has completed.

**Article 13**

1. The normal working hours of any person from whom forced or compulsory labour is exacted shall be the same as those prevailing in the case of voluntary labour, and the hours worked in excess of the normal working hours shall be remunerated at the rates prevailing in the case of overtime for voluntary labour.
2. A weekly day of rest shall be granted to all persons from whom forced or compulsory labour of any kind is exacted and this day shall coincide as far as possible with the day fixed by tradition or custom in the territories or regions concerned.

**Article 14**

1. With the exception of the forced or compulsory labour provided for in Article 10 of this Convention, forced or compulsory labour of all kinds shall be remunerated in cash at rates not less than those prevailing for similar kinds of work either in the district in which the labour is employed or in the district from which the labour is recruited, whichever may be the higher.
2. In the case of labour to which recourse is had by chiefs in the exercise of their administrative functions, payment of wages in accordance with the provisions of the preceding paragraph shall be introduced as soon as possible.
3. The wages shall be paid to each worker individually and not to his tribal chief or to any other authority.
4. For the purpose of payment of wages the days spent in travelling to and from the place of work shall be counted as working days.
5. Nothing in this Article shall prevent ordinary rations being given as a part of wages, such rations to be at least equivalent in value to the money payment they are taken to represent, but deductions from wages shall not be made either for the payment of taxes or for special food, clothing or accommodation supplied to a worker for the purpose of maintaining him in a fit condition to carry on his work under the special conditions of any employment, or for the supply of tools.

**Article 15**

1. Any laws or regulations relating to workmen's compensation for accidents or sickness arising out of the employment of the worker and any laws or regulations providing

compensation for the dependants of deceased or incapacitated workers which are or shall be in force in the territory concerned shall be equally applicable to persons from whom forced or compulsory labour is exacted and to voluntary workers.

2. In any case it shall be an obligation on any authority employing any worker on forced or compulsory labour to ensure the subsistence of any such worker who, by accident or sickness arising out of his employment, is rendered wholly or partially incapable of providing for himself, and to take measures to ensure the maintenance of any persons actually dependent upon such a worker in the event of his incapacity or decease arising out of his employment.

**Article 16**

1. Except in cases of special necessity, persons from whom forced or compulsory labour is exacted shall not be transferred to districts where the food and climate differ so considerably from those to which they have been accustomed as to endanger their health.
2. In no case shall the transfer of such workers be permitted unless all measures relating to hygiene and accommodation which are necessary to adapt such workers to the conditions and to safeguard their health can be strictly applied.
3. When such transfer cannot be avoided, measures of gradual habituation to the new conditions of diet and of climate shall be adopted on competent medical advice.
4. In cases where such workers are required to perform regular work to which they are not accustomed, measures shall be taken to ensure their habituation to it, especially as regards progressive training, the hours of work and the provision of rest intervals, and any increase or amelioration of diet which may be necessary.

**Article 17**

Before permitting recourse to forced or compulsory labour for works of construction or maintenance which entail the workers remaining at the workplaces for considerable periods, the competent authority shall satisfy itself:

1. that all necessary measures are taken to safeguard the health of the workers and to guarantee the necessary medical care, and, in particular, (a) that the workers are medically examined before commencing the work and at fixed intervals during the period of service, (b) that there is an adequate medical staff, provided with the dispensaries, infirmaries, hospitals and equipment necessary to meet all requirements, and (c) that the sanitary conditions of the workplaces, the supply of drinking water, food, fuel, and cooking utensils, and, where necessary, of housing and clothing, are satisfactory;
2. that definite arrangements are made to ensure the subsistence of the families of the workers, in particular by facilitating the remittance, by a safe method, of part of the wages to the family, at the request or with the consent of the workers;
3. that the journeys of the workers to and from the work-places are made at the expense and under the responsibility of the administration, which shall facilitate such journeys by making the fullest use of all available means of transport;
4. that, in case of illness or accident causing incapacity to work of a certain duration, the worker is repatriated at the expense of the administration;

5. that any worker who may wish to remain as a voluntary worker at the end of his period of forced or compulsory labour is permitted to do so without, for a period of two years, losing his right to repatriation free of expense to himself.

**Article 18**

1. Forced or compulsory labour for the transport of persons or goods, such as the labour of porters or boatmen, shall be abolished within the shortest possible period. Meanwhile the competent authority shall promulgate regulations determining, *inter alia*, (a) that such labour shall only be employed for the purpose of facilitating the movement of officials of the administration, when on duty, or for the transport of Government stores, or, in cases of very urgent necessity, the transport of persons other than officials, (b) that the workers so employed shall be medically certified to be physically fit, where medical examination is possible, and that where such medical examination is not practicable the person employing such workers shall be held responsible for ensuring that they are physically fit and not suffering from any infectious or contagious disease, (c) the maximum load which these workers may carry, (d) the maximum distance from their homes to which they may be taken, (e) the maximum number of days per month or other period for which they may be taken, including the days spent in returning to their homes, and (f) the persons entitled to demand this form of forced or compulsory labour and the extent to which they are entitled to demand it.
2. In fixing the maxima referred to under (c), (d) and (e) in the foregoing paragraph, the competent authority shall have regard to all relevant factors, including the physical development of the population from which the workers are recruited, the nature of the country through which they must travel and the climatic conditions.
3. The competent authority shall further provide that the normal daily journey of such workers shall not exceed a distance corresponding to an average working day of eight hours, it being understood that account shall be taken not only of the weight to be carried and the distance to be covered, but also of the nature of the road, the season and all other relevant factors, and that, where hours of journey in excess of the normal daily journey are exacted, they shall be remunerated at rates higher than the normal rates.

**Article 19**

1. The competent authority shall only authorise recourse to compulsory cultivation as a method of precaution against famine or a deficiency of food supplies and always under the condition that the food or produce shall remain the property of the individuals or the community producing it.
2. Nothing in this Article shall be construed as abrogating the obligation on members of a community, where production is organised on a communal basis by virtue of law or custom and where the produce or any profit accruing from the sale thereof remain the property of the community, to perform the work demanded by the community by virtue of law or custom.

**Article 21**

Forced or compulsory labour shall not be used for work underground in mines.

**Article 23**

1. To give effect to the provisions of this Convention the competent authority shall issue complete and precise regulations governing the use of forced or compulsory labour.
2. These regulations shall contain, *inter alia*, rules permitting any person from whom forced or compulsory labour is exacted to forward all complaints relative to the conditions of labour to the authorities and ensuring that such complaints will be examined and taken into consideration.

**Article 25**

The illegal exaction of forced or compulsory labour shall be punishable as a penal offence . . .

# 28. ILO: Convention No 105 (1957) Concerning the Abolition of Forced Labour (entry into force 1959)

**Commentary**: Although the two forced labour conventions are among the most highly ratified conventions, the Committee of Experts on the Application of Conventions and Recommendations continues to observe instances of the practice. For ILO perspectives, see ILO (1968), 'Summary of Reports on Unratified Conventions and Recommendations (Article 19 of the Constitution): Forced Labour', Geneva and ILO (2001), 'Stopping Forced Labour: Global Report under the Follow-up to the ILO Declaration on Fundamental Principles and Rights at Work', Report of the Director-General, Geneva. For a case study, see Solla P. (1998), 'Supervising labour standards and human rights: the case of forced labour in Myanmar (Burma)', *International Labour Review*, **137**, 391–409. On the question of compensation, see Fassbender B. (2005), 'Compensation for forced labour in World War II: the German Compensation Law of 2 August 2000', *Journal of International Criminal Justice*, **3**, 243–52.

**Article 1**
Each Member of the ILO which ratifies this Convention undertakes to suppress and not to make use of any form of forced or compulsory labour:

(a) as a means of political coercion or education or as a punishment for holding or expressing political views or views ideologically opposed to the established political, social or economic system;
(b) as a method of mobilising and using labour for purposes of economic development;
(c) as a means of labour discipline;
(d) as a punishment for having participated in strikes;
(e) as a means of racial, social, national or religious discrimination.

**Article 2**
Each Member of the ILO which ratifies this Convention undertakes to take effective measures to secure the immediate and complete abolition of forced or compulsory labour as specified in Article 1 of this Convention.

# 29. ILO: Convention No 182 (1999) Concerning the Prohibition and Immediate Action for the Elimination of the Worst Forms of Child Labour (entry into force 2000)

**Commentary**: See further, Recommendation No 190 (1999) concerning the prohibition and immediate action for the elimination of the worst forms of child labour. On the position of employers, see IOE General Council (1996), Resolution on Child Labour, 73rd Session, Geneva. On joint IOE/ILO initiatives, see IOE/ILO (1998), 'An Employer's Handbook on Child Labour: A Guide for Taking Action', Geneva; IOE/ILO (1999), 'An Employer's Initiative for Ratification of the Worst Forms of Child Labour Convention 1999 (No 182)', Geneva. For academic commentary, see Krug N.J. (1998), 'Exploiting child labour: corporate responsibility and the role of corporate codes of conduct', *New York Law School Journal of Human Rights*, **14**, 651–76.

**Article 1**

Each Member which ratifies this Convention shall take immediate and effective measures to secure the prohibition and elimination of the worst forms of child labour as a matter of urgency.

**Article 2**

For the purposes of this Convention, the term child shall apply to all persons under the age of 18.

**Article 3**

For the purposes of this Convention, the term the worst forms of child labour comprises:

(a) all forms of slavery or practices similar to slavery, such as the sale and trafficking of children, debt bondage and serfdom and forced or compulsory labour, including forced or compulsory recruitment of children for use in armed conflict;
(b) the use, procuring or offering of a child for prostitution, for the production of pornography or for pornographic performances;
(c) the use, procuring or offering of a child for illicit activities, in particular for the production and trafficking of drugs as defined in the relevant international treaties;
(d) work which, by its nature or the circumstances in which it is carried out, is likely to harm the health, safety or morals of children.

**Article 4**

1. The types of work referred to under Article 3(d) shall be determined by national laws or regulations or by the competent authority, after consultation with the organizations of employers and workers concerned, taking into consideration relevant international standards, in particular Paragraphs 3 and 4 of the Worst Forms of Child Labour Recommendation, 1999.
2. The competent authority, after consultation with the organizations of employers and workers concerned, shall identify where the types of work so determined exist.
3. The list of the types of work determined under paragraph 1 of this Article shall be periodically examined and revised as necessary, in consultation with the organizations of employers and workers concerned.

**Article 5**

Each Member shall, after consultation with employers' and workers' organizations, establish or designate appropriate mechanisms to monitor the implementation of the provisions giving effect to this Convention.

**Article 6**

1. Each Member shall design and implement programmes of action to eliminate as a priority the worst forms of child labour.
2. Such programmes of action shall be designed and implemented in consultation with relevant government institutions and employers' and workers' organizations, taking into consideration the views of other concerned groups as appropriate.

# 30. ILO: Convention No 138 (1973) Concerning Minimum Age for Admission to Employment (entry into force 1976)

**Commentary**: This Convention revised earlier Minimum Age Conventions and Recommendations with respect to Industry (1919 & 1937), Sea (1920 & 1936), Agriculture (1921), Trimmers and Stokers (1921), Non-Industrial Employment (1932 & 1937), Fishermen (1959) and Underground Work (1965). See further, Recommendation No 146 (1973) concerning the Minimum Age. See also, ILO Convention No 79 (1946) concerning Night Work of Young Persons (Non-Industrial Occupations) (entry into force 1950); Convention No 90 (1948) concerning Night Work of Young Persons (Industry) (entry into force 1951) as revised.

**Article 1**

Each Member for which this Convention is in force undertakes to pursue a national policy designed to ensure the effective abolition of child labour and to raise progressively the minimum age for admission to employment or work to a level consistent with the fullest physical and mental development of young persons.

**Article 2**

1. Each Member which ratifies this Convention shall specify, in a declaration appended to its ratification, a minimum age for admission to employment or work within its territory and on means of transport registered in its territory; subject to Articles 4 to 8 of this Convention, no one under that age shall be admitted to employment or work in any occupation.
3. The minimum age specified in pursuance of paragraph 1 of this Article shall not be less than the age of completion of compulsory schooling and, in any case, shall not be less than 15 years.
4. Notwithstanding the provisions of paragraph 3 of this Article, a Member whose economy and educational facilities are insufficiently developed may, after consultation with the organisations of employers and workers concerned, where such exist, initially specify a minimum age of 14 years . . .

**Article 3**

1. The minimum age for admission to any type of employment or work which by its nature or the circumstances in which it is carried out is likely to jeopardise the health, safety or morals of young persons shall not be less than 18 years.

2. The types of employment or work to which paragraph 1 of this Article applies shall be determined by national laws or regulations or by the competent authority, after consultation with the organisations of employers and workers concerned, where such exist.
3. Notwithstanding the provisions of paragraph 1 of this Article, national laws or regulations or the competent authority may, after consultation with the organisations of employers and workers concerned, where such exist, authorise employment or work as from the age of 16 years on condition that the health, safety and morals of the young persons concerned are fully protected and that the young persons have received adequate specific instruction or vocational training in the relevant branch of activity.

**Article 4**

1. In so far as necessary, the competent authority, after consultation with the organisations of employers and workers concerned, where such exist, may exclude from the application of this Convention limited categories of employment or work in respect of which special and substantial problems of application arise . . .

**Article 5**

1. A Member whose economy and administrative facilities are insufficiently developed may, after consultation with the organisations of employers and workers concerned, where such exist, initially limit the scope of application of this Convention.
3. The provisions of the Convention shall be applicable as a minimum to the following: mining and quarrying; manufacturing; construction; electricity, gas and water; sanitary services; transport, storage and communication; and plantations and other agricultural undertakings mainly producing for commercial purposes, but excluding family and small-scale holdings producing for local consumption and not regularly employing hired workers . . .

**Article 6**

This Convention does not apply to work done by children and young persons in schools for general, vocational or technical education or in other training institutions, or to work done by persons at least 14 years of age in undertakings, where such work is carried out in accordance with conditions prescribed by the competent authority, after consultation with the organisations of employers and workers concerned, where such exist, and is an integral part of:

(a) a course of education or training for which a school or training institution is primarily responsible;
(b) a programme of training mainly or entirely in an undertaking, which programme has been approved by the competent authority; or
(c) a programme of guidance or orientation designed to facilitate the choice of an occupation or of a line of training.

**Article 7**

1. National laws or regulations may permit the employment or work of persons 13 to 15 years of age on light work which is:

(a) not likely to be harmful to their health or development; and
(b) not such as to prejudice their attendance at school, their participation in vocational orientation or training programmes approved by the competent authority or their capacity to benefit from the instruction received.

2. National laws or regulations may also permit the employment or work of persons who are at least 15 years of age but have not yet completed their compulsory schooling on work which meets the requirements set forth in sub-paragraphs (a) and (b) of paragraph 1 of this Article.
4. Notwithstanding the provisions of paragraphs 1 and 2 of this Article, a Member which has availed itself of the provisions of paragraph 4 of Article 2 may, for as long as it continues to do so, substitute the ages 12 and 14 for the ages 13 and 15 in paragraph 1 and the age 14 for the age 15 in paragraph 2 of this Article.

**Article 8**

1. After consultation with the organisations of employers and workers concerned, where such exist, the competent authority may, by permits granted in individual cases, allow exceptions to the prohibition of employment or work provided for in Article 2 of this Convention, for such purposes as participation in artistic performances.
2. Permits so granted shall limit the number of hours during which and prescribe the conditions in which employment or work is allowed.

# 31. ILO: Convention No 111 (1958) Concerning Discrimination in Respect of Employment and Occupation (entry into force 1960)

**Commentary**: See further, Recommendation No 111 (1958) concerning Discrimination (Employment and Occupation). See also, ILO Convention No 122 (1964, entry into force 1966) & Recommendation No 122 (1964) concerning Employment Policy; ILO Convention No 3 (1919) concerning Maternity Protection as revised by Convention No 103 (1952), No 183 (2000, entry into force 2002) and Recommendation No 191 (2000); ILO Convention No 156 (1981, entry into force 1983) & Recommendation No 165 (1981) concerning Equal Opportunities and Equal Treatment for Men and Women Workers (Workers with Family Responsibilities).

**Article 1**

1. For the purpose of this Convention the term discrimination includes:

   (a) any distinction, exclusion or preference made on the basis of race, colour, sex, religion, political opinion, national extraction or social origin, which has the effect of nullifying or impairing equality of opportunity or treatment in employment or occupation;

   (b) such other distinction, exclusion or preference which has the effect of nullifying or impairing equality of opportunity or treatment in employment or occupation as may be determined by the Member concerned after consultation with representative employers' and workers' organisations, where such exist, and with other appropriate bodies.

2. Any distinction, exclusion or preference in respect of a particular job based on the inherent requirements thereof shall not be deemed to be discrimination.
3. For the purpose of this Convention the terms employment and occupation include access to vocational training, access to employment and to particular occupations, and terms and conditions of employment.

**Article 2**

Each Member for which this Convention is in force undertakes to declare and pursue a national policy designed to promote, by methods appropriate to national conditions and practice, equality of opportunity and treatment in respect of employment and occupation, with a view to eliminating any discrimination in respect thereof.

**Article 3**

Each Member for which this Convention is in force undertakes, by methods appropriate to national conditions and practice:

(a) to seek the co-operation of employers' and workers' organisations and other appropriate bodies in promoting the acceptance and observance of this policy . . .

**Article 5**

1. Special measures of protection or assistance provided for in other Conventions or Recommendations adopted by the International Labour Conference shall not be deemed to be discrimination.
2. Any Member may, after consultation with representative employers' and workers' organisations, where such exist, determine that other special measures designed to meet the particular requirements of persons who, for reasons such as sex, age, disablement, family responsibilities or social or cultural status, are generally recognised to require special protection or assistance, shall not be deemed to be discrimination.

# 32. ILO: Convention No 100 (1951) Concerning Equal Remuneration for Men and Women Workers for Work of Equal Value (entry into force 1953)

**Commentary**: See further, Recommendation No 90 (1951) concerning Equal Remuneration. See also, ILO Convention No 95 (1949, entry into force 1952) and Recommendation No 85 (1949) Concerning the Protection of Wages; ILO Convention No 1 (1919) Limiting the Hours of Work in Industrial Undertakings to Eight in the Day and Forty-Eight in the Week (entry into force 1921); ILO Convention No 30 (1930) Concerning the Regulation of Hours of Work in Commerce and Offices (entry into force 1932); ILO Recommendation No 7 (1920) concerning Hours of Work (Fishing); ILO Recommendation No 8 (1920) concerning Hours of Work (Inland Navigation).

**Article 1**

For the purpose of this Convention:

(a) the term remuneration includes the ordinary, basic or minimum wage or salary and any additional emoluments whatsoever payable directly or indirectly, whether in cash or in kind, by the employer to the worker and arising out of the worker's employment;

(b) the term equal remuneration for men and women workers for work of equal value refers to rates of remuneration established without discrimination based on sex.

**Article 2**

1. Each Member shall, by means appropriate to the methods in operation for determining rates of remuneration, promote and, in so far as is consistent with such methods, ensure the application to all workers of the principle of equal remuneration for men and women workers for work of equal value.
2. This principle may be applied by means of:

   (a) national laws or regulations;
   (b) legally established or recognised machinery for wage determination;
   (c) collective agreements between employers and workers; or
   (d) a combination of these various means.

**Article 3**

1. Where such action will assist in giving effect to the provisions of this Convention measures shall be taken to promote objective appraisal of jobs on the basis of the work to be performed.
2. The methods to be followed in this appraisal may be decided upon by the authorities responsible for the determination of rates of remuneration, or, where such rates are determined by collective agreements, by the parties thereto.
3. Differential rates between workers which correspond, without regard to sex, to differences, as determined by such objective appraisal, in the work to be performed shall not be considered as being contrary to the principle of equal remuneration for men and women workers for work of equal value.

**Article 4**

Each Member shall co-operate as appropriate with the employers' and workers' organisations concerned for the purpose of giving effect to the provisions of this Convention.

# 33. ILO: Tripartite Declaration of Principles concerning Multinational Enterprises and Social Policy, 2001

**Commentary**: In 1972 the International Labour Conference became concerned by the social problems raised by MNEs, and convened a tripartite meeting of experts to 'explore and submit recommendations to the Governing Body on the desirability and possible scope of ILO action in this area'. In 1976 a Tripartite Advisory Meeting on the Relationship of MNEs and Social Policy reviewed the ILO research programme. The resulting Tripartite Declaration was adopted in 1977 with a second edition issued in 1991. The third edition (*OB* Vol LXXXIII, 2000, Series A, No 3; extracted below with footnotes omitted) was updated to include the 1998 ILO Declaration on Fundamental Principles and Rights at Work: see ILO, 'Updating of references annexed to the Tripartite Declaration of Principles concerning MNEs and Social Policy', Doc GB.277/MNE/3 (2000).

Drawing upon relevant principles in ILO Conventions and Recommendations (see Annex One), the Declaration calls for voluntary commitments in the areas of development policy, rights at work, employment, training, conditions of work and life and industrial relations: ILO, 'A Guide to the Tripartite Declaration of Principles concerning MNEs and Social Policy, Knowing and Using Universal Guidelines for Social Responsibility', Geneva, 2002. Since 1985, quadrennial surveys have been issued to governments and employers' and workers' organisations to monitor the effect given to the instrument. Following the fifth survey in 1990, questionnaires were sent to employers' and workers' organisations and their periodicity adjusted from three to four years. The Seventh Survey covers the 1996–99 period: see Summary of Reports (ILO Doc GB.280/MNE/1/2), Analysis (ILO Doc GB.280/MNE/1/1) and Conclusions (GB.280/MNE/13).

Interpretations are also rendered by the ILO Subcommittee on Multinational Enterprises. As of 1999, the Subcommittee had received over 23 such requests but very few passed the test of receivability, thereby disqualifying opportunities for interpretations: see ILO Subcommittee on MNEs, 'Follow-up and Promotion', ILO Doc GB.277/MNE/1 (2000).

Relevant ILO Governing Body documents include promoting the MNE Declaration: the 2003 activities report (ILO Doc GB.289/MNE/1), developments in other organisations (GB.289/MNE/2 (2004)) and a 2003 information note on corporate social responsibility and international labour standards (GB.288/WP/SDG/3). Relevant ILO Working Papers include Gunter H. (1981), 'The Tripartite Declaration of Principles concerning MNEs and Social Policy (history, contents, follow-up and relationship with relevant instruments of other organisations)', ILO WP18; Gunter H. (1982), 'ILO research on MNEs and social policy: an overview', ILO WP15; Morawetz R. (1991), 'Recent foreign direct investment in Eastern Europe: towards a possible role for the Tripartite Declaration of Principles concerning MNEs and Social Policy', ILO WP71.

**Preamble**

1. MNEs play an important part in the economies of most countries and in international economic relations. This is of increasing interest to governments as well as to employers and workers and their respective organizations. Through international direct investment and other means such enterprises can bring substantial benefits to home and host countries by contributing to the more efficient utilization of capital, technology and labour. Within the framework of development policies established by governments, they can also make an important contribution to the promotion of economic and social welfare; to the improvement of living standards and the satisfaction of basic needs; to the creation of employment opportunities, both directly and indirectly; and to the enjoyment of basic human rights, including freedom of association, throughout the world. On the other hand, the advances made by MNEs in organizing their operations beyond the national framework may lead to abuse of concentrations of economic power and to conflicts with national policy objectives and with the interest of the workers. In addition, the complexity of MNEs and the difficulty of clearly perceiving their diverse structures, operations and policies sometimes give rise to concern either in the home or in the host countries, or in both.
2. The aim of this Tripartite Declaration of Principles is to encourage the positive contribution which MNEs can make to economic and social progress and to minimize and resolve the difficulties to which their various operations may give rise, taking into account the UN resolutions advocating the establishment of a NIEO.
3. This aim will be furthered by appropriate laws and policies, measures and actions adopted by the governments and by cooperation among the governments and the employers' and workers' organizations of all countries.
4. The principles set out in this Declaration are commended to the governments, the employers' and workers' organizations of home and host countries and to the MNEs themselves.
5. These principles are intended to guide the governments, the employers' and workers' organizations and the MNEs in taking such measures and actions and adopting such social policies, including those based on the principles laid down in the Constitution and the relevant Conventions and Recommendations of the ILO, as would further social progress.
6. To serve its purpose this Declaration does not require a precise legal definition of MNEs; this paragraph is designed to facilitate the understanding of the Declaration and not to provide such a definition. MNEs include enterprises, whether they are of public, mixed or private ownership, which own or control production, distribution, services or other facilities outside the country in which they are based. The degree of autonomy of entities within MNEs in relation to each other varies widely from one such enterprise to another, depending on the nature of the links between such entities and their fields of activity and having regard to the great diversity in the form of ownership, in the size, in the nature and location of the operations of the enterprises concerned. Unless otherwise specified, the term 'MNE' is used in this Declaration to designate the various entities (parent companies or local entities or both or the organization as a whole) according to the distribution of responsibilities among them, in the expectation that they will cooperate and provide assistance to one another as necessary to facilitate observance of the principles laid down in the Declaration.
7. This Declaration sets out principles in the fields of employment, training, conditions of work and life and industrial relations which governments, employers' and workers'

organizations and MNEs are recommended to observe on a voluntary basis; its provisions shall not limit or otherwise affect obligations arising out of ratification of any ILO Convention.

**General Policies**

8. All the parties concerned by this Declaration should respect the sovereign rights of States, obey the national laws and regulations, give due consideration to local practices and respect relevant international standards. They should respect the Universal Declaration of Human Rights and the corresponding International Covenants adopted by the General Assembly of the UN as well as the Constitution of the ILO and its principles according to which freedom of expression and association are essential to sustained progress. They should contribute to the realization of the ILO Declaration on Fundamental Principles and Rights at Work and its Follow-up, adopted in 1998. They should also honour commitments which they have freely entered into, in conformity with the national law and accepted international obligations.
9. Governments which have not yet ratified Conventions Nos. 87, 98, 111, 122, 138 and 182 are urged to do so and in any event to apply, to the greatest extent possible, through their national policies, the principles embodied therein and in Recommendations Nos. 111, 119, 122, 146 and 190. Without prejudice to the obligation of governments to ensure compliance with Conventions they have ratified, in countries in which the Conventions and Recommendations cited in this paragraph are not complied with, all parties should refer to them for guidance in their social policy.
10. MNEs should take fully into account established general policy objectives of the countries in which they operate. Their activities should be in harmony with the development priorities and social aims and structure of the country in which they operate. To this effect, consultations should be held between MNEs, the government and, wherever appropriate, the national employers' and workers' organizations concerned.
11. The principles laid down in this Declaration do not aim at introducing or maintaining inequalities of treatment between multinational and national enterprises. They reflect good practice for all. Multinational and national enterprises, wherever the principles of this Declaration are relevant to both, should be subject to the same expectations in respect of their conduct in general and their social practices in particular.
12. Governments of home countries should promote good social practice in accordance with this Declaration of Principles, having regard to the social and labour law, regulations and practices in host countries as well as to relevant international standards. Both host and home country governments should be prepared to have consultations with each other, whenever the need arises, on the initiative of either.

**Employment**

*Employment Promotion*

13. With a view to stimulating economic growth and development, raising living standards, meeting manpower requirements and overcoming unemployment and underemployment, governments should declare and pursue, as a major goal, an active policy designed to promote full, productive and freely chosen employment.

14. This is particularly important in the case of host country governments in developing areas of the world where the problems of unemployment and underemployment are at their most serious. In this connection, the general conclusions adopted by the Tripartite World Conference on Employment, Income Distribution and Social Progress and the International Division of Labour (Geneva, June 1976) should be kept in mind.
15. Paragraphs 13 and 14 above establish the framework within which due attention should be paid, in both home and host countries, to the employment impact of MNEs.
16. MNEs, particularly when operating in developing countries, should endeavour to increase employment opportunities and standards, taking into account the employment policies and objectives of the governments, as well as security of employment and the long-term development of the enterprise.
17. Before starting operations, MNEs should, wherever appropriate, consult the competent authorities and the national employers' and workers' organizations in order to keep their manpower plans, as far as practicable, in harmony with national social development policies. Such consultation, as in the case of national enterprises, should continue between the MNEs and all parties concerned, including the workers' organizations.
18. MNEs should give priority to the employment, occupational development, promotion and advancement of nationals of the host country at all levels in cooperation, as appropriate, with representatives of the workers employed by them or of the organizations of these workers and governmental authorities.
19. MNEs, when investing in developing countries, should have regard to the importance of using technologies which generate employment, both directly and indirectly. To the extent permitted by the nature of the process and the conditions prevailing in the economic sector concerned, they should adapt technologies to the needs and characteristics of the host countries. They should also, where possible, take part in the development of appropriate technology in host countries.
20. To promote employment in developing countries, in the context of an expanding world economy, MNEs, wherever practicable, should give consideration to the conclusion of contracts with national enterprises for the manufacture of parts and equipment, to the use of local raw materials and to the progressive promotion of the local processing of raw materials. Such arrangements should not be used by MNEs to avoid the responsibilities embodied in the principles of this Declaration.

*Equality of Opportunity and Treatment*

21. All governments should pursue policies designed to promote equality of opportunity and treatment in employment, with a view to eliminating any discrimination based on race, colour, sex, religion, political opinion, national extraction or social origin.
22. MNEs should be guided by this general principle throughout their operations without prejudice to the measures envisaged in paragraph 18 or to government policies designed to correct historical patterns of discrimination and thereby to extend equality of opportunity and treatment in employment. MNEs should accordingly make qualifications, skill and experience the basis for the recruitment, placement, training and advancement of their staff at all levels.
23. Governments should never require or encourage MNEs to discriminate on any of the grounds mentioned in paragraph 21, and continuing guidance from governments, where appropriate, on the avoidance of such discrimination in employment is encouraged.

*Security of Employment*

24. Governments should carefully study the impact of MNEs on employment in different industrial sectors. Governments, as well as MNEs themselves, in all countries should take suitable measures to deal with the employment and labour market impacts of the operations of MNEs.
25. MNEs equally with national enterprises, through active manpower planning, should endeavour to provide stable employment for their employees and should observe freely negotiated obligations concerning employment stability and social security. In view of the flexibility which MNEs may have, they should strive to assume a leading role in promoting security of employment, particularly in countries where the discontinuation of operations is likely to accentuate long-term unemployment.
26. In considering changes in operations (including those resulting from mergers, takeovers or transfers of production) which would have major employment effects, MNEs should provide reasonable notice of such changes to the appropriate government authorities and representatives of the workers in their employment and their organizations so that the implications may be examined jointly in order to mitigate adverse effects to the greatest possible extent. This is particularly important in the case of the closure of an entity involving collective lay-offs or dismissals.
27. Arbitrary dismissal procedures should be avoided.
28. Governments, in cooperation with multinational as well as national enterprises, should provide some form of income protection for workers whose employment has been terminated.

*Training*

29. Governments, in cooperation with all the parties concerned, should develop national policies for vocational training and guidance, closely linked with employment. This is the framework within which MNEs should pursue their training policies.
30. In their operations, MNEs should ensure that relevant training is provided for all levels of their employees in the host country, as appropriate, to meet the needs of the enterprise as well as the development policies of the country. Such training should, to the extent possible, develop generally useful skills and promote career opportunities. This responsibility should be carried out, where appropriate, in cooperation with the authorities of the country, employers' and workers' organizations and the competent local, national or international institutions.
31. MNEs operating in developing countries should participate, along with national enterprises, in programmes, including special funds, encouraged by host governments and supported by employers' and workers' organizations. These programmes should have the aim of encouraging skill formation and development as well as providing vocational guidance, and should be jointly administered by the parties which support them. Wherever practicable, MNEs should make the services of skilled resource personnel available to help in training programmes organized by governments as part of a contribution to national development.
32. MNEs, with the cooperation of governments and to the extent consistent with the efficient operation of the enterprise, should afford opportunities within the enterprise as a whole to broaden the experience of local management in suitable fields such as industrial relations.

## Conditions of Work and Life

*Wages, Benefits and Conditions of Work*

33. Wages, benefits and conditions of work offered by MNEs should be not less favourable to the workers than those offered by comparable employers in the country concerned.
34. When MNEs operate in developing countries, where comparable employers may not exist, they should provide the best possible wages, benefits and conditions of work, within the framework of government policies. These should be related to the economic position of the enterprise, but should be at least adequate to satisfy basic needs of the workers and their families. Where they provide workers with basic amenities such as housing, medical care or food, these amenities should be of a good standard.
35. Governments, especially in developing countries, should endeavour to adopt suitable measures to ensure that lower income groups and less developed areas benefit as much as possible from the activities of MNEs.

*Minimum Age*

36. MNEs, as well as national enterprises, should respect the minimum age for admission to employment or work in order to secure the effective abolition of child labour.

*Safety and Health*

37. Governments should ensure that both multinational and national enterprises provide adequate safety and health standards for their employees. Those governments which have not yet ratified the ILO Conventions on Guarding of Machinery (No. 119), Ionising Radiation (No. 115), Benzene (No. 136) and Occupational Cancer (No. 139) are urged nevertheless to apply to the greatest extent possible the principles embodied in these Conventions and in their related Recommendations (Nos. 118, 114, 144 and 147). The codes of practice and guides in the current list of publications on occupational safety and health should also be taken into account.
38. MNEs should maintain the highest standards of safety and health, in conformity with national requirements, bearing in mind their relevant experience within the enterprise as a whole, including any knowledge of special hazards. They should also make available to the representatives of the workers in the enterprise, and upon request, to the competent authorities and the workers' and employers' organizations in all countries in which they operate, information on the safety and health standards relevant to their local operations, which they observe in other countries. In particular, they should make known to those concerned any special hazards and related protective measures associated with new products and processes. They, like comparable domestic enterprises, should be expected to play a leading role in the examination of causes of industrial safety and health hazards and in the application of resulting improvements within the enterprise as a whole.
39. MNEs should cooperate in the work of international organizations concerned with the preparation and adoption of international safety and health standards.
40. In accordance with national practice, MNEs should cooperate fully with the competent safety and health authorities, the representatives of the workers and their organizations, and established safety and health organizations. Where appropriate, matters relating to safety and health should be incorporated in agreements with the representatives of the workers and their organizations.

**Industrial Relations**

41. MNEs should observe standards of industrial relations not less favourable than those observed by comparable employers in the country concerned.

*Freedom of Association and the Right to Organize*

42. Workers employed by MNEs as well as those employed by national enterprises should, without distinction whatsoever, have the right to establish and, subject only to the rules of the organization concerned, to join organizations of their own choosing without previous authorisation. They should also enjoy adequate protection against acts of anti-union discrimination in respect of their employment.
43. Organizations representing MNEs or the workers in their employment should enjoy adequate protection against any acts of interference by each other or each other's agents or members in their establishment, functioning or administration.
44. Where appropriate, in the local circumstances, MNEs should support representative employers' organizations.
45. Governments, where they do not already do so, are urged to apply the principles of Convention No. 87, Article 5, in view of the importance, in relation to MNEs, of permitting organizations representing such enterprises or the workers in their employment to affiliate with international organizations of employers and workers of their own choosing.
46. Where governments of host countries offer special incentives to attract foreign investment, these incentives should not include any limitation of the workers' freedom of association or the right to organize and bargain collectively.
47. Representatives of the workers in MNEs should not be hindered from meeting for consultation and exchange of views among themselves, provided that the functioning of the operations of the enterprise and the normal procedures which govern relationships with representatives of the workers and their organizations are not thereby prejudiced.
48. Governments should not restrict the entry of representatives of employers' and workers' organizations who come from other countries at the invitation of the local or national organizations concerned for the purpose of consultation on matters of mutual concern, solely on the grounds that they seek entry in that capacity.

*Collective Bargaining*

49. Workers employed by MNEs should have the right, in accordance with national law and practice, to have representative organizations of their own choosing recognized for the purpose of collective bargaining.
50. Measures appropriate to national conditions should be taken, where necessary, to encourage and promote the full development and utilization of machinery for voluntary negotiation between employers or employers' organizations and workers' organizations, with a view to the regulation of terms and conditions of employment by means of collective agreements.
51. MNEs, as well as national enterprises, should provide workers' representatives with such facilities as may be necessary to assist in the development of effective collective agreements.
52. MNEs should enable duly authorized representatives of the workers in their employment in each of the countries in which they operate to conduct negotiations with representatives of management who are authorized to take decisions on the matters under negotiation.

53. MNEs, in the context of bona fide negotiations with the workers' representatives on conditions of employment, or while workers are exercising the right to organize, should not threaten to utilize a capacity to transfer the whole or part of an operating unit from the country concerned in order to influence unfairly those negotiations or to hinder the exercise of the right to organize; nor should they transfer workers from affiliates in foreign countries with a view to undermining bona fide negotiations with the workers' representatives or the workers' exercise of their right to organize.
54. Collective agreements should include provisions for the settlement of disputes arising over their interpretation and application and for ensuring mutually respected rights and responsibilities.
55. MNEs should provide workers' representatives with information required for meaningful negotiations with the entity involved and, where this accords with local law and practice, should also provide information to enable them to obtain a true and fair view of the performance of the entity or, where appropriate, of the enterprise as a whole.
56. Governments should supply to the representatives of workers' organizations on request, where law and practice so permit, information on the industries in which the enterprise operates, which would help in laying down objective criteria in the collective bargaining process. In this context, multinational as well as national enterprises should respond constructively to requests by governments for relevant information on their operations.

*Consultation*

57. In multinational as well as in national enterprises, systems devised by mutual agreement between employers and workers and their representatives should provide, in accordance with national law and practice, for regular consultation on matters of mutual concern. Such consultation should not be a substitute for collective bargaining.

*Examination of Grievances*

58. Multinational as well as national enterprises should respect the right of the workers whom they employ to have all their grievances processed in a manner consistent with the following provision: any worker who, acting individually or jointly with other workers, considers that he has grounds for a grievance should have the right to submit such grievance without suffering any prejudice whatsoever as a result, and to have such grievance examined pursuant to an appropriate procedure. This is particularly important whenever the MNEs operate in countries which do not abide by the principles of ILO Conventions pertaining to freedom of association, to the right to organize and bargain collectively and to forced labour.

*Settlement of Industrial Disputes*

59. Multinational as well as national enterprises jointly with the representatives and organizations of the workers whom they employ should seek to establish voluntary conciliation machinery, appropriate to national conditions, which may include provisions for voluntary arbitration, to assist in the prevention and settlement of industrial disputes between employers and workers. The voluntary conciliation machinery should include equal representation of employers and workers.

**Other Documents**

Addendum One lists ILO Conventions and Recommendations adopted since 1977 which contain provisions relevant to the Tripartite Declaration. It also states that:

A number of international labour Conventions and Recommendations containing provisions relevant to the Declaration are referred to in footnotes in the Declaration as well as in an Annex. These footnotes do not affect the meaning of the provisions of the Declaration to which they refer. They should be considered as references to relevant instruments adopted by the ILO in the corresponding subject areas, which have helped shape the provisions of the Declaration. In keeping with the voluntary nature of the Declaration all of its provisions, whether derived from ILO Conventions and Recommendations or other sources, are recommendatory, except of course for provisions in Conventions which are binding on the Member States which have ratified them.

Addendum Two, adopted by the Governing Body in 2000, provides that:

the interpretation and application of the Tripartite Declaration of Principles concerning MNEs and Social Policy should fully take into account the objectives of the ILO Declaration on Fundamental Principles and Rights at Work. This reference does not in any way affect the voluntary character or the meaning of the provisions of the Tripartite Declaration of Principles concerning MNEs and Social Policy.

As noted above, several paragraphs of the Tripartite Declaration (namely, paragraphs 1–7, 8, 10, 25, 26 & 52) have been interpreted pursuant to a Procedure (first established in 1981 and since amended) for examining disputes concerning its application: see the ILO's Procedure for the Examination of Disputes concerning the Application of the Tripartite Declaration of Principles concerning MNEs and Social Policy by means of Interpretation of its Provisions, ILO *OB* 1986, Vol LXIX, Series A, No. 3: 196–7 (extracted below). To date, five cases have been the subject of Governing Body decisions (two originating from governments and three from workers' organisations). Four were declared receivable: the BIFU case (ILO Doc GB.229/13/13/Appendix), the Belgian Case No. 1 (GB.239/14/24/Appendix), the ICEF case (GB.264/MNE/2) and the Belgian Case No. 2 (GB.270/MNE/1Confidential). The IUF case (GB.255/10/12) was adjudged non-receivable and did not reach the interpretation stage.

*Procedure for the Examination of Disputes concerning the Application of the Tripartite Declaration of Principles concerning Multinational Enterprises and Social Policy by means of Interpretation of its Provisions*

1. The purpose of the procedure is to interpret the provisions of the Declaration when needed to resolve a disagreement on their meaning, arising from an actual situation, between parties to whom the Declaration is commended.
2. The procedure should in no way duplicate or conflict with existing national or ILO procedures. Thus, it cannot be invoked:

    (a) in respect of national law and practice;
    (b) in respect of international labour Conventions and Recommendations;
    (c) in respect of matters falling under the freedom of association procedure.

The above means that questions regarding national law and practice should be considered through appropriate national machinery; that questions regarding international labour Conventions and Recommendations should be examined through the various procedures provided for in articles 19, 22, 24 and 26 of the Constitution of the ILO, or through government requests to the Office for informal interpretation; and that questions concerning freedom of association should be considered through the special ILO procedures applicable to that area.

3. When a request for interpretation of the Declaration is received by the ILO, the Office shall acknowledge receipt and bring it before the Officers of the Committee on Multinational Enterprises. The Office will inform the government and the central organizations of employers and workers concerned of any request for interpretation received directly from an organization under paragraph 5(b) and (c).
4. The Officers of the Committee on MNEs shall decide unanimously after consultations in the groups whether the request is receivable under the procedure. If they cannot reach agreement the request shall be referred to the full Committee for decision.
5. Requests for interpretation may be addressed to the Office:

   (a) as a rule by the government of a member State acting either on its own initiative or at the request of a national organization of employers or workers;
   (b) by a national organization of employers or workers, which is representative at the national and/or sectoral level, subject to the conditions set out in paragraph 6. Such requests should normally be channelled through the central organizations in the country concerned;
   (c) by an international organization of employers or workers on behalf of a representative national affiliate.

6. In the case of 5(b) and (c), requests may be submitted if it can be demonstrated:

   (a) that the government concerned has declined to submit the request to the Office; or
   (b) that three months have elapsed since the organization addressed the government without a statement of the government's intention.

7. In the case of receivable requests the Office shall prepare a draft reply in consultation with the Officers of the Committee on MNEs. All appropriate sources of information shall be used, including government, employers' and workers' sources in the country concerned. The Officers may ask the Office to indicate a period within which the information should be provided.
8. The draft reply to a receivable request shall be considered and approved by the Committee on MNEs prior to submission to the Governing Body for approval.
9. The reply when approved by the Governing Body shall be forwarded to the parties concerned and published in the *Official Bulletin* of the ILO.

# 34. ILO: Code of Practice on Managing Disability in the Workplace, 2002

**Commentary**: Primarily addressed to employers within the private or public sectors irrespective of size or location, the Code encourages them to adopt positive strategies in managing disability-related issues within the workplace (www.ilo.org/public/english/employment/skills/disability/download/code.pdf). It is not legally binding and does not supersede national legislation. The Preface observes that the Code 'outlines best practices which enable employers to utilize the skills and potential of people with disabilities within existing national conditions'. Appendix 1 lists relevant international disability initiatives and Appendix 2 other related ILO Conventions and Recommendations. See also, Declaration on the Rights of Mentally Retarded Persons, UNGA Resolution 2856 (1971); Declaration on the Rights of Disabled Persons, UNGA Resolution 3447 (1975). Although also delineating the responsibilities of competent authorities and workers' organisations, the extracts below are limited to identifying the roles and responsibilities envisaged for employers and employers' organisations.

**1. General provisions**

1.1. The objective of this code is to provide practical guidance on the management of disability issues in the workplace with a view to:

(a) ensuring that people with disabilities have equal opportunities in the workplace;
(b) improving employment prospects for persons with disabilities by facilitating recruitment, return to work, job retention and opportunities for advancement;
(c) promoting a safe, accessible and healthy workplace;
(d) assuring that employer costs associated with disability among employees are minimized – including health care and insurance payments, in some instances;
(e) maximizing the contribution which workers with disabilities can make to the enterprise.

1.2.3. The code is based on the conviction that employers benefit from the employment of people with disabilities, who can make a significant contribution at their place of employment, in jobs matched to their skills and abilities, if disability-related issues are appropriately managed. It is also based on evidence that enterprises may gain from the retention of experienced workers who become disabled, and on indications that significant savings can be made in terms of health costs, insurance payments and time lost, if an effective disability management strategy is in place.

1.2.5. Disability management practices are most effective when based on positive cooperation among governments, employers' organizations, workers' representatives, workers' organizations and organizations of persons with disabilities.

1.3.1. The code is intended to be of benefit to:

(i) private and public sector employers of different sizes, located in urban and rural areas of industrialized countries, developing countries and countries in transition;
(ii) employers' organizations in their role as providers of information, advisory and other services to their members, as well as advocates of employment opportunities for disabled persons . . .

1.3.2. The provisions of the code should be considered as basic ingredients for the effective management of disability issues in the workplace. They can assist employers in maximizing the benefits to be gained through employing or retaining workers with disabilities. They can contribute to ensuring that workers with disabilities can make a valued contribution, and that they have equal opportunity and are not subject to discrimination, within the legal framework set by national legislation.

1.4. Definitions.

Adjustment or accommodation: Adaptation of the job, including adjustment and modification of machinery and equipment and/or modification of the job content, working time and work organization, and the adaptation of the work environment to provide access to the place of work, to facilitate the employment of individuals with disabilities.

Disability management: A process in the workplace designed to facilitate the employment of persons with a disability through a coordinated effort and taking into account individual needs, work environment, enterprise needs and legal responsibilities.

Disabled person: An individual whose prospects of securing, returning to, retaining and advancing in suitable employment are substantially reduced as a result of a duly recognized physical, sensory, intellectual or mental impairment.

Discrimination: Any distinction, exclusion or preference based on certain grounds which nullifies or impairs equality of opportunity or treatment in employment or occupation. General standards that establish distinctions based on prohibited grounds constitute discrimination in law. The specific attitude of a public authority or a private individual that treats unequally persons or members of a group on a prohibited ground constitutes discrimination in practice. Indirect discrimination refers to apparently neutral situations, regulations or practices which in fact result in unequal treatment of persons with certain characteristics. Distinction or preferences that may result from application of special measures of protection and assistance taken to meet the particular requirements of disabled persons are not considered discriminatory.

Employer: A person or organization employing workers under a written or verbal contract of employment which establishes the rights and duties of both parties, in accordance with national law and practice. Governments, public authorities and private companies as well as individuals may be employers.

Employee assistance programme: A programme – either jointly operated by an employer and a workers' organization, or by an employer alone, or a workers' organization alone – that offers assistance to workers and frequently also to their family members, with problems liable to cause personal distress, which affect or could eventually affect job productivity.

Employers' organization: An organization whose membership consists of individual employers, other associations of employers or both, formed primarily to protect and promote the interests of members and to provide services to its members in employment-related matters.

Equal opportunity: Equal access to and opportunities for all persons in employment, vocational training and particular occupations, without discrimination, consistent with Article 4 of Convention No. 159.

Impairment: Any loss or abnormality of a psychological, physiological or physical function.

Job adaptation: The adaptation or redesign of tools, machines, workstations and the work environment to an individual's needs. It may also include adjustments in work organization, work schedules, sequences of work and in breaking down work tasks to their basic elements.

Job analysis: Making a detailed list of the duties that a particular job involves and the skills required . . .

Job retention: Remaining with the same employer, with the same or different duties or conditions of employment, including return after a period of paid or unpaid absence.

Mainstreaming: Including people with disabilities in employment, education, training and all sectors of society.

Occupational health services (OHS): Health services which have essentially a preventive function and which are responsible for advising the employer, as well as the workers and their representatives, on the requirements for establishing and maintaining a safe and healthy working environment to facilitate optimal physical and mental health in relation to work . . .

Return to work: The process by which a worker is supported in resuming work after an absence due to injury or illness.

Vocational rehabilitation: A process which enables disabled persons to secure, retain and advance in suitable employment and thereby furthers their integration or reintegration into society.

Works council/workplace committee: A committee of workers within the enterprise with which the employer cooperates and which is consulted by the employer on matters of mutual concern.

Worker/employee: Any person who works for a wage or salary and performs services for an employer.

Working conditions: The factors determining the circumstances in which the worker works. These include hours of work, work organization, job content, welfare services and the measures taken to protect the occupational safety and health of the worker.

Working environment: The facilities and circumstances in which work takes place and the environmental factors which may affect workers' health.

Workplace: All the places where people in employment need to be or to go to carry out their work and which are under the direct or indirect control of the employer. Examples include offices, factories, plantations, construction sites, ships and private residences.

Workstation: The part of the office or factory where an individual works, including desk or work surface used, chair, equipment and other items.

Work trial: Work activity to provide experience in or test suitability for a particular job.

## 2. General Duties of Employers and Workers' Representatives, and Responsibilities of Competent Authorities

2.1.1. To manage disability-related issues in the workplace, employers should adopt a strategy for managing disability as an integral part of their overall employment policy and specifically as part of the human resources development strategy. This disability management strategy may be linked to employee assistance programmes, where they exist.

2.1.2. The disability management strategy should include provision for:

(a) recruiting jobseekers with disabilities, including those who have not worked before and those who wish to return to work after a period of non-employment;
(b) equal opportunity for employees with disabilities;
(c) job retention by employees who acquire a disability.

2.1.3. The disability management strategy should be linked to a workplace-level policy on promoting a safe and healthy workplace, including provision for occupational safety and health measures, risk analysis of any adaptation adjustment or accommodation, early intervention and referral to treatment and rehabilitation of those who acquire a disability while in employment and a mentoring system to ensure that integration of new employees is fostered.

2.1.4. The strategy should be in accordance with national policy and legislation and incorporate the principles of equal opportunity and mainstreaming, underpinning the relevant ILO Conventions and in particular Convention No. 159.

2.1.5. The programme should be formulated in cooperation with workers' representatives, in consultation with individual disabled employees, occupational health services, where they exist, and, where possible, with organizations of persons with disabilities. In developing the programme, employers may also benefit from consultation with the competent authorities and expert agencies with specialist knowledge regarding disability-related issues.

2.1.6. The disability management strategy within the workplace should be coordinated utilizing existing representational structures or by a new structure established for the purpose. The person or persons responsible for the coordination of the programme should receive training in disability management or have access to qualified personnel.

2.1.7. Employers should seek to cooperate with the employment services in matching jobseekers with disabilities to jobs suited to their ability, work capacity and interest.

2.1.8. Employers should ensure that, in their employment, people with disabilities are treated equally with non-disabled workers in terms of benefits in kind such as transport or housing.

2.1.9. Employers' organizations should act as advocates, among their members, for the promotion of employment opportunities for disabled persons and job retention of those who acquire a disability while in employment. They may do this, for example, by providing practical information and advisory services, particularly to small companies, publicizing the advantages to business of managing disability in the workplace, promoting partnerships between employers in relation to disability management and by advocating disability management strategies in consultation processes at national and international levels.

2.1.10. To promote the introduction of disability management strategies in the workplace, employers' organizations should introduce and implement such a strategy for their own employees.

**3. Framework for the Management of Disability Issues in the Workplace**

3.1.1. Employers should consider the management of disability issues in the workplace a priority task which contributes to business success, and regard it as an integral part of the workplace human resources development strategy.

3.1.2. The disability management strategy should be formulated in accordance with national legislation, policy and practice, taking account of national institutions and organizations in the field.

3.1.3. In formulating a strategy for managing disability issues in the workplace, employers should collaborate with worker representatives and consult with disabled workers or their representatives.

3.1.4. The strategy at workplace level should complement the human resources development strategy in its aim to maximize the contributions and abilities of all staff, including those with disabilities and support adherence to occupational safety and health standards and related early intervention and referral procedures in accordance with the principles of this code.

3.1.5. The disability management strategy could consider provision for workers who hold family responsibility for a disabled person or persons.

3.1.6. The disability management strategy in the workplace should include provision for consultation from the employment service or other specialist agencies, where necessary, to ensure that the individual with a disability is well matched to the job in terms of ability, work capacity and interest, as is usual in recruitment procedures.

3.2.1. The disability management strategy in the workplace should be brought to the attention of all employees, in a language which can be easily understood, in cooperation with worker representatives.

3.2.2. General information on disability in the workplace should be provided to all employees, along with specific information about the enterprise strategy, and about any adaptations which may be needed in a working environment, workstation and work schedules to enable workers with disabilities to optimize their effectiveness . . . In conjunction, an opportunity should be given to all employees to raise any questions which they may have about the prospect of working with a disabled co-worker.

3.2.3. Inputs from specialist agencies, which may include organizations of persons with disabilities, should be sought, if necessary, in planning these information and awareness-raising sessions in the workplace.

3.2.4. Employers, including senior managers, should signal their commitment to the disability management strategy, through such measures as they consider appropriate regarding the recruitment of people with disabilities and the retention of employees who acquire a disability.

3.2.5. Employers, employers' organizations, workers' organizations, competent authorities and organizations of persons with disabilities should consider collaboratively publicizing strategies on disability issues and information on the implementation of these policies.

3.2.6. Employers should inform their suppliers and sources of procurement of their strategies on disability management, with a view to encouraging good practice.

3.2.7. In promoting strategies on managing disability in the workplace, groups of employers and employer organizations should consider arranging exchanges of information and training on the subject with relevant public sector agencies, expert bodies and other competent agencies.

3.3.1. Employers should evaluate the effectiveness of their workplace strategy on the management of disability at regular intervals and make improvements where required.

3.3.2. Worker representatives at the workplace should have access to the evaluation and participate in it.

3.3.3. Competent authorities, in order to assess the effectiveness of their support, if any, to these programmes, may require information from the employer.

3.3.4. All information regarding the disability management programme should be made anonymous and confidentiality protected, before being distributed.

## 4. Recruitment

4.1.1. The principle of non-discrimination should be respected throughout the recruitment process, to ensure maximal benefit to the employer and equitable opportunities for candidates with and without disabilities . . .

4.1.2. Employers should ensure that the recruitment process attracts applications from as many qualified people with disabilities as possible . . .

4.1.3. Where employers rely on agencies for the management of recruitment, the competent authorities could collaborate with employers' organizations, relevant organizations of persons with disabilities and advertising associations to develop advertising practices which attract applications from jobseekers with disabilities.

4.1.4. Competent authorities should assist employers by facilitating the recruitment of disabled persons through the use of effective job placement services . . .

4.1.5. Organizations of employers and workers, and competent authorities, where appropriate, could prepare guidelines to assist in the employment of people with disabilities in urban and rural areas . . .

4.1.6. Employers' organizations could support the recruitment of workers with disabilities by working with service agencies, employment services and organizations of persons with disabilities to ensure that the services provided effectively meet employer needs.

4.1.7. In considering a candidate with a disability for a specific job, employers should be open to making adjustments, if required, in the workplace, workstation and work conditions, to maximize the ability of this candidate to perform the job ... Adjustments, where required, should be planned in consultation with disabled and non disabled workers, and be made with the agreement of workers' representatives and the disabled worker(s) involved.

4.2.1. Pre-employment tests and selection criteria should focus on the specific skills, knowledge and abilities regarded as essential to the functions of the vacant job. Care should be taken in selecting the tests to ensure that they are in a format which is accessible to disabled applicants ...

4.2.2. Members of interview panels in the private and public sectors should be provided with guidance on the interview and selection process of persons with disabilities.

4.2.3. Employers should consider ways of enabling candidates with disabilities to participate and perform at interviews on an equal basis with other candidates, for example by permitting a sign language interpreter or an advocate to be present.

4.2.4. In issuing invitations to interview, employers could encourage candidates to state in advance any specific needs or accommodations they may require in order to participate in the interview.

4.2.5. Adjustments in the recruitment process to take account of the different needs of disabled jobseekers, and the rationale for such adjustments, should be communicated to disabled candidates and to employees.

4.3.1. Employers should arrange an orientation to the company or service, the work environment and the job for each newly recruited worker with a disability, in the same way as for non-disabled workers.

4.3.2. Employers should ensure that information essential to the job and workplace, such as job instructions, works manuals, information on staff rules, grievance procedures and health and safety procedures are communicated to employees with disabilities in a format which assures that they are fully informed.

4.3.3. In offering a job to a disabled candidate, the employer should indicate any disability-related adjustments to the work environment, workstation, work schedules or training which are proposed and consult with the candidate further on the subject ...

4.3.4. Workers' representatives and co-workers should be consulted about any substantial adjustments made or planned, to take account of specific needs of an employee with a disability.

4.3.5. Employers should cooperate with the competent authorities or other relevant agencies in facilitating courses for management, supervisors, or co-workers who wish to learn alternative communication techniques, to better communicate with colleagues who have difficulty speaking, hearing or understanding verbal language.

4.3.6. Once the recruitment of a person with a disability has taken place, follow-up services may be important in ensuring that any problems which may arise are swiftly identified and resolved ...

4.4.1. Where employers are not immediately in a position to employ a disabled worker, they could consider providing work experience opportunities to jobseekers with disabilities, to enable them to acquire the skills, knowledge and work attitude required for specific jobs in the workplace ...

4.4.2. Where work experience is provided, employers may assign a supervisor or senior worker to assist the person. Alternatively, the services of a job coach may be provided through the employment services.

4.5.1. The competent authorities should facilitate work experience, work trials and supported employment by providing employers and persons with disabilities with technical advice, as required, and by informing them of incentive schemes available to subsidize any costs involved, such as wage costs or costs of adaptations to premises, tools or equipment.

4.5.2. As an alternative to immediate recruitment or the provision of work experience opportunities, employers could consider giving a disabled person a work trial or a supported employment placement, in accordance with national law and practice . . .

4.5.3. In the case of supported employment, the competent authorities could facilitate the provision of job-coach services and ongoing follow-up throughout the placement, either directly through the public employment services, or through other specialist agencies.

4.5.4. On completion of work trials, the competent authorities or other specialist agencies could follow up with the employer, to review the trial's success and make other arrangements, if necessary . . .

4.6.1. Employers should keep their recruitment process under review, in order to ensure that it is accessible to people with different types of disability.

**5. Promotion**

5.1.1. Workers with disabilities should be afforded equal opportunities with other workers at the workplace to acquire the skills and experience necessary to advance in their careers.

5.1.2. Information about career development and promotional opportunities should be made available and communicated in a range of formats accessible to workers with different disabilities in the enterprise . . .

5.1.3. Workers with disabilities should be encouraged to apply for promotion, particularly where it appears that they may be reluctant to do so, because of an impairment or other obstacle arising from their disability, or perceived obstacles in their working environment.

5.1.4. In considering workers for promotion, employers should take account of their prior experience, if any, competencies, present performance and capabilities, in addition to formal qualifications suitable to the essential requirements of the job.

5.2.1. Opportunities for workers with disabilities to avail of in-service training programmes should be developed and publicized . . .

5.2.2. Employers should consider adjusting time schedules, venues and programmes to facilitate and maximize the participation of persons with disabilities in measures intended for the career development of all employees.

5.2.3. In developing training opportunities, employers or groups of employers should ensure that these are accessible to disabled persons.

5.2.4. Workplace training handbooks and materials should be accessible to persons with communication impairments and intellectual disabilities, including, when the need arises, alternative formats for printed materials and use of visual illustrations, in place of text.

5.3.1. A policy of equal opportunity should be implemented in workplace-based enrolment for vocational training by making courses available and accessible to all employees, including those with disabilities and modifying course manuals and materials, where necessary.

5.3.3. In selecting external training services and opportunities, employers should take account of the venue accessibility for workers with disabilities.

5.4.1. The performance appraisal of workers with disabilities should take place according to the same criteria applied to holders of the same or similar jobs.

**6. Job retention**

6.1.1. Where existing employees acquire a disability while in employment, employers can continue to benefit from their accumulated expertise and experience by taking steps to enable them to retain their employment. In developing a strategy for managing disability in the workplace, employers should include measures for job retention including:

(a) early intervention and referral to appropriate services;
(b) measures for a gradual resumption of work;
(c) opportunities for workers with disabilities to test work or obtain experience in an alternative job if they are unable to resume their previous jobs;
(d) the use of support and technical advice to identify any opportunities and any adjustments which might be required.

6.1.2. In seeking to facilitate job retention or return to work by a disabled employee, employers should be aware of the range of possible options . . .

6.1.3. In developing measures for the redeployment of workers with disabilities, employers should take into account the occupational preferences of those workers and consult with worker representatives, if necessary.

6.1.4. When a worker acquires a disability, the employer should ensure that accommodation measures are fully considered in order to utilize the residual potential and skills of that worker, before other steps are taken.

6.1.5. The competent authorities should provide guidance, services and incentives to employers, groups of employers and employers' organizations, in order to maximize opportunities for people with disabilities to retain their employment, and to resume work speedily following an accident, injury, disease, changed capacity or disabling condition . . .

6.2.1. The competent authorities, upon request of the employer, should facilitate employers to assess the abilities and work experience of workers who have acquired a disability or reduced capacity for their job, with a view to their continuing in the same job, if necessary with some modification of their job tasks, the working environment or work schedule, or through retraining . . .

**7. Adjustments**

In recruiting or retaining workers with disabilities, employers may need to make an adjustment or adjustments in some cases to enable the individual to perform the job effectively . . .

7.1.1. To facilitate the recruitment of persons with disabilities and job retention by workers who acquire a disability, employers should take steps to improve the accessibility of the work premises to people with different types of disability. This should include consideration of entrance to and movement around the premises and of toilet and washroom facilities.

7.1.2. Accessibility should also be understood to include signage in use, manuals, workplace instructions and electronic information . . .

7.1.3. Accessibility for people with hearing impairment includes access to information frequently conveyed by sound – such as the ringing of a bell, a fire alarm, whistle or siren . . .

7.1.4. In planning to improve accessibility, employers should consult with the disabled worker and with specialist technical advisory services, which might include organizations of persons with disabilities, and refer to any criteria established by the competent authorities.

7.1.5. Emergency planning should ensure that persons with disabilities are able to safely and effectively evacuate the workplace to an area of safety.

7.2.1. Adaptations may be required to the workstation to enable the worker with a disability to perform the job effectively. In planning adaptations, employers should consult with the disabled worker involved and with worker representatives.

7.2.2. Similarly, adaptations may be required to tools and equipment to facilitate optimal job performance. These, too, should be planned in consultation with the disabled worker, and worker representatives.

7.2.3. For some workers with disabilities, it may be necessary to review the job description and make changes – for example by deleting a part of the job which the person is unable to perform and replacing this with another task or tasks.

7.2.4. Flexibility of work schedules can be a significant factor in enabling some individuals with disabilities to perform a job satisfactorily. This too should be considered, in consultation with the workers concerned and their representatives.

7.2.5. Performance requirements may need to be reviewed, in consultation with the disabled workers and their representatives, particularly at an early stage after recruitment, or after an existing employee has acquired a disability.

7.3.1. The competent authorities should make available to employers incentives for workplace adjustments, as well as a technical advisory service which provides up-to-date advice and information on adjustments to the workplace or to the organization of job tasks, as required.

### 8. Confidentiality of information

8.1. With the consent of the person concerned, any relevant information relating to a disabled worker's reduced function or impaired health status should be assembled and kept by the employer, in a manner that maintains confidentiality.

## Additional Instruments

*i. ILO: Code of Practice on HIV/AIDS and the World of Work, 2001*

**Commentary**: The Preface to this Code observes that HIV/AIDS 'is imposing huge costs on enterprises in all sectors through declining productivity, increasing labour costs and loss of skills and experience'. See further, Lisk F. (2002), 'Labour market and employment implications of HIV/AIDS', ILO WP1. The Code is the product of collaboration between the ILO, its tripartite constituents and international partners: ILO (1999), *Proceedings of the Regional Tripartite Workshop on Strategies to Tackle the Social and Labour Implications of HIV/AIDS*, Windhoek. It applies to all employers and workers (including applicants therefor) in both the public and private sectors as well as work within the formal and informal sectors. The Code of Practice with respect to HIV/AIDS (www.ilo.org/public/english/protection/trav/aids) follows a similar template to that of managing disability (extracted above) in so far as it outlines the respective responsibilities of governments, employers and workers, occupational health personnel, HIV/AIDS specialists and all relevant stakeholders (including community-based organisations and NGOs). The Appendices provide basic facts about the epidemic (1), infection control measures within the workplace (2) and a checklist for planning and implementing workplace policies (3). The ILO's work programme on the topic includes conducting workshops and issuing newsletters: ILO (2002), 'Implementing the ILO Code of Practice on HIV/AIDS and the world of work: an education and training manual'. See further, ILO/IOE/UNAIDS (2002), 'Employers' Handbook on HIV/AIDS: a guide for action'; Joint UN Programme on HIV/AIDS (UNAIDS)/PWBLF/The Global Business Council on HIV & AIDS (2000), 'The Business Response to HIV/AIDS: Impact and Lessons Learned', Geneva & London; The Conference Board (1997), *Corporate Response to HIV/AIDS*, New York. See also, Declaration of Commitment on HIV/AIDS, UNGA Resolution S-26/2 (2001).

# 35. ILO: Convention No 174 (1993) Concerning the Prevention of Major Industrial Accidents (entry into force 1997)

**Commentary**: This Convention delimits the roles and responsibilities of employers, employees, competent authorities and exporting States. It builds upon the ILO Code of Practice on the Prevention of Major Industrial Accidents (1991), the work of the ILO's International Programme on Chemical Safety and ILO (1988), 'Major Hazard Control: A Practical Manual'. See further, Recommendation No 31 (1929) concerning the Prevention of Industrial Accidents and Recommendation No 181 (1993) concerning the Prevention of Major Industrial Accidents. See also, ILO Convention No 155 (1981) & Recommendation No 164 (1981) Concerning Occupational Safety and Health as well as the 2002 Protocol; ILO Convention No 148 (1977) & Recommendation No 156 (1977) concerning the Working Environment; ILO Convention No 148 (1977) concerning the Working Environment (Air Pollution, Noise and Vibration); ILO Convention No 170 (1990) & Recommendation No 177 (1990) Concerning Chemicals. Additional ILO Conventions of relevance specifically address production techniques (No 115 (1960) on Radiation Protection, No 119 (1963) concerning the Guarding of Machinery and No 127 (1967) on Maximum Weight), occupational health and safety (No 120 (1964) on Hygiene in Commerce and Offices and No 139 (1974) on Occupational Cancer), particular products (such as No 162 (1986) on Asbestos or No 136 (1971) concerning Benzene) and occupations (including No 147 (1976) on Merchant Shipping, No 161 (1985) on Occupational Health Services, No 110 (1958) on Plantations, No 167 (1988) on Safety and Health in Construction and No 176 (1995) concerning Safety and Health in Mines).

**Article 1**

1. The purpose of this Convention is the prevention of major accidents involving hazardous substances and the limitation of the consequences of such accidents.
2. This Convention applies to major hazard installations.
3. This Convention does not apply to:

   (a) nuclear installations and plants processing radioactive substances except for facilities handling non-radioactive substances at these installations;
   (b) military installations;
   (c) transport outside the site of an installation other than by pipeline.

4. A Member ratifying this Convention may, after consulting the representative organizations of employers and workers concerned and other interested parties who may be

affected, exclude from the application of the Convention installations or branches of economic activity for which equivalent protection is provided.

**Article 2**
Where special problems of a substantial nature arise so that it is not immediately possible to implement all the preventive and protective measures provided for in this Convention, a Member shall draw up plans, in consultation with the most representative organizations of employers and workers and with other interested parties who may be affected, for the progressive implementation of the said measures within a fixed time frame.

**Article 3**
For the purposes of this Convention:

(a) the term 'hazardous substance' means a substance or mixture of substances which by virtue of chemical, physical or toxicological properties, either singly or in combination, constitutes a hazard;
(b) the term 'threshold quantity' means for a given hazardous substance or category of substances that quantity, prescribed in national laws and regulations by reference to specific conditions, which if exceeded identifies a major hazard installation;
(c) the term 'major hazard installation' means one which produces, processes, handles, uses, disposes of or stores, either permanently or temporarily, one or more hazardous substances or categories of substances in quantities which exceed the threshold quantity;
(d) the term 'major accident' means a sudden occurrence – such as a major emission, fire or explosion – in the course of an activity within a major hazard installation, involving one or more hazardous substances and leading to a serious danger to workers, the public or the environment, whether immediate or delayed;
(e) the term 'safety report' means a written presentation of the technical, management and operational information covering the hazards and risks of a major hazard installation and their control and providing justification for the measures taken for the safety of the installation;
(f) the term 'near miss' means any sudden event involving one or more hazardous substances which, but for mitigating effects, actions or systems, could have escalated to a major accident.

**Article 4**
1. In the light of national laws and regulations, conditions and practices, and in consultation with the most representative organizations of employers and workers and with other interested parties who may be affected, each Member shall formulate, implement and periodically review a coherent national policy concerning the protection of workers, the public and the environment against the risk of major accidents.
2. This policy shall be implemented through preventive and protective measures for major hazard installations and, where practicable, shall promote the use of the best available safety technologies.

**Article 5**

1. The competent authority, or a body approved or recognized by the competent authority, shall, after consulting the most representative organizations of employers and workers and other interested parties who may be affected, establish a system for the identification of major hazard installations as defined in Article 3 (c), based on a list of hazardous substances or of categories of hazardous substances or of both, together with their respective threshold quantities, in accordance with national laws and regulations or international standards.
2. The system mentioned in paragraph 1 above shall be regularly reviewed and updated.

**Article 6**

The competent authority, after consulting the representative organizations of employers and workers concerned, shall make special provision to protect confidential information transmitted or made available to it in accordance with Articles 8, 12, 13 or 14, whose disclosure would be liable to cause harm to an employer's business, so long as this provision does not lead to serious risk to the workers, the public or the environment.

**Article 7**

Employers shall identify any major hazard installation within their control on the basis of the system referred to in Article 5.

**Article 8**

1. Employers shall notify the competent authority of any major hazard installation which they have identified:

   (a) within a fixed time-frame for an existing installation;
   (b) before it is put into operation in the case of a new installation.

2. Employers shall also notify the competent authority before any permanent closure of a major hazard installation.

**Article 9**

In respect of each major hazard installation employers shall establish and maintain a documented system of major hazard control which includes provision for:

(a) the identification and analysis of hazards and the assessment of risks including consideration of possible interactions between substances;
(b) technical measures, including design, safety systems, construction, choice of chemicals, operation, maintenance and systematic inspection of the installation;
(c) organizational measures, including training and instruction of personnel, the provision of equipment in order to ensure their safety, staffing levels, hours of work, definition of responsibilities, and controls on outside contractors and temporary workers on the site of the installation;
(d) emergency plans and procedures, including:

   (i) the preparation of effective site emergency plans and procedures, including emergency medical procedures, to be applied in case of major accidents or threat thereof, with periodic testing and evaluation of their effectiveness and revision as necessary;
   (ii) the provision of information on potential accidents and site emergency plans to authorities and bodies responsible for the preparation of emergency plans and procedures for the protection of the public and the environment outside the site of the installation;
   (iii) any necessary consultation with such authorities and bodies;

(e) measures to limit the consequences of a major accident;
(f) consultation with workers and their representatives;
(g) improvement of the system, including measures for gathering information and analysing accidents and near misses. The lessons so learnt shall be discussed with the workers and their representatives and shall be recorded in accordance with national law and practice.

**Article 10**
1. Employers shall prepare a safety report based on the requirements of Article 9.
2. The report shall be prepared:

   (a) in the case of existing major hazard installations, within a period after notification prescribed by national laws or regulations;
   (b) in the case of any new major hazard installation, before it is put into operation.

**Article 11**
Employers shall review, update and amend the safety report:

(a) in the event of a modification which has a significant influence on the level of safety in the installation or its processes or in the quantities of hazardous substances present;
(b) when developments in technical knowledge or in the assessment of hazards make this appropriate;
(c) at intervals prescribed by national laws or regulations;
(d) at the request of the competent authority.

**Article 12**
Employers shall transmit or make available to the competent authority the safety reports referred to in Articles 10 and 11.

**Article 13**
Employers shall inform the competent authority and other bodies designated for this purpose as soon as a major accident occurs.

**Article 14**

1. Employers shall, within a fixed time-frame after a major accident, present a detailed report to the competent authority containing an analysis of the causes of the accident and describing its immediate on-site consequences, and any action taken to mitigate its effects.
2. The report shall include recommendations detailing actions to be taken to prevent a recurrence.

**Article 15**

Taking into account the information provided by the employer, the competent authority shall ensure that emergency plans and procedures containing provisions for the protection of the public and the environment outside the site of each major hazard installation are established, updated at appropriate intervals and coordinated with the relevant authorities and bodies.

**Article 18**

2. Representatives of the employer and representatives of the workers of a major hazard installation shall have the opportunity to accompany inspectors supervising the application of the measures prescribed in pursuance of this Convention, unless the inspectors consider, in the light of the general instructions of the competent authority, that this may be prejudicial to the performance of their duties.

**Article 19**

The competent authority shall have the right to suspend any operation which poses an imminent threat of a major accident.

**Article 20**

The workers and their representatives at a major hazard installation shall be consulted through appropriate cooperative mechanisms in order to ensure a safe system of work. In particular, the workers and their representatives shall:

(f) discuss with the employer any potential hazards they consider capable of generating a major accident and have the right to notify the competent authority of those hazards.

# 36. ILO: Convention No 169 (1989) Concerning Indigenous and Tribal Peoples in Independent Countries (entry into force 1991)

**Commentary**: This Convention was formulated by the FAO, UNESCO, WHO and the Inter-American Indian Institute and is intended to remove the 'assimilationist orientation' of ILO Convention No 107 (1957) and Recommendation No 104 (1957) concerning Indigenous and Tribal Populations. In addition to extracts below, the Convention also contains provisions with respect to *inter alia* enjoying human rights without discrimination (Article 3), special protective measures (4), respect for social, cultural, religious and spiritual values (5), independent economic, social and cultural development (including improving conditions of work and life, conducting social, spiritual, cultural and environmental impact assessments and environmental protection) (7), due regard for local customs or customary laws (8), recognising cultural and spiritual relationships with territory (13), relocation and compensation (16), transmitting land rights (17), national agrarian programmes (19), health services (25) and educational programmes (27). Provisions of commercial interest pertain to land ownership (including natural resources), employment conditions, handicrafts and rural industries. See also, Sub-Commission on Prevention of Discrimination and Protection of Minorities Resolution 1990/26; UNCTC (1994), 'Discrimination against indigenous peoples, transnational investments and operations on the lands of indigenous peoples'. For academic commentary, see Macklem P. (2001), 'Indigenous rights and MNCs at international law', *Hastings International and Comparative Law Review*, **24** (3), 475–84; Wagner M. (2001), 'The international legal rights of indigenous peoples affected by natural resource exploitation: a brief case study', *Hastings International and Comparative Law Review*, **24** (3), 491–502.

**Article 1**

1. This Convention applies to:

   (a) tribal peoples in independent countries whose social, cultural and economic conditions distinguish them from other sections of the national community, and whose status is regulated wholly or partially by their own customs or traditions or by special laws or regulations;

   (b) peoples in independent countries who are regarded as indigenous on account of their descent from the populations which inhabited the country, or a geographical region to which the country belongs, at the time of conquest or colonisation or the establishment of present state boundaries and who, irrespective of their legal status, retain some or all of their own social, economic, cultural and political institutions.

2. Self-identification as indigenous or tribal shall be regarded as a fundamental criterion for determining the groups to which the provisions of this Convention apply.

**Article 11**

The exaction from members of the peoples concerned of compulsory personal services in any form, whether paid or unpaid, shall be prohibited and punishable by law, except in cases prescribed by law for all citizens.

**Article 14**

1. The rights of ownership and possession of the peoples concerned over the lands which they traditionally occupy shall be recognised. In addition, measures shall be taken in appropriate cases to safeguard the right of the peoples concerned to use lands not exclusively occupied by them, but to which they have traditionally had access for their subsistence and traditional activities. Particular attention shall be paid to the situation of nomadic peoples and shifting cultivators in this respect . . .

**Article 15**

1. The rights of the peoples concerned to the natural resources pertaining to their lands shall be specially safeguarded. These rights include the right of these peoples to participate in the use, management and conservation of these resources.
2. In cases in which the State retains the ownership of mineral or sub-surface resources or rights to other resources pertaining to lands, governments shall establish or maintain procedures through which they shall consult these peoples, with a view to ascertaining whether and to what degree their interests would be prejudiced, before undertaking or permitting any programmes for the exploration or exploitation of such resources pertaining to their lands. The peoples concerned shall wherever possible participate in the benefits of such activities, and shall receive fair compensation for any damages which they may sustain as a result of such activities.

**Article 18**

Adequate penalties shall be established by law for unauthorised intrusion upon, or use of, the lands of the peoples concerned, and governments shall take measures to prevent such offences.

**Article 20**

1. Governments shall, within the framework of national laws and regulations, and in co operation with the peoples concerned, adopt special measures to ensure the effective protection with regard to recruitment and conditions of employment of workers belonging to these peoples, to the extent that they are not effectively protected by laws applicable to workers in general.
2. Governments shall do everything possible to prevent any discrimination between workers belonging to the peoples concerned and other workers, in particular as regards:

(a) admission to employment, including skilled employment, as well as measures for promotion and advancement;
(b) equal remuneration for work of equal value;
(c) medical and social assistance, occupational safety and health, all social security benefits and any other occupationally related benefits, and housing;
(d) the right of association and freedom for all lawful trade union activities, and the right to conclude collective agreements with employers or employers' organisations.

3. The measures taken shall include measures to ensure:

(a) that workers belonging to the peoples concerned, including seasonal, casual and migrant workers in agricultural and other employment, as well as those employed by labour contractors, enjoy the protection afforded by national law and practice to other such workers in the same sectors, and that they are fully informed of their rights under labour legislation and of the means of redress available to them;
(b) that workers belonging to these peoples are not subjected to working conditions hazardous to their health, in particular through exposure to pesticides or other toxic substances;
(c) that workers belonging to these peoples are not subjected to coercive recruitment systems, including bonded labour and other forms of debt servitude;
(d) that workers belonging to these peoples enjoy equal opportunities and equal treatment in employment for men and women, and protection from sexual harassment.

4. Particular attention shall be paid to the establishment of adequate labour inspection services in areas where workers belonging to the peoples concerned undertake wage employment, in order to ensure compliance with the provisions of this Part of this Convention.

**Article 23**

1. Handicrafts, rural and community-based industries, and subsistence economy and traditional activities of the peoples concerned, such as hunting, fishing, trapping and gathering, shall be recognised as important factors in the maintenance of their cultures and in their economic self-reliance and development . . .

# 37. UN: International Convention on the Rights of all Migrant Workers and Members of their Families, 1990

**Commentary**: The Convention (UN Doc A/45/49 (1990), entry into force 2003) seeks to end the illegal or clandestine recruitment and trafficking of migrant workers and to discourage their employment in irregular or undocumented situations. Article 2 identifies various categories of migrant worker. Under Part 3, the rights extending to all migrant workers and their families include non-discriminatory treatment (Articles 1 & 7), freedom of movement (8), life (9), freedom from torture (10), freedom of thought and expression (12 & 13), privacy (14), equality before the law (18), consular assistance (23), social security (27), medical care (28), cultural identity (31) and information access (33). Certain rights apply to the children of migrant workers (Articles 29 & 30). It is prohibited to destroy identity documents (Article 21).

Part 4 identifies additional rights for migrant workers and their families who are in documented or regular situations (Article 36). These pertain to full information (Article 37), temporary absences (38), freedom of movement (39), participation in public affairs (41), representation in procedures or institutions (42) and transferring earnings abroad (47). Such workers are also entitled to protective measures for family units (44), exemption from import and export duties or taxes in certain circumstances (46) and protection from double taxation (48) and expulsion (56). Particular categories of migrant workers and their families enjoy these rights to the extent that they have not been modified by Part 5 (Article 57). These modifications apply to frontier workers (Article 58), seasonal workers (59), itinerant workers (60), project-tied workers (61), specified-employment workers (62) and self-employed workers (63).

Under Part 6, governments must promote sound, equitable and humane conditions for the international migration of workers and their families (Article 64). Under Part 7, compliance is monitored by the Committee on the Protection of the Rights of All Migrant Workers and Members of their Families (CMW), a body of independent experts which assesses national reports, issues general comments on thematic issues and considers individual complaints alleging violations of their Convention rights by State Parties: see further, www.ohchr.org. See also, ILO Convention No 143 (1975) concerning Migrations in Abusive Conditions and the Promotion of Equality of Opportunity and Treatment of Migrant Workers (entry into force 1978); Recommendation No 151 (1975) concerning Migrant Workers; Convention No 97 (1949) (entry into force 1952) & Recommendation No 86 (1949) concerning Migration for Employment; Recommendation No 100 (1955) concerning Protection of Migrant Workers (Underdeveloped Countries).

## Part 1 Scope and Definitions

*Article 2*
For the purposes of the present Convention:

1. The term 'migrant worker' refers to a person who is to be engaged, is engaged or has been engaged in a remunerated activity in a State of which he or she is not a national.
2. (a) The term 'frontier worker' refers to a migrant worker who retains his or her habitual residence in a neighbouring State to which he or she normally returns every day or at least once a week;
   (b) The term 'seasonal worker' refers to a migrant worker whose work by its character is dependent on seasonal conditions and is performed only during part of the year;
   (c) The term 'seafarer', which includes a fisherman, refers to a migrant worker employed on board a vessel registered in a State of which he or she is not a national;
   (d) The term 'worker on an offshore installation' refers to a migrant worker employed on an offshore installation that is under the jurisdiction of a State of which he or she is not a national;
   (e) The term 'itinerant worker' refers to a migrant worker who, having his or her habitual residence in one State, has to travel to another State or States for short periods, owing to the nature of his or her occupation;
   (f) The term 'project-tied worker' refers to a migrant worker admitted to a State of employment for a defined period to work solely on a specific project being carried out in that State by his or her employer;
   (g) The term 'specified-employment worker' refers to a migrant worker:

      (i) Who has been sent by his or her employer for a restricted and defined period of time to a State of employment to undertake a specific assignment or duty; or
      (ii) Who engages for a restricted and defined period of time in work that requires professional, commercial, technical or other highly specialized skill; or
      (iii) Who, upon the request of his or her employer in the State of employment, engages for a restricted and defined period of time in work whose nature is transitory or brief; and who is required to depart from the State of employment either at the expiration of his or her authorized period of stay, or earlier if he or she no longer undertakes that specific assignment or duty or engages in that work;

   (h) The term 'self-employed worker' refers to a migrant worker who is engaged in a remunerated activity otherwise than under a contract of employment and who earns his or her living through this activity normally working alone or together with members of his or her family, and to any other migrant worker recognized as self-employed by applicable legislation of the State of employment or bilateral or multilateral agreements.

*Article 3*
The present Convention shall not apply to:

(a) Persons sent or employed by international organizations and agencies or persons sent or employed by a State outside its territory to perform official functions, whose admission and status are regulated by general international law or by specific international agreements or conventions;
(b) Persons sent or employed by a State or on its behalf outside its territory who participate in development programmes and other co-operation programmes, whose admission and status are regulated by agreement with the State of employment and who, in accordance with that agreement, are not considered migrant workers;
(c) Persons taking up residence in a State different from their State of origin as investors;
(d) Refugees and stateless persons, unless such application is provided for in the relevant national legislation of, or international instruments in force for, the State Party concerned;
(e) Students and trainees;
(f) Seafarers and workers on an offshore installation who have not been admitted to take up residence and engage in a remunerated activity in the State of employment.

*Article 5*
For the purposes of the present Convention, migrant workers and members of their families:

(a) Are considered as documented or in a regular situation if they are authorized to enter, to stay and to engage in a remunerated activity in the State of employment pursuant to the law of that State and to international agreements to which that State is a party;
(b) Are considered as non-documented or in an irregular situation if they do not comply with the conditions provided for in subparagraph (a) of the present article.

## Part 2 Non-discrimination with respect to Rights

*Article 7*
States Parties undertake, in accordance with the international instruments concerning human rights, to respect and to ensure to all migrant workers and members of their families within their territory or subject to their jurisdiction the rights provided for in the present Convention without distinction of any kind such as to sex, race, colour, language, religion or conviction, political or other opinion, national, ethnic or social origin, nationality, age, economic position, property, marital status, birth or other status.

## Part 3 Human Rights of All Migrant Workers and Members of Their Families

*Article 11*
1. No migrant worker or member of his or her family shall be held in slavery or servitude.
2. No migrant worker or member of his or her family shall be required to perform forced or compulsory labour.
3. Paragraph 2 of the present article shall not be held to preclude, in States where imprisonment with hard labour may be imposed as a punishment for a crime, the performance of hard labour in pursuance of a sentence to such punishment by a competent court.
4. For the purpose of the present article the term 'forced or compulsory labour' shall not include:

(a) Any work or service not referred to in paragraph 3 of the present article normally required of a person who is under detention in consequence of a lawful order of a court or of a person during conditional release from such detention;
(b) Any service exacted in cases of emergency or calamity threatening the life or well being of the community;
(c) Any work or service that forms part of normal civil obligations so far as it is imposed also on citizens of the State concerned.

*Article 15*
No migrant worker or member of his or her family shall be arbitrarily deprived of property, whether owned individually or in association with others. Where, under the legislation in force in the State of employment, the assets of a migrant worker or a member of his or her family are expropriated in whole or in part, the person concerned shall have the right to fair and adequate compensation.

*Article 16*
1. Migrant workers and members of their families shall have the right to liberty and security of person.
2. Migrant workers and members of their families shall be entitled to effective protection by the State against violence, physical injury, threats and intimidation, whether by public officials or by private individuals, groups or institutions . . .
9. Migrant workers and members of their families who have been victims of unlawful arrest or detention shall have an enforceable right to compensation.

*Article 18*
1. Migrant workers and members of their families shall have the right to equality with nationals of the State concerned before the courts and tribunals. In the determination of any criminal charge against them or of their rights and obligations in a suit of law, they shall be entitled to a fair and public hearing by a competent, independent and impartial tribunal established by law . . .

*Article 20*
1. No migrant worker or member of his or her family shall be imprisoned merely on the ground of failure to fulfil a contractual obligation.
2. No migrant worker or member of his or her family shall be deprived of his or her authorization of residence or work permit or expelled merely on the ground of failure to fulfil an obligation arising out of a work contract unless fulfilment of that obligation constitutes a condition for such authorization or permit.

*Article 22*
1. Migrant workers and members of their families shall not be subject to measures of collective expulsion . . .
6. In case of expulsion, the person concerned shall have a reasonable opportunity before or after departure to settle any claims for wages and other entitlements due to him or her and any pending liabilities.
9. Expulsion from the State of employment shall not in itself prejudice any rights of a migrant worker or a member of his or her family acquired in accordance with the law of that State, including the right to receive wages and other entitlements due to him or her.

*Article 25*

1. Migrant workers shall enjoy treatment not less favourable than that which applies to nationals of the State of employment in respect of remuneration and:

   (a) Other conditions of work, that is to say, overtime, hours of work, weekly rest, holidays with pay, safety, health, termination of the employment relationship and any other conditions of work which, according to national law and practice, are covered by these terms;
   (b) Other terms of employment, that is to say, minimum age of employment, restriction on home work and any other matters which, according to national law and practice, are considered a term of employment.

2. It shall not be lawful to derogate in private contracts of employment from the principle of equality of treatment referred to in paragraph 1 of the present article.
3. States Parties shall take all appropriate measures to ensure that migrant workers are not deprived of any rights derived from this principle by reason of any irregularity in their stay or employment. In particular, employers shall not be relieved of any legal or contractual obligations, nor shall their obligations be limited in any manner by reason of such irregularity.

*Article 26*

1. States Parties recognize the right of migrant workers and members of their families:

   (a) To take part in meetings and activities of trade unions and of any other associations established in accordance with law, with a view to protecting their economic, social, cultural and other interests, subject only to the rules of the organization concerned;
   (b) To join freely any trade union and any such association as aforesaid, subject only to the rules of the organization concerned;
   (c) To seek the aid and assistance of any trade union and of any such association as aforesaid.

2. No restrictions may be placed on the exercise of these rights other than those that are prescribed by law and which are necessary in a democratic society in the interests of national security, public order (*ordre public*) or the protection of the rights and freedoms of others.

*Article 27*

1. With respect to social security, migrant workers and members of their families shall enjoy in the State of employment the same treatment granted to nationals in so far as they fulfil the requirements provided for by the applicable legislation of that State and the applicable bilateral and multilateral treaties. The competent authorities of the State or origin and the State of employment can at any time establish the necessary arrangements to determine the modalities of application of this norm . . .

*Article 32*

Upon the termination of their stay in the State of employment, migrant workers and members of their families shall have the right to transfer their earnings and savings and, in accordance with the applicable legislation of the States concerned, their personal effects and belongings.

## Part 4 Other Rights of Migrant Workers and Members of their Families who are Documented or in a Regular Situation

*Article 40*

1. Migrant workers and members of their families shall have the right to form associations and trade unions in the State of employment for the promotion and protection of their economic, social, cultural and other interests.
2. No restrictions may be placed on the exercise of this right other than those that are prescribed by law and are necessary in a democratic society in the interests of national security, public order (*ordre public*) or the protection of the rights and freedoms of others.

*Article 43*

1. Migrant workers shall enjoy equality of treatment with nationals of the State of employment in relation to:

   (c) Access to vocational training and retraining facilities and institutions;

   (f) Access to co-operatives and self-managed enterprises, which shall not imply a change of their migration status and shall be subject to the rules and regulations of the bodies concerned . . .

*Article 49*

1. Where separate authorizations to reside and to engage in employment are required by national legislation, the States of employment shall issue to migrant workers authorization of residence for at least the same period of time as their authorization to engage in remunerated activity.
2. Migrant workers who in the State of employment are allowed freely to choose their remunerated activity shall neither be regarded as in an irregular situation nor shall they lose their authorization of residence by the mere fact of the termination of their remunerated activity prior to the expiration of their work permits or similar authorizations.
3. In order to allow migrant workers referred to in paragraph 2 of the present article sufficient time to find alternative remunerated activities, the authorization of residence shall not be withdrawn at least for a period corresponding to that during which they may be entitled to unemployment benefits.

*Article 51*

Migrant workers who in the State of employment are not permitted freely to choose their remunerated activity shall neither be regarded as in an irregular situation nor shall they lose their authorization of residence by the mere fact of the termination of their remunerated activity prior to the expiration of their work permit, except where the authorization of residence is expressly dependent upon the specific remunerated activity for which they were admitted. Such migrant workers shall have the right to seek alternative employment, participation in public work schemes and retraining during the remaining period of their authorization to work, subject to such conditions and limitations as are specified in the authorization to work.

*Article 52*

1. Migrant workers in the State of employment shall have the right freely to choose their remunerated activity, subject to the following restrictions or conditions.

2. For any migrant worker a State of employment may:

   (a) Restrict access to limited categories of employment, functions, services or activities where this is necessary in the interests of this State and provided for by national legislation;
   (b) Restrict free choice of remunerated activity in accordance with its legislation concerning recognition of occupational qualifications acquired outside its territory. However, States Parties concerned shall endeavour to provide for recognition of such qualifications.

3. For migrant workers whose permission to work is limited in time, a State of employment may also:

   (a) Make the right freely to choose their remunerated activities subject to the condition that the migrant worker has resided lawfully in its territory for the purpose of remunerated activity for a period of time prescribed in its national legislation that should not exceed two years;
   (b) Limit access by a migrant worker to remunerated activities in pursuance of a policy of granting priority to its nationals or to persons who are assimilated to them for these purposes by virtue of legislation or bilateral or multilateral agreements. Any such limitation shall cease to apply to a migrant worker who has resided lawfully in its territory for the purpose of remunerated activity for a period of time prescribed in its national legislation that should not exceed five years.

4. States of employment shall prescribe the conditions under which a migrant worker who has been admitted to take up employment may be authorized to engage in work on his or her own account. Account shall be taken of the period during which the worker has already been lawfully in the State of employment.

*Article 53*

1. Members of a migrant worker's family who have themselves an authorization of residence or admission that is without limit of time or is automatically renewable shall be permitted freely to choose their remunerated activity under the same conditions as are applicable to the said migrant worker in accordance with article 52 of the present Convention.
2. With respect to members of a migrant worker's family who are not permitted freely to choose their remunerated activity, States Parties shall consider favourably granting them priority in obtaining permission to engage in a remunerated activity over other workers who seek admission to the State of employment, subject to applicable bilateral and multilateral agreements.

*Article 54*

1. Without prejudice to the terms of their authorization of residence or their permission to work and the rights provided for in articles 25 and 27 of the present Convention, migrant workers shall enjoy equality of treatment with nationals of the State of employment in respect of:

   (a) Protection against dismissal;
   (b) Unemployment benefits;

(c) Access to public work schemes intended to combat unemployment;
(d) Access to alternative employment in the event of loss of work or termination of other remunerated activity, subject to article 52 of the present Convention.

2. If a migrant worker claims that the terms of his or her work contract have been violated by his or her employer, he or she shall have the right to address his or her case to the competent authorities of the State of employment, on terms provided for in article 18, paragraph 1, of the present Convention.

*Article 55*
Migrant workers who have been granted permission to engage in a remunerated activity, subject to the conditions attached to such permission, shall be entitled to equality of treatment with nationals of the State of employment in the exercise of that remunerated activity.

## Part 5 Provisions applicable to Particular Categories of Migrant Workers and of their Families

*Article 61*
2. If a project-tied worker claims that the terms of his or her work contract have been violated by his or her employer, he or she shall have the right to address his or her case to the competent authorities of the State which has jurisdiction over that employer, on terms provided for in article 18, paragraph 1, of the present Convention . . .

## Part 6 Promotion of Sound, Equitable, Humane and Lawful Conditions in Connection with International Migration of Workers and Members of their Families

*Article 65*
1. States Parties shall maintain appropriate services to deal with questions concerning international migration of workers and members of their families. Their functions shall include, *inter alia*:

(c) The provision of appropriate information, particularly to employers, workers and their organizations on policies, laws and regulations relating to migration and employment, on agreements concluded with other States concerning migration and on other relevant matters . . .

*Article 66*
1. Subject to paragraph 2 of the present article, the right to undertake operations with a view to the recruitment of workers for employment in another State shall be restricted to:

(a) Public services or bodies of the State in which such operations take place;
(b) Public services or bodies of the State of employment on the basis of agreement between the States concerned;
(c) A body established by virtue of a bilateral or multilateral agreement.

2. Subject to any authorization, approval and supervision by the public authorities of the States Parties concerned as may be established pursuant to the legislation and practice of those States, agencies, prospective employers or persons acting on their behalf may also be permitted to undertake the said operations.

*Article 68*

1. States Parties, including States of transit, shall collaborate with a view to preventing and eliminating illegal or clandestine movements and employment of migrant workers in an irregular situation. The measures to be taken to this end within the jurisdiction of each State concerned shall include:

   (a) Appropriate measures against the dissemination of misleading information relating to emigration and immigration;
   (b) Measures to detect and eradicate illegal or clandestine movements of migrant workers and members of their families and to impose effective sanctions on persons, groups or entities which organize, operate or assist in organizing or operating such movements;
   (c) Measures to impose effective sanctions on persons, groups or entities which use violence, threats or intimidation against migrant workers or members of their families in an irregular situation.

2. States of employment shall take all adequate and effective measures to eliminate employment in their territory of migrant workers in an irregular situation, including, whenever appropriate, sanctions on employers of such workers. The rights of migrant workers *vis-à-vis* their employer arising from employment shall not be impaired by these measures . . .

# 38. World Federation of the Sporting Goods Industry: Code of Conduct – Guiding Principles, 2000

**Commentary**: Established in 1978, the World Federation of the Sporting Goods Industry (WFSGI, www.wfsgi.org) consists of large international sports companies, smaller national companies and national federations from over 50 States. The WFSGI Committee on Ethics and Fair Trade first developed this Model Code in 1997 following consultation with constituent federations, other members, international organisations and NGOs. This version of the Code, endorsed by the WFSGI General Assembly in 2000, serves as a model for companies to develop individual codes and ensure 'that their operations satisfy the highest ethical standards in the global marketplace'. Additional instruments include WFSGI (1995), 'Code of Best Practice concerning Child Labour', Verbier and WFSGI/International Olympic Committee (IOC) (2004), 'Code of Conduct'. See further, Fédération Internationale de Football Association/International Confederation of Free Trade Unions/International Federation of Commercial, Clerical, Professional and Technical Employees/ International Textile, Garment and Leather Workers Federation (1996), 'Code of Labour Practice'. Compare also the International Council of Toy Industries (1995, revised 2001), 'Code of Business Practices', New York (www.toy-icti.org/info/code.htm) with the Toy Industry of Europe (1997), 'Code of Business Practices', Brussels (www.tietoyorg).

**Preamble**

The ideals of the WFSGI are the ideals of sport, and the organization seeks to promote fairness, honesty, mutual understanding and high ethical standards not only on the sports field but also in the factories which make sports products. WFSGI members recognize the important role they play in the global economy and their influence on the social and economic conditions under which sporting goods are manufactured and produced. That influence is exercised both through their actions as employers and far more profoundly through their decisions as customers of companies that serve as suppliers of goods and services.

The relationship between WFSGI member companies and their suppliers, and in turn any sub contractors involved in the production process, must be based on trust, mutual respect and common values. WFSGI is committed to fostering a sports industry in which member companies actively build business partnerships with those who share the values of sport and take responsibility for making the values real through active engagement.

These Principles are based on the international labour standards outlined in the relevant Conventions of the ILO. WFSGI also acknowledges that companies operate under different legal, economic, social and cultural environments and these differences merit understanding and respect. Members must ensure that all activities related to the production of their goods at least comply with all relevant applicable mandatory legal requirements.

**Legal Compliance**
Member companies and the companies that produce goods for them ('employers') should operate in full compliance with national and local laws, rules and regulations relevant to their business operations.

**Working Conditions**
Local industry standards should prevail when higher than the local legal requirements. In countries where the legal requirements fall short of internationally recognized standards, it is recommended that members should apply the following minimum criteria:

*i. Forced Labour*
Employers shall not use forced labour, whether in the form of prison labour, indentured labour, bonded labour, or otherwise. No employee can be compelled to work through force, the threat of force, or intimidation of any form.

*ii. Non-discrimination*
No person shall be subject to any discrimination in employment, included in hiring, salary, benefits, advancement, disciplines, termination or retirement, on the basis of gender, race, religion, age, disability, sexual orientation, nationality, political opinion, or social or ethnic origin.

*iii. Freedom of Association and Collective Bargaining*
Employers shall recognize and respect the rights of workers to join workers' organizations and associations of their own choosing, and to bargain collectively. Where the right to freedom of association and collective bargaining is restricted under law, the employer shall consider the development of parallel means for independent and free association and bargaining.

*iv. Wages*
Employers recognize that wages are essential to meeting employees' basic needs and that employees should be fully compensated for all time worked. In all cases, wages must equal or exceed the minimum wage or the prevailing industry wage, whichever is higher.

In addition to their compensation for regular hours of work, employees shall be compensated for overtime hours at the premium rate legally required in the country of manufacture or, in those countries where such laws do not exist, at a rate exceeding their regular hourly compensation rate.

*v. Hours of Work*
Workers shall not be required, except in extraordinary business circumstances, to work in excess of 60 hours per week, including overtime, or the local legal requirement, whichever is less. Employees shall be entitled to at least one day off for every seven day period.

*vi. Benefits and Leave*
Each employee will be provided all legally mandated benefits. These may include meals or meal subsidies; transportation or transportation subsidies; other cash allowances; health care;

child care; emergency, pregnancy or sick leave; religious, or bereavement leave; and contributions for social security and other insurance, including life, health and employees compensation.

*vii. Child Labour*

No person shall be employed at an age younger than 15 (or 14 where the law of the country of manufacture allows) or younger than the age for completing compulsory education in the country of manufacture where such age is higher than 15.

*viii. Health and Safety*

A safe and hygienic working environment shall be provided, and occupational health and safety practices which prevent accidents and injury to health arising out of, linked with, or occurring in the course of work or as a result of the operation of employer facilities shall be promoted.

This includes protection from fire, accidents, and toxic substances. Lighting, heating and ventilation systems should be adequate. Employees should have access at all times to sanitary facilities, which should be adequate and clean. The factory must have safety and health policies and procedures that are clearly communicated to the workers. These should apply to employee residential facilities, where provided by employers.

*ix. Harassment or Abuse*

Every employee should be treated with respect and dignity and have the right to a workplace free from physical, sexual, psychological or verbal harassment or abuse.

**Environment**

Members should aim for progressive improvement in their environmental performance, not only in their own operations, but also in their relationships with partners, suppliers and subcontractors.

This includes:

(i) Integrating principles of sustainability into business decisions.
(ii) Responsible use of natural resources such as land, soil, energy and water.
(iii) Reducing, minimizing and avoiding pollution and waste including solid, liquid and atmospheric conditions.
(iv) Designing and developing products, materials and technologies according to the principles of sustainability.

**Community Involvement**

Employers recognize the economic and social impact of their work and are committed to improving conditions in the wider community.

**Company Specific Standards**

Members are encouraged to draw up their own specific code of ethical conduct, if they have not already done so, building on the above standards.

**Verification**

These Principles have been adopted by WFSGI to provide guidance for individual companies in ensuring that their products are made under fair factory conditions. Members are encouraged to establish their own internal management systems to monitor the standards outlined in their own code of conduct and to implement action plans for continuous improvements in factory working conditions in their own operations and those who supply them. Members are also encouraged to have factories monitored by appropriately qualified external third party organizations.

**Compliance**

Members shall take steps to ensure compliance with these standards in their own operations and those who supply them. Where there are instances of non compliance (e.g. significant and/or persistent breaches) whether found by internal or external monitors, members shall ensure timely and reasonable remediation of such non compliance; and ensure that adequate steps are taken to prevent recurrence and/or occurrence in other factories.

# 39. Ethical Trading Initiative: Base Code and Principles of Implementation, 1998

**Commentary**: The Ethical Trading Initiative (ETI, www.ethicaltrade.org/) is an alliance of companies, NGOs and trade union organisations concerned with the labour issues arising from international supply chains. The Initiative is intended to promote ethical sourcing, a concept defined as 'a company taking responsibility to work with its suppliers to implement internationally-accepted labour standards in the workplace'. The Base Code draws upon ILO Conventions with respect to workers' rights as well as international human rights standards. ETI member companies are expected to adopt this code of labour practice or formulate their own, provided that it incorporates the Base Code. However, member companies may limit the application of the Code by division or product line and ETI accepts that some non-compliances may take time to fix, for example, if there are constraints arising beyond the supplier's control, if they are constrained by national law or if the Code is otherwise not realisable. The ETI does not audit or certify corporate compliance, but member companies share experiences. See further, ETI (1997), 'Eliminating World Poverty: A Challenge for the Twenty-First Century', White Paper, Cmnd 3789; ETI (2004), 'Putting Ethics to Work: Annual Report', London.

**The Base Code**

*1. Employment is Freely Chosen*

1.1 There is no forced, bonded or involuntary prison labour.

1.2 Workers are not required to lodge 'deposits' or their identity papers with their employer and are free to leave their employer after reasonable notice.

*2. Freedom of Association and the Right to Collective Bargaining are Respected*

2.1 Workers, without distinction, have the right to join or form trade unions of their own choosing and to bargain collectively.

2.2 The employer adopts an open attitude towards the activities of trade unions and their organisational activities.

2.3 Workers' representatives are not discriminated against and have access to carry out their representative functions in the workplace.

2.4 Where the right to freedom of association and collective bargaining is restricted under law, the employer facilitates, and does not hinder, the development of parallel means for independent and free association and bargaining.

*3. Working Conditions are Safe and Hygienic*

3.1 A safe and hygienic working environment shall be provided, bearing in mind the prevailing knowledge of the industry and of any specific hazards. Adequate steps shall be taken to prevent accidents and injury to health arising out of, associated with, or occurring in the course of work, by minimising, so far as is reasonably practicable, the causes of hazards inherent in the working environment.

3.2 Workers shall receive regular and recorded health and safety training, and such training shall be repeated for new or reassigned workers.

3.3 Access to clean toilet facilities and to potable water, and, if appropriate, sanitary facilities for food storage shall be provided.

3.4 Accommodation, where provided, shall be clean, safe, and meet the basic needs of the workers.

3.5 The company observing the code shall assign responsibility for health and safety to a senior management representative.

*4. Child Labour Shall Not Be Used*

4.1 There shall be no new recruitment of child labour.

4.2 Companies shall develop or participate in and contribute to policies and programmes which provide for the transition of any child found to be performing child labour to enable her or him to attend and remain in quality education until no longer a child; 'child' and 'child labour' being defined in the appendices.

4.3 Children and young persons under 18 shall not be employed at night or in hazardous conditions.

4.4 These policies and procedures shall conform to the provisions of the relevant ILO standards.

*5. Living Wages Are Paid*

5.1 Wages and benefits paid for a standard working week meet, at a minimum, national legal standards or industry benchmark standards, whichever is higher. In any event wages should always be enough to meet basic needs and to provide some discretionary income.

5.2 All workers shall be provided with written and understandable information about their employment conditions in respect to wages before they enter employment and about the particulars of their wages for the pay period concerned each time that they are paid.

5.3 Deductions from wages as a disciplinary measure shall not be permitted nor shall any deductions from wages not provided for by national law be permitted without the expressed permission of the worker concerned. All disciplinary measures should be recorded.

*6. Working Hours Are Not Excessive*

6.1 Working hours comply with national laws and benchmark industry standards, whichever affords greater protection.

6.2 In any event, workers shall not on a regular basis be required to work in excess of 48 hours per week and shall be provided with at least one day off for every 7 day period on average. Overtime shall be voluntary, shall not exceed 12 hours per week, shall not be demanded on a regular basis and shall always be compensated at a premium rate.

*7. No Discrimination is Practiced*

7.1 There is no discrimination in hiring, compensation, access to training, promotion, termination or retirement based on race, caste, national origin, religion, age, disability, gender, marital status, sexual orientation, union membership or political affiliation.

8. *Regular Employment is Provided*
8.1 To every extent possible work performed must be on the basis of a recognised employment relationship established through national law and practice.
8.2 Obligations to employees under labour or social security laws and regulations arising from the regular employment relationship shall not be avoided through the use of labour-only contracting, sub-contracting, or home-working arrangements, or through apprenticeship schemes where there is no real intent to impart skills or provide regular employment, nor shall any such obligations be avoided through the excessive use of fixed-term contracts of employment.

9. *No Harsh or Inhumane Treatment Is Allowed*
9.1 Physical abuse or discipline, the threat of physical abuse, sexual or other harassment and verbal abuse or other forms of intimidation shall be prohibited.

The provisions of this code constitute minimum and not maximum standards, and this code should not be used to prevent companies from exceeding these standards.

Companies applying this code are expected to comply with national and other applicable law and, where the provisions of law and this Base Code address the same subject, to apply that provision which affords the greater protection.

**ETI Principles of Implementation**

The purpose of ETI is to identify, develop and promote good practice with respect to implementing codes of labour practice. Critical areas include monitoring and verification, and transparency and disclosure, to determine and communicate whether standards embodied in the code are being achieved. ETI members accept the following as general principles upon which to develop or refine their search for best practice.

1. *Commitment*
1.1 The company gives its membership of ETI, the code and its implementation process an informed and explicit endorsement.
1.2 This commitment is communicated throughout the company and to its suppliers and sub-contractors (including closely associated self-employed staff).
1.3 A member of senior management is assigned responsibility for the implementation of compliance with the code.
1.4 The code and the implementation process is integrated into the core business relationships and culture.
1.5 The company will ensure that human and financial resources are made available to enable it to meet its stated commitments.

2. *Monitoring, Independent Verification and Reporting*
2.1 Member companies accept the principle that the implementation of codes will be assessed through monitoring and independent verification; and that performance with regard to monitoring practice and implementation of codes will be reported annually.
2.2 Companies will engage with other members in the design, implementation and analysis of pilot schemes to identify good practice in monitoring and independent verification and share this experience with other members.

2.3 Company members will draw on this experience in establishing where relevant with other ETI members' work plans to implement programmes of monitoring, independent verification, and reporting, and will report progress against these programmes to and through the ETI in a format and timing to be agreed.

2.4 Workers covered by the code shall be provided with a confidential means to report failure to observe the code and shall be otherwise protected in this respect.

*3. Awareness-Raising and Training*

3.1 All relevant personnel are provided appropriate training and guidelines that will enable them to apply the code in their work.

3.2 Suppliers are made aware of the code, and the company's commitment to sourcing from suppliers who observe the standards in the code.

3.3 Workers whose work is covered by the code are, where possible, made aware of the code and implementation principles or procedures.

*4. Corrective Actions*

4.1 Member companies commit themselves, on the basis of knowledge gained from monitoring to; (a) negotiate and implement agreed schedules for corrective actions with suppliers failing to observe the terms of the code, i.e. a continuous improvement approach; (b) require the immediate cessation of serious breaches of the code, and; (c) where serious breaches of the code persist, to terminate any business relationship with the supplier concerned.

*5. Management Procedures, Pricing and Incentives*

5.1 Negotiations with suppliers shall take into account the costs of observing the code.

5.2 Understanding and implementation of company policy with respect to its code of labour practice shall constitute a positive performance measure when assessing appropriate personnel.

# 40. Clean Clothes Campaign: Code of Labour Practices for the Apparel Industry including Sportswear, 1998

**Commentary**: The Clean Clothes Campaign (CCC, www.cleanclothes.org) is a global network of more than 200 NGOs, trade unions and individuals with an international secretariat located in Amsterdam. The Code of Labour Practices seeks to improve working conditions in the global garment and sportswear industries. On the history of the Code, see Ascoly N. and Zeldenrust I. (1999), 'The Code Debate in Context: A Decade of Campaigning for Clean Clothes', working paper, The Netherlands (available at www.cleanclothes.org/codes/99-3-11.htm, 2 May 2005). See also, Ascoly N., Zeldenrust I. and Oldenziel J. (2001), 'Overview of recent developments on monitoring and verification in the garment and sportswear industry in Europe', Center for Research on MNCs, Amsterdam, 2nd edn (www.somo.nl). For a comparable initiative, see the American Apparel Manufacturers Association (1997), Worldwide Responsible Apparel Production Principles, Arlington, VA (www.wrapapparel.org). For comment, see Sajhau J.P. (1997), 'Business Ethics in the Textile, Clothing and Footwear (TCF) Industries: Code of Conduct', ILO Doc SAP 2.60/WP. 110.

## Part I Introduction

*Statement of Purpose*

The Clean Clothes Campaign is dedicated to advancing the interests of workers in the apparel and sportswear industry and the concerns of consumers who purchase products made and sold by this industry. The Campaign seeks an end to the oppression, exploitation and abuse of workers in this industry, most of who are women. The Campaign also seeks to provide consumers with accurate information concerning the working conditions under which the apparel and sports wear they purchase are made. The Clean Clothes Campaign seeks to achieve its aims through a variety of means including a code of labour practice that would be adopted and implemented by companies, industry associations and employer organisations. The code, which is a concise statement of minimum standards with respect to labour practices, is meant to be accompanied by a commitment by the companies adopting it to take positive actions in applying it. Companies are expected to insist on compliance with the code by any of their contractors, subcontractors, suppliers and licensees organising production that would fall under the scope of the code.

Companies adopting the code will be expected to engage an independent institution established for the purpose of monitoring compliance with the code, in assisting companies in implementing the code and in providing consumers with information concerning the labour practices in the industry.

This code of labour practice sets forth minimum standards for wages, working time and working conditions and provides for observance of all of the core standards of the ILO including Conventions 29, 87, 98, 100, 105, 111 and 138. These are minimum standards that are meant to apply throughout the industry and in all countries. The code is not a trade protectionist measure. It is not meant to be used as a means to close the markets of some countries at the expense of workers in other countries.

The code is not meant to be a substitute for international intergovernmental co-operation nor for international legislation. Although the code does seek to afford workers protection from oppression, abuse and exploitation where national laws are inadequate or are not enforced, it does not seek to become a substitute for national laws or the national labour inspectorate. The code is not a substitute for secure and independent trade unions nor should it be used as a substitute for collective bargaining.

*Scope of Application*

The code is intended for retailers as well as manufacturers and all companies positioned in between those in the apparel and sportswear supply chain. It can also be used by industry associations or employer organisations.

The code applies to all of the company's apparel and sportswear products (including sport shoes). The code specifically applies to the following general industrial classification of economic activities within the European Community (NACE) classification codes:

436 knitting industry
451 manufacture of mass-produced footwear
452 production of hand-made footwear
453 manufacture of ready-made clothing and accessories
454 bespoke tailoring, dressmaking and hatmaking
456 manufacture of furs and of fur goods

Through the code retailers and manufacturers declare their responsibility for the working conditions under which the apparel, sportswear and shoes they sell are produced. This responsibility extends to all workers producing products for the company, regardless of their status or relationship to the company and whether or not they are employees of the company. The code would therefore apply to home-based workers and to workers who are engaged either informally or on a contracted basis. The code applies to all of the companies' contractors, subcontractors, suppliers and licensees world-wide. The terms 'contractor', 'subcontractor', 'supplier' mean any natural or legal person who contracts with the company and is engaged in a manufacturing process, including CMT (cut-make-and-trim), assembly and packaging, which result in a finished product for the consumer. A licensee means any natural or legal person who contracts with a company to produce or distribute finished products using the name or brand image of that company.

Observance of the code must be an enforceable and enforced part of any agreement between the company and its contractors, subcontractors, suppliers and licensees.

## Part II Code of Labour Practices

*Introduction*

The code provides a concise statement of minimum labour standards together with a pledge by the company to observe these standards and to require its contractors, subcontractors, suppliers and licensees to observe these standards. The code is concise in order to display it in workplaces and in order to avoid any confusion between basic principles and the application of principles. An independent institution, established to provide independent monitoring of compliance with the code and to assist companies in implementing the code, will provide an auditable check-list of practices and conditions that are consistent with the standards set forth in the code. This independent organisation will also provide a means by which questions over the meaning of the code can be resolved.

The preamble establishes three principles: First, the company accepts responsibility for its workers, including workers involved in contracting and subcontracting agreements. Second, the company pledges to observe the core ILO labour standards and to ensure that workers are provided with living wages and decent working conditions. Third, the company pledges to make observance of the code a condition of any agreements that it makes with contractors and suppliers and to require them to extend this obligation to their subcontractors.

The body of the code is based on the same core ILO conventions including prohibitions against child labour, forced or bonded labour, discrimination, freedom of association and the right to collective bargaining. This is followed by the basic labour conditions – wages, hours and working conditions (including health and safety) – and their formulation in the code, also derived from ILO standards.

This section also addresses the issue of regular employment relationships. Increasingly employers avoid the obligations of the employment relationship by treating workers as 'independent contractors' when in fact their situation is the same as that of regular employees. The ILO is in the process of developing an international standard on this subject.

The closing section sets out the most important obligations contractors, subcontractors, suppliers and licensees must undertake in implementing the code and pledges the company to enforce its code using a range of sanctions up to and including termination of any agreements. The closing section pledges all employers concerned to refrain from disciplinary action, dismissal or otherwise discriminating against any worker for providing information concerning observance of the code.

This part also states that the code establishes only minimum standards that must not be used as a ceiling or to discourage collective bargaining. The text of the code, when meant to be posted where workers can see it, shall also include a means by which workers can report failure to comply with the code in a confidential manner.

*Preamble*

(name of company) recognises its responsibilities to workers for the conditions under which its products or services are made and that these responsibilities extend to all workers producing products or services for (name of company) whether or not they are employees of (name of company).

Any workers producing products or services manufactured, sold or distributed by (name of company) must be provided with living wages and decent working conditions, and the international labour standards established by Conventions 29, 87, 98, 100, 105, 111 and 138 of the ILO must be observed.

(name of company) will require its contractors, their sub-contractors, suppliers and licensees to provide these conditions and observe these standards when producing or distributing products or components of products for (name of company). (name of company) will, prior to placing orders with suppliers, engaging contractors and subcontractors or granting licenses, assess whether the provisions of this code can be met.

For the purposes of this code the term 'contractor', 'subcontractor' or 'supplier' shall mean any natural or legal person who contracts with (name of company), either directly or indirectly via another natural or legal person who contracts with (name of company) and is engaged in a manufacturing process, including CMT (cut-make-and-trim), assembly and packaging, which result in a finished product for the consumer. The term 'licensee' means any natural or legal person who as part of a contractual arrangement with (name of company) uses for any purpose the name of (name of company) or its recognised brand names or images.

*Content*

(i) Employment is freely chosen:
There shall be no use of forced, including bonded or prison, labour (ILO Conventions 29 and 105). Nor shall workers be required to lodge 'deposits' or their identity papers with their employer.

(ii) There is no discrimination in employment:
Equality of opportunity and treatment regardless of race, colour, sex, religion, political opinion, nationality, social origin or other distinguishing characteristic shall be provided (ILO conventions 100 and 111).

(iii) Child labour is not used:
There shall be no use of child labour. Only workers above the age of 15 years or above the compulsory school-leaving age shall be engaged (ILO Convention 138). Adequate transitional economic assistance and appropriate educational opportunities shall be provided to any replaced child workers.

(iv) Freedom of association and the right to collective bargaining are respected:
The right of all workers to form and join trade unions and to bargain collectively shall be recognised (ILO Conventions 87 and 98). Workers' representatives shall not be the subject of discrimination and shall have access to all workplaces necessary to enable them to carry out their representation functions (ILO Convention 135 and Recommendation 143). Employers shall adopt a positive approach towards the activities of trade unions and an open attitude towards their organisational activities.

(v) Living wages are paid:
Wages and benefits paid for a standard working week shall meet at least legal or industry minimum standards and always be sufficient to meet basic needs of workers and their families and to provide some discretionary income. Deductions from wages for disciplinary measures shall not be permitted nor shall any deductions from wages not provided for by national law be permitted without the expressed permission of the worker concerned. All workers shall be provided with written and understandable information about the conditions in respect of wages before they enter employment and of the particulars of their wages for the pay period concerned each time that they are paid.

(vi) Hours of work are not excessive:
Hours of work shall comply with applicable laws and industry standards. In any event, workers shall not on a regular basis be required to work in excess of 48 hours per week and shall be provided with at least one day off for every 7 day period. Overtime shall be voluntary, shall not exceed 12 hours per week, shall not be demanded on a regular basis and shall always be compensated at a premium rate.

(vii) Working conditions are decent:
A safe and hygienic working environment shall be provided, and best occupational health and safety practice shall be promoted, bearing in mind the prevailing

knowledge of the industry and of any specific hazards. Physical abuse, threats of physical abuse, unusual punishments or discipline, sexual and other harassment, and intimidation by the employer is strictly prohibited.

(viii) The employment relationship is established:
Obligations to employees under labour or social security laws and regulations arising from the regular employment relationship shall not be avoided through the use of labour-only contracting arrangements, or through apprenticeship schemes where there is no real intent to impart skills or provide regular employment. Younger workers shall be given the opportunity to participate in education and training programmes.

*Closing Section*
Contractors, subcontractors, suppliers and licensees shall undertake to support and co operate in the implementation and monitoring of this code by:

(i) providing (name of company) with relevant information concerning their operations;
(ii) permitting inspection at any time of their workplaces and operations by approved inspectors;
(iii) maintaining records of the name, age, hours worked and wages paid for each worker and making these available to approved inspectors on request;
(iv) informing, verbally and in writing, the workers concerned of the provisions of this code; and,
(v) refraining from disciplinary action, dismissal or otherwise discriminating against any worker for providing information concerning observance of this code.

Contractors, subcontractors, suppliers and licensees found to be in breach of one or more terms of this Code of Labour Practices may lose the right to produce or organise production of goods for (name of company).

Questions as to the interpretation of the meaning of the provisions of this code shall be resolved according to the procedure set forth by an independent institution established for this purpose.

The provisions of this code constitute only minimum standards and conditions for the purpose of preventing exploitation. (name of company) does not intend, will not use, and will not allow any contractor, subcontractor, supplier or licensee to use these minimum standards and conditions as maximum standards or as the only conditions permitted by (name of company) or to serve as the basis for any claim as to what standards or conditions of employment should be provided.

*Specific Industry Standards*
Specific industry standards, especially with respect to health and safety (including access to medical services) and workers' accommodation may be incorporated into the code or attached separately and referenced in the code under section vii 'working conditions are decent'. These standards may be formally recognised standards or established best practice.

## Part III Implementation

*Introduction*
Implementation refers to the whole range of activities that could be taken by a company to give effect to the Code of Labour Practices. In the past some companies have adopted codes

as a public relations response to reports of exploitation but have failed to implement them. Companies adopting the Code of Labour Practices for the apparel and sportswear industry will be expected to agree to certain minimum conditions with respect to implementing the code. One of the most important ways in which a code can be implemented is for it to become an enforceable and enforced part of agreements with contractors, subcontractors suppliers and licensees.

Implementation and monitoring are often confused. Monitoring, which means to watch or check that the terms of the code are being respected is one aspect of implementing a code. It is expected that companies adopting the code will in their relationship with their contractors, sub-contractors, suppliers and licensees monitor their compliance with the code.

Companies adopting the code are also expected to co-operate and support a system of independent monitoring of compliance with the code. This section concerns the general obligations of the company to implement the code. The obligations of the company with respect to independent monitoring are considered in Part IV.

A. OBLIGATIONS OF THE COMPANY TO IMPLEMENT THE CODE

(i) The company agrees to take positive actions to implement the code, to incorporate the code into all of its operations and to make the code an integral part of its overall philosophy and general policy.

(ii) The company will assign responsibility for all matters pertaining to the code within its organisation and inform the independent institution and other relevant bodies where this responsibility is assigned.

(iii) The Board of Directors (or other governing body) of the company shall periodically review the operation of the code, including the reports of internal and external monitoring.

(iv) The company accepts responsibility for observing the code with respect to all employees and workers that it supervises and agrees to:

   (a) assign responsibility for implementing this code at each place that it owns or controls;
   (b) ensure that all workers are aware of the contents of the code by clearly displaying an authorised text of the code at all workplaces and by orally informing these employees in a language understood by them of the provisions of the code;
   (c) refrain from disciplining, dismissing or otherwise discriminating against any employee for providing information concerning observance of this code.

(v) The company will make observance of the code a condition of all agreements that it enters into with contractors, suppliers and licensees. These agreements will obligate these contractors, suppliers and licensees to require observance of the code in all agreements that they make with their respective subcontractors and suppliers in fulfilling their agreement with the company. Such agreements shall also oblige these contractors, subcontractors, suppliers and licensees to undertake the same obligations to implement the code as found in the preceding point.

B. OBLIGATIONS OF THE COMPANY TO ENFORCE THE CODE

Observance of the code by contractors, sub-contractors and suppliers must be an enforceable and enforced condition of agreement with the company.

In order to achieve this:

(i) The company will ensure that all agreements it enters into concerning the production of apparel and sportswear allow for the termination of the agreement for failure to observe the code by any contractors, sub-contractors and suppliers.

(ii) The company shall authorise a procedure with fixed time limits to rectify situations where its code is not being fully observed by a contractor, sub-contractor or supplier. The agreement by the contractor, sub-contractor or supplier to abide by this procedure would enable the continuation of the agreement with the company. The company shall require contractors or suppliers to institute similar procedures with respect to their contractors, sub-contractors or suppliers.

(iii) Such procedures shall be authorised only where:

  (a) there is a reasonable expectation that the situation will be corrected and that the code will be observed in the future;
  (b) the period specified for correcting the situation is reasonable;
  (c) recognisable and unmistakable violations of the code are ceased immediately;
  (d) such procedures shall not be authorised more than once for the same contractor, sub contractor or supplier for the same or similar failure to comply with the code; and
  (e) such procedures are consistent with any recommendations or procedures set forth by the independent institution established to assist in implementing this code.

(iv) With respect to child labour, such procedures shall require that there be no further engagement of children and that temporary measures to assist child workers such as the reduction in working time, the provision of educational opportunities and transitional economic support be instituted. In the end, child workers must be replaced by adults and, where possible, from the same family. Procedures should also include measures to assist the children concerned through provision of educational opportunities and transitional economic support.

(v) Contractors, sub-contractors and suppliers must, as part of their agreement with the company, agree to terminate any contract or agreement for the supply or production of goods by any contractor, sub-contractor or supplier that they engage not fully observing the code, or they must seek and receive approval from the company to institute a procedure with fixed time limits to rectify situations where the code is not being fully observed.

(vi) Where there is repeated failure to observe or to ensure observance of the code by a particular contractor, sub-contractor, supplier or licensee, the agreement should be terminated. Guidelines or procedures for determining when it is necessary to terminate a contract for failure to observe the code shall be set forth by an independent institution established for this purpose.

In situations where it is not clear whether a particular practice constitutes a violation of the code, relevant international labour standards of the ILO and any recommendations provided by the independent institution established to assist companies in implementing this code shall be sought for guidance.

## Part IV Independent Monitoring, Accreditation and Certification

*Introduction*

When a sufficient number of companies, industry associations or employers' organisations have adopted the code of labour practice for the apparel and sportswear industry, then they, in conjunction with appropriate trade union organisations and NGOs, shall establish jointly an independent institution, referred to in this document as 'the Foundation'.

The purpose of the Foundation shall be to:

(i) conduct, directly or indirectly through other organisations, the independent monitoring of compliance with the code;
(ii) assist companies in implementing the code; and
(iii) provide a means to inform consumers about observance of the code and more generally about labour conditions in the industry.

To these ends the Foundation shall:

(i) establish standards for the independent monitoring and for the accreditation of independent monitors;
(ii) train, or to arrange for the training, of independent monitors;
(iii) prepare an auditable checklist of labour practices to be used in monitoring the code;
(iv) conduct or otherwise cause to be conducted independent monitoring of compliance by specific companies with the code of labour practice;
(v) receive reports of such independent monitoring and make effective recommendations based on these reports to the companies concerned;
(vi) investigate any substantiated reports concerning compliance by participating companies and make effective recommendations based on the findings of such investigations;
(vii) prepare and publish guidelines for participating companies on the implementation of the code;
(viii) provide other technical assistance to companies in implementing the code, including the training of company personnel;
(ix) prepare and publish the authorised version of the code in various languages and in sufficient quantities as required by participating companies;
(x) establish a means to interpret the provisions of the code, provided that this means is based on the recognised jurisprudence of the ILO;
(xi) provide a means by which workers and any others can report on a confidential basis observance of the code;
(xii) establish, based on independent monitoring, a system of certification concerning labour practices which can be used by consumers;
(xiii) collect information from any source on working conditions in the apparel and sportswear industry and make this information available to consumers;
(xiv) promote the code of labour practice and encourage all companies operating in the industry to adopt it; and
(xv) establish a mechanism that can make effective recommendations with respect to any disputes arising out of the implementation or the certification process.

The Foundation shall be governed by a board consisting of equal representatives of appropriate trade union organisations and NGOs on one hand and of appropriate representatives of retailers and manufactures on the other hand. The Foundation shall be financed by contributions from participating organisations and by payments for services from contracting companies.

The principal means by which the Foundation shall conduct its work will be based on contracts with specific companies to independently monitor and certify their compliance with the code and by contracts with individuals and organisations to conduct monitoring. It is understood that the standards for independent monitoring established by the Foundation shall be based on the best practice of the two existing professions that monitor labour practices – the labour inspectorate and the contract-enforcement practices of trade unions. It is also understood that these standards shall include ethical practices for monitors, including respect for any confidential commercial information. It is also understood that any individuals engaged to conduct monitoring shall receive training for this purpose.

*Relation between the Company and the Foundation*

Companies adopting the code of labour practice for the apparel and sportswear industry shall enter into an agreement with the Foundation. This agreement shall provide for the following:

(a) the time-frame in which the production in the different facilities should comply with all the standards in the code;
(b) the information the company has to give to the Monitoring Foundation;
(c) the payments the company should make to the Monitoring Foundation;
(d) the procedures for the actual monitoring and the obligations of the different parties; and
(e) the use of the Foundation contract by the company in its public relations.

With respect to (b) the company assumes the following obligations:

(i) to maintain full and up-to-date information on all contractors, sub-contractors, suppliers and licensees obliged to observe this code, including the nature and location of all workplaces, and to provide this information to the Foundation or its accredited monitors in a timely manner upon request.
(ii) to require contractors, sub-contractors, suppliers and licensees to maintain records of the names, ages, hours worked, and wages paid for each worker, and make these records available for inspection by accredited monitors, and to allow the Foundation or its accredited monitors to conduct confidential interviews with workers.
(iii) to ensure that the code is clearly displayed in all places where apparel and sportswear are produced and/or distributed by or under agreement with or for the company and provide authorised texts of the code to contractors and suppliers for their use, and the use by any contractors, sub-contractors and suppliers obliged to observe this code. In all cases the text of the code so displayed shall be in languages so that the workers concerned are able to understand it. The text of the code shall be provided to each worker covered by its provisions and all workers so covered shall be orally informed in a language that they can understand of the provisions of the code.
(iv) the code so displayed must provide information to assist workers in reporting violations of the code to the Foundation or its agents taking into account the difficulties that workers will face in doing this and the need for confidentiality in order to protect workers.
(v) to allow for the necessary access to independent monitors and provide them with any and all relevant information upon demand.

(vi) to ensure and clearly demonstrate that the code is being observed by all parties obliged to observe the code, the company must allow the Foundation and its agents access to all information pertaining to the implementation of the code, and ensure that its contractors, sub-contractors and suppliers give similar access to the Foundation and its agents.

*Monitoring: Basic Principles*

(i) monitoring must be by the actual observance of working conditions through unannounced inspection visits ('spot checks') to all workplaces covered by the code;
(ii) the frequency of inspections must be established;
(iii) accredited monitors must be permitted to interview workers on a confidential basis;
(iv) in addition to regular or routine inspections, inspections shall be undertaken at specific locations following substantiated complaints, where there is sufficient reason to believe that the code is not being observed;
(v) inspections shall be conducted in a way which does not cause undue disruption to the performance of work in the premises being inspected;
(vi) written reports shall be provided by accredited monitors to all parties and to the participating company concerned following each visit.

The Foundation may seek other sources of information concerning compliance with the code including consulting appropriate trade union organisations, human rights organisations, religious and other similar institutions in order to obtain additional information on a certain company or in order to investigate a certain complaint.

If violations of the code are found, the company must agree to accept the recommendation of the Foundation. This recommendation shall in the first instance be aimed at improving the existing situation. Where such improvement is not possible or satisfactory, then the Foundation can oblige companies to re-negotiate, terminate or refuse to renew their contracts with certain contractors, subcontractors and/or suppliers.

Where companies fail to observe their agreement with the Foundation it is understood that the Foundation may release any relevant information to the public and may terminate the contract between the company and the Foundation.

The independent monitoring process shall form the basis for any public claims by the Foundation or by participating companies as to the operation of the code or concerning the actual labour practices covered by the code.

# 41. Global Exchange/International Labour Rights Fund: US Business Principles for Human Rights of Workers in China, 1999

**Commentary**: Global Exchange is a human rights NGO. The Business Principles (www.globalexchange.org/campaigns/sweatshops/china/principles.html) arose in response to a 1998 report by the National Labor Committee documenting links between leading US corporations and working conditions within China. They have since been endorsed *inter alia* by Amnesty International USA, the Consumers' Federation of America and the Fair Trade Foundation. For academic commentary, see Orentlicher D. and Gelatt T. (1992), 'Public law, private actors: the impact of human rights on business investors in China', *Northwestern Journal of International Law and Business*, **14**, 66–129. For an analogous initiative, see Coalition for Justice in the Maquiladoras, 'The Maquiladora Standards of Conduct', San Antonio, Texas, 1991 in (1992) *The CJM Newsletter* 1. For academic commentary, see Compa L. and Hinchliffe-Darricarrere T. (1995), 'Enforcing international labor rights through corporate codes of conduct', *Columbia Journal of Transnational Law*, **33**, 663–716.

As companies doing business in China, we seek to hear and respond to the concerns of workers making our products. We want to ensure that our business practices in China respect basic labour standards defined by the ILO, and basic human rights defined by the UN Covenants on Economic, Social and Cultural Rights, and Civil and Political Rights, signed by the Chinese government, as well as China's national laws. To this end, we agree to implement and to promote the following principles in the People's Republic of China:

No goods or products produced within our company-owned facilities or those of our suppliers shall be manufactured by bonded labour, forced labour, within prison camps or as part of reform-through-labour or re-education-through-labour programs.

Our facilities and suppliers shall adhere to wages that meet workers' basic needs, and to fair and decent working hours, at a minimum adhering to the wage and hour guidelines provided by China's labour laws and policies.

Our facilities and suppliers shall prohibit the use of corporal punishment, as well as any physical, sexual or verbal abuse or harassment of workers.

Our facilities and suppliers shall use production methods that do not negatively affect the occupational safety and health of workers.

Our facilities and suppliers shall not call on the police or military to enter their premises to prevent workers from exercising their rights.

We shall undertake to promote the following freedoms among our employees and the employees of our suppliers: freedom of association and assembly, including the rights to form unions and to bargain collectively; freedom of expression, and freedom from arbitrary arrest or detention.

Employees working in our facilities and those of our suppliers shall not face discrimination in hiring, remuneration or promotion based on age, gender, marital status, pregnancy, ethnicity or region of origin.

Employees working in our facilities and those of our suppliers shall not face discrimination in hiring, remuneration or promotion based on labour, political or religious activity, or on involvement in demonstrations, past records of arrests or internal exile for peaceful protest, or membership in organizations committed to non violent social or political change.

Our facilities and suppliers shall use environmentally responsible methods of production that have minimum adverse impact on land, air and water quality.

Our facilities and suppliers shall prohibit child labour, at a minimum complying with guidelines on minimum age for employment within China's labour laws.

We will work cooperatively with human rights organizations both to ensure that our enterprises and suppliers are respecting these principles, and more broadly to promote respect for these principles in China. We will issue an annual statement to the Human Rights for Workers in China Working Group detailing our efforts to uphold these principles and to promote these basic freedoms.

# 42. Irish National Caucus: the MacBride Principles for Northern Ireland, 1986

**Commentary**: The MacBride Principles were first proposed in 1984 by Dr Sean MacBride, founder of Amnesty International. They are a set of nine equal opportunity guidelines for commercial operations within Northern Ireland. Some 65 companies agreed to 'make all possible lawful efforts to implement and/or increase activity on each of the nine MacBride Principles'. See further, www.irishnationalcaucus.org. For academic commentary, see McCrudden C. (1999), 'Human rights codes for TNCs: what can the Sullivan and McBride Principles tell us?', *Oxford Journal of Legal Studies*, **19**, 167–202.

1. Increasing the representation of individuals from underrepresented religious groups in the workforce including managerial, supervisory, administrative, clerical and technical jobs.
2. Adequate security for the protection of minority employees both at the workplace and while travelling to and from work.
3. The banning of provocative religious or political emblems from the workplace.
4. All job openings should be publicly advertised and special recruitment efforts should be made to attract applicants from underrepresented religious groups.
5. Layoff, recall, and termination procedures should not in practice, favour particular religious groupings.
6. The abolition of job reservations, apprenticeship restrictions, and differential employment criteria, which discriminate on the basis of religion or ethnic origin.
7. The development of training programs that will prepare substantial numbers of current minority employees for skilled jobs, including the expansion of existing programs and the creation of new programs to train, upgrade, and improve the skills of minority employees.
8. The establishment of procedures to assess, identify and actively recruit minority employees with potential for further advancement.
9. The appointment of a senior management staff member to oversee the company's affirmative action efforts and the setting up of timetables to carry out affirmative action principles.

# 43. Reverend Sullivan: the Global Sullivan Principles of Social Responsibility, 1997

**Commentary**: Reverend Leon H. Sullivan first formulated the Sullivan Statement of Principles for US Corporations Operating in South Africa during 1977 to counter racial discrimination in the workplace under South African apartheid. They called for corporate divestment with any entity engaged in discriminatory practices and were subsequently amplified on four occasions: see 24 *ILM* 1486 (1985). For comparable intergovernmental codes, see the Code of Conduct concerning the Employment Practices of Canadian Companies Operating in South Africa 24 *ILM* 1464 (1985); the European Community Code of Conduct for Enterprises having Affiliates, Subsidiaries or Agencies in South Africa (1977) 9 *EC Bulletin* 2.2.4. Following the abolition of apartheid, Reverend Sullivan announced the Global Sullivan Principles as guidelines for ethical business practices within developing countries: www.globalsullivanprinciples.org. Formulated with input from several corporations and business associations, corporate endorsers commit to implementing appropriate internal policies and procedures, undertaking effective training, completing publicly available annual reports and sharing experiences at annual meetings: see further, Global Sullivan Principles Endorser List.

As a company which endorses the Global Sullivan Principles we will respect the law, and as a responsible member of society we will apply these Principles with integrity consistent with the legitimate role of business. We will develop and implement company policies, procedures, training and internal reporting structures to ensure commitment to these Principles throughout our organization. We believe the application of these Principles will achieve greater tolerance and better understanding among peoples, and advance the culture of peace.

Accordingly, we will:

(i) Express our support for universal human rights and, particularly, those of our employees, the communities within which we operate, and parties with whom we do business.

(ii) Promote equal opportunity for our employees at all levels of the company with respect to issues such as colour, race, gender, age, ethnicity or religious beliefs, and operate without unacceptable worker treatment such as the exploitation of children, physical punishment, female abuse, involuntary servitude, or other forms of abuse.

(iii) Respect our employees' voluntary freedom of association.

(iv) Compensate our employees to enable them to meet at least their basic needs and provide the opportunity to improve their skill and capability in order to raise their social and economic opportunities.

(v) Provide a safe and healthy workplace; protect human health and the environment; and promote sustainable development.

(vi) Promote fair competition including respect for intellectual and other property rights, and not offer, pay or accept bribes.

(vii) Work with governments and communities in which we do business to improve the quality of life in those communities – their educational, cultural, economic and social well being – and seek to provide training and opportunities for workers from disadvantaged backgrounds.

(viii) Promote the application of these Principles by those with whom we do business. We will be transparent in our implementation of these Principles and provide information which demonstrates publicly our commitment to them.

# 44. International Union of Food, Agricultural, Hotel, Restaurant, Catering, Tobacco and Allied Workers' Associations (IUF)/Danone: Joint Declaration on Trade Union Rights, 1994

**Commentary**: Since 1985, Danone's central management and IUF-affiliated unions have discussed industrial relations at the international level. In 1989, two agreements were concluded concerning enhanced information disclosure for economic and social matters and on employment equality for men and women. An agreement on skills training was also signed during 1992. In 1997, the Danone group (formerly BSN) and the IUF signed a joint understanding in the event of changes of business activity affecting employment or working conditions. The Joint Declaration on Trade Union Rights below (available through www.iuf.org) is an illustration of a framework agreement concluded between a corporation and a trade union and applicable throughout the corporate structure irrespective of the territorial location of operations. Such arrangements may not be attributable to governments: *Arriba Ltd v Petroleos Mexicanos* 962 *F.2d* 528 (1992). See also, IUF (1995), Code of Conduct for the Tea Sector, Petit-Lancy, Switzerland.

**BSN and the IUF**

(i) recalling the fundamental right of each employee to be represented and defended by the trade union organization of her/his choice;

(ii) affirming that the counterweight represented by the trade union organizations contributes to the respect of the needs and aspirations of the workforce by company executives;

(iii) mutually recognizing the legitimacy of each party and their right to participate in the social as well as economic spheres, each mindful of their respective responsibilities as far as these conform with laws, collective agreements or other contractual agreement in effect;

(iv) are convinced that reinforcing democratic forms of co-operation in the enterprise is the responsibility of both parties, and that this implies the recognition of divergent approaches and differences in judgement as well as the search for negotiated solutions;

(v) note that achieving this objective requires efforts to provide economic and social education and information to the entire workforce as well as their representatives to better understand the problems, the limitations faced by the company, and what it has at stake;

In this spirit, BSN and the IUF undertake to:

1. Monitor proper compliance throughout all BSN subsidiaries with ILO Conventions 87, 98 and 135, which concern respectively:

    (a) the right of all employees to join the trade union organization of their choice;
    (b) the right of all workers to be free from any act of discrimination leading to the restriction of trade union rights;
    (c) the protection of all workers' representatives from all prejudicial measures, including firing, resulting from their status or activity as representatives of the workforce in accordance with the law, collective agreements, or other forms of contractual agreement in effect;

2. Encourage management and trade unions to negotiate agreements (concerning trade union rights), where possible for fixed durations, and to seek to publicize these agreements among the workforce to the widest possible extent;
3. Encourage management and employee representatives to negotiate and conclude agreements seeking to ensure that trade union and employee representatives benefit, with comparable ability, from the same opportunities of access to training, salary progression and promotion as other employees, and that the remainder of their professional development is taken care of when they decide to stand down from office. Within the continuity of the BSN/IUF framework agreements (equality of men and women, economic and social information, vocational training), BSN and the IUF confirm that the process of informing and educating trade union and worker representatives should develop within each BSN subsidiary with the goal of ensuring effective implementation.

A first review of the implementation of this declaration will be undertaken in a concerted way during the plenary meeting in 1995.

# 45. Additional initiatives

## i. The International Confederation of Free Trade Unions/International Trade Secretariat: Basic Code of Labour Practice, 1997

**Commentary**: This Code was developed by the ICFTU/ITS Working Party on Multinational Companies in consultation with trade union organisations and other interested individuals or organisations prior to final adoption by the ICFTU Executive Board (www.icftu.org). Its scope of application extends to the labour practices of corporate contractors, subcontractors, principal suppliers, licensees and franchise holders involved in producing and/or distributing goods or services. The Code is a standard-form template enabling individual corporations to commit to freely chosen employment, non-discrimination, avoiding child labour, respecting freedom of association and the right to collective bargaining, paying living wages, non-excessive working hours, decent working conditions and appropriate employment relationships. The Code contemplates inspections, record-keeping and losing business in the event of violations. See also, ICFTU, 'Charter of Trade Union Demands for the Legislative Control of MNCs', ICFTU Doc D/1976/0403/13.

## ii. US Department of Labour Apparel Industry Partnership: Workplace Code of Conduct and Principles of Monitoring, 1997

**Commentary**: The AIP (www.itcilo.it/actrav/actrav-english/telearn/global/ilo/guide/apparell.htm) aims to implement higher labour standards within supply chain contractors. The Code of Conduct prohibits forced and child labour, harassment or abuse and discrimination. Consistent with applicable local law, employers must provide safe and healthy working environments, recognise freedom of association and collective bargaining, pay minimum wages, require less than 48 hours per week and compensate overtime. The Principles of Monitoring require companies to establish clear standards, create informed workplaces, develop information databases, establish training programmes and provide appropriate means of remediation. Employees can report non-adherence to local human rights NGOs, labour unions, religious organisations or other institutions. Member companies become subject to periodic independent audits and unannounced visits are confidentially conducted by the Fair Labour Association, an organisation composed of industry, labour and NGO representatives. Independent external monitors must establish clear evaluation criteria, review information databases, verify the creation by companies of informed workplaces and communications channels and conduct confidential employee interviews.

The Principles of Monitoring also apply to contractors where companies are manufacturers and to suppliers where companies are retailers. A 'contractor' or 'supplier' means an entity engaged in the manufacturing process (including cutting, sewing, assembling and packaging) which results in finished products for consumers. See further, US Department of Labour (1996), 'The Apparel Industry and Codes of Conduct: A Solution to the International Child Labour Problem?', Washington, DC (www.dol.gov).

# PART VI

# International Environmental Standards

# 46. Council of Europe: Convention on Civil Liability for Damage Resulting from Activities Dangerous to the Environment, 1993

**Commentary**: The Lugano Convention (1993) *ETS* 150 (not yet in force) covers all types of damage (including environmental damage) and is not limited to that of a trans-boundary nature. Hence its provisions go further than several governments are prepared to accept. Article 14 provides that any person may access environmental information held by 'public authorities' (further defined in Article 13) without having to prove an interest but that this right may be restricted where it affects *inter alia* commercial or industrial confidentiality, including intellectual property. Article 18 provides that environmental protection associations or foundations may request the prohibition of dangerous activities which are unlawful and pose grave threats of environmental damage or that operators be ordered to adopt preventive or reinstatement measures. Article 19 concerning jurisdiction provides that compensation actions may only be brought before the national courts of the State where damage was suffered, where dangerous activities were conducted or where defendants have their habitual residence. Annex I lists criteria and methods for several categories of dangerous substances and Annex II identifies installations or sites for incinerating, treating, handling or recycling waste.

On laws, regulations and administrative provisions relating to classifying, packaging and labelling dangerous substances, see EC Directives 67/548/EEC (1967) (*OJEC* No. L196/1), 88/379/EEC (1988) (*OJEC* No. L187/14), 90/492/EEC (1990) (*OJEC* No. L275/35), 92/32/EEC (1992) (*OJEC* No. L154/1) & 92/37/EEC (1992) (*OJEC* No. L154/30). See also, EC Commission Proposal for a Council Directive on Civil Liability for Damage Caused by Waste (1989) *OJEC* 251, 3 as amended (1991) *OJEC* 192; CEFIC, 'CEFIC Comments on the Amended Proposal for a Council Directive on Civil Liability for Damage Caused by Waste', Brussels, 1991.

**Article 1: Object and Purpose**

This Convention aims at ensuring adequate compensation for damage resulting from activities dangerous to the environment and also provides for means of prevention and reinstatement.

**Article 2: Definitions**

For the purpose of this Convention:

1. 'Dangerous activity' means one or more of the following activities provided that it is performed professionally, including activities conducted by public authorities:

(a) the production, handling, storage, use or discharge of one or more dangerous substances or any operation of a similar nature dealing with such substances;
(b) the production, culturing, handling, storage, use, destruction, disposal, release or any other operation dealing with one or more:

(i) genetically modified organisms which as a result of the properties of the organism, the genetic modification and the conditions under which the operation is exercised, pose a significant risk for man, the environment or property;
(ii) micro-organisms which as a result of their properties and the conditions under which the operation is exercised pose a significant risk for man, the environment or property, such as those micro-organisms which are pathogenic or which produce toxins;

(c) the operation of an installation or site for the incineration, treatment, handling or recycling of waste, such as those installations or sites specified in Annex II, provided that the quantities involved pose a significant risk for man, the environment or property;
(d) the operation of a site for the permanent deposit of waste.

2. 'Dangerous substance' means:

(a) substances or preparations which have properties which constitute a significant risk for man, the environment or property. A substance or preparation which is explosive, oxidizing, extremely flammable, highly flammable, flammable, very toxic, toxic, harmful, corrosive, irritant, sensitizing, carcinogenic, mutagenic, toxic for reproduction or dangerous for the environment within the meaning of Annex I, Part A to this Convention shall in any event be deemed to constitute such a risk;
(b) substances specified in Annex I, Part B to this Convention . . .

3. 'Genetically modified organism' means any organism in which the genetic material has been altered in a way which does not occur naturally by mating and/or natural recombination.

However, the following genetically modified organisms are not covered by the Convention:

(i) organisms obtained by mutagenesis on condition that the genetic modification does not involve the use of genetically modified organisms as recipient organisms; and
(ii) plants obtained by cell fusion (including protoplast fusion) if the resulting plant can also be produced by traditional breeding methods and on condition that the genetic modification does not involve the use of genetically modified organisms as parental organisms.

'Organism' refers to any biological entity capable of replication or of transferring genetic material.

4. 'Micro-organism' means any microbiological entity, cellular or non cellular, capable of replication or of transferring genetic material.

5. 'Operator' means the person who exercises the control of a dangerous activity.
6. 'Person' means any individual or partnership or any body governed by public or private law, whether corporate or not, including a State or any of its constituent subdivisions.
7. 'Damage' means:

   (a) loss of life or personal injury;
   (b) loss of or damage to property other than to the installation itself or property held under the control of the operator, at the site of the dangerous activity;
   (c) loss or damage by impairment of the environment in so far as this is not considered to be damage within the meaning of sub-paragraphs (a) or (b) above provided that compensation for impairment of the environment, other than for loss of profit from such impairment, shall be limited to the costs of measures of reinstatement actually undertaken or to be undertaken;
   (d) the costs of preventive measures and any loss or damage caused by preventive measures,

   to the extent that the loss or damage referred to in sub-paragraphs (a) to (c) of this paragraph arises out of or results from the hazardous properties of the dangerous substances, genetically modified organisms or micro organisms or arises or results from waste.

8. 'Measures of reinstatement' means any reasonable measures aiming to reinstate or restore damaged or destroyed components of the environment, or to introduce, where reasonable, the equivalent of these components into the environment. Internal law may indicate who will be entitled to take such measures.
9. 'Preventive measures' means any reasonable measures taken by any person, after an incident has occurred to prevent or minimise loss or damage as referred to in paragraph 7, sub-paragraphs (a) to (c) of this article.
10. 'Environment' includes:

    (i) natural resources both abiotic and biotic, such as air, water, soil, fauna and flora and the interaction between the same factors;
    (ii) property which forms part of the cultural heritage; and
    (iii) the characteristic aspects of the landscape.

11. 'Incident' means any sudden occurrence or continuous occurrence or any series of occurrences having the same origin, which causes damage or creates a grave and imminent threat of causing damage.

**Article 3: Geographical Scope**
Without prejudice to the provisions of Chapter III, this Convention shall apply:

(a) when the incident occurs in the territory of a Party, as determined in accordance with Article 34, regardless of where the damage is suffered;
(b) when the incident occurs outside the territory referred to in sub-paragraph (a) above and the conflict of laws rules lead to the application of the law in force for the territory referred to in sub-paragraph (a) above.

**Article 4: Exceptions**

1. This Convention shall not apply to damage arising from carriage; carriage includes the period from the beginning of the process of loading until the end of the process of unloading. However, the Convention shall apply to carriage by pipeline, as well as to carriage performed entirely in an installation or on a site unaccessible to the public where it is accessory to other activities and is an integral part thereof.
2. This Convention shall not apply to damage caused by a nuclear substance:

   (a) arising from a nuclear incident the liability of which is regulated either by the Paris Convention of 29 July 1960 on third party liability in the field of nuclear energy, and its Additional Protocol of 28 January 1964, or the Vienna Convention of 21 May 1963 on civil liability for nuclear damage; or
   (b) if liability for such damage is regulated by a specific internal law, provided that such law is as favourable, with regard to compensation for damage, as any of the instruments referred to under sub-paragraph (a) above . . .

**Article 6: Liability in Respect of Substances, Organisms and Certain Waste Installations or Sites**

1. The operator in respect of a dangerous activity mentioned under Article 2, paragraph 1, sub-paragraphs (a) to (c) shall be liable for the damage caused by the activity as a result of incidents at the time or during the period when he was exercising the control of that activity.
2. If an incident consists of a continuous occurrence, all operators successively exercising the control of the dangerous activity during that occurrence shall be jointly and severally liable. However, the operator who proves that the occurrence during the period when he was exercising the control of the dangerous activity caused only a part of the damage shall be liable for that part of the damage only.
3. If an incident consists of a series of occurrences having the same origin, the operators at the time of any such occurrence shall be jointly and severally liable. However, the operator who proves that the occurrence at the time when he was exercising the control of the dangerous activity caused only a part of the damage shall be liable for that part of the damage only.
4. If the damage resulting from a dangerous activity becomes known after all such dangerous activity in the installation or on the site has ceased, the last operator of this activity shall be liable for that damage unless he or the person who suffered damage proves that all or part of the damage resulted from an incident which occurred at a time before he became the operator. If it is so proved, the provisions of paragraphs 1 to 3 of this article shall apply.
5. Nothing in this Convention shall prejudice any right of recourse of the operator against any third party.

**Article 7: Liability in Respect of Sites for the Permanent Deposit of Waste**

1. The operator of a site for the permanent deposit of waste at the time when damage caused by waste deposited at that site becomes known, shall be liable for this damage. Should the damage caused by waste deposited before the closure of such a site become known after that closure, the last operator shall be liable.

2. Liability under this article shall apply to the exclusion of any liability of the operator under Article 6, irrespective of the nature of the waste.
3. Liability under this article shall apply to the exclusion of any liability of the operator under Article 6 if the same operator conducts another dangerous activity on the site for the permanent deposit of waste.

   However, if this operator or the person who has suffered damage proves that only a part of the damage was caused by the activity concerning the permanent deposit of waste, this article shall only apply to that part of the damage.
4. Nothing in this Convention shall prejudice any right of recourse of the operator against any third party.

**Article 8: Exemptions**

The operator shall not be liable under this Convention for damage which he proves:

(a) was caused by an act of war, hostilities, civil war, insurrection or a natural phenomenon of an exceptional, inevitable and irresistible character;
(b) was caused by an act done with the intent to cause damage by a third party, despite safety measures appropriate to the type of dangerous activity in question;
(c) resulted necessarily from compliance with a specific order or compulsory measure of a public authority;
(d) was caused by pollution at tolerable levels under local relevant circumstances; or
(e) was caused by a dangerous activity taken lawfully in the interests of the person who suffered the damage, whereby it was reasonable towards this person to expose him to the risks of the dangerous activity.

**Article 9: Fault of the Person who Suffered the Damage**

If the person who suffered the damage or a person for whom he is responsible under internal law, has, by his own fault, contributed to the damage, the compensation may be reduced or disallowed having regard to all the circumstances.

**Article 10: Causality**

When considering evidence of the causal link between the incident and the damage or, in the context of a dangerous activity as defined in Article 2, paragraph 1, sub-paragraph (d), between the activity and the damage, the court shall take due account of the increased danger of causing such damage inherent in the dangerous activity.

**Article 11: Plurality of Installations or Sites**

When damage results from incidents which have occurred in several installations or on several sites where dangerous activities are conducted or from dangerous activities under Article 2, paragraph 1, sub-paragraph (d), the operators of the installations or sites concerned shall be jointly and severally liable for all such damage. However, the operator who proves that only part of the damage was caused by an incident in the installation or on the site where he conducts the dangerous activity or by a dangerous activity under Article 2, paragraph 1, sub-paragraph (d), shall be liable for that part of the damage only.

**Article 12: Compulsory Financial Security Scheme**
Each Party shall ensure that where appropriate, taking due account of the risks of the activity, operators conducting a dangerous activity on its territory be required to participate in a financial security scheme or to have and maintain a financial guarantee up to a certain limit, of such type and terms as specified by internal law, to cover the liability under this Convention.

**Article 14: Access to Information Held by Public Authorities**

1. Any person shall, at his request and without his having to prove an interest, have access to information relating to the environment held by public authorities. The Parties shall define the practical arrangements under which such information is effectively made available.
2. The right of access may be restricted under internal law where it affects:

    (a) the confidentiality of the proceedings of public authorities, international relations and national defence;
    (b) public security;
    (c) matters which are or have been sub judice, or under enquiry (including disciplinary enquiries), or which are the subject of preliminary investigation proceedings;
    (d) commercial and industrial confidentiality, including intellectual property;
    (e) the confidentiality of personal data and/or files;
    (f) material supplied by a third party without that party being under a legal obligation to do so; or
    (g) material, the disclosure of which would make it more likely that the environment to which that material related would be damaged.

    Information held by public authorities shall be supplied in part where it is possible to separate out information on items concerning the interests referred to above.
3. A request for information may be refused where it would involve the supply of unfinished documents or data or internal communications, or where the request is manifestly unreasonable or formulated in too general a manner.
4. A public authority shall respond to a person requesting information as soon as possible and at the latest within two months. The reasons for a refusal to provide the information requested must be given.
5. A person who considers that his request for information has been unreasonably refused or ignored, or has been inadequately answered by a public authority, may seek a judicial or administrative review of the decision, in accordance with the relevant internal legal system.
6. The Parties may make a charge for supplying the information, but such a charge may not exceed a reasonable cost.

**Article 16: Access to Specific Information Held by Operators**

1. The person who suffered the damage may, at any time, request the court to order an operator to provide him with specific information, in so far as this is necessary to establish the existence of a claim for compensation under this Convention.
2. Where, under this Convention, a claim for compensation is made to an operator, whether or not in the framework of judicial proceedings, this operator may request the court to

order another operator to provide him with specific information, in so far as this is necessary to establish the extent of his possible obligation to compensate the person who has suffered the damage, or of his own right to compensation from the other operator.

3. The operator shall be required to provide information under paragraphs 1 and 2 of this article concerning the elements which are available to him and dealing essentially with the particulars of the equipment, the machinery used, the kind and concentration of the dangerous substances or waste as well as the nature of genetically modified organisms or micro-organisms.
5. The court may refuse a request which places a disproportionate burden on the operator, taking into account all the interests involved.
6. In addition to the restrictions under Article 14, paragraph 2 of this Convention, which shall apply *mutatis mutandis*, the operator may refuse to provide information where such information would incriminate him.
7. Any reasonable charge shall be paid by the person requesting the information . . .

**Article 17: Limitation Periods**

1. Actions for compensation under this Convention shall be subject to a limitation period of three years from the date on which the claimant knew or ought reasonably to have known of the damage and of the identity of the operator. The laws of the Parties regulating suspension or interruption of limitation periods shall apply to the limitation period prescribed in this paragraph.
2. However, in no case shall actions be brought after thirty years from the date of the incident which caused the damage . . .

# 47. European Community: Proposed Directive on the Protection of the Environment through Criminal Law, 2001 and 2002

**Commentary**: For the purpose of criminalising acts causing or likely to cause environmental damage, the Council of Europe in 1998 concluded the European Convention on the Protection of the Environment through Criminal Law (*ETS* No 172 (1998), not yet in force). No Member State signed it. In 2000, Denmark extracted its main elements and proposed a Council Framework Decision based upon the so-called third pillar of the EU Treaty (intergovernmental cooperation): Council Framework Decision 2003/80/JHA and *OJEC* L29/55 (2003). In 2001, the Commission proposed a Directive based upon the first pillar (EC law): EC Proposal for a Directive on the protection of the environment through criminal law COM(2001)139 and COM(2002)544FINAL as amended. In addition to the provisions extracted below, Article 5 contemplates governments reporting on implementation every three years. The Annex identifies EC provisions concerning environmental protection. In 2003, the Commission commenced proceedings (still ongoing) against the Council before the European Court of Justice alleging that it had breached the division of powers under the EU Treaty: Case C176/03 *OJEC* C135/21 (2003). See also, 'Criminal Penalties in EU Member States' Environmental Law', Study 1 (2002) and Study 2 (2003); europa.eu.int/comm/environment/crime.

**Article 1 – Purpose**

The purpose of this Directive is to ensure a more effective application of Community law on the protection of the environment by establishing throughout the Community a minimum set of criminal offences.

**Article 2 – Definitions**

For the purpose of this Directive

(a) 'legal person' means any legal entity having such status under the applicable national law, except for States or other public bodies acting in the exercise of their sovereign rights and for public international organisations.
(b) 'activities' means active behaviour and failure to act, insofar as there is a legal duty to act.

**Article 3 – Offences**
Member States shall ensure that the following activities are criminal offences, when committed intentionally or with serious negligence, as far as they breach the rules of Community law protecting the environment as set out in the Annex and/or rules adopted by Member States in order to comply with such Community law:

(a) the discharge of hydrocarbons, waste oils or sewage sludge into water;
(b) the discharge, emission or introduction of a quantity of materials into air, soil or water and the treatment, disposal, storage, transport, export or import of hazardous waste;
(c) the discharge of waste on or into land or into water, including the operation of a landfill;
(d) the possession, taking, damaging, killing or trading of or in protected wild fauna and flora species or parts thereof;
(e) the significant deterioration of a protected habitat;
(f) trade in ozone-depleting substances;
(g) the operation of a plant in which a dangerous activity is carried out or in which dangerous substances or preparations are stored or used.

**Article 4 – Sanctions**
Member States shall ensure that the offences referred to in Article 3, and the participation in or instigation of such offences are punishable by effective, proportionate and dissuasive sanctions.

a) As concerns natural persons, Member States shall provide for criminal penalties, involving in serious cases deprivation of liberty.
b) As concerns natural and legal persons, where appropriate, Member States shall provide for fines, exclusion from entitlement to public benefits or aid, temporary or permanent disqualification from the practice of commercial activities, placing under judicial supervision or judicial winding-up orders.

# 48. European Community: Directive 2004/35/EC of the European Parliament and of the Council of 21 April 2004 on Environmental Liability with Regard to the Prevention and Remedying of Environmental Damage

**Commentary**: For a considerable period the EC has sought to implement the polluter pays principle within a Community regime: see the Commission's Green Paper COM(93)47FINAL (1993) and White Paper on Environmental Liability COM(2000)66FINAL. Thereafter followed a Joint Hearing with the European Parliament in 1993, two Opinions of the Economic and Social Committee (1994 & 2002 *OJEC* 241, 162), an Opinion of the Committee of the Regions and a public consultation process: see, for example, CEFIC, 'CEFIC Comments and Suggestions on the Commission's White Paper on Environmental Liability', Brussels, 2000. The legislative proposal was finalised during 2002: see (2002) *OJEC* 151E, 132. The subsequent process included an Opinion of the European Parliament in 2003, a Common Position of the Council of Ministers (*OJEC* 277E, 10 (2003)), an EC Communication to the European Parliament during 2003 and a Commission Opinion on the European Parliament's amendments to the Council's Common Position: see COM(2004)55FINAL. The conciliation process concluded in 2004 with the adoption of a joint text by the Conciliation Committee which was subsequently approved by the Council and the European Parliament. Member States have three years in which to implement the Environmental Liability Directive (*OJEC* L143 (2004), entry into force 2004) into national law. In addition to the provisions extracted below, Article 12 enables natural or legal persons having sufficient interests in environmental decision-making to submit observations and request action by competent authorities. Annex I elaborates upon the criteria required by Article 2(1)(a), Annex II outlines the common framework for remedying environmental damage, Annex III identifies the activities referred to in Article 3(1), Annex IV lists the international conventions referred to by Article 4(2), Annex V lists those international instruments referred to in Article 4(4) and Annex VI identifies the information required by Article 18(1). See also the EC's Sixth Environment Action Programme, 'Environment 2010: Our Future, Our Choice'.

**Article 1: Subject Matter**

The purpose of this Directive is to establish a framework of environmental liability based on the 'polluter-pays' principle, to prevent and remedy environmental damage.

**Article 2: Definitions**

For the purpose of this Directive the following definitions shall apply:

1. 'environmental damage' means:

   (a) damage to protected species and natural habitats, which is any damage that has significant adverse effects on reaching or maintaining the favourable conservation status of such habitats or species . . .
   (b) water damage, which is any damage that significantly adversely affects the ecological, chemical and/or quantitative status and/or ecological potential, as defined in Directive 2000/60/EC, of the waters concerned, with the exception of adverse effects where Article 4(7) of that Directive applies;
   (c) land damage, which is any land contamination that creates a significant risk of human health being adversely affected as a result of the direct or indirect introduction, in, on or under land, of substances, preparations, organisms or micro-organisms;

2. 'damage' means a measurable adverse change in a natural resource or measurable impairment of a natural resource service which may occur directly or indirectly;
3. 'protected species and natural habitats' means:

   (a) the species mentioned in Article 4(2) of Directive 79/409/EEC or listed in Annex I thereto or listed in Annexes II and IV to Directive 92/43/EEC;
   (b) the habitats of species mentioned in Article 4(2) of Directive 79/409/EEC or listed in Annex I thereto or listed in Annex II to Directive 92/43/EEC, and the natural habitats listed in Annex I to Directive 92/43/EEC and the breeding sites or resting places of the species listed in Annex IV to Directive 92/43/EEC; and
   (c) where a Member State so determines, any habitat or species, not listed in those Annexes which the Member State designates for equivalent purposes as those laid down in these two Directives;

4. 'conservation status' means:

   (a) in respect of a natural habitat, the sum of the influences acting on a natural habitat and its typical species that may affect its long-term natural distribution, structure and functions as well as the long-term survival of its typical species . . .
   (b) in respect of a species, the sum of the influences acting on the species concerned that may affect the long-term distribution and abundance of its populations . . .

5. 'waters' mean all waters covered by Directive 2000/60/EC;
6. 'operator' means any natural or legal, private or public person who operates or controls the occupational activity or, where this is provided for in national legislation, to whom decisive economic power over the technical functioning of such an activity has been delegated, including the holder of a permit or authorisation for such an activity or the person registering or notifying such an activity;
7. 'occupational activity' means any activity carried out in the course of an economic activity, a business or an undertaking, irrespectively of its private or public, profit or non-profit character;

8. 'emission' means the release in the environment, as a result of human activities, of substances, preparations, organisms or micro-organisms;
9. 'imminent threat of damage' means a sufficient likelihood that environmental damage will occur in the near future;
10. 'preventive measures' means any measures taken in response to an event, act or omission that has created an imminent threat of environmental damage, with a view to preventing or minimising that damage;
11. 'remedial measures' means any action, or combination of actions, including mitigating or interim measures to restore, rehabilitate or replace damaged natural resources and/or impaired services, or to provide an equivalent alternative to those resources or services as foreseen in Annex II;
12. 'natural resource' means protected species and natural habitats, water and land;
13. 'services' and 'natural resources services' mean the functions performed by a natural resource for the benefit of another natural resource or the public;
14. 'baseline condition' means the condition at the time of the damage of the natural resources and services that would have existed had the environmental damage not occurred, estimated on the basis of the best information available;
15. 'recovery', including 'natural recovery', means, in the case of water, protected species and natural habitats the return of damaged natural resources and/or impaired services to baseline condition and in the case of land damage, the elimination of any significant risk of adversely affecting human health;
16. 'costs' means costs which are justified by the need to ensure the proper and effective implementation of this Directive including the costs of assessing environmental damage, an imminent threat of such damage, alternatives for action as well as the administrative, legal, and enforcement costs, the costs of data collection and other general costs, monitoring and supervision costs.

**Article 3: Scope**

1. This Directive shall apply to:

   (a) environmental damage caused by any of the occupational activities listed in Annex III, and to any imminent threat of such damage occurring by reason of any of those activities;

   (b) damage to protected species and natural habitats caused by any occupational activities other than those listed in Annex III, and to any imminent threat of such damage occurring by reason of any of those activities, whenever the operator has been at fault or negligent.

3. Without prejudice to relevant national legislation, this Directive shall not give private parties a right of compensation as a consequence of environmental damage or of an imminent threat of such damage.

**Article 4: Exceptions**

1. This Directive shall not cover environmental damage or an imminent threat of such damage caused by:

(a) an act of armed conflict, hostilities, civil war or insurrection;
(b) a natural phenomenon of exceptional, inevitable and irresistible character.

2. This Directive shall not apply to environmental damage or to any imminent threat of such damage arising from an incident in respect of which liability or compensation falls within the scope of any of the International Conventions listed in Annex IV . . .
3. This Directive shall be without prejudice to the right of the operator to limit his liability in accordance with national legislation implementing the Convention on Limitation of Liability for Maritime Claims (LLMC), 1976, including any future amendment to the Convention, or the Strasbourg Convention on Limitation of Liability in Inland Navigation (CLNI), 1988, including any future amendment to the Convention.
4. This Directive shall not apply to such nuclear risks or environmental damage or imminent threat of such damage as may be caused by the activities covered by the Treaty establishing the European Atomic Energy Community or caused by an incident or activity in respect of which liability or compensation falls within the scope of any of the international instruments listed in Annex V, including any future amendments thereof.
5. This Directive shall only apply to environmental damage or to an imminent threat of such damage caused by pollution of a diffuse character, where it is possible to establish a causal link between the damage and the activities of individual operators . . .

**Article 5: Preventive Action**

1. Where environmental damage has not yet occurred but there is an imminent threat of such damage occurring, the operator shall, without delay, take the necessary preventive measures.
2. Member States shall provide that, where appropriate, and in any case whenever an imminent threat of environmental damage is not dispelled despite the preventive measures taken by the operator, operators are to inform the competent authority of all relevant aspects of the situation, as soon as possible.
3. The competent authority may, at any time:

   (a) require the operator to provide information on any imminent threat of environmental damage or in suspected cases of such an imminent threat;
   (b) require the operator to take the necessary preventive measures;
   (c) give instructions to the operator to be followed on the necessary preventive measures to be taken; or
   (d) itself take the necessary preventive measures.

4. The competent authority shall require that the preventive measures are taken by the operator. If the operator fails to comply with the obligations laid down in paragraph 1 or 3(b) or (c), cannot be identified or is not required to bear the costs under this Directive, the competent authority may take these measures itself.

**Article 6: Remedial Action**

1. Where environmental damage has occurred the operator shall, without delay, inform the competent authority of all relevant aspects of the situation and take:

(a) all practicable steps to immediately control, contain, remove or otherwise manage the relevant contaminants and/or any other damage factors in order to limit or to prevent further environmental damage and adverse effects on human health or further impairment of services and
(b) the necessary remedial measures, in accordance with Article 7.

2. The competent authority may, at any time:

(a) require the operator to provide supplementary information on any damage that has occurred;
(b) take, require the operator to take or give instructions to the operator concerning, all practicable steps to immediately control, contain, remove or otherwise manage the relevant contaminants and/or any other damage factors in order to limit or to prevent further environmental damage and adverse effect on human health, or further impairment of services;
(c) require the operator to take the necessary remedial measures;
(d) give instructions to the operator to be followed on the necessary remedial measures to be taken; or
(e) itself take the necessary remedial measures.

3. The competent authority shall require that the remedial measures are taken by the operator. If the operator fails to comply with the obligations laid down in paragraph 1 or 2(b), (c) or (d), cannot be identified or is not required to bear the costs under this Directive, the competent authority may take these measures itself, as a means of last resort.

**Article 7: Determination of Remedial Measures**

1. Operators shall identify, in accordance with Annex II, potential remedial measures and submit them to the competent authority for its approval, unless the competent authority has taken action under Article 6(2)(e) and (3).
2. The competent authority shall decide which remedial measures shall be implemented in accordance with Annex II, and with the cooperation of the relevant operator, as required.
3. Where several instances of environmental damage have occurred in such a manner that the competent authority cannot ensure that the necessary remedial measures are taken at the same time, the competent authority shall be entitled to decide which instance of environmental damage must be remedied first. In making that decision, the competent authority shall have regard, *inter alia*, to the nature, extent and gravity of the various instances of environmental damage concerned, and to the possibility of natural recovery. Risks to human health shall also be taken into account.
4. The competent authority shall invite the persons referred to in Article 12(1) and in any case the persons on whose land remedial measures would be carried out to submit their observations and shall take them into account.

**Article 8: Prevention and Remediation Costs**

1. The operator shall bear the costs for the preventive and remedial actions taken pursuant to this Directive.

2. Subject to paragraphs 3 and 4, the competent authority shall recover, *inter alia*, via security over property or other appropriate guarantees from the operator who has caused the damage or the imminent threat of damage, the costs it has incurred in relation to the preventive or remedial actions taken under this Directive. However, the competent authority may decide not to recover the full costs where the expenditure required to do so would be greater than the recoverable sum or where the operator cannot be identified.
3. An operator shall not be required to bear the cost of preventive or remedial actions taken pursuant to this Directive when he can prove that the environmental damage or imminent threat of such damage:

   (a) was caused by a third party and occurred despite the fact that appropriate safety measures were in place; or
   (b) resulted from compliance with a compulsory order or instruction emanating from a public authority other than an order or instruction consequent upon an emission or incident caused by the operator's own activities. In such cases Member States shall take the appropriate measures to enable the operator to recover the costs incurred.

4. The Member States may allow the operator not to bear the cost of remedial actions taken pursuant to this Directive where he demonstrates that he was not at fault or negligent and that the environmental damage was caused by:

   (a) an emission or event expressly authorised by, and fully in accordance with the conditions of, an authorisation conferred by or given under applicable national laws and regulations which implement those legislative measures adopted by the Community specified in Annex III, as applied at the date of the emission or event;
   (b) an emission or activity or any manner of using a product in the course of an activity which the operator demonstrates was not considered likely to cause environmental damage according to the state of scientific and technical knowledge at the time when the emission was released or the activity took place.

5. Measures taken by the competent authority in pursuance of Article 5(3) and (4) and Article 6(2) and (3) shall be without prejudice to the liability of the relevant operator under this Directive and without prejudice to Articles 87 and 88 of the Treaty.

**Article 9: Cost Allocation in Cases of Multiple Party Causation**
This Directive is without prejudice to any provisions of national regulations concerning cost allocation in cases of multiple party causation especially concerning the apportionment of liability between the producer and the user of a product.

**Article 10: Limitation Period for Recovery of Costs**
The competent authority shall be entitled to initiate cost recovery proceedings against the operator, or if appropriate, a third party who has caused the damage or the imminent threat of damage in relation to any measures taken in pursuance of this Directive within five years from the date on which those measures have been completed or the liable operator, or third party, has been identified, whichever is the later.

**Article 12: Request for Action**

1. Natural or legal persons:

    (a) affected or likely to be affected by environment damage or
    (b) having a sufficient interest in environmental decision making relating to the damage or, alternatively,
    (c) alleging the impairment of a right, where administrative procedural law of a Member State requires this as a precondition, shall be entitled to submit to the competent authority any observations relating to instances of environmental damage or an imminent threat of such damage of which they are aware and shall be entitled to request the competent authority to take action under this Directive.

    What constitutes a 'sufficient interest' and 'impairment of a right' shall be determined by the Member States.
    To this end, the interest of any non-governmental organisation promoting environmental protection and meeting any requirements under national law shall be deemed sufficient for the purpose of subparagraph (b). Such organisations shall also be deemed to have rights capable of being impaired for the purpose of subparagraph (c).
2. The request for action shall be accompanied by the relevant information and data supporting the observations submitted in relation to the environmental damage in question.
3. Where the request for action and the accompanying observations show in a plausible manner that environmental damage exists, the competent authority shall consider any such observations and requests for action. In such circumstances the competent authority shall give the relevant operator an opportunity to make his views known with respect to the request for action and the accompanying observations.
4. The competent authority shall, as soon as possible and in any case in accordance with the relevant provisions of national law, inform the persons referred to in paragraph 1, which submitted observations to the authority, of its decision to accede to or refuse the request for action and shall provide the reasons for it.
5. Member States may decide not to apply paragraphs 1 and 4 to cases of imminent threat of damage.

**Article 14: Financial Security**

1. Member States shall take measures to encourage the development of financial security instruments and markets by the appropriate economic and financial operators, including financial mechanisms in case of insolvency, with the aim of enabling operators to use financial guarantees to cover their responsibilities under this Directive . . .

**Article 17: Temporal Application**

This Directive shall not apply to:

(i) damage caused by an emission, event or incident that took place before the date referred to in Article 19(1),

(ii) damage caused by an emission, event or incident which takes place subsequent to the date referred to in Article 19(1) when it derives from a specific activity that took place and finished before the said date,

(iii) damage, if more than 30 years have passed since the emission, event or incident, resulting in the damage, occurred.

**Article 19: Implementation**

1. Member States shall bring into force the laws, regulations and administrative provisions necessary to comply with this Directive by 30 April 2007 . . .

# 49. UN Economic Commission for Europe: Convention on the Transboundary Effects of Industrial Accidents, 1992

**Commentary**: The Convention (31 *ILM* 1330 (1992), entry into force 2000) protects human health and the environment by preventing industrial accidents as far as possible, reducing their frequency and severity and by mitigating their effects. Article 7 provides that Parties of origin shall establish policies on the siting of new hazardous activities and on significant modifications to existing hazardous activities. Article 9 contemplates providing information to the public, opportunities for procedural participation and commencing legal actions. The Convention leaves national law unaffected, thereby protecting information related to industrial and commercial secrecy, including intellectual property (Article 22). Relevant Annexes include hazardous substances for the purposes of defining hazardous activities (Annex I), preventive measures pursuant to Article 6 (Annex IV), decision-making on siting pursuant to Article 7 (Annex VII), emergency preparedness measures pursuant to Article 8 (Annex VIII), industrial accident notification systems pursuant to Article 10 (Annex IX) and exchanging information pursuant to Article 15 (Annex XI). See COP Decision 2002/3 for the long-term programme of work. See further, the 2003 Protocol on Civil Liability for Damage and Compensation for Damage Caused by Transboundary Effects of Industrial Accidents on Transboundary Waters.

Additionally relevant instruments include the UN ECE Code of Conduct on Accidental Pollution of Transboundary Inland Waters; the UN ECE Convention on Long-Range Transboundary Air Pollution, 1979 (entry into force 1983) and its eight protocols. For intergovernmental responses to industrial accidents, see UNEP Industry and Environment Programme (1988), 'Awareness and Preparedness for Emergencies at the Local Level (APELL): A Process for Responding to Technological Accidents', Paris (www.uneptie.org/pc/apell/home.html); OECD (1992), 'Guiding Principles for Chemical Accident Prevention, Preparedness and Response: Guidance for Public Authorities, Industry, Labour and Others for the Establishment of Programmes and Policies related to Prevention of, Preparedness for, and Response to Accidents involving Hazardous Substances', OECD Environment Monograph No 51. For academic comment, see Muchlinski P.T. (1993), 'The accountability of MNEs and the right to development: the compensation of industrial accident victims from developing countries', *Third World Legal Studies*, 189–201.

**Article 1: Definitions**

For the purposes of this Convention,

(a) 'Industrial accident' means an event resulting from an uncontrolled development in the course of any activity involving hazardous substances either:

   (i) In an installation, for example during manufacture, use, storage, handling, or disposal; or
   (ii) During transportation in so far as it is covered by paragraph 2 (d) of Article 2;

(b) 'Hazardous activity' means any activity in which one or more hazardous substances are present or may be present in quantities at or in excess of the threshold quantities listed in Annex I hereto, and which is capable of causing transboundary effects;

(c) 'Effects' means any direct or indirect, immediate or delayed adverse consequences caused by an industrial accident on, *inter alia*:

   (i) Human beings, flora and fauna;
   (ii) Soil, water, air and landscape;
   (iii) The interaction between the factors in (i) and (ii);
   (iv) Material assets and cultural heritage, including historical monuments;

(d) 'Transboundary effects' means serious effects within the jurisdiction of a Party as a result of an industrial accident occurring within the jurisdiction of another Party;

(e) 'Operator' means any natural or legal person, including public authorities, in charge of an activity, e.g. supervising, planning to carry out or carrying out an activity;

(g) 'Party of origin' means any Party or Parties under whose jurisdiction an industrial accident occurs or is capable of occurring;

(h) 'Affected Party' means any Party or Parties affected or capable of being affected by transboundary effects of an industrial accident;

(j) 'The public' means one or more natural or legal persons.

**Article 2: Scope**

1. This Convention shall apply to the prevention of, preparedness for and response to industrial accidents capable of causing transboundary effects, including the effects of such accidents caused by natural disasters, and to international cooperation concerning mutual assistance, research and development, exchange of information and exchange of technology in the area of prevention of, preparedness for and response to industrial accidents.
2. This Convention shall not apply to:

   (a) Nuclear accidents or radiological emergencies;
   (b) Accidents at military installations;
   (c) Dam failures, with the exception of the effects of industrial accidents caused by such failures;
   (d) Land-based transport accidents with the exception of:

      (i) Emergency response to such accidents;
      (ii) Transportation on the site of the hazardous activity;

   (e) Accidental release of genetically modified organisms;

(f) Accidents caused by activities in the marine environment, including seabed exploration or exploitation;
(g) Spills of oil or other harmful substances at sea.

**Article 3: General Provisions**

1. The Parties shall, taking into account efforts already made at national and international levels, take appropriate measures and cooperate within the framework of this Convention, to protect human beings and the environment against industrial accidents by preventing such accidents as far as possible, by reducing their frequency and severity and by mitigating their effects. To this end, preventive, preparedness and response measures, including restoration measures, shall be applied.
2. The Parties shall, by means of exchange of information, consultation and other cooperative measures and without undue delay, develop and implement policies and strategies for reducing the risks of industrial accidents and improving preventive, preparedness and response measures, including restoration measures, taking into account, in order to avoid unnecessary duplication, efforts already made at national and international levels.
3. The Parties shall ensure that the operator is obliged to take all measures necessary for the safe performance of the hazardous activity and for the prevention of industrial accidents . . .

**Article 4: Identification, Consultation and Advice**

1. For the purpose of undertaking preventive measures and setting up preparedness measures, the Party of origin shall take measures, as appropriate, to identify hazardous activities within its jurisdiction and to ensure that affected Parties are notified of any such proposed or existing activity.
2. Parties concerned shall, at the initiative of any such Party, enter into discussions on the identification of those hazardous activities that are, reasonably, capable of causing transboundary effects. If the Parties concerned do not agree on whether an activity is such a hazardous activity, any such Party may, unless the Parties concerned agree on another method of resolving the question, submit that question to an inquiry commission in accordance with the provisions of Annex II hereto for advice . . .

**Article 6: Prevention**

1. The Parties shall take appropriate measures for the prevention of industrial accidents, including measures to induce action by operators to reduce the risk of industrial accidents. Such measures may include, but are not limited to those referred to in Annex IV hereto.
2. With regard to any hazardous activity, the Party of origin shall require the operator to demonstrate the safe performance of the hazardous activity by the provision of information such as basic details of the process, including but not limited to, analysis and evaluation as detailed in Annex V hereto.

**Article 8: Emergency Preparedness**

1. The Parties shall take appropriate measures to establish and maintain adequate emergency preparedness to respond to industrial accidents. The Parties shall ensure that

preparedness measures are taken to mitigate transboundary effects of such accidents, on-site duties being undertaken by operators. These measures may include, but are not limited to those referred to in Annex VII hereto. In particular, the Parties concerned shall inform each other of their contingency plans.

2. The Party of origin shall ensure for hazardous activities the preparation and implementation of on-site contingency plans, including suitable measures for response and other measures to prevent and minimize transboundary effects. The Party of origin shall provide to the other Parties concerned the elements it has for the elaboration of contingency plans.
3. Each Party shall ensure for hazardous activities the preparation and implementation of off-site contingency plans covering measures to be taken within its territory to prevent and minimize transboundary effects . . .
4. Contingency plans should be reviewed regularly, or when circumstances so require, taking into account the experience gained in dealing with actual emergencies.

**Article 10: Industrial Accident Notification Systems**

1. The Parties shall, with the aim of obtaining and transmitting industrial accident notifications containing information needed to counteract transboundary effects, provide for the establishment and operation of compatible and efficient industrial accident notification systems at appropriate levels.
2. In the event of an industrial accident, or imminent threat thereof, which causes or is capable of causing transboundary effects, the Party of origin shall ensure that affected Parties are, without delay, notified at appropriate levels through the industrial accident notification systems . . .

**Article 16: Exchange of Technology**

1. The Parties shall, consistent with their laws, regulations and practices, facilitate the exchange of technology for the prevention of, preparedness for and response to the effects of industrial accidents, particularly through the promotion of:

   (a) Exchange of available technology on various financial bases;
   (b) Direct industrial contacts and cooperation;
   (c) Exchange of information and experience;
   (d) Provision of technical assistance.

2. In promoting the activities specified in paragraph 1, subparagraphs (a) to (d) of this Article, the Parties shall create favourable conditions by facilitating contacts and cooperation among appropriate organizations and individuals in both the private and the public sectors that are capable of providing technology, design and engineering services, equipment or finance.

# 50. UN Economic Commission for Europe: Espoo Convention on Environmental Impact Assessment in a Transboundary Context, 1991

**Commentary**: The Convention (30 *ILM* 800 (1991), entry into force 1997) contemplates obligations of notification and consultation for all major projects likely to have significant adverse transboundary environmental impacts. Article 5 provides for consultation with affected Parties concerning the potential transboundary impact of proposed activities on the basis of environmental impact assessments without undue delay. Appendix I lists activities including crude oil refineries, thermal power stations, nuclear and chemical installations, constructing motorways, oil and gas pipelines, trading ports, waste-disposal, large dams and reservoirs, pulp and paper manufacturing, major mining projects and offshore hydrocarbon production. The criteria used to determine the environmental significance of activities not identified by Appendix I includes their size, location and effects (Appendix III). Appendix II outlines the content of environmental impact assessments and Appendix IV envisages an inquiry procedure providing *inter alia* for information confidentiality. See further, the 2003 Protocol on Strategic Environmental Assessment under the Espoo Convention (www.unece.org/env/eia/documents/protocolenglish.pdf). See also, EC Directives 85/337/EEC & 97/11/EC concerning Environmental Impact Assessment for individual projects and Directive 2001/42/EC concerning Strategic Environmental Assessment for plans, programmes and policies.

**Article 1: Definitions**

For the purposes of this Convention,

(ii) 'Party of origin' means the Contracting Party or Parties to this Convention under whose jurisdiction a proposed activity is envisaged to take place;

(iii) 'Affected Party' means the Contracting Party or Parties to this Convention likely to be affected by the transboundary impact of a proposed activity;

(iv) 'Concerned Parties' means the Party of origin and the affected Party of an environmental impact assessment pursuant to this Convention;

(v) 'Proposed activity' means any activity or any major change to an activity subject to a decision of a competent authority in accordance with an applicable national procedure;

(vi) 'Environmental impact assessment' means a national procedure for evaluating the likely impact of a proposed activity on the environment;

(vii) 'Impact' means any effect caused by a proposed activity on the environment including human health and safety, flora, fauna, soil, air, water, climate, landscape and historical monuments or other physical structures or the interaction among these factors; it also includes effects on cultural heritage or socio-economic conditions resulting from alterations to those factors;

(viii) 'Transboundary impact' means any impact, not exclusively of a global nature, within an area under the jurisdiction of a Party caused by a proposed activity the physical origin of which is situated wholly or in part within the area under the jurisdiction of another Party;

(x) 'The Public' means one or more natural or legal persons.

**Article 2: General Provisions**

1. The Parties shall, either individually or jointly, take all appropriate and effective measures to prevent, reduce and control significant adverse transboundary environmental impact from proposed activities.
3. The Party of origin shall ensure that in accordance with the provisions of this Convention an environmental impact assessment is undertaken prior to a decision to authorize or undertake a proposed activity listed in Appendix I that is likely to cause a significant adverse transboundary impact.
6. The Party of origin shall provide, in accordance with the provisions of this Convention, an opportunity to the public in the areas likely to be affected to participate in relevant environmental impact assessment procedures regarding proposed activities and shall ensure that the opportunity provided to the public of the affected Party is equivalent to that provided to the public of the Party of origin.
7. Environmental impact assessments as required by this Convention shall, as a minimum requirement, be undertaken at the project level of the proposed activity. To the extent appropriate, the Parties shall endeavour to apply the principles of environmental impact assessment to policies, plans and programmes.
8. The provisions of this Convention shall not affect the right of Parties to implement national laws, regulations, administrative provisions or accepted legal practices protecting information the supply of which would be prejudicial to industrial and commercial secrecy or national security . . .

**Article 3: Notification**

1. For a proposed activity listed in Appendix I that is likely to cause a significant adverse transboundary impact, the Party of origin shall, for the purposes of ensuring adequate and effective consultations under Article 5, notify any Party which it considers may be an affected Party as early as possible and no later than when informing its own public about that proposed activity.
8. The concerned Parties shall ensure that the public of the affected Party in the areas likely to be affected be informed of, and be provided with possibilities for making comments or objections on, the proposed activity, and for the transmittal of these comments or objections to the competent authority of the Party of origin, either directly to this authority or, where appropriate, through the Party of origin.

### Article 4: Preparation of the Environmental Impact Assessment Documentation

1. The environmental impact assessment documentation to be submitted to the competent authority of the Party of origin shall contain, as a minimum, the information described in Appendix II.
2. The Party of origin shall furnish the affected Party, as appropriate through a joint body where one exists, with the environmental impact assessment documentation. The concerned Parties shall arrange for distribution of the documentation to the authorities and the public of the affected Party in the areas likely to be affected and for the submission of comments to the competent authority of the Party of origin, either directly to this authority or, where appropriate, through the Party of origin within a reasonable time before the final decision is taken on the proposed activity.

### Article 5: Consultations on the Basis of the Environmental Impact Assessment Documentation

The Party of origin shall, after completion of the environmental impact assessment documentation, without undue delay enter into consultations with the affected Party concerning, *inter alia*, the potential transboundary impact of the proposed activity and measures to reduce or eliminate its impact. Consultations may relate to:

(a) Possible alternatives to the proposed activity, including the no-action alternative and possible measures to mitigate significant adverse transboundary impact and to monitor the effects of such measures at the expense of the Party of origin;

(b) Other forms of possible mutual assistance in reducing any significant adverse transboundary impact of the proposed activity; and

(c) Any other appropriate matters relating to the proposed activity.

The Parties shall agree, at the commencement of such consultations, on a reasonable time-frame for the duration of the consultation period. Any such consultations may be conducted through an appropriate joint body, where one exists.

# 51. UNEP: Basel Convention on the Control of Transboundary Movements of Hazardous Wastes and Their Disposal, 1989

**Commentary**: The Convention (28 *ILM* 652 (1989), entry into force 1992) seeks to prevent uncontrolled movements and dumping of hazardous wastes in developing States by companies from developed countries. Such a practice was undertaken by 'toxic traders' during the 1980s in response to tighter environmental regulations within industrialised States. The Cairo Guidelines and Principles for the Environmentally Sound Management of Hazardous Wastes introduced notification systems for receiving or transit States and it was the exporter's responsibility to ensure that disposal sites met specified safety requirements: UNEP Governing Council Decision 14/30 (1987).

The Basel Convention addresses hazardous waste at source and espouses environmentally sound management and an integrated life-cycle approach. In addition to the extracts below, Article 7 provides that Article 6(1) applies *mutatis mutandis* to transboundary movements of hazardous wastes from Parties to non-Parties. Article 10 contemplates international cooperation to harmonise technical standards and waste management practices as well as implementing new environmentally sound low-waste technologies. Article 13 contemplates information exchange. Article 16 provides that the Secretariat may receive information from NGOs and can provide governments with information on consulting firms possessing the necessary technical competence.

Annex I lists categories of waste streams to be controlled and wastes with particular constituents. Annex II identifies categories of waste requiring special consideration. Annex III lists hazardous characteristics (explosive, flammable, oxidising, poisonous, infectious, corrosive, toxic, ecotoxic) corresponding to the hazard classification system of the UN (1993) 'Recommendations on the Transport of Dangerous Goods' (8th edn). Annex IV identifies disposal operations leading to resource recovery, recycling, reclamation, direct re-use or alternative uses. Annex VA identifies the notification information provided by exporters and Annex VB the information necessary for movement documents. Annex VI contemplates inter-State arbitration. Annex VII was adopted as a result of the 'Basel Ban' (see below). Annex VIII List A identifies wastes characterised as hazardous under Article 1 and Annex IX List B those wastes not covered by the Convention.

Governments have since banned the export of hazardous wastes intended for final disposal from Annex VII States (members of the EU, the OECD and Liechtenstein) to non-Annex VII States (all other Parties): COP Decision 3/1 (1995) on an Amendment to the Basel Convention (the 'Basel Ban', not yet in force). Governments also agreed to ban from 1997 the export of wastes intended for recovery and recycling: COP Decision 2/12 (1994).

The Strategic Plan for the Implementation of the Basel Convention 2000–2010 includes *inter alia* preventing illegal traffic and promoting cleaner production methods: see further, the 1999 Ministerial Declaration on Environmentally Sound Management. The secretariat (www.basel.int) offers training and technical assistance to private companies and industry associations. Additionally relevant instruments include the 1992 UNECE Convention on the Protection and Use of Transboundary Watercourses and International Lakes (www.unece.org/env/water/text/text.htm); the Bamako Convention on the Ban of the Import into Africa and the Control of Transboundary Movement and Management of Hazardous Wastes within Africa (1991) 30 *ILM* 773; EC Directive 96/61/EC concerning Integrated Pollution Prevention and Control; and EC Directive 2003/105/EC amending Council Directive 96/82/EC on the control of major-accident hazards involving dangerous substances. See also, EC Commission Communication towards a thematic strategy on the prevention and recycling of waste COM(2003)301.

**Article 1: Scope of the Convention**

1. The following wastes that are subject to transboundary movement shall be 'hazardous wastes' for the purposes of this Convention:

   (a) Wastes that belong to any category contained in Annex I, unless they do not possess any of the characteristics contained in Annex III; and
   (b) Wastes that are not covered under paragraph (a) but are defined as, or are considered to be, hazardous wastes by the domestic legislation of the Party of export, import or transit.

2. Wastes that belong to any category contained in Annex II that are subject to transboundary movement shall be 'other wastes' for the purposes of this Convention.
3. Wastes which, as a result of being radioactive, are subject to other international control systems, including international instruments, applying specifically to radioactive materials, are excluded from the scope of this Convention.
4. Wastes which derive from the normal operations of a ship, the discharge of which is covered by another international instrument, are excluded from the scope of this Convention.

**Article 2: Definitions**

For the purposes of this Convention:

1. 'Wastes' are substances or objects which are disposed of or are intended to be disposed of or are required to be disposed of by the provisions of national law;
2. 'Management' means the collection, transport and disposal of hazardous wastes or other wastes, including after-care of disposal sites;
3. 'Transboundary movement' means any movement of hazardous wastes or other wastes from an area under the national jurisdiction of one State to or through an area under the national jurisdiction of another State or to or through an area not under the national jurisdiction of any State, provided at least two States are involved in the movement;

4. 'Disposal' means any operation specified in Annex IV to this Convention;
5. 'Approved site or facility' means a site or facility for the disposal of hazardous wastes or other wastes which is authorized or permitted to operate for this purpose by a relevant authority of the State where the site or facility is located;
8. 'Environmentally sound management of hazardous wastes or other wastes' means taking all practicable steps to ensure that hazardous wastes or other wastes are managed in a manner which will protect human health and the environment against the adverse effects which may result from such wastes;
9. 'Area under the national jurisdiction of a State' means any land, marine area or air space within which a State exercises administrative and regulatory responsibility in accordance with international law in regard to the protection of human health or the environment;
14. 'Person' means any natural or legal person;
15. 'Exporter' means any person under the jurisdiction of the State of export who arranges for hazardous wastes or other wastes to be exported;
16. 'Importer' means any person under the jurisdiction of the State of import who arranges for hazardous wastes or other wastes to be imported;
17. 'Carrier' means any person who carries out the transport of hazardous wastes or other wastes;
18. 'Generator' means any person whose activity produces hazardous wastes or other wastes or, if that person is not known, the person who is in possession and/or control of those wastes;
19. 'Disposer' means any person to whom hazardous wastes or other wastes are shipped and who carries out the disposal of such wastes;
21. 'Illegal traffic' means any transboundary movement of hazardous wastes or other wastes as specified in Article 9.

**Article 3: National Definitions of Hazardous Wastes**

1. Each Party shall, within six months of becoming a Party to this Convention, inform the Secretariat of the Convention of the wastes, other than those listed in Annexes I and II, considered or defined as hazardous under its national legislation and of any requirements concerning transboundary movement procedures applicable to such wastes . . .

**Article 4: General Obligations**

1. (a) Parties exercising their right to prohibit the import of hazardous wastes or other wastes for disposal shall inform the other Parties of their decision pursuant to Article 13.
   (b) Parties shall prohibit or shall not permit the export of hazardous wastes and other wastes to the Parties which have prohibited the import of such wastes, when notified pursuant to subparagraph (a) above.
   (c) Parties shall prohibit or shall not permit the export of hazardous wastes and other wastes if the State of import does not consent in writing to the specific import, in the case where that State of import has not prohibited the import of such wastes.

2. Each Party shall take the appropriate measures to:

(a) Ensure that the generation of hazardous wastes and other wastes within it is reduced to a minimum, taking into account social, technological and economic aspects;
(b) Ensure the availability of adequate disposal facilities, for the environmentally sound management of hazardous wastes and other wastes, that shall be located, to the extent possible, within it, whatever the place of their disposal;
(c) Ensure that persons involved in the management of hazardous wastes or other wastes within it take such steps as are necessary to prevent pollution due to hazardous wastes and other wastes arising from such management and, if such pollution occurs, to minimize the consequences thereof for human health and the environment;
(d) Ensure that the transboundary movement of hazardous wastes and other wastes is reduced to the minimum consistent with the environmentally sound and efficient management of such wastes, and is conducted in a manner which will protect human health and the environment against the adverse effects which may result from such movement;
(e) Not allow the export of hazardous wastes or other wastes to a State or group of States belonging to an economic and/or political integration organization that are Parties, particularly developing countries, which have prohibited by their legislation all imports, or if it has reason to believe that the wastes in question will not be managed in an environmentally sound manner, according to criteria to be decided on by the Parties at their first meeting;
(f) Require that information about a proposed transboundary movement of hazardous wastes and other wastes be provided to the States concerned, according to Annex VA, to state clearly the effects of the proposed movement on human health and the environment;
(g) Prevent the import of hazardous wastes and other wastes if it has reason to believe that the wastes in question will not be managed in an environmentally sound manner;
(h) Co-operate in activities with other Parties and interested organizations, directly and through the Secretariat, including the dissemination of information on the transboundary movement of hazardous wastes and other wastes, in order to improve the environmentally sound management of such wastes and to achieve the prevention of illegal traffic.

3. The Parties consider that illegal traffic in hazardous wastes or other wastes is criminal.
4. Each Party shall take appropriate legal, administrative and other measures to implement and enforce the provisions of this Convention, including measures to prevent and punish conduct in contravention of the Convention.
5. A Party shall not permit hazardous wastes or other wastes to be exported to a non-Party or to be imported from a non-Party.
6. The Parties agree not to allow the export of hazardous wastes or other wastes for disposal within the area south of 60° South latitude, whether or not such wastes are subject to transboundary movement.
7. Furthermore, each Party shall:

(a) Prohibit all persons under its national jurisdiction from transporting or disposing of hazardous wastes or other wastes unless such persons are authorized or allowed to perform such types of operations;

(b) Require that hazardous wastes and other wastes that are to be the subject of a transboundary movement be packaged, labelled, and transported in conformity with generally accepted and recognized international rules and standards in the field of packaging, labelling, and transport, and that due account is taken of relevant internationally recognized practices;

(c) Require that hazardous wastes and other wastes be accompanied by a movement document from the point at which a transboundary movement commences to the point of disposal.

8. Each Party shall require that hazardous wastes or other wastes, to be exported, are managed in an environmentally sound manner in the State of import or elsewhere. Technical guidelines for the environmentally sound management of wastes subject to this Convention shall be decided by the Parties at their first meeting.

9. Parties shall take the appropriate measures to ensure that the transboundary movement of hazardous wastes and other wastes only be allowed if:

(a) The State of export does not have the technical capacity and the necessary facilities, capacity or suitable disposal sites in order to dispose of the wastes in question in an environmentally sound and efficient manner; or

(b) The wastes in question are required as a raw material for recycling or recovery industries in the State of import; or

(c) The transboundary movement in question is in accordance with other criteria to be decided by the Parties, provided those criteria do not differ from the objectives of this Convention.

10. The obligation under this Convention of States in which hazardous wastes and other wastes are generated to require that those wastes are managed in an environmentally sound manner may not under any circumstances be transferred to the States of import or transit . . .

**Article 6: Transboundary Movement between Parties**

1. The State of export shall notify, or shall require the generator or exporter to notify, in writing, through the channel of the competent authority of the State of export, the competent authority of the States concerned of any proposed transboundary movement of hazardous wastes or other wastes . . .

2. The State of import shall respond to the notifier in writing, consenting to the movement with or without conditions, denying permission for the movement, or requesting additional information . . .

3. The State of export shall not allow the generator or exporter to commence the transboundary movement until it has received written confirmation that:

(a) The notifier has received the written consent of the State of import; and

(b) The notifier has received from the State of import confirmation of the existence of a contract between the exporter and the disposer specifying environmentally sound management of the wastes in question.

4. Each State of transit which is a Party shall promptly acknowledge to the notifier receipt of the notification. It may subsequently respond to the notifier in writing, within 60

days, consenting to the movement with or without conditions, denying permission for the movement, or requesting additional information. The State of export shall not allow the transboundary movement to commence until it has received the written consent of the State of transit. However, if at any time a Party decides not to require prior written consent, either generally or under specific conditions, for transit transboundary movements of hazardous wastes or other wastes, or modifies its requirements in this respect, it shall forthwith inform the other Parties of its decision pursuant to Article 13. In this latter case, if no response is received by the State of export within 60 days of the receipt of a given notification by the State of transit, the State of export may allow the export to proceed through the State of transit.

5. In the case of a transboundary movement of wastes where the wastes are legally defined as or considered to be hazardous wastes only:

   (a) By the State of export, the requirements of paragraph 9 of this Article that apply to the importer or disposer and the State of import shall apply *mutatis mutandis* to the exporter and State of export, respectively;
   (b) By the State of import, or by the States of import and transit which are Parties, the requirements of paragraphs 1, 3, 4 and 6 of this Article that apply to the exporter and State of export shall apply *mutatis mutandis* to the importer or disposer and State of import, respectively; or
   (c) By any State of transit which is a Party, the provisions of paragraph 4 shall apply to such State.

6. The State of export may, subject to the written consent of the States concerned, allow the generator or the exporter to use a general notification where hazardous wastes or other wastes having the same physical and chemical characteristics are shipped regularly to the same disposer via the same customs office of exit of the State of export via the same customs office of entry of the State of import, and, in the case of transit, via the same customs office of entry and exit of the State or States of transit.
7. The States concerned may make their written consent to the use of the general notification referred to in paragraph 6 subject to the supply of certain information, such as the exact quantities or periodical lists of hazardous wastes or other wastes to be shipped.
8. The general notification and written consent referred to in paragraphs 6 and 7 may cover multiple shipments of hazardous wastes or other wastes during a maximum period of 12 months.
9. The Parties shall require that each person who takes charge of a transboundary movement of hazardous wastes or other wastes sign the movement document either upon delivery or receipt of the wastes in question. They shall also require that the disposer inform both the exporter and the competent authority of the State of export of receipt by the disposer of the wastes in question and, in due course, of the completion of disposal as specified in the notification. If no such information is received within the State of export, the competent authority of the State of export or the exporter shall so notify the State of import.
11. Any transboundary movement of hazardous wastes or other wastes shall be covered by insurance, bond or other guarantee as may be required by the State of import or any State of transit which is a Party.

**Article 8: Duty to Re-import**

When a transboundary movement of hazardous wastes or other wastes to which the consent of the States concerned has been given, subject to the provisions of this Convention, cannot be completed in accordance with the terms of the contract, the State of export shall ensure that the wastes in question are taken back into the State of export, by the exporter, if alternative arrangements cannot be made for their disposal in an environmentally sound manner, within 90 days from the time that the importing State informed the State of export and the Secretariat, or such other period of time as the States concerned agree . . .

**Article 9: Illegal Traffic**

1. For the purpose of this Convention, any transboundary movement of hazardous wastes or other wastes:

   (a) without notification pursuant to the provisions of this Convention to all States concerned; or
   (b) without the consent pursuant to the provisions of this Convention of a State concerned; or
   (c) with consent obtained from States concerned through falsification, misrepresentation or fraud; or
   (d) that does not conform in a material way with the documents; or
   (e) that results in deliberate disposal (e.g. dumping) of hazardous wastes or other wastes in contravention of this Convention and of general principles of international law, shall be deemed to be illegal traffic.

2. In case of a transboundary movement of hazardous wastes or other wastes deemed to be illegal traffic as the result of conduct on the part of the exporter or generator, the State of export shall ensure that the wastes in question are:

   (a) taken back by the exporter or the generator or, if necessary, by itself into the State of export, or, if impracticable,
   (b) are otherwise disposed of in accordance with the provisions of this Convention, within 30 days from the time the State of export has been informed about the illegal traffic or such other period of time as States concerned may agree . . .

3. In the case of a transboundary movement of hazardous wastes or other wastes deemed to be illegal traffic as the result of conduct on the part of the importer or disposer, the State of import shall ensure that the wastes in question are disposed of in an environmentally sound manner by the importer or disposer or, if necessary, by itself within 30 days from the time the illegal traffic has come to the attention of the State of import or such other period of time as the States concerned may agree . . .
4. In cases where the responsibility for the illegal traffic cannot be assigned either to the exporter or generator or to the importer or disposer, the Parties concerned or other Parties, as appropriate, shall ensure, through co-operation, that the wastes in question are disposed of as soon as possible in an environmentally sound manner either in the State of export or the State of import or elsewhere as appropriate . . .

**Article 13: Transmission of Information**

1. The Parties shall, whenever it comes to their knowledge, ensure that, in the case of an accident occurring during the transboundary movement of hazardous wastes or other wastes or their disposal, which are likely to present risks to human health and the environment in other States, those States are immediately informed . . .

## Additional Instruments

*Basel Protocol on Liability and Compensation for Damage Resulting from Transboundary Movements of Hazardous Wastes and their Disposal, 1999*

**Commentary**: A Protocol on Liability and Compensation as contemplated by Article 12 was adopted at COP-5 (1999) but is yet to enter into force. It establishes liability rules and compensation for damage caused by accidental spills of hazardous waste during export, import or disposal. In addition to the extracts below, Article 12 states that the financial limits for liability contemplated under Article 4 are specified in Annex B whereas there are no financial limits on liability under Article 5. Article 13 provides that compensation claims must be brought within ten years from the date of the incident or five years from the date claimants knew or ought reasonably to have known of the damage. Article 14 provides that persons liable under Article 4 shall establish and maintain insurance, bonds or other financial guarantees and that proof of coverage for notifiers, exporters and importers shall accompany notifications of Article 6. Article 15 contemplates additional financial measures where compensation does not cover all damage costs. Article 17 locates the national courts competent to determine compensation claims in States where damage was suffered, where incidents occur or where defendants have their habitual residence or principal place of business.

ARTICLE 1: OBJECTIVE

The objective of the Protocol is to provide for a comprehensive regime for liability and for adequate and prompt compensation for damage resulting from the transboundary movement of hazardous wastes and other wastes and their disposal including illegal traffic in those wastes.

ARTICLE 2: DEFINITIONS

2. For the purposes of the Protocol:

   (c) 'Damage' means:

      (i) Loss of life or personal injury;
      (ii) Loss of or damage to property other than property held by the person liable in accordance with the present Protocol;
      (iii) Loss of income directly deriving from an economic interest in any use of the environment, incurred as a result of impairment of the environment, taking into account savings and costs;

(iv) The costs of measures of reinstatement of the impaired environment, limited to the costs of measures actually taken or to be undertaken; and

(v) The costs of preventive measures, including any loss or damage caused by such measures, to the extent that the damage arises out of or results from hazardous properties of the wastes involved in the transboundary movement and disposal of hazardous wastes and other wastes subject to the Convention;

(d) 'Measures of reinstatement' means any reasonable measures aiming to assess, reinstate or restore damaged or destroyed components of the environment. Domestic law may indicate who will be entitled to take such measures;

(e) 'Preventive measures' means any reasonable measures taken by any person in response to an incident, to prevent, minimize, or mitigate loss or damage, or to effect environmental clean-up;

(h) 'Incident' means any occurrence, or series of occurrences having the same origin that causes damage or creates a grave and imminent threat of causing damage . . .

ARTICLE 3: SCOPE OF APPLICATION

1. The Protocol shall apply to damage due to an incident occurring during a transboundary movement of hazardous wastes and other wastes and their disposal, including illegal traffic, from the point where the wastes are loaded on the means of transport in an area under the national jurisdiction of a State of export. Any Contracting Party may by way of notification to the Depositary exclude the application of the Protocol, in respect of all transboundary movements for which it is the State of export, for such incidents which occur in an area under its national jurisdiction, as regards damage in its area of national jurisdiction . . .

ARTICLE 4: STRICT LIABILITY

1. The person who notifies in accordance with Article 6 of the Convention, shall be liable for damage until the disposer has taken possession of the hazardous wastes and other wastes. Thereafter the disposer shall be liable for damage. If the State of export is the notifier or if no notification has taken place, the exporter shall be liable for damage until the disposer has taken possession of the hazardous wastes and other wastes. With respect to Article 3, subparagraph 6 (b), of the Protocol, Article 6, paragraph 5, of the Convention shall apply *mutatis mutandis*. Thereafter the disposer shall be liable for damage.
2. Without prejudice to paragraph 1, with respect to wastes under Article 1, subparagraph 1 (b), of the Convention that have been notified as hazardous by the State of import in accordance with Article 3 of the Convention but not by the State of export, the importer shall be liable until the disposer has taken possession of the wastes, if the State of import is the notifier or if no notification has taken place. Thereafter the disposer shall be liable for damage.
3. Should the hazardous wastes and other wastes be re-imported in accordance with Article 8 of the Convention, the person who notified shall be liable for damage from the time the hazardous wastes leave the disposal site, until the wastes are taken into possession by the exporter, if applicable, or by the alternate disposer.
4. Should the hazardous wastes and other wastes be re-imported under Article 9, subparagraph 2 (a), or Article 9, paragraph 4, of the Convention, subject to Article 3

of the Protocol, the person who re-imports shall be held liable for damage until the wastes are taken into possession by the exporter if applicable, or by the alternate disposer.

5. No liability in accordance with this Article shall attach to the person referred to in paragraphs 1 and 2 of this Article, if that person proves that the damage was:

   (a) The result of an act of armed conflict, hostilities, civil war or insurrection;
   (b) The result of a natural phenomenon of exceptional, inevitable, unforeseeable and irresistible character;
   (c) Wholly the result of compliance with a compulsory measure of a public authority of the State where the damage occurred; or
   (d) Wholly the result of the wrongful intentional conduct of a third party, including the person who suffered the damage.

6. If two or more persons are liable according to this Article, the claimant shall have the right to seek full compensation for the damage from any or all of the persons liable.

ARTICLE 5: FAULT-BASED LIABILITY

Without prejudice to Article 4, any person shall be liable for damage caused or contributed to by his lack of compliance with the provisions implementing the Convention or by his wrongful intentional, reckless or negligent acts or omissions . . .

ARTICLE 6: PREVENTIVE MEASURES

1. Subject to any requirement of domestic law any person in operational control of hazardous wastes and other wastes at the time of an incident shall take all reasonable measures to mitigate damage arising therefrom.
2. Notwithstanding any other provision in the Protocol, any person in possession and/or control of hazardous wastes and other wastes for the sole purpose of taking preventive measures, provided that this person acted reasonably and in accordance with any domestic law regarding preventive measures, is not thereby subject to liability under the Protocol.

ARTICLE 7: COMBINED CAUSE OF THE DAMAGE

1. Where damage is caused by wastes covered by the Protocol and wastes not covered by the Protocol, a person otherwise liable shall only be liable according to the Protocol in proportion to the contribution made by the wastes covered by the Protocol to the damage.
2. The proportion of the contribution to the damage of the wastes referred to in paragraph 1 shall be determined with regard to the volume and properties of the wastes involved, and the type of damage occurring.
3. In respect of damage where it is not possible to distinguish between the contribution made by wastes covered by the Protocol and wastes not covered by the Protocol, all damage shall be considered to be covered by the Protocol.

ARTICLE 8: RIGHT OF RECOURSE

1. Any person liable under the Protocol shall be entitled to a right of recourse in accordance with the rules of procedure of the competent court:

(a) Against any other person also liable under the Protocol; and
(b) As expressly provided for in contractual arrangements . . .

ARTICLE 9: CONTRIBUTORY FAULT

Compensation may be reduced or disallowed if the person who suffered the damage, or a person for whom he is responsible under the domestic law, by his own fault, has caused or contributed to the damage having regard to all circumstances.

# 52. UNEP: Stockholm Convention on Persistent Organic Pollutants, 2001

**Commentary**: The Stockholm Convention (UN Doc UNEP/POPS/CONF/2 (2001), entry into force 2004) aims to protect human health and the environment from persistent organic pollutants (POPs). POPs are chemicals which remain intact for long periods, are toxic to humans and wildlife and become widely distributed. In addition to the extracts below, Article 4 envisages a specific exemptions register open to the public. The process for listing chemicals in Annexes A, B and C through the POPs Review Committee under Article 8 contemplates soliciting technical comments from observers and taking these comments into account when completing risk profiles. Article 9 provides for information exchange including from NGOs subject to confidentiality but information on human health and safety or the environment is deemed non-confidential. Under Article 11, governments agree to support research, development and monitoring. Article 13(2) encourages voluntary financial contributions 'from other sources'. Article 15 imposes reporting obligations, Article 16 lists mechanisms for evaluating effectiveness and Article 17 envisages a non-compliance mechanism. Annexes to the Convention pertain to chemicals for elimination (Annex A) and restriction (B), unintentional production (C), the screening criteria (D), risk profile (E) and socio-economic information (F).

See further, UNEP (1999), Guidelines for the identification of PCBs and materials containing PCBs; UNEP (2002), 'Reducing and Eliminating the use of Persistent Organic Pesticides: Guidance on alternative strategies for sustainable pest and vector management'; UNEP (2002), 'Ridding the world of POPs: A guide to the Stockholm Convention on Persistent Organic Pollutants'; UNEP (2003), 'Standardized Toolkit for Identification and Quantification of Dioxin and Furan Release'. See also, UNEP, 'Guidelines on Best Available Techniques and Provisional Guidance on Best Environmental Practices relevant to Article 5 and Annex C of the Convention' and the work programme of the Intergovernmental Forum on Chemicals Safety (IFCS)/Ad hoc Working Group on Persistent Organic Pollutants. For commercial perspectives, see ICCA (2000), 'UNEP Global POPs Treaty-INC5: Statement on Key Issues', Virginia; CEFIC/Euro Chlor (2000), 'Comments on Persistent Organic Pollutants (POPs)', Brussels.

**Article 1: Objective**

Mindful of the precautionary approach as set forth in Principle 15 of the Rio Declaration on Environment and Development, the objective of this Convention is to protect human health and the environment from persistent organic pollutants.

**Article 3: Measures to Reduce or Eliminate Releases from Intentional Production and Use**

1. Each Party shall:

   (a) Prohibit and/or take the legal and administrative measures necessary to eliminate:

      (i) Its production and use of the chemicals listed in Annex A subject to the provisions of that Annex; and
      (ii) Its import and export of the chemicals listed in Annex A in accordance with the provisions of paragraph 2; and

   (b) Restrict its production and use of the chemicals listed in Annex B in accordance with the provisions of that Annex.

2. Each Party shall take measures to ensure:

   (a) That a chemical listed in Annex A or Annex B is imported only:

      (i) For the purpose of environmentally sound disposal as set forth in paragraph 1(d) of Article 6; or
      (ii) For a use or purpose which is permitted for that Party under Annex A or Annex B;

   (b) That a chemical listed in Annex A for which any production or use specific exemption is in effect or a chemical listed in Annex B for which any production or use specific exemption or acceptable purpose is in effect, taking into account any relevant provisions in existing international prior informed consent instruments, is exported only:

      (i) For the purpose of environmentally sound disposal as set forth in paragraph 1(d) of Article 6;
      (ii) To a Party which is permitted to use that chemical under Annex A or Annex B; or
      (iii) To a State not Party to this Convention which has provided an annual certification to the exporting Party. Such certification shall specify the intended use of the chemical and include a statement that, with respect to that chemical, the importing State is committed to:

         a. Protect human health and the environment by taking the necessary measures to minimize or prevent releases;
         b. Comply with the provisions of paragraph 1 of Article 6; and
         c. Comply, where appropriate, with the provisions of paragraph 2 of Part II of Annex B.

   The certification shall also include any appropriate supporting documentation, such as legislation, regulatory instruments, or administrative or policy guidelines . . .

   (c) That a chemical listed in Annex A, for which production and use specific exemptions are no longer in effect for any Party, is not exported from it except for the purpose of environmentally sound disposal as set forth in paragraph 1 (d) of Article 6 . . .

3. Each Party that has one or more regulatory and assessment schemes for new pesticides or new industrial chemicals shall take measures to regulate with the aim of preventing the production and use of new pesticides or new industrial chemicals which, taking into consideration the criteria in paragraph 1 of Annex D, exhibit the characteristics of persistent organic pollutants.
4. Each Party that has one or more regulatory and assessment schemes for pesticides or industrial chemicals shall, where appropriate, take into consideration within these schemes the criteria in paragraph 1 of Annex D when conducting assessments of pesticides or industrial chemicals currently in use.
5. Except as otherwise provided in this Convention, paragraphs 1 and 2 shall not apply to quantities of a chemical to be used for laboratory-scale research or as a reference standard.
6. Any Party that has a specific exemption in accordance with Annex A or a specific exemption or an acceptable purpose in accordance with Annex B shall take appropriate measures to ensure that any production or use under such exemption or purpose is carried out in a manner that prevents or minimizes human exposure and release into the environment. For exempted uses or acceptable purposes that involve intentional release into the environment under conditions of normal use, such release shall be to the minimum extent necessary, taking into account any applicable standards and guidelines.

**Article 5: Measures to Reduce or Eliminate Releases from Unintentional Production**

Each Party shall at a minimum take the following measures to reduce the total releases derived from anthropogenic sources of each of the chemicals listed in Annex C, with the goal of their continuing minimization and, where feasible, ultimate elimination:

(a) Develop an action plan or, where appropriate, a regional or subregional action plan within two years of the date of entry into force of this Convention . . .
(b) Promote the application of available, feasible and practical measures that can expeditiously achieve a realistic and meaningful level of release reduction or source elimination;
(c) Promote the development and, where it deems appropriate, require the use of substitute or modified materials, products and processes to prevent the formation and release of the chemicals listed in Annex C, taking into consideration the general guidance on prevention and release reduction measures in Annex C and guidelines to be adopted by decision of the Conference of the Parties;
(d) Promote and, in accordance with the implementation schedule of its action plan, require the use of best available techniques for new sources within source categories which a Party has identified as warranting such action in its action plan, with a particular initial focus on source categories identified in Part II of Annex C. In any case, the requirement to use best available techniques for new sources in the categories listed in Part II of that Annex shall be phased in as soon as practicable but no later than four years after the entry into force of the Convention for that Party. For the identified categories, Parties shall promote the use of best environmental practices. When applying best available techniques and best environmental practices, Parties should take into

consideration the general guidance on prevention and release reduction measures in that Annex and guidelines on best available techniques and best environmental practices to be adopted by decision of the Conference of the Parties;

(e) Promote, in accordance with its action plan, the use of best available techniques and best environmental practices:

   (i) For existing sources, within the source categories listed in Part II of Annex C and within source categories such as those in Part III of that Annex; and
   (ii) For new sources, within source categories such as those listed in Part III of Annex C which a Party has not addressed under subparagraph (d).

   When applying best available techniques and best environmental practices, Parties should take into consideration the general guidance on prevention and release reduction measures in Annex C and guidelines on best available techniques and best environmental practices to be adopted by decision of the Conference of the Parties;

(f) For the purposes of this paragraph and Annex C:

   (i) 'Best available techniques' means the most effective and advanced stage in the development of activities and their methods of operation which indicate the practical suitability of particular techniques for providing in principle the basis for release limitations designed to prevent and, where that is not practicable, generally to reduce releases of chemicals listed in Part I of Annex C and their impact on the environment as a whole. In this regard:
   (ii) 'Techniques' includes both the technology used and the way in which the installation is designed, built, maintained, operated and decommissioned;
   (iii) 'Available' techniques means those techniques that are accessible to the operator and that are developed on a scale that allows implementation in the relevant industrial sector, under economically and technically viable conditions, taking into consideration the costs and advantages; and
   (iv) 'Best' means most effective in achieving a high general level of protection of the environment as a whole;
   (v) 'Best environmental practices' means the application of the most appropriate combination of environmental control measures and strategies;
   (vi) 'New source' means any source of which the construction or substantial modification is commenced at least one year after the date of:

      a. Entry into force of this Convention for the Party concerned; or
      b. Entry into force for the Party concerned of an amendment to Annex C where the source becomes subject to the provisions of this Convention only by virtue of that amendment.

(g) Release limit values or performance standards may be used by a Party to fulfil its commitments for best available techniques under this paragraph.

**Article 6: Measures to Reduce or Eliminate Releases from Stockpiles and Wastes**

1. In order to ensure that stockpiles consisting of or containing chemicals listed either in Annex A or Annex B and wastes, including products and articles upon becoming

wastes, consisting of, containing or contaminated with a chemical listed in Annex A, B or C, are managed in a manner protective of human health and the environment, each Party shall:

(a) Develop appropriate strategies for identifying:

   (i) Stockpiles consisting of or containing chemicals listed either in Annex A or Annex B; and
   (ii) Products and articles in use and wastes consisting of, containing or contaminated with a chemical listed in Annex A, B or C;

(b) Identify, to the extent practicable, stockpiles consisting of or containing chemicals listed either in Annex A or Annex B on the basis of the strategies referred to in subparagraph (a);
(c) Manage stockpiles, as appropriate, in a safe, efficient and environmentally sound manner. Stockpiles of chemicals listed either in Annex A or Annex B, after they are no longer allowed to be used according to any specific exemption specified in Annex A or any specific exemption or acceptable purpose specified in Annex B, except stockpiles which are allowed to be exported according to paragraph 2 of Article 3, shall be deemed to be waste and shall be managed in accordance with subparagraph (d);
(d) Take appropriate measures so that such wastes, including products and articles upon becoming wastes, are:

   (i) Handled, collected, transported and stored in an environmentally sound manner;
   (ii) Disposed of in such a way that the persistent organic pollutant content is destroyed or irreversibly transformed so that they do not exhibit the characteristics of persistent organic pollutants or otherwise disposed of in an environmentally sound manner when destruction or irreversible transformation does not represent the environmentally preferable option or the persistent organic pollutant content is low, taking into account international rules, standards, and guidelines, including those that may be developed pursuant to paragraph 2, and relevant global and regional regimes governing the management of hazardous wastes;
   (iii) Not permitted to be subjected to disposal operations that may lead to recovery, recycling, reclamation, direct reuse or alternative uses of persistent organic pollutants; and
   (iv) Not transported across international boundaries without taking into account relevant international rules, standards and guidelines;

(e) Endeavour to develop appropriate strategies for identifying sites contaminated by chemicals listed in Annex A, B or C; if remediation of those sites is undertaken it shall be performed in an environmentally sound manner.

2. The Conference of the Parties shall cooperate closely with the appropriate bodies of the Basel Convention on the Control of Transboundary Movements of Hazardous Wastes and their Disposal to, *inter alia*:

(a) Establish levels of destruction and irreversible transformation necessary to ensure that the characteristics of persistent organic pollutants as specified in paragraph 1 of Annex D are not exhibited . . .

**Article 7: Implementation Plans**

1. Each Party shall:

   (a) Develop and endeavour to implement a plan for the implementation of its obligations under this Convention . . .

2. The Parties shall, where appropriate, cooperate directly or through global, regional and subregional organizations, and consult their national stakeholders, including women's groups and groups involved in the health of children, in order to facilitate the development, implementation and updating of their implementation plans . . .

**Article 9: Information Exchange**

1. Each Party shall facilitate or undertake the exchange of information relevant to:

   (a) The reduction or elimination of the production, use and release of persistent organic pollutants; and
   (b) Alternatives to persistent organic pollutants, including information relating to their risks as well as to their economic and social costs.

5. For the purposes of this Convention, information on health and safety of humans and the environment shall not be regarded as confidential. Parties that exchange other information pursuant to this Convention shall protect any confidential information as mutually agreed.

**Article 10: Public Information, Awareness and Education**

1. Each Party shall, within its capabilities, promote and facilitate:

   (a) Awareness among its policy and decision makers with regard to persistent organic pollutants;
   (b) Provision to the public of all available information on persistent organic pollutants, taking into account paragraph 5 of Article 9;
   (c) Development and implementation, especially for women, children and the least educated, of educational and public awareness programmes on persistent organic pollutants, as well as on their health and environmental effects and on their alternatives;
   (d) Public participation in addressing persistent organic pollutants and their health and environmental effects and in developing adequate responses, including opportunities for providing input at the national level regarding implementation of this Convention;
   (e) Training of workers, scientists, educators and technical and managerial personnel;

(f) Development and exchange of educational and public awareness materials at the national and international levels; and
(g) Development and implementation of education and training programmes at the national and international levels.

2. Each Party shall, within its capabilities, ensure that the public has access to the public information referred to in paragraph 1 and that the information is kept up-to-date.
3. Each Party shall, within its capabilities, encourage industry and professional users to promote and facilitate the provision of the information referred to in paragraph 1 at the national level and, as appropriate, subregional, regional and global levels.
4. In providing information on persistent organic pollutants and their alternatives, Parties may use safety data sheets, reports, mass media and other means of communication, and may establish information centres at national and regional levels . . .

# 53. UNEP: Rotterdam Convention on the Prior Informed Consent Procedure for Certain Hazardous Chemicals and Pesticides in International Trade, 1998

**Commentary**: The Rotterdam Convention (UN Doc UNEP/FAO/PIC/CONF/5 (1998), entry into force 2004) builds upon Agenda 21 Chapter 19, UNEP's Amended London Guidelines for exchanging information on chemicals in international trade, UNEP's Code of Ethics on the international chemicals trade and the FAO's International Code of Conduct on distributing and using pesticides (see below). Prior informed consent (PIC) requires exporters trading in specified hazardous substances to obtain importer consent before proceeding with trade. Importing governments require tools and information to identify potential hazards and exclude chemicals they cannot safely manage. Where a government imports chemicals, the Convention promotes safe use through labelling standards, technical assistance and other support. In addition to the extracts below, Article 6 provides that developing country Parties or those with transition economies can propose listing a severely hazardous pesticide formulation under Annex III, drawing upon 'technical expertise from any relevant source'. Article 7 envisages a draft decision guidance document being prepared by the Chemical Review Committee for chemicals recommended for listing under Annex III. The Conference of the Parties ultimately decides whether chemicals become subject to the PIC procedure. Article 9 contemplates removing chemicals from Annex III, Article 12 provides for export notifications and Article 17 envisages a non-compliance procedure. Annexes specify the information required for notifications pursuant to Article 5 (Annex I), the criteria for listing banned or severely restricted chemicals under Annex III (Annex II), identified chemicals subject to the PIC procedure (Annex III), information and criteria for listing severely hazardous pesticide formulations under Annex III (Annex IV) and information required for export notification (Annex V). See further, the Severely Hazardous Pesticide Formulation Report Form, the Decision Guidance Documents for chemicals subject to the PIC procedure and the Report of the First Conference of the Parties, UN Doc UNEP/FAO/RC/COP.1/33 (2004). See also, FAO/UNEP (1991), 'Guidance for Governments: Operation of the PIC Procedure for Banned or Severely Restricted Chemicals in International Trade'.

**Article 1: Objective**

The objective of this Convention is to promote shared responsibility and cooperative efforts among Parties in the international trade of certain hazardous chemicals in order to protect human health and the environment from potential harm and to contribute to their environmentally sound use, by facilitating information exchange about their characteristics, by providing for a national decision-making process on their import and export and by disseminating these decisions to Parties.

**Article 2: Definitions**
For the purposes of this Convention:

(a) 'Chemical' means a substance whether by itself or in a mixture or preparation and whether manufactured or obtained from nature, but does not include any living organism. It consists of the following categories: pesticide (including severely hazardous pesticide formulations) and industrial;
(b) 'Banned chemical' means a chemical all uses of which within one or more categories have been prohibited by final regulatory action, in order to protect human health or the environment. It includes a chemical that has been refused approval for first-time use or has been withdrawn by industry either from the domestic market or from further consideration in the domestic approval process and where there is clear evidence that such action has been taken in order to protect human health or the environment;
(c) 'Severely restricted chemical' means a chemical virtually all use of which within one or more categories has been prohibited by final regulatory action in order to protect human health or the environment, but for which certain specific uses remain allowed. It includes a chemical that has, for virtually all use, been refused for approval or been withdrawn by industry either from the domestic market or from further consideration in the domestic approval process, and where there is clear evidence that such action has been taken in order to protect human health or the environment;
(d) 'Severely hazardous pesticide formulation' means a chemical formulated for pesticidal use that produces severe health or environmental effects observable within a short period of time after single or multiple exposure, under conditions of use;
(e) 'Final regulatory action' means an action taken by a Party, that does not require subsequent regulatory action by that Party, the purpose of which is to ban or severely restrict a chemical;
(f) 'Export' and 'import' mean, in their respective connotations, the movement of a chemical from one Party to another Party, but exclude mere transit operations . . .

**Article 3: Scope of the Convention**
1. This Convention applies to:

   (a) Banned or severely restricted chemicals; and
   (b) Severely hazardous pesticide formulations.

2. This Convention does not apply to:

   (a) Narcotic drugs and psychotropic substances;
   (b) Radioactive materials;
   (c) Wastes;
   (d) Chemical weapons;
   (e) Pharmaceuticals, including human and veterinary drugs;

(f) Chemicals used as food additives;
(g) Food;
(h) Chemicals in quantities not likely to affect human health or the environment provided they are imported:

(i) For the purpose of research or analysis; or
(ii) By an individual for his or her own personal use in quantities reasonable for such use.

**Article 5: Procedures for Banned or Severely Restricted Chemicals**

1. Each Party that has adopted a final regulatory action shall notify the Secretariat in writing of such action. Such notification shall be made as soon as possible, and in any event no later than ninety days after the date on which the final regulatory action has taken effect, and shall contain the information required by Annex I, where available.
5. When the Secretariat has received at least one notification from each of two Prior Informed Consent regions regarding a particular chemical that it has verified meet the requirements of Annex I, it shall forward them to the Chemical Review Committee. The composition of the Prior Informed Consent regions shall be defined in a decision to be adopted by consensus at the first meeting of the Conference of the Parties.
6. The Chemical Review Committee shall review the information provided in such notifications and, in accordance with the criteria set out in Annex II, recommend to the Conference of the Parties whether the chemical in question should be made subject to the Prior Informed Consent procedure and, accordingly, be listed in Annex III.

**Article 6: Procedures for Severely Hazardous Pesticide Formulations**

1. Any Party that is a developing country or a country with an economy in transition and that is experiencing problems caused by a severely hazardous pesticide formulation under conditions of use in its territory, may propose to the Secretariat the listing of the severely hazardous pesticide formulation in Annex III. In developing a proposal, the Party may draw upon technical expertise from any relevant source. The proposal shall contain the information required by part 1 of Annex IV.
2. The Secretariat shall, as soon as possible, and in any event no later than six months after receipt of a proposal under paragraph 1, verify whether the proposal contains the information required by part 1 of Annex IV. If the proposal contains the information required, the Secretariat shall forthwith forward to all Parties a summary of the information received. If the proposal does not contain the information required, it shall inform the proposing Party accordingly.
3. The Secretariat shall collect the additional information set out in part 2 of Annex IV regarding the proposal forwarded under paragraph 2.
4. When the requirements of paragraphs 2 and 3 above have been fulfilled with regard to a particular severely hazardous pesticide formulation, the Secretariat shall forward the proposal and the related information to the Chemical Review Committee.
5. The Chemical Review Committee shall review the information provided in the proposal and the additional information collected and, in accordance with the criteria set out in part 3 of Annex IV, recommend to the conference of the Parties whether the severely

hazardous pesticide formulation in question should be made subject to the Prior Informed Consent procedure and, accordingly, be listed in Annex III.

**Article 7: Listing of Chemicals in Annex III**

1. For each chemical that the Chemical Review Committee has decided to recommend for listing in Annex III, it shall prepare a draft decision guidance document. The decision guidance document should, at a minimum, be based on the information specified in Annex I, or, as the case may be, Annex IV, and include information on uses of the chemical in a category other than the category for which the final regulatory action applies.
2. The recommendation referred to in paragraph 1 together with the draft decision guidance document shall be forwarded to the conference of the Parties. The Conference of the Parties shall decide whether the chemical should be made subject to the Prior Informed Consent procedure and, accordingly, list the chemical in Annex III and approve the draft decision guidance document.
3. When a decision to list a chemical in Annex III has been taken and the related decision guidance document has been approved by the Conference of the Parties, the Secretariat shall forthwith communicate this information to all Parties.

**Article 10: Obligations in Relation to Imports of Chemicals Listed in Annex III**

1. Each Party shall implement appropriate legislative or administrative measures to ensure timely decisions with respect to the import of chemicals listed in Annex III.
2. Each Party shall transmit to the Secretariat, as soon as possible, and in any event no later than nine months after the date of dispatch of the decision guidance document referred to in paragraph 3 of Article 7, a response concerning the future import of the chemical concerned. If a Party modifies this response, it shall forthwith submit the revised response to the Secretariat.
4. A response under paragraph 2 shall consist of either:

   (a) A final decision, pursuant to legislative or administrative measures:

      (i) To consent to import;
      (ii) Not to consent to import; or
      (iii) To consent to import only subject to specified conditions; or

   (b) An interim response, which may include:

      (i) An interim decision consenting to import with or without specified conditions, or not consenting to import during the interim period;
      (ii) A statement that a final decision is under active consideration;
      (iii) A request to the Secretariat, or to the Party that notified the final regulatory action, for further information;
      (iv) A request to the Secretariat for assistance in evaluating the chemical.

5. A response under subparagraphs (a) or (b) of paragraph 4 shall relate to the category or categories specified for the chemical in Annex III.

6. A final decision should be accompanied by a description of any legislative or administrative measures upon which it is based.
8. Each Party shall make its responses under this Article available to those concerned within its jurisdiction, in accordance with its legislative or administrative measures.
9. A Party that, pursuant to paragraphs 2 and 4 above and paragraph 2 of Article 11, takes a decision not to consent to import of a chemical or to consent to its import only under specified conditions shall, if it has not already done so, simultaneously prohibit or make subject to the same conditions:

   (a) Import of the chemical from any source; and
   (b) Domestic production of the chemical for domestic use . . .

10. Every six months the Secretariat shall inform all Parties of the responses it has received. Such information shall include a description of the legislative or administrative measures on which the decisions have been based, where available. The Secretariat shall, in addition, inform the Parties of any cases of failure to transmit a response.

**Article 11: Obligations in Relation to Exports of Chemicals listed in Annex III**

1. Each exporting Party shall:

   (a) Implement appropriate legislative or administrative measures to communicate the responses forwarded by the Secretariat in accordance with paragraph 10 of Article 10 to those concerned within its jurisdiction;
   (b) Take appropriate legislative or administrative measures to ensure that exporters within its jurisdiction comply with decisions in each response no later than six months after the date on which the Secretariat first informs the Parties of such response in accordance with paragraph 10 of Article 10 . . .

2. Each Party shall ensure that a chemical listed in Annex III is not exported from its territory to any importing Party that, in exceptional circumstances, has failed to transmit a response or has transmitted an interim response that does not contain an interim decision, unless:

   (a) It is a chemical that, at the time of import, is registered as a chemical in the importing Party; or
   (b) It is a chemical for which evidence exists that it has previously been used in, or imported into, the importing Party and in relation to which no regulatory action to prohibit its use has been taken; or
   (c) Explicit consent to the import has been sought and received by the exporter through a designated national authority of the importing Party. The importing Party shall respond to such a request within sixty days . . .

**Article 13: Information to Accompany Exported Chemicals**

1. The Conference of the Parties shall encourage the World Customs Organization to assign specific Harmonized System customs codes to the individual chemicals or groups of chemicals listed in Annex III, as appropriate. Each Party shall require that, whenever

a code has been assigned to such a chemical, the shipping document for that chemical bears the code when exported.

2. Without prejudice to any requirements of the importing Party, each Party shall require that both chemicals listed in Annex III and chemicals banned or severely restricted in its territory are, when exported, subject to labelling requirements that ensure adequate availability of information with regard to risks and/or hazards to human health or the environment, taking into account relevant international standards.
3. Without prejudice to any requirements of the importing Party, each Party may require that chemicals subject to environmental or health labelling requirements in its territory are, when exported, subject to labelling requirements that ensure adequate availability of information with regard to risks and/or hazards to human health or the environment, taking into account relevant international standards.
4. With respect to the chemicals referred to in paragraph 2 that are to be used for occupational purposes, each exporting Party shall require that a safety data sheet that follows an internationally recognized format, setting out the most up-to-date information available, is sent to each importer . . .

**Article 14: Information Exchange**

2. Parties that exchange information pursuant to this Convention shall protect any confidential information as mutually agreed.
3. The following information shall not be regarded as confidential for the purposes of this Convention:

   (a) The information referred to in Annexes I and IV, submitted pursuant to Articles 5 and 6 respectively;
   (b) The information contained in the safety data sheet referred to in paragraph 4 of Article 13;
   (c) The expiry date of the chemical;
   (d) Information on precautionary measures, including hazard classification, the nature of the risk and the relevant safety advice; and
   (e) The summary results of the toxicological and ecotoxicological tests.

4. The production date of the chemical shall generally not be considered confidential for the purposes of this Convention . . .

**Article 15: Implementation of the Convention**

1. Each Party shall take such measures as may be necessary to establish and strengthen its national infrastructures and institutions for the effective implementation of this Convention. These measures may include, as required, the adoption or amendment of national legislative or administrative measures and may also include:

   (b) The encouragement of initiatives by industry to promote chemical safety; and
   (c) The promotion of voluntary agreements, taking into consideration the provisions of Article 16.

2. Each Party shall ensure, to the extent practicable, that the public has appropriate access to information on chemical handling and accident management and on alternatives

that are safer for human health or the environment than the chemicals listed in Annex III . . .

**Article 16: Technical Assistance**

The Parties shall, taking into account in particular the needs of developing countries and countries with economies in transition, cooperate in promoting technical assistance for the development of the infrastructure and the capacity necessary to manage chemicals to enable implementation of this Convention. Parties with more advanced programmes for regulating chemicals should provide technical assistance, including training, to other Parties in developing their infrastructure and capacity to manage chemicals throughout their life-cycle.

# 54. UNEP: Code of Ethics on the International Trade in Chemicals, 1994

**Commentary**: The Code (www.chem.unep.ch/ethics/) was a product of UNEP Governing Council Decision 16/35 (1991) on toxic chemicals and UNGA Resolution 47/190 (1992). It is intended to complement existing international instruments, intergovernmental codes, PVIs and industry programmes. The private sector is expected to ensure chemical safety throughout the product life cycle, introduce safer packaging including clear labelling, reduce their reliance upon hazardous chemicals, undertake quality assurance and promote safety education and training. Although it permits flexible application in the light of national conditions, the Code should not be used 'to sustain or create tariff or non-tariff barriers to trade in chemicals'. By 1998, several chemical industry associations (for example, the European Chemical Industry Council, the Japanese Responsible Care Council and the Spanish Chemical Industry Federation) had expressed their support and seven governments agreed to promote voluntary implementation by national industry: UNEP (1998), 'Report on the Status of the Application of the Code of Ethics'. See also, UN (1991), 'Consolidated List of Products whose Consumption and/or Sale have been Banned, Withdrawn, Severely Restricted or Not Approved' (4th edn); UNEP (1993), 'International Register of Potentially Toxic Chemicals'. The Code does not preclude adopting additional action: hence several provisions address chemicals dedicated towards domestic use. For chemical use and employment, see ILO Convention No 170 (1990) and Recommendation No 177 (1990) on Safety in the Use of Chemicals at Work; ILO (1993), 'Code of Practice on Safety in the Use of Chemicals at Work'.

## Part I. General Provisions

*I. Objective*

1. The objective of this code is to set forth principles and guidance for private sector parties, governing standards of conduct in the production and management of chemicals in international trade, taking into account their entire life cycle, with the purpose of reducing risks to human health and the environment which might be posed by such chemicals.

*II. Definitions*

2. For purposes of the code:

(a) 'Banned chemical' means a chemical which has, for health or environmental reasons, been prohibited for all uses by final governmental regulatory action;

(b) 'Severely restricted chemical' means a chemical for which, for health or environmental reasons, virtually all uses have been prohibited nationally by final government regulatory action, but for which certain specific uses remain authorized;
(c) 'Hazardous chemical' means a chemical which represents a threat to human or animal health or to the environment.
(d) 'Private sector parties' means industry, workers and their representatives, environmental and consumer groups and other NGOs, and the public.
(e) 'Industry' means all segments involved in production and management of chemicals, taking into account their entire life cycle, including producers, formulators, importers and exporters, traders, and transporters.
(f) 'International trade in chemicals' means export or import of chemicals.
(g) 'Export' and 'import' mean, in their respective connotations, the movement of a chemical from one State to another State, but exclude mere transit operations.
(h) 'Management' means the handling, supply transport, storage, treatment, application or other use of a chemical subsequent to its initial manufacture or formulation.
(i) 'Prior informed consent' (PIC) refers to the principle that international shipment of a chemical that is banned or severely restricted in order to protect human health and the environment should not proceed without the agreement, where such agreement exists, or contrary to the decision of, the designated national authority in the importing country . . .
(j) 'Prior informed consent procedure' (PIC procedure) means the procedure for formally obtaining and disseminating the decisions of importing countries as to whether they wish to receive future shipments of chemicals which have been banned or severely restricted, being carried out by UNEP and FAO.
(k) 'PIC decision' means a decision by a importing country of a chemical subject to the PIC procedure with respect to the future import of chemicals.

*III. Exemptions*

3. The code should not apply to:

(a) Pharmaceuticals, including narcotics, drugs and psychotropic substances;
(b) Radioactive materials;
(c) Chemicals imported for the purpose of research or analysis in quantities not likely to affect the environment or human health;
(d) Chemicals imported as personal or household effects, in quantities reasonable for these uses;
(e) Food additives.

*IV. The Commitment to Improved Health, Safety and Environmental Protection Related to the International Trade in Chemicals*

4. Private sector parties involved in the international trade in chemicals should make a commitment to undertake self-regulatory measures to meet the standards of conduct set out in the principles and guidance contained in Part II below in order to ensure the safe production and management of chemicals in domestic and international trade, taking into account their entire life cycle.
5. Private sector parties should recognize in the commitment their shared responsibility, along with the governments of chemical exporting and importing countries, for the

protection of human health and the environment. In particular, business and industry should recognize their responsibility for fully participating in the implementation and evaluation of activities related to Agenda 21.

6. The private sector parties that have already entered into the commitment under 'Responsible Care' or a similar instrument consistent with this code, such as the FAO Code of Conduct, are encouraged to make a declaration, expressing that existing commitments are consistent with this code. The parties that have not made commitment under 'Responsible Care' or a similar instrument should demonstrate their commitment by making an appropriate declaration in a written statement and publish such declaration.
7. Private sector parties making such written declaration should notify UNEP of their respective decisions to enter into commitment to meet the standards of conduct set out in the principles and guidance contained in the code.
8. The parties that have made such written declaration under paragraph 5 and entered into voluntary commitment under the code should initiate necessary action to meet the standards of conduct set out in the principles and guidance below within 180 days after the commitment is notified to UNEP.
9. The commitment by the private sector parties should include the following elements:

   (a) Increase chemical safety and enhance the sound production and management of chemicals, taking into account their entire life cycle, in all countries by providing government authorities and relevant private sector parties with relevant information on chemicals in domestic and international trade.
   (b) Comply with the PIC procedure being carried out by UNEP and FAO to the extent applicable to private sector parties.

10. Enterprises/companies involved in the production or management of chemicals in domestic and international trade, taking into account their entire life cycle, should demonstrate this commitment at all levels of their enterprises/companies, starting with the highest level of management. This commitment should be communicated throughout the enterprises/companies.

## Part II. General Principles and Guidance for the Implementation of the General Principles

11. Having agreed to take appropriate actions to protect human health and the environment from adverse effects from the production and management of chemicals in international trade, taking into account their entire life cycle, and to promote chemical safety, private sector parties should:

   (a) Act in accordance with the guidance set out in this code, and develop the means for applying the guidance in a manner appropriate to local circumstances;
   (b) Allocate the resources necessary for the application of the guidance to their own activities;
   (c) Enhance co-operation among private sector parties as well as with government agencies and relevant international organizations for the promotion of the code;
   (d) Cooperate with the local community to address problems related to chemicals in international trade and solving such problems, including the provision of relevant information.

12. Enterprises/companies involved in the international trade in chemicals, such as producers, formulators, transporters, traders including exporters and importers, should:

    (a) Develop management systems to enable the proper production and management of chemicals, taking into account their entire life cycle;
    (b) To the extent practicable, evaluate and do business with suppliers, contract manufacturers, transporters, traders and professional users who meet applicable safety, health and environmental criteria.

13. Private sector parties should promote the application of the guidance set out in the code by:

    (a) Establishing the means for sharing experience with various private sector parties, including those parties in different countries or regions, and, as appropriate, with relevant government authorities, concerning measures taken in accordance with the code;
    (b) Offering assistance to others who produce and manage chemicals, taking into account their entire life cycle.

14. Private sector parties should work with government authorities responsible for health and environmental protection from the harmful effect of chemicals in international trade, including customs offices, in accordance with the principles and guidance in the code.
15. Private sector parties should take initiatives to assist in the implementation of internationally agreed instruments related to chemicals in international trade, in particular the prior informed consent procedure being carried out by UNEP and FAO, as well as those instruments related to chemical accident prevention, preparedness and response.
16. Private sector parties, in co-operation with Governments and relevant international organizations, should establish a procedure for reviewing and revising the code, as appropriate.

*II. Guidance for the Implementation of the General Principles*

17. The following guidance, set out in seven categories, represent the standards of conduct which should be undertaken in order to fulfil the commitment and general principles set out above. Private sector parties should apply the paragraphs relevant to them, in a way which will be effective under their particular circumstances.

A. REDUCING RISKS

18. Chemical producers and formulators should:

    (a) Make every reasonable effort, to the extent practicable, to reduce risks by:

        (i) Introducing appropriate procedures to minimize adverse health and environmental effects from chemicals being manufactured and managed, taking into account their entire life cycle, under both normal operating conditions as well as emergency situations.
        (ii) Developing safer packaging, and using clear and concise labelling, taking into account existing international schemes with respect to packaging and labelling.

(iii) Take initiatives, to the extent possible, in following chemicals to the ultimate consumer, keeping track of any problems arising in actual use of the chemicals, as a basis for changes in labelling, directions and packaging.

(b) When safe manufacture and management of a chemical, taking into account its entire life cycle, does not seem possible, voluntarily take corrective action and help find solutions to difficulties.
(c) Halt manufacturing and trade, and recall products when appropriate due to the unacceptable risks associated with the product.

19. Chemical producers, formulators and traders should:

(a) Co-operate with relevant government authorities of importing countries and comply with their PIC decisions, recognizing that this might be dependent upon the governments of exporting countries fulfilling their responsibility to transmit to their industry the PIC decisions of importing countries under the PIC procedure.
(b) Co-operate with government authorities in order to ensure implementation of the export notification procedures for banned or severely restricted chemicals, where applicable.

20. Industry should:

(a) Whenever possible, endeavour to reduce the quantity of hazardous chemicals used.
(b) Co-operate with government authorities in activities related to chemical accident prevention, preparedness and response, including the development of emergency preparedness plans and support international activities in this area.
(c) In co operation with the Government, ensure safe management and disposal of chemicals, taking into account their entire life cycle.

21. Private sector parties should ensure that transfer of know-how for the production of chemicals be subject to the standards of conduct set out in the code.

B. TESTING AND ASSESSMENT

22. Chemical producers and formulators should:

(a) As regards new chemicals, produce and commercialize only the chemicals that are known to have gone through a process of testing and assessment that is conducted in accordance with national laws and regulations or internationally accepted procedures and updated where appropriate, and where necessary, taking into account the specific conditions of intended use. This testing and assessment should provide the necessary basis for an evaluation of the risks of the chemical in order to allow appropriate actions to protect human health and the environment.
(b) Provide summaries of the reports of such testing and assessment to government authorities and, upon request, provide these authorities with the full reports in accordance with applicable national laws and regulations, where such laws and regulations have been in force.

(c) Identify reasonably foreseeable uses and misuses of chemicals and, in order to do so, seek feedback from occupational users on use and misuse of chemicals. To the extent appropriate, undertake additional testing and revision of assessment taking into account the information on uses and misuses of chemicals.

(d) Ensure that proposed uses, labelling, information and advertising reflect the results of the testing and assessment.

(e) Provide, as appropriate, chemical producers and formulators in other countries or government authorities with advice and assistance related to testing and assessment, including assistance in the interpretation and evaluation of data.

(f) Ensure that contract manufacturers are kept informed of new significant health, safety and environmental data on chemicals in international trade.

C. QUALITY ASSURANCE

23. Chemical producers and formulators should:

(a) Maintain quality assurance procedures to ensure that chemicals comply with relevant human health and environmental standards and specifications, including non-exploitation of products which are out of date and, to this end, co-operate with government authorities, as appropriate.

(b) Ensure, to the extent possible, that chemicals manufactured or formulated by a subsidiary company or a contract manufacturer meets appropriate human health and environmental requirements and standards which are consistent with the requirements of the country of manufacture as well as those of the parent or contracting company.

24. Chemical producers, formulators and traders should ensure that the quality of a chemical complies with the information in the attached label and with the literature and specifications published by a chemical's manufacturer.

D. CLASSIFICATION, PACKAGING AND LABELLING

25. Chemical producers, formulators and traders should:

(a) Ensure that:

(i) chemicals are labelled;
(ii) labels include appropriate recommendations, instructions, warnings, precautions and first aid information;
(iii) labels show appropriate hazard classifications;
(iv) labels provide appropriate lot or batch information;
(v) labels are in a format appropriate for traders, transporters and occupational users with respect to, for example the language used and the use of symbols and pictograms.

(b) Ensure that classification, packaging and labelling of chemicals conform to applicable international rules, regulations and guidelines, such as the FAO Guidelines, including, for example those dealing with transportation. Where no such international rules, regulations or guidelines are available, an appropriate national or regional system for classification, packaging and labelling should be applied. Labelling requirements should cover:

(i) information to be given in the label;
(ii) legibility, durability and size of the label;
(iii) uniformity of labels and symbols, including colours.

26. Traders and transporters should ensure that chemicals are handled and transported safely in accordance with the information in the labels attached to the packages.

E. PROVISION OF INFORMATION

27. Chemical producers and formulators should:

(a) Provide occupational users, traders, transporters and contract manufacturers with appropriate information and guidance, which should be kept up-dated, to enable proper development, manufacture and management of all chemicals, taking into account their entire life cycle. Safety data sheets (or material safety data sheets) should be prepared for hazardous chemicals and be provided to occupational users, traders, and contract manufacturers to the extent that this could improve safety in the handling and use of the chemicals.
(b) Provide information and instructions in a form and language which will ensure safe and effective use of a chemical.
(c) Ensure consistency of all safety information provided on a given chemical.
(d) Provide government authorities and consumers with relevant information on:

(i) health and environmental hazards which might be posed by chemicals in international trade;
(ii) recommended protective measures;
(iii) first aid measures.

In providing such information, claims for protection of confidential and proprietary information should not compromise the overriding objective of protecting health and the environment and promoting safety.
(e) Provide the information on safe handling of chemicals when they are outdated or expired.

28. Industry should:

(a) Make reasonable efforts to ensure that the information relevant to health and environmental protection from harmful effects of chemicals reaches the occupational users or traders in importing countries. The information should be included in the labels attached to the packages whenever possible.
(b) Co-operate with governments and competent international organizations for the purpose of information exchange, including the provision of information, upon request, to a government authority in an importing country concerning banned or severely restricted chemicals and alternatives to such chemicals.
(c) Communicate on health, safety and environmental matters to government authorities and other interested parties. In this regard, industry should establish and implement policies to ensure openness in health, safety and environmental information in a manner appropriate to local circumstances.

(d) Assist UNEP to establish databases to be used by designated national authorities for registration and monitoring of chemicals, taking into account their entire life cycle, and for attention to emergencies.

F. EDUCATION AND TRAINING

29. For the purpose of preventing harmful effects of chemicals in international trade to health and the environment, industry should continue to:

(a) Educate and train employees at all levels on the proper management of chemicals, taking into account their entire life cycle.
(b) Provide employees with safety data sheets or similar relevant information.
(c) Educate and train relevant employees so that they can advise occupational users and traders on the proper management of chemicals, taking into account their entire life cycle.
(d) Disseminate educational information to, *inter alia*, chemical handlers and consumers, as well as other interested parties such as medical personnel and customs officials, through a coordinated effort of Governments, international organizations and industry.
(e) Provide support for training of occupational users and government authorities in importing countries, including training for emergency responses.

G. ADVERTISING AND MARKETING

30. Recognizing difference in countries, and with a view to providing accurate information of chemicals to ultimate consumers, such as occupational users, industry should:

(a) Ensure that advertising is consistent with the standards of conduct set out in the code. Statements used in advertising should be capable of technical substantiation. Advertising should not be likely to mislead any buyer, in particular with regard to safety or suitability of use. Advertisements should not encourage uses inconsistent with approved labels or at variance with generally-accepted recommendations. Advertising should draw attention to warnings and should encourage careful reading of labels.
(b) Encourage importing enterprises/companies and relevant trade associations to cooperate in order to achieve fair and safe marketing and trade practices and to help government authorities to stamp out malpractice.

**Part III. Monitoring and Follow-up**

31. Industry, NGOs, workers and consumers unions, and other relevant public interest groups, in cooperation with Governments and international organizations, should:

(a) Take an active role to monitor the activities of industry and other private sector parties involved in the international trade in chemicals as to whether those activities are in compliance with the standards of conduct set out in the principles and guidance above.
(b) Report the results of the monitoring to government authorities and competent international organizations, such as UNEP, with a view to:

(i) Improving performance of industry and other private sector parties involved in the international trade in chemicals;
(ii) Assisting Governments to adopt or amend national laws, regulations and administrative measures governing activities in the international trade in chemicals.
(iii) Co-operating with Governments and international organizations to develop relevant international instruments.

(c) Communicate on health, safety and environmental matters related to chemicals in international trade with other interested parties.

32. Industry is encouraged to cooperate with UNEP and NGOs in the implementation and monitoring of the standards of conduct set out in the principles and guidance above.
33. Industry should ensure that workers and others are not punished for monitoring and reporting its performance to Governments, international organizations and relevant private sector parties.
34. Private sector parties are encouraged to enter into voluntary agreements with Governments for the application of the standards of conduct set out in the principles and guidance above.
35. Private sector parties, in cooperation with Governments and international organizations such as UNEP, should promote the code to extend the parties committed to apply the standards of conduct set out in the principles and guidance above.
36. Private sector parties should develop procedures for self-evaluation to assess performance in undertaking self-regulatory measures to meet the standards of conduct set out in the principles and guidance above.
37. Private sector parties, in cooperation with Governments and international organizations, should periodically monitor compliance, review and revise, as appropriate, the code at international fora which will be convened by UNEP subject to the availability of resources.
38. UNEP will, within available resources:

(a) maintain, up-date and publish a list of those private sector parties that have entered into commitment under the code;
(b) compile and publish reports on progress in the application of the standards of conduct set out in the principles and guidance above.

# 55. UNEP: London Guidelines for the Exchange of Information on Chemicals in International Trade, 1989

**Commentary**: The London Guidelines were adopted through UNEP Governing Council Decision 15/30 (1989). Since they are primarily addressed to governments with a view to increasing chemical safety and information exchange, the extracts below are limited to commercial roles and responsibilities (footnotes also omitted). The Annexes contain various forms including a PIC decision guidance document.

**Introduction to the Guidelines**

5. These Guidelines provide a mechanism for importing countries to formally record and disseminate their decisions regarding the future importation of chemicals which have been banned or severely restricted and outlines the shared responsibilities of importing and exporting countries and exporting industries in ensuring that these decisions are heeded . . .

## Part 1: General Provisions

*1. Definitions*

For the purposes of the Guidelines:

(a) 'Chemical' means a chemical substance whether by itself or in a mixture or preparation, whether manufactured or obtained from nature and includes such substances used as industrial chemicals and pesticides;

(b) 'Banned chemical' means a chemical which has, for health or environmental reasons, been prohibited for all uses by final governmental regulatory actions;

(c) 'Severely restricted chemical' means a chemical for which, for health or environmental reasons, virtually all uses have been prohibited nationally by final government regulatory action, but for which certain specific uses remain authorized;

(d) 'International trade' means export or import of chemicals;

(e) 'Export' and 'import' mean, in their respective connotations, the movement of a chemical from one State to another State, but exclude mere transit operations;

(f) 'Management' means the handling, supply transport, storage, treatment, application, or other use of a chemical subsequent to its initial manufacture or formulation;

(g) 'Prior informed consent' (PIC) refers to the principle that international shipment of a chemical that is banned or severely restricted in order to protect human health or the environment should not proceed without the agreement, where such agreement exists, or contrary to the decision, of the designated national authority in the importing country;

(h) 'Prior informed consent procedure' (PIC procedure) means the procedure for formerly obtaining and disseminating the decisions of importing countries as to whether they wish to receive future shipments of chemicals which have been banned or severely restricted . . .

*3. Exemptions*

These Guidelines should not apply to:

(a) Pharmaceuticals, including narcotics, drugs and psychotropic substances;
(b) Radioactive materials;
(c) Chemicals imported for the purposes of research or analysis in quantities not likely to affect the environment or human health;
(d) Chemicals imported as personal or household effects, in quantities reasonable for these uses;
(e) Food additives.

*5. Institutional Arrangements*

5.7 States should as soon as possible make available the name and address of their designated national authority to the International Register of Potentially Toxic Chemicals (IRPTC), as well as subsequent changes;

5.9 IRPTC should, in addition:

(c) Maintain liaison with other concerned intergovernmental and non-governmental organizations;

*7. Operation of the PIC Procedure*

7.4 Dissemination of information.

(a) IRPTC will inform designated national authorities of decisions taken by participating importing countries in a timely fashion and should also make these available to industry and other interested parties on request, preferably through a computer data base. This information should also be included in the regular updates of the UN Consolidated List of Products whose Consumption and/or Sale have been Banned, Withdrawn or Severely Restricted by Governments . . .

(b) Governments of exporting countries shall, upon receipt of importing countries' decisions, transmit them to their industry.

*12. Functions of Designated National Authorities*

(c) Exports. It should be the function of designated national authorities, with regard to exports of banned or severely restricted chemicals:

(iii) To communicate PIC decisions to their export industry;

(d) Other functions. Designated national authorities should also consider the need:

(ii) To ensure the provision of appropriate precautionary information to persons using or handling the chemicals concerned;

(iii) To keep records of notifications and information received, issued and transmitted which could be open for public inspection in accordance with national law, except for information classified as confidential or proprietary;

*13. Information, Advice and Assistance*

(c) With regard to the use of imported chemicals, States of import should, on the basis of notification and information provided by States of export, take the necessary measures to ensure that users are provided with information, advice and assistance for the sound management of such chemicals, including appropriate precautionary information;

*14. Classification, Packaging and Labelling*

(c) In the absence of other standards in the State of import, States should ensure that the classification, packaging and labelling of chemicals exported from their territories conform to recognized and, where appropriate, internationally harmonized procedures and practices for ensuring the protection of human health and the environment during use of these chemicals.

*15. Technical Assistance*

(d) Essential elements of technical assistance needed by developing countries for the management of chemicals include:

(iii) Training to include:

b. Awareness campaigns on the safe management of chemicals for industrial and agricultural workers, customs officials and doctors . . .

# 56. FAO: International Code of Conduct on the Distribution and Use of Pesticides, 2002

**Commentary**: The Code is a reference point for all public and private sector entities engaged in distributing and using pesticides. It was first adopted by the FAO Conference at its Twenty-Fifth Session, approved by UNGA Resolution 39/248 (1985) and amended in 1989 to include provisions concerning the prior informed consent (PIC) procedure. In 1999, the FAO revised the Code in the light of the 1998 Rotterdam Convention (above), the changing international policy framework, persistent pesticide management problems within developing States and the recommendations of an FAO expert panel. Governments, NGOs, the pesticide industry and other UN organisations participated in the revision process prior to its final approval by FAO Council Resolution 1/123 (2002). Pesticide management involves reducing risk, protecting human and environmental health, supporting sustainable agriculture, employing the life-cycle concept and applying integrated pest management (IPM) strategies. Implementation of the Code is overseen by the FAO Pesticide Management Group in the light of information provided by governments, the pesticide industry, NGOs and other interested parties: FAO (2003), 'Report of the 18th Session of the FAO Panel of Experts on Pesticide Specifications, Registration Requirements, Application Standards and Prior Informed Consent', Rome. See further, FAO/OECD Pesticide Risk Reduction Survey; FAO Global Monitoring of Pesticide Management Practices; and FAO Pesticide Management Guidelines. Although the Code delimits the roles and responsibilities of all relevant actors, the extracts below focus upon those of industry and footnotes are omitted. Annex I identifies several relevant international policy instruments pertaining to chemical management, protecting human and environmental health, sustainable development and international trade. See also, FAO (1995), 'Revised guidelines on good labelling practice for pesticides', Rome; FAO (1988), 'Guidelines for retail distribution of pesticides with particular reference to storage and handling at the point of supply to users in developing countries', Rome; WHO/ILO/UNEP, 'The IPCS INTOX system', Geneva; WHO (1997), 'Specifications for pesticides used in public health', Geneva (7th edn). See further, www.fao.org/ag/AGP/AGPP/Pesticid/Default.htm.

**Article 1: Objectives of the Code**

1.1 The objectives of this Code are to establish voluntary standards of conduct for all public and private entities engaged in or associated with the distribution and use of pesticides, particularly where there is inadequate or no national legislation to regulate pesticides.

1.2 The Code is designed for use within the context of national legislation as a basis whereby government authorities, pesticide manufacturers, those engaged in trade and any citizens concerned may judge whether their proposed actions and the actions of others constitute acceptable practices.

1.3 The Code describes the shared responsibility of many sectors of society to work together so that the benefits to be derived from the necessary and acceptable use of pesticides are achieved without significant adverse effects on human health or the environment . . .

1.4 The Code addresses the need for a cooperative effort between governments of pesticide exporting and importing countries to promote practices that minimize potential health and environmental risks associated with pesticides, while ensuring their effective use.

1.5 The entities which are addressed by this Code include international organizations, governments of exporting and importing countries, pesticide industry, application equipment industry, traders, food industry, users, and public-sector organizations such as environmental groups, consumer groups and trade unions.

1.6 The Code recognizes that training at all appropriate levels is an essential requirement in implementing and observing its provisions. Therefore, governments, pesticide industry, users of pesticides, international organizations, NGOs and other parties concerned should give high priority to training activities related to each Article of the Code.

1.7 The standards of conduct set forth in this Code:

1.7.1 encourage responsible and generally accepted trade practices;

1.7.3 promote practices which reduce risks in the handling of pesticides, including minimizing adverse effects on humans and the environment and preventing accidental poisoning resulting from improper handling;

1.7.4 ensure that pesticides are used effectively and efficiently for the improvement of agricultural production and of human, animal and plant health;

1.7.5 adopt the 'life-cycle' concept to address all major aspects related to the development, regulation, production, management, packaging, labelling, distribution, handling, application, use and control, including post registration activities and disposal of all types of pesticides, including used pesticide containers;

1.7.6 are designed to promote Integrated Pest Management (IPM) (including integrated vector management for public health pests) . . .

**Article 2: Terms and Definitions**

For the purpose of this Code:

'Active ingredient' means the biologically active part of the pesticide.

'Advertising' means the promotion of the sale and use of pesticides by printed and electronic media, signs, displays, gift, demonstration or word of mouth.

'Application equipment' means any technical aid, equipment, implement or machinery which is used for the application of pesticides.

'Application technology' means the actual physical delivery and distribution process of a pesticide to the target organism or to the place where the target organism comes into contact with the pesticide.

'Banned pesticide' means a pesticide for which all uses have been prohibited by final regulatory action, in order to protect human health or the environment. The term includes a pesticide that has been refused approval for first-time use, or has been withdrawn by industry either from the domestic market or from further consideration in the domestic approval process, and where there is clear evidence that such action has been taken in order to protect human health or the environment.

'Disposal' means any operation to recycle, neutralize, destruct or isolate pesticide waste, used containers and contaminated materials.

'Distribution' means the process by which pesticides are supplied through trade channels to local or international markets.

'Environment' means surroundings, including water, air, soil and their interrelationship as well as all relationships between them and any living organisms.

'Equivalence' means the determination of the similarity of the impurity and toxicological profile, as well as of the physical and chemical properties, presented by supposedly similar technical material originating from different manufacturers, in order to assess whether they present similar levels of risk.

'Extension service' means those entities in the country responsible for the transfer of information, technology and advice regarding the improvement of agricultural practices, including production, handling, storage and marketing of agricultural commodities.

'Formulation' means the combination of various ingredients designed to render the product useful and effective for the purpose claimed; the form of the pesticide as purchased by users.

'Good Agricultural Practice (GAP) in the use of pesticides' includes the officially recommended or nationally authorized uses of pesticides under actual conditions necessary for effective and reliable pest control. It encompasses a range of levels of pesticide applications up to the highest authorized use, applied in a manner which leaves a residue which is the smallest amount practicable.

'Hazard' means the inherent property of a substance, agent or situation having the potential to cause undesirable consequences (e.g. properties that can cause adverse effects or damage to health, the environment or property).

'Integrated Pest Management (IPM)' means the careful consideration of all available pest control techniques and subsequent integration of appropriate measures that discourage the development of pest populations and keep pesticides and other interventions to levels that are economically justified and reduce or minimize risks to human health and the environment. IPM emphasizes the growth of a healthy crop with the least possible disruption to agro-ecosystems and encourages natural pest control mechanisms.

'Label' means the written, printed or graphic matter on, or attached to, the pesticide or the immediate container thereof and also to the outside container or wrapper of the retail package of the pesticide.

'Manufacturer' means a corporation or other entity in the public or private sector or any individual engaged in the business or function (whether directly or through an agent or entity controlled by or under contract with it) of manufacturing a pesticide active ingredient or preparing its formulation or product.

'Marketing' means the overall process of product promotion, including advertising, product public relations and information services as well as the distribution and sale on local or international markets.

'Maximum Residue Limit (MRL)' means the maximum concentration of a residue that is legally permitted or recognized as acceptable in or on a food or agricultural commodity or animal feedstuff.

'Packaging' means the container together with the protective wrapping used to carry pesticide products via wholesale or retail distribution to users.

'Personal protective equipment' means any clothes, materials or devices that provide protection from pesticide exposure during handling and application. In the context of this Code, it includes both specifically designed protective equipment and clothing reserved for pesticide application and handling.

'Pesticide' means any substance or mixture of substances intended for preventing, destroying or controlling any pest, including vectors of human or animal disease, unwanted species of plants or animals causing harm during or otherwise interfering with the production, processing, storage, transport or marketing of food, agricultural commodities, wood and wood products or animal feedstuffs, or substances which may be administered to animals for the control of insects, arachnids or other pests in or on their bodies. The term includes substances intended for use as a plant growth regulator, defoliant, desiccant or agent for thinning fruit or preventing the premature fall of fruit, and substances applied to crops either before or after harvest to protect the commodity from deterioration during storage and transport.

'Pesticide industry' means all those organizations and individuals engaged in manufacturing, formulating or marketing pesticides and pesticide products.

'Pesticide legislation' means any laws or regulations introduced to regulate the manufacture, marketing, distribution, labelling, packaging, use and disposal of pesticides in their qualitative, quantitative, health and environmental aspects.

'Poison' means a substance that can cause disturbance of structure or function, leading to injury or death when absorbed in relatively small amounts by human beings, plants or animals.

'Poisoning' means occurrence of damage or disturbance caused by a poison, and includes intoxication.

'Product (or pesticide product)' means the pesticide active ingredient(s) and other components, in the form in which it is packaged and sold.

'Product stewardship' means the responsible and ethical management of a pesticide product from its discovery through to its ultimate use and beyond.

'Public sector groups' means (but is not limited to) scientific associations, farmer groups, citizens' organizations, labour unions and environmental, consumer and health organizations.

'Registration' means the process whereby the responsible national government or regional authority approves the sale and use of a pesticide following the evaluation of comprehensive scientific data demonstrating that the product is effective for the intended purposes and does not pose an unacceptable risk to human or animal health or the environment.

'Repackaging' means the authorized transfer of a pesticide from any commercial package into any other, usually smaller, container for subsequent sale.

'Residue' means any specified substances in or on food, agricultural commodities or animal feed resulting from the use of a pesticide. The term includes any derivatives of a pesticide, such as conversion products, metabolites, reaction products and impurities considered to be of toxicological significance. The term 'pesticide residue' includes residues from unknown or unavoidable sources (e.g. environmental) as well as known uses of the chemical.

'Risk' is a function of the probability of an adverse health or environmental effect, and the severity of that effect, following exposure to a pesticide.

'Severely restricted pesticide' means a pesticide for which virtually all use has been prohibited by final regulatory action in order to protect human health or the environment, but for which certain specific uses remain allowed. It includes a pesticide that has, for virtually all use, been refused for approval or been withdrawn by industry either from the domestic market or from further consideration in the domestic approval process, and where there is clear evidence that such action has been taken in order to protect human health or the environment.

'Tender' means request for bids in purchasing of pesticides.

'Toxicity' means a physiological or biological property which determines the capacity of a chemical to do harm or produce injury to a living organism by other than mechanical means.

'Trader' means anyone engaged in trade, including export, import and domestic distribution.

'Use pattern' means the combination of all factors involved in the use of a pesticide, including the concentration of active ingredient in the preparation being applied, rate of application, time of treatment, number of treatments, use of adjuvants and methods and sites of application which determine the quantity applied, timing of treatment and interval before harvest.

**Article 3: Pesticide Management**

3.2 Pesticide industry should adhere to the provisions of this Code as a standard for the manufacture, distribution and advertising of pesticides, particularly in countries lacking appropriate legislation and advisory services.

3.4 Pesticide industry and traders should observe the following practices in pesticide management, especially in countries without legislation or means of implementing regulations:

3.4.1 supply only pesticides of adequate quality, packaged and labelled as appropriate for each specific market;

3.4.2 in close cooperation with procurers of pesticides, adhere closely to provisions of FAO guidelines on tender procedures;

3.4.3 pay special attention to the choice of pesticide formulations and to presentation, packaging and labelling in order to reduce risks to users and minimize adverse effects on the environment;

3.4.4 provide, with each package of pesticide, information and instructions in a form and language adequate to ensure effective use and reduce risks during handling;

3.4.5 be capable of providing effective technical support, backed up by full product stewardship to field level, including advice on disposal of pesticides and used pesticide containers, if necessary;

3.4.6 retain an active interest in following their products to the end-user, keeping track of major uses and the occurrence of any problems arising from the use of their products, as a basis for determining the need for changes in labelling, directions for use, packaging, formulation or product availability.

3.5 Pesticides whose handling and application require the use of personal protective equipment that is uncomfortable, expensive or not readily available should be avoided, especially in the case of small-scale users in tropical climates. Preference should be given to pesticides that require inexpensive personal protective and application equipment and to procedures appropriate to the conditions under which the pesticides are to be handled and used.

3.6 National and international organizations, governments and pesticide industry should take coordinated action to disseminate educational materials of all types to pesticide users, farmers, farmer organizations, agricultural workers, unions and other interested parties. Similarly, users should seek and understand educational materials before applying pesticides and should follow proper procedures.

3.8 All stakeholders, including farmers and farmer associations, IPM researchers, extension agents, crop consultants, food industry, manufacturers of biological and chemical pesticides and application equipment, environmentalists and representatives of consumer groups should play a proactive role in the development and promotion of IPM.

3.10 Governments and the application equipment industry should develop and promote the use of pesticide application methods and equipment that pose low risks to human health and the environment and that are more efficient and cost-effective, and should conduct ongoing practical training in such activities.

3.11 Governments, pesticide industry and national and international organizations should collaborate in developing and promoting resistance management strategies to prolong the useful life of valuable pesticides and reduce the adverse effects resulting from the development of resistance of pests to pesticides.

**Article 4: Testing of Pesticides**

4.1 Pesticide industry should:

4.1.1 ensure that each pesticide and pesticide product is adequately and effectively tested by recognized procedures and test methods so as to fully evaluate its efficacy, behaviour, fate, hazard and risk with regard to the various anticipated conditions in regions or countries of use;

4.1.2 ensure that such tests are conducted in accordance with sound scientific procedures and the principles of good laboratory practice;

4.1.3 make available copies or summaries of the original reports of such tests for assessment by responsible government authorities in all countries where the pesticide is to be offered for sale. Evaluation of the data should be carried out by qualified experts. If translated documents are provided, their accuracy should be validated;

4.1.4 ensure that the proposed use pattern, label claims and directions, packages, technical literature and advertising truly reflect the outcome of these scientific tests and assessments;

4.1.5 provide, at the request of a country, methods for the analysis of any active ingredient or formulation that they manufacture, and provide the necessary analytical standards;

4.1.6 provide advice and assistance in the training of technical staff involved in the relevant analytical work. Formulators should actively support this effort;

4.1.7 conduct residue trials prior to marketing, at least in accordance with Codex Alimentarius and FAO guidelines on good analytical practice and on crop residue data in order to provide a basis for establishing appropriate maximum residue limits.

4.5 Pesticide industry and governments should collaborate in post registration surveillance or conducting monitoring studies to determine the fate of pesticides and their health and environmental effects under field conditions.

**Article 5: Reducing Health and Environmental Risks**

5.1 Governments should:

5.1.8 ensure, with the cooperation of pesticide industry, that where pesticides are available through outlets which also deal in food, clothing, medicines or other products for consumption or topical application, they are physically segregated from other merchandise to prevent contamination and/or mistaken identity. Where appropriate, they should be clearly marked as hazardous materials. Every effort should be made to publicize the dangers of storing foodstuffs and pesticides together;

5.2 Even where a control scheme is in operation, pesticide industry should:

5.2.1 cooperate in the periodic reassessment of the pesticides which are marketed;

5.2.2 provide poison-control centres and medical practitioners with information about pesticide hazards and on suitable treatment of pesticide poisoning;

5.2.3 make every reasonable effort to reduce risks posed by pesticides by:

5.2.3.1 making less toxic formulations available;

5.2.3.2 introducing products in ready-to-use packages;

5.2.3.3 developing application methods and equipment that minimize exposure to pesticides;

5.2.3.4 using returnable and refillable containers where effective container collection systems are in place;

5.2.3.5 using containers that are not attractive for subsequent reuse and promoting programmes to discourage their reuse, where effective container collection systems are not in place;

5.2.3.6 using containers that are not attractive to or easily opened by children, particularly for domestic use products;

5.2.3.7 using clear and concise labelling.
5.2.4 halt sale and recall products when handling or use pose an unacceptable risk under any use directions or restrictions.
5.3 Government and industry should cooperate in further reducing risks by:
5.3.1 promoting the use of proper and affordable personal protective equipment;
5.3.2 making provisions for safe storage of pesticides at both warehouse and farm level;
5.3.3 establishing services to collect and safely dispose of used containers and small quantities of left-over pesticides;
5.3.4 protecting biodiversity and minimizing adverse effects of pesticides on the environment (water, soil and air) and on non-target organisms.
5.4 To avoid unjustified confusion and alarm among the public, concerned parties should consider all available facts and should promote responsible information dissemination on pesticides and their uses.
5.5 In establishing production facilities of a suitable standard in developing countries, manufacturers and governments should cooperate to:
5.5.1 adopt engineering standards and operating practices appropriate to the nature of the manufacturing operations and the hazards involved, and ensure the availability of appropriate protective equipment;
5.5.2 take all necessary precautions to protect workers, bystanders, surrounding communities and the environment;
5.5.3 ensure the proper siting of manufacturing and formulating plants and adequately control wastes and effluents;
5.5.4 maintain quality-assurance procedures to ensure compliance with the relevant standards of purity, performance, stability and safety.

**Article 6: Regulatory and Technical Requirements**

6.2 Pesticide industry should:
6.2.1 provide an objective pesticide data assessment together with the necessary supporting data on each product, including sufficient data to support risk assessment and to allow a risk management decision to be made;
6.2.2 provide national regulatory authorities with any new or updated information that could change the regulatory status of the pesticide, as soon as it becomes available;
6.2.3 ensure that the active ingredient and other ingredients of pesticide products being marketed correspond in identity, quality, purity and composition to the substances tested, evaluated and cleared for toxicological and environmental acceptability;
6.2.4 ensure that active ingredients, and formulated products for pesticides for which international specifications have been developed, conform with the relevant FAO specifications for agricultural pesticides, and with WHO pesticide specifications for public health pesticides;
6.2.5 verify the quality and purity of pesticides offered for sale;
6.2.6 when problems occur, voluntarily take corrective action and, when requested by governments, help find solutions to difficulties;
6.2.7 provide their national governments with clear and concise data on export, import, manufacture, formulation, sales, quality and quantity of pesticides . . .

**Article 7: Availability and Use**

7.4 Governments and industry should ensure that all pesticides made available to the general public are packaged and labelled in a manner which is consistent with the FAO guidelines on packaging and labelling and with appropriate national regulations.

**Article 8: Distribution and Trade**

8.2 Pesticide industry should:

8.2.1 take all necessary steps to ensure that pesticides entering international trade conform at least to:

8.2.1.1 relevant FAO, WHO or equivalent specifications (where such specifications have been developed);

8.2.1.2 principles embodied in relevant FAO guidelines on classification, packaging, marketing, labelling, procurement and documentation;

8.2.1.3 rules and regulations laid down by the UN Recommendations on the Transport of Dangerous Goods, and by international organizations concerned with specific modes of transport (e.g. ICAO, IMO, RID, ADR and IATA).

8.2.2 endeavour to ensure that pesticides manufactured for export are subject to the same quality requirements and standards as those applied to comparable domestic products;

8.2.3 ensure that pesticides manufactured or formulated by a subsidiary company meet appropriate quality requirements and standards. These should be consistent with the requirements of the host country and of the parent company;

8.2.4 encourage importing agencies, national or regional formulators and their respective trade organizations to cooperate in order to achieve fair practices as well as marketing and distribution practices that reduce the risks posed by pesticides, and to collaborate with authorities in stamping out any malpractice within the industry;

8.2.5 recognize that a pesticide may need to be recalled by a manufacturer and distributor when its use, as recommended, represents an unacceptable risk to human and animal health or the environment, and act accordingly;

8.2.6 endeavour to ensure that pesticides are traded by and purchased from reputable traders, who should preferably be members of a recognized trade organization;

8.2.7 ensure that persons involved in the sale of pesticides are trained adequately, hold appropriate government licences (where such licences exist) and have access to sufficient information, such as material safety data sheets, so that they are capable of providing buyers with advice on risk reduction and efficient use;

8.2.8 provide, consistent with national requirements, a range of pack sizes and types that are appropriate for the needs of small-scale farmers and other local users, in order to reduce risks and to discourage sellers from repackaging products in unlabelled or inappropriate containers.

**Article 9: Information Exchange**

9.4 All parties should:

9.4.1 support the process of information exchange and facilitate access to information regarding pesticide residues in food and related regulatory actions;

9.4.2 encourage collaboration between public sector groups, international organizations, governments and other interested stakeholders to ensure that countries are provided with the information they need to meet the objectives of the Code.

**Article 10: Labelling, Packaging, Storage and Disposal**

10.1 All pesticide containers should be clearly labelled in accordance with applicable guidelines, at least in line with the FAO guidelines on good labelling practice.

10.2 Industry should use labels that:

10.2.1 comply with registration requirements and include recommendations consistent with those of the recognized research and advisory agencies in the country of sale;

10.2.2 include appropriate symbols and pictograms whenever possible, in addition to written instructions, warnings and precautions in the appropriate language or languages;

10.2.3 comply with national or international labelling requirements for dangerous goods in international trade and, if appropriate, clearly show the appropriate WHO hazard classification of the contents;

10.2.4 include, in the appropriate language or languages, a warning against the reuse of containers and instructions for the safe disposal or decontamination of used containers;

10.2.5 identify each lot or batch of the product in numbers or letters that can be understood without the need for additional code references;

10.2.6 clearly show the release date (month and year) of the lot or batch and contain relevant information on the storage stability of the product.

10.3 Pesticide industry, in cooperation with government, should ensure that:

10.3.1 packaging, storage and disposal of pesticides conform in principle to the relevant FAO, UNEP, WHO guidelines or regulations or to other international guidelines, where applicable;

10.3.2 packaging or repackaging is carried out only on licensed premises where the responsible authority is satisfied that staff are adequately protected against toxic hazards, that the resulting product will be properly packaged and labelled, and that the content will conform to the relevant quality standards.

10.5 Governments, with the help of pesticide industry and with multilateral cooperation, should inventory obsolete or unusable stocks of pesticides and used containers, establish and implement an action plan for their disposal, or remediation in the case of contaminated sites, and record these activities.

10.6 Pesticide industry should be encouraged, with multilateral cooperation, to assist in disposing of any banned or obsolete pesticides and of used containers, in an environmentally sound manner, including reuse with minimal risk where approved and appropriate.

10.7 Governments, pesticide industry, international organizations and the agricultural community should implement policies and practices to prevent the accumulation of obsolete pesticides and used containers.

**Article 11: Advertising**

11.2 Pesticide industry should ensure that:

11.2.1 all statements used in advertising are technically justified;

11.2.2 advertisements do not contain any statement or visual presentation which, directly or by implication, omission, ambiguity or exaggerated claim, is likely to mislead the buyer, in particular with regard to the 'safety' of the product, its nature, composition or suitability for use, official recognition or approval;

11.2.3 pesticides which are legally restricted to use by trained or registered operators are not publicly advertised through journals other than those catering for such operators, unless the restricted availability is clearly and prominently shown;

11.2.4 no company or individual in any one country simultaneously markets different pesticide active ingredients or combinations of ingredients under a single brand name;

11.2.5 advertising does not encourage uses other than those specified on the approved label;

11.2.6 promotional material does not include recommendations at variance with those of the recognized research and advisory agencies;

11.2.7 advertisements do not misuse research results, quotations from technical and scientific literature or scientific jargon to make claims appear to have a scientific basis they do not possess;

11.2.8 claims as to safety, including statements such as 'safe', 'non-poisonous', 'harmless', 'non-toxic' or 'compatible with IPM', are not made without a qualifying phrase such as 'when used as directed'. [However, reference to use within specified IPM programmes may be included if validated by the regulating authority and the claim qualified accordingly];

11.2.9 statements comparing the risk, hazard or 'safety' of different pesticides or other substances are not made;

11.2.10 misleading statements are not made concerning the effectiveness of the product;

11.2.11 no guarantees or implied guarantees, such as 'more profits with . . .' or 'guarantees high yields', are given unless definite evidence to substantiate such claims is available;

11.2.12 advertisements do not contain any visual representation of potentially dangerous practices, such as mixing or application without sufficient protective clothing, use near food or use by or in the vicinity of children;

11.2.13 advertising or promotional material draws attention to the appropriate warning phrases and symbols as laid down in the FAO labelling guidelines;

11.2.14 technical literature provides adequate information on correct practices, including the observance of recommended application rates, frequency of applications and pre-harvest intervals;

11.2.15 false or misleading comparisons with other pesticides are not made;

11.2.16 all staff involved in sales promotion are adequately trained and possess sufficient technical knowledge to present complete, accurate and valid information on the products sold;

11.2.17 advertisements encourage purchasers and users to read the label carefully, or have the label read to them if they cannot read;

11.2.18 advertisements and promotional activities should not include inappropriate incentives or gifts to encourage the purchase of pesticides.

### Article 12: Monitoring and Observance of the Code

12.1 The Code should be published and should be observed through collaborative action on the part of governments, individually or in regional groupings, appropriate organizations and bodies of the UN system, international, governmental and non-governmental organizations and the pesticide industry.

12.2 The Code should be brought to the attention of all concerned in the regulation, manufacture, distribution and use of pesticides, so that governments, individually or in regional groupings, pesticide industry, international institutions, pesticide user organizations, agricultural commodity industries and food industry groups (such as supermarkets) that are in a position to influence good agricultural practices, understand their shared responsibilities in working together to ensure that the objectives of the Code are achieved.

12.3 All parties should observe this Code and should promote the principles and ethics expressed by the Code, irrespective of other parties' ability to observe the Code. Pesticide industry should cooperate fully in the observance of the Code and promote the principles and ethics expressed by the Code, irrespective of a government's ability to observe the Code.

12.8 Pesticide industry is invited to provide reports to the Director-General of FAO on its product stewardship activities related to observance of the Code.

12.9 NGOs and other interested parties are invited to monitor activities related to the implementation of the Code and report these to the Director General of FAO . . .

# 57. UN: Framework Convention on Climate Change, 1992

**Commentary**: The UNFCCC (1771 *UNTS* 107) seeks to stabilise greenhouse gas emissions 'at a level that would prevent dangerous anthropogenic (human induced) interference with the climate system'. The contributions made by corporations to climate change is also of interest: UNCTC (1992), 'Climate Change and TNCs: Analysis and Trends', New York, UN Doc ST/CTC/112. In 1995, the Intergovernmental Panel on Climate Change confirmed the discernible human influence upon the global climate. As a framework agreement, the UNFCCC identifies commitments to be augmented over time such as updated inventories of greenhouse gas emissions. It also places the heaviest burdens upon industrialised States (Annex II countries). Annex I countries are industrialised economies and those States undergoing economic transition. In addition to the provisions below, all governments undertake to provide public access to information and ensure public participation in addressing climate change and its effects (Article 6). The financial mechanism contemplated by Article 11 includes modalities ensuring that projects funded to address climate change conform with accepted policies, programme priorities and eligibility criteria. See further, UNFCCC (2002), 'A Guide to the Climate Change Convention Process', Bonn (http://unfccc.int); UNFCCC/UNEP (2002), 'Climate Change Information Kit'. For commercial perspectives, see European Roundtable of Industrialists (ERT) (2000), 'Climate Change: How Governments and Industry Can Work Together', Brussels; ICC (2003), 'Climate Change: The Business View', Paris.

**Article 1: Definitions**

For the purposes of this Convention:

1. 'Adverse effects of climate change' means changes in the physical environment or biota resulting from climate change which have significant deleterious effects on the composition, resilience or productivity of natural and managed ecosystems or on the operation of socio-economic systems or on human health and welfare.
2. 'Climate change' means a change of climate which is attributed directly or indirectly to human activity that alters the composition of the global atmosphere and which is in addition to natural climate variability observed over comparable time periods.
3. 'Climate system' means the totality of the atmosphere, hydrosphere, biosphere and geosphere and their interactions.
4. 'Emissions' means the release of greenhouse gases and/or their precursors into the atmosphere over a specified area and period of time.
5. 'Greenhouse gases' means those gaseous constituents of the atmosphere, both natural and anthropogenic, that absorb and re-emit infrared radiation.

7. 'Reservoir' means a component or components of the climate system where a greenhouse gas or a precursor of a greenhouse gas is stored.
8. 'Sink' means any process, activity or mechanism which removes a greenhouse gas, an aerosol or a precursor of a greenhouse gas from the atmosphere.
9. 'Source' means any process or activity which releases a greenhouse gas, an aerosol or a precursor of a greenhouse gas into the atmosphere.

**Article 2: Objective**

The ultimate objective of this Convention and any related legal instruments that the Conference of the Parties may adopt is to achieve, in accordance with the relevant provisions of the Convention, stabilization of greenhouse gas concentrations in the atmosphere at a level that would prevent dangerous anthropogenic interference with the climate system. Such a level should be achieved within a time-frame sufficient to allow ecosystems to adapt naturally to climate change, to ensure that food production is not threatened and to enable economic development to proceed in a sustainable manner.

**Article 3: Principles**

In their actions to achieve the objective of the Convention and to implement its provisions, the Parties shall be guided, *inter alia*, by the following:

1. The Parties should protect the climate system for the benefit of present and future generations of humankind, on the basis of equity and in accordance with their common but differentiated responsibilities and respective capabilities. Accordingly, the developed country Parties should take the lead in combating climate change and the adverse effects thereof.
2. The specific needs and special circumstances of developing country Parties, especially those that are particularly vulnerable to the adverse effects of climate change, and of those Parties, especially developing country Parties, that would have to bear a disproportionate or abnormal burden under the Convention, should be given full consideration.
3. The Parties should take precautionary measures to anticipate, prevent or minimize the causes of climate change and mitigate its adverse effects. Where there are threats of serious or irreversible damage, lack of full scientific certainty should not be used as a reason for postponing such measures, taking into account that policies and measures to deal with climate change should be cost-effective so as to ensure global benefits at the lowest possible cost. To achieve this, such policies and measures should take into account different socio-economic contexts, be comprehensive, cover all relevant sources, sinks and reservoirs of greenhouse gases and adaptation, and comprise all economic sectors. Efforts to address climate change may be carried out cooperatively by interested Parties.
4. The Parties have a right to, and should, promote sustainable development. Policies and measures to protect the climate system against human-induced change should be appropriate for the specific conditions of each Party and should be integrated with national development programmes, taking into account that economic development is essential for adopting measures to address climate change.
5. The Parties should cooperate to promote a supportive and open international economic system that would lead to sustainable economic growth and development in all Parties,

particularly developing country Parties, thus enabling them better to address the problems of climate change. Measures taken to combat climate change, including unilateral ones, should not constitute a means of arbitrary or unjustifiable discrimination or a disguised restriction on international trade.

**Article 4: Commitments**

1. All Parties, taking into account their common but differentiated responsibilities and their specific national and regional development priorities, objectives and circumstances, shall:

   (a) Develop, periodically update, publish and make available to the Conference of the Parties, in accordance with Article 12, national inventories of anthropogenic emissions by sources and removals by sinks of all greenhouse gases not controlled by the Montreal Protocol, using comparable methodologies to be agreed upon by the Conference of the Parties;
   (b) Formulate, implement, publish and regularly update national and, where appropriate, regional programmes containing measures to mitigate climate change by addressing anthropogenic emissions by sources and removals by sinks of all greenhouse gases not controlled by the Montreal Protocol, and measures to facilitate adequate adaptation to climate change;
   (c) Promote and cooperate in the development, application and diffusion, including transfer, of technologies, practices and processes that control, reduce or prevent anthropogenic emissions of greenhouse gases not controlled by the Montreal Protocol in all relevant sectors, including the energy, transport, industry, agriculture, forestry and waste management sectors;
   (d) Promote sustainable management, and promote and cooperate in the conservation and enhancement, as appropriate, of sinks and reservoirs of all greenhouse gases not controlled by the Montreal Protocol, including biomass, forests and oceans as well as other terrestrial, coastal and marine ecosystems;
   (f) Take climate change considerations into account, to the extent feasible, in their relevant social, economic and environmental policies and actions, and employ appropriate methods, for example impact assessments, formulated and determined nationally, with a view to minimizing adverse effects on the economy, on public health and on the quality of the environment, of projects or measures undertaken by them to mitigate or adapt to climate change;
   (h) Promote and cooperate in the full, open and prompt exchange of relevant scientific, technological, technical, socio-economic and legal information related to the climate system and climate change, and to the economic and social consequences of various response strategies;
   (i) Promote and cooperate in education, training and public awareness related to climate change and encourage the widest participation in this process, including that of NGOs; and
   (j) Communicate to the Conference of the Parties information related to implementation, in accordance with Article 12.

2. The developed country Parties and other Parties included in Annex I commit themselves specifically as provided for in the following:

(a) Each of these Parties shall adopt national policies and take corresponding measures on the mitigation of climate change, by limiting its anthropogenic emissions of greenhouse gases and protecting and enhancing its greenhouse gas sinks and reservoirs. These policies and measures will demonstrate that developed countries are taking the lead in modifying longer-term trends in anthropogenic emissions consistent with the objective of the Convention, recognizing that the return by the end of the present decade to earlier levels of anthropogenic emissions of carbon dioxide and other greenhouse gases not controlled by the Montreal Protocol would contribute to such modification, and taking into account the differences in these Parties' starting points and approaches, economic structures and resource bases, the need to maintain strong and sustainable economic growth, available technologies and other individual circumstances, as well as the need for equitable and appropriate contributions by each of these Parties to the global effort regarding that objective. These Parties may implement such policies and measures jointly with other Parties and may assist other Parties in contributing to the achievement of the objective of the Convention and, in particular, that of this subparagraph;

(b) In order to promote progress to this end, each of these Parties shall communicate, within six months of the entry into force of the Convention for it and periodically thereafter, and in accordance with Article 12, detailed information on its policies and measures referred to in subparagraph (a) above, as well as on its resulting projected anthropogenic emissions by sources and removals by sinks of greenhouse gases not controlled by the Montreal Protocol for the period referred to in subparagraph (a), with the aim of returning individually or jointly to their 1990 levels these anthropogenic emissions of carbon dioxide and other greenhouse gases not controlled by the Montreal Protocol. This information will be reviewed by the Conference of the Parties, at its first session and periodically thereafter, in accordance with Article 7;

(e) Each of these Parties shall:

(i) Coordinate as appropriate with other such Parties, relevant economic and administrative instruments developed to achieve the objective of the Convention; and

(ii) Identify and periodically review its own policies and practices which encourage activities that lead to greater levels of anthropogenic emissions of greenhouse gases not controlled by the Montreal Protocol than would otherwise occur;

3. The developed country Parties and other developed Parties included in Annex II shall provide new and additional financial resources to meet the agreed full costs incurred by developing country Parties in complying with their obligations under Article 12, paragraph 1. They shall also provide such financial resources, including for the transfer of technology, needed by the developing country Parties to meet the agreed full incremental costs of implementing measures that are covered by paragraph 1 of this Article and that are agreed between a developing country Party and the international entity or entities referred to in Article 11, in accordance with that Article. The implementation of these commitments shall take into account the need for adequacy and predictability in the flow of funds and the importance of appropriate burden sharing among the developed country Parties.

5. The developed country Parties and other developed Parties included in Annex II shall take all practicable steps to promote, facilitate and finance, as appropriate, the transfer of, or access to, environmentally sound technologies and know-how to other Parties, particularly developing country Parties, to enable them to implement the provisions of the Convention. In this process, the developed country Parties shall support the development and enhancement of endogenous capacities and technologies of developing country Parties. Other Parties and organizations in a position to do so may also assist in facilitating the transfer of such technologies.
7. The extent to which developing country Parties will effectively implement their commitments under the Convention will depend on the effective implementation by developed country Parties of their commitments under the Convention related to financial resources and transfer of technology and will take fully into account that economic and social development and poverty eradication are the first and overriding priorities of the developing country Parties.
8. In the implementation of the commitments in this Article, the Parties shall give full consideration to what actions are necessary under the Convention, including actions related to funding, insurance and the transfer of technology, to meet the specific needs and concerns of developing country Parties arising from the adverse effects of climate change and/or the impact of the implementation of response measures, especially on:

   (a) Small island countries;
   (b) Countries with low-lying coastal areas;
   (c) Countries with arid and semi-arid areas, forested areas and areas liable to forest decay;
   (d) Countries with areas prone to natural disasters;
   (e) Countries with areas liable to drought and desertification;
   (f) Countries with areas of high urban atmospheric pollution;
   (g) Countries with areas with fragile ecosystems, including mountainous ecosystems;
   (h) Countries whose economies are highly dependent on income generated from the production, processing and export, and/or on consumption of fossil fuels and associated energy-intensive products; and
   (i) Land-locked and transit countries . . .

9. The Parties shall take full account of the specific needs and special situations of the least developed countries in their actions with regard to funding and transfer of technology.
10. The Parties shall, in accordance with Article 10, take into consideration in the implementation of the commitments of the Convention the situation of Parties, particularly developing country Parties, with economies that are vulnerable to the adverse effects of the implementation of measures to respond to climate change. This applies notably to Parties with economies that are highly dependent on income generated from the production, processing and export, and/or consumption of fossil fuels and associated energy-intensive products and/or the use of fossil fuels for which such Parties have serious difficulties in switching to alternatives.

**Article 7: Conference of the Parties**

1. A Conference of the Parties is hereby established.

2. The Conference of the Parties, as the supreme body of this Convention, shall keep under regular review the implementation of the Convention and any related legal instruments that the Conference of the Parties may adopt, and shall make, within its mandate, the decisions necessary to promote the effective implementation of the Convention. To this end, it shall:

   (1) Seek and utilize, where appropriate, the services and cooperation of, and information provided by, competent international organizations and intergovernmental and non-governmental bodies;

6. The United Nations, its specialized agencies and the International Atomic Energy Agency, as well as any State member thereof or observers thereto not Party to the Convention, may be represented at sessions of the Conference of the Parties as observers. Any body or agency, whether national or international, governmental or non-governmental, which is qualified in matters covered by the Convention, and which has informed the secretariat of its wish to be represented at a session of the Conference of the Parties as an observer, may be so admitted unless at least one third of the Parties present object. The admission and participation of observers shall be subject to the rules of procedure adopted by the Conference of the Parties.

**Article 10: Subsidiary Body for Implementation**

1. A subsidiary body for implementation is hereby established to assist the Conference of the Parties in the assessment and review of the effective implementation of the Convention. This body shall be open to participation by all Parties and comprise government representatives who are experts on matters related to climate change. It shall report regularly to the Conference of the Parties on all aspects of its work . . .

**Article 11: Financial Mechanism**

1. A mechanism for the provision of financial resources on a grant or concessional basis, including for the transfer of technology, is hereby defined. It shall function under the guidance of and be accountable to the Conference of the Parties, which shall decide on its policies, programme priorities and eligibility criteria related to this Convention. Its operation shall be entrusted to one or more existing international entities . . .

**Article 12: Communication of Information related to Implementation**

1. In accordance with Article 4, paragraph 1, each Party shall communicate to the Conference of the Parties, through the secretariat, the following elements of information:

   (a) A national inventory of anthropogenic emissions by sources and removals by sinks of all greenhouse gases not controlled by the Montreal Protocol, to the extent its capacities permit, using comparable methodologies to be promoted and agreed upon by the Conference of the Parties;
   (b) A general description of steps taken or envisaged by the Party to implement the Convention; and

(c) Any other information that the Party considers relevant to the achievement of the objective of the Convention and suitable for inclusion in its communication, including, if feasible, material relevant for calculations of global emission trends.

9. Information received by the secretariat that is designated by a Party as confidential, in accordance with criteria to be established by the Conference of the parties, shall be aggregated by the secretariat to protect its confidentiality before being made available to any of the bodies involved in the communication and review of information.

# 58. UN: Kyoto Protocol to the UN Framework Convention on Climate Change, 1997

**Commentary**: Commercial roles under the Kyoto Protocol (37 *ILM* 22 (1998), entry into force 2005) are not limited to technology transfer. The private sector can participate within three 'flexibility mechanisms'. First, international emissions trading under Article 17 allows Annex I Parties (developed States) to buy or sell assigned emission amounts with other Annex I Parties. Second, Annex I Parties may acquire carbon credits (credits for emissions avoided or emission reduction units) by investing in projects within Annex I States (joint implementation arising under Articles 3, 4 & 6). Third, Annex I Parties may acquire certified emissions reductions by investing within non-Annex I Parties (developing States) in projects leading to 'real, measurable and long-term' greenhouse gas reductions through the clean development mechanism of Article 12. In addition to the provisions below, Articles 7 and 8 contemplate a compliance procedure and periodical review pursuant to Article 9 'in the light of the best available scientific information and assessments on climate change and its impacts, as well as relevant technical, social and economic information'. Article 11 envisages developed country Parties providing financial resources to developing country Parties for technology transfer purposes. Article 15 provides for a Subsidiary Body for Scientific and Technological Advice and a Subsidiary Body for Implementation. Annex A identifies several greenhouse gases, energy sources, industrial processes, agricultural techniques and waste. Annex B contains a list of the Party Quantified emission limitation or reduction commitment. Of the decisions adopted at Marrakech during 2001, see in particular those concerning technology transfer (Decision 4/CP.7), the clean development mechanism (Decision 17/CP.17) and emissions trading (Decision 18/CP.7). On emissions trading, see EC Directive 2003/87/EC as amended by Directive 2004/101/EC establishing a scheme for greenhouse gas emission allowance trading within the Community. For commercial perspectives, see US BRT (1998), 'The Kyoto Protocol: A Gap Analysis', Washington, DC; US BRT (1999), 'Trade and Industry Impacts of the Kyoto Protocol', Washington, DC; ICC (1999), 'Monitoring, compliance, enforcement and liability under the Kyoto Protocol: an international perspective', Paris; ICC/USCIB (1999), 'The Kyoto Mechanisms: A Business Perspective', Paris; ICC (2003), 'The Role of Companies in Kyoto Mechanisms', Paris; IPIECA (2000), 'Summary Text of the IPIECA Workshop on the Kyoto Mechanisms: Practical Application of the Kyoto Mechanisms–Opportunities and Issues', Milan; IPIECA (2000), 'Opportunities, Issues and Barriers to the Practical Application of the Kyoto Mechanisms', London; IPIECA/International Association of Oil and Gas Producers/American Petroleum Institute (2003), 'Petroleum Industry Guidelines for Reporting Greenhouse Gas Emissions' (available through www.ipieca.org). See also, International Conference for Renewable Energies, 'Policy Recommendations for Renewable Energies', 2004 (www.renewables2004.de/en/2004/outcome_recommendations.asp) especially Chapter V(2) on the role of energy producers and the financial industry.

**Article 2**

1. Each Party included in Annex I, in achieving its quantified emission limitation and reduction commitments under Article 3, in order to promote sustainable development, shall:

   (a) Implement and/or further elaborate policies and measures in accordance with its national circumstances, such as:

      (i) Enhancement of energy efficiency in relevant sectors of the national economy;
      (ii) Protection and enhancement of sinks and reservoirs of greenhouse gases not controlled by the Montreal Protocol, taking into account its commitments under relevant international environmental agreements; promotion of sustainable forest management practices, afforestation and reforestation;
      (iii) Promotion of sustainable forms of agriculture in light of climate change considerations;
      (iv) Research on, and promotion, development and increased use of, new and renewable forms of energy, of carbon dioxide sequestration technologies and of advanced and innovative environmentally sound technologies;
      (v) Progressive reduction or phasing out of market imperfections, fiscal incentives, tax and duty exemptions and subsidies in all greenhouse gas emitting sectors that run counter to the objective of the Convention and application of market instruments;
      (vi) Encouragement of appropriate reforms in relevant sectors aimed at promoting policies and measures which limit or reduce emissions of greenhouse gases not controlled by the Montreal Protocol;
      (vii) Measures to limit and/or reduce emissions of greenhouse gases not controlled by the Montreal Protocol in the transport sector;
      (viii) Limitation and/or reduction of methane emissions through recovery and use in waste management, as well as in the production, transport and distribution of energy . . .

2. The Parties included in Annex I shall pursue limitation or reduction of emissions of greenhouse gases not controlled by the Montreal Protocol from aviation and marine bunker fuels, working through the International Civil Aviation Organization and the International Maritime Organization, respectively . . .

**Article 3**

1. The Parties included in Annex I shall, individually or jointly, ensure that their aggregate anthropogenic carbon dioxide equivalent emissions of the greenhouse gases listed in Annex A do not exceed their assigned amounts, calculated pursuant to their quantified emission limitation and reduction commitments inscribed in Annex B and in accordance with the provisions of this Article, with a view to reducing their overall emissions of such gases by at least 5 per cent below 1990 levels in the commitment period 2008 to 2012.
2. Each Party included in Annex I shall, by 2005, have made demonstrable progress in achieving its commitments under this Protocol.

3. The net changes in greenhouse gas emissions by sources and removals by sinks resulting from direct human-induced land-use change and forestry activities, limited to afforestation, reforestation and deforestation since 1990, measured as verifiable changes in carbon stocks in each commitment period, shall be used to meet the commitments under this Article of each Party included in Annex I . . .
5. The Parties included in Annex I undergoing the process of transition to a market economy whose base year or period was established pursuant to decision 9/CP.2 of the Conference of the Parties at its second session shall use that base year or period for the implementation of their commitments under this Article.
7. In the first quantified emission limitation and reduction commitment period, from 2008 to 2012, the assigned amount for each Party included in Annex I shall be equal to the percentage inscribed for it in Annex B of its aggregate anthropogenic carbon dioxide equivalent emissions of the greenhouse gases listed in Annex A in 1990, or the base year or period determined in accordance with paragraph 5 above, multiplied by five. Those Parties included in Annex I for whom land-use change and forestry constituted a net source of greenhouse gas emissions in 1990 shall include in their 1990 emissions base year or period the aggregate anthropogenic carbon dioxide equivalent emissions by sources minus removals by sinks in 1990 from land-use change for the purposes of calculating their assigned amount.
8. Any Party included in Annex I may use 1995 as its base year for hydrofluorocarbons, perfluorocarbons and sulphur hexafluoride, for the purposes of the calculation referred to in paragraph 7 above . . .

**Article 5**

1. Each Party included in Annex I shall have in place, no later than one year prior to the start of the first commitment period, a national system for the estimation of anthropogenic emissions by sources and removals by sinks of all greenhouse gases not controlled by the Montreal protocol . . .

**Article 6**

1. For the purpose of meeting its commitments under Article 3, any Party included in Annex I may transfer to, or acquire from, any other such Party emission reduction units resulting from projects aimed at reducing anthropogenic emissions by sources or enhancing anthropogenic removals by sinks of greenhouse gases in any sector of the economy, provided that:

   (a) Any such project has the approval of the Parties involved;
   (b) Any such project provides a reduction in emissions by sources, or an enhancement of removals by sinks, that is additional to any that would otherwise occur;
   (c) It does not acquire any emission reduction units if it is not in compliance with its obligations under Articles 5 and 7; and
   (d) The acquisition of emission reduction units shall be supplemental to domestic actions for the purposes of meeting commitments under Article 3.

3. A Party included in Annex I may authorize legal entities to participate, under its responsibility, in actions leading to the generation, transfer or acquisition under this Article of emission reduction units.

**Article 7**

1. Each Party included in Annex I shall incorporate in its annual inventory of anthropogenic emissions by sources and removals by sinks of greenhouse gases not controlled by the Montreal Protocol submitted in accordance with the relevant decisions of the Conference of the Parties, the necessary supplementary information for the purposes of ensuring compliance with Article 3 . . .

**Article 10**

All Parties, taking into account their common but differentiated responsibilities and their specific national and regional development priorities, objectives and circumstances, without introducing any new commitments for Parties not included in Annex I, but reaffirming existing commitments under Article 4, paragraph 1, of the Convention, and continuing to advance the implementation of these commitments in order to achieve sustainable development, taking into account Article 4, paragraphs 3, 5 and 7, of the Convention, shall:

(b) Formulate, implement, publish and regularly update national and, where appropriate, regional programmes containing measures to mitigate climate change and measures to facilitate adequate adaptation to climate change:

  (i) Such programmes would, *inter alia*, concern the energy, transport and industry sectors as well as agriculture, forestry and waste management. Furthermore, adaptation technologies and methods for improving spatial planning would improve adaptation to climate change . . .

(c) Cooperate in the promotion of effective modalities for the development, application and diffusion of, and take all practicable steps to promote, facilitate and finance, as appropriate, the transfer of, or access to, environmentally sound technologies, know how, practices and processes pertinent to climate change, in particular to developing countries, including the formulation of policies and programmes for the effective transfer of environmentally sound technologies that are publicly owned or in the public domain and the creation of an enabling environment for the private sector, to promote and enhance the transfer of, and access to, environmentally sound technologies;

**Article 12**

1. A clean development mechanism is hereby defined.
2. The purpose of the clean development mechanism shall be to assist Parties not included in Annex I in achieving sustainable development and in contributing to the ultimate objective of the Convention, and to assist Parties included in Annex I in achieving compliance with their quantified emission limitation and reduction commitments under Article 3.
3. Under the clean development mechanism:

   (a) Parties not included in Annex I will benefit from project activities resulting in certified emission reductions; and
   (b) Parties included in Annex I may use the certified emission reductions accruing from such project activities to contribute to compliance with part of their quanti-

fied emission limitation and reduction commitments under Article 3, as determined by the Conference of the Parties serving as the meeting of the Parties to this Protocol.

5. Emission reductions resulting from each project activity shall be certified by operational entities to be designated by the Conference of the Parties serving as the meeting of the Parties to this Protocol, on the basis of:

   (a) Voluntary participation approved by each Party involved;
   (b) Real, measurable, and long-term benefits related to the mitigation of climate change; and
   (c) Reductions in emissions that are additional to any that would occur in the absence of the certified project activity.

6. The clean development mechanism shall assist in arranging funding of certified project activities as necessary.
9. Participation under the clean development mechanism, including in activities mentioned in paragraph 3(a) above and in the acquisition of certified emission reductions, may involve private and/or public entities, and is to be subject to whatever guidance may be provided by the executive board of the clean development mechanism . . .

**Article 17**
The Conference of the Parties shall define the relevant principles, modalities, rules and guidelines, in particular for verification, reporting and accountability for emissions trading. The Parties included in Annex B may participate in emissions trading for the purposes of fulfilling their commitments under Article 3. Any such trading shall be supplemental to domestic actions for the purpose of meeting quantified emission limitation and reduction commitments under that Article.

# 59. UNEP: Vienna Convention for the Protection of the Ozone Layer, 1985

**Commentary**: The ozone layer is situated between 10 and 50 km above the earth's surface and absorbs harmful ultraviolet-B (UV-B) solar radiation. The possibility of ozone depletion arising from human activity was first considered by UNEP in 1976 in reaction to scientific concerns: Molina M.J. and Rowland F.S. (1974), 'Stratospheric sink for chlorofluoromethanes: chlorine atom-catalysed destruction of ozone', *Nature*, **249**, 810–12. The Vienna Convention (1513 *UNTS* 293 (1985), extracts appearing below) encourages intergovernmental cooperation on research, systematic observation, monitoring CFC production and information exchange. However, it contains no obligation to reduce CFC production or consumption: see the Declarations made when adopting the Final Act at the Conference of Plenipotentiaries. Annex I identifies major scientific issues warranting further research and identifies chemical substances 'thought to have the potential to modify the chemical and physical properties of the ozone layer'. Annex II (below) contemplates exchanging commercial information. See also, Andersen S.O. and Madhava Sarma K. (2002), *Protecting the Ozone Layer: The UN History*, UNEP; UNEP (2002), 'Scientific Assessment of Ozone Depletion'; Technology & Economic Assessment Panel reports (available through www.unep.org/ozone/index.asp).

**Article 1: Definitions**

For the purposes of this Convention:

1. 'The ozone layer' means the layer of atmospheric ozone above the planetary boundary layer.
2. 'Adverse effects' means changes in the physical environment or biota, including changes in climate, which have significant deleterious effects on human health or on the composition, resilience and productivity of natural and managed ecosystems, or on materials useful to mankind.
3. 'Alternative technologies or equipment' means technologies or equipment the use of which makes it possible to reduce or effectively eliminate emissions of substances which have or are likely to have adverse effects on the ozone layer.
4. 'Alternative substances' means substances which reduce, eliminate or avoid adverse effects on the ozone layer.

**Article 2: General obligations**

1. The Parties shall take appropriate measures in accordance with the provisions of this Convention and of those protocols in force to which they are party to protect human

health and the environment against adverse effects resulting or likely to result from human activities which modify or are likely to modify the ozone layer.

2. To this end the Parties shall, in accordance with the means at their disposal and their capabilities:

   (a) Co-operate by means of systematic observations, research and information exchange in order to better understand and assess the effects of human activities on the ozone layer and the effects on human health and the environment from modification of the ozone layer;
   (b) Adopt appropriate legislative or administrative measures and co-operate in harmonizing appropriate policies to control, limit, reduce or prevent human activities under their jurisdiction or control should it be found that these activities have or are likely to have adverse effects resulting from modification or likely modification of the ozone layer . . .

4. The application of this article shall be based on relevant scientific and technical considerations.

**Article 3: Research and systematic observations**

1. The Parties undertake, as appropriate, to initiate and co-operate in, directly or through competent international bodies, the conduct of research and scientific assessments on:

   (a) The physical and chemical processes that may affect the ozone layer;
   (b) The human health and other biological effects deriving from any modifications of the ozone layer, particularly those resulting from changes in ultra-violet solar radiation having biological effects (UV-B);
   (c) Climatic effects deriving from any modifications of the ozone layer;
   (d) Effects deriving from any modifications of the ozone layer and any consequent change in UV-B radiation on natural and synthetic materials useful to mankind;
   (e) Substances, practices, processes and activities that may affect the ozone layer, and their cumulative effects;
   (f) Alternative substances and technologies;
   (g) Related socio-economic matters;

   and as further elaborated in annexes I and II . . .

**Article 4: Co-operation in the Legal, Scientific and Technical Fields**

1. The Parties shall facilitate and encourage the exchange of scientific, technical, socio-economic, commercial and legal information relevant to this Convention as further elaborated in annex II. Such information shall be supplied to bodies agreed upon by the Parties. Any such body receiving information regarded as confidential by the supplying Party shall ensure that such information is not disclosed and shall aggregate it to protect its confidentiality before it is made available to all Parties.
2. The Parties shall co-operate, consistent with their national laws, regulations and practices and taking into account in particular the needs of the developing countries, in

promoting, directly or through competent international bodies, the development and transfer of technology and knowledge . . .

**Annex II: Information Exchange**

1. The Parties to the Convention recognize that the collection and sharing of information is an important means of implementing the objectives of this Convention and of assuring that any actions that may be taken are appropriate and equitable. Therefore, Parties shall exchange scientific, technical, socio-economic, business, commercial and legal information.
2. The Parties to the Convention, in deciding what information is to be collected and exchanged, should take into account the usefulness of the information and the costs of obtaining it. The Parties further recognize that co-operation under this annex has to be consistent with national laws, regulations and practices regarding patents, trade secrets, and protection of confidential and proprietary information.
3. Scientific information
   This includes information on:

   (a) Planned and ongoing research, both governmental and private, to facilitate the coordination of research programmes so as to make the most effective use of available national and international resources;

4. Technical information
   This includes information on:

   (a) The availability and cost of chemical substitutes and of alternative technologies to reduce the emissions of ozone modifying substances and related planned and ongoing research;
   (b) The limitations and any risks involved in using chemical or other substitutes and alternative technologies.

5. Socio-economic and commercial information on the substances referred to in annex I
   This includes information on:

   (a) Production and production capacity;
   (b) Use and use patterns;
   (c) Imports/exports;
   (d) The costs, risks and benefits of human activities which may indirectly modify the ozone layer and of the impacts of regulatory actions taken or being considered to control these activities.

6. Legal information
   This includes information on:

   (c) Methods and terms of licensing and availability of patents relevant to the protection of the ozone layer.

# 60. UNEP: Montreal Protocol on Substances that Deplete the Ozone Layer, 1987

**Commentary**: The Montreal Protocol (1522 *UNTS* 3 (1987), entry into force 1989) is a Protocol to the preceding Vienna Convention. It was formulated so that phase-out schedules could be revised on the basis of periodic scientific and technological assessments. Article 2A (below) illustrates the consumption and production schedule for CFCs. Similar consumption and production schedules are contemplated with respect to halons (Article 2B), other fully halogenated CFCs (2C), carbon tetrachloride (2D), trichloroethane or methyl chloroform (2E), hydrochlorofluorocarbons (2F), hydrobromofluorocarbons (2G), methyl bromide (2H) and bromochloromethane (2I). Article 3 identifies the method for calculating control levels. Articles 4 and 4A specify a schedule for banning the import of those controlled substances identified in the Annexes from Parties and non-Parties. Article 4B establishes a licensing system for importing and exporting new, used, recycled or reclaimed controlled substances listed in Annexes A, B, C and E. Article 5 provides that to meet domestic needs developing States may delay compliance for ten years. Article 6 contemplates assessing and reviewing control measures every four years by panels of appropriately qualified experts on the basis of available scientific, environmental, technical and economic information. Article 7 envisages reporting statistical data to the secretariat, Article 8 concerns non-compliance and Article 10 establishes a Multilateral Financing Fund. The Protocol was adjusted and/or amended to introduce new control measures and add other controlled substances in London (1990), Copenhagen (1992), Vienna (1995), Montreal (1997) and Beijing (1999). Annex A lists controlled substances having ozone-depleting potential based upon existing knowledge. Annexes B and C list controlled substances with ozone-depleting potential including the most commercially viable substances. Annex D lists products containing the controlled substances identified in Annex A and includes domestic or commercial refrigeration units, air conditioning systems and aerosol products. See further, UNEP (2000), 'Production and Consumption of Ozone Depleting Substances under the Montreal Protocol 1986–2000'; UNEP (2003), 'Synthesis of the 2002 Assessments of the Assessment Panels of the Montreal Protocol', UN Doc UNEP/OzL.Pro/WG.1/23/3. For a commercial perspective, see Alliance for Responsible CFC Policy (1987), *The Montreal Protocol: A Briefing Book*, Arlington, VA.

**Article 1: Definitions**
For the purposes of this Protocol:

4. 'Controlled substance' means a substance in Annex A, Annex B, Annex C or Annex E to this Protocol, whether existing alone or in a mixture. It includes the isomers of any

such substance, except as specified in the relevant Annex, but excludes any controlled substance or mixture which is in a manufactured product other than a container used for the transportation or storage of that substance.

5. 'Production' means the amount of controlled substances produced, minus the amount destroyed by technologies to be approved by the Parties and minus the amount entirely used as feedstock in the manufacture of other chemicals. The amount recycled and reused is not to be considered as 'production'.
6. 'Consumption' means production plus imports minus exports of controlled substances.
7. 'Calculated levels' of production, imports, exports and consumption means levels determined in accordance with Article 3.
8. 'Industrial rationalization' means the transfer of all or a portion of the calculated level of production of one Party to another, for the purpose of achieving economic efficiencies or responding to anticipated shortfalls in supply as a result of plant closures.

**Article 2: Control Measures**

5. Any Party may, for one or more control periods, transfer to another Party any portion of its calculated level of production set out in Articles 2A to 2F, and Article 2H [Articles 2B–2F, 2H not reproduced], provided that the total combined calculated levels of production of the Parties concerned for any group of controlled substances do not exceed the production limits set out in those Articles for that group . . .
9. (a) Based on the assessments made pursuant to Article 6, the Parties may decide whether:

   (i) Adjustments to the ozone depleting potentials specified in Annex A, Annex B, Annex C and/or Annex E should be made and, if so, what the adjustments should be; and
   (ii) Further adjustments and reductions of production or consumption of the controlled substances should be undertaken and, if so, what the scope, amount and timing of any such adjustments and reductions should be . . .

**Article 2A: CFCs**

1. Each Party shall ensure that for the twelve-month period commencing on the first day of the seventh month following the date of entry into force of this Protocol, and in each twelve-month period thereafter, its calculated level of consumption of the controlled substances in Group I of Annex A does not exceed its calculated level of consumption in 1986. By the end of the same period, each Party producing one or more of these substances shall ensure that its calculated level of production of the substances does not exceed its calculated level of production in 1986, except that such level may have increased by no more than ten per cent based on the 1986 level. Such increase shall be permitted only so as to satisfy the basic domestic needs of the Parties operating under Article 5 and for the purposes of industrial rationalization between Parties.
2. Each Party shall ensure that for the period from 1 July 1991 to 31 December 1992 its calculated levels of consumption and production of the controlled substances in Group I of Annex A do not exceed 150 per cent of its calculated levels of production and consumption of those substances in 1986 . . .

3. Each Party shall ensure that for the twelve-month period commencing on 1 January 1994, and in each twelve-month period thereafter, its calculated level of consumption of the controlled substances in Group I of Annex A does not exceed, annually, twenty-five per cent of its calculated level of consumption in 1986. Each Party producing one or more of these substances shall, for the same periods, ensure that its calculated level of production of the substances does not exceed, annually, twenty-five per cent of its calculated level of production in 1986. However, in order to satisfy the basic domestic needs of the Parties operating under paragraph 1 of Article 5, its calculated level of production may exceed that limit by up to ten per cent of its calculated level of production in 1986.
4. Each Party shall ensure that for the twelve-month period commencing on 1 January 1996, and in each twelve-month period thereafter, its calculated level of consumption of the controlled substances in Group I of Annex A does not exceed zero. Each Party producing one or more of these substances shall, for the same periods, ensure that its calculated level of production of the substances does not exceed zero. However, in order to satisfy the basic domestic needs of the Parties operating under paragraph 1 of Article 5, its calculated level of production may exceed that limit by a quantity equal to the annual average of its production of the controlled substances in Group I of Annex A for basic domestic needs for the period 1995 to 1997 inclusive. This paragraph will apply save to the extent that the Parties decide to permit the level of production or consumption that is necessary to satisfy uses agreed by them to be essential.
5. Each Party shall ensure that for the twelve-month period commencing on 1 January 2003 and in each twelve-month period thereafter, its calculated level of production of the controlled substances in Group I of Annex A for the basic domestic needs of the Parties operating under paragraph 1 of Article 5 does not exceed eighty per cent of the annual average of its production of those substances for basic domestic needs for the period 1995 to 1997 inclusive.
6. Each Party shall ensure that for the twelve-month period commencing on 1 January 2005 and in each twelve-month period thereafter, its calculated level of production of the controlled substances in Group I of Annex A for the basic domestic needs of the Parties operating under paragraph 1 of Article 5 does not exceed fifty per cent of the annual average of its production of those substances for basic domestic needs for the period 1995 to 1997 inclusive.
7. Each Party shall ensure that for the twelve-month period commencing on 1 January 2007 and in each twelve-month period thereafter, its calculated level of production of the controlled substances in Group I of Annex A for the basic domestic needs of the Parties operating under paragraph 1 of Article 5 does not exceed fifteen per cent of the annual average of its production of those substances for basic domestic needs for the period 1995 to 1997 inclusive.
8. Each Party shall ensure that for the twelve-month period commencing on 1 January 2010 and in each twelve-month period thereafter, its calculated level of production of the controlled substances in Group I of Annex A for the basic domestic needs of the Parties operating under paragraph 1 of Article 5 does not exceed zero.
9. For the purposes of calculating basic domestic needs under paragraphs 4 to 8 of this Article, the calculation of the annual average of production by a Party includes any production entitlements that it has transferred in accordance with paragraph 5 of Article 2, and excludes any production entitlements that it has acquired in accordance with paragraph 5 of Article 2.

**Article 5: Special Situation of Developing Countries**

1. Any Party that is a developing country and whose annual calculated level of consumption of the controlled substances in Annex A is less than 0.3 kilograms per capita on the date of the entry into force of the Protocol for it, or any time thereafter until 1 January 1999, shall, in order to meet its basic domestic needs, be entitled to delay for ten years its compliance with the control measures set out in Articles 2A to 2E, provided that any further amendments to the adjustments or Amendment adopted at the Second Meeting of the Parties in London, 29 June 1990, shall apply to the Parties operating under this paragraph after the review provided for in paragraph 8 of this Article has taken place and shall be based on the conclusions of that review . . .

**Article 6: Assessment and Review of Control Measures**

Beginning in 1990, and at least every four years thereafter, the Parties shall assess the control measures provided for in Article 2 and Article 2A to 2I on the basis of available scientific, environmental, technical and economic information. At least one year before each assessment, the Parties shall convene appropriate panels of experts qualified in the fields mentioned and determine the composition and terms of reference of any such panels. Within one year of being convened, the panels will report their conclusions, through the Secretariat, to the Parties.

**Article 9: Research, Development, Public Awareness and Exchange of Information**

1. The Parties shall co-operate, consistent with their national laws, regulations and practices and taking into account in particular the needs of developing countries, in promoting, directly or through competent international bodies, research, development and exchange of information on:

   (a) best technologies for improving the containment, recovery, recycling, or destruction of controlled substances or otherwise reducing their emissions;
   (b) possible alternatives to controlled substances, to products containing such substances, and to products manufactured with them; and
   (c) costs and benefits of relevant control strategies . . .

**Article 10A: Transfer of Technology**

Each Party shall take every practicable step, consistent with the programmes supported by the financial mechanism, to ensure:

(a) that the best available, environmentally safe substitutes and related technologies are expeditiously transferred to Parties operating under paragraph 1 of Article 5; and
(b) that the transfers referred to in subparagraph (a) occur under fair and most favourable conditions.

# 61. UNEP: Convention on Biological Diversity, 1992

**Commentary**: The CBD (31 *ILM* 818 (1992), entry into force 1994) seeks to preserve the variety of life on earth and promote sustainable development. For the views of the US during negotiations, see Declaration made at the UNEP Conference for the Adoption of the Agreed Text of the CBD (1992) 31 *ILM* 848. In addition to the provisions below, Article 7 contemplates identifying and monitoring biodiversity components. Article 8 addresses measures promoting *in situ* biodiversity conservation whereas Article 9 applies to *ex situ* conservation. States Parties under Article 11 shall adopt economically and socially sound incentive measures for conserving and sustainably using biodiversity. Article 12 envisages governments promoting research and training. Under Article 13, governments will promote the importance of biodiversity through the media. Article 14 provides for environmental impact assessments for those projects likely to have significant adverse effects upon biodiversity, public participation therein and notification, information exchange and consultation for activities under national jurisdiction or control. Article 14 moreover envisages governments examining questions of liability, redress, restoration and compensation. For commercial perspectives, see ICC (1992), 'Comments on the UN CBD', Paris; WBCSD/World Conservation Union (1997), 'Business and Biodiversity: A Guide for the Private Sector', Geneva. See further, www.biodiv.org.

### Article 1. Objectives

The objectives of this Convention, to be pursued in accordance with its relevant provisions, are the conservation of biological diversity, the sustainable use of its components and the fair and equitable sharing of the benefits arising out of the utilization of genetic resources, including by appropriate access to genetic resources and by appropriate transfer of relevant technologies, taking into account all rights over those resources and to technologies, and by appropriate funding.

### Article 2. Use of Terms

For the purposes of this Convention:

'Biological diversity' means the variability among living organisms from all sources including, *inter alia*, terrestrial, marine and other aquatic ecosystems and the ecological complexes of which they are part; this includes diversity within species, between species and of ecosystems.

'Biological resources' includes genetic resources, organisms or parts thereof, populations, or any other biotic component of ecosystems with actual or potential use or value for humanity.

'Biotechnology' means any technological application that uses biological systems, living organisms, or derivatives thereof, to make or modify products or processes for specific use.

'Country of origin of genetic resources' means the country which possesses those genetic resources in *in-situ* conditions.

'Country providing genetic resources' means the country supplying genetic resources collected from *in-situ* sources, including populations of both wild and domesticated species, or taken from *ex-situ* sources, which may or may not have originated in that country.

'Domesticated or cultivated species' means species in which the evolutionary process has been influenced by humans to meet their needs.

'Ecosystem' means a dynamic complex of plant, animal and micro-organism communities and their non-living environment interacting as a functional unit.

'*Ex-situ* conservation' means the conservation of components of biological diversity outside their natural habitats.

'Genetic material' means any material of plant, animal, microbial or other origin containing functional units of heredity.

'Genetic resources' means genetic material of actual or potential value.

'Habitat' means the place or type of site where an organism or population naturally occurs.

'*In-situ* conditions' means conditions where genetic resources exist within ecosystems and natural habitats, and, in the case of domesticated or cultivated species, in the surroundings where they have developed their distinctive properties.

'*In-situ* conservation' means the conservation of ecosystems and natural habitats and the maintenance and recovery of viable populations of species in their natural surroundings and, in the case of domesticated or cultivated species, in the surroundings where they have developed their distinctive properties.

'Protected area' means a geographically defined area which is designated or regulated and managed to achieve specific conservation objectives.

'Sustainable use' means the use of components of biological diversity in a way and at a rate that does not lead to the long-term decline of biological diversity, thereby maintaining its potential to meet the needs and aspirations of present and future generations.

'Technology' includes biotechnology.

**Article 10. Sustainable Use of Components of Biological Diversity**
Each Contracting Party shall, as far as possible and as appropriate:

(e) Encourage cooperation between its governmental authorities and its private sector in developing methods for sustainable use of biological resources.

**Article 15. Access to Genetic Resources**

2. Each Contracting Party shall endeavour to create conditions to facilitate access to genetic resources for environmentally sound uses by other Contracting Parties and not to impose restrictions that run counter to the objectives of this Convention . . .
7. Each Contracting Party shall take legislative, administrative or policy measures, as appropriate, and in accordance with Articles 16 and 19 and, where necessary, through the financial mechanism established by Articles 20 and 21 with the aim of sharing in a fair and equitable way the results of research and development and the benefits arising from the commercial and other utilization of genetic resources with the Contracting Party providing such resources. Such sharing shall be upon mutually agreed terms.

**Article 16. Access to and Transfer of Technology**

1. Each Contracting Party, recognizing that technology includes biotechnology, and that both access to and transfer of technology among Contracting Parties are essential elements for the attainment of the objectives of this Convention, undertakes subject to the provisions of this Article to provide and/or facilitate access for and transfer to other Contracting Parties of technologies that are relevant to the conservation and sustainable use of biological diversity or make use of genetic resources and do not cause significant damage to the environment.
2. Access to and transfer of technology referred to in paragraph 1 above to developing countries shall be provided and/or facilitated under fair and most favourable terms, including on concessional and preferential terms where mutually agreed, and, where necessary, in accordance with the financial mechanism established by Articles 20 and 21. In the case of technology subject to patents and other intellectual property rights, such access and transfer shall be provided on terms which recognize and are consistent with the adequate and effective protection of intellectual property rights. The application of this paragraph shall be consistent with paragraphs 3, 4 and 5 below.
3. Each Contracting Party shall take legislative, administrative or policy measures, as appropriate, with the aim that Contracting Parties, in particular those that are developing countries, which provide genetic resources are provided access to and transfer of technology which makes use of those resources, on mutually agreed terms, including technology protected by patents and other intellectual property rights, where necessary, through the provisions of Articles 20 and 21 and in accordance with international law and consistent with paragraphs 4 and 5 below.
4. Each Contracting Party shall take legislative, administrative or policy measures, as appropriate, with the aim that the private sector facilitates access to, joint development and transfer of technology referred to in paragraph 1 above for the benefit of both governmental institutions and the private sector of developing countries and in this regard shall abide by the obligations included in paragraphs 1, 2 and 3 above.

5. The Contracting Parties, recognizing that patents and other intellectual property rights may have an influence on the implementation of this Convention, shall cooperate in this regard subject to national legislation and international law in order to ensure that such rights are supportive of and do not run counter to its objectives.

**Article 19. Handling of Biotechnology and Distribution of its Benefits**

1. Each Contracting Party shall take legislative, administrative or policy measures, as appropriate, to provide for the effective participation in biotechnological research activities by those Contracting Parties, especially developing countries, which provide the genetic resources for such research, and where feasible in such Contracting Parties.
2. Each Contracting Party shall take all practicable measures to promote and advance priority access on a fair and equitable basis by Contracting Parties, especially developing countries, to the results and benefits arising from biotechnologies based upon genetic resources provided by those Contracting Parties. Such access shall be on mutually agreed terms.
3. The Parties shall consider the need for and modalities of a protocol setting out appropriate procedures, including in particular, advance informed agreement, in the field of the safe transfer, handling and use of any living modified organism resulting from biotechnology that may have adverse effect on the conservation and sustainable use of biological diversity.
4. Each Contracting Party shall, directly or by requiring any natural or legal person under its jurisdiction providing the organisms referred to in paragraph 3 above, provide any available information about the use and safety regulations required by that Contracting Party in handling such organisms, as well as any available information on the potential adverse impact of the specific organisms concerned to the Contracting Party into which those organisms are to be introduced.

**Article 20: Financial Resources**

1. Each Contracting Party undertakes to provide, in accordance with its capabilities, financial support and incentives in respect of those national activities which are intended to achieve the objectives of this Convention, in accordance with its national plans, priorities and programmes.
2. The developed country Parties shall provide new and additional financial resources to enable developing country Parties to meet the agreed full incremental costs to them of implementing measures which fulfil the obligations of this Convention and to benefit from its provisions and which costs are agreed between a developing country Party and the institutional structure referred to in Article 21, in accordance with policy, strategy, programme priorities and eligibility criteria and an indicative list of incremental costs established by the Conference of the Parties . . .
3. The developed country Parties may also provide, and developing country Parties avail themselves of, financial resources related to the implementation of this Convention through bilateral, regional and other multilateral channels.
4. The extent to which developing country Parties will effectively implement their commitments under this Convention will depend on the effective implementation by developed country Parties of their commitments under this Convention related to financial resources and transfer of technology and will take fully into account the fact that

economic and social development and eradication of poverty are the first and overriding priorities of the developing country Parties . . .

**Article 21: Financial Mechanism**

1. There shall be a mechanism for the provision of financial resources to developing country Parties for purposes of this Convention on a grant or concessional basis the essential elements of which are described in this Article . . . Voluntary contributions may also be made by the developed country Parties and by other countries and sources . . .

# 62. CBD: Cartagena Protocol on Biosafety to the Convention on Biological Diversity, 2000

**Commentary**: Furthering Article 19(3) of the CBD, the Protocol (39 *ILM* 1027 (2000), entry into force 2003) was formulated over three years by an Open-ended Ad Hoc Working Group on Biosafety established under COP Decision II/5 (1995). The Protocol was finally adopted through COP Decision EM-I/3 (2000) and seeks to protect biodiversity from the risks posed by living modified organisms (LMOs) resulting from modern biotechnology. It contemplates an advance informed agreement (AIA) procedure so that importing governments make informed decisions. The AIA procedure does not apply to LMOs in transit or destined for contained use in accordance with the standards of the importing Party (Article 6). The procedure applies to the first intentional transboundary movement of LMOs (Article 7). Importing Parties acknowledge receipt of notifications in writing within 90 days and the failure to do so does not imply consent (Article 9). Article 10 outlines the decision-making procedure for importing Parties to provide written consent, the terms thereof, applicable time-frames and reasons for decisions. Article 11 contemplates governments notifying the Biosafety Clearing House in respect of LMOs intended for direct use as food or feed or for processing. This process does not apply to decisions regarding field trials. Article 12 contemplates decision-making review including initiation by notifiers where a change in circumstances may influence the outcome of risk assessments or where additional relevant scientific or technical information is available. Article 13 provides for a simplified import procedure. Under Article 16, governments undertake risk assessments including ensuring that LMOs have undergone observation periods commensurate with their life-cycle or generation time before being put to their intended use. Governments under Article 17 notify affected ones when they know of occurrences which may lead to unintentional transboundary movements and consultation to determine appropriate responses including emergency measures. Under Article 18, governments ensure that LMOs are handled, packaged and transported under safe conditions including *inter alia* providing accompanying documentation which identifies importers and exporters. Under Article 23, governments are to promote public awareness, education and participation in decision-making. Annex I identifies information required for notifications under Articles 8, 10 and 13. Annex II identifies information required with respect to LMOs intended for direct use as food or feed or for processing under Article 11. Annex III describes the objectives, methodology and considerations relevant to risk assessment. For commercial perspectives, see USCIB (1992), 'Business Statement on the Biosafety Protocol', New York.

**Article 1: Objective**

In accordance with the precautionary approach contained in Principle 15 of the Rio Declaration on Environment and Development, the objective of this Protocol is to contribute to ensuring an adequate level of protection in the field of the safe transfer, handling and use of living modified organisms resulting from modern biotechnology that may have adverse effects on the conservation and sustainable use of biological diversity, taking also into account risks to human health, and specifically focusing on transboundary movements.

**Article 2: General Provisions**

3. Nothing in this Protocol shall affect in any way the sovereignty of States over their territorial sea established in accordance with international law, and the sovereign rights and the jurisdiction which States have in their exclusive economic zones and their continental shelves in accordance with international law, and the exercise by ships and aircraft of all States of navigational rights and freedoms as provided for in international law and as reflected in relevant international instruments.
5. The Parties are encouraged to take into account, as appropriate, available expertise, instruments and work undertaken in international forums with competence in the area of risks to human health.

**Article 3: Use of Terms**

For the purposes of this Protocol:

(b) 'Contained use' means any operation, undertaken within a facility, installation or other physical structure, which involves living modified organisms that are controlled by specific measures that effectively limit their contact with, and their impact on, the external environment;
(c) 'Export' means intentional transboundary movement from one Party to another Party;
(d) 'Exporter' means any legal or natural person, under the jurisdiction of the Party of export, who arranges for a living modified organism to be exported;
(e) 'Import' means intentional transboundary movement into one Party from another Party;
(f) 'Importer' means any legal or natural person, under the jurisdiction of the Party of import, who arranges for a living modified organism to be imported;
(g) 'Living modified organism' means any living organism that possesses a novel combination of genetic material obtained through the use of modern biotechnology;
(h) 'Living organism' means any biological entity capable of transferring or replicating genetic material, including sterile organisms, viruses and viroids;
(i) 'Modern biotechnology' means the application of:

a) In vitro nucleic acid techniques, including recombinant deoxyribonucleic acid (DNA) and direct injection of nucleic acid into cells or organelles, or
b) Fusion of cells beyond the taxonomic family, that overcome natural physiological reproductive or recombination barriers and that are not techniques used in traditional breeding and selection;

(k) 'Transboundary movement' means the movement of a living modified organism from one Party to another Party, save that for the purposes of Articles 17 and 24 transboundary movement extends to movement between Parties and non-Parties.

**Article 4: Scope**

This Protocol shall apply to the transboundary movement, transit, handling and use of all living modified organisms that may have adverse effects on the conservation and sustainable use of biological diversity, taking also into account risks to human health.

**Article 5: Pharmaceuticals**

Notwithstanding Article 4 and without prejudice to any right of a Party to subject all living modified organisms to risk assessment prior to the making of decisions on import, this Protocol shall not apply to the transboundary movement of living modified organisms which are pharmaceuticals for humans that are addressed by other relevant international agreements or organizations.

**Article 7: Application of the Advance Informed Agreement Procedure**

1. Subject to Articles 5 and 6, the advance informed agreement procedure in Articles 8 to 10 and 12 shall apply prior to the first intentional transboundary movement of living modified organisms for intentional introduction into the environment of the Party of import.
2. 'Intentional introduction into the environment' in paragraph 1 above, does not refer to living modified organisms intended for direct use as food or feed, or for processing.
3. Article 11 shall apply prior to the first transboundary movement of living modified organisms intended for direct use as food or feed, or for processing.
4. The advance informed agreement procedure shall not apply to the intentional transboundary movement of living modified organisms identified in a decision of the Conference of the Parties serving as the meeting of the Parties to this Protocol as being not likely to have adverse effects on the conservation and sustainable use of biological diversity, taking also into account risks to human health.

**Article 8: Notification**

1. The Party of export shall notify, or require the exporter to ensure notification to, in writing, the competent national authority of the Party of import prior to the intentional transboundary movement of a living modified organism that falls within the scope of Article 7, paragraph 1. The notification shall contain, at a minimum, the information specified in Annex I.
2. The Party of export shall ensure that there is a legal requirement for the accuracy of information provided by the exporter.

**Article 10: Decision Procedure**

1. Decisions taken by the Party of import shall be in accordance with Article 15.
2. The Party of import shall, within the period of time referred to in Article 9, inform the notifier, in writing, whether the intentional transboundary movement may proceed:

   (a) Only after the Party of import has given its written consent; or
   (b) After no less than ninety days without a subsequent written consent.

3. Within two hundred and seventy days of the date of receipt of notification, the Party of import shall communicate, in writing, to the notifier and to the Biosafety Clearing-House the decision referred to in paragraph 2 (a) above:

   (a) Approving the import, with or without conditions, including how the decision will apply to subsequent imports of the same living modified organism;
   (b) Prohibiting the import;
   (c) Requesting additional relevant information in accordance with its domestic regulatory framework or Annex I; in calculating the time within which the Party of import is to respond, the number of days it has to wait for additional relevant information shall not be taken into account; or
   (d) Informing the notifier that the period specified in this paragraph is extended by a defined period of time.

4. Except in a case in which consent is unconditional, a decision under paragraph 3 above, shall set out the reasons on which it is based.
5. A failure by the Party of import to communicate its decision within two hundred and seventy days of the date of receipt of the notification shall not imply its consent to an intentional transboundary movement.
6. Lack of scientific certainty due to insufficient relevant scientific information and knowledge regarding the extent of the potential adverse effects of a living modified organism on the conservation and sustainable use of biological diversity in the Party of import, taking also into account risks to human health, shall not prevent that Party from taking a decision, as appropriate, with regard to the import of the living modified organism in question as referred to in paragraph 3 above, in order to avoid or minimize such potential adverse effects . . .

**Article 11: Procedure for Living Modified Organisms Intended for Direct Use as Food or Feed, or For Processing**

1. A Party that makes a final decision regarding domestic use, including placing on the market, of a living modified organism that may be subject to transboundary movement for direct use as food or feed, or for processing shall, within fifteen days of making that decision, inform the Parties through the Biosafety Clearing-House. This information shall contain, at a minimum, the information specified in Annex II. The Party shall provide a copy of the information, in writing, to the national focal point of each Party that informs the Secretariat in advance that it does not have access to the Biosafety Clearing-House. This provision shall not apply to decisions regarding field trials.
2. The Party making a decision under paragraph 1 above, shall ensure that there is a legal requirement for the accuracy of information provided by the applicant . . .

**Article 15: Risk Assessment**

1. Risk assessments undertaken pursuant to this Protocol shall be carried out in a scientifically sound manner, in accordance with Annex III and taking into account recognized risk assessment techniques. Such risk assessments shall be based, at a minimum, on information provided in accordance with Article 8 and other available scientific evidence in order to identify and evaluate the possible adverse effects of living modified

organisms on the conservation and sustainable use of biological diversity, taking also into account risks to human health.

2. The Party of import shall ensure that risk assessments are carried out for decisions taken under Article 10. It may require the exporter to carry out the risk assessment.
3. The cost of risk assessment shall be borne by the notifier if the Party of import so requires.

**Article 17: Unintentional Transboundary Movements and Emergency Measures**

1. Each Party shall take appropriate measures to notify affected or potentially affected States, the Biosafety Clearing-House and, where appropriate, relevant international organizations, when it knows of an occurrence under its jurisdiction resulting in a release that leads, or may lead, to an unintentional transboundary movement of a living modified organism that is likely to have significant adverse effects on the conservation and sustainable use of biological diversity, taking also into account risks to human health in such States. The notification shall be provided as soon as the Party knows of the above situation . . .

**Article 21: Confidential Information**

1. The Party of import shall permit the notifier to identify information submitted under the procedures of this Protocol or required by the Party of import as part of the advance informed agreement procedure of the Protocol that is to be treated as confidential. Justification shall be given in such cases upon request.
2. The Party of import shall consult the notifier if it decides that information identified by the notifier as confidential does not qualify for such treatment and shall, prior to any disclosure, inform the notifier of its decision, providing reasons on request, as well as an opportunity for consultation and for an internal review of the decision prior to disclosure.
3. Each Party shall protect confidential information received under this Protocol, including any confidential information received in the context of the advance informed agreement procedure of the Protocol. Each Party shall ensure that it has procedures to protect such information and shall protect the confidentiality of such information in a manner no less favourable than its treatment of confidential information in connection with domestically produced living modified organisms.
4. The Party of import shall not use such information for a commercial purpose, except with the written consent of the notifier.
5. If a notifier withdraws or has withdrawn a notification, the Party of import shall respect the confidentiality of commercial and industrial information, including research and development information as well as information on which the Party and the notifier disagree as to its confidentiality.
6. Without prejudice to paragraph 5 above, the following information shall not be considered confidential:

   (a) The name and address of the notifier;
   (b) A general description of the living modified organism or organisms;
   (c) A summary of the risk assessment of the effects on the conservation and sustainable use of biological diversity, taking also into account risks to human health; and
   (d) Any methods and plans for emergency response.

**Article 22: Capacity Building**

1. The Parties shall cooperate in the development and/or strengthening of human resources and institutional capacities in biosafety, including biotechnology to the extent that it is required for biosafety, for the purpose of the effective implementation of this Protocol, in developing country Parties, in particular the least developed and small island developing States among them, and in Parties with economies in transition, including through existing global, regional, subregional and national institutions and organizations and, as appropriate, through facilitating private sector involvement . . .

**Article 24: Non-Parties**

1. Transboundary movements of living modified organisms between Parties and non-Parties shall be consistent with the objective of this Protocol. The Parties may enter into bilateral, regional and multilateral agreements and arrangements with non-Parties regarding such transboundary movements . . .

**Article 25: Illegal Transboundary Movements**

1. Each Party shall adopt appropriate domestic measures aimed at preventing and, if appropriate, penalizing transboundary movements of living modified organisms carried out in contravention of its domestic measures to implement this Protocol. Such movements shall be deemed illegal transboundary movements.
2. In the case of an illegal transboundary movement, the affected Party may request the Party of origin to dispose, at its own expense, of the living modified organism in question by repatriation or destruction, as appropriate.

# 63. CBD: Bonn Guidelines on Access to Genetic Resources and Fair and Equitable Sharing of the Benefits Arising out of their Utilisation, 2002

**Commentary**: Adopted by COP Decision VI/24 (2002), the Bonn Guidelines build upon Article 15 of the CBD. They were formulated in the light of their voluntary nature, ease of use, practicality, acceptability, complementarity, evolutionary approach, flexibility and transparency (para 7). Note that the terms defined under Article 2 CBD also apply to these Guidelines (para 8). National focal points are responsible for informing applicants for access to genetic resources on the procedures for acquiring prior informed consent and mutually agreed terms, including benefit-sharing (para 13). Appendix I to the Bonn Guidelines lists suggested elements for material transfer agreements, Appendix II identifies monetary and non-monetary benefits and the Annex outlines draft elements for an action plan on capacity building including intellectual property rights. COP Decision VII/19 (2004) recognised 'that the Guidelines are making a useful contribution to the development of national regimes and contractual arrangements for access and benefit-sharing and to the implementation of the objectives of the Convention'. See further, COP Decision VII/19 (2004). The Ad Hoc Open-ended Working Group on Access and Benefit-sharing has since prepared a prospective international regime on the topic: UN Doc UNEP/CBD/COP/7/6 (2004). For commercial perspectives, see CEFIC (2000), 'The Chemical Industry Comments on the Legal Protection of Traditional Knowledge and Access to Genetic Resources-Patenting', Brussels. For academic commentary, see Tully S. (2003), 'The Bonn Guidelines on Access to Genetic Resources and Benefit-Sharing', *Review of European Community and International Environmental Law*, **12** (1), 84–98. See also, FAO Conference Resolution 3/2001, International Treaty on Plant Genetic Resources for Food and Agriculture, Resolution adopted at the Thirty-First Session.

**General Provisions**

1. These Guidelines may serve as inputs when developing and drafting legislative, administrative or policy measures on access and benefit-sharing with particular reference to provisions under Articles 8(j), 10(c), 15, 16 and 19; and contracts and other arrangements under mutually agreed terms for access and benefit-sharing.

5. Nothing in these Guidelines, including the use of terms such as 'provider', 'user', and 'stakeholder', should be interpreted to assign any rights over genetic resources beyond those provided in accordance with the Convention;

6. Nothing in these Guidelines should be interpreted as affecting the rights and obligations relating to genetic resources arising out of the mutually agreed terms under which the resources were obtained from the country of origin.
9. All genetic resources and associated traditional knowledge, innovations and practices covered by the Convention on Biological Diversity and benefits arising from the commercial and other utilization of such resources should be covered by the guidelines, with the exclusion of human genetic resources.
11. The objectives of the Guidelines are the following:

    b) To provide Parties and stakeholders with a transparent framework to facilitate access to genetic resources and ensure fair and equitable sharing of benefits;
    d) To inform the practices and approaches of stakeholders (users and providers) in access and benefit-sharing arrangements;
    g) To promote the adequate and effective transfer of appropriate technology to providing Parties, especially developing countries, in particular least developed countries and small island developing States among them, stakeholders and indigenous and local communities . . .

**Roles and Responsibilities in Access and Benefit-sharing Pursuant to Article 15 of the Convention on Biological Diversity**

16. Recognizing that Parties and stakeholders may be both users and providers, the following balanced list of roles and responsibilities provides key elements to be acted upon:

    b) In the implementation of mutually agreed terms, users should:

        i) Seek informed consent prior to access to genetic resources, in conformity with Article 15, paragraph 5, of the Convention;
        ii) Respect customs, traditions, values and customary practices of indigenous and local communities;
        iii) Respond to requests for information from indigenous and local communities;
        iv) Only use genetic resources for purposes consistent with the terms and conditions under which they were acquired;
        v) Ensure that uses of genetic resources for purposes other than those for which they were acquired, only take place after new prior informed consent and mutually agreed terms are given;
        vi) Maintain all relevant data regarding the genetic resources, especially documentary evidence of the prior informed consent and information concerning the origin and the use of genetic resources and the benefits arising from such use;
        vii) As much as possible endeavour to carry out their use of the genetic resources in, and with the participation of, the providing country;
        viii) When supplying genetic resources to third parties, honour any terms and conditions regarding the acquired material. They should provide this third party with relevant data on their acquisition, including prior informed consent and conditions of use and record and maintain data on their supply to third parties . . .

ix) Ensure the fair and equitable sharing of benefits, including technology transfer to providing countries, pursuant to Article 16 of the Convention arising from the commercialization or other use of genetic resources, in conformity with the mutually agreed terms they established with the indigenous and local communities or stakeholders involved;

c) Providers should:

i) Only supply genetic resources and/or traditional knowledge when they are entitled to do so;
ii) Strive to avoid imposition of arbitrary restrictions on access to genetic resources . . .

**Participation of Stakeholders**

17. Involvement of relevant stakeholders is essential to ensure the adequate development and implementation of access and benefit-sharing arrangements. However, due to the diversity of stakeholders and their diverging interests, their appropriate involvement can only be determined on a case-by-case basis.
18. Relevant stakeholders should be consulted and their views taken into consideration in each step of the process, including:

a) When determining access, negotiating and implementing mutually agreed terms, and in the sharing of benefits;
b) In the development of a national strategy, policies or regimes on access and benefit-sharing.

19. To facilitate the involvement of relevant stakeholders, including indigenous and local communities, appropriate consultative arrangements, such as national consultative committees, comprising relevant stakeholder representatives, should be made.
20. The involvement of relevant stakeholders should be promoted by:

a) Providing information, especially regarding scientific and legal advice, in order for them to be able to participate effectively;
b) Providing support for capacity-building, in order for them to be actively engaged in various stages of access and benefit-sharing arrangements, such as in the development and implementation of mutually agreed terms and contractual arrangements.

21. The stakeholders involved in access to genetic resources and benefit-sharing may wish to seek the support of a mediator or facilitator when negotiating mutually agreed terms.

**Steps in the Access and Benefit-sharing Process**

*Prior Informed Consent*

24. . . . In accordance with Article 15, paragraph 5, of the Convention on Biological Diversity, access to genetic resources shall be subject to prior informed consent of the contracting Party providing such resources, unless otherwise determined by that Party.

26. The basic principles of a prior informed consent system should include:

    a) Legal certainty and clarity;
    b) Access to genetic resources should be facilitated at minimum cost;
    c) Restrictions on access to genetic resources should be transparent, based on legal grounds, and not run counter to the objectives of the Convention;
    d) Consent of the relevant competent national authority(ies) in the provider country. The consent of relevant stakeholders, such as indigenous and local communities, as appropriate to the circumstances and subject to domestic law, should also be obtained.

27. Elements of a prior informed consent system may include:

    a) Competent authority(ies) granting or providing for evidence of prior informed consent;
    b) Timing and deadlines;
    c) Specification of use;
    d) Procedures for obtaining prior informed consent;
    e) Mechanism for consultation of relevant stakeholders;
    f) Process.

30. National procedures should facilitate the involvement of all relevant stakeholders from the community to the government level, aiming at simplicity and clarity.
33. Prior informed consent is to be sought adequately in advance to be meaningful both for those seeking and for those granting access. Decisions on applications for access to genetic resources should also be taken within a reasonable period of time.
34. Prior informed consent should be based on the specific uses for which consent has been granted . . .
35. Prior informed consent is linked to the requirement of mutually agreed terms.
36. An application for access could require the following information to be provided, in order for the competent authority to determine whether or not access to a genetic resource should be granted . . .

    a) Legal entity and affiliation of the applicant and/or collector and contact person when the applicant is an institution;
    b) Type and quantity of genetic resources to which access is sought;
    c) Starting date and duration of the activity;
    d) Geographical prospecting area;
    e) Evaluation of how the access activity may impact on conservation and sustainable use of biodiversity, to determine the relative costs and benefits of granting access;
    f) Accurate information regarding intended use (e.g.: taxonomy, collection, research, commercialization);
    g) Identification of where the research and development will take place;
    h) Information on how the research and development is to be carried out;
    i) Identification of local bodies for collaboration in research and development;
    j) Possible third party involvement;
    k) Purpose of the collection, research and expected results;

l) Kinds/types of benefits that could come from obtaining access to the resource, including benefits from derivatives and products arising from the commercial and other utilization of the genetic resource;
m) Indication of benefit-sharing arrangements;
n) Budget;
o) Treatment of confidential information.

38. Applications for access to genetic resources through prior informed consent and decisions by the competent authority(ies) to grant access to genetic resources or not shall be documented in written form.
39. The competent authority could grant access by issuing a permit or licence or following other appropriate procedures . . .
40. The procedures for obtaining an access permit/licence should be transparent and accessible by any interested party.

*Mutually Agreed Terms*

41. In accordance with Article 15, paragraph 7, of the Convention on Biological Diversity, each Contracting Party shall 'take legislative, administrative or policy measures, as appropriate . . . with the aim of sharing in a fair and equitable way the results of research and development and the benefits arising from the commercial and other utilization of genetic resources with the Contracting Party providing such resources. Such sharing shall be upon mutually agreed terms' . . .
42. The following principles or basic requirements could be considered for the development of mutually agreed terms:

a) Legal certainty and clarity;
b) Minimization of transaction costs, by, for example:

    i) Establishing and promoting awareness of the Government's and relevant stakeholders' requirements for prior informed consent and contractual arrangements;
    ii) Ensuring awareness of existing mechanisms for applying for access, entering into arrangements and ensuring the sharing of benefits;
    iii) Developing framework agreements, under which repeat access under expedited arrangements can be made;
    iv) Developing standardized material transfer agreements and benefit-sharing arrangements for similar resources and similar uses (see Appendix I for suggested elements of such an agreement);

c) Inclusion of provisions on user and provider obligations;
d) Development of different contractual arrangements for different resources and for different uses and development of model agreements;
e) Different uses may include, *inter alia*, taxonomy, collection, research, commercialization;
f) Mutually agreed terms should be negotiated efficiently and within a reasonable period of time;
g) Mutually agreed terms should be set out in a written agreement.

43. The following elements could be considered as guiding parameters in contractual agreements. These elements could also be considered as basic requirements for mutually agreed terms:

   a) Regulating the use of resources in order to take into account ethical concerns of the particular Parties and stakeholders, in particular indigenous and local communities concerned;
   b) Making provision to ensure the continued customary use of genetic resources and related knowledge;
   c) Provision for the use of intellectual property rights include joint research, obligation to implement rights on inventions obtained and to provide licences by common consent;
   d) The possibility of joint ownership of intellectual property rights according to the degree of contribution.

44. The following provides an indicative list of typical mutually agreed terms:

   a) Type and quantity of genetic resources, and the geographical/ecological area of activity;
   b) Any limitations on the possible use of the material;
   c) Recognition of the sovereign rights of the country of origin;
   d) Capacity-building in various areas to be identified in the agreement;
   e) A clause on whether the terms of the agreement in certain circumstances (e.g. change of use) can be renegotiated;
   f) Whether the genetic resources can be transferred to third parties and conditions to be imposed in such cases . . .
   g) Whether the knowledge, innovations and practices of indigenous and local communities have been respected, preserved and maintained, and whether the customary use of biological resources in accordance with traditional practices has been protected and encouraged;
   h) Treatment of confidential information;
   i) Provisions regarding the sharing of benefits arising from the commercial and other utilization of genetic resources and their derivatives and products.

45. Mutually agreed terms could cover the conditions, obligations, procedures, types, timing, distribution and mechanisms of benefits to be shared . . .

47. Near-term, medium-term and long-term benefits should be considered, including up front payments, milestone payments and royalties. The time-frame of benefit-sharing should be definitely stipulated . . .

48. Pursuant to mutually agreed terms established following prior informed consent, benefits should be shared fairly and equitably with all those who have been identified as having contributed to the resource management, scientific and/or commercial process . . .

49. Mechanisms for benefit-sharing may vary depending upon the type of benefits, the specific conditions in the country and the stakeholders involved . . .

50. Mechanisms for sharing benefits should include full cooperation in scientific research and technology development, as well as those that derive from commercial products including trust funds, joint ventures and licences with preferential terms.

**Other Provisions**

51. The following incentive measures exemplify measures which could be used in the implementation of the guidelines:

    d) The creation and use of markets should be considered as a way of efficiently achieving conservation and sustainable use of biological diversity.

52. Parties should endeavour to establish mechanisms to promote accountability by all stakeholders involved in access and benefit-sharing arrangements.
53. To promote accountability, Parties may consider establishing requirements regarding:

    a) Reporting; and
    b) Disclosure of information.

54. The individual collector or institution on whose behalf the collector is operating should, where appropriate, be responsible and accountable for the compliance of the collector.
55. Depending on the terms of access and benefit-sharing, national monitoring may include:

    c) Applications for intellectual property rights relating to the material supplied.

58. A system of voluntary certification could serve as a means to verify the transparency of the process of access and benefit-sharing . . .
59. As most obligations arising under mutually agreed arrangements will be between providers and users, disputes arising in these arrangements should be solved in accordance with the relevant contractual arrangements on access and benefit-sharing and the applicable law and practices.

# 64. International Atomic Energy Agency: Vienna Convention on Civil Liability for Nuclear Damage, 1963

**Commentary**: The Convention (IAEA Doc INFCIRC/500 (1996), entry into force 1977) establishes the liability of operators for nuclear damage. The extracts below derive from the consolidated text of the Convention as amended by a 1997 Protocol: IAEA Doc INFCIRC/566 (1998). The Protocol provides for coastal State jurisdiction, limits operator liability at no less than 300 million special drawing rights (SDRs) and extends the definition of nuclear damage, the geographical scope of the Convention and the period in which to recover claims. Article VD contemplates governments amending the liability limits of Article V in the light of the risk of damage resulting from nuclear incidents, changes in monetary value or the capacity of insurance markets. The nature, form and extent of compensation are governed by national law and priority in the equitable distribution thereof is given to claims in respect of loss of life or personal injury (Article VIII). Jurisdiction rests with the courts of the State where the nuclear incident occurred (Article XI). See further, IAEA (1990), 'General Conference Resolution on a Code of Practice on the International Transboundary Movement of Radioactive Waste', IAEA Doc GC(34)/RES/530; www.iaea.org. On the liability of nuclear operators, see *Duke Power Co v Carolina Environmental Study Group Inc* 438 *US* 59 (1978); *Merlin v British Nuclear Fuels Ltd* [1990] 3 *All ER* 711; *Blue Circle Industries PLC v Ministry of Defence* [1998] 3 *All ER* 385.

**Article I**

1. For the purposes of this Convention:

   a) 'Person' means any individual, partnership, any private or public body whether corporate or not, any international organization enjoying legal personality under the law of the Installation State, and any State or any of its constituent sub-divisions.
   b) 'National of a Contracting Party' includes a Contracting Party or any of its constituent sub-divisions, a partnership, or any private or public body whether corporate or not established within the territory of a Contracting Party.
   c) 'Operator', in relation to a nuclear installation, means the person designated or recognized by the Installation State as the operator of that installation.
   d) 'Installation State', in relation to a nuclear installation, means the Contracting Party within whose territory that installation is situated or, if it is not situated within the territory of any State, the Contracting Party by which or under the authority of which the nuclear installation is operated.

f) 'Nuclear fuel' means any material which is capable of producing energy by a self sustaining chain process of nuclear fission.

g) 'Radioactive products or waste' means any radioactive material produced in, or any material made radioactive by exposure to the radiation incidental to, the production or utilization of nuclear fuel, but does not include radioisotopes which have reached the final stage of fabrication so as to be usable for any scientific, medical, agricultural, commercial or industrial purpose.

h) 'Nuclear material' means:

   i) nuclear fuel, other than natural uranium and depleted uranium, capable of producing energy by a self-sustaining chain process of nuclear fission outside a nuclear reactor, either alone or in combination with some other material; and
   ii) radioactive products or waste.

i) 'Nuclear reactor' means any structure containing nuclear fuel in such an arrangement that a self-sustaining chain process of nuclear fission can occur therein without an additional source of neutrons.

j) 'Nuclear installation' means:

   i) any nuclear reactor other than one with which a means of sea or air transport is equipped for use as a source of power, whether for propulsion thereof or for any other purpose;
   ii) any factory using nuclear fuel for the production of nuclear material, or any factory for the processing of nuclear material, including any factory for the re-processing of irradiated nuclear fuel; and
   iii) any facility where nuclear material is stored, other than storage incidental to the carriage of such material; and
   iv) such other installations in which there are nuclear fuel or radioactive products or waste as the Board of Governors of the International Atomic Energy Agency shall from time to time determine; . . .

k) 'Nuclear damage' means:

   i) loss of life, any personal injury;
   ii) loss of or damage to property;

and each of the following to the extent determined by the law of the competent court:

   iii) economic loss arising from loss or damage referred to in sub-paragraph (i) or (ii) . . .
   iv) the costs of measures of reinstatement of impaired environment, unless such impairment is insignificant, if such measures are actually taken or to be taken . . .
   v) loss of income deriving from an economic interest in any use or enjoyment of the environment, incurred as a result of a significant impairment of that environment . . .
   vi) the costs of preventive measures, and further loss or damage caused by such measures;

vii) any other economic loss, other than any caused by the impairment of the environment, if permitted by the general law on civil liability of the competent court, in the case of sub-paragraphs (i) to (v) and (vii) above, to the extent that the loss or damage arises out of or results from ionizing radiation emitted by any source of radiation inside a nuclear installation, or emitted from nuclear fuel or radioactive products or waste in, or of nuclear material coming from, originating in, or sent to, a nuclear installation, whether so arising from the radioactive properties of such matter, or from a combination of radioactive properties with toxic, explosive or other hazardous properties of such matter.

l) 'Nuclear incident' means any occurrence or series of occurrences having the same origin which causes nuclear damage or, but only with respect to preventive measures, creates a grave and imminent threat of causing such damage.
m) 'Measures of reinstatement' means any reasonable measures which have been approved by the competent authorities of the State where the measures were taken, and which aim to reinstate or restore damaged or destroyed components of the environment, or to introduce, where reasonable, the equivalent of these components into the environment. The law of the State where the damage is suffered shall determine who is entitled to take such measures.
n) 'Preventive measures' means any reasonable measures taken by any person after a nuclear incident has occurred to prevent or minimize damage referred to in sub-paragraphs (k)(i) to (v) or (vii), subject to any approval of the competent authorities required by the law of the State where the measures were taken.
o) 'Reasonable measures' means measures which are found under the law of the competent court to be appropriate and proportionate having regard to all the circumstances, for example:

   i) the nature and extent of the damage incurred or, in the case of preventive measures, the nature and extent of the risk of such damage;
   ii) the extent to which, at the time they are taken, such measures are likely to be effective; and
   iii) relevant scientific and technical expertise.

2. An Installation State may, if the small extent of the risks involved so warrants, exclude any nuclear installation or small quantities of nuclear material from the application of this Convention . . .

**Article IA**

1. This Convention shall apply to nuclear damage wherever suffered.
2. However, the legislation of the Installation State may exclude from the application of this Convention damage suffered:

   a) in the territory of a non-Contracting State; or
   b) in any maritime zones established by a non-Contracting State in accordance with the international law of the sea.

3. An exclusion pursuant to paragraph 2 of this Article may apply only in respect of a non-Contracting State which at the time of the incident:

a) has a nuclear installation in its territory or in any maritime zones established by it in accordance with the international law of the sea; and
b) does not afford equivalent reciprocal benefits . . .

**Article II**

1. The operator of a nuclear installation shall be liable for nuclear damage upon proof that such damage has been caused by a nuclear incident:

a) in his nuclear installation; or
b) involving nuclear material coming from or originating in his nuclear installation, and occurring:

i) before liability with regard to nuclear incidents involving the nuclear material has been assumed, pursuant to the express terms of a contract in writing, by the operator of another nuclear installation;
ii) in the absence of such express terms, before the operator of another nuclear installation has taken charge of the nuclear material; or
iii) where the nuclear material is intended to be used in a nuclear reactor with which a means of transport is equipped for use as a source of power, whether for propulsion thereof or for any other purpose, before the person duly authorized to operate such reactor has taken charge of the nuclear material; but
iv) where the nuclear material has been sent to a person within the territory of a non-Contracting State, before it has been unloaded from the means of transport by which it has arrived in the territory of that non-Contracting State;

c) involving nuclear material sent to his nuclear installation, and occurring:

i) after liability with regard to nuclear incidents involving the nuclear material has been assumed by him, pursuant to the express terms of a contract in writing, from the operator of another nuclear installation;
ii) in the absence of such express terms, after he has taken charge of the nuclear material; or
iii) after he has taken charge of the nuclear material from a person operating a nuclear reactor with which a means of transport is equipped for use as a source of power, whether for propulsion thereof or for any other purpose; but
iv) where the nuclear material has, with the written consent of the operator, been sent from a person within the territory of a non-Contracting State, only after it has been loaded on the means of transport by which it is to be carried from the territory of that State;

provided that, if nuclear damage is caused by a nuclear incident occurring in a nuclear installation and involving nuclear material stored therein incidentally to the carriage of such material, the provisions of sub-paragraph (a) of this paragraph shall not apply where another operator or person is solely liable pursuant to the provisions of sub-paragraph (b) or (c) of this paragraph.

2. The Installation State may provide by legislation that, in accordance with such terms as may be specified therein, a carrier of nuclear material or a person handling radioactive waste may, at his request and with the consent of the operator concerned, be designated or recognized as operator in the place of that operator in respect of such nuclear material or radioactive waste respectively . . .

3. a) Where nuclear damage engages the liability of more than one operator, the operators involved shall, in so far as the damage attributable to each operator is not reasonably separable, be jointly and severally liable . . .
   b) Where a nuclear incident occurs in the course of carriage of nuclear material, either in one and the same means of transport, or, in the case of storage incidental to the carriage, in one and the same nuclear installation, and causes nuclear damage which engages the liability of more than one operator, the total liability shall not exceed the highest amount applicable with respect to any one of them pursuant to Article V.
   c) In neither of the cases referred to in sub-paragraphs (a) and (b) of this paragraph shall the liability of any one operator exceed the amount applicable with respect to him pursuant to Article V.

4. Subject to the provisions of paragraph 3 of this Article, where several nuclear installations of one and the same operator are involved in one nuclear incident, such operator shall be liable in respect of each nuclear installation involved up to the amount applicable with respect to him pursuant to Article V . . .
5. Except as otherwise provided in this Convention, no person other than the operator shall be liable for nuclear damage . . .
7. Direct action shall lie against the person furnishing financial security pursuant to Article VII, if the law of the competent court so provides.

**Article III**
The operator liable in accordance with this Convention shall provide the carrier with a certificate issued by or on behalf of the insurer or other financial guarantor furnishing the financial security required pursuant to Article VII . . .

**Article IV**
1. The liability of the operator for nuclear damage under this Convention shall be absolute.
2. If the operator proves that the nuclear damage resulted wholly or partly either from the gross negligence of the person suffering the damage or from an act or omission of such person done with intent to cause damage, the competent court may, if its law so provides, relieve the operator wholly or partly from his obligation to pay compensation in respect of the damage suffered by such person.
3. No liability under this Convention shall attach to an operator if he proves that the nuclear damage is directly due to an act of armed conflict, hostilities, civil war or insurrection.
4. Whenever both nuclear damage and damage other than nuclear damage have been caused by a nuclear incident or jointly by a nuclear incident and one or more other occurrences, such other damage shall, to the extent that it is not reasonably separable

from the nuclear damage, be deemed, for the purposes of this Convention, to be nuclear damage caused by that nuclear incident . . .

5. The operator shall not be liable under this Convention for nuclear damage:

    a) to the nuclear installation itself or any other nuclear installation, including a nuclear installation under construction, on the site where that installation is located; and
    b) to any property on that same site which is used or to be used in connection with any such installation.

6. Compensation for damage caused to the means of transport upon which the nuclear material is involved was at the time of the nuclear incident shall not have the effect of reducing the liability of the operator in respect of other damage to an amount less than either 150 million SDRs, or any higher amount established by the legislation of a Contracting Party, or an amount established pursuant to sub-paragraph (c) of paragraph 1 of Article V.
7. Nothing in this Convention shall affect the liability of any individual for nuclear damage for which the operator, by virtue of paragraph 3 or 5 of this Article, is not liable under this Convention and which that individual caused by an act or omission done with intent to cause damage.

**Article V**

1. The liability of the operator may be limited by the Installation State for any one nuclear incident, either:

    a) to not less than 300 million SDRs; or
    b) to not less than 150 million SDRs provided that in excess of that amount and up to at least 300 million SDRs public funds shall be made available by that State to compensate nuclear damage; or
    c) for a maximum of 15 years from the date of entry into force of this Protocol, to a transitional amount of not less than 100 million SDRs in respect of a nuclear incident occurring within that period. An amount lower than 100 million SDRs may be established, provided that public funds shall be made available by that State to compensate nuclear damage between that lesser amount and 100 million SDRs.

2. Notwithstanding paragraph 1 of this Article, the Installation State, having regard to the nature of the nuclear installation or the nuclear substances involved and to the likely consequences of an incident originating therefrom, may establish a lower amount of liability of the operator, provided that in no event shall any amount so established be less than 5 million SDRs, and provided that the Installation State ensures that public funds shall be made available up to the amount established pursuant to paragraph 1.
3. The amounts established by the Installations State of the liable operator in accordance with paragraphs 1 and 2 of this Article and paragraph 6 of Article IV shall apply wherever the nuclear incident occurs.

**Article VA**

1. Interest and costs awarded by a court in actions for compensation of nuclear damage shall be payable in addition to the amounts referred to in Article V . . .

**Article VB**

1. Each Contracting Party shall ensure that persons suffering damage may enforce their rights to compensation without having to bring separate proceedings according to the origin of the funds provided for such compensation.

**Article VI**

1. a) Rights of compensation under this Convention shall be extinguished if an action is not brought within:

   i) with respect to loss of life and personal injury, thirty years from the date of the nuclear incident;
   ii) with respect to other damage, ten years from the date of the nuclear incident.

   b) If, however, under the law of the Installation State, the liability of the operator is covered by insurance or other financial security including State funds for a longer period, the law of the competent court may provide that rights of compensation against the operator shall only be extinguished after such a longer period which shall not exceed the period for which his liability is so covered under the law of the Installation State.

3. Rights of compensation under the Convention shall be subject to prescription or extinction, as provided by the law of the competent court, if an action is not brought within three years from the date on which the person suffering damage had knowledge or ought reasonably to have had knowledge of the damage and of the operator liable for the damage, provided that the periods established pursuant to sub-paragraphs (a) and (b) of paragraph 1 of this Article shall not be exceeded . . .

**Article VII**

1. a) The operator shall be required to maintain insurance or other financial security covering his liability for nuclear damage in such amount, of such type and in such terms as the Installation State shall specify. The Installation State shall ensure the payment of claims for compensation for nuclear damage which have been established against the operator by providing the necessary funds to the extent that the yield of insurance or other financial security is inadequate to satisfy such claims, but not in excess of the limit, if any, established pursuant to Article V. Where the liability of the operator is unlimited, the Installation State may establish a limit of the financial security of the operator liable, provided that such limit is not lower than 300 million SDRs . . .

   b) Notwithstanding sub-paragraph (a) of this paragraph, where the liability of the operator is unlimited, the Installation State, having regard to the nature of the nuclear installation or the nuclear substances involved and to the likely consequences of an incident originating therefrom, may establish a lower amount of financial security of the operator, provided that in no event shall any amount so established be less than 5 million SDRs, and provided that the Installation State ensures the payment of claims for compensation for nuclear damage which have been established against the operator by providing necessary funds to the extent that the yield of insurance or other financial security is inadequate to satisfy such claims, and up to the limit provided pursuant to sub-paragraph (a) of this paragraph.

4. No insurer or other financial guarantor shall suspend or cancel the insurance or other financial security provided pursuant to paragraph 1 of this Article without giving notice in writing of at least two months to the competent public authority or, in so far as such insurance or other financial security relates to the carriage of nuclear material, during the period of the carriage in question.

**Article IX**

1. a) If a person who is a national of a Contracting Party, other than the operator, has paid compensation for nuclear damage under an international convention or under the law of a non-Contracting State, such person shall, up to the amount which he has paid, acquire by subrogation the rights under this Convention of the person so compensated. No rights shall be so acquired by any person to the extent that the operator has a right of recourse against such person under this Convention.
   b) Nothing in this Convention shall preclude an operator who has paid compensation for nuclear damage out of funds other than those provided pursuant to paragraph 1 of Article VII from recovering from the person providing financial security pursuant to that paragraph or from the Installation State, up to the amount he has paid, the sum which the person so compensated would have obtained under this Convention.

**Article X**

The operator shall have a right of recourse only:

a) if this is expressly provided for by a contract in writing; or
b) if the nuclear incident results from an act or omission done with intent to cause damage, against the individual who has acted or omitted to act with such intent . . .

**Additional Instruments**

*i. OECD: Convention on Third Party Liability in the Field of Nuclear Energy of 29th July 1960, as Amended by the Additional Protocol of 28th January 1964 and by the Protocol of 16th November 1982*

**Commentary**: The 'Paris Convention' (956 *UNTS* 251, entry into force 1968) has been twice amended (1964 & 1982) and a 2004 Protocol has recently been issued: www.nea.fr/html/law/legal-documents.html. The Paris Convention adopts a similar template to the Vienna Convention extracted above. Under Article 7, operator liability in respect of nuclear damage is not less than 700 million euros. See further, OECD Council (1982), 'Recommendations with Respect to the Paris Convention' C(82)181 & C(82)182; OECD Nuclear Energy Agency (1990), 'Paris Convention: Decisions, Recommendations, Interpretations'. The 1963 ('Brussels') Convention Supplementary to the Paris Convention (1041 *UNTS* 358, entry into force 1974) increases the compensation for damage resulting from using nuclear energy for peaceful purposes. It has been similarly amended in 1964, 1982 and 2004. See further, OECD Council (1992), Recommendation on the application of the Brussels Supplementary Convention C(92)166/FINAL.

The 1997 Convention on Supplementary Compensation for Nuclear Damage IAEA Doc INFCIRC/567 (1998, not yet in force) identifies additional amounts provided by governments. Any State may adhere to this Convention irrespective of whether it is Party to an existing nuclear liability regime or has nuclear installations on its territory. Following the Chernobyl accident, a Joint Protocol Relating to the Application of the Vienna Convention and the Paris Convention was adopted in 1988. It links these two Conventions within one expanded liability regime: States Parties to the Joint Protocol are treated as though they are Parties to both Conventions and a choice of law rule determines which Convention applies to the exclusion of the other in respect of the same incident.

# 65. International Maritime Organisation: Convention on the Prevention of Marine Pollution by Dumping of Wastes and other Matter, 1972

**Commentary**: Dumping waste generated on land at sea was undertaken for several years by industrialised States until action in the early 1970s. The London Convention (1046 *UNTS* 120, entry into force 1975) prohibits dumping particular hazardous materials (the 'black' list) and requires permits for dumping other materials provided certain conditions are satisfied (the 'grey' list). The extracts below contain all amendments which have entered into force. Annex I identifies various compounds, plastics, crude oil and other matter and also defines 'industrial waste' and 'incineration at sea'. Annex II lists substances or materials requiring special care. Annex III identifies characteristics of the waste matter, dumping sites, methods of deposit and general criteria for issuing permits. See further, IMO, 'Guidelines for the Assessment of Wastes or Other Matter that May Be Considered for Dumping' (generic guidelines applicable to all material which is acceptable for ocean disposal) and complementary waste-specific guidelines: www.londonconvention.org.

A 1996 Protocol (IMO Doc LC/SM1/6, not yet in force) will replace the London Convention with several major changes. Article 3 thereof introduces the precautionary approach to ensure that 'appropriate preventative measures are taken when there is reason to believe that wastes or other matter introduced into the marine environment are likely to cause harm even when there is no conclusive evidence to prove a causal relation between inputs and their effects'. Article 3 also provides that 'the polluter should, in principle, bear the cost of pollution'. Article 4 contemplates governments prohibiting the dumping of any wastes or other matter with the exception of those listed under Annex I. These include dredged material, sewage sludge, fish waste, vessels, platforms or other man-made structures at sea, inert or inorganic geological material, organic material of natural origin and bulky items comprising iron, steel, concrete or similar non-harmful materials. Article 8 permits dumping 'in cases of force majeure caused by stress of weather, or in any case which constitutes a danger to human life or a real threat to vessels'.

For land-based sources of marine pollution, see UNEP, 'Global Programme of Action for the Protection of the Marine Environment from Land-based Activities', UN Doc UNEP(OCA)/LBA/IG.2/7 (1995) and Intergovernmental Conference Report, UN Doc UNEP Doc UNEP(OCA)/LBA/IG.2/6 (1995).

**Article I**
Contracting Parties shall individually and collectively promote the effective control of all sources of pollution of the marine environment, and pledge themselves especially to take all practicable steps to prevent the pollution of the sea by the dumping of waste and other matter that is liable to create hazards to human health, to harm living resources and marine life, to damage amenities or to interfere with other legitimate uses of the sea.

**Article III**
For the purposes of this Convention:

1. (a) 'Dumping' means:

   (i) any deliberate disposal at sea of wastes or other matter from vessels, aircraft, platforms or other man-made structures at sea;
   (ii) any deliberate disposal at sea of vessels, aircraft, platforms or other man-made structures at sea.

   (b) 'Dumping' does not include:

   (i) the disposal at sea of wastes or other matter incidental to, or derived from the normal operations of vessels, aircraft, platforms or other man-made structures at sea and their equipment, other than wastes or other matter transported by or to vessels, aircraft, platforms or other man-made structures at sea, operating for the purpose of disposal of such matter or derived from the treatment of such wastes or other matter on such vessels, aircraft, platforms or structures;
   (ii) placement of matter for a purpose other than the mere disposal thereof, provided that such placement is not contrary to the aims of this Convention.

   (c) The disposal of wastes or other matter directly arising from, or related to the exploration, exploitation and associated off-shore processing of sea-bed mineral resources will not be covered by the provisions of this Convention.

2. 'Vessels and aircraft' means waterborne or airborne craft of any type whatsoever. This expression includes air cushioned craft and floating craft, whether self-propelled or not.
3. 'Sea' means all marine waters other than the internal waters of States.
4. 'Wastes or other matter' means material and substance of any kind, form or description.
5. 'Special permit' means permission granted specifically on application in advance and in accordance with Annex II and Annex III.
6. 'General permit' means permission granted in advance and in accordance with Annex III.

**Article IV**
1. In accordance with the provisions of this Convention Contracting Parties shall prohibit the dumping of any wastes or other matter in whatever form or condition except as otherwise specified below:

(a) the dumping of wastes or other matter listed in Annex I is prohibited;
(b) the dumping of wastes or other matter listed in Annex II requires a prior special permit;
(c) the dumping of all other wastes or matter requires a prior general permit.

2. Any permit shall be issued only after careful consideration of all the factors set forth in Annex III, including prior studies of the characteristics of the dumping site, as set forth in sections B and C of that Annex . . .

**Article V**

1. The provisions of article IV shall not apply when it is necessary to secure the safety of human life or of vessels, aircraft, platforms or other man-made structures at sea in cases of force majeure caused by stress of weather, or in any case which constitutes a danger to human life or a real threat to vessels, aircraft, platforms or other man-made structures at sea, if dumping appears to be the only way of averting the threat and if there is every probability that the damage consequent upon such dumping will be less than would otherwise occur. Such dumping shall be so conducted as to minimize the likelihood of damage to human or marine life and shall be reported forthwith to the Organization.
2. A Contracting Party may issue a special permit as an exception to article IV(1)(a), in emergencies, posing unacceptable risk relating to human health and admitting no other feasible solution . . .

**Article VI**

1. Each Contracting Party shall designate an appropriate authority or authorities to:

(a) issue special permits which shall be required prior to, and for, the dumping of matter listed in Annex II and in the circumstances provided for in article V(2);
(b) issue general permits which shall be required prior to, and for, the dumping of all other matter;
(c) keep records of the nature and quantities of all matter permitted to be dumped and the location, time and method of dumping;
(d) monitor individually, or in collaboration with other Parties and competent international organizations, the condition of the seas for the purposes of this Convention.

2. The appropriate authority or authorities of a contracting Party shall issue prior special or general permits in accordance with paragraph (1) in respect of matter intended for dumping:

(a) loaded in its territory;
(b) loaded by a vessel or aircraft registered in its territory or flying its flag, when the loading occurs in the territory of a State not party to this Convention.

**Article VII**

1. Each Contracting Party shall apply the measures required to implement the present Convention to all:

(a) vessels and aircraft registered in its territory or flying its flag;
(b) vessels and aircraft loading in its territory or territorial seas matter which is to be dumped;
(c) vessels and aircraft and fixed or floating platforms under its jurisdiction believed to be engaged in dumping.

3. The Parties agree to co-operate in the development of procedures for the effective application of this Convention particularly on the high seas, including procedures for the reporting of vessels and aircraft observed dumping in contravention of the Convention.

**Article XII**
The Contracting Parties pledge themselves to promote, within the competent specialized agencies and other international bodies, measures to protect the marine environment against pollution caused by:

(a) hydrocarbons, including oil and their wastes;
(b) other noxious or hazardous matter transported by vessels for purposes other than dumping;
(c) wastes generated in the course of operation of vessels, aircraft, platforms and other man-made structures at sea;
(d) radio-active pollutants from all sources, including vessels;
(e) agents of chemical and biological warfare;
(f) wastes or other matter directly arising from, or related to the exploration, exploitation and associated off-shore processing of sea-bed mineral resources.

The Parties will also promote, within the appropriate international organization, the codification of signals to be used by vessels engaged in dumping.

**Additional Instruments**
The 1969 International Convention Relating to Intervention on the High Seas in Cases of Oil Pollution Casualties (970 *UNTS* 211, entry into force 1975) followed the 1967 *Torrey Canyon* disaster. The Convention affirms the right of coastal States to adopt such measures on the high seas as may be necessary following a maritime casualty to prevent, mitigate or eliminate danger to its coastline or related interests from oil pollution or the threat thereof. Coastal States are empowered to take such action only after due consultation with appropriate interests including flag States, the owners of the ships or cargoes in question and circumstances requiring independent experts. See further, 1973 Protocol relating to Intervention on the High Seas in Cases of Marine Pollution by Substances other than Oil (1313 *UNTS* 3, entry into force 1983).

The 1969 International Convention on Civil Liability for Oil Pollution Damage (the CLC Convention, 973 *UNTS* 3, entry into force 1975) ensures that adequate compensation is available to persons who suffer oil pollution damage resulting from maritime casualties involving oil-carrying ships. Strict liability is imposed upon shipowners from whose ships polluting oil escaped or was discharged. Shipowners cannot limit liability where incidents occur through the owner's personal fault. Ships are required to maintain insurance or other financial security. The 1969 Convention is currently being replaced by a 1992 Protocol (86 *UKTS* (1996), entry into force 1996) which extends the scope of the Convention to cover pollution damage caused in the exclusive economic zone (EEZ) and applicable to both laden and unladen tankers (including bunker oil spills). Compensation for environmental damage is limited to costs incurred for reasonable measures to reinstate contaminated environments. Shipowners cannot limit liability where pollution damage results from personal acts or omissions committed with intent to cause damage, or recklessly and with knowledge that such damage would probably result.

The 1971 International Convention on the Establishment of an International Fund for Compensation for Oil Pollution Damage (1110 *UNTS* 57, entry into force 1978 and ceasing to be in force 2002) provided compensation for pollution damage where protection under the 1969 Civil Liability Convention proved inadequate. The International Fund paid compensation to States and persons who suffered pollution damage where they are unable to secure compensation from shipowners or where the compensation was insufficient. A 1992 Protocol (87 *UKTS* (1996), entry into force 1996) replaces the 1971 Convention with a separate, 1992 International Oil Pollution Compensation Fund (the 1992 Fund). It moreover modifies entry into force requirements and increases compensation amounts. An additional, third tier of compensation is provided through a 2003 Protocol which establishes an International Oil Pollution Compensation Supplementary Fund (IMO Doc LEG/CONF.14/20 (2003), not yet in force).

The 1973 International Convention for the Prevention of Pollution from Ships (1340 *UNTS* 184, not yet in force) prevents pollution of marine environments by ships from operational or accidental causes. A 1978 Protocol (1340 *UNTS* 61, entry into force 1983) absorbed the parent Convention. MARPOL 73/78 also has Annexes containing regulations to prevent oil pollution (Annex I), to control pollution by bulk noxious liquid substances (II), to prevent pollution by harmful substances carried by sea in packaged form (III), to prevent pollution by ship sewage (IV), to prevent pollution by ship garbage (V) and to prevent air pollution from ships (VI).

Following the *Torrey Canyon* and *Exxon Valdez* disasters, oil companies and the shipping industry formulated voluntary contractual regimes providing for additional compensation mechanisms: see Tanker Owners Voluntary Agreement concerning Liability for Oil Pollution (TOVALOP) 8 *ILM* 497 (1969); Contract Regarding an Interim Supplement to Tanker Liability for Oil Pollution (CRISTAL) 10 *ILM* 137 (1971); Offshore Pollution Liability Agreement (OPAL) 13 *ILM* 1409 (1974). See further, *International Association of Independent Tanker Owners v Locke* 148 *F.3d* 1053 (1990).

The 1976 Convention on Limitation of Liability for Maritime Claims (the LLMC Convention, 1456 *UNTS* 221, entry into force 1986) imposes limits with respect to two types of claim: claims for loss of life or personal injury and property claims (including damage to other ships, property or harbour works). An individual is unable to limit liability if 'it is proved that the loss resulted from his personal act or omission, committed with the intent to cause such a loss, or recklessly and with knowledge that such loss would probably result'. A 1996 Protocol (35 *ILM* 1433, entry into force 2004) increases the compensation payable and introduces a 'tacit acceptance' procedure for updating this amount.

The 1990 International Convention on Oil Pollution Preparedness, Response and Co-operation (the OPRC Convention, 30 *ILM* 735, entry into force 1995) requires ships and operators of offshore units to formulate oil pollution emergency plans. Ships are also required to report pollution incidents to coastal authorities. The Convention calls for stockpiling oil spill combating equipment, conducting oil spill combating exercises and developing detailed plans for addressing pollution incidents.

The 1996 International Convention on Liability and Compensation for Damage in Connection with the Carriage of Hazardous and Noxious Substances by Sea (the HNS Convention, IMO Doc LEG/CONF.10/8/2 (1996), not yet in force) goes further than the CLC and Fund Conventions (above) to cover not only pollution damage but also the risk of fire or explosion. Damage includes loss of life or personal injury, loss of or damage to property outside the ship, loss or damage by environmental contamination and preventive costs. HNS includes oils, other liquid substances defined as noxious or dangerous, liquefied gases, dangerous, hazardous and harmful materials or substances carried in packaged form, solid bulk materials which possess chemical hazards and residues thereof. The Convention introduces strict shipowner liability, establishes liability limits and compulsory insurance systems. This first tier of liability is supplemented by a second, the HNS Fund, which is financed by cargo interests. For commercial perspectives, see CEFIC (1995), 'Consideration of a Draft International Convention on Liability and Compensation for Damage in Connection with the Carriage of Hazardous and Noxious Substances by Sea (HNS)', Brussels; CEFIC (1997 & 1998), 'Consideration of a Draft International Convention on Liability and Compensation for Damage resulting from Transboundary Movements of Hazardous Wastes and their Disposal', Brussels. A 2000 Protocol on Preparedness, Response and Co-operation to Pollution Incidents by Hazardous and Noxious Substances (the OPRC–HNS Protocol, IMO Doc HNS-OPRC/CONF/11/Rev 1 (2000), not yet in force) seeks to ensure that ships carrying hazardous and noxious liquid substances are already covered by oil incident regimes. It requires governments to establish measures which address pollution incidents or major threats of marine pollution. Ships are required to carry emergency pollution plans.

The 2004 International Convention for the Control and Management of Ships' Ballast Water and Sediments (IMO Doc BWM/CONF/36 (2004), not yet in force) aims to prevent, minimise and eliminate the transfer of harmful aquatic organisms and pathogens. Under Article 5, governments are to provide adequate reception facilities and ships may be surveyed, certified (Article 7) and inspected by port State control officers (Article 9).

# 66. International Seabed Authority: Regulations on Prospecting and Exploration for Polymetallic Nodules in the Area, 2000

**Commentary**: The UN Convention on the Law of the Sea (UNCLOS, UN Doc A/CONF.62/122 (1982), entry into force 1994) defines the roles and responsibilities of national vessels to utilise living marine resources including fishing rights. It also envisages that exploring and exploiting the seabed, ocean floor and subsoil thereof shall be carried out for the benefit of humanity. Commercial exploitation of the deep seabed and the position of pioneer investors became the subject of lengthy intergovernmental negotiations: see further, Resolution II Governing Preparatory Investment in Pioneer Activities Relating to Polymetallic Nodules 21 *ILM* 1254 (1982); Agreement concerning Interim Arrangements relating to Polymetallic Nodules of the Deep Sea-Bed 21 *ILM* 950 (1982); Provisional Understanding Regarding Deep Seabed Mining 23 *ILM* 1354 (1984); Declaration adopted by the UNCLOS Preparatory Commission, UN Doc LOS/PCN/72 (1985); New York Agreement Relating to the Implementation of Part XI of the 1982 Convention on the Law of the Sea 33 *ILM* 1309 (1994). For academic comment, see Dubow M. (1982), 'The Third United Nations Conference on the Law of the Sea: questions of equity for American business', *Northwestern Journal of International Law and Business*, **4**, 172. Consideration was ultimately given to formulating an intergovernmental code of conduct: see UN (1998), 'Seabed Council Receives Mining Code Draft', Press Release SEA/1578; UN (1998), 'International Seabed Authority to Resume Work on Mining Code', Press Release SEA/1573. Finally, the International Seabed Authority (ISBA) approved these Regulations after three years of negotiations: ISBA Doc ISBA/6/A/18 (2000). See further, www.isa.org.jm.

In addition to those regulations extracted below (footnotes omitted), Regulation 19 identifies the applicable application fee as US$250,000. Regulation 20 contemplates the receipt, acknowledgement and safe custody of applications (including assurances of confidentiality). Under Regulation 21, the Legal and Technical Commission considers *inter alia* whether proposed work plans effectively protect human health or safety and the marine environment. The Commission also considers whether there will be any interference to recognised sea lanes essential to international navigation or to areas of intense fishing activity. Where the Commission does not recommend approval, it shall inform applicants and provide them with further opportunities to make representations. Regulation 28 contemplates periodic review every five years by the contractor and Secretary-General of the implementation of the work plan for exploration. Under Regulation 33, the rights of coastal States are unaffected. However, contractors must have reasonable opportunities to respond where coastal States believe that activities are likely to cause serious environmental harm. Regulation 37 identifies when notice in writing is considered effective. Regulation 38 enables the Legal and Technical Commission to issue technical or administrative recommendations to guide contractors. Under Regulation 39, disputes concerning the interpretation or application of these Regulations are settled in accordance with UNCLOS, Part XI, section 5. Where prospectors or contractors locate resources other than polymetallic nodules in the Area, under Regulation 40, subsequent prospecting, exploration and exploitation are subject to the rules, regulations and procedures of the ISBA. Annex 1 identifies factual details which constitute a notification of intention to engage in prospecting. Annex 2 specifies information to accompany applications for approval of work plans for exploration with a view to obtaining a contract. Annex 3 contains a sample exploration contract and Annex 4 contains standard clauses thereof. See also, ISBA Council Decision relating to the regulations on prospecting and exploration for polymetallic nodules in the Area, ISBA Doc ISBA/6/C/12.

## Part I: Introduction

REGULATION 1: USE OF TERMS AND SCOPE

3. For the purposes of these Regulations:

(a) 'Exploitation' means the recovery for commercial purposes of polymetallic nodules in the Area and the extraction of minerals therefrom, including the construction and operation of mining, processing and transportation systems, for the production and marketing of metals;
(b) 'Exploration' means searching for deposits of polymetallic nodules in the Area with exclusive rights, the analysis of such deposits, the testing of collecting systems and equipment, processing facilities and transportation systems, and the carrying out of studies of the environmental, technical, economic, commercial and other appropriate factors that must be taken into account in exploitation;
(c) 'Marine environment' includes the physical, chemical, geological and biological components, conditions and factors which interact and determine the productivity, state, condition and quality of the marine ecosystem, the waters of the seas and oceans and the airspace above those waters, as well as the seabed and ocean floor and subsoil thereof;
(d) 'Polymetallic nodules' means one of the resources of the Area consisting of any deposit or accretion of nodules, on or just below the surface of the deep seabed, which contain manganese, nickel, cobalt and copper;
(e) 'Prospecting' means the search for deposits of polymetallic nodules in the Area, including estimation of the composition, sizes and distributions of polymetallic nodule deposits and their economic values, without any exclusive rights;
(f) 'Serious harm to the marine environment' means any effect from activities in the Area on the marine environment which represents a significant adverse change in the marine environment determined according to the rules, regulations and procedures adopted by the Authority on the basis of internationally recognized standards and practices . . .

## Part II: Prospecting

REGULATION 2: PROSPECTING

1. Prospecting shall be conducted in accordance with the Convention and these Regulations and may commence only after the prospector has been informed by the Secretary-General that its notification has been recorded pursuant to regulation 4, paragraph 2.
2. Prospecting shall not be undertaken if substantial evidence indicates the risk of serious harm to the marine environment.
3. Prospecting shall not be undertaken in an area covered by an approved plan of work for exploration for polymetallic nodules or in a reserved area; nor may there be prospecting in an area which the Council has disapproved for exploitation because of the risk of serious harm to the marine environment.
4. Prospecting shall not confer on the prospector any rights with respect to resources. A prospector may, however, recover a reasonable quantity of minerals, being the quantity necessary for testing, and not for commercial use.
5. There shall be no time limit on prospecting except that prospecting in a particular area shall cease upon written notification to the prospector by the Secretary-General that a plan of work for exploration has been approved with regard to that area.
6. Prospecting may be conducted simultaneously by more than one prospector in the same area or areas.

REGULATION 3: NOTIFICATION OF PROSPECTING.

1. A proposed prospector shall notify the Authority of its intention to engage in prospecting.
2. Each notification of prospecting shall be in the form prescribed in Annex 1 to these Regulations, addressed to the Secretary-General, and shall conform to the requirements of these Regulations.
3. Each notification shall be submitted:

   (a) In the case of a State, by the authority designated for that purpose by it;
   (b) In the case of an entity, by its designated representative; and
   (c) In the case of the Enterprise, by its competent authority.

4. Each notification shall be in one of the languages of the Authority and shall contain:

   (a) The name, nationality and address of the proposed prospector and its designated representative;
   (b) The coordinates of the broad area or are as within which prospecting is to be conducted, in accordance with the most recent generally accepted international standard used by the Authority;
   (c) A general description of the prospecting programme, including the proposed date of commencement and its approximate duration;
   (d) A satisfactory written undertaking that the proposed prospector will:

      (i) Comply with the Convention and the relevant rules, regulations and procedures of the Authority concerning:

a. Cooperation in the training programmes in connection with marine scientific research and transfer of technology referred to in articles 143 and 144 of the Convention; and
b. Protection and preservation of the marine environment; and

(ii) Accept verification by the Authority of compliance there with.

REGULATION 4: CONSIDERATION OF NOTIFICATIONS

1. The Secretary-General shall acknowledge in writing receipt of each notification submitted under regulation 3, specifying the date of receipt.
2. The Secretary-General shall review and act on the notification within 45 days of its receipt. If the notification conforms with the requirements of the Convention and these Regulations, the Secretary-General shall record the particulars of the notification in a register maintained for that purpose and shall inform the prospector in writing that the notification has been so recorded.
3. The Secretary-General shall, within 45 days of receipt of the notification, inform the proposed prospector in writing if the notification includes any part of an area included in an approved plan of work for exploration or exploitation of any category of resources, or any part of a reserved area, or any part of an area which has been disapproved by the Council for exploitation because of the risk of serious harm to the marine environment, or if the written undertaking is not satisfactory, and shall provide the proposed prospector with a written statement of reasons. In such cases, the proposed prospector may, within 90 days, submit an amended notification. The Secretary-General shall, within 45 days, review and act upon such amended notification.
4. A prospector shall inform the Secretary-General in writing of any change in the information contained in the notification.
5. The Secretary-General shall not release any particulars contained in the notification except with the written consent of the prospector. The Secretary-General shall, however, from time to time inform all members of the Authority of the identity of prospectors and the general areas in which prospecting is being conducted.

REGULATION 5: ANNUAL REPORT

1. A prospector shall, within 90 days of the end of each calendar year, submit a report to the Authority on the status of prospecting . . . Each such report shall contain:

   (a) A general description of the status of prospecting and of the results obtained; and
   (b) Information on compliance with the undertakings referred to in regulation 3, paragraph (4)(d).

2. If the prospector intends to claim expenditures for prospecting as part of the development costs incurred prior to the commencement of commercial production, the prospector shall submit an annual statement, in conformity with internationally accepted accounting principles and certified by a duly qualified firm of public accountants, of the actual and direct expenditures incurred by the prospector in carrying out prospecting.

REGULATION 6: CONFIDENTIALITY OF DATA AND INFORMATION FROM PROSPECTING CONTAINED IN THE ANNUAL REPORT

1. The Secretary-General shall ensure the confidentiality of all data and information contained in the reports submitted under regulation 5 in accordance with the provisions of regulations 35 and 36.
2. The Secretary-General may, at any time, with the consent of the prospector concerned, release data and information relating to prospecting in an area in respect of which a notification has been submitted. If the Secretary-General determines that the prospector no longer exists or cannot be located, the Secretary-General may release such data and information.

REGULATION 7: NOTIFICATION OF INCIDENTS CAUSING SERIOUS HARM TO THE MARINE ENVIRONMENT

A prospector shall immediately notify the Secretary-General in writing, using the most effective means, of any incident arising from prospecting which causes serious harm to the marine environment. Upon receipt of such notification the Secretary-General shall act in a manner consistent with regulation 32.

REGULATION 8: OBJECTS OF AN ARCHAEOLOGICAL OR HISTORICAL NATURE

A prospector shall immediately notify the Secretary-General in writing of any finding in the Area of an object of an archaeological or historical nature and its location . . .

## Part III: Applications for Approval of Plans of Work for Exploration in the Form of Contracts

### *Section 1: General Provisions*

REGULATION 9: GENERAL

Subject to the provisions of the Convention, the following may apply to the Authority for approval of plans of work for exploration:

(a) The Enterprise, on its own behalf or in a joint arrangement;
(b) States Parties, state enterprises or natural or juridical persons which possess the nationality of States Parties or are effectively controlled by them or their nationals, when sponsored by such States, or any group of the foregoing which meets the requirements of these Regulations.

### *Section 2: Content of Applications*

REGULATION 10: FORM OF APPLICATIONS

1. Each application for approval of a plan of work for exploration shall be in the form prescribed in Annex 2 to these Regulations, shall be addressed to the Secretary-General, and shall conform to the requirements of these Regulations.
2. Each application shall be submitted:

   (a) In the case of a State Party, by the authority designated for that purpose by it;
   (b) In the case of an entity, by its designated representative or the authority designated for that purpose by the sponsoring State or States; and
   (c) In the case of the Enterprise, by its competent authority.

3. Each application by a state enterprise or one of the entities referred to in subparagraph (b) of regulation 9 shall also contain:

   (a) Sufficient information to determine the nationality of the applicant or the identity of the State or States by which, or by whose nationals, the applicant is effectively controlled; and
   (b) The principal place of business or domicile and, if applicable, place of registration of the applicant.

4. Each application submitted by a partnership or consortium of entities shall contain the required information in respect of each member of the partnership or consortium.

REGULATION 11: CERTIFICATE OF SPONSORSHIP

1. Each application by a state enterprise or one of the entities referred to in subparagraph (b) of regulation 9 shall be accompanied by a certificate of sponsorship issued by the State of which it is a national or by which or by whose nationals it is effectively controlled . . .
3. Each certificate of sponsorship shall be duly signed on behalf of the State by which it is submitted and shall contain:

   (a) The name of the applicant;
   (b) The name of the sponsoring State;
   (c) A statement that the applicant is:

      (i) A national of the sponsoring State; or
      (ii) Subject to the effective control of the sponsoring State or its nationals;

   (d) A statement by the sponsoring State that it sponsors the applicant;
   (f) A declaration that the sponsoring State assumes responsibility in accordance with article 139, article 153, paragraph 4, and Annex III, article 4, paragraph 4, of the Convention.

4. States or entities in a joint arrangement with the Enterprise shall also comply with this regulation.

REGULATION 12: FINANCIAL AND TECHNICAL CAPABILITIES

1. Each application for approval of a plan of work for exploration shall contain specific and sufficient information to enable the Council to determine whether the applicant is financially and technically capable of carrying out the proposed plan of work for exploration and of fulfilling its financial obligations to the Authority.
2. An application for approval of a plan of work for exploration submitted on behalf of a State or entity, or any component of such entity, referred to in resolution II, paragraph 1(a)(ii) or (iii), other than a registered pioneer investor, which has already undertaken substantial activities in the Area prior to the entry into force of the Convention, or its successor in interest, shall be considered to have met the financial and technical qualifications necessary for approval of a plan of work for exploration if the sponsoring State or States certify that the applicant has expended an amount equivalent to at least US$ 30 million in research and exploration activities and has expended no less than 10 per cent

of that amount in the location, survey and evaluation of the area referred to in the plan of work for exploration.

3. An application for approval of a plan of work for exploration by the Enterprise shall include a statement by its competent authority certifying that the Enterprise has the necessary financial resources to meet the estimated costs of the proposed plan of work for exploration.
5. An application for approval of a plan of work for exploration by an entity, other than a registered pioneer investor or an entity referred to in resolution II, paragraph 1(a)(ii) or (iii), shall include copies of its audited financial statements, including balance sheets and profit-and-loss statements, for the most recent three years, in conformity with internationally accepted accounting principles and certified by a duly qualified firm of public accountants; and

   (a) If the applicant is a newly organized entity and a certified balance sheet is not available, a pro forma balance sheet certified by an appropriate official of the applicant;
   (b) If the applicant is a subsidiary of another entity, copies of such financial statements of that entity and a statement from that entity, in conformity with internationally accepted accounting principles and certified by a duly qualified firm of public accountants, that the applicant will have the financial resources to carry out the plan of work for exploration;
   (c) If the applicant is controlled by a State or a state enterprise, a statement from the State or state enterprise certifying that the applicant will have the financial resources to carry out the plan of work for exploration.

6. Where an applicant referred to in paragraph 5 intends to finance the proposed plan of work for exploration by borrowings, its application shall include the amount of such borrowings, the repayment period and the interest rate.
7. Except as provided for in paragraph 2, all applications shall include:

   (a) A general description of the applicant's previous experience, knowledge, skills, technical qualifications and expertise relevant to the proposed plan of work for exploration;
   (b) A general description of the equipment and methods expected to be used in carrying out the proposed plan of work for exploration and other relevant non-proprietary information about the characteristics of such technology; and
   (c) A general description of the applicant's financial and technical capability to respond to any incident or activity which causes serious harm to the marine environment.

8. Where the applicant is a partnership or consortium of entities in a joint arrangement, each member of the partnership or consortium shall provide the information required by this regulation.

REGULATION 13: PREVIOUS CONTRACTS WITH THE AUTHORITY

Where the applicant or, in the case of an application by a partnership or consortium of entities in a joint arrangement, any member of the partnership or consortium, has previously been awarded any contract with the Authority, the application shall include:

(a) The date of the previous contract or contracts;
(b) The dates, reference numbers and titles of each report submitted to the Authority in connection with the contract or contracts; and
(c) The date of termination of the contract or contracts, if applicable.

REGULATION 14: UNDERTAKINGS

Each applicant, including the Enterprise, shall, as part of its application for approval of a plan of work for exploration, provide a written undertaking to the Authority that it will:

(a) Accept as enforceable and comply with the applicable obligations created by the provisions of the Convention and the rules, regulations and procedures of the Authority, the decisions of the relevant organs of the Authority and the terms of its contracts with the Authority;
(b) Accept control by the Authority of activities in the Area, as authorized by the Convention; and
(c) Provide the Authority with a written assurance that its obligations under the contract will be fulfilled in good faith.

REGULATION 15: TOTAL AREA COVERED BY THE APPLICATION

Each application for approval of a plan of work for exploration shall define the boundaries of the area under application by a list of coordinates in accordance with the most recent generally accepted international standard used by the Authority. Applications other than those under regulation 17 shall cover a total area, which need not be a single continuous area, sufficiently large and of sufficient estimated commercial value to allow two mining operations. The applicant shall indicate the coordinates dividing the area into two parts of equal estimated commercial value. The area to be allocated to the applicant shall be subject to the provisions of regulation 25.

REGULATION 16: DATA AND INFORMATION TO BE SUBMITTED BEFORE THE DESIGNATION OF A RESERVED AREA

1. Each application shall contain sufficient data and information, as prescribed in Section II of Annex 2 to these Regulations, with respect to the area under application to enable the Council, on the recommendation of the Legal and Technical Commission, to designate a reserved area based on the estimated commercial value of each part . . .

REGULATION 17: APPLICATIONS FOR APPROVAL OF PLANS OF WORK WITH RESPECT TO A RESERVED AREA

1. Any State which is a developing State or any natural or juridical person sponsored by it and effectively controlled by it or by any other developing State, or any group of the foregoing, may notify the Authority that it wishes to submit a plan of work for exploration with respect to a reserved area. The Secretary-General shall forward such notification to the Enterprise, which shall inform the Secretary-General in writing within six months whether or not it intends to carry out activities in that area. If the Enterprise intends to carry out activities in that area, it shall, pursuant to paragraph 4, also inform in writing the contractor whose application for approval of a plan of work for exploration originally included that area.
2. An application for approval of a plan of work for exploration in respect of a reserved area may be submitted at any time after such an area becomes available following a

decision by the Enterprise that it does not intend to carry out activities in that area or where the Enterprise has not, within six months of the notification by the Secretary-General, either taken a decision on whether it intends to carry out activities in that area or notified the Secretary-General in writing that it is engaged in discussions regarding a potential joint venture. In the latter instance, the Enterprise shall have one year from the date of such notification in which to decide whether to conduct activities in that area.

3. If the Enterprise or a developing State or one of the entities referred to in paragraph 1 does not submit an application for approval of a plan of work for exploration for activities in a reserved area within 15 years of the commencement by the Enterprise of its functions independent of the Secretariat of the Authority or within 15 years of the date on which that area is reserved for the Authority, whichever is the later, the contractor whose application for approval of a plan of work for exploration originally included that area shall be entitled to apply for a plan of work for exploration for that area provided it offers in good faith to include the Enterprise as a joint venture partner.
4. A contractor has the right of first refusal to enter into a joint venture arrangement with the Enterprise for exploration of the area which was included in its application for approval of a plan of work for exploration and which was designated by the Council as a reserved area.

REGULATION 18: DATA AND INFORMATION TO BE SUBMITTED FOR APPROVAL OF THE PLAN OF WORK FOR EXPLORATION

After the Council has designated the reserved area, the applicant, if it has not already done so, shall submit, with a view to receiving approval of the plan of work for exploration in the form of a contract, the following information:

(a) A general description and a schedule of the proposed exploration programme, including the programme of activities for the immediate five year period, such as studies to be undertaken in respect of the environmental, technical, economic and other appropriate factors that must be taken into account in exploration;
(b) A description of the programme for oceanographic and environmental baseline studies in accordance with these Regulations and any environmental rules, regulations and procedures established by the Authority that would enable an assessment of the potential environmental impact of the proposed exploration activities, taking into account any recommendations issued by the Legal and Technical Commission;
(c) A preliminary assessment of the possible impact of the proposed exploration activities on the marine environment;
(d) A description of proposed measures for the prevention, reduction and control of pollution and other hazards, as well as possible impacts, to the marine environment;
(e) Data necessary for the Council to make the determination it is required to make in accordance with regulation 12, paragraph 1; and
(f) A schedule of anticipated yearly expenditures in respect of the programme of activities for the immediate five-year period.

## Part IV: Contracts for Exploration

REGULATION 23: THE CONTRACT

1. After a plan of work for exploration has been approved by the Council, it shall be prepared in the form of a contract between the Authority and the applicant as prescribed

in Annex 3 to these Regulations. Each contract shall incorporate the standard clauses set out in Annex 4 in effect at the date of entry into force of the contract.

3. In accordance with the principle of non-discrimination, a contract with a State or entity or any component of such entity referred to in paragraph 6(a)(i) of section 1 of the annex to the Agreement shall include arrangements that shall be similar to and no less favourable than those agreed with any registered pioneer investor . . .

REGULATION 24: RIGHTS OF THE CONTRACTOR

1. The contractor shall have the exclusive right to explore an area covered by a plan of work for exploration in respect of polymetallic nodules. The Authority shall ensure that no other entity operates in the same area for resources other than polymetallic nodules in a manner that might interfere with the operations of the contractor.
2. A contractor who has an approved plan of work for exploration only shall have a preference and a priority among applicants submitting plans of work for exploitation of the same area and resources. Such preference or priority may be withdrawn by the Council if the contractor has failed to comply with the requirements of its approved plan of work for exploration within the time period specified in a written notice or notices from the Council to the contractor indicating which requirements have not been complied with by the contractor. The time period specified in any such notice shall not be unreasonable. The contractor shall be accorded a reasonable opportunity to be heard before the withdrawal of such preference or priority becomes final. The Council shall provide the reasons for its proposed withdrawal of preference or priority and shall consider any contractor's response. The decision of the Council shall take account of that response and shall be based on substantial evidence.
3. A withdrawal of preference or priority shall not become effective until the contractor has been accorded a reasonable opportunity to exhaust the judicial remedies available to it pursuant to Part XI, section 5, of the Convention.

REGULATION 25: SIZE OF AREA AND RELINQUISHMENT

1. The total area allocated to the contractor under the contract shall not exceed 150,000 square kilometres. The contractor shall relinquish portions of the area allocated to it to revert to the Area, in accordance with the following schedule:

   (a) 20 per cent of the area allocated by the end of the third year from the date of the contract;
   (b) An additional 10 per cent of the area allocated by the end of the fifth year from the date of the contract; and
   (c) An additional 20 per cent of the area allocated or such larger amount as would exceed the exploitation area decided upon by the Authority, after eight years from the date of the contract,

   provided that a contractor shall not be required to relinquish any portion of such area when the total area allocated to it does not exceed 75,000 square kilometres.
2. In the case of a registered pioneer investor, the contract shall take into account the schedule of relinquishment, where applicable, in accordance with the terms of its registration as a registered pioneer investor.
3. The Council may, at the request of the contractor, and on the recommendation of the Commission, in exceptional circumstances, defer the schedule of relinquishment. Such

exceptional circumstances shall be determined by the Council and shall include, *inter alia*, consideration of prevailing economic circumstances or other unforeseen exceptional circumstances arising in connection with the operational activities of the Contractor.

REGULATION 26: DURATION OF CONTRACTS

1. A plan of work for exploration shall be approved for a period of 15 years. Upon expiration of a plan of work for exploration, the contractor shall apply for a plan of work for exploitation unless the contractor has already done so, has obtained an extension for the plan of work for exploration or decides to renounce its rights in the area covered by the plan of work for exploration.
2. Not later than six months before the expiration of a plan of work for exploration, a contractor may apply for extensions for the plan of work for exploration for periods of not more than five years each. Such extensions shall be approved by the Council, on the recommendation of the Commission, if the contractor has made efforts in good faith to comply with the requirements of the plan of work but for reasons beyond the contractor's control has been unable to complete the necessary preparatory work for proceeding to the exploitation stage or if the prevailing economic circumstances do not justify proceeding to the exploitation stage.

REGULATION 27: TRAINING

1. Pursuant to article 15 of Annex III to the Convention, each contract shall include as a schedule a practical programme for the training of personnel of the Authority and developing States and drawn up by the contractor in cooperation with the Authority and the sponsoring State or States. Training programmes shall focus on training in the conduct of exploration, and shall provide for full participation by such personnel in all activities covered by the contract . . .

REGULATION 29: TERMINATION OF SPONSORSHIP

1. Each contractor shall have the required sponsorship throughout the period of the contract.
2. If a Stage terminates its sponsorship it shall promptly notify the Secretary-General in writing. The sponsoring State should also inform the Secretary-General of the reasons for terminating its sponsorship. Termination of sponsorship shall take effect six months after the date of receipt of the notification by the Secretary-General unless the notification specifies a later date.
3. In the event of termination of sponsorship the contractor shall, within the period referred to in paragraph 2, obtain another sponsor. Such sponsor shall submit a certificate of sponsorship in accordance with regulation 11. Failure to obtain a sponsor within the required period shall result in the termination of the contract.
4. A sponsoring State shall not be discharged by reason of the termination of its sponsorship from any obligations accrued while it was a sponsoring State, nor shall such termination affect any legal rights and obligations created during such sponsorship.

REGULATION 30: RESPONSIBILITY AND LIABILITY

Responsibility and liability of the contractor and of the Authority shall be in accordance with the Convention. The contractor shall continue to have responsibility for any damage arising out of wrongful acts in the conduct of its operations, in particular damage to the marine environment, after the completion of the exploration phase.

## Part V: Protection and Preservation of the Marine Environment

REGULATION 31: PROTECTION AND PRESERVATION OF THE MARINE ENVIRONMENT

1. The Authority shall, in accordance with the Convention and the Agreement, establish and keep under periodic review environmental rules, regulations and procedures to ensure effective protection for the marine environment from harmful effects which may arise from activities in the Area.
2. In order to ensure effective protection for the marine environment from harmful effects which may arise from activities in the Area, the Authority and sponsoring States shall apply a precautionary approach, as reflected in principle 15 of the Rio Declaration, to such activities . . .
3. Pursuant to article 145 of the Convention and paragraph 2 of this regulation, each contractor shall take necessary measures to prevent, reduce and control pollution and other hazards to the marine environment arising from its activities in the Area as far as reasonably possible using the best technology available to it.
4. Each contract shall require the contractor to gather environmental baseline data and to establish environmental baselines, taking into account any recommendations issued by the Legal and Technical Commission pursuant to regulation 38, against which to assess the likely effects of its programme of activities under the plan of work for exploration on the marine environment and a programme to monitor and report on such effects.
5. The contractor shall report annually in writing to the Secretary-General on the implementation and results of the monitoring programme referred to in paragraph 4 and shall submit data and information, taking into account any recommendations issued by the Commission pursuant to regulation 38 . . .
6. Contractors, sponsoring States and other interested States or entities shall cooperate with the Authority in the establishment and implementation of programmes for monitoring and evaluating the impacts of deep seabed mining on the marine environment.
7. If the Contractor applies for exploitation rights, it shall propose areas to be set aside and used exclusively as impact reference zones and preservation reference zones. 'Impact reference zones' means areas to be used for assessing the effect of each contractor's activities in the Area on the marine environment and which are representative of the environmental characteristics of the Area. 'Preservation reference zones' means areas in which no mining shall occur to ensure representative and stable biota of the seabed in order to assess any changes in the flora and fauna of the marine environment.

REGULATION 32: EMERGENCY ORDERS

1. When the Secretary-General has been notified by a contractor or otherwise becomes aware of an incident resulting from or caused by a contractor's activities in the Area that has caused, or is likely to cause, serious harm to the marine environment, the Secretary-General shall issue a general notification of the incident, shall notify in writing the contractor and the sponsoring State or States, and shall report immediately to the Legal and Technical Commission and to the Council . . .
2. Pending any action by the Council, the Secretary-General shall take such immediate measures of a temporary nature as are practical and reasonable in the circumstances to prevent, contain and minimize serious harm to the marine environment . . .
3. After having received the report of the Secretary-General, the Commission shall determine, based on the evidence provided to it and taking into account the measures already taken by the contractor, which measures are necessary to respond effectively to the

incident in order to prevent, contain and minimize the serious harm, and shall make its recommendations to the Council.

5. The Council, taking into account the recommendations of the Commission and any information provided by the Contractor, may issue emergency orders, which may include orders for the suspension or adjustment of operations, as may be reasonably necessary to prevent, contain and minimize serious harm to the marine environment arising out of activities in the Area.
6. If a contractor does not promptly comply with an emergency order to prevent serious harm to the marine environment arising out of its activities in the Area, the Council shall take by itself or through arrangements with others on its behalf, such practical measures as are necessary to prevent, contain and minimize any such serious harm to the marine environment.
7. In order to enable the Council, when necessary, to take immediately the practical measures to prevent, contain and minimize serious harm to the marine environment referred to in paragraph 6, the contractor, prior to the commencement of testing of collecting systems and processing operations, will provide the Council with a guarantee of its financial and technical capability to comply promptly with emergency orders or to assure that the Council can take such emergency measures . . .

## Part VI: Confidentiality

REGULATION 35: PROPRIETARY DATA AND INFORMATION AND CONFIDENTIALITY

1. Data and information submitted or transferred to the Authority or to any person participating in any activity or programme of the Authority pursuant to these Regulations or a contract issued under these Regulations, and designated by the contractor, in consultation with the Secretary-General, as being of a confidential nature, shall be considered confidential unless it is data and information which:

   (a) Is generally known or publicly available from other sources;
   (b) Has been previously made available by the owner to others without an obligation concerning its confidentiality; or
   (c) Is already in the possession of the Authority with no obligation concerning its confidentiality.

2. Confidential data and information may only be used by the Secretary-General and staff of the Secretariat, as authorized by the Secretary-General, and by the members of the Legal and Technical Commission as necessary for and relevant to the effective exercise of their powers and functions.
3. Ten years after the date of submission of confidential data and information to the Authority or the expiration of the contract for exploration, whichever is the later, and every five years thereafter, the Secretary-General and the contractor shall review such data and information to determine whether they should remain confidential. Such data and information shall remain confidential if the contractor establishes that there would be a substantial risk of serious and unfair economic prejudice if the data and information were to be released. No such data and information shall be released until the contractor has been accorded a reasonable opportunity to exhaust the judicial remedies available to it pursuant to Part XI, section 5, of the Convention.

4. If, at any time following the expiration of the contract for exploration, the contractor enters into a contract for exploitation in respect of any part of the exploration area, confidential data and information relating to that part of the area shall remain confidential in accordance with the contract for exploitation.
5. The contractor may at any time waive confidentiality of data and information.

REGULATION 36: PROCEDURES TO ENSURE CONFIDENTIALITY

1. The Secretary-General shall be responsible for maintaining the confidentiality of all confidential data and information and shall not, except with the prior written consent of the contractor, release such data and information to any person external to the Authority. To ensure the confidentiality of such data and information, the Secretary-General shall establish procedures, consistent with the provisions of the Convention, governing the handling of confidential information by members of the Secretariat, members of the Legal and Technical Commission and any other person participating in any activity or programme of the Authority. Such procedures shall include:

   (a) Maintenance of confidential data and information in secure facilities and development of security procedures to prevent unauthorized access to or removal of such data and information;
   (b) Development and maintenance of a classification, log and inventory system of all written data and information received, including its type and source and routing from the time of receipt until final disposition.

2. A person who is authorized pursuant to these Regulations to have access to confidential data and information shall not disclose such data and information except as permitted under the Convention and these Regulations. The Secretary-General shall require any person who is authorized to have access to confidential data and information to make a written declaration witnessed by the Secretary-General or his or her authorized representative to the effect that the person so authorized:

   (a) Acknowledges his or her legal obligation under the Convention and these Regulations with respect to the non-disclosure of confidential data and information;
   (b) Agrees to comply with the applicable regulations and procedures established to ensure the confidentiality of such data and information.

3. The Legal and Technical Commission shall protect the confidentiality of confidential data and information submitted to it pursuant to these Regulations or a contract issued under these Regulations. In accordance with the provisions of article 163, paragraph 8, of the Convention, members of the Commission shall not disclose, even after the termination of their functions, any industrial secret, proprietary data which are transferred to the Authority in accordance with Annex III, article 14, of the Convention, or any other confidential information coming to their knowledge by reason of their duties for the Authority.
4. The Secretary-General and staff of the Authority shall not disclose, even after the termination of their functions with the Authority, any industrial secret, proprietary data which are transferred to the Authority in accordance with Annex III, article 14, of the Convention, or any other confidential information coming to their knowledge by reason of their employment with the Authority.

5. Taking into account the responsibility and liability of the Authority pursuant to Annex III, article 22, of the Convention, the Authority may take such action as may be appropriate against any person who, by reason of his or her duties for the Authority, has access to any confidential data and information and who is in breach of the obligations relating to confidentiality contained in the Convention and these Regulations.

REGULATION 38: RECOMMENDATIONS FOR THE GUIDANCE OF CONTRACTORS

1. The Legal and Technical Commission may from time to time issue recommendations of a technical or administrative nature for the guidance of contractors to assist them in the implementation of the rules, regulations and procedures of the Authority.
2. The full text of such recommendations shall be reported to the Council. Should the Council find that a recommendation is inconsistent with the intent and purpose of these Regulations, it may request that the recommendation be modified or withdrawn.

# 67. FAO: Code of Conduct for Responsible Fisheries, 1995

**Commentary**: The UN Convention on the Law of the Sea (UNCLOS, UN Doc A/CONF.62/122 (1982), entry into force 1994) grants coastal States rights and responsibilities for sustainably managing and using fishery resources within their exclusive economic zones (EEZs). By the late 1980s, it was apparent that fisheries resources would be unable to satisfy international demand for fish and fish products. In 1991 the FAO Committee on Fisheries (COFI) called for new management approaches embracing sustainable exploitation, conservation and environmental protection. The 1992 International Conference on Responsible Fishing in Cancun requested the FAO to prepare an international Code of Conduct addressing these concerns. Developing this instrument was carried out in collaboration with FAO members, interested non-Members, relevant UN Agencies, other international organisations and NGOs. Negotiations included a Technical Consultation in 1994 and a Working Group and Technical Committee during 1995: see Annex I concerning background information on the origin and elaboration of the Code. Negotiators were mindful of the desirability of harmonising Articles 6 and 7 of the Code with the Agreement for the Implementation of the Provisions of UNCLOS Relating to the Conservation and Management of Straddling Fish Stocks and Highly Migratory Fish Stocks and the 1993 FAO Agreement to Promote Compliance with International Conservation and Management Measures by Fishing Vessels on the High Seas. Article 3 of the Code states that it is to be interpreted and applied in conformity with these and other relevant international legal rules.

The FAO Conference Resolution adopting the Code called upon 'States, International Organizations, whether Governmental or Non-Governmental, and all those involved in fisheries to collaborate in the fulfilment and implementation of the objectives and principles contained in this Code': FAO Conference Resolution of 31 October 1995 (28th Session), Annex 2, para 2. Although the Code identifies the responsibilities of governments, subregional and regional fisheries management organisations, the extracts below focus upon expectations for the fishing industry.

See further, FAO Ministerial Meeting on Fisheries (1999), 'Rome Declaration on the Implementation of the Code of Conduct for Responsible Fisheries'; COFI (2001), 'Progress Report on the Code of Conduct for Responsible Fisheries', 24th Session, Rome. The FAO Fisheries Department is entrusted with monitoring implementation and has formulated Technical Guidelines for Responsible Fisheries and a strategy in support of implementation: see FAO Doc COFI/99/INF.6 (1999). See further, the four International Plans of Action and the Strategy for Improving Information on Status and Trends of Capture Fisheries, 2003. See also, www.fao.org/fi. The FAO Code forms the basis for the Australian Seafood Industry Council's Code of Conduct for a Responsible Seafood Industry and the US National Marine Fisheries Service's Implementation Plan for the Code of Conduct for Responsible Fisheries.

**Article 1: Nature and Scope of the Code**

1.1. This Code is voluntary . . . The Code also contains provisions that may be or have already been given binding effect by means of other obligatory legal instruments amongst the Parties . . .

1.2. The Code is global in scope, and is directed toward members and non-members of FAO, fishing entities, subregional, regional and global organizations, whether governmental or non-governmental, and all persons concerned with the conservation of fishery resources and management and development of fisheries, such as fishers, those engaged in processing and marketing of fish and fishery products and other users of the aquatic environment in relation to fisheries.

1.3. The Code provides principles and standards applicable to the conservation, management and development of all fisheries. It also covers the capture, processing and trade of fish and fishery products, fishing operations, aquaculture, fisheries research and the integration of fisheries into coastal area management.

**Article 2: Objectives of the Code**

The objectives of the Code are to:

a) establish principles, in accordance with the relevant rules of international law, for responsible fishing and fisheries activities, taking into account all their relevant biological, technological, economic, social, environmental and commercial aspects;
e) facilitate and promote technical, financial and other cooperation in conservation of fisheries resources and fisheries management and development;
f) promote the contribution of fisheries to food security and food quality, giving priority to the nutritional needs of local communities;
g) promote protection of living aquatic resources and their environments and coastal areas;
h) promote the trade of fish and fishery products in conformity with relevant international rules and avoid the use of measures that constitute hidden barriers to such trade;
j) provide standards of conduct for all persons involved in the fisheries sector.

**Article 4: Implementation, Monitoring and Updating**

4.1. All members and non-members of FAO, fishing entities and relevant subregional, regional and global organizations, whether governmental or non-governmental, and all persons concerned with the conservation, management and utilization of fisheries resources and trade in fish and fishery products should collaborate in the fulfilment and implementation of the objectives and principles contained in this Code.

4.2. FAO, in accordance with its role within the UN system, will monitor the application and implementation of the Code and its effects on fisheries and the Secretariat will report accordingly to the Committee on Fisheries (COFI). All States, whether members or non-members of FAO, as well as relevant international organizations, whether governmental or non-governmental should actively cooperate with FAO in this work.

4.4. States and international organizations, whether governmental or non-governmental, should promote the understanding of the Code among those involved in fisheries, including, where practicable, by the introduction of schemes which would promote voluntary acceptance of the Code and its effective application.

**Article 5: Special Requirements of Developing Countries**

5.2. . . . States, relevant intergovernmental and non-governmental organizations and financial institutions should work for the adoption of measures to address the needs of developing countries, especially in the areas of financial and technical assistance, technology transfer, training and scientific cooperation and in enhancing their ability to develop their own fisheries as well as to participate in high seas fisheries, including access to such fisheries.

**Article 6: General Principles**

6.1. States and users of living aquatic resources should conserve aquatic ecosystems. The right to fish carries with it the obligation to do so in a responsible manner so as to ensure effective conservation and management of the living aquatic resources.

6.2. Fisheries management should promote the maintenance of the quality, diversity and availability of fishery resources in sufficient quantities for present and future generations in the context of food security, poverty alleviation and sustainable development. Management measures should not only ensure the conservation of target species but also of species belonging to the same ecosystem or associated with or dependent upon the target species.

6.4. Conservation and management decisions for fisheries should be based on the best scientific evidence available, also taking into account traditional knowledge of the resources and their habitat, as well as relevant environmental, economic and social factors . . .

6.5. States and subregional and regional fisheries management organizations should apply a precautionary approach widely to conservation, management and exploitation of living aquatic resources in order to protect them and preserve the aquatic environment, taking account of the best scientific evidence available . . .

6.6. Selective and environmentally safe fishing gear and practices should be further developed and applied, to the extent practicable, in order to maintain biodiversity and to conserve the population structure and aquatic ecosystems and protect fish quality . . .

6.7. The harvesting, handling, processing and distribution of fish and fishery products should be carried out in a manner which will maintain the nutritional value, quality and safety of the products, reduce waste and minimize negative impacts on the environment.

6.9. States should ensure that their fisheries interests, including the need for conservation of the resources, are taken into account in the multiple uses of the coastal zone and are integrated into coastal area management, planning and development.

6.11. States authorizing fishing and fishing support vessels to fly their flags should exercise effective control over those vessels so as to ensure the proper application of this Code . . .

6.13. . . . States, in accordance with appropriate procedures, should facilitate consultation and the effective participation of industry, fishworkers, environmental and other interested organizations in decision making with respect to the development of laws and policies related to fisheries management, development, international lending and aid.

6.14. International trade in fish and fishery products should be conducted in accordance with the principles, rights and obligations established in the World Trade Organization (WTO) Agreement and other relevant international agreements . . .

6.16. States, recognizing the paramount importance to fishers and fishfarmers of understanding the conservation and management of the fishery resources on which they depend, should promote awareness of responsible fisheries through education and training. They should ensure that fishers and fishfarmers are involved in the policy formulation and implementation process, also with a view to facilitating the implementation of the Code.

6.17. States should ensure that fishing facilities and equipment as well as all fisheries activities allow for safe, healthy and fair working and living conditions and meet internationally agreed standards adopted by relevant international organizations.

**Article 7: Fisheries Management**

7.1.1. States and all those engaged in fisheries management should, through an appropriate policy, legal and institutional framework, adopt measures for the long term conservation and sustainable use of fisheries resources. Conservation and management measures, whether at local, national, subregional or regional levels, should be based on the best scientific evidence available and be designed to ensure the long-term sustainability of fishery resources at levels which promote the objective of their optimum utilization and maintain their availability for present and future generations; short term considerations should not compromise these objectives.

7.1.2. Within areas under national jurisdiction, States should seek to identify relevant domestic parties having a legitimate interest in the use and management of fisheries resources and establish arrangements for consulting them to gain their collaboration in achieving responsible fisheries.

7.1.6. Representatives from relevant organizations, both governmental and non-governmental, concerned with fisheries should be afforded the opportunity to take part in meetings of subregional and regional fisheries management organizations and arrangements as observers or otherwise, as appropriate, in accordance with the procedures of the organization or arrangement concerned. Such representatives should be given timely access to the records and reports of such meetings, subject to the procedural rules on access to them.

7.1.10. States and subregional or regional fisheries management organizations and arrangements should give due publicity to conservation and management measures and ensure that laws, regulations and other legal rules governing their implementation are effectively disseminated . . .

7.2.2. Such measures should provide *inter alia* that:

a) excess fishing capacity is avoided and exploitation of the stocks remains economically viable;
b) the economic conditions under which fishing industries operate promote responsible fisheries;
c) the interests of fishers, including those engaged in subsistence, small-scale and artisanal fisheries, are taken into account;
d) biodiversity of aquatic habitats and ecosystems is conserved and endangered species are protected;
e) depleted stocks are allowed to recover or, where appropriate, are actively restored;

f) adverse environmental impacts on the resources from human activities are assessed and, where appropriate, corrected; and
g) pollution, waste, discards, catch by lost or abandoned gear, catch of non-target species, both fish and non-fish species, and impacts on associated or dependent species are minimized, through measures including, to the extent practicable, the development and use of selective, environmentally safe and cost-effective fishing gear and techniques.

7.4.7. Subregional or regional fisheries management organizations or arrangements should compile data and make them available, in a manner consistent with any applicable confidentiality requirements, in a timely manner and in an agreed format to all members of these organizations and other interested parties in accordance with agreed procedures.

7.5.1. States should apply the precautionary approach widely to conservation, management and exploitation of living aquatic resources in order to protect them and preserve the aquatic environment. The absence of adequate scientific information should not be used as a reason for postponing or failing to take conservation and management measures . . .

7.6.4. The performance of all existing fishing gear, methods and practices should be examined and measures taken to ensure that fishing gear, methods and practices which are not consistent with responsible fishing are phased out and replaced with more acceptable alternatives . . .

7.6.7. In the evaluation of alternative conservation and management measures, their cost-effectiveness and social impact should be considered.

7.8.1. Without prejudice to relevant international agreements, States should encourage banks and financial institutions not to require, as a condition of a loan or mortgage, fishing vessels or fishing support vessels to be flagged in a jurisdiction other than that of the State of beneficial ownership where such a requirement would have the effect of increasing the likelihood of non-compliance with international conservation and management measures.

**Article 8: Fishing Operations**

8.1.5. States should ensure that health and safety standards are adopted for everyone employed in fishing operations. Such standards should be not less than the minimum requirements of relevant international agreements on conditions of work and service.

8.1.10. States, with the assistance of relevant international organizations, should endeavour to ensure through education and training that all those engaged in fishing operations be given information on the most important provisions of this Code, as well as provisions of relevant international conventions and applicable environmental and other standards that are essential to ensure responsible fishing operations.

8.2.5. Flag States should ensure compliance with appropriate safety requirements for fishing vessels and fishers in accordance with international conventions, internationally agreed codes of practice and voluntary guidelines.

8.2.7. Flag States should take enforcement measures in respect of fishing vessels entitled to fly their flag which have been found by them to have contravened applicable conservation and management measures, including, where appropriate, making the contravention of such measures an offence under national legislation . . .

8.2.8. Flag States should promote access to insurance coverage by owners and charterers of fishing vessels. Owners or charterers of fishing vessels should carry sufficient insurance cover to protect the crew of such vessels and their interests, to indemnify third parties against loss or damage and to protect their own interests.

8.4.1. States should ensure that fishing is conducted with due regard to the safety of human life and the International Maritime Organization International Regulations for Preventing Collisions at Sea, as well as International Maritime Organization requirements relating to the organization of marine traffic, protection of the marine environment and the prevention of damage to or loss of fishing gear.

8.4.2. States should prohibit dynamiting, poisoning and other comparable destructive fishing practices.

8.4.3. States should make every effort to ensure that documentation with regard to fishing operations, retained catch of fish and non-fish species and, as regards discards, the information required for stock assessment as decided by relevant management bodies, is collected and forwarded systematically to those bodies.

8.4.4. States should promote the adoption of appropriate technology, taking into account economic conditions, for the best use and care of the retained catch.

8.4.5. States, with relevant groups from industry, should encourage the development and implementation of technologies and operational methods that reduce discards . . .

8.4.7. States should ensure that assessments of the implications of habitat disturbance are carried out prior to the introduction on a commercial scale of new fishing gear, methods and operations to an area.

8.5.1. States should require that fishing gear, methods and practices, to the extent practicable, are sufficiently selective so as to minimize waste, discards, catch of non-target species, both fish and non-fish species, and impacts on associated or dependent species and that the intent of related regulations is not circumvented by technical devices. In this regard, fishers should cooperate in the development of selective fishing gear and methods . . .

8.5.2. In order to improve selectivity, States should, when drawing up their laws and regulations, take into account the range of selective fishing gear, methods and strategies available to the industry.

8.6.2. States should promote the development and transfer of technology in relation to energy optimization within the fisheries sector and, in particular, encourage owners, charterers and managers of fishing vessels to fit energy optimization devices to their vessels.

8.7.2. Owners, charterers and managers of fishing vessels should ensure that their vessels are fitted with appropriate equipment as required by MARPOL 73/78 and should consider fitting a shipboard compactor or incinerator to relevant classes of vessels in order to treat garbage and other shipboard wastes generated during the vessel's normal service.

8.7.3. Owners, charterers and managers of fishing vessels should minimize the taking aboard of potential garbage through proper provisioning practices.

8.7.4. The crew of fishing vessels should be conversant with proper shipboard procedures in order to ensure discharges do not exceed the levels set by MARPOL 73/78. Such procedures should, as a minimum, include the disposal of oily waste and the handling and storage of shipboard garbage.

8.8.2. Owners, charterers and managers of fishing vessels should ensure that their vessels are fitted with equipment to reduce emissions of ozone depleting substances. The responsible crew members of fishing vessels should be conversant with the proper running and maintenance of machinery on board.

8.8.3. Competent authorities should make provision for the phasing out of the use of chlorofluorocarbons (CFCs) and transitional substances such as hydrochlorofluorocarbons (HCFCs) in the refrigeration systems of fishing vessels and should ensure that the shipbuilding industry and those engaged in the fishing industry are informed of and comply with such provisions.

8.8.4. Owners or managers of fishing vessels should take appropriate action to refit existing vessels with alternative refrigerants to CFCs and HCFCs and alternatives to Halons in fire fighting installations. Such alternatives should be used in specifications for all new fishing vessels.

8.8.5. States and owners, charterers and managers of fishing vessels as well as fishers should follow international guidelines for the disposal of CFCs, HCFCs and Halons.

### Article 9: Aquaculture Development

9.1.2. States should promote responsible development and management of aquaculture, including an advance evaluation of the effects of aquaculture development on genetic diversity and ecosystem integrity, based on the best available scientific information.

9.2.1. States should protect transboundary aquatic ecosystems by supporting responsible aquaculture practices within their national jurisdiction and by cooperation in the promotion of sustainable aquaculture practices.

9.4.1. States should promote responsible aquaculture practices in support of rural communities, producer organizations and fish farmers.

9.4.2. States should promote active participation of fishfarmers and their communities in the development of responsible aquaculture management practices.

### Article 10: Integration of Fisheries into Coastal Area Management

10.1.2. In view of the multiple uses of the coastal area, States should ensure that representatives of the fisheries sector and fishing communities are consulted in the decision-making processes and involved in other activities related to coastal area management planning and development.

10.1.3. States should develop, as appropriate, institutional and legal frameworks in order to determine the possible uses of coastal resources and to govern access to them taking into account the rights of coastal fishing communities and their customary practices to the extent compatible with sustainable development.

10.1.5. States should promote the establishment of procedures and mechanisms at the appropriate administrative level to settle conflicts which arise within the fisheries sector and between fisheries resource users and other users of the coastal area.

10.2.1. States should promote the creation of public awareness of the need for the protection and management of coastal resources and the participation in the management process by those affected.

10.2.2. In order to assist decision-making on the allocation and use of coastal resources, States should promote the assessment of their respective value taking into account economic, social and cultural factors.

10.4.2. States should ensure that the authority or authorities representing the fisheries sector in the coastal management process have the appropriate technical capacities and financial resources.

**Article 11: Post-Harvest Practices and Trade**

11.1.1. States should adopt appropriate measures to ensure the right of consumers to safe, wholesome and unadulterated fish and fishery products.

11.1.2. States should establish and maintain effective national safety and quality assurance systems to protect consumer health and prevent commercial fraud.

11.1.3. States should set minimum standards for safety and quality assurance and make sure that these standards are effectively applied throughout the industry . . .

11.1.5. States should give due consideration to the economic and social role of the post-harvest fisheries sector when formulating national policies for the sustainable development and utilization of fishery resources.

11.1.7. States, noting the existence of different production methods, should through cooperation and by facilitating the development and transfer of appropriate technologies, ensure that processing, transporting and storage methods are environmentally sound.

11.1.8. States should encourage those involved in fish processing, distribution and marketing to:

a) reduce post-harvest losses and waste;
b) improve the use of by-catch to the extent that this is consistent with responsible fisheries management practices; and
c) use the resources, especially water and energy, in particular wood, in an environmentally sound manner.

11.1.11. States should ensure that international and domestic trade in fish and fishery products accords with sound conservation and management practices through improving the identification of the origin of fish and fishery products traded.

11.1.12. States should ensure that environmental effects of post-harvest activities are considered in the development of related laws, regulations and policies without creating any market distortions.

11.2.3. States should ensure that measures affecting international trade in fish and fishery products are transparent, based, when applicable, on scientific evidence, and are in accordance with internationally agreed rules.

11.2.4. Fish trade measures adopted by States to protect human or animal life or health, the interests of consumers or the environment, should not be discriminatory and should be in accordance with internationally agreed trade rules, in particular the principles, rights and obligations established in the Agreement on the Application of Sanitary and Phytosanitary Measures and the Agreement on Technical Barriers to Trade of the WTO.

11.2.6. States should not directly or indirectly create unnecessary or hidden barriers to trade which limit the consumer's freedom of choice of supplier or that restrict market access.

11.3.2. States, in accordance with their national laws, should facilitate appropriate consultation with and participation of industry as well as environmental and consumer groups in the development and implementation of laws and regulations related to trade in fish and fishery products.

11.3.4. When a State introduces changes to its legal requirements affecting trade in fish and fishery products with other States, sufficient information and time should be given to allow the States and producers affected to introduce, as appropriate, the changes needed in their processes and procedures . . .

**Article 12: Fisheries Research**

12.1. States should recognize that responsible fisheries requires the availability of a sound scientific basis to assist fisheries managers and other interested parties in making decisions . . .

12.3. States should ensure that data generated by research are analyzed, that the results of such analyses are published, respecting confidentiality where appropriate, and distributed in a timely and readily understood fashion, in order that the best scientific evidence is made available as a contribution to fisheries conservation, management and development.

12.9. States should ensure that the economic, social, marketing and institutional aspects of fisheries are adequately researched and that comparable data are generated for ongoing monitoring, analysis and policy formulation.

12.11. States should ensure that before the commercial introduction of new types of gear, a scientific evaluation of their impact on the fisheries and ecosystems where they will be used should be undertaken. The effects of such gear introductions should be monitored.

# 68. Marine Stewardship Council: Principles and Criteria for Sustainable Fishing, 2002

**Commentary**: The Marine Stewardship Council (MSC, www.msc.org) was established in 1997 by Unilever and the World Wide Fund for Nature. It is currently supported by approximately 100 organisations in more than 20 States. Fisheries irrespective of size voluntarily conforming to the MSC Principles and Criteria are eligible for certification by independent MSC-accredited organisations. The Principles and Criteria seek to promote sustainable and effective fisheries management, ecosystem integrity and legal compliance.

## Introduction

At the centre of the MSC is a set of Principles and Criteria for Sustainable Fishing which are used as a standard in a third party, independent and voluntary certification programme. These were developed by means of an extensive, international consultative process through which the views of stakeholders in fisheries were gathered.

These Principles reflect a recognition that a sustainable fishery should be based upon:

(i) The maintenance and re-establishment of healthy populations of targeted species;
(ii) The maintenance of the integrity of ecosystems;
(iii) The development and maintenance of effective fisheries management systems, taking into account all relevant biological, technological, economic, social, environmental and commercial aspects; and
(iv) Compliance with relevant local and national local laws and standards and international understandings and agreements.

The Principles and Criteria are further designed to recognise and emphasise that management efforts are most likely to be successful in accomplishing the goals of conservation and sustainable use of marine resources when there is full co-operation among the full range of fisheries stakeholders, including those who are dependent on fishing for their food and livelihood.

On a voluntary basis, fisheries which conform to these Principles and Criteria will be eligible for certification by independent MSC-accredited certifiers. Fish processors, traders and retailers will be encouraged to make public commitments to purchase fish products only from certified sources. This will allow consumers to select fish products with the confidence that they come from sustainable, well managed sources. It will also benefit the fishers and the fishing industry who depend on the abundance of fish stocks, by providing market incentives to work towards sustainable practices. Fish processors, traders and retailers who buy from certified sustainable sources will in turn benefit from the assurance of continuity of future supply and hence sustainability of their own businesses.

The MSC promotes equal access to its certification programme irrespective of the scale of the fishing operation. The implications of the size, scale, type, location and intensity of the fishery, the uniqueness of the resources and the effects on other ecosystems will be considered in every certification.

The MSC further recognises the need to observe and respect the long-term interests of people dependent on fishing for food and livelihood to the extent that it is consistent with ecological sustainability, and also the importance of fisheries management and operations being conducted in a manner consistent with established local, national, and international rules and standards as well as in compliance with the MSC Principles and Criteria.

*Preamble*

The following Principles & Criteria are intended to guide the efforts of the Marine Stewardship Council towards the development of sustainable fisheries on a global basis. They were developed assuming that a sustainable fishery is defined, for the purposes of MSC certification, as one that is conducted in such a way that:

(i) it can be continued indefinitely at a reasonable level;
(ii) it maintains and seeks to maximise, ecological health and abundance;
(iii) it maintains the diversity, structure and function of the ecosystem on which it depends as well as the quality of its habitat, minimising the adverse effects that it causes;
(iv) it is managed and operated in a responsible manner, in conformity with local, national and international laws and regulations;
(v) it maintains present and future economic and social options and benefits;
(vi) it is conducted in a socially and economically fair and responsible manner.

The Principles represent the overarching philosophical basis for this initiative in stewardship of marine resources: the use of market forces to promote behaviour which helps achieve the goal of sustainable fisheries. They form the basis for detailed Criteria which will be used to evaluate each fishery seeking certification under the MSC programme. Although the primary focus is the ecological integrity of world fisheries, the principles also embrace the human and social elements of fisheries. Their successful implementation depends upon a system which is open, fair, based upon the best information available and which incorporates all relevant legal obligations. The certification programme in which these principles will be applied is intended to give any fishery the opportunity to demonstrate its commitment to sustainable fishing and ultimately benefit from this commitment in the market place.

*Scope*

The scope of the MSC Principles and Criteria relates to marine fisheries activities up to but not beyond the point at which the fish are landed. However, MSC-accredited certifiers may be informed of serious concerns associated with post-landing practices.[1]

The MSC Principles and Criteria apply at this stage only to wildcapture fisheries (including, but not limited to shellfish, crustaceans and cephalopods). Aquaculture and the harvest of other species are not currently included.

Issues involving allocation of quotas and access to marine resources are considered to be beyond the scope of these Principles and Criteria.

PRINCIPLE 1

A fishery must be conducted in a manner that does not lead to over-fishing or depletion of the exploited populations and, for those populations that are depleted, the fishery must be conducted in a manner that demonstrably leads to their recovery.[2]

Intent:

The intent of this principle is to ensure that the productive capacities of resources are maintained at high levels and are not sacrificed in favour of short term interests. Thus, exploited populations would be maintained at high levels of abundance designed to retain their productivity, provide margins of safety for error and uncertainty, and restore and retain their capacities for yields over the long term.

Criteria:

1. The fishery shall be conducted at catch levels that continually maintain the high productivity of the target population(s) and associated ecological community relative to its potential productivity.
2. Where the exploited populations are depleted, the fishery will be executed such that recovery and rebuilding is allowed to occur to a specified level consistent with the precautionary approach and the ability of the populations to produce long-term potential yields within a specified time frame.
3. Fishing is conducted in a manner that does not alter the age or genetic structure or sex composition to a degree that impairs reproductive capacity.

PRINCIPLE 2

Fishing operations should allow for the maintenance of the structure, productivity, function and diversity of the ecosystem (including habitat and associated dependent and ecologically related species) on which the fishery depends.

Intent:

The intent of this principle is to encourage the management of fisheries from an ecosystem perspective under a system designed to assess and restrain the impacts of the fishery on the ecosystem.

Criteria:

1. The fishery is conducted in a way that maintains natural functional relationships among species and should not lead to trophic cascades or ecosystem state changes.
2. The fishery is conducted in a manner that does not threaten biological diversity at the genetic, species or population levels and avoids or minimises mortality of, or injuries to endangered, threatened or protected species.
3. Where exploited populations are depleted, the fishery will be executed such that recovery and rebuilding is allowed to occur to a specified level within specified time frames, consistent with the precautionary approach and considering the ability of the population to produce long-term potential yields.

PRINCIPLE 3

The fishery is subject to an effective management system that respects local, national and international laws and standards and incorporates institutional and operational frameworks that require use of the resource to be responsible and sustainable.

Intent:
The intent of this principle is to ensure that there is an institutional and operational framework for implementing Principles 1 and 2, appropriate to the size and scale of the fishery.

A. Management System Criteria
1. The fishery shall not be conducted under a controversial unilateral exemption to an international agreement.

The management system shall:
2. demonstrate clear long-term objectives consistent with MSC Principles and Criteria and contain a consultative process that is transparent and involves all interested and affected parties so as to consider all relevant information, including local knowledge. The impact of fishery management decisions on all those who depend on the fishery for their livelihoods, including, but not confined to subsistence, artisanal, and fishing dependent communities shall be addressed as part of this process;
3. be appropriate to the cultural context, scale and intensity of the fishery – reflecting specific objectives, incorporating operational criteria, containing procedures for implementation and a process for monitoring and evaluating performance and acting on findings;
4. observe the legal and customary rights and long term interests of people dependent on fishing for food and livelihood, in a manner consistent with ecological sustainability;
5. incorporates an appropriate mechanism for the resolution of disputes arising within the system;[3]
6. provide economic and social incentives that contribute to sustainable fishing and shall not operate with subsidies that contribute to unsustainable fishing;
7. act in a timely and adaptive fashion on the basis of the best available information using a precautionary approach particularly when dealing with scientific uncertainty;
8. incorporate a research plan – appropriate to the scale and intensity of the fishery – that addresses the information needs of management and provides for the dissemination of research results to all interested parties in a timely fashion;
9. require that assessments of the biological status of the resource and impacts of the fishery have been and are periodically conducted;
10. specify measures and strategies that demonstrably control the degree of exploitation of the resource, including, but not limited to:

    a) setting catch levels that will maintain the target population and ecological community's high productivity relative to its potential productivity, and account for the non-target species (or size, age, sex) captured and landed in association with, or as a consequence of, fishing for target species;
    b) identifying appropriate fishing methods that minimise adverse impacts on habitat, especially in critical or sensitive zones such as spawning and nursery areas;
    c) providing for the recovery and rebuilding of depleted fish populations to specified levels within specified time frames;
    d) mechanisms in place to limit or close fisheries when designated catch limits are reached;
    e) establishing no-take zones where appropriate;

11. contains appropriate procedures for effective compliance, monitoring, control, surveillance and enforcement which ensure that established limits to exploitation are not exceeded and specifies corrective actions to be taken in the event that they are.

B. Operational Criteria

Fishing operation shall:

12. make use of fishing gear and practices designed to avoid the capture of non-target species (and non-target size, age, and/or sex of the target species); minimise mortality of this catch where it cannot be avoided, and reduce discards of what cannot be released alive;
13. implement appropriate fishing methods designed to minimise adverse impacts on habitat, especially in critical or sensitive zones such as spawning and nursery areas;
14. not use destructive fishing practices such as fishing with poisons or explosives;
15. minimise operational waste such as lost fishing gear, oil spills, on-board spoilage of catch, etc;
16. be conducted in compliance with the fishery management system and all legal and administrative requirements; and
17. assist and co-operate with management authorities in the collection of catch, discard, and other information of importance to effective management of the resources and the fishery.

## Notes

1. Other complementary certification programmes (e.g., ISO 14000) provide opportunities for documenting and evaluating impacts of post landing activities related to fisheries products certified to MSC standards. Constructive solutions to address these concerns through appropriate measures should be sought through dialogue with certification organisations and other relevant bodies.
2. The sequence in which the Principles and Criteria appear does not represent a ranking of their significance, but is rather intended to provide a logical guide to certifiers when assessing a fishery. The criteria by which the MSC Principles will be implemented will be reviewed and revised as appropriate in light of relevant new information, technologies and additional consultations.
3. Outstanding disputes of substantial magnitude involving a significant number of interests will normally disqualify a fishery from certification.

# 69. UN: Treaty on Principles Governing the Activities of States in the Exploration and Use of Outer Space, including the Moon and Other Celestial Bodies, 1967

**Commentary**: The Outer Space Treaty (610 *UNTS* 205, entry into force 1967) derives from UNGA Resolution 1962 (1963). The exploration and use of outer space is for the benefit of all States (Article I) and is therefore not subject to national appropriation (Article II). In addition to the provisions below, governments undertake consultations where they believe that activities by their nationals would cause potentially harmful interference to others (Article IX). See further, UNGA Resolution 51/122 (1996) concerning a Declaration on International Cooperation in the Exploration and Use of Outer Space for the Benefit and in the Interest of All States, Taking into Particular Account the Needs of Developing Countries and the Report of the Legal Subcommittee on the work of its forty-third session, UN Doc A/AC.105/826 (2004). For academic commentary, see Williams S.M. (1987), 'International law and the exploration of outer space: a new market for private enterprise?', in Snyder F.E. and Sathirathai S. (eds), *Third World Attitudes toward International Law*, Dordrecht: Martinus Nijhoff, 787. See also, UN Office for Outer Space Affairs: www.oosa.unvienna.org.

**Article VI**

States Parties to the Treaty shall bear international responsibility for national activities in outer space, including the moon and other celestial bodies, whether such activities are carried on by governmental agencies or by non-governmental entities, and for assuring that national activities are carried out in conformity with the provisions set forth in the present Treaty. The activities of non-governmental entities in outer space, including the moon and other celestial bodies, shall require authorization and continuing supervision by the appropriate State Party to the Treaty . . .

**Article VII**

Each State Party to the Treaty that launches or procures the launching of an object into outer space, including the moon and other celestial bodies, and each State Party from whose territory or facility an object is launched, is internationally liable for damage to another State Party to the Treaty or to its natural or juridical persons by such object or its component parts on the Earth, in air or in outer space, including the moon and other celestial bodies.

# 70. UN: Agreement Governing the Activities of States on the Moon and Other Celestial Bodies, 1979

**Commentary**: The Moon Agreement (1986 *ATS* No 14, entry into force 1984) provides that the moon and its natural resources are the common heritage of mankind and contemplates a future international regime governing exploitation. Article 4 provides that exploration and use of the moon is for the benefit of all States with due regard to development and the interests of present and future generations. Article 6 establishes freedom of scientific investigation and Article 12 envisages governments retaining jurisdiction and control over their personnel, vehicles, equipment, facilities, stations and installations.

**Article 1**

1. The provisions of this Agreement relating to the moon shall also apply to other celestial bodies within the solar system, other than the earth, except in so far as specific legal norms enter into force with respect to any of these celestial bodies.
2. For the purposes of this Agreement reference to the moon shall include orbits around or other trajectories to or around it.
3. This Agreement does not apply to extraterrestrial materials which reach the surface of the earth by natural means.

**Article 11**

1. The moon and its natural resources are the common heritage of mankind . . .
2. The moon is not subject to national appropriation by any claim of sovereignty, by means of use or occupation, or by any other means.
3. Neither the surface nor the subsurface of the moon, nor any part thereof or natural resources in place, shall become property of any State, international intergovernmental or non-governmental organization, national organization or non-governmental entity or of any natural person. The placement of personnel, space vehicles, equipment, facilities, stations and installations on or below the surface of the moon, including structures connected with its surface or subsurface, shall not create a right of ownership over the surface or the subsurface of the moon or any areas thereof.
5. States Parties to this Agreement hereby undertake to establish an international regime, including appropriate procedures, to govern the exploitation of the natural resources of the moon as such exploitation is about to become feasible . . .
7. The main purposes of the international regime to be established shall include:

(a) The orderly and safe development of the natural resources of the moon;
(b) The rational management of those resources;
(c) The expansion of opportunities in the use of those resources;
(d) An equitable sharing by all States Parties in the benefits derived from those resources, whereby the interests and needs of the developing countries, as well as the efforts of those countries which have contributed either directly or indirectly to the exploration of the moon, shall be given special consideration . . .

**Article 14**

1. States Parties to this Agreement shall bear international responsibility for national activities on the moon, whether such activities are carried on by governmental agencies or by non-governmental entities, and for assuring that national activities are carried out in conformity with the provisions set forth in this Agreement. States Parties shall ensure that non-governmental entities under their jurisdiction shall engage in activities on the moon only under the authority and continuing supervision of the appropriate State Party . . .

# 71. UN: Convention on International Liability for Damage Caused by Space Objects, 1972

**Commentary**: The Liability Convention (961 *UNTS* 187, entry into force 1972) furthers Article 7 of the Outer Space Treaty (above). Launching States are absolutely liable to pay compensation for damage caused by their space objects on the earth's surface or to aircraft and become liable where at fault for damage in space. Compensation claims under Article X must ordinarily be presented within one year following the date of damage or identification of the launching State. Under Article XI, the prior exhaustion of local remedies is not required and nothing precludes governments or the natural or juridical persons they represent from pursuing claims before the national courts of launching States. Article XIV envisages a Claims Commission where diplomatic settlements cannot be concluded.

**Article I**

For the purposes of this Convention:

(a) The term 'damage' means loss of life, personal injury or other impairment of health; or loss of or damage to property of States or of persons, natural or juridical, or property of international intergovernmental organizations;

(b) The term 'launching' includes attempted launching;

(d) The term 'space object' includes component parts of a space object as well as its launch vehicle and parts thereof.

**Article II**

A launching State shall be absolutely liable to pay compensation for damage caused by its space object on the surface of the earth or to aircraft flight.

**Article III**

In the event of damage being caused elsewhere than on the surface of the earth to a space object of one launching State or to persons or property on board such a space object by a space object of another launching State, the latter shall be liable only if the damage is due to its fault or the fault of persons for whom it is responsible.

**Article IV**

1. In the event of damage being caused elsewhere than on the surface of the earth to a space object of one launching State or to persons or property on board such a space object by

a space object of another launching State, and of damage thereby being caused to a third State or to its natural or juridical persons, the first two States shall be jointly and severally liable to the third State, to the extent indicated by the following:

(a) If the damage has been caused to the third State on the surface of the earth or to aircraft in flight, their liability to the third State shall be absolute;
(b) If the damage has been caused to a space object of the third State or to persons or property on board that space object elsewhere than on the surface of the earth, their liability to the third State shall be based on the fault of either of the first two States or on the fault of persons for whom either is responsible . . .

**Article VI**

1. Subject to the provisions of paragraph 2 of this Article, exoneration from absolute liability shall be granted to the extent that a launching State establishes that the damage has resulted either wholly or partially from gross negligence or from an act or omission done with intent to cause damage on the part of a claimant State or of natural or juridical persons it represents . . .
2. No exoneration whatever shall be granted in cases where the damage has resulted from activities conducted by a launching State which are not in conformity with international law including, in particular, the Charter of the United Nations and the Treaty on Principles Governing the Activities of States in the Exploration and Use of Outer Space, including the Moon and Other Celestial Bodies.

**Article VII**

The provisions of this Convention shall not apply to damage caused by a space object of a launching State to:

(a) nationals of that launching State;
(b) foreign nationals during such time as they are participating in the operation of that space object from the time of its launching or at any stage thereafter until its descent, or during such time as they are in the immediate vicinity of a planned launching or recovery area as the result of an invitation by that launching State.

**Article VIII**

1. A State which suffers damage, or whose natural or juridical persons suffer damage, may present to a launching State a claim for compensation for such damage.
2. If the State of nationality has not presented a claim, another State may, in respect of damage sustained in its territory by any natural or juridical person, present a claim to a launching State.
3. If neither the State of nationality nor the State in whose territory the damage was sustained has presented a claim or notified its intention of presenting a claim, another State may, in respect of damage sustained by its permanent residents, present a claim to a launching State.

**Article XII**

The compensation which the launching State shall be liable to pay for damage under this Convention shall be determined in accordance with international law and the principles of justice and equity, in order to provide such reparation in respect of the damage as will restore the person, natural or juridical, State or international organization on whose behalf the claim is presented to the condition which would have existed if the damage had not occurred.

# 72. Australian–Asian Pacific Mining Network: Principles for the Conduct of Company Operations within the Minerals Industry, 1997

**Commentary**: The Principles are not a code of conduct but rather guidelines from which groups and organisations may draw information to develop mining agreements. They are not final or definitive but form the basis for ongoing negotiations. The Principles represent the collective views of the Australian Asia-Pacific Mining Network as at 1997 and are not necessarily the current views of any particular NGO, partner group or grassroot community network affected by mining within the Asia-Pacific region. See further, mining declarations arising from meetings in Bali (part of the World Summit on Sustainable Development); Manado, Indonesia (the first international conference on submarine tailings disposal); Madang, Papua New Guinea (PNG–specific mining); and India (concerning Women and Mining).

The Network includes the Australian Conservation Foundation (ACF), the Australian Council for Overseas Aid, the Australian Red Cross, Amnesty International, Community Aid Abroad, the Mineral Policy Institute, the World Wide Fund for Nature and the Uniting Church–Social Responsibility & Justice. These organisations do not endorse those Principles falling outside their mandate. The Network considers that where legislative implementation or international treaties are not viable enforcement options, possible sanctions include removing tax concessions, access to government loans and/or insurance. Only the Principles are reproduced below (available through www.natural-resources.org/minerals/csr/practices.htm) and the useful explanatory commentary, quotations, further references and bibliography are omitted.

For other NGO initiatives, see ACF (1995), 'Principles for the Conduct of Australian Mining Companies operating in Papua New Guinea'; Friends of the Earth (1997), 'Draft Model Code for Mining Projects'. For business initiatives, see Keidanren (Japan Federation of Economic Organisations) (1991), 'The Global Environment Charter and the Ten Point Environmental Guidelines for Japanese Enterprises Operating Abroad'. For intergovernmental initiatives, see UNEP (1992), 'Guidelines for the Environmental Management of Aluminium Production'; UNIDO (1994), 'Pollution Prevention and Abatement Guidelines for the Alumina Industry'; World Bank (1995), 'Environment, Health and Safety Guidelines: Milling and Open Pit Mining'.

**Definitions**

Landowners: The term landowners is used in this document to include both legally recognised landowners under the prevailing land tenure and traditional owners of land regardless of whether their land rights are recognised under prevailing land tenure.

Disjunctive process: A process whereby the company and landowners make separate agreements to cover the exploration phase and the mining phase.

Conjunctive process: A process whereby the company and landowners make an agreement that covers both the exploration and mining phases. That is landowners agree to mining if a workable deposit is found as a result of the exploration.

Independent: Not selected by or connected with a company or any body having a vested (financial or ownership) interest in the company or the minerals industry.

Participation: As equal partners in any process, with full access to all necessary information and a share in the decision making process, including the right to publish dissenting reports.

Affected people: Any person, persons or community affected either financially, socially or environmentally by a project.

Community: A term defining all those parties with an interest in a project or an area or issue affected by a project. The nature and extent of community will vary from place to place and time to time.

Involuntary resettlement: Is resettlement that is agreed to by the community, as a result of their agreement to a project proceeding on their land(s). Not to be confused with forced resettlement to which people have not consented.

International best practice: The standards by which a project should be operated, as defined jointly by the company, independent experts and the community. Hopefully this will keep changing and improving.

Tailing(s): Waste materials generated at the end of milling and separation of metal from ore.

Ore: material containing both the metal to be extracted and waste materials.

Stakeholders: Those individuals, community groups or other organisations whose interests are affected by a company's actions. Among the most important of these stakeholders are: residents of local communities in which companies have production facilities or offices; competitors in the related small business fields; business and trade associations; state and national governments; regional and international intergovernmental organisations; local, regional and international not-for-profit, non-governmental organisations working for human rights, education, welfare, economic or cultural development, environmental protection, and various other humane objectives; employees and contractors who work for the company.

Non-Governmental Organisation: Refers to organisations or special interest groups that represent grass roots people's movements and concerns as opposed to government or business interests.

Ecologically Sustainable Development: There is no clear and unambiguous definition of ESD. At best it is regarded as a process of change designed to effectively integrate ecological, social and economic considerations such that the needs of future generations are protected in the process of meeting the needs of the present generations. It is based upon a series of principles regarding such matters as resource use, global equity, intergenerational equity and the nature of development.

Environmental Impact Assessment: The identification, assessment and evaluation of the potential environmental effects associated with any particular policy, program, project or development proposal. To this definition it is important to add processes of monitoring and follow up.

Socio-economic Impact Assessment: The identification, assessment and evaluation of the natural, or biophysical, environmental impacts to include the social and socioeconomic impacts that may be associated with any particular policy, program, project or development proposal.

Code of Conduct: A statement of universal principles and ethical guidelines for the way that a company will regulate a whole range of relationships between the company and the stakeholders who are affected by its activities. Other organisations such as NGOs need similar codes.

**Terms Used**

1. 'the must': The legal obligations, prescriptions and proscriptions under which mining companies operate.
2. 'the should': The moral obligations under which mining companies operate.

**Principles for the Conduct of Company Operations within the Minerals Industry**

*Background*

The following position paper has been prepared by Australian based NGOs, with a view to providing a basic set of principles which should be followed by minerals companies regardless of where they are operating or under what circumstances. It is intended to have a general application for the operations of mining and oil and gas companies. In addition we hope that the paper will provide a useful resource document for governments, communities and non-government organisations which are dealing with minerals companies, environmental and human rights issues.

It is important to stress that this paper is primarily directed at providing a broad set of principles. It cannot and does not attempt to set prescriptive standards for individual projects which minerals companies may undertake. Nevertheless there are aspects of these principles that provide definitive guidelines (as opposed to technical standards) which companies should follow, such as the guidelines applying to the management of tailings, waste rock and acid mine drainage.

*General/Overriding Principles*

2.1. Extraterritoriality: Companies should be bound by the jurisdiction of the territory in which they have their headquarters, regardless of where they are operating (The principle of extraterritoriality).

Australian companies operating overseas should adhere, at all stages of operations to the highest standards of environmental protection and management that are required and practised in Australia.

Companies should comply with local and international standards where these are higher than in Australia.

2.2. Public Disclosure/Community Right to Know: Companies should fully disclose all commissioned reports by governments, companies and other stakeholders relating to environmental, social, human, political, civil and social rights and health and safety issues.

2.3. Community Participation: Companies should include community participation at all stages of project identification, development and monitoring.

Companies should include NGOs/communities and/or their nominated representatives, in the community's right to know and participation in the development of environmental impact statements and social impact statements.

2.4. Confidentiality Clauses and Issues: Companies should avoid binding parties to extensive confidentiality clauses.

2.5. Company Involvement in Legislative and Political Issues: Companies should not becoming involved in the drafting of legislation for governments in which they have a vested interest.

2.6. Standards for Lending, Insurance and Investment: Companies involved in the mining industry, including banks, insurance companies, investment funds, superannuation funds should establish ethical guidelines which preclude investing, insuring or lending to companies which are not prepared to abide by acceptable codes of conduct. Such codes should be in line with community standards and endorsed by community groups.

2.7. Funding for Community Participation (trusts etc.): Companies should establish trust accounts in order to ensure resources to enable adequate levels of community and NGO participation when requesting such organisation to help them in their work. Such trusts should be administered independently of either company or NGOs by a Board of trustees, which should include representatives of companies, and of community groups but which has a majority of independent representatives.

2.8. International Treaties and Codes, including Compliance: Companies should abide by all relevant international treaties and codes such as mentioned in this document.

2.9. Community (Local) Employment: Companies should implement programs for the employment of the local people.

2.10. Education and Training (eg Cultural Awareness): All employees involved (including CEOs etc.) in decision-making should be required to undertake appropriate training/cultural awareness and environmental workshops. Employees should be bound by codes of conduct as a condition of employment with appropriate penalties for breaches.

2.11. Conduct of Annual General Meetings (AGMs): Companies should accept AGMs as suitable forums for discussions and questioning on key matters of public interest and should extend a broad invitation to affected communities and community groups to send representatives.

*Land Rights, Land Ownership and Indigenous Issues*

3.1. Resettlement: Companies should not forcibly remove or be a party to others who want to remove indigenous people from their land or territories. No relocation shall take place without free and informed consent of the indigenous peoples concerned and after agreement on just and fair compensation

Companies should not operate any project in areas where any forced removals from land have occurred.

Companies should ensure that if the development of a mine means that people have to be moved off the mining site, then the resettlement and rehabilitation of those people, should be agreed to by the people of the affected community. Such removals should be carefully planned and implemented by the mining company, so that no affected person, group or community has their standard of living, economic, culture and social cohesion diminished as a result.

3.2. Royalty and Compensation Agreements: Companies should ensure that all royalties and compensation agreements are based on international best practice in terms of terms and conditions being the highest achievable by landowners for equity, participation, employment, royalties and compensation.

3.3. Traditional Land Rights: Companies must recognise indigenous people and their traditional or customary ownership of land especially where a host government does not recognise the legal status of customary land.

3.4. Protocols for Negotiations: Mining companies should develop and publish a code of practice for negotiations over exploration and mining with communities and NGOs.

3.5. Right to Negotiate and Veto: Companies must recognise that every community has a right to negotiate over the use of its land and impose a veto on development that it does not support.

3.6. Negotiations With and Participation of other Land Owners: Companies must ensure that all landowners are fully involved in any negotiations concerning any minerals operations which affects or has the potential to affect them.

3.7. Disjunctive versus Conjunctive Agreements: All agreements with indigenous people or other landowners should be based on the disjunctive agreement process whereby a separate agreement is required at both mining and exploration stages.

3.8. Small Scale Mining: Companies should recognise the legitimate role and rights of small-scale miners and not seek to obtain minerals leases that involve their dispossession. Where appropriate companies should negotiate agreements with small-scale miners for compensation, where such miners are prepared to relinquish their land. Where the activities of large companies adversely affect small-scale miners appropriate compensation should be paid.

*Environmental Standards*

Companies must abide by the following Principles based on International Treaties or Conventions.

4.1. Baseline Data Establishment: Companies should establish baseline monitoring programs at a very early stage.

4.2. Waste Management, Treatment and Disposal: Companies must recognise and take action to prevent any type of ocean and/or riverine tailings disposal that is not acceptable. Companies should recognise that mineral deposits must not be developed unless tailings containment is available and acceptable, from safety and other perspectives.

Companies must ensure that pollution of riverine, ground-water and marine environments does not occur from waste rock dumps.

4.3. Areas Closed to Exploration and Mining: Companies must ensure that they make a firm commitment to putting various areas off limits to both exploration and mining. These should include all world heritage listed areas, all national parks, conservation reserves, international sites (such as Ramsar sites) and most areas listed for indigenous cultural reasons. Where possible there should be buffer areas around such parks and reserves.

4.4. Precautionary Principle: All companies should operate according to the precautionary principle, which provides that in the event of doubt about the potential impacts of an action or operation, the company should avoid taking that course of action . . .

4.5. Intergenerational Equity: Companies should ensure that all mining operations adhere to the principle of intergenerational equity.

Companies should adhere to the following Principles at all times even where there may be no relevant International Treaty or Obligation.

4.6. Sustainable Development: Companies must publicly recognise that mining in its basic form of simple extraction of a non-renewable resource cannot be considered sustainable and should not be portrayed as such.

Companies that are vertically integrated companies, should produce reports showing how the company is achieving recycling of metal products. Non-vertically integrated companies (ie mining companies without manufacturing/retailing arms) should demonstrate agreements with other companies which set out goals for metals recycling targets of goods produced from company minerals.

Companies should set goals for waste minimisation, recycling and life cycle targets for minerals/mineral products.

4.7. Acid Mine Drainage: Companies should not mine high sulphide ore-bodies unless steps are in place to prevent the effects of Acid Mine Drainage (AMD).

4.8. Uranium and Nuclear Fuel Cycle: Companies should not be involved in the mining, milling or processing of uranium.

4.9. Definitions of Environmental Best Practice: Companies should agree to best practice targets being defined not by companies, but by independent committees comprising scientists, other experts (eg social scientists) NGOs community representatives, and company representatives.

4.10. Rehabilitation and Rehabilitation Bonds: Companies should be required to rehabilitate land as closely as possible to its pre-mining condition.

4.11. Social Value of Minerals: Companies should include in their assessment of investment options the social usefulness of minerals to be extracted.

4.12. Transport and Trade: Companies should identify mechanisms by which all the environmental and social costs involved in transport and trade operations can be avoided or minimised.

4.13. Polluter Pays: Companies should ensure that all environmental costs involved in mining, milling, transport and processing of minerals should be borne by the company as polluter/generator and should include these costs as part of their feasibility assessment. These should include all external costs such as impacts on recreational values or tourism, costs of remediating accidents and other associated social costs. Advance compensation agreements should be negotiated, where appropriate. Full costs of rehabilitation and ongoing monitoring should be borne by the developer.

4.14. Continuous Environmental Improvement: Companies should operate under the concept of continuous environmental improvement. This concept provides for continual annual review of environmental targets. Community groups should be involved in setting these targets at all levels.

4.15. Hazards and Contingency Planning: Companies should prepare a plan to deal with a range of potential accidents and environmental emergencies associated with mining. These should include off-site activities such as transport.

4.16. Environmental Cost Accounting: Companies should ensure that accounting practices identify all costs, such as environmental and social costs, associated with company operations and these are taken into account in actual pricing of resources and, where appropriate lodged in trust funds for post mine rehabilitation.

4.17. Environmental and Social Impact Assessment: Companies should carry out environmental and social impact assessment for both exploration and mining activities. The company using independent consultants agreed to by both the company and the community, or the representative organisation of the community's choice should pay for studies. All EIAs should include the option for mining not to proceed at all if environmental and social impacts are found to be sufficiently severe.

*Human Rights Issues including Civil, Political and Social Rights*

5.1. General Principles:

Mining companies have a responsibility to contribute to the promotion and protection of human rights.

All mining companies have a direct responsibility to respect human rights in their own operations.

The mining industry, as a business community, also has a wider responsibility in both moral and legal terms to use its influence to promote respect for human rights.

Protecting and promoting human rights is good for effective and profitable mining business.

Mining companies should acknowledge the potential for human rights abuse through the environmental impacts of development, and should further seek to minimise environmental impact for human rights promotion.

5.2. Best Practice for Human Rights for Mining Companies:

Mining companies should develop a Company Policy for human rights.

Mining companies should prescribe and enforce a set of operational principles relating to all aspects of mining operations for the protection and promotion of human rights.

In practice, achieving the above would mean that the company is committed to a number of practical steps laid out in the following operational principles checklist.

(i) Ensure Appropriate Security Arrangements.
(ii) Ensure Effective Community Engagement.
(iii) Ensure Freedom From Discrimination.
(iv) Ensure Freedom From Slavery.
(v) Ensure Effective Health and Safety.
(vi) Ensure Freedom Of Association And The Right To Collective Bargaining.
(vii) Ensure Fair Working Conditions.
(viii) Monitoring Human Rights.

5.3. Economic Considerations For Human Rights Promotion and Protection.

While it is not our place to prescribe effective mining practice on economic grounds, we believe the following to be worthy considerations for the joint goal of effective business and human rights promotion and protection:

Mining companies which uphold their obligations on human rights as previously described will be likely to build a stronger reputation which is important for business in several ways.
Mining companies enhance their reputation amongst shareholders, corporate colleagues, and potential government partners by pursuing a human rights agenda as part of core business.
Protecting human rights helps to build a stronger and more stable community and society within which company operations must take place.
Mining Companies that demonstrate moral leadership by supporting such issues as human rights are more likely to have an enthusiastic and committed work force.

5.4. International Humanitarian Law (IHL) with respect to Armed Conflict:
Mining companies must do all that is reasonable within their power to avoid exacerbating the social, political and cultural climate, which might lead to armed conflict.
It is recognised that mining companies have legitimate concerns to protect themselves and their employees.
Mining companies should not operate in areas where such operations require the use of military forces or excessive security in order to maintain the operation.
Companies must not hire mercenaries to protect their business interests.
Companies must be mindful of important IHL treaties, such as the Geneva Conventions of 1949 and the Additional Protocols to those Conventions of 1977.

*Labour Standards and Workers' Rights*

6.2. The Must-Obligations of Companies:
Companies must observe not only the labour laws applicable in the countries in which they operate but also International Human Rights law and the ILO conventions, regardless of whether such laws have been ratified by the states within which companies operate.
Companies must recognise that basic workers' rights is of fundamental importance and in the legitimate interests of employees and contractors adhere to the following conventions:

6.3. The Right and Freedom to Work: Companies must recognise that everyone has the right to work, to free choice of employment, to just and favourable conditions of work and to protection against unemployment.

6.4. Equal Pay for Equal Work: Companies must recognise that 'everyone without discrimination has the right to equal pay for equal work'.

6.5. Just Reward: Companies must recognise that 'everyone who works has a right to just and favourable remuneration ensuring for him/herself and his/her family an existence worthy of human dignity supplemented, if necessary, by other means of social protection'.

6.6. Right to Holidays and Leisure: Companies must recognise that 'everyone has the right to rest and leisure, including reasonable limitations of working hours and periodic holidays'.

6.7. Standard of Living/Income: Companies must recognise that 'everyone has the right to a standard of living adequate for health and well-being of him/herself and his/her family, including food, clothing, housing and medical care and necessary social services, and the right to security in the event of unemployment, sickness, disability, widowhood, old age or lack of livelihood in circumstances beyond his/her control'.

6.8. No Slave or Forced Labour: Companies must recognise that forced labour is unacceptable, and therefore, 'no one shall be required to perform forced or compulsory labour' and 'no one shall be held in slavery; slavery and the slave trade in all their forms shall be prohibited'.

6.9. Non Discrimination: Companies must recognise that all people have the right to work 'without discrimination of any kind as to race, colour, sex, language, religion, political or other opinion, nationality or social origin, property, birth or other status'.

6.10. Vocational Training: Companies must recognise that all people have the right to 'technical and vocational guidance and training programs, policies and techniques to achieve steady economic, social and cultural development and full and productive employment under conditions safeguarding fundamental political and economic freedoms'.

6.11. Conditions of Employment: Companies must recognise the right of everyone to the enjoyment of just and favourable conditions of work which ensure, in particular:

(i) fair wages and equal remuneration for work of equal value without distinction of any kind, in particular women being guaranteed conditions of work nor inferior to those by men, with equal pay for equal work;
(ii) a decent living for themselves and their families in accordance with the provisions of the present Covenant;
(iii) equal opportunity for everyone to be promoted in his/her employment to an appropriate higher level. Subject to no considerations other those of seniority and competence;
(iv) rest, leisure and reasonable limitations of working hours and periodic holidays with pay, as well as remuneration for public holidays.

6.12. Trade Union Rights:
Companies must recognise the right of everyone to form trade unions and join the trade union of his/her choice, subject only to the rules of the organisation concerned, for the promotion and protection of his/her economic and social interests. No restrictions may be placed on the exercise of this right other than those prescribed by law, which are necessary in a democratic society in the interests of national security or public order or for the protection of the rights and freedoms of others.
Companies must recognise the right of trade unions to establish national federations or confederations and the right of the latter to form or join international trade-union organisations.
Companies must recognise the right of trade unions to freely operate subject to no limitations other than those prescribed by law and which are necessary in a democratic society in the interests of national security or public order or for the protection of the rights and freedoms of others.
Companies must recognise the right to strike provided that it is exercised in conformity with the laws of the particular country.
Companies should promote collective bargaining as the most fair way for the employer–employee relationship.

6.13. The Elimination of Discrimination against Women:
Companies must not discriminate against women and therefore must recognise:

(i) the right to work as an inalienable right of all human beings;
(ii) all people have the right to the same employment opportunities, including the application of the same criteria for selection in matters of employment;
(iii) the right to free choice of profession and employment, the right to promotion, job security and all benefits and conditions of service and the right to receive vocational training and retraining, including apprenticeships, advance vocational training and recurrent training;
(iv) the right to equal remuneration including benefits, and to equal treatment in respect of work of equal value, as well as equality of treatment in the evaluation of the quality of work;
(v) the right to social security, particularly in cases of retirement, unemployment, sickness, invalidity and old age and other incapacity to work, as well as the right to paid leave;
(vi) the right to protection of health and safety in working conditions, including the safeguarding of the function of reproduction.

6.14. Discrimination on the Basis of Marriage or Maternity:
Companies must recognise the special needs of women and thus:

(i) insure against 'dismissal on the grounds of pregnancy or of maternity leave and discrimination in dismissal on the basis of marital status';
(ii) introduce 'maternity leave with pay or with comparable social benefits without loss of former employment, seniority or social allowances';
(iii) support clauses which 'encourage provision of the necessary supporting social services to enable parents to combine family obligations with work responsibilities . . . in particular through promoting the establishment and development of a network of child care facilities';
(iv) recognise the need 'to provide special protection to women during pregnancy in types of work proved to be harmful to them.'

6.15. Children and Work:
Companies must recognise 'the right of the child to be protected from economic exploitation from performing any work that is likely to be hazardous or to interfere with the child's education, or be harmful to the child's health or physical, mental, spiritual, moral or social development.'
Companies must 'respect the minimum age for admission to employment'.

*Independent Monitoring, Auditing and Reporting*

7.1. Codes of Conduct including Enforcement:
Companies should adhere to codes of conduct that are acceptable to NGOs and landowners groups/communities in the host countries (where projects are occurring). Codes should include:

(i) the company's position in relation to issues: its philosophy and rationale.
(ii) the mechanisms by which the company will fulfil its obligations.
(iii) the nature and format of a regular, open and candid reporting system.
(iv) provision for independent monitoring, undertaken in consultation with NGOs with expertise.

7.2. Independent Monitoring:
Companies should allow an ongoing process of independent transparent monitoring of their operations, including the impact of company operations on environmental, labour, human, civil, political and social rights.
The company shall appoint a director for human rights. This director will have a direct line of mutual communication with local management and the Board of Directors. The director shall have staff support in the form of human rights experts.

7.3. Promoting Compliance: The company must recognise that if the code of human rights conduct is to be complied with then a regular and independent external review of the policy as practised must be implemented.

7.4. Independent Auditing: Companies should have regular and independent audits of their operations carried out by independent auditors, which include representatives nominated by relevant stakeholders.

7.5. Design and Implementation of Monitoring and Auditing: Companies must recognise that design and implementation of the independent monitoring and auditing should be jointly designed by the company in consultation with representatives of communities and NGOs.

7.6. Independent Verification and Reporting: Companies must report the results of auditing and monitoring programs in an annual report prepared and verified by an independent auditor agreed to by stakeholder representatives.

7.7. Complaints Mechanism: Companies should support the establishment of an independent and accessible complaint mechanism, to which communities who feel that the industry's standards have been breached by a particular mine can bring complaints.

# 73. Ceres: The Ceres Principles, 1989

**Commentary**: Originally formulated following the *Exxon Valdez* oil disaster, the Ceres Principles currently promote responsible corporate environmental conduct irrespective of industry sector by encouraging continuous improvement, ongoing dialogue and annual reporting. Ceres was formerly known as the Coalition for Environmentally Responsible Economies. Approximately 70 companies to date (principally US based) have endorsed the Principles which *inter alia* commit them to addressing stakeholder concerns. See further, www.ceres.org.

**Introduction**

By endorsing the Ceres Principles, companies not only formalize their dedication to environmental awareness and accountability, but also actively commit to an ongoing process of continuous improvement, dialogue and comprehensive, systematic public reporting. Endorsing companies have access to the diverse array of experts in our network, from investors to policy analysts, energy experts, scientists, and others.

**Principles**

*1. Protection of the Biosphere*

We will reduce and make continual progress toward eliminating the release of any substance that may cause environmental damage to the air, water, or the earth or its inhabitants. We will safeguard all habitats affected by our operations and will protect open spaces and wilderness, while preserving biodiversity.

*2. Sustainable Use of Natural Resources*

We will make sustainable use of renewable natural resources, such as water, soils and forests. We will conserve non-renewable natural resources through efficient use and careful planning.

*3. Reduction and Disposal of Wastes*

We will reduce and where possible eliminate waste through source reduction and recycling. All waste will be handled and disposed of through safe and responsible methods.

*4. Energy Conservation*

We will conserve energy and improve the energy efficiency of our internal operations and of the goods and services we sell. We will make every effort to use environmentally safe and sustainable energy sources.

*5. Risk Reduction*
We will strive to minimize the environmental, health and safety risks to our employees and the communities in which we operate through safe technologies, facilities and operating procedures, and by being prepared for emergencies.

*6. Safe Products and Services*
We will reduce and where possible eliminate the use, manufacture or sale of products and services that cause environmental damage or health or safety hazards. We will inform our customers of the environmental impacts of our products or services and try to correct unsafe use.

*7. Environmental Restoration*
We will promptly and responsibly correct conditions we have caused that endanger health, safety or the environment. To the extent feasible, we will redress injuries we have caused to persons or damage we have caused to the environment and will restore the environment.

*8. Informing the Public*
We will inform in a timely manner everyone who may be affected by conditions caused by our company that might endanger health, safety or the environment. We will regularly seek advice and counsel through dialogue with persons in communities near our facilities. We will not take any action against employees for reporting dangerous incidents or conditions to management or to appropriate authorities.

*9. Management Commitment*
We will implement these Principles and sustain a process that ensures that the Board of Directors and Chief Executive Officer are fully informed about pertinent environmental issues and are fully responsible for environmental policy. In selecting our Board of Directors, we will consider demonstrated environmental commitment as a factor.

*10. Audits and Reports*
We will conduct an annual self-evaluation of our progress in implementing these Principles. We will support the timely creation of generally accepted environmental audit procedures. We will annually complete the Ceres Report, which will be made available to the public.

**Disclaimer**
These Principles establish an environmental ethic with criteria by which investors and others can assess the environmental performance of companies. Companies that endorse these Principles pledge to go voluntarily beyond the requirements of the law. The terms 'may' and 'might' in Principles one and eight are not meant to encompass every imaginable consequence, no matter how remote. Rather, these Principles obligate endorsers to behave as prudent persons who are not governed by conflicting interests and who possess a strong commitment to environmental excellence and to human health and safety. These Principles are not intended to create new legal liabilities, expand existing rights or obligations, waive legal defences, or otherwise affect the legal position of any endorsing company, and are not intended to be used against an endorser in any legal proceeding for any purpose.

**Endorsing Company Statement**

By adopting these Principles, we publicly affirm our belief that corporations have a responsibility for the environment, and must conduct all aspects of their business as responsible stewards of the environment by operating in a manner that protects the Earth. We believe that corporations must not compromise the ability of future generations to sustain themselves. We will update our practices constantly in light of advances in technology and new understandings in health and environmental science. In collaboration with Ceres, we will promote a dynamic process to ensure that the Principles are interpreted in a way that accommodates changing technologies and environmental realities. We intend to make consistent, measurable progress in implementing these Principles and to apply them to all aspects of our operations throughout the world.

# 74. Additional initiatives

## i. UN: World Charter for Nature, 1982

**Commentary**: UNGA Resolution 37/7 (1982), paragraph 21, provides *inter alia* that: States and, to the extent that they are able, other public authorities, international organisations, individuals, groups and corporations shall:

(a) Co-operate in the task of conserving nature through common activities and other relevant actions, including information exchange and consultations;
(b) Establish standards for products and manufacturing processes that may have adverse effects on nature, as well as agreed methodologies for assessing these effects;
(c) Implement the applicable international legal provisions for the conservation of nature and the protection of the environment;
(d) Ensure that activities within their jurisdictions or control do not cause damage to the natural systems located within other States or in the areas beyond the limits of national jurisdiction;
(e) Safeguard and conserve nature in areas beyond national jurisdiction.

The Charter also refers to the precautionary principle. See further, EC (2000), 'Commission Communication on the Precautionary Principle', COM (2000)/1FINAL. For commercial perspectives, see CEFIC (1995), 'The Precautionary Principle, Industry and Law-making, Brussels'; ICC (1997), 'A Precautionary Approach: An ICC Business Perspective', Policy Statement, Paris; CEFIC (2000), 'Views on the Precautionary Principle', Brussels; CEFIC (2000), 'Comments on the Commission Communication on the Precautionary Principle of 2 February 2000', Brussels; ICCA (2000), 'Comments on the Application of the Precautionary Principle in Regulatory Decision-making', Arlington, VA; ACC (2001), 'The Precautionary Principle: An Industry Perspective on Domestic and International Developments in Precaution', Arlington, VA. On the application of the principle in the context of insolvency, see *Official Receiver as Liquidator of Celtic Extraction Ltd and Bluestone Chemicals Ltd v Environmental Agency* [1999] 1 *All ER* 746; *Re Wilmott Trading Ltd (in liquidation) (Nos 1 & 2)* [1999] 2 *BCLC* 541.

## ii. UN: Draft Declaration of Principles on Human Rights and the Environment, 1994

**Commentary**: The Declaration was formulated by human rights and environmental protection experts at the invitation of the Sierra Club Legal Defense Fund, the

Association mondiale pour l'école instrument de paix and the Société suisse pour la protection de l'environement. It forms an Annex to the Final Report of the Special Rapporteur on Human Rights and the Environment, Ms Ksentini, to the UN Sub-Commission on the Prevention of Discrimination and Protection of Minorities, UN Doc E/CN.4/Sub.2/1994/9. All persons, individually and in association with others, have duties of environmental protection and preservation (Article 21). In particular, governments must adopt administrative, legislative and other measures to ensure *inter alia* that corporations, wherever they operate, implement their duties of environmental protection, sustainable development and respect for human rights (Article 22).

### iii. UNEP: International Declaration on Cleaner Production, 1998

**Commentary**: Originally launched with 67 inaugural signatories, the Declaration (www.uneptie.org/pc/cp/declaration) currently has over 1700 signatories. The Declaration is a voluntary commitment to the strategy and practice of cleaner production and open to adoption by governments, corporations, business associations, NGOs and community organisations. Cleaner production means continuously applying integrated, preventive strategies to processes, products and services in the pursuit of economic, social, health, safety and environmental benefits. Signatories moreover recognise the virtues of eco-efficiency, green productivity and preventing pollution, and employ tools such as environmental performance evaluation, environmental accounting, environmental impact assessments, environmentally sound technology and life-cycle analysis. To ensure sustainable production and consumption practices, signatories undertake to demonstrate leadership, education and training, research and development, communication and implementation.

### iv. American Chemistry Council: Responsible Care, 1999

**Commentary**: The American Chemistry Council (ACC, formerly the CMA; www.americanchemistry.com) obligates member companies to participate in the Responsible Care programme and make good faith compliance efforts through a management systems verification protocol. Implementation costs are justifiable by reference to reduced insurance premiums, improved regulatory compliance, forging consumer and employee relationships, limiting production losses and prolonging the chemical industry's long-term viability. Responsible Care has since been incorporated into voluntary agreements with governments, integrated into national regulatory programmes and used to minimise health liability to employees: see further, ACC (2000), 'Responsible Care Progress Report 2000', Arlington, VA; ICCA (2000), 'Responsible Care Status Report 2000', Geneva. The first status report was presented to governments at the UN Intergovernmental Forum on Chemical Safety (IFCS) during 1997 and showcased before UNGA's Special Session on Rio + 5: see CMA (1997), 'Responsible Care Progress Report 1997: Meeting Expectations and Achieving

Goals', Arlington, VA. The second and third reports described how Responsible Care had initiated partnership agreements between corporate suppliers and memorandums of understanding with intergovernmental organisations: see CEFIC (2001), 'Responsible Care Status Report 2000', Brussels. Responsible Care has spawned additional codes pertaining to employee health, process safety, pollution prevention, distribution, product stewardship, community awareness and emergency response. Each code translates government controls into management processes to enable systematic review of environmental, health and safety regulations. See also, ICCA (2000), 'Responsible Care Code of Conduct' (www.icca-chem.org/section02a.html).

### v. Various: Responsible Use Principles for Hydrofluorocarbons, 2002

**Commentary**: The Principles are the product of a partnership between the US Environmental Protection Agency, the Japanese Ministry of Economy, Trade and Industry, UNEP and the Alliance for Responsible Atmospheric Policy (www.arap.org/). They contemplate various environmental commitments with respect to fire suppression, air conditioning, refrigeration and HFC production. See also WRI/WBCSD (2001), Greenhouse Gas (GhG) Protocol: www.ghgprotocol.org.

### vi. The Permanent Peoples' Tribunal: Charter on Industrial Hazards and Human Rights, 1995

**Commentary**: The Permanent Peoples' Tribunal is an NGO established in 1979 and located in Rome. It fills international legal gaps through adjudicative processes such as receiving testimony, hearing arguments from legal counsel and private deliberations. The Charter (www.globalpolicy.org/socecon/envronmt/charter.htm) was drafted over five years with public hearings conducted in New Haven (1991), Bangkok (1991), Bhopal (1992) and London (1994). Its content encompasses the right to life, occupational health and safety, environmental protection, risk management and reducing damage with respect to hazardous production. Provisions relevant to corporations include parent company liability for the actions of subsidiaries (the right to accountability under Article 3), non-intervention in the internal affairs of host States (Article 7(4)) and the right of individuals adversely affected by hazardous activities to commence litigation within their chosen forum (Article 29).

# PART VII

# Sustainable Development

# 75. UNCED: Agenda 21, 1992

**Commentary**: Although initially contemplating tighter regulatory control, the 1992 Rio Conference on Environment and Development (UNCED) acknowledged the positive contributions of business to sustainable development, supported free market mechanisms and promoted self-regulatory approaches: UNTCMD (1992), 'TNCs and Sustainable Development: A Review of Agenda 21', New York; UNTCMD (1993), 'Follow-up to UNCED as Related to TNCs', New York, UN Doc E/C.10/1993/13. For commercial perspectives, see Schmidheiny S./WBCSD (1992), *Changing Course: A Global Business Perspective on Development and the Environment*, Cambridge, MA: MIT Press; Willums J.-O. and Goluke U. (1992), *From Ideas to Action: Business and Sustainable Development, The Greening of Enterprise*, Oslo: ICC International Environmental Bureau.

UNCED's principal outcome – Agenda 21 (UNCED Report, UN Doc A/CONF.151/26/Rev.1 (1992), Vol 1) – is a comprehensive global plan of action for intergovernmental organisations, governments and others with respect to poverty reduction, consumption, human health and settlement, deforestation, managing ecosystems, agriculture, biodiversity and protecting the atmospheres, seas, land and freshwater resources. The roles and responsibilities of 'industry', 'the private sector', 'business' and 'transnational corporations' feature prominently throughout Agenda 21. See further, Integrating Environment and Development in Decision-making (Chapter 8); Environmentally Sound Management of Biotechnology (Chapter 16); Environmentally Sound Management of Toxic Chemicals (Chapter 19); Environmentally Sound Management of Hazardous Wastes including Prevention of Illegal International Traffic in Hazardous Wastes (Chapter 20); Environmentally Sound Management of Solid Wastes and Sewerage-Related Issues (Chapter 21); Safe and Environmentally Sound Management of Radioactive Wastes (Chapter 22); and the Transfer of Environmentally Sound Technology, Cooperation and Capacity-Building (Chapter 34).

At UNGA's Special Session (UNGASS) for the Review and Appraisal of Agenda 21, New York, 1997 (Earth Summit + 5), it was observed that achievements were limited to large corporations with small and medium-sized enterprises (SMEs), particularly from developing countries, yet to be engaged: UNGA Resolution S/19-2 (1997) on a Programme for the Further Implementation of Agenda 21; UN Secretary-General (2001), 'Implementing Agenda 21', UN Doc E/CN.17/2002/PC.2/7 (2001); CSD (1997), 'Dialogue Sessions with Major Groups: Summary Report of the Dialogue Session with Business and Industry', UN Doc E/CN.17/1997/L.10. Greater resort to environmental management systems (EMSs) which transpose environmental performance into routine commercial decision-making have since been promoted: CSD (1998), 'ICC/WBCSD Submission on Corporate Management Tools for Sustainable Development', Background Paper No 5, Sixth Session.

## Chapter 30: Strengthening the Role of Business and Industry

30.1. Business and industry, including TNCs, play a crucial role in the social and economic development of a country. A stable policy regime enables and encourages business and industry to operate responsibly and efficiently and to implement longer-term policies. Increasing prosperity, a major goal of the development process, is contributed primarily by the activities of business and industry. Business enterprises, large and small, formal and informal, provide major trading, employment and livelihood opportunities. Business opportunities available to women are contributing towards their professional development, strengthening their economic role and transforming social systems. Business and industry, including TNCs, and their representative organizations should be full participants in the implementation and evaluation of activities related to Agenda 21.

30.2. Through more efficient production processes, preventive strategies, cleaner production technologies and procedures throughout the product life cycle, hence minimizing or avoiding wastes, the policies and operations of business and industry, including TNCs, can play a major role in reducing impacts on resource use and the environment. Technological innovations, development, applications, transfer and the more comprehensive aspects of partnership and cooperation are to a very large extent within the province of business and industry.

30.3. Business and industry, including TNCs, should recognize environmental management as among the highest corporate priorities and as a key determinant to sustainable development. Some enlightened leaders of enterprises are already implementing 'responsible care' and product stewardship policies and programmes, fostering openness and dialogue with employees and the public and carrying out environmental audits and assessments of compliance. These leaders in business and industry, including TNCs, are increasingly taking voluntary initiatives, promoting and implementing self-regulations and greater responsibilities in ensuring their activities have minimal impacts on human health and the environment. The regulatory regimes introduced in many countries and the growing consciousness of consumers and the general public and enlightened leaders of business and industry, including TNCs, have all contributed to this. A positive contribution of business and industry, including TNCs, to sustainable development can increasingly be achieved by using economic instruments such as free market mechanisms in which the prices of goods and services should increasingly reflect the environmental costs of their input, production, use, recycling and disposal subject to country-specific conditions.

30.4. The improvement of production systems through technologies and processes that utilize resources more efficiently and at the same time produce less wastes – achieving more with less – is an important pathway towards sustainability for business and industry. Similarly, facilitating and encouraging inventiveness, competitiveness and voluntary initiatives are necessary for stimulating more varied, efficient and effective options. To address these major requirements and strengthen further the role of business and industry, including TNCs, the following two programmes are proposed.

*Programme Areas*

A. PROMOTING CLEANER PRODUCTION

30.5. There is increasing recognition that production, technology and management that use resources inefficiently form residues that are not reused, discharge wastes that have adverse impacts on human health and the environment and manufacture products that when used have further impacts and are difficult to recycle, need to be replaced with technologies, good engineering and management practices and know-how that would minimize waste throughout the product life cycle. The concept of cleaner production implies striving for optimal efficiencies at every stage of the product life cycle. A result would be the improvement of the overall competitiveness of the enterprise. The need for a transition towards cleaner production policies was recognized at the UNIDO organized ministerial-level Conference on Ecologically Sustainable Industrial Development, held at Copenhagen in October 1991.

30.6. Governments, business and industry, including TNCs, should aim to increase the efficiency of resource utilization, including increasing the reuse and recycling of residues, and to reduce the quantity of waste discharge per unit of economic output.

Activities

30.7. Governments, business and industry, including TNCs, should strengthen partnerships to implement the principles and criteria for sustainable development.

30.8. Governments should identify and implement an appropriate mix of economic instruments and normative measures such as laws, legislations and standards, in consultation with business and industry, including TNCs, that will promote the use of cleaner production, with special consideration for small and medium-sized enterprises. Voluntary private initiatives should also be encouraged.

30.9. Governments, business and industry, including TNCs, academia and international organizations, should work towards the development and implementation of concepts and methodologies for the internalization of environmental costs into accounting and pricing mechanisms.

30.10. Business and industry, including TNCs, should be encouraged:

(a) To report annually on their environmental records, as well as on their use of energy and natural resources;
(b) To adopt and report on the implementation of codes of conduct promoting the best environmental practice, such as the Business Charter on Sustainable Development of the ICC and the chemical industry's responsible care initiative.

30.11. Governments should promote technological and know-how cooperation between enterprises, encompassing identification, assessment, research and development, management marketing and application of cleaner production.

30.12. Industry should incorporate cleaner production policies in its operations and investments, taking also into account its influence on suppliers and consumers.

30.13. Industry and business associations should cooperate with workers and trade unions to continuously improve the knowledge and skills for implementing sustainable development operations.

30.14. Industry and business associations should encourage individual companies to undertake programmes for improved environmental awareness and responsibility at all levels to make these enterprises dedicated to the task of improving environmental performance based on internationally accepted management practices.

30.15. International organizations should increase education, training and awareness activities relating to cleaner production, in collaboration with industry, academia and relevant national and local authorities.

30.16. International and non-governmental organizations, including trade and scientific associations, should strengthen cleaner production information dissemination by expanding existing databases, such as the UNEP International Cleaner Production Clearing House, the UNIDO Industrial and Technological Information Bank and the ICC International Environment Bureau, and should forge networking of national and international information systems.

### B. PROMOTING RESPONSIBLE ENTREPRENEURSHIP

30.17. Entrepreneurship is one of the most important driving forces for innovations, increasing market efficiencies and responding to challenges and opportunities. Small and medium-sized entrepreneurs, in particular, play a very important role in the social and economic development of a country. Often, they are the major means for rural development, increasing off-farm employment and providing the transitional means for improving the livelihoods of women. Responsible entrepreneurship can play a major role in improving the efficiency of resource use, reducing risks and hazards, minimizing wastes and safeguarding environmental qualities.

#### Objectives

30.18. The following objectives are proposed:

(a) To encourage the concept of stewardship in the management and utilization of natural resources by entrepreneurs;

(b) To increase the number of entrepreneurs engaged in enterprises that subscribe to and implement sustainable development policies.

30.19. Governments should encourage the establishment and operations of sustainably managed enterprises. The mix would include regulatory measures, economic incentives and streamlining of administrative procedures to assure maximum efficiency in dealing with applications for approval in order to facilitate investment decisions, advice and assistance with information, infrastructural support and stewardship responsibilities.

30.20. Governments should encourage, in cooperation with the private sector, the establishment of venture capital funds for sustainable development projects and programmes.

30.21. In collaboration with business, industry, academia and international organizations, Governments should support training in the environmental aspects of enterprise management. Attention should also be directed towards apprenticeship schemes for youth.

30.22. Business and industry, including TNCs, should be encouraged to establish worldwide corporate policies on sustainable development, arrange for environmentally sound technologies to be available to affiliates owned substantially by their parent company in developing countries without extra external charges, encourage overseas affiliates to modify procedures in order to reflect local ecological conditions and share experiences with local authorities, national Governments and international organizations.

30.23. Large business and industry, including TNCs, should consider establishing partnership schemes with small and medium-sized enterprises to help facilitate the exchange of experience in managerial skills, market development and technological know-how, where appropriate, with the assistance of international organizations.

30.24. Business and industry should establish national councils for sustainable development and help promote entrepreneurship in the formal and informal sectors. The inclusion of women entrepreneurs should be facilitated.

30.25. Business and industry, including TNCs, should increase research and development of environmentally sound technologies and environmental management systems, in collaboration with academia and the scientific/engineering establishments, drawing upon indigenous knowledge, where appropriate.

30.26. Business and industry, including TNCs, should ensure responsible and ethical management of products and processes from the point of view of health, safety and environmental aspects. Towards this end, business and industry should increase self-regulation, guided by appropriate codes, charters and initiatives integrated into all elements of business planning and decision-making, and fostering openness and dialogue with employees and the public.

30.27. Multilateral and bilateral financial aid institutions should continue to encourage and support small- and medium-scale entrepreneurs engaged in sustainable development activities.

30.28. UN organizations and agencies should improve mechanisms for business and industry inputs, policy and strategy formulation processes, to ensure that environmental aspects are strengthened in foreign investment.

30.29. International organizations should increase support for research and development on improving the technological and managerial requirements for sustainable development, in particular for small and medium-sized enterprises in developing countries.

# 76. Commission on Sustainable Development: Decision 6/2 on Industry and Sustainable Development, 1998

**Commentary**: The UN Commission on Sustainable Development (CSD) ensures the overall implementation of Agenda 21: UNGA Res 47/191 (1992) & www.un.org/esa/sustdev/csd. However, public participation in implementation is also a prerequisite for sustainable development. The nine major constituency groups from civil society recognised by Agenda 21 and entitled to participate within CSD deliberations are women, children, indigenous people, NGOs, local authorities, trade unions, business and industry, the scientific and technological community and farmers. The extracts below (see further, CSD (1998), 'Report on the Sixth Session') highlight the roles and responsibilities envisaged for business and industry for economic and social development as well as environmental protection. Part C of the Annex (paragraphs 17–40; recommendations for governments) and Part E (paragraphs 51–66; recommendations for the international community) are omitted. Future work envisaged for the CSD includes establishing industry dialogues, reviewing the effectiveness of PVIs and encouraging financial sector contributions: Decision, paragraphs 17–19. It also involves enhanced voluntary reporting: see Annex, paragraphs 67–69. See further CSD, 'Report of the Sixth Session concerning the Relationship between Industry and Sustainable Development', UN Doc E/CN.17/1998/4; CSD (1998), 'Report of the Inter-Sessional Ad Hoc Working Group on Industry and Sustainable Development', New York. On the concept of responsible entrepreneurship, see UNCSD (1998), 'ICC/WBCSD Submission on Responsible Entrepreneurship', Background Paper No 1, Sixth Session.

## A. Industry and Economic Development

6. The Commission recognized that industry plays a critical role in technological innovations and research and development activities, which are crucial for the economic and social development of any country, as well as in the development, diffusion and transfer of environmentally sound technologies and management techniques, which constitute a key element of sustainable development.
7. The Commission emphasized that it was important for the achievement of sustainable development for Governments to develop and maintain an enabling policy framework based on a sound regulatory foundation complemented with a judicious mix of economic instruments, voluntary initiatives and agreements and public–private partnerships.

**B. Industry and Social Development**

9. The Commission recognized that industry contributes to social development objectives through, *inter alia*, the creation of productive employment, compliance with labour standards, corporate social initiatives and attention to human resources development and worker welfare. Industry continues to face such challenges, which can be addressed through better dialogue with trade unions and Governments.

**C. Industry and Environmental Protection**

15. The Commission called upon industry to increase its efforts, as appropriate, in the areas of responsible entrepreneurship and employment of various corporate management tools, including environmental management systems and environmental reporting, to improve its environmental performance.

**Annex: Report of the Inter-sessional Ad Hoc Working Group on Industry and Sustainable Development, 1998**

*A. Background*

*B. General Recommendations*

6. Further action is needed to adjust policy approaches that have unintended adverse environmental or social effects and to establish a policy framework that fosters sustainability, including encouragement to companies of all sizes and in all sectors to integrate sustainable development into their business strategies, planning and operations . . .
8. Since the role of the private sector has expanded in most economies, effective sustainable development policies require constructive dialogue and partnerships between Government at all levels, industry, trade unions and civil society, including women's organizations . . .
9. Consistent with Agenda 21, the development and further elaboration of national policies and strategies and integrated approaches, particularly in industrialized countries, are needed to encourage changes in unsustainable consumption and production patterns, while strengthening, as appropriate, international approaches and policies that promote sustainable consumption patterns on the basis of the principle of common but differentiated responsibilities, applying the 'polluter pays' principle and encouraging producer responsibility and greater consumer awareness.
10. Governments, industry and organizations of civil society should, as appropriate, use the media, advertising, marketing and other means to promote greater producer and consumer awareness of sustainable development in order to encourage a shift to more sustainable consumption and production patterns . . .
11. Sustainable development should be encouraged with continuous innovation and the adoption of environmentally sound technologies to change current production and consumption patterns. The challenge is to implement measures that will have a significant long-term impact on preventing and mitigating pollution and resource consumption alongside continued growth in gross domestic product. Eco-efficiency, cost internalization and policies for products and services are important tools for making consumption and production patterns more sustainable.

13. Business and industry should be encouraged to develop and implement voluntary guidelines and codes of conduct which can help to promote and disseminate best practices in environmentally and socially responsible entrepreneurship, and to develop further those that already exist. To be effective, business and industry need to develop and implement such codes by themselves, for that will ensure their commitment to the process. Equally important, their credibility with stakeholders requires that the codes stimulate positive action that goes well beyond 'business as usual'. Therefore, an essential element is transparency in monitoring and public reporting of progress.
14. Governments at all levels, industry, trade unions and other organizations of civil society, in particular women's organizations, should work together towards the elimination of discrimination against women in employment, education, property ownership and access to credit and to ensure that women have effective equal access to economic opportunities and social participation . . .
15. Particular efforts are needed to promote small and medium-sized enterprises and entrepreneurial potential, in, *inter alia*, the informal sector in developing countries . . . Large companies and TNCs can provide support by working through the supply chain, including local suppliers.
16. Training should be utilized by all sectors and societies to promote cleaner production . . .

*D. Recommendations for Industry*

42. Companies can enable consumers to make more informed choices by providing reliable and accurate information on the impacts, and where possible, conditions of production and qualities of products and services, through their marketing and advertising activities, environmental reporting and improved stakeholder dialogue.
43. Industry and civil society should work with Governments to strengthen secondary, vocational and advanced education and to ensure that it meets the developmental needs of society and the economy. This includes fair treatment of employees and constructive training programmes.
44. Environmentally oriented management should aim at both preventing environmental damage and encouraging sustainable use of natural resources through, for example, more efficient use of energy, water and raw materials; the reduction of emissions into the air, water and soil; the reduction of noise impacts; the reduction of waste; and the development of environmentally sound products and services. Environmental management systems and practices suitable to particular circumstances can enable business to control its environmental impacts and stimulate awareness of sustainability as a key business issue. To maintain and enhance competitiveness over the longer term, companies need to integrate environmental and social sustainability into their strategic planning. This includes developing cleaner products and processes that use resources more efficiently and minimize environmental impacts.
45. Industry should act to improve its environmental performance through appropriate implementation of environmental management systems. For example, TNCs should consider setting a time-frame within which to fully implement such systems. At the same time, Governments and industry must also work together to develop policies to ensure that compliance with standards is not too costly or difficult to achieve for companies in developing countries. National certification schemes should be based upon the principles of transparency and non-discrimination and should not be used as non-tariff trade barriers.

46. Large corporations should apply best practice in their own branches, both domestically and abroad. Companies are encouraged to provide environmentally sound technologies, supported by appropriate management techniques and training, *inter alia*, so as to help companies in other countries, particularly developing countries, to develop and implement environmentally sound policies. Those companies and corporations should also be proactive in promoting the implementation of core labour standards of the ILO.
47. Chambers of commerce and business organizations in developed and developing countries should be encouraged to cooperate in the transfer of technology and in the development of management tools and institutional frameworks for sustainable development.
48. There is a growing trend among a variety of stakeholders to hold industry accountable and responsible for the environmental impact of its operations and products throughout their entire life cycle. The industry and business sectors should respond positively to these demands by continuing to develop voluntary codes of conduct, charters and codes of practices. Industry and business should observe these codes when operating in developing countries and in economies in transition, in particular where environmental enforcement is still being developed.
49. The financial sector has an important role to play in promoting sustainable development. Voluntary commitments and initiatives taken by the financial sector (banks, savings and micro-credit institutions, and insurance companies) which promote sustainable development should be further developed and implemented, and strategies for monitoring progress should be developed. Since financial institutions play an important role in sustainable development in developing countries, their policies may include requirements and incentives to stimulate sustainable development and to report on their progress.

# 77. UN World Summit on Sustainable Development (WSSD): Johannesburg Declaration and Plan of Implementation, 2002

**Commentary**: The Johannesburg Declaration and Programme of Action (see WSSD Report, UN Doc A/CONF.199/20 (2002)) builds upon the Copenhagen Declaration on Social Development and Programme of Action of the 1995 World Summit on Social Development (UN Doc A/CONF.166/9 (1995)) and the 1992 Rio Earth Summit. The UN Secretary-General in his Opening Statement observed that: 'Without the private sector, sustainable development will remain only a distant dream. We are not asking corporations to do something different from their normal business: we are asking them to do their normal business differently'. See also, UN Secretary-General Report (2001), 'Business and development', UN Doc A/56/442. Specific economic sectors prepared reports in preparation for the WSSD: see UNEP (2001), 'Guidelines for Industry Sector Reports for the WSSD 2002', Paris; WRI/UNEP/WBCSD (2002), 'Tomorrow's Markets: Global Trends and Their Implications for Business', Washington, DC. These were subsequently evaluated by UNEP: see UNEP (2002), 'Industry as a Partner for Sustainable Development, 10 Years After Rio: The UNEP Assessment', Paris. During the Summit itself, business statements were submitted at roundtable sessions, the Chairman of Business Action for Sustainable Development (BASD) addressed the multistakeholder event and BASD hosted '*Lekgotla* [a dialogue of leaders]: a business day'.

Public–private partnerships were the dominant means of implementation. The Plan of Implementation also contemplated *inter alia* private sector contributions to a world solidarity fund to eradicate poverty (paragraph 7) and efforts to change unsustainable consumption and production patterns (14). Stakeholders were encouraged to improve energy efficiency, affordability and accessibility, disseminate alternative technologies, employ cleaner fossil fuel technologies, encourage the transition to renewable energies and reduce gas flaring (20). Private sector involvement was encouraged for protecting the natural resource base (38), strengthening agricultural research capacity (40) and ensuring sustainable forest management (45). The means of implementation envisaged *inter alia* private sector contributions of financial and technical assistance to developing countries (83), joint public/private sector financing mechanisms which are sufficiently transparent and accountable and involving the private sector in debt reduction (89). Governments are expected to establish regulatory frameworks which expedite the transfer of environmentally sound technology in a cost-effective manner by the private sector to developing countries on favourable terms, including concessional and preferential terms as mutually agreed (105). Partnerships conducive to investment and sharing best practice, particularly with the scientific community (108), could enhance industrial efficiency, agricultural productivity, environmental management and competitiveness (106). For these purposes the CSD was encouraged to enhance major group participation within its programme of work (149, 168).

For assessments of the WSSD, see UN Secretary-General (2003), 'Follow-up to the WSSD and the Future Role of the CSD: The Implementation Track', UN Doc E/CN.17/2003/2; UN Division for Sustainable Development (2003), 'The Road from Johannesburg–What Was Achieved and the Way Forward'. On sustainable development partnerships, see PWBLF (1994), 'Partnerships for Sustainable Development: The Role of Business and Industry', London; PWBLF/UNDP/IBRD (1996), 'Business as Partners in Development: Creating Wealth for Countries, Companies and Communities', London; PWBLF (1998), 'Managing Partnerships: Tools for Mobilising the Public Sector, Business and Civil Society as Partners in Development', London; 'Partnerships/Initiatives to Strengthen the Implementation of Agenda 21', UN Doc A/C.2/57/L.83 (2002); ICC (2002), 'Sustainable Development: A Vision for Partnership', ICC Doc 213/4. On the concept of eco-efficiency, see WBCSD (2000), 'Eco-efficiency: Creating more Value with Less Impact', Geneva; WBCSD (2000), 'Measuring Eco-Efficiency: A Guide for Companies to Report Performance', Geneva; Desimone L.D. and Popoff F. (2000), *Eco-Efficiency: The Business Link to Sustainable Development*, Cambridge, MA: MIT Press; UNCTAD (2004), 'A Manual for the Preparers and Users of Eco-Efficiency Indicators', Geneva. For commercial perspectives, see CEFIC (2000), 'Statement on an Integrated Approach towards Sustainable Development', Brussels; UNEP (2002), 'Catalysing Change: How Industry Associations Can Promote Sustainable Development', Paris.

## Chapter I: Resolutions adopted by the Summit

*Johannesburg Declaration on Sustainable Development*

26. We recognize that sustainable development requires a long-term perspective and broad-based participation in policy formulation, decision-making and implementation at all levels . . .
27. We agree that in pursuit of its legitimate activities the private sector, including both large and small companies, has a duty to contribute to the evolution of equitable and sustainable communities and societies.
29. We agree that there is a need for private sector corporations to enforce corporate accountability, which should take place within a transparent and stable regulatory environment.

*Plan of Implementation of the World Summit on Sustainable Development*

III. CHANGING UNSUSTAINABLE PATTERNS OF CONSUMPTION AND PRODUCTION

18. Enhance corporate environmental and social responsibility and accountability. This would include actions at all levels to:

    (a) Encourage industry to improve social and environmental performance through voluntary initiatives, including environmental management systems, codes of conduct, certification and public reporting on environmental and social issues, taking into account such initiatives as the International Organization for Standardization standards and Global Reporting Initiative guidelines on sustainability reporting, bearing in mind principle 11 of the Rio Declaration on Environment and Development;

(b) Encourage dialogue between enterprises and the communities in which they operate and other stakeholders;

(c) Encourage financial institutions to incorporate sustainable development considerations into their decision-making processes;

(d) Develop workplace-based partnerships and programmes, including training and education programmes.

V. SUSTAINABLE DEVELOPMENT IN A GLOBALIZING WORLD

49. Actively promote corporate responsibility and accountability, based on the Rio principles, including through the full development and effective implementation of intergovernmental agreements and measures, international initiatives and public–private partnerships and appropriate national regulations, and support continuous improvement in corporate practices in all countries.

XI. INSTITUTIONAL FRAMEWORK FOR SUSTAINABLE DEVELOPMENT

140. The international community should:

(f) Promote corporate responsibility and accountability and the exchange of best practices in the context of sustainable development, including, as appropriate, through multi-stakeholder dialogue, such as through the Commission on Sustainable Development, and other initiatives;

**Chapter III: Partnership Events**

45. The summary of the partnerships plenary meetings prepared by the ex officio Vice-President of the summit (A/CONF.199/16/Add.2) read as follows:

5. The issues:
The importance of the role of the private sector, but with transparency and clarity of roles and standards, corporate responsibility and social contribution.

35. The role of the private sector as a provider of technology, management and finance. It is most effective when there is a strong public sector assigning allocation priorities and where standards of accountability are present for all sectors.

52. A notable difference between Rio and Johannesburg is the more conspicuous presence of business at the latter. Business has taken more interest in sustainable development issues; industries in some countries have realized that it might be more profitable to produce more sustainably . . .

53. TNCs have the potential to contribute to sustainable development and to guide good practices in countries where they invest. Companies are interested in new technology, and many are aware of the need for capacity-building in developing countries. Pressures on them to adopt sustainable practices could come from host countries and

NGOs through such means as environmental accounting and reporting requirements. Local authorities could promote green procurement policies to push industries to produce in environmentally friendly and fair manners.

55. Other issues highlighted include:

(i) Perspectives of small and medium enterprises to be considered;
(ii) Seeking corporate social responsibility and accountability;
(iii) The possibility that Government control may lead corporations to seek lowest common denominators thus, good governance is important.

60. . . . In order to be effective, partnerships must be based on the principles of transparency, ownership, sustainability and major-group participation, and underpinned with new, more and better-directed financial resources.

53. The summary of the partnership plenary meeting on regional implementation prepared by the ex officio Vice-President of the summit (A/CONF. 199/16/Add.3) read as follows:

6. Awareness has increased within the private sector on the importance of sustainable development issues. However, the notion of profits must be addressed for business and industry to become truly committed to undertaking private initiatives towards sustainable development. Markets and profits should be effectively directed to alleviate poverty and attain other Millennium development goals through market incentives.

**Chapter V: Multi-stakeholder Event**

6. The trade unions noted that workers were central to the social pillar of sustainable development . . . They urged . . . active government effort to build upon existing international instruments addressing the behaviour of MNCs.
7. Business and industry expressed appreciation to Governments in voicing confidence in the ability of business to play a role in sustainable development through market mechanisms, and noted the need for cooperation in technology transfer and the role of consumers, especially youth. They noted awareness of the high standards by which business would be judged in undertaking partnership initiatives and grass-roots projects, and supported systems for business input into international institutions to create an environment of cooperation. Recognizing the need for accountability and open reporting initiatives to build support and trust, they reiterated their willingness to work together with other major groups and governments in that regard.

**Chapter VI: Roundtable Sessions**

*Roundtable 1*

4. Clear goals, accountability, peer review, trust in partnerships and addressing corruption in both the private sector and Government were emphasized as keys to success in attracting investment for poverty reduction. The private sector can be a positive agent for change, but it needs reassurance that legal and political frameworks will promote stability for investments, as well as support from the public sector.

*Roundtable 3*

7. . . . The private sector, for its part, should stimulate community action through the planning of social and economic development efforts . . .
8. . . . Recognizing that States represent national interests and private organizations answer primarily to their shareholders, there was support for the creation of a global NGO that could pragmatically address poverty, health, education and other issues on a voluntary basis, with contributions from the private sector, including resources, technology and support for free and fair trade.

*Roundtable 4*

5. The recognition that business can and should be part of the solution is a positive outcome of the Summit, as was discussed in detail by a number of participants. Some shortcomings of NGOs, such as difficulty in obtaining long term funding, were noted. Regarding forestry, for example, the private sector can more effectively address reforestation by working with small farmers, and through land and forest stewardship, providing incentives for conservation. Companies are potential partners not just for funding but also as a means for implementing environmental projects.
6. Many private companies want to demonstrate that they have become environmentally and socially responsible. They face questions about legitimacy and are increasingly seen to establish links to environmental activity, and developing countries should try to take advantage of this. Businesses are acknowledging that trust and responsibility are essential to credible efforts in meaningful partnership, such as the Global Compact Initiative. The representative of the business community noted that sustainability for business is an opportunity; responsibility is the standard by which countries will be judged; accountability is an obligation they must assume; and partnership is the pathway that they will pursue in the future.
8. There is a need to create small- and medium-scale entrepreneurs and jobs, especially in least developed countries . . .

**Chapter IX: Adoption of the Plan of Implementation of the World Summit on Sustainable Development**

20. The representative of the United States of America submitted the following written statement:

    Corporate responsibility.

    During the conference, the Chairman of the Main Committee stated that it was 'the collective understanding' of the contact group on means of implementation that paragraph 49 of the Plan of Implementation, regarding corporate responsibility and accountability, refers to existing intergovernmental agreements and international initiatives, and that this understanding should be reflected in the final report of the conference. The United States associates itself with this statement and notes that this understanding is of critical importance to the proper understanding and implementation of paragraph 49.

# 78. UNEP: Statement by Financial Institutions on the Environment and Sustainable Development, 1992 (revised 1997)

**Commentary**: UNEP has collaborated closely with industry to develop environmental management strategies since its inception at the 1972 Stockholm Conference on the Human Environment. This Bank Statement was launched in New York during 1992 in the run-up to UNCED and by 2002 had been endorsed by 197 banks from more than 50 States. Participants commit themselves to integrating sustainable development into all operational and service aspects, supporting a precautionary approach to environmental management, recognising that environmental risks identification and quantification should be part of risk management and pursuing best environmental practice. The Financial Institutions Initiative (http://unepfi.net) conducts roundtable sessions, holds annual general meetings and produces fact sheets, discussion papers, surveys, reports and newsletters: see, for example, UNEP Finance Initiative (2004), 'The Materiality of Social, Environmental and Corporate Governance Issues to Equity Pricing', Geneva. See further, UNEP (1995), 'Report of UNEP Advisory Group Meeting on Commercial Banks and the Environment', Geneva; UNEP (1998), 'Voluntary Industry Codes of Conduct for the Environment', Technical Report No 40, Paris. See also the Equator Principles developed in 2003 by financial institutions under the auspices of the International Finance Corporation (http://equatorprinciples.ifc.org/ifcext/equatorprinciples.nsf).

## 1. Commitment to sustainable development

1.1 We regard sustainable development as a fundamental aspect of sound business management.

1.2 We believe that sustainable development can best be achieved by allowing markets to work within an appropriate framework of cost-efficient regulations and economic instruments. Governments in all countries have a leadership role in establishing and enforcing long-term common environmental priorities and values.

1.3 We regard the financial services sector as an important contributor towards sustainable development, in association with other economic sectors.

1.4 We recognize that sustainable development is a corporate commitment and an integral part of our pursuit of good corporate citizenship.

## 2. Environmental management and financial institutions

2.1 We support the precautionary approach to environmental management, which strives to anticipate and prevent potential environmental degradation.

2.2 We are committed to complying with local, national, and international environmental regulations applicable to our operations and business services. We will work towards integrating environmental considerations into our operations, asset management, and other business decisions, in all markets.

2.3 We recognize that identifying and quantifying environmental risks should be part of the normal process of risk assessment and management, both in domestic and international operations. With regard to our customers, we regard compliance with applicable environmental regulations and the use of sound environmental practices as important factors in demonstrating effective corporate management.

2.4 We will endeavour to pursue the best practice in environmental management, including energy efficiency, recycling and waste reduction. We will seek to form business relations with partners, suppliers, and subcontractors who follow similarly high environmental standards.

2.5 We intend to update our practices periodically to incorporate relevant developments in environmental management. We encourage the industry to undertake research in these and related areas.

2.6 We recognize the need to conduct internal environmental reviews on a periodic basis, and to measure our activities against our environmental goals.

2.7 We encourage the financial services sector to develop products and services which will promote environmental protection.

**3. Public awareness and communication**

3.1 We recommend that financial institutions develop and publish a statement of their environmental policy and periodically report on the steps they have taken to promote integration of environmental considerations into their operations.

3.2 We will share information with customers, as appropriate, so that they may strengthen their own capacity to reduce environmental risk and promote sustainable development.

3.3 We will foster openness and dialogue relating to environmental matters with relevant audiences, including shareholders, employees, customers, governments, and the public.

3.4 We ask the UN Environment Programme (UNEP) to assist the industry to further the principles and goals of this Statement by providing, within its capacity, relevant information relating to sustainable development.

3.5 We will encourage other financial institutions to support this Statement. We are committed to share with them our experiences and knowledge in order to extend best practices.

3.6 We will work with UNEP periodically to review the success in implementing this Statement and will revise it as appropriate.

We, the undersigned, endorse the principles set forth in the above statement and will endeavour to ensure that our policies and business actions promote the consideration of the environment and sustainable development.

# 79. UNEP: Statement of Environmental Commitment by the Insurance Industry, 2002

**Commentary**: First formulated in 1995, approximately 90 companies from 27 States have since signed the Statement. Noting important contributions to be made by the insurance industry, the signatories support insurance products and services which promote environmentally sound practices and undertake to include environmental considerations within asset management. The Insurance Industry Initiative (http://unepfi.net/iii/index.htm) also considers the impact of climate change, multilateral environmental agreements and environmental reporting. It produces reports, holds annual general meetings and arranges conferences. See also, UNEP's Insurance Industry Initiative (1996), 'Final Report on Implementing Environmental Commitment in the Insurance Industry', London.

**Preamble**

The insurance industry recognizes that economic development needs to be compatible with human welfare and a healthy environment. To ignore this is to risk increasing social, environmental and financial costs. Our Industry plays an important role in managing and reducing environmental risk, in conjunction with governments, individuals and organizations. We are committed to work together to address key issues such as pollution reduction, the efficient use of resources, and climate change. We endeavour to identify realistic, sustainable solutions.

**1. General Principles of Sustainable Development**

1.1 We regard sustainable development, defined as development that meets the needs of the present without compromising the ability of future generations to meet their own needs, as a fundamental aspect of sound business management.

1.2 We believe that sustainable development is best achieved by allowing markets to work within an appropriate framework of cost efficient regulations and economic instruments. Government has a leadership role in establishing and enforcing long term priorities and values.

1.3 We regard a strong, proactive insurance industry as an important contributor to sustainable development, through its interaction with other economic sectors and consumers.

1.4 We believe that the existing skills and techniques of our industry in understanding uncertainty, identifying and quantifying risk, and responding to risk, are core strengths in managing environmental problems.

1.5 We recognize the precautionary principle, in that it is not possible to quantify some concerns sufficiently, nor indeed to reconcile all impacts in purely financial terms. Research is needed to reduce uncertainty but cannot eliminate it entirely.

## 2. Environmental Management

2.1 We will reinforce the attention given to environmental risks in our core activities. These activities include risk management, loss prevention, product design, claims handling and asset management.

2.2 We are committed to manage internal operations and physical assets under our control in a manner that reflects environmental considerations.

2.3 We will periodically review our management practices, to integrate relevant developments of environmental management in our planning, marketing, employee communications and training as well as our other core activities.

2.4 We encourage research in these and related issues. Responses to environmental issues can vary in effectiveness and cost. We encourage research that identifies creative and effective solutions.

2.5 We support insurance products and services that promote sound environmental practice through measures such as loss prevention and contract terms and conditions. While satisfying requirements for security and profitability, we will seek to include environmental considerations in our asset management.

2.6 We will conduct regular internal environmental reviews, and will seek to create measurable environmental goals and standards.

2.7 We shall comply with all applicable local, national and international environmental regulations. Beyond compliance, we will strive to develop and adopt best practices in environmental management. We will support our clients, partners and suppliers to do likewise.

## 3. Public Awareness and Communications

3.1 Bearing in mind commercial confidence, we are committed to share relevant information with our stakeholders, including clients, intermediaries, shareholders, employees and regulators. By doing so we will improve society's response to environmental challenges.

3.2 Through dialogue with public authorities and other bodies we aim to contribute to the creation of a more effective framework for sustainable development.

3.3 We will work with the UN Environment Programme to further the principles and goals of this Statement, and look for UNEP's active support.

3.4 We will encourage other insurance institutions to support this Statement. We are committed to share with them our experiences and knowledge in order to extend best practices.

3.5 We will actively communicate our environmental activities to the public, review the success of this Statement periodically, and we expect all signatories to make real progress.

# 80. International Chamber of Commerce: Business Charter for Sustainable Development, 1991

**Commentary**: The International Chamber of Commerce (ICC, www.iccwbo.org) first published the Business Charter in 1987 with a view to assisting business following the release of the Brundtland Commission Report. See also, ICC (1974), 'Environmental Guidelines for World Industry', Publication No 435, Paris. Commencing in 1989, numerous companies and business organisations contributed input over a two-year period to the ICC Working Party for Sustainable Development. A revised Charter was adopted by the ICC Executive Board in 1990 and formally launched in 1991 as a Declaration on Environmental Management at the Second World Industry Conference on Environmental Management in Rotterdam just prior to UNCED. The Charter is promoted as a set of good practices from which companies may formulate their own environmental management system (EMS) and continuously improve environmental performance. The ICC does not attempt to 'enforce' compliance but features corporate endorsers in a 'Company Showcase' and regularly publishes Charter bulletins. See further, ICC (1985), 'MNEs: Their Contribution to Economic Growth and Development', Paris; ICC (2000), 'Responsible Business Conduct: An ICC Approach', Paris. See also the Bundesverband der Deutschen Industrie eV (1992), 'Perspectives 2000', Berlin.

**Introduction**

Sustainable development involves meeting the needs of the present without compromising the ability of future generations to meet their own needs. Economic growth provides the conditions in which protection of the environment can best be achieved, and environmental protection, in balance with other human goals, is necessary to achieve growth that is sustainable. In turn, versatile, dynamic, responsive and profitable businesses are required as the driving force for sustainable economic development and for providing the managerial, technical and financial resources to contribute to the resolution of environmental challenges. Market economies, characterised by entrepreneurial initiatives, are essential to achieve this. Business thus shares the view that there should be a common goal, not a conflict, between economic development and environmental protection, both now and for future generations. Making market forces work in this way to protect and improve the quality of the environment – with the help of standards such as ISO 14000, and judicious use of economic instruments in a harmonious regulatory framework is an on-going challenge that the world faces in entering the 21st century. This challenge was recognised by the nations of the world at the 1992 UN Conference on Environment and Development, which called on the co-operation of business in tackling it. To this end, business leaders have launched initiatives in their individual enterprises as well as through sectoral and cross-sectoral associations. In order that more businesses join this effort and that their environmental performance continues to improve, the International Chamber of Commerce continues to call upon enterprises and their associations to use the following Principles as a basis for pursuing such improvement and to express publicly their support for them. Individual programmes to implement these Principles will reflect the wide diversity among enterprises in size and function. The objective remains that the widest range of enterprises commit themselves to improving their environmental performance in accordance with these Principles, to having in place management practices to effect such improvement, to measuring their progress, and to reporting this progress as appropriate internally and externally.

## Principles for Environmental Management

*1. Corporate Priority*
To recognise environmental management as among the highest corporate priorities and as a key determinant to sustainable development; to establish policies, programmes and practices for conducting operations in an environmentally sound manner.

*2. Integrated Management*
To integrate these policies, programmes and practices fully into each business as an essential element of management in all its functions.

*3. Process of Improvement*
To continue to improve corporate policies, programmes and environmental performance, taking into account technical developments, scientific understanding, consumer needs and community expectations, with legal regulations as a starting point; and to apply the same environmental criteria internationally.

*4. Employee Education*
To educate, train and motivate employees to conduct their activities in an environmentally responsible manner.

*5. Prior Assessment*
To assess environmental impacts before starting a new activity or project and before decommissioning a facility or leaving a site.

*6. Products and Services*
To develop and provide products or services that have no undue environmental impact and are safe in their intended use, that are efficient in their consumption of energy and natural resources, and that can be recycled, reused, or disposed of safely.

*7. Customer Advice*
To advise, and where relevant educate, customers, distributors and the public in the safe use, transportation, storage and disposal of products provided; and to apply similar considerations to the provision of services.

*8. Facilities and Operations*
To develop, design and operate facilities and conduct activities taking into consideration the efficient use of energy and materials, the sustainable use of renewable resources, the

minimisation of adverse environmental impact and waste generation, and the safe and responsible disposal of residual wastes.

*9. Research*

To conduct or support research on the environmental impacts of raw materials, products, processes, emissions and wastes associated with the enterprise and on the means of minimizing such adverse impacts.

*10. Precautionary Approach*

To modify the manufacture, marketing or use of products or services or the conduct of activities, consistent with scientific and technical understanding, to prevent serious or irreversible environmental degradation.

*11. Contractors and Suppliers*

To promote the adoption of these principles by contractors acting on behalf of the enterprise, encouraging and, where appropriate, requiring improvements in their practices to make them consistent with those of the enterprise; and to encourage the wider adoption of these principles by suppliers.

*12. Emergency Preparedness*

To develop and maintain, where significant hazards exist, emergency preparedness plans in conjunction with the emergency services, relevant authorities and the local community, recognising potential transboundary impacts.

*13. Transfer of Technology*

To contribute to the transfer of environmentally sound technology and management methods throughout the industrial and public sectors.

*14. Contributing to the Common Effort*

To contribute to the development of public policy and to business, governmental and intergovernmental programmes and educational initiatives that will enhance environmental awareness and protection.

*15. Openness to Concerns*

To foster openness and dialogue with employees and the public, anticipating and responding to their concerns about the potential hazards and impacts of operations, products, wastes or services, including those of transboundary or global significance.

*16. Compliance and Reporting*

To measure environmental performance; to conduct regular environmental audits and assessments of compliance with company requirements, legal requirements and these principles; and periodically to provide appropriate information to the Board of Directors, shareholders, employees, the authorities and the public.

NB The term environment as used in this document also refers to environmentally related aspects of health, safety and product stewardship.

# 81. Minerals Council of Australia: Enduring Value – The Australian Minerals Industry Framework for Sustainable Development, 2004

**Commentary**: To harness the global mining industry's commitment to sustainable development within a strategic framework, in 2003 the International Council on Mining and Metals (ICMM; www.icmm.com) adopted ten sustainable development principles underpinned by 48 supporting elements. The Minerals Council of Australia (MCA; www.minerals.org.au) represents the exploration, mining and minerals processing sectors in Australia. Enduring Value, the MCA's Operational Framework for Sustainable Development Implementation, assists companies implement the ICMM's Sustainable Development Framework at site level while also providing a regional framework for those companies not engaged in the ICMM process: MCA (2003), 'Annual Report'. Enduring Value builds upon the MCA's earlier Environmental Management Code (noted below) and identifies several 'pigeon-holes' for capturing and extending leading social, environmental and economic management practices across industry. The Global Reporting Initiative (GRI) 2002 Sustainability Reporting Guidelines as well as the Mining and Metals Sector Supplement are the reporting tools for demonstrating compliance with both the ICMM Framework and the Australian-led initiative.

Enduring Value is compulsory for MCA members and open to adoption by others. All exploration, mining and minerals processing companies and contractors are eligible to become signatories provided that they commit to implementation in writing. Obligations include progressively implementing the ICMM Principles and Elements, annual public reporting of site-level performance (reporting metrics are selected from either the GRI or self-developed) and internal or external risk assessment. The Code applies to all activities wherever signatories operate as well as those of contractors. Signatories will moreover encourage the Code's application to operations where they hold a non-controlling interest. Companies are removed as signatories in the event of non-conformity and where negotiations to correct the behaviour by the MCA have proved unsuccessful. A review of Enduring Value is envisaged for 2008. The extracts below are drawn from the MCA's 'Guidance for Implementation' (www.minerals.org.au/enduringvalue) which provides operational statements for each ICMM Principle and Element. This Operational Framework is also accompanied by 'guidance statements', web-based tool kits and company or site-based case studies. For ICMM materials, see International Council on Mining and the Environment (ICME) (1993 & 1997), 'Environmental Charter', London; ICMM (1998), 'Charter on Sustainable Development', London; ICMM (2002), 'Toronto Declaration & Implementation Process', London; ICMM (2002), 'The Mining and Metals Industries: Progress in Contributing to Sustainable Development', Working Paper, London. See also, the Global Mining Initiative (GMI, www.icmm.com/gmi.php) concluded during 2002. For related private initiatives, see the Mining Minerals and Sustainable Development (MMSD, www.iied.org/mmsd) project including MMSD (2002), *Breaking New Ground*, London: Earthscan.

Industry Vision: A valued Australian minerals industry achieving outstanding environmental, social and economic performance

Industry Mission: To achieve continual improvement in the environmental, social and economic performance and accountability of the Australian minerals industry through implementation of the Principles and Elements of Enduring Value

## Principle 1: Implement and Maintain Ethical Business Practices and Sound Systems of Corporate Governance

*Element 1.1: Develop and Implement Company Statements of Ethical Business Principles and Practices that Management is Committed to Enforcing*

IMPLEMENTATION GUIDANCE

(i) Develop a company statement of ethical business principles and practices that the board of directors endorses and monitors.

(ii) This statement should reflect the ten ICMM principles and their supporting elements, which are intended to deliver sustainable shareholder value through commitment to improving social, health, safety, environmental and economic performance.

(iii) This statement could establish a business code of conduct for employees consistent with sustainable development principles, and mandate mechanisms for reporting on adherence to the code.

(a) This code might cover expectations of behaviour in relation to elements of the principles.

(iv) This statement should commit the company at every level to enabling its people to learn how to behave in principled ways and account for their performance.

(a) For examples of learning requirements that may impact on most or many employees and contractors, refer to 1.2, 2.5, 3.4, 5.3 and 9.2.

*Element 1.2: Implement Policies and Practices that Seek to Prevent Bribery and Corruption*

IMPLEMENTATION GUIDANCE

(i) Bribery includes making promises as well as actual paying money or providing goods, services or favours to illicitly influence official decisions or acts. Implement a 'no-bribery' policy based on an informed view of relevant law, regulations and international conventions.

(a) Competent legal advice is useful (see element 1.3).

(ii) Some payments that may be seen as attempts to influence official decisions and acts may be legal and regarded as proper within particular jurisdictions and recognised conventions. Transparency is a key issue, so policy should be developed and systems should be put in place to record and report on decisions and transactions related to:

(a) political contributions, including direct or indirect contributions to political parties, organisations or individuals involved in politics;
(b) 'facilitation payments' to low-ranking officials for processing licences or other functions;
(c) charitable contributions and sponsorships;
(d) payments made to comply with particular statutes (see elements 1.1, 1.3, 3.4, 10.1).

(iii) Train employees to apply the 'no-bribery' policy and use systems to ensure relevant issues are recognised, recorded, managed and reported transparently.

(a) Implement systems for managing allegations or suspicions of business misconduct in confidential, professional ways consistent with due process (see elements 3.2, 3.4).

*Element 1.3: Comply with or Exceed the Requirements of Host Country Laws and Regulations*

IMPLEMENTATION GUIDANCE

(i) Obtain competent legal advice.
(ii) Create a register of relevant legal requirements.
(iii) Ensure responsibility and accountability for particular compliance requirements is clearly assigned and understood, and employees responsible for compliance have appropriate training (see elements 2.5, 3.4, 8.5).
(iv) Regularly review legal compliance, identify instances of non-compliance, implement a system for documenting and tracking instances of non-compliance, document action plans to achieve compliance and take prompt action to implement these plans.
(v) Once compliance is established, move to exceed requirements where this equates to good industry practice (see element 2.3).

*Element 1.4: Work with Governments, Industry and Other Stakeholders to Achieve Appropriate and Effective Public Policy, Laws, Regulations and Procedures that Facilitate the Mining, Minerals and Metals Sector's Contribution to Sustainable Development Within National Sustainable Development Strategies*

IMPLEMENTATION GUIDANCE

(i) Participate openly, honestly and constructively in public policy development (see elements 1.2, 2.6, 3.6, 4.1, 4.3, 7.2–7.3, 8.4–8.5).
(ii) Develop research programs both in-house and collaboratively to address relevant knowledge gaps (see elements 6.1, 7.2–7.3, 8.1–8.2).
(iii) Provide scientific and technical advice and case studies to assist development of appropriate standards and controls (see elements 8.1–8.5).

(iv) Promote the sustainable development performance of smaller companies in the minerals industry and of businesses that supply to or buy from the industry (see element 2.4).

**Principle 2: Integrate Sustainable Development Considerations within the Corporate Decision-making Process**

*Element 2.1: Integrate sustainable development principles into company policies and practices*

IMPLEMENTATION GUIDANCE

(i) Establish a business case for including sustainable development principles in policy and practice and gain management commitment.
(ii) Embed sustainable development principles in planning, designing, constructing, managing and closing operations (see element 2.2).
(iii) Allocate clear roles, responsibilities, accountabilities and resources to facilitate the implementation of company policies and practices.
(iv) Provide all employees with relevant information, performance targets, training, resources and management support across all dimensions of sustainable development.
(v) Ensure appropriate environmental and social accounting is embedded in the reporting system (see elements 4.1, 4.3, 5.4, 6.1, 8.3–8.4, 9.2, 10.1–10.3).

*Element 2.2: Plan, Design, Operate and Close Operations in a manner that Enhances Sustainable Development*

IMPLEMENTATION GUIDANCE

(i) Use consultative methods and a life-cycle approach in applying the sustainable development principles during planning and design phases; and in managing operations and closure of operations. In particular refer to various elements from Principles 3 to 10 within this Framework.
(ii) Reporting on sustainable development criteria may require benchmark or baseline information to be collected early in the cycle and used in developing metrics and targets (see elements 4.1, 6.1).
(iii) Operational plans should set targets for performance on financial, social, health, safety, environmental and economic criteria. Operational performance should be reviewed regularly against those targets (see elements 3.3, 4.2, 5.1–5.2, 6.2, 7.3, 9.3, 10.1).

*Element 2.3: Implement Good Practice and Innovate to Improve Social, Environmental and Economic Performance whilst Enhancing Shareholder Value*

IMPLEMENTATION GUIDANCE

(i) In partnership with relevant stakeholders, periodically benchmark operations against good industry practice for sustainable development (see element 2.2).
(ii) Implement a system to identify and pursue sustainable development opportunities in relation to:

    (a) improving relations with employees (see elements 3.1–3.4), local communities (see elements 3.5–3.6, 4.1, 4.3, 5.1, 9.1–9.5, 10.3) and other stakeholders;

(b) improving risk management (see elements 4.1–4.4);
(c) improving health and safety performance on site and locally (see elements 5.1–5.5) and through the supply chain (see elements 1.4, 2.4, 8.1–8.5);
(d) improving environmental management on site, locally and through the supply chain (see elements 4.1, 4.3, 6.1–6.5, 7.1–7.3, 8.1–8.5);
(e) improving business and financial performance.

*Element 2.4: Encourage Customers, Business Partners and Suppliers of Goods and Services to Adopt Principles and Practices that Are Comparable to Our Own*

IMPLEMENTATION GUIDANCE

(i) Implement a procurement policy that includes sustainable development performance outcomes in key contracts (see elements 1.4, 2.4, 6.4, 8.2–8.5).
(ii) Promote product stewardship initiatives throughout the supply chain through partnerships with contractors, suppliers and customers (see elements 1.4, 8.1–8.5).
(iii) Encourage customers, contractors, suppliers and business partners to adopt sustainable development policies and practices.
(iv) Establish 'suppliers of choice' which include sustainable development criteria, such as the role of local employment, service and supply to foster local economies (see elements 1.4, 8.1–8.5).

*Element 2.5: Provide Sustainable Development Training to Ensure Adequate Competency at All Levels among Our Own Employees and Those of Our Contractors*

IMPLEMENTATION GUIDANCE

(i) Identify the training needs of employees and contractors to ensure adequate understanding and competency. In particular assess the knowledge and skills they need to learn in order to fulfill their responsibilities for:

(a) understanding the sustainable development principles, adhering to the company's code of conduct, carrying out its anti-bribery and corruption policy, complying with relevant legal requirements and supporting responsible corporate citizenship (see elements 1.1–1.4, 2.6, 7.1);
(b) acquiring competencies required to apply the principles in supporting and making management decisions, implementing good practice and encouraging good practice throughout the supply chain (see elements 2.1–2.4);
(c) minimising harassment and unfair discrimination; upholding human rights and respecting the cultures, customs and values of affected parties (see element 3.4);
(d) participating effectively in risk management and emergency response based on sustainable development principles (see elements 4.1–4.4);
(e) taking responsibility for working in a safe, healthy manner; and managing health and safety issues in the workplace (see element 5.3);
(f) managing environmental issues through the operational cycle, especially continual improvement (see elements 6.1–6.5);
(g) understanding the life-cycle effects of minerals and metals and the implications of the integrated materials management concept in their work and applying these concepts competently (see elements 2.4, 8.1–8.5);

(h) contributing appropriately to the development of communities affected by operations (see elements 9.2–9.5);
(i) providing timely, accurate and relevant reports on economic, social and environmental as well as financial performance (see elements 10.1–10.3);

(ii) Liaise with training providers and educational institutions to ensure that training delivered to current and potential employees is consistent with SD principles.

*Element 2.6: Support Public Policies that Foster Open and Competitive Markets*

IMPLEMENTATION GUIDANCE

(i) Participate in, and contribute to, relevant activities undertaken at company, industry and government levels.
(ii) Do not participate in or condone anti-competitive activities, including corruption (see element 1.2).

### Principle 3: Uphold Fundamental Human Rights and Respect Cultures, Customs and Values in dealings with Employees and Others Who Are Affected by Our Activities

*Element 3.1: Ensure Fair Remuneration and Work Conditions for All Employees and Do Not Use Forced, Compulsory or Child Labour*

IMPLEMENTATION GUIDANCE

(i) Implement policies and practices that attract and retain high quality staff.

(a) Many of the elements can contribute to recruiting, retention and development (see elements 1.1–1.2, 2.1, 3.1–3.3, 5.2).

(ii) Provide equal opportunity and remuneration for work of equal value relative to local economic conditions (see element 3.2).
(iii) Understand, respect and actively support human rights within the company (see elements 1.1, 3.4).
(iv) Develop and communicate clear retrenchment and re-skilling guidelines (see elements 3.2, 4.3).
(v) Promote a safe work culture that recognises that no job needs to be done if it cannot be done safely (see elements 4.1, 4.3, 5.2–5.3, 5.5).

*Element 3.2: Provide for the Constructive Engagement of Employees on Matters of Mutual Concern*

IMPLEMENTATION GUIDANCE

(i) Engage employees proactively about their work-related concerns:

(a) Listen actively and document the issues employees raise fairly and accurately;
(b) Discuss the issues in timely, open and culturally appropriate ways;
(c) Recognise employee freedom of association;

(ii) Seek agreed resolutions, including:

(a) flexible working arrangements where this benefits both company and employee;
(b) protection of entitlements in divestment and closure situations (see element 9.2).

*Element 3.3: Implement Policies and Practices Designed to Eliminate Harassment and Unfair Discrimination in All Aspects of Our Activities*

IMPLEMENTATION GUIDANCE

(i) Educate and train employees in anti-harassment and anti-discrimination policies and practices.
(ii) Establish and monitor mechanisms to register, resolve and report on incidents and complaints.
(iii) Encourage open discussion of workplace issues and address root causes of discrimination.
(iv) Where appropriate, establish special measures intended to reduce harassment and achieve fairness.

*Element 3.4: Ensure that All Relevant Staff, Including Security Personnel, Are Provided with Appropriate Cultural and Human Rights Training and Guidance*

IMPLEMENTATION GUIDANCE

(i) Provide employees and contractors with cultural awareness and human rights training that:

(a) is relevant to their areas of work;
(b) includes conflict and dispute resolution skills;
(c) provides examples of the difficult choices that individuals may need to make;
(d) reinforces the importance of viewing the project within its local cultural context;

(ii) Where security personnel are involved, maintain the safety and security of company operations within a framework that ensures respect for human rights.

*Element 3.5: Minimise Involuntary Resettlement, and Compensate Fairly for Adverse Effects on the Community Where This Cannot Be Avoided*

IMPLEMENTATION GUIDANCE

(i) Minimise resettlement and compensate fairly for unavoidable impacts (see elements 1.2, 2.2–2.3, 4.1, 6.1, 8.1, 9.1–9.5).
(ii) Provide compensation in a form that helps to build sustainable capacity within affected communities and delivers benefits to both current and future generations (see elements 2.3, 9.1–9.5, 10.3).
(iii) As far as practicable, ensure that the communities that experience the most adverse impacts receive the most benefit from compensation arrangements (see elements 1.2, 1.4, 2.2, 4.1, 6.1, 9.1).
(iv) Seek a consensus about relocation through a transparent process that includes the communities that will receive relocated people (see elements 1.2–1.4, 2.2, 4.1, 6.1, 9.1, 10.3).

*Element 3.6: Respect the Culture and Heritage of Local Communities, Including Indigenous Peoples*

IMPLEMENTATION GUIDANCE

(i) Recognise and respect the culture and heritage of local communities including:

(a) the culture and traditions of Indigenous peoples and their relationships with lands and waters;
(b) sites and objects of local, regional and national significance (see element 9.2);

(ii) Engage with local and Indigenous communities in culturally appropriate ways, respecting their customs and beliefs.

(a) Work with communities to develop appropriate, cooperative strategies to protect and manage sites of special significance to those communities on lands within and adjacent to our operations.
(b) Where appropriate, incorporate local and traditional environmental knowledge and land management practices into company operations.
(c) Work with communities to develop employment, education, training and business development and other opportunities.

## Principle 4: Implement Risk Management Strategies Based on Valid Data and Sound Science

*Element 4.1: Consult with Interested and Affected Parties in the Identification, Assessment and Management of All Significant Social, Health, Safety, Environmental and Economic Impacts associated with Our Activities*

IMPLEMENTATION GUIDANCE

(i) Use appropriate risk assessment methods to identify the potential social, health, safety, environmental and economic impacts of the intended operations.
(ii) Identify communities and organisations that may be affected by the operations:

(a) Undertake desktop baseline socio-economic assessments;
(b) Use the outcomes of these assessments to plan appropriate communications before engaging stakeholders;
(c) Where appropriate extend socio-economic assessment through stakeholder engagement;
(d) Explain company intentions honestly, accurately and succinctly;
(e) Engage stakeholders to identify their interests, concerns and aspirations;
(f) Incorporate what is learned into company planning and provide feedback on outcomes to relevant stakeholders;

(iii) Manage issues commensurate with the level of risk.[1]
(iv) Develop, implement and maintain systems to manage both chronic and acute risks.
(v) Maintain a risk register that documents the control philosophy, status and associated actions of all identified major risks.

(vi) Involve members of the workforce and other relevant stakeholders in risk assessment and risk management processes (see elements 3.2, 4.3–4.4, 5.1, 6.1, 8.1, 9.1).

(vii) The right and requirement to stop work when conditions become unsafe should be communicated and understood by employees and contractors and acted on (see elements 1.1, 3.1, 4.3).

*Element 4.2: Ensure Regular Review and Updating of Risk Management Systems*

IMPLEMENTATION GUIDANCE

(i) Implement a system of risk management and internal control that incorporates:

- (a) management commitment;
- (b) demonstrable systematic risk identification and mitigation;
- (c) documented risk communication;
- (d) documented cost-estimates of non-compliances and losses;
- (e) assurance reporting on programs aimed at achieving or maintaining conformance with the relevant risk profile;
- (f) documented key risks and opportunities that could impact on shareholder and relevant stakeholder interests;

(ii) Regularly review and continually improve risk management systems and practices in consultation with relevant stakeholders and with due consideration to regional and local effects.

(iii) Review and update the risk register periodically; and whenever changes in the operating environment or the operations alter risks and ensure necessary change management practices are in place.

*Element 4.3: Inform Potentially Affected Parties of Significant Risks from Mining, Minerals and Metals Operations and of the Measures that Will Be Taken to Manage the Potential Risks Effectively*

IMPLEMENTATION GUIDANCE

(i) Facilitate open and transparent dialogue on risk management measures conducted in the appropriate form for the particular audience (see elements, 4.1, 4.4, 5.4, 9.1–9.2, 10.3).

(ii) Inform the workforce of the hazards and risks to which they may be exposed prior to commencing employment and on continuing basis during employment (see elements 3.2, 5.2–5.4, 8.1, 9.1, 10.1–10.3).

(iii) Communicate with stakeholders on significant risks and their corresponding management plans in a culturally appropriate manner (see elements 4.1, 4.4, 9.1–9.2, 10.1–10.3).

(iv) Inform regulators, industry bodies and affected parties as soon as practicable of significant incidents, associated risks and the steps taken to remedy their impacts.

*Element 4.4: Develop, Maintain and Test Effective Emergency Response Procedures in Collaboration with Potentially Affected Parties*

IMPLEMENTATION GUIDANCE

(i) Identify potential emergencies and develop appropriate emergency response strategies and capabilities (see elements 2.1–2.3, 3.2, 4.1, 5.2, 6.2, 6.4, 9.1–9.5, 10.3).

(ii) Ensure adequate resources are available to respond to identified emergency scenarios (see elements 1.3, 5.2, 5.5, 6.5, 8.3).

(iii) Conduct training and periodically test the effectiveness of emergency response strategies and capabilities. Capture the learnings from this process (see elements 5.2–5.3).

(iv) Develop partnerships with local emergency services to provide mutual aid, for example, sharing mine rescue equipment with bush fire brigades (see elements 4.1, 4.3, 8.1, 9.3–9.4).

**Principle 5: Seek Continual Improvement of Our Health and Safety Performance**

*Element 5.1: Implement a Management System Focused on Continual Improvement of All Aspects of Operations that Could Have a Significant Impact on the Health and Safety of Our Own Employees, Those of Contractors and Communities Where We Operate*

IMPLEMENTATION GUIDANCE

(i) Implement an occupational and community health management system consistent with recognised quality standards that includes:

  (a) an occupational and community health and safety policy statement;
  (b) documented procedures for hazard identification, hazard/risk assessment and control of hazards/risks of activities, products and services over which the organisation has control, including the activities, products and services of contractors and suppliers;
  (c) an assessment of legal and voluntary obligations;
  (d) documented occupational and community health and safety objectives and targets and programs and timeframes to achieve them;
  (e) identified management structures, responsibilities, resources, training, awareness and competencies;
  (f) a communication system which includes employees and other interested parties, and provides for the relevant and timely reporting of performance;
  (g) document and data control procedures;
  (h) monitoring and measurement of key characteristics of operations that can cause illness and injury;
  (i) documented procedures for incident investigation, corrective and preventative action;
  (j) a series of periodic internal audits and management review;
  (k) continual improvement objectives (see elements 1.1, 2.1);

(ii) Involve employees and other relevant stakeholders in auditing management systems and in management reviews (see elements 3.2, 4.3, 9.2, 10.3).

*Element 5.2: Take All Practical and Reasonable Measures to Eliminate Workplace Fatalities, Injuries and Diseases among Our Employees and Those of Our Contractors*

IMPLEMENTATION GUIDANCE

(i) Set zero illness and injuries as the goal and monitor progress towards its achievement (see elements 1.1, 2.1–2.3):

- (a) Establish targets and timelines for key safety and health performance measures;
- (b) Use both leading and lagging performance measures.

(ii) Establish and maintain safe behaviours:

- (a) Promote a safe work culture – no job should be done if it cannot be done safely;
- (b) Encourage employees and contractors to take responsibility for their own safety and their workmates' safety;
- (c) Implement a Fitness for Work Program which may address factors such as substance abuse, stress and lack of physical capability;
- (d) Implement a program to address employee fatigue and implement working conditions that protect employee health and safety;
- (e) Utilise permit to work systems for designated hazardous work;
- (f) Implement safety behaviour principles and observation systems with management and employee participation (see element 3.2);

(iii) Establish and maintain safe conditions and processes:

- (a) Identify fatality-potential hazards and agents and implement appropriate controls (see elements 4.1–4.5, 6.4);
- (b) Operate and maintain plant and equipment according to established safe work procedures;
- (c) Utilise task-based risk assessment processes where appropriate;
- (d) Conduct systematic inspections of the workplace, record the results and ensure that any deficiencies are addressed.

(iv) Implement a comprehensive incident management process with management and employee participation:

- (a) Implement improvements based on investigating each incident (see element 4.2).

(v) Proactively manage changes that have the potential to impact on the safety and health of employees and contractors (see elements 4.1–4.4, 6.4).

*Element 5.3: Provide All Employees with Health and Safety Training, and Require Employees of Contractors to Have Undergone Such Training*

IMPLEMENTATION GUIDANCE

(i) Document and regularly review the OHS responsibilities, skills, knowledge and experience requirements associated with all roles in the organisation (see elements 2.4, 4.1–4.4, 8.1, 8.3).

(ii) Assess employees and contractors against the requirements of their roles before they are permitted to undertake work.
(iii) Provide general induction, area and task-specific training for all employees and contractors (see elements 2.4–2.5, 3.2).
(iv) Review training in and compliance with safe work procedures; implement the necessary improvements arising out of reviews (see elements 5.1, 4.4).
(v) Maintain records for all training and competency assessments, including compliance with mandatory training requirements; report appropriately (see element 10.1).

*Element 5.4: Implement Regular Health Surveillance and Risk-based Monitoring of Employees*

IMPLEMENTATION GUIDANCE

(i) Conduct relevant and risk-based initial and ongoing occupational medical surveillance of employees to ensure they are fit for their jobs and to enable early detection of any work-related health problems, including diseases (see elements 3.1–3.2).
(ii) Minimise exposures to harmful substances and conditions (see elements 5.1–5.3). Use internationally recognised standards to assess exposures; report against those standards (see elements 4.3, 6.4, 8.1–8.5). Monitor the workplace for exposures and conditions that could cause harm (see elements 3.1, 4.1, 4.3–4.4, 6.4).
(iii) Ensure work practices are ergonomically safe, that workers are fit for their work roles and are not asked to do work that may injure them or aggravate pre-existing medical conditions (see elements 3.1–3.2).
(iv) Establish targets to drive improvements in the management of occupational health hazards, and report performance against these targets (see elements 3.2, 4.1–4.5, 8.2, 10.1–10.3).
(v) Inform relevant employees of the results of their occupational health monitoring (see element 4.3).
(vi) Fully inform all employees and contractors about any substances or conditions that could have long-term impacts on their health (see elements 3.2, 4.3, 8.1, 8.3).
(vii) Promote the health and well being of the workforce through access to health information, including general health patterns, and programs (see element 8.1).

*Element 5.5: Rehabilitate and Reintegrate Employees into Operations Following Illness or Injury, where Feasible*

IMPLEMENTATION GUIDANCE

(i) Implement an injury management system to improve the health and safety of all employees and contractors (see elements 1.1, 2.3, 3.1–3.4, 5.1).
(ii) Establish rehabilitation processes to promote rapid recovery from work-related injuries and early return to work (see elements 1.1, 1.3, 2.3, 3.1–3.2).
(iii) Provide all practical and reasonable opportunities to people who are injured and cannot, as a result of their injury or illness, return to their previous employment (see elements 3.1–3.4, 5.1).

## Principle 6: Seek Continual Improvement of Our Environmental Performance

### *Element 6.1: Assess the Positive, Negative and Indirect and the Cumulative Impacts of New Projects – from Exploration through Closure*

IMPLEMENTATION GUIDANCE

(i) Assess and manage environmental impacts for the whole project cycle.

(ii) Predict, assess and monitor emissions to air, land and water, including noise, odour and vibration; ensure design emissions are within standards and guidelines; make project changes as necessary to ensure commissioned site can meet emission standards; provide a basis for future improvements.

(iii) Predict, assess and monitor impacts on visual amenity prior to development and make necessary project changes to reduce such impacts.

(iv) Annually review operations and implement management plans to mitigate the potential impact of emissions to air, land and water:

- (a) Use environmental impact assessments, change management and/or risk management approaches to evaluate and mitigate impact from new or altered processes;

(v) Predict, assess and monitor impacts on biodiversity and heritage issues (see element 7.3).

(vi) Where appropriate, contribute to total watershed and airshed management in partnership with relevant external organisations (see elements 1.3, 7.1–7.3, 8.1–8.4).

### *Element 6.2: Implement an Environmental Management System Focused on Continual Improvement to Review, Prevent, Mitigate or Ameliorate Adverse Environmental Impacts*

IMPLEMENTATION GUIDANCE

(i) Implement an environmental management system consistent with recognised quality standards that includes:

- (a) an environmental policy statement;
- (b) an assessment of environmental aspects and impacts of operations, products and services;
- (c) an assessment of legal and voluntary obligations;
- (d) documented environmental objectives and targets and programs to achieve them;
- (e) identified management structures, responsibilities, training, awareness and competencies;
- (f) a communication system with document control;
- (g) emergency preparedness and response procedures;
- (h) checking and corrective action for non-conformance;
- (i) a series of periodic internal audits and management review;
- (j) continual improvement objectives;

(ii) The environmental management system is a component of the sustainable development system (see elements 1.3, 4.1–4.2, 5.1, 7.1–7.3, 8.3, 10.3).

*Element 6.3: Rehabilitate Land Disturbed or Occupied by Operations in Accordance with Appropriate Post-mining Land Uses*

IMPLEMENTATION GUIDANCE

(i) Consult relevant stakeholders and develop a closure plan that clearly defines the post-closure land use.
(ii) Where appropriate, rehabilitate progressively over the life of the operation.
(iii) Monitor success criteria agreed with relevant stakeholders:

  (a) Report performance;

(iv) Undertake and support research into land and water rehabilitation practices.
(v) Use appropriate technologies to reduce negative environmental impacts and improve site rehabilitation techniques.
(vi) Manage and, where appropriate, rehabilitate historical disturbances to an appropriate standard (see elements 4.1, 6.3–6.4, 7.1, 7.3, 9.1, 10.3).

*Element 6.4: Provide for Safe Storage and Disposal of Residual Wastes and Process Residues*

IMPLEMENTATION GUIDANCE

(i) Design processes and facilities to minimise contamination and decrease closure costs:

  (a) Monitor the supply and use of significant chemicals over the life of the mine to identify losses and potential opportunities for recovery;
  (b) Identify opportunities for beneficial use of end wastes with other relevant stakeholders.

(ii) Document and apply effective process for:

  (a) materials handling, containment and control processes for all by-products and residues;
  (b) identification, assessment monitoring, management and/or remediation of contaminated sites.

(iii) Review, continually improve and introduce good industry practice (see elements 4.1–4.4, 5.1–5.2, 5.4, 8.1–8.5).

*Element 6.5: Design and Plan All Operations so that Adequate Resources are Available to Meet the Closure Requirements of All Operations*

IMPLEMENTATION GUIDANCE

(i) Plan operations to minimise costs and risks; comply with relevant law, standards and guidelines; maximise sustainable development opportunities; and deliver postclosure landforms that are safe and stable from physical, geochemical and ecological perspectives (see elements 5.1, 7.3, 8.3–8.5).
(ii) Provide adequate resources to achieve social objectives of closure including any costs associated with community dislocation (see elements 1.3, 2.2–2.3, 3.5, 7.1, 8.1).

(iii) Set aside funds externally held and not accessible for other purposes to implement the closure plan and to undertake post closure monitoring and maintenance, taking risk into account.

(iv) Periodically review closure plans in the light of changing regulatory requirements and community expectations (see elements 2.2, 3.5, 4.1–4.4, 9.1–9.3).

## Principle 7: Contribute to Conservation of Biodiversity and Integrated Approaches to Land Use Planning

### *Element 7.1: Respect Legally Designated Protected Areas*

IMPLEMENTATION GUIDANCE

(i) Plan exploration activities and operations to avoid and/or minimise impacts on ecological and cultural values of legally protected areas.

(ii) Work with key stakeholders to optimise the ecosystem integrity of protected areas proximal to the company's operations.

### *Element 7.2: Disseminate Scientific Data on and Promote Practices and Experiences in Biodiversity Assessment and Management*

IMPLEMENTATION GUIDANCE

(i) Share scientific and technical information regarding biodiversity assessment and management with key stakeholders, including academia and government.

(ii) Make biodiversity information collected for the environmental impact assessment process publicly available.

(iii) Collect, collate and analyse scientific data, and disseminate final reports to stakeholders in a suitable format.

(iv) Work with key stakeholders (including government) to protect endangered species and their habitat.

(v) Work with neighbouring communities and key stakeholders to minimise the impacts of feral animals and the spread of weeds and pests.

(vi) Involve stakeholders from local and scientific communities in monitoring and reporting of information regarding biodiversity assessment and management where appropriate.

(vii) Where feasible, work with stakeholders to optimise ecosystem integrity (including habitat protection) on a regional basis by addressing these issues proactively in mine planning and buffer zone management, and specifically in rehabilitation/closure planning (see elements 2.2–2.5, 4.1, 6.1–6.5, 8.1–8.3).

### *Element 7.3: Support the Development and Implementation of Scientifically Sound, Inclusive and Transparent Procedures for Integrated Approaches to Land Use Planning, Biodiversity Conservation and Mining*

IMPLEMENTATION GUIDANCE

(i) Produce credible and timely information regarding land-use issues, involving the input of independent assessment as necessary, to address stakeholder and community concerns and expectations (see elements 4.1, 6.1).

(ii) Find ways to maintain, enhance and restore (where appropriate) habitats in and around operations, including buffer zones.
(iii) Enhance biodiversity monitoring through the use of bioindicators.
(iv) Minimise the likelihood of localised extinctions and minimise impacts of feral animals, weeds and pests.
(v) Promote and apply the principles of multiple and sequential land use within the operation's sphere of influence.
(vi) Where feasible, work with key stakeholders to optimise the ecosystem integrity of protected areas adjacent to operations.
(vii) Where feasible, work with stakeholders to optimise ecosystem integrity (including habitat protection) on a regional basis.
(viii) Use offsetting programs to increase net conservation benefits where these are feasible and agreed with government.
(ix) Seek to achieve a net positive environmental gain through partnership activities and resourcing of local biodiversity groups.
(x) Engage with state-based planning authorities to ensure that operations are consistent with regional or catchment scale land use planning priorities.
(xi) Educate employees and contractors regarding the importance of biodiversity conservation values of the area subject to disturbance (see elements 2.2–2.5, 6.1–6.5, 8.1–8.5).

**Principle 8: Facilitate and Encourage Responsible Product Design, Use, Re-use, Recycling and Disposal of Our Products**

*Element 8.1: Advance Understanding of the Properties of Metals and Minerals and Their Life-cycle Effects on Human Health and the Environment*

IMPLEMENTATION GUIDANCE

(i) Where appropriate, support research that improves understanding of the life cycle effects of minerals and metal products on human and environmental health.
(ii) Monitor and review the impacts of exploration and operations on occupational, community and environmental health, taking into account advances in the understanding of life cycle issues (see elements 1.4, 2.4, 4.1, 6.1, 7.2–7.3, 8.3).

*Element 8.2: Conduct or Support Research and Innovation that Promotes the Use of Products and Technologies that are Safe and Efficient in Their Use of Energy, Natural Resources and Other Materials*

IMPLEMENTATION GUIDANCE

(i) Where appropriate support research to improve eco-efficiency of production processes and products.
(ii) Review and innovate to reduce waste through cleaner production processes, recycling and reuse of materials.
(iii) Review usage and innovate to improve efficiency in the use of energy and water. Take other users' present and future requirements into account, including air and water quality and environmental flows of water.
(iv) Involve suppliers identifying opportunities to reduce energy consumption or use renewable sources to reduce production of greenhouse gases and other emissions.

(v) Where feasible, collaborate in industrial ecology activities to develop synergies in resource usage (see elements 1.4, 2.4, 4.1, 6.1, 7.2–7.3, 8.3).

*Element 8.3: Develop and Promote the Concept of Integrated Materials Management Throughout the Metals and Minerals Value Chain*

IMPLEMENTATION GUIDANCE

(i) Track business inputs and outputs in a communicable and reportable format.
(ii) Promote safe handling, storage and use of materials throughout the supply chain.
(iii) Inform customers about the safe and responsible use of mineral products and options for their reuse (see element 2.4).
(iv) Develop preferred safe and responsible suppliers of materials and resources (see element 2.4).

*Element 8.4: Provide Regulators and Other Stakeholders with Scientifically Sound Data and Analysis Regarding Our Products and Operations as a Basis for Regulatory Decisions*

IMPLEMENTATION GUIDANCE

(i) Understand the precautionary principle and its application in policy development; and integrate this understanding into planning, design and the cycle of management review (see elements 1.3, 2.1).
(ii) As appropriate, provide regulators and the scientific community with scientific and technical advice about our products and operations, including the outcomes of site-based monitoring (see elements 1.4, 4.1, 6.4, 7.2–7.3, 10.1–10.3).
(iii) Collaborate in research on life cycle impacts of processes, products and by-products as appropriate (see elements 2.4, 4.1, 6.3, 7.2–7.3, 10.3).
(iv) Encourage collaboration between government, industry and the scientific community in research and demonstration programs to foster improved science and informed policy development (see elements 1.4, 4.1, 6.4, 7.2–7.3, 10.1–10.3).

*Element 8.5: Support the Development of Scientifically Sound Policies, Regulations, Product Standards and Material Choice Decisions that Encourage the Safe Use of Mineral Products*

IMPLEMENTATION GUIDANCE

(i) At industry, company, site and supply chain level, participate in creating and sharing knowledge about relevant disciplines such as:

   (a) materials handling regulations, standards or requirements;
   (b) management of hazardous substances;
   (c) risk assessment and identification;
   (d) controls on the selection of materials;
   (e) establishment and regulation of product standards.

(ii) At industry, company, site and supply chain level, participate constructively in policy development in relevant jurisdictions (see elements 1.4, 4.1, 6.4, 8.4, 10.1–10.3).

## Principle 9: Contribute to the Social, Economic and Institutional Development of the Communities in Which We Operate

*Element 9.1: Engage at the Earliest Practical Stage with Likely Affected Parties to Discuss and Respond to Issues and Conflicts Concerning the Management of Social Impacts*

IMPLEMENTATION GUIDANCE

(i) Engage communities and stakeholder groups in areas that may be affected by operations early – if possible before exploration.
(ii) Establish a stakeholder register to assist in the identification of relevant stakeholders, and keep this current over the whole cycle.
(iii) Undertake engagement in a culturally-appropriate manner throughout the life of the operation.
(iv) Implement systems to appropriately manage issues and effects, positive and negative, of mining (see elements 2.2–2.3, 3.2, 3.6, 4.1, 4.3, 5.4, 8.3, 10.1–10.3).

*Element 9.2: Ensure that Appropriate Systems Are in Place for Ongoing Interaction with Affected Parties, Making Sure that Minorities and Other Marginalised Groups Have Equitable and Culturally Appropriate Means of Engagement*

IMPLEMENTATION GUIDANCE

(i) Establish fair and equitable processes for engagement with Indigenous and local communities.
(ii) Establish processes to ensure ongoing interaction with communities regarding issues of interest to the mining operation and/or to the community.
(iii) Understand and respect directly affected peoples' decision-making and dispute resolution processes and their time frames for going through these processes.
(iv) Develop partnerships that provide opportunities for reciprocal learning and mutual understanding.
(v) Identify historically marginalised groups and implement strategies to address the special needs of individuals or groups in the community to ensure their effective participation.
(vi) In engaging the community ensure that proper consideration is given to community views and that they are considered in the company decision-making process (see elements 2.2–2.3, 3.2, 3.6, 4.1, 5.1, 8.1, 10.1–10.3).

*Element 9.3: Contribute to Community Development from Project Development through Closure in Collaboration with Host Communities and Their Representatives*

IMPLEMENTATION GUIDANCE

(i) Contribute to the development of sustainable communities. Apply a development model which identifies communities' current strengths and long-term needs for economic, social and institutional security.
(ii) Strengthen and diversify the local and regional economy by supporting local businesses and products when this is feasible and consistent with sound business practices.

(iii) Identify and work to realise training and other opportunities for capacity building and community development. Work in partnership with relevant institutions and organisations.
(iv) Ensure that exit strategies are in place for all programs, particularly if they will terminate before mine closure.
(v) Engage the community in defining the intended post mining land-use in mine closure plans.
(vi) Contribute to the professional development of young people in local communities through capacity building and mentoring programs.
(vii) Meet community development commitments prior to divestment, or seek to ensure that these commitments are transferred to the asset purchaser (see elements 1.2–1.3, 2.2, 3.5–3.6, 4.1, 6.1, 7.3).

*Element 9.4: Encourage Partnerships with Governments and Non-government Organisations to Ensure that Programmes (such as Community Health, Education, Local Business Development) Are Well Designed and Effectively Delivered*

IMPLEMENTATION GUIDANCE

(i) Undertake social and economic research and assessment in partnership with communities and appropriate organisations to support planning and development of operations with subsequent management review of social and economic effects through the whole cycle.
(ii) Recognise existing community planning processes and utilise these where feasible to achieve mutually beneficial social outcomes. Develop community partnerships and work to secure community ownership of the processes and outcomes.
(iii) Develop partnerships (including government, NGOs and other relevant organisations) where appropriate to facilitate program design and delivery.
(iv) Implement programs (including apprenticeships and cadetships) to build skills and experience and to secure a skilled future workforce (see elements 1.2–1.3, 2.2, 3.5–3.6, 4.1, 6.1, 7.3).

*Element 9.5: Enhance Social and Economic Development by Seeking Opportunities to Address Poverty*

IMPLEMENTATION GUIDANCE

(i) Plan and operate in ways that support the sustainable social, economic and environmental development of the host country, region and local communities.
(ii) Work to realise education and training opportunities for local people to increase their employment options.
(iii) Identify opportunities for skill development and training and implement these in collaboration with employees to increase their employment options following mine closure.
(iv) In conjunction with local communities, support the development and improvement of sustainable infrastructure.
(v) Seek to ensure the fair and equitable distribution of resources provided to host and local communities (see elements 1.2–1.3, 2.2, 3.5–3.6, 4.1, 6.1, 7.3).

**Principle 10: Implement Effective and Transparent Engagement, Communication and Independently Verified Reporting Arrangements with Our Stakeholders**

*Element 10.1: Report on Our Economic, Social and Environmental Performance and Contribution to Sustainable Development*

IMPLEMENTATION GUIDANCE

(i) Produce an annual report on sustainable development performance against company targets and make this publicly available.
(ii) Provide information in a manner that is culturally appropriate and easily understood. Reporting should be undertaken in a way that is useful, legible, and accessible to those receiving the information.
(iii) Undertake financial reporting in accordance with relevant accounting standards (see elements 3.6, 4.3, 5.2, 6.1–6.2, 7.2, 8.1–8.5, 9.2).

*Element 10.2: Provide Information that is Timely, Accurate and Relevant*

IMPLEMENTATION GUIDANCE

(i) Provide information within appropriate timeframes and contexts and identify the reporting period.
(ii) Validate data, information and processes in performance reports.
(iii) Utilise appropriate verification processes for reports to provide public confidence in the information being reported.
(iv) Systematically identify stakeholder information needs to ensure that information provided is relevant.
(v) Utilise stakeholder feedback on the reporting structure, format, timeframes and verification to continually improve the reporting processes (see elements 3.6, 4.3, 5.2, 6.1–6.2, 7.2, 8.1–8.5, 9.2).

*Element 10.3: Engage with and Respond to Stakeholders through Open Consultation Processes*

IMPLEMENTATION GUIDANCE

(i) Ensure all stakeholders have been identified in an open and transparent manner.
(ii) Conduct a stakeholder analysis to identify rights and interests, and periodically review this throughout the life of the operation.
(iii) Utilise transparent and consultative communication processes to engage key stakeholders and provide feedback on issues raised.
(iv) Apply appropriate mechanisms for hearing and resolving stakeholder feedback within transparent and defined timeframes.
(v) Maintain a complaint and comment register. Provide open and transparent grievance mechanisms. Publish reports about complaints and disputes and their resolutions (see elements 3.2, 3.6, 4.1, 4.3–4.4, 7.2, 8.1, 8.4, 9.1–9.2, 10.1–10.2).

## Glossary

Baseline Information: A baseline is an information reference point against which performance is measured or compared. In social and environmental impact assessment, the baseline would be the state of the ecosystem or community without the proposed development. In applying the concept of continuous improvement, the baseline is typically the performance of the preceding year for a particular measure.

Benchmark: Benchmarking is a method by which organisations compare their processes, practices and performance with those of others – either through direct comparison with other companies or comparison with industry standards. Benchmarking processes identify, interpret and adapt outstanding practices from anywhere in the world to help an organisation improve its performance.

Capacity Building: Capacity building is working with a community to increase their ability to determine and manage their own future. Capacity building projects are most relevant where a host community might not capture the benefits of a project without new skills and resources. Effective capacity building is driven by the needs of the community – not the company. A company can use its resources to work with a host community to build its skills, knowledge and institutions so that the benefits of the project are captured in the community for the long-term. An example of this might be where a company provides training in project planning, budgeting and management – at the request of the community – so that project royalties can fund more viable and sustainable community projects.

Chronic and Acute Risk: Risk is the likelihood of a hazard occurring. A risk is a function of a number of factors, including the nature of the hazard, the likelihood of occurrence, characteristics of the exposed population, the route, frequency and extent of exposure, the seriousness of the consequences and the public perception of the risk. Acute risks are those that result in immediate harmful effects and result from a single exposure. Chronic risks are those that cause harmful effects to show up after prolonged or repeated exposure – potentially over years.

Community (including local and affected community): A community is a group of people living in a particular area or region. In mining industry terms, community is generally applied to the inhabitants of immediate and surrounding areas who are affected by a company's activities. The term local or host community is usually applied to those living in the immediate vicinity of an operation, being indigenous or non indigenous people, who may have cultural affinity or claim, or direct ownership of an area in which a company has an interest. Affected community refers to the members of the community affected by a company's activities. The effects are most commonly social (resettlement, changed services such as education and health), economic (compensation, job prospects, creation of local wealth), environmental and political. Whilst the economic and associated social impacts of a company may be extensive and operate at provincial, state or national levels, these broader impacts would not typically be used to define the affected community.

Corporate Governance: Corporate governance is a broad term that refers to the manner in which a company is directed, and the laws, customs and behaviours affecting that direction. Corporate governance influences how the objectives of the company are set and achieved, how risk is monitored and assessed and how performance is optimised. Governance structures oversee the role of management and the board, decision making, financial reporting and disclosure, risk management, the rights of shareholders, company performance, remuneration and the interests of stakeholders. Good corporate governance structures will monitor the integrity and ethical values of a company and make it accountable for its actions.

Discrimination: Discrimination is treating people unfairly or unequally because of their age, sex, race, religion, disability or sexual orientation. Two kinds or discrimination are generally recognised. Direct discrimination means receiving less favourable treatment than another person in the same or similar circumstances on any grounds of unlawful discrimination in any areas of public life covered by the relevant laws. An example is not awarding a candidate a job because of their nationality. Indirect discrimination is when apparently neutral rules, policies or practices can impact negatively on a particular group in an unreasonable manner. An example of this would be providing a company uniform that couldn't be worn by employees that practised a particular religion. In Australia, discrimination is covered by numerous Commonwealth and State Acts. Grounds of unlawful discrimination in Australia vary from State to State, but at least include sex, marital status, pregnancy, race and disability.

Employee Entitlements: Employee entitlements are the benefits that employees are owed by their employer as a result of their employment. The main types of employee entitlements are salaries and wages, performance pay, annual leave, sick leave, long service leave and superannuation.

Engagement: At its simplest, engagement is communicating effectively with the people who affect and are affected by a company's activities (its stakeholders). A good engagement process typically involves identifying and prioritising stakeholders, conducting a two-way dialogue with them to understand their particular interest in an issue and any concerns they may have, exploring with them ways to address these issues, and providing feedback to stakeholders on actions taken. At a more complex level, engagement is a means of negotiating agreed outcomes over issues of concern or mutual interest.

Ethical Business Practice: Ethics are a set of moral principles, standards or rules that govern the conduct of the members of a group. Ethical business practice is doing business based on a set of ethical principles developed by the company. It is commonly a commitment to conduct business in an honest and ethical manner and fulfill commitments with integrity. The principles or rules of conduct will outline behaviour that is accepted by members of society, taking into consideration such factors as host country laws and regulations and industry regulations and procedures.

Facilitation Payments: Facilitation payments are small payments to low-level public officials to expedite routine approvals. An example of this would be paying a government official a fee to have a license or permit processed. There are differing views on the acceptability of facilitation payments irrespective of their legality in some countries, with some considering them to be a form of bribery. Facilitation payments are permissible under US law for foreign transactions and under the OECD Convention on Combating Bribery of Foreign Public Officials in International Business Transactions. The International Chamber of Commerce (ICC) does not condone facilitation payments, and some companies including Shell and BP have policies banning facilitation payments in keeping with the ICC stance. Many resource companies address stakeholder concerns about the ethics of facilitation payments through ensuring payments are fully disclosed and reported publicly.

Harassment: Harassment is unwelcome or offensive behaviour by one person to another. Examples of harassment include unwanted sexual attention, bullying, intimidation and abuse of power. The Australian Government National Occupational Health and Safety Commission defines harassment as 'any form of behaviour that is not wanted and humiliates you, offends you or intimidates you'. To 'harass' is to irritate or torment persistently. Harassment is often about one person (or a group of people) using power inappropriately over another person/group of people. Throughout Australia, it is against the law for you to be harassed because of your gender, pregnancy, race, marital status, or disability.

Hazard: A hazard is anything that has the potential to cause harm. A more technical definition of hazard is the intrinsic property of a dangerous substance or physical situation, with a potential for creating damage to human health and/or the environment. (Joint Research Centre for the European Commission).

Human Rights: Human rights are the rights and freedoms shared by all members of the human family. These are often referred to as being 'equal rights'. Human rights are protected by law and apply even if the individual is prepared to relinquish them. Hence, they are considered 'inalienable rights'. The UN Universal Declaration of Human Rights includes in the basic set of human rights: equality, life, liberty and security of person, access to education and the law, freedom of movement, asylum, nationality, freedom to marry and have a family, freedom to choose and practice religion, freedom of expression and opinion, the right to work and leisure, minimum standard of living, duties to and enjoyment of community. For the full version of the UN Universal Declaration of Human Rights, go to www.un.org/Overview/rights.html.

Integrated Materials Management: Integrated materials management (IMM), often called product stewardship, is an approach that seeks to reduce the environmental impacts of products from mining. It requires an understanding of the impacts and drivers along the whole extraction–production–use–waste management chain, that is, applying a life-cycle approach to natural resource production. Integrated materials management improves efficiency and reduces waste. In an IMM system, products are recycled to the greatest extent possible and wastes remain valuable materials unless, and until, their useful life is expended. Successful IMM requires the involvement and cooperation of companies throughout the supply chain.

Multiple and Sequential Land Use: Multiple and sequential land use means that, if land is not of high environmental or social value, it can be used for different purposes at the same time (multiple) and for a different purpose after a land use has finished (sequential). While multiple and sequential land use policy in Australia recognises that access to land may be partially or wholly restricted due to high conservation and social values (e.g. national park or native title), the objective of the policy is to facilitate access to resources for exploration and resource development, providing these activities are not in conflict with the values to be protected. An example of multiple and sequential land use would be where part of a grazing property is mined for resources whilst the balance of the property continues to operate. Once the mine has closed and appropriate rehabilitation has been undertaken, the land returns to its previous use.

Offsetting: Where native vegetation clearing is permitted, an offset is an action taken to partially recover both the extent and quality of vegetation lost. This action may include protecting vegetation of equivalent type, quality and extent to that being cleared, acquiring additional land with comparable biodiversity values, or re-vegetating cleared land. Often, it involves a combination of these actions. Offsets are typically guided by policies aimed at improving the overall extent and quality of native vegetation and associated biodiversity. Offsets are typically applied in situations where a company cannot avoid an impact on native vegetation because of the location of the ore body or operational constraints.

Permit-to-work System (for designated hazardous work): A permit-to-work system is a formal written system used to control potentially hazardous types of work. A permit to work is a document that specifies the work to be done and the precautions to be taken. The purpose of a permit-to-work system is to ensure that proper consideration is given to the risks of particular work and that these are assessed and controlled before work starts. It is a system to ensure that managers and supervisors understand the identity, nature and extent of a job, the hazards involved and the precautions to be taken.

Precautionary Principle: The Precautionary Principle means that action to avert serious or irreversible environmental damage may be needed before there is scientific certainty that the harm exists. The Precautionary Principle was first recognised at an international level in the World Charter for Nature, adopted by the UN General Assembly in 1982. It was enshrined at the 1992 Rio Conference on the Environment through Principle 15 of the Rio Declaration which states that: 'in order to protect the environment, the precautionary approach shall be widely applied by States according to their capability. Where there are threats of serious or irreversible damage, lack of full scientific certainty shall not be used as a reason for postponing cost-effective measures to prevent environmental degradation'. This principle has since become progressively consolidated in international environmental law. An example of the Precautionary Principle would be the international response by governments to tackle global climate change through reduced greenhouse gas emissions while there was still considerable uncertainty about both its cause and likely impacts.

Risk Assessment: Risk assessment is determining how likely and how extensive a risk might be to an operation. It can be defined as 'the process by which one attempts to evaluate and predict the likelihood and extent of harm (in quantitative [how many] and qualitative [descriptive] terms) that may result from a perceived health or safety hazard'. (The National Mining Association (USA)). Good risk assessments, and resulting risk management procedures, enable an organisation to allocate appropriate resources for sustainable reduction of risk exposure and potential crises. Whilst risk assessment has traditionally been considered an objective, science-based process, more contemporary approaches consider both science and societal values, and incorporate objective and subjective data in the analysis.

Socio-economic Assessment: Socio-economic assessments seek to estimate and appraise in advance the social and economic consequences that are likely to follow from specific policies or project developments. Impacts that might be considered in a socio-economic assessment include: direct and indirect economic (includes employment), demographic, housing, social infrastructure and services, and socio-cultural (e.g. quality of life, crime, conflict etc). Note: For the purposes of the implementation guidance, socio-economic assessment and socio-economic impact assessment should be considered to be the same.

Special Measures: Special measures are programs that aim to promote groups, or individual members of groups, who are affected by historic disadvantage because of laws and rules, stereotypes and attitudes. For example, Australian Commonwealth programs that aim to increase Aboriginal school retention and achievement rates, such as the Aboriginal Student Support and Parent Awareness funding program, are 'special measures'.

Stakeholder: At Earth Summit 2002, stakeholders were defined as 'those who have an interest in a particular decision, either as individuals or representatives of a group. This includes people who influence a decision, or can influence it, as well as those affected by it'. Stakeholders might include local community members, non-government organisations, governments, shareholders and employees.

Traditionally Marginalised Groups: Traditionally marginalised groups are those that are excluded from mainstream society. Traditionally, groups have been oppressed or marginalised for their gender, ethnicity, cultural or indigenous identity, poverty or disability. Marginalisation can affect basic rights, such as access to education, health services, water and food (see Human Rights) For example, the 8–10 million Roma/Gypsies of Europe are seldom recognised by the majority of society as fully-fledged European people. As a result of centuries of rejection, they live in very difficult conditions, often on the fringes of society and their participation in public life is very limited.

Verification: Verification is independent analysis and authentication, performed by an external auditor or verifier, of information presented about a company's environmental, social and economic performance and how this may support a company's claims about progress towards sustainability. Verification is sought to provide evidence that specified requirements have been fulfilled, generally to improve third-party confidence in the veracity of the information. Note: to date, there is no universally agreed method for verifying social, environmental and economic data. There exist many methodologies and verifying agencies.

## Note

1. Importantly the risk assessment process should take into account the precautionary principle.

## Additional Instrument

*i. MCA: Code for Environmental Management, 2000*

**Commentary**: The MCA first introduced this Code in 1996 and subsequently reviewed it during 1999. 'The industry determined that regulation only prescribed the bare minimum, that our communities expected more, and in response established the Code as a voluntary adjunct to regulation requiring companies to move beyond a compliance mentality, which can stifle innovation and the pursuit of excellence': Mr M.H. Hooke, Chief Executive, MCA, 'The Australian Minerals Industry Code for Environmental Management', Presentation to the Global Mining Industry Conference, Toronto, 2002. The Code was a principles-based framework document to enable companies to improve environmental performance. Signatories (39 as at 2002) committed themselves to continuous improvement with the assistance of an External Environmental Advisory Group: see further, 'Guidance Note on the Australian Minerals Industry External Environmental Advisory Group: Terms of Reference and

Roles and Responsibilities'. They also undertook to complete annual public environmental reports and an annual self-assessment of performance against the Code principles (the Code Implementation Survey) which was verified every three years by an accredited internal or external auditor. The overall implementation record was then annually aggregated by the MCA secretariat in an industry-wide performance analysis against the code principles. Consistent with its voluntary nature, signatories could withdraw at any stage. Implementation guidance was provided by MCA Code Guidance Notes and policy statements, a series of Best Practice Environmental Management in Mining modules available from the Australian Minerals and Energy Environment Foundation (www.ameef.com.au), environmental management standards from Standards Australia (www.standards.com.au) and technical guidance provided by the Australian Centre for Mining Environmental Research (www.acmer.com.au). The Environmental Code was superseded in 2005 by Enduring Value (extracted above).

# 82. International Gas Union: Guiding Principles for Sustainable Development, 2003

**Commentary**: Founded in 1931, the International Gas Union (IGU, www.igu.org) is a global non-profit organisation registered in Switzerland with a secretariat located in Denmark. The IGU's objective is to promote technical and economic progress within the gas industry and its membership consists of associations and entities from 67 States. The IGU formulates an action programme at World Gas conferences held every three years for subsequent implementation by working committees. See also IGU (2003), *Seven Decades with IGU*, Hoersholm: Denmark. For other sectoral approaches, see International Fertilizer Industry Association (1992, 2000), 'Mission Statements on Sustainable Development', Vancouver (www.fertilizer.org/ifa); the International Hotel Environmental Initiative (1992), 'Charter for Environmental Action in the Hotel Industry', London (www.ihei.org).

The underlying tenet of the IGU Guiding Principles for Sustainable Development is that the gas industry integrates economic, environmental and social factors in all its business practices. The gas industry further recognises that continuous improvement of corporate performance towards sustainable development is critical for successful business.

The gas industry's corporate performance for Sustainable Development is guided by the following declarations:

(i) The Universal Declaration of Human Rights, 1948.
(ii) The ILO Declaration on Fundamental Principles and Rights at Works, 1998.
(iii) The Rio Declaration on Sustainable Development and its Agenda for the 21st century, 1992.

**Environmentally Sound by Making Choices Today that Work Tomorrow**
Continuous improvement in the performance of the gas industry is of vital importance as the world moves towards a sustainable energy future. The gas industry shall:

(i) co-operate with all parties involved in the gas chain to minimise environmental impact;
(ii) assess environmental impacts of activities and adopt a precautionary approach to prevent serious or irreversible environmental degradation;
(iii) fulfil all operations in an environmentally responsible manner and commit to improving industry wide environmental performance taking legal obligations as minimum reference criteria;
(iv) develop and maintain emergency preparedness plans to be prepared for and respond to emergencies in a timely and effective manner;

(v) incorporate environmental values into purchasing decisions;
(vi) educate and motivate employees and customers to conduct their activities in an environmentally responsible manner;
(vii) encourage clean and efficient gas utilisation to improve local conditions and contribute to a reduction of greenhouse gas emissions;
(viii) support research on the environmental impacts from the gas industry's activities and on the means of minimising such adverse impacts;
(ix) support efficient and combined utilisation of renewable energy and natural gas by investing in research and pilot programmes;
(x) communicate in an open, transparent and objective manner on environmental matters to employees, authorities, customers, shareholders and the public.

**Socially Responsible by Supporting Healthy Communities**

The gas industry is committed to ensuring the health and safety of its employees, subcontractors, customers and the public affected by its operations, products and services. The gas industry in IGU member countries shall recognise the responsibility to support healthy employees, contractors and communities by:

(i) continuously improving Environment, Health & Safety (EHS) performance through effective implementation of EHS Management Systems;
(ii) implementing leading-edge employment standards and practices;
(iii) investing in employment training programmes that benefit the industry and communities;
(iv) prioritise local employment and suppliers, when possible technically, economically and legally;
(v) developing an open dialogue with interested parties such as customers, employees, governments and non-government organisations;
(vi) gathering and promptly responding to community complaints;
(vii) partnering with community-based organisations that support business success;
(viii) incorporating human rights and labour standards in the purchasing policy;
(ix) promoting technology transfer of highly efficient and low emissions technologies to developing countries.

**Economically Viable by Supporting Sustainable Developments**

A sustainable future needs a strong economy to support the social, environmental and other programmes. The gas industry in IGU member countries shall support viable economies by:

(i) providing meaningful and fairly paid employment to communities;
(ii) delivering reliable, competitively priced energy to local industry;
(iii) contributing revenue from sales, property and income taxes;
(iv) supporting transparency;
(v) developing and adhering to well-designed anti-corruption policies and implementation strategies;
(vi) maintaining economically viable conditions for necessary investments.

**Means of Implementation**

The work on sustainable development is based on a plan, do, check and act approach to achieve continuous improvements.

Environmental, social and economic considerations are integrated into the process of planning, construction and operation.

All employees receive education on environmentally sound, socially responsible and economically viable behaviour and decision-making to assure effective implementation of a sustainable development approach.

A comprehensive view, from 'cradle to grave', is applied in the evaluation of the impacts and benefits of the activities, when establishing and implementing corporate policies, goals, programmes and procedures.

Assessments of compliance with the legal requirements as a minimum, but also with company procedures, is guaranteed by regular audits and relevant reports are provided to government, employees and other interested parties.

Sustainable development is measured and reported using performance indicators as a reference for improvements.

# 83. Oxfam–Community Aid Abroad: Principles on a Human Rights Approach to Development, 2001

**Commentary**: The Oxfam Principles (Policy Serial No 2.2) illustrate NGO expectations for greater commercial contributions to realising a human rights-oriented approach to sustainable development. See further, Community Aid Abroad (2004), 'Mining Ombudsman Report'; www.oxfam.org.au.

Oxfam Community Aid Abroad acknowledges that without a respect for, and an understanding and promotion of human rights, there can be no real solution to poverty. While governments and various sectors of society fail to provide the frameworks to support the realisation of human rights for people and communities, there can be no long-term eradication of poverty.

**Oxfam Community Aid Abroad Principles**

In recent times Oxfam Community Aid Abroad has emphasised the use of a human rights framework in our work. A rights based approach to development empowers people to demand justice as a right, not as charity. We believe that the following human rights are central for true and sustainable development:

(i) The right to a sustainable livelihood.
(ii) The right to basic services.
(iii) The right to life and security.
(iv) The right to be heard.
(v) The right to an identity: gender and diversity.

These human rights must be seen in the context of the international human rights instruments including (but not limited to) the Universal Declaration on Human Rights (UDHR), International Covenant on Civil and Political Rights (ICCPR), International Covenant on Economic, Social and Cultural Rights (ICESCR); Convention on the Elimination of All Forms of Discrimination against Women (CEDAW), Convention on the Elimination of All Forms of Racial Discrimination, and the Convention on the Rights of the Child (CROC). The rights in these documents are interconnected, indivisible and universal.

Oxfam Community Aid Abroad employs a multifaceted approach to the realisation of human rights including working towards the empowerment of communities to determine their own futures, lobbying and advocating for fairer policies and practices, and educating and raising awareness in the Australian community of the myriad occurrences of poverty, and the fundamental factors behind its institutionalisation and ongoing spread throughout the world.

Consequently, Oxfam Community Aid Abroad calls for principled leadership by government and legislators, who must provide the framework for the establishment of a culture which sets a high store on human rights. National governments have a responsibility to legislate domestically in support of the international human rights instruments and play a proactive role with neighbours, regional partners and the like in the promotion, protection and institutionalising of rights. Through leadership and support for human rights, governments lay the necessary foundations for civil society to take up the mantle of human rights education and awareness. We also call on corporations, the business and community sector to ensure that the development that they are involved in are supportive of the realisation of human rights. A human rights approach necessitates a consistent and wide-reaching commitment to the realisation of a just and equitable society, free from prejudice and discrimination of any kind.

# 84. Additional initiatives

## i. UNCED: Rio Declaration on Environment and Development, 1992

**Commentary**: One of the many positive and longstanding contributions made by business is the economic development of States: UNCTC (1988), *TNCs in World Development: Trends and Prospects*, New York. 'Sustainable development' is defined as development which meets the needs of present generations without compromising the ability of future ones to satisfy their own requirements: Brundtland, G. (ed.) (1987), *Our Common Future: The World Commission on Environment and Development*, Oxford: Oxford University Press (the Brundtland Commission). The Rio Declaration (see UNCED Report, UN Doc A/CONF.151/26 (1992) Vol I) builds upon the 1972 Stockholm Declaration from the UN Conference on the Human Environment, UN Doc A/CONF.48/14/Rev.1 (1973). Of the 27 Principles, Principle 16 provides that: 'National authorities should endeavour to promote the internalization of environmental costs and the use of economic instruments, taking into account the approach that the polluter should, in principle, bear the cost of pollution, with due regard to the public interest and without distorting international trade and investment'.

Also emanating from UNCED was the 'Non-legally Binding Authoritative Statement of Principles for a Global Consensus on the Management, Conservation and Sustainable Development of All Types of Forests', UNCED Report, UN Doc A/CONF.151/26 (Vol. III) (1992). See further, EC proposal for the development of a code of conduct for European logging companies COM(89)0410. For PVIs in this field, see the Forest Stewardship Council (FSC, www.fsc.org) and the FSC 'Principles and Criteria', Document 1.2 (1993) (revised 2000); American Forest and Paper Association (1994), 'Sustainable Forestry Initiative' (www.afandpa.org).

## ii. UN General Assembly: Resolution 50/106 (1995) on Business and Development, 1995

**Commentary**: The General Assembly in UNGA Resolution 50/106 (1996) stated that it:

1. Values the promotion of entrepreneurship in the development of small and medium-sized enterprises and industries by various actors throughout civil society, and of privatization, demonopolization and the simplification of administrative procedures;
2. Invites Member States, requests the Secretary-General and calls upon and encourages the relevant organs, organizations and programmes of the UN system

to continue to foster active participation in support of entrepreneurship, privatization, demonopolization and the simplification of administrative procedures, as described in UNGA Resolution 48/180;

3. Also invites Member States, requests the Secretary-General and calls upon and encourages the relevant organs, organizations and programmes of the UN system, in their respective activities for the provision of infrastructure services, to encourage private-sector cost-effective involvement in the efficient construction, use and maintenance of infrastructure.

See further, UNGA Resolution 48/180 (1993) concerning Entrepreneurship and Privatisation for Economic Growth and Sustainable Development; UN Secretary-General (1995), 'Report concerning policies and activities related to entrepreneurship, privatization, demonopolization and administrative deregulation', UN Doc A/50/417.

### iii. UNDP: Monterrey Consensus on Financing for Development, 2002

**Commentary**: The Monterrey Consensus (see 'Report of the International Conference on Financing for Development', UN Doc A/CONF.198/11; www.undp.org/ffd) is relevant to corporations in several important respects. Governments emphasised continued reliance upon public–private partnerships for achieving sustainable development objectives (paragraph 24). They also committed themselves to mobilising private savings (paragraph 10), encouraging private sector initiatives which foster dynamic and well-functioning business sectors (12), welcoming financial sector contributions in providing access to capital (17 and 18), encouraging foreign direct investment (20) and securing fair debt burden-sharing between the public and private sectors (51 and 58). Governments would provide transparent, stable and predictable investment climates which enable proper contractual enforcement and respect for property rights (paragraph 21). It was envisaged that international institutions would provide *inter alia* export credits, risk guarantees, information concerning investment opportunities and business development services (paragraph 22). Careful attention will be devoted to capital flows (paragraph 25) and official development assistance (39). Finally, governments encouraged active private sector involvement when preparing intergovernmental development assessments (paragraph 71).

Particularly noteworthy is that:

23. While Governments provide the framework for their operation, businesses, for their part, are expected to engage as reliable and consistent partners in the development process. We urge businesses to take into account not only the economic and financial but also the developmental, social, gender and environmental implications of their undertakings. In that spirit, we invite banks and other financial institutions, in developing countries as well as developed countries, to foster innovative developmental financing approaches. We welcome all efforts to encourage good corporate citizenship and note the initiative undertaken in the UN to promote global partnerships.

The International Business Forum, chaired by the ICC and including *inter alia* the UN Business Council and the World Economic Forum, developed several practical policy proposals predicated upon public/private initiatives for prospective adoption by governments (see Conference Report, Annex III, paras 6–8). The Ministerial segment of the Conference considered reports from the business and civil society forums and heard an ICC statement delivered on behalf of the International Business Forum.

By way of follow-up, the UNGA held a High-level Dialogue on Financing for Development in New York during 2003: see UNGA President Summary, UN Doc A/58/555 (2003); UNGA Resolution 58/230 (2003). See further, Report of the UN-sanctioned business interlocutors to the International Conference on Financing for Development (2002), 'Strengthening Financing for Development: Proposals from the Private Sector'; UNDP/Commission on the Private Sector and Development (2004), 'Unleashing Entrepreneurship: Making business work for the poor'.

# PART VIII

# Roles and Responsibilities in Zones of Conflict

# 85. Articles Common to the Geneva Conventions

**Commentary**: For the roles and responsibilities of corporations in zones of conflict, see further, International Alert/Council on Economic Priorities/PWBLF (2000), 'The Business of Peace: The Private Sector as a Partner in Conflict Prevention and Resolution', London; OHCHR (2001), 'Global Compact Dialogue on the Role of the Private Sector in Zones of Conflict', Palais Wilson; Global Compact Office (2002), 'Business Guide for Conflict Impact Assessment and Risk Management'; Global Compact Office (2005), *Enabling Economies of Peace: Public Policy for Conflict-Sensitive Business*, New York; World Bank (2005), 'International Companies and Post-Conflict Reconstruction; Cross-Sectoral Comparisons', Paper No. 22, Washington, DC. See also, the activities of the International Committee of the Red Cross (ICRC; www.icrc.org) and the Business Humanitarian Forum (BHF; www.bhforum.ch). For academic commentary, see Carbonnier G. (2001), 'Corporate responsibility and humanitarian principles: what relations between the business and humanitarian worlds?', *International Review of the Red Cross*, **83** (844), 947–68; Fort T.L. and Schipani C.A. (2002), 'The role of the corporation in fostering sustainable peace', *Vanderbilt Journal of Transnational Law*, **35**, 389–436; Orts E.W. (2002), 'War and the business corporation', *Vanderbilt Journal of Transnational Law*, **35**, 549–84.

Extracted below, the First Geneva Convention (75 *UNTS* 31), Second (75 *UNTS* 85), Third (75 *UNTS* 135) and Fourth (75 *UNTS* 287) were concluded in 1949 and entered into force during 1950. Collectively they constitute (together with the two Additional Protocols – see below) the legal regime with respect to international humanitarian law. The legal character of hostilities (international or non-international armed conflicts) may be relevant to the enforcement of insurance contracts: *Janson v Driefontein Consolidated Mines Ltd* [1902] *AC* 484. Occupying powers may not be liable under international humanitarian law in the event of property damage for failure to maintain law and order: *Industria Panificadora SA v US* 957 *F.2d* 886 (1992); *Goldstar (Panama) SA v US* 967 *F.2d* 965 (1992). However, compensation may be more readily obtainable under bilateral investment treaties: ICSID, *American Manufacturing & Trading Inc v Republic of Zaire*, Case ARB/93/1 (1997); ICSID, *Asian Agricultural Products Ltd v Republic of Sri Lanka* (1997) 106 *ILR* 416, 451–64.

**Article 2**

In addition to the provisions which shall be implemented in peacetime, the present Convention shall apply to all cases of declared war or of any other armed conflict which may arise between two or more of the High Contracting Parties, even if the state of war is not recognized by one of them.

**Article 3**

In the case of armed conflict not of an international character occurring in the territory of one of the High Contracting Parties, each Party to the conflict shall be bound to apply, as a minimum, the following provisions:

1. Persons taking no active part in the hostilities, including members of armed forces who have laid down their arms and those placed *hors de combat* by sickness, wounds, detention, or any other cause, shall in all circumstances be treated humanely, without any adverse distinction founded on race, colour, religion or faith, sex, birth or wealth, or any other similar criteria. To this end, the following acts are and shall remain prohibited at any time and in any place whatsoever with respect to the above-mentioned persons:

    (a) Violence to life and person. in particular murder of all kinds, mutilation, cruel treatment and torture;
    (b) Taking of hostages;
    (c) Outrages upon personal dignity, in particular humiliating and degrading treatment;
    (d) The passing of sentences and the carrying out of executions without previous judgment pronounced by a regularly constituted court, affording all the judicial guarantees which are recognized as indispensable by civilized peoples . . .

**Article 13/4**[1]

[The present Convention shall apply to the wounded and sick belonging to the following categories]/[ The present Convention shall apply to the wounded, sick and shipwrecked at sea belonging to the following categories]/[Prisoners of war, in the sense of the present Convention, are persons belonging to one of the following categories, who have fallen into the power of the enemy]:

4. Persons who accompany the armed forces without actually being members thereof, such as civil members of military aircraft crews, war correspondents, supply contractors, members of labour units or of services responsible for the welfare of the armed forces, provided that they have received authorization from the armed forces which they accompany . . .
5. Members of crews, including masters, pilots and apprentices of the merchant marine and the crews of civil aircraft of the Parties to the conflict, who do not benefit by more favourable treatment under any other provisions in international law.

## Annex I: Draft Agreement Relating to Hospital [and Safety] Zones and Localities[2]

*Article 2*

No persons residing, in whatever capacity, in a hospital [and safety] zone shall perform any work, either within or without the zone, directly connected with military operations or the production of war material.

*Article 4*

Hospital [and safety] zones shall fulfil the following conditions:

(c) They shall be far removed and free from all military objectives, or large industrial or administrative establishments.

## Notes

1. Article 13, Geneva Convention for the Amelioration of the Condition of the Wounded and Sick in Armed Forces in the Field; Article 13, Geneva Convention for the Amelioration of the Condition of Wounded, Sick and Shipwrecked Members of Armed Forces at Sea; Article 4, Geneva Convention relative to the Treatment of Prisoners of War.
2. Geneva Convention for the Amelioration of the Condition of the Wounded and Sick in Armed Forces in the Field, 1949; Geneva Convention relative to the Protection of Civilian Persons in Time of War, 1949.

# 86. UN: Geneva Convention for the Amelioration of the Condition of the Wounded and Sick in Armed Forces in the Field, 1949

### Chapter IV: Personnel

*Article 28*
Personnel designated in Articles 24 and 26 [medical personnel and members of voluntary aid societies] who fall into the hands of the adverse Party shall be retained only in so far as the state of health, the spiritual needs and the number of prisoners of war require . . . They shall further enjoy the following facilities for carrying out their medical or spiritual duties:

(c) Although retained personnel in a camp shall be subject to its internal discipline, they shall not, however, be required to perform any work outside their medical or religious duties . . .

### Chapter VI: Medical Transports

*Article 35*
Transports of wounded and sick or of medical equipment shall be respected and protected in the same way as mobile medical units . . . The civilian personnel and all means of transport obtained by requisition shall be subject to the general rules of international law.

### Chapter VII: The Distinctive Emblem

*Article 38*
As a compliment to Switzerland, the heraldic emblem of the red cross on a white ground, formed by reversing the Federal colours, is retained as the emblem and distinctive sign of the Medical Service of armed forces. Nevertheless, in the case of countries which already use as emblem, in place of the red cross, the red crescent or the red lion and sun on a white ground, those emblems are also recognized by the terms of the present Convention.

### Chapter IX: Repression of Abuses and Infractions

*Article 53*
The use by individuals, societies, firms or companies either public or private, other than those entitled thereto under the present Convention, of the emblem or the designation 'Red Cross' or 'Geneva Cross', or any sign or designation constituting an imitation there of, whatever the

object of such use, and irrespective of the date of its adoption, shall be prohibited at all times. By reason of the tribute paid to Switzerland by the adoption of the reversed Federal colours, and of the confusion which may arise between the arms of Switzerland and the distinctive emblem of the Convention, the use by private individuals, societies or firms, of the arms of the Swiss Confederation, or of marks constituting an imitation thereof, whether as trade-marks or commercial marks, or as parts of such marks, or for a purpose contrary to commercial honesty, or in circumstances capable of wounding Swiss national sentiment, shall be prohibited at all times.

# 87. UN: Geneva Convention for the Amelioration of the Condition of Wounded, Sick and Shipwrecked Members of Armed Forces at Sea, 1949

**Commentary**: Article 43 of this Convention specifies the identification system for hospital ships (white exterior surfaces, large dark red crosses and national flags). See further, Hague Convention (VI) relating to the Status of Enemy Merchant Ships at the Outbreak of Hostilities 205 *Consol TS* 305 (entry into force 1910); Hague Convention (VII) relating to the Conversion of Merchant Ships into War-Ships, 205 *Consol TS* 319 (entry into force 1910).

## Chapter II: Wounded, Sick and Shipwrecked

*Article 14*
All warships of a belligerent Party shall have the right to demand that the wounded, sick or shipwrecked on board military hospital ships, and hospital ships belonging to relief societies or to private individuals, as well as merchant vessels, yachts and other craft shall be surrendered, whatever their nationality, provided that the wounded and sick are in a fit state to be moved and that the warship can provide adequate facilities for necessary medical treatment.

*Article 21*
The Parties to the conflict may appeal to the charity of commanders of neutral merchant vessels, yachts or other craft, to take on board and care for wounded, sick or shipwrecked persons, and to collect the dead. Vessels of any kind responding to this appeal, and those having of their own accord collected wounded, sick or shipwrecked persons, shall enjoy special protection and facilities to carry out such assistance. They may, in no case, be captured on account of any such transport; but, in the absence of any promise to the contrary, they shall remain liable to capture for any violations of neutrality they may have committed.

## Chapter III: Hospital Ships

*Article 22*
Military hospital ships, that is to say, ships built or equipped by the Powers especially and solely with a view to assisting the wounded, sick and shipwrecked, to treating them and to transporting them, may in no circumstances be attacked or captured, but shall at all times be respected and protected, on condition that their names and descriptions have been notified to

the Parties to the conflict ten days before those ships are employed. The characteristics which must appear in the notification shall include registered gross tonnage, the length from stem to stern and the number of masts and funnels.

*Article 24*
Hospital ships utilized by National Red Cross Societies, by officially recognized relief societies or by private persons shall have the same protection as military hospital ships and shall be exempt from capture, if the Party to the conflict on which they depend has given them an official commission and in so far as the provisions of Article 22 concerning notification have been complied with . . .

*Article 25*
Hospital ships utilized by National Red Cross Societies, officially recognized relief societies, or private persons of neutral countries shall have the same protection as military hospital ships and shall be exempt from capture, on condition that they have placed themselves under the control of one of the Parties to the conflict, with the previous consent of their own governments and with the authorization of the Party to the conflict concerned, in so far as the provisions of Article 22 concerning notification have been complied with.

*Article 26*
The protection mentioned in Articles 22, 24 and 25 shall apply to hospital ships of any tonnage and to their lifeboats, wherever they are operating . . .

*Article 33*
Merchant vessels which have been transformed into hospital ships cannot be put to any other use throughout the duration of hostilities.

*Article 35*
The following conditions shall not be considered as depriving hospital ships or sick bays of vessels of the protection due to them:

1. The fact that the crews of ships or sick bays are armed for the maintenance of order, for their own defence or that of the sick and wounded.
2. The presence on board of apparatus exclusively intended to facilitate navigation or communication.
3. The discovery on board hospital ships or in sick-bays of portable arms and ammunition taken from the wounded, sick and shipwrecked and not yet handed to the proper service.
4. The fact that the humanitarian activities of hospital ships and sickbays of vessels or of the crews extend to the care of wounded, sick or shipwrecked civilians.
5. The transport of equipment and of personnel intended exclusively for medical duties, over and above the normal requirements.

## Chapter V: Medical Transports

*Article 38*
Ships chartered for that purpose shall be authorized to transport equipment exclusively intended for the treatment of wounded and sick members of armed forces or for the

prevention of disease, provided that the particulars regarding their voyage have been notified to the adverse Power and approved by the latter. The adverse Power shall preserve the right to board the carrier ships, but not to capture them or seize the equipment carried . . .

*Article 39*
Medical aircraft, that is to say, aircraft exclusively employed for the removal of wounded, sick and shipwrecked, and for the transport of medical personnel and equipment, may not be the object of attack, but shall be respected by the Parties to the conflict, while flying at heights, at times and on routes specifically agreed upon between the Parties to the conflict concerned. They shall be clearly marked with the distinctive emblem prescribed in Article 41, together with their national colours, on their lower, upper and lateral surfaces. Unless agreed otherwise, flights over enemy or enemy-occupied territory are prohibited. Medical aircraft shall obey every summons to alight on land or water . . .

*Article 40*
Subject to the provisions of the second paragraph, medical aircraft of Parties to the conflict may fly over the territory of neutral Powers, land thereon in case of necessity, or use it as a port of call. They shall give neutral Powers prior notice of their passage over the said territory, and obey every summons to alight, on land or water. They will be immune from attack only when flying on routes, at heights and at times specifically agreed upon between the Parties to the conflict and the neutral Power concerned . . .

### Chapter VI: The Distinctive Emblem

*Article 41*
Under the direction of the competent military authority, the emblem of the red cross on a white ground shall be displayed on the flags, armlets and on all equipment employed in the Medical Service. Nevertheless, in the case of countries which already use as emblem, in place of the red cross, the red crescent or the red lion and sun on a white ground, these emblems are also recognized by the terms of the present Convention.

# 88. UN: Geneva Convention relative to the Treatment of Prisoners of War, 1949

**Commentary**: Article 4A defines prisoners of war as including members of the armed forces of Parties to the conflict (paragraph 1), members of militias or volunteer corps provided certain conditions are met (2), the armed forces of unrecognised governments (3), persons who accompany armed forces 'without actually being members thereof, such as civilian members of military aircraft crews, war correspondents, supply contractors, members of labour units or of services responsible for the welfare of the armed forces, provided that they have received authorization from the armed forces which they accompany, who shall provide them for that purpose with an identity card' (4), the crews of merchant marine vessels and civil aircraft (5) and local inhabitants acting spontaneously (6). Article 4B also identifies the armed forces of occupied countries (paragraph 1) and individuals received by neutral or non-belligerent Powers (2) as entitled to prisoners of war status.

## Chapter II: Quarters, Food and Clothing of Prisoners of War

*ARTICLE 26*

The basic daily food rations shall be sufficient in quantity, quality and variety to keep prisoners of war in good health and to prevent loss of weight or the development of nutritional deficiencies. Account shall also be taken of the habitual diet of the prisoners. The Detaining Power shall supply prisoners of war who work with such additional rations as are necessary for the labour on which they are employed.

*ARTICLE 27*

Clothing, underwear and footwear shall be supplied to prisoners of war in sufficient quantities by the Detaining Power, which shall make allowance for the climate of the region where the prisoners are detained . . . In addition, prisoners of war who work shall receive appropriate clothing, wherever the nature of the work demands.

## Chapter III: Hygiene and Medical Attention

*ARTICLE 30*

Prisoners of war suffering from serious disease, or whose condition necessitates special treatment, a surgical operation or hospital care, must be admitted to any military or civilian medical unit where such treatment can be given, even if their repatriation is contemplated in the near future . . .

## Chapter IV: Medical Personnel and Chaplains Retained to Assist Prisoners of War

*ARTICLE 33*

Members of the medical personnel and chaplains while retained by the Detaining Power with a view to assisting prisoners of war, shall not be considered as prisoners of war. They shall, however, receive as a minimum the benefits and protection of the present Convention, and shall also be granted all facilities necessary to provide for the medical care of, and religious ministration to prisoners of war . . . They shall also benefit by the following facilities in the exercise of their medical or spiritual functions:

(c) Although they shall be subject to the internal discipline of the camp in which they are retained, such personnel may not be compelled to carry out any work other than that concerned with their medical or religious duties.

## Chapter V: Religious, Intellectual and Physical Activities

*ARTICLE 36*

Prisoners of war who are ministers of religion, without having officiated as chaplains to their own forces, shall be at liberty, whatever their denomination, to minister freely to the members of their community . . . They shall not be obliged to do any other work.

### SECTION III: LABOUR OF PRISONERS OF WAR

*ARTICLE 49*

The Detaining Power may utilize the labour of prisoners of war who are physically fit, taking into account their age, sex, rank and physical aptitude, and with a view particularly to maintaining them in a good state of physical and mental health. Non-commissioned officers who are prisoners of war shall only be required to do supervisory work. Those not so required may ask for other suitable work which shall, so far as possible, be found for them. If officers or persons of equivalent status ask for suitable work, it shall be found for them, so far as possible, but they may in no circumstances be compelled to work.

*ARTICLE 50*

Besides work connected with camp administration, installation or maintenance, prisoners of war may be compelled to do only such work as is included in the following classes:

(a) Agriculture;
(b) Industries connected with the production or the extraction of raw materials, and manufacturing industries, with the exception of metallurgical, machinery and chemical industries; public works and building operations which have no military character or purpose;
(c) Transport and handling of stores which are not military in character or purpose;
(d) Commercial business, and arts and crafts;
(e) Domestic service;
(f) Public utility services having no military character or purpose.

Should the above provisions be infringed, prisoners of war shall be allowed to exercise their right of complaint, in conformity with Article 78.

*ARTICLE 51*

Prisoners of war must be granted suitable working conditions, especially as regards accommodation, food, clothing and equipment; such conditions shall not be inferior to those enjoyed by nationals of the Detaining Power employed in similar work; account shall also be taken of climatic conditions. The Detaining Power, in utilizing the labour of prisoners of war, shall ensure that in areas in which prisoners are employed, the national legislation concerning the protection of labour, and, more particularly, the regulations for the safety of workers, are duly applied. Prisoners of war shall receive training and be provided with the means of protection suitable to the work they will have to do and similar to those accorded to the nationals of the Detaining Power. Subject to the provisions of Article 52, prisoners may be submitted to the normal risks run by these civilian workers. Conditions of labour shall in no case be rendered more arduous by disciplinary measures.

*ARTICLE 52*

Unless he be a volunteer, no prisoner of war may be employed on labour which is of an unhealthy or dangerous nature. No prisoner of war shall be assigned to labour which would be looked upon as humiliating for a member of the Detaining Power's own forces . . .

*ARTICLE 53*

The duration of the daily labour of prisoners of war, including the time of the journey to and fro, shall not be excessive, and must in no case exceed that permitted for civilian workers in the district, who are nationals of the Detaining Power and employed on the same work. Prisoners of war must be allowed, in the middle of the day's work, a rest of not less than one hour. This rest will be the same as that to which workers of the Detaining Power are entitled, if the latter is of longer duration. They shall be allowed in addition a rest of twenty-four consecutive hours every week, preferably on Sunday or the day of rest in their country of origin. Furthermore, every prisoner who has worked for one year shall be granted a rest of eight consecutive days, during which his working pay shall be paid him. If methods of labour such as piece-work are employed, the length of the working period shall not be rendered excessive thereby.

*ARTICLE 54*

The working pay due to prisoners of war shall be fixed in accordance with the provisions of Article 62 of the present Convention. Prisoners of war who sustain accidents in connection with work, or who contract a disease in the course, or in consequence of their work, shall receive all the care their condition may require. The Detaining Power shall furthermore deliver to such prisoners of war a medical certificate enabling them to submit their claims to the Power on which they depend, and shall send a duplicate to the Central Prisoners of War Agency provided for in Article 123.

*ARTICLE 55*

The fitness of prisoners of war for work shall be periodically verified by medical examinations at least once a month. The examinations shall have particular regard to the nature of the work which prisoners of war are required to do. If any prisoner of war considers himself incapable of working, he shall be permitted to appear before the medical authorities of his camp. Physicians or surgeons may recommend that the prisoners who are, in their opinion, unfit for work, be exempted therefrom.

*ARTICLE 56*

The organization and administration of labour detachments shall be similar to those of prisoner of war camps. Every labour detachment shall remain under the control of and administratively part of a prisoner of war camp. The military authorities and the commander of the said camp shall be responsible, under the direction of their government, for the observance of the provisions of the present Convention in labour detachments . . .

*ARTICLE 57*

The treatment of prisoners of war who work for private persons, even if the latter are responsible for guarding and protecting them, shall not be inferior to that which is provided for by the present Convention. The Detaining Power, the military authorities and the commander of the camp to which such prisoners belong shall be entirely responsible for the maintenance, care, treatment, and payment of the working pay of such prisoners of war. Such prisoners of war shall have the right to remain in communication with the prisoners' representatives in the camps on which they depend.

SECTION IV: FINANCIAL RESOURCES OF PRISONERS OF WAR

*ARTICLE 60*

The Detaining Power shall grant all prisoners of war a monthly advance of pay, the amount of which shall be fixed by conversion, into the currency of the said power, of the following amounts . . .

*ARTICLE 62*

Prisoners of war shall be paid a fair working rate of pay by the detaining authorities direct. The rate shall be fixed by the said authorities, but shall at no time be less than one-fourth of one Swiss franc for a full working day. The Detaining Power shall inform prisoners of war, as well as the Power on which they depend, through the intermediary of the Protecting Power, of the rate of daily working pay that it has fixed. Working pay shall likewise be paid by the detaining authorities to prisoners of war permanently detailed to duties or to a skilled or semi-skilled occupation in connection with the administration, installation or maintenance of camps, and to the prisoners who are required to carry out spiritual or medical duties on behalf of their comrades. The working pay of the prisoners' representative, of his advisers, if any, and of his assistants, shall be paid out of the fund maintained by canteen profits. The scale of this working pay shall be fixed by the prisoners, representative and approved by the camp commander. If there is no such fund, the detaining authorities shall pay these prisoners a fair working rate of pay.

*ARTICLE 64*

The Detaining Power shall hold an account for each prisoner of war, showing at least the following:

1. The amounts due to the prisoner or received by him as advances of pay, as working pay or derived from any other source . . .

*ARTICLE 68*

Any claim by a prisoner of war for compensation in respect of any injury or other disability arising out of work shall be referred to the Power on which he depends, through the Protecting Power . . .

SECTION VI: RELATIONS BETWEEN PRISONERS OF WAR AND THE AUTHORITIES

*ARTICLE 78*

Prisoners of war shall have the right to make known to the military authorities in whose power they are, their requests regarding the conditions of captivity to which they are subjected. They shall also have the unrestricted right to apply to the representatives of the Protecting Powers either through their prisoners' representative or, if they consider it necessary, direct, in order to draw their attention to any points on which they may have complaints to make regarding their conditions of captivity . . .

*ARTICLE 89*

The disciplinary punishments applicable to prisoners of war are the following:

1. A fine which shall not exceed 50 per cent of the advances of pay and working pay which the prisoner of war would otherwise receive under the provisions of Articles 60 and 62 during a period of not more than thirty days . . .

*Part IV: Termination of Captivity*

*ARTICLE 123*

A Central Prisoners of War Information Agency shall be created in a neutral country . . . The function of the Agency shall be to collect all the information it may obtain through official or private channels respecting prisoners of war, and to transmit it as rapidly as possible to the country of origin of the prisoners of war or to the Power on which they depend . . .

*Part VI: Execution of the Convention*

*ARTICLE 129*

The High Contracting Parties undertake to enact any legislation necessary to provide effective penal sanctions for persons committing, or ordering to be committed, any of the grave breaches of the present Convention defined in the following Article.

*ARTICLE 130*

Grave breaches to which the preceding Article relates shall be those involving any of the following acts, if committed against persons or property protected by the Convention: wilful killing, torture or inhuman treatment, including biological experiments, wilfully causing great suffering or serious injury to body or health, compelling a prisoner of war to serve in the forces of the hostile Power, or wilfully depriving a prisoner of war of the rights of fair and regular trial prescribed in this Convention.

# 89. UN: Geneva Convention relative to the Protection of Civilian Persons in Time of War, 1949

## Part II: General Protection of Populations against Certain Consequences of War

ARTICLE 18

Civilian hospitals organized to give care to the wounded and sick, the infirm and maternity cases, may in no circumstances be the object of attack, but shall at all times be respected and protected by the Parties to the conflict . . . Civilian hospitals shall be marked by means of the emblem provided for in Article 38 of the Geneva Convention for the Amelioration of the Condition of the Wounded and Sick in Armed Forces in the Field of August 12, 1949, but only if so authorized by the State . . .

ARTICLE 20

Persons regularly and solely engaged in the operation and administration of civilian hospitals, including the personnel engaged in the search for, removal and transporting of and caring for wounded and sick civilians, the infirm and maternity cases, shall be respected and protected. In occupied territory and in zones of military operations, the above personnel shall be recognizable by means of an identity card certifying their status, bearing the photograph of the holder and embossed with the stamp of the responsible authority, and also by means of a stamped, water-resistant armlet which they shall wear on the left arm while carrying out their duties . . . Other personnel who are engaged in the operation and administration of civilian hospitals shall be entitled to respect and protection and to wear the armlet, as provided in and under the conditions prescribed in this Article, while they are employed on such duties. The identity card shall state the duties on which they are employed . . .

ARTICLE 22

Aircraft exclusively employed for the removal of wounded and sick civilians, the infirm and maternity cases, or for the transport of medical personnel and equipment, shall not be attacked, but shall be respected while flying at heights, times and on routes specifically agreed upon between all the Parties to the conflict concerned. They may be marked with the distinctive emblem . . . Unless agreed otherwise, flights over enemy or enemy-occupied territory are prohibited. Such aircraft shall obey every summons to land. In the event of a landing thus imposed, the aircraft with its occupants may continue its flight after examination, if any.

## Part III: Status and Treatment of Protected Persons

*Section I: Provisions Common to the Territories of the Parties of the Conflict and to Occupied Territories*

ARTICLE 30

Protected persons shall have every facility for making application to the Protecting Powers, the International Committee of the Red Cross, the National Red Cross (Red Cresent, Red Lion and Sun) Society of the country where they may be, as well as to any organization that might assist them . . .

ARTICLE 32

The High Contracting Parties specifically agree that each of them is prohibited from taking any measure of such a character as to cause the physical suffering or extermination of protected persons in their hands. This prohibition applies not only to murder, torture, corporal punishment, mutilation and medical or scientific experiments not necessitated by the medical treatment of a protected person but also to any other measures of brutality whether applied by civilian or military agents.

*Section II: Aliens in the Territory of a Party to the Conflict*

ARTICLE 39

Protected persons who, as a result of the war, have lost their gainful employment, shall be granted the opportunity to find paid employment. That opportunity shall, subject to security considerations and to the provisions of Article 40, be equal to that enjoyed by the nationals of the Power in whose territory they are. Where a Party to the conflict applies to a protected person methods of control which result in his being unable to support himself, and especially if such a person is prevented for reasons of security from finding paid employment on reasonable conditions, the said Party shall ensure his support and that of his dependents . . .

ARTICLE 40

Protected persons may be compelled to work only to the same extent as nationals of the Party to the conflict in whose territory they are. If protected persons are of enemy nationality, they may only be compelled to do work which is normally necessary to ensure the feeding, sheltering, clothing, transport and health of human beings and which is not directly related to the conduct of military operations. In the cases mentioned in the two preceding paragraphs, protected persons compelled to work shall have the benefit of the same working conditions and of the same safeguards as national workers, in particular as regards wages, hours of labour, clothing and equipment, previous training and compensation for occupational accidents and diseases. If the above provisions are infringed, protected persons shall be allowed to exercise their right of complaint in accordance with Article 30.

*Section III: Occupied Territories*

ARTICLE 51

. . . The Occupying Power may not compel protected persons to work unless they are over eighteen years of age, and then only on work which is necessary either for the needs of the army of occupation, or for the public utility services, or for the feeding, sheltering, clothing, transportation or health of the population of the occupied country. Protected persons may not be compelled to undertake any work which would involve them in the obligation of taking part in military operations. The Occupying Power may not compel protected persons to employ forcible means to ensure the security of the installations where they are performing compulsory labour. The work shall be carried out only in the occupied territory where the persons whose services have been requisitioned are. Every such person shall, so far as possible, be kept in his usual place of employment. Workers shall be paid a fair wage and the work shall be proportionate to their physical and intellectual capacities. The legislation in force in the occupied country concerning working conditions, and safeguards as regards, in particular, such matters as wages, hours of work, equipment, preliminary training and compensation for occupational accidents and diseases, shall be applicable to the protected persons assigned to the work referred to in this Article. In no case shall requisition of labour lead to a mobilization of workers in an organization of a military or semi-military character.

ARTICLE 52

No contract, agreement or regulation shall impair the right of any worker, whether voluntary or not and wherever he may be, to apply to the representatives of the Protecting Power in order to request the said Power's intervention. All measures aiming at creating unemployment or at restricting the opportunities offered to workers in an occupied territory, in order to induce them to work for the Occupying Power, are prohibited.

ARTICLE 53

Any destruction by the Occupying Power of real or personal property belonging individually or collectively to private persons, or to the State, or to other public authorities, or to social or cooperative organizations, is prohibited, except where such destruction is rendered absolutely necessary by military operations.

ARTICLE 56

To the fullest extent of the means available to it, the Occupying Power has the duty of ensuring and maintaining, with the cooperation of national and local authorities, the medical and hospital establishments and services, public health and hygiene in the occupied territory, with particular reference to the adoption and application of the prophylactic and preventive measures necessary to combat the spread of contagious diseases and epidemics. Medical personnel of all categories shall be allowed to carry out their duties . . .

ARTICLE 63

Subject to temporary and exceptional measures imposed for urgent reasons of security by the Occupying Power:

(a) Recognized National Red Cross (Red Crescent, Red Lion and Sun) Societies shall be able to pursue their activities in accordance with Red Cross principles, as defined by the International Red Cross Conferences . . .
(b) The Occupying Power may not require any changes in the personnel or structure of these societies, which would prejudice the aforesaid activities.

The same principles shall apply to the activities and personnel of special organizations of a non-military character, which already exist or which may be established, for the purpose of ensuring the living conditions of the civilian population by the maintenance of the essential public utility services, by the distribution of relief and by the organization of rescues.

*Section IV: Regulations for the Treatment of Internees*

ARTICLE 82

The Detaining Power shall, as far as possible, accommodate the internees according to their nationality, language and customs . . . Throughout the duration of their internment, members of the same family, and in particular parents and children, shall be lodged together in the same place of internment, except when separation of a temporary nature is necessitated for reasons of employment or health or for the purposes of enforcement . . .

ARTICLE 89

Internees who work shall receive additional rations in proportion to the kind of labour which they perform . . .

ARTICLE 90

Workers shall receive suitable working outfits, including protective clothing, whenever the nature of their work so requires . . .

ARTICLE 95

The Detaining Power shall not employ internees as workers, unless they so desire. Employment which, if undertaken under compulsion by a protected person not in internment, would involve a breach of Articles 40 or 51 of the present Convention, and employment on work which is of a degrading or humiliating character are in any case prohibited. After a working period of six weeks, internees shall be free to give up work at any moment, subject to eight days' notice. These provisions constitute no obstacle to the right of the Detaining Power to employ interned doctors, dentists and other medical personnel in their professional capacity on behalf of their fellow internees, or to employ internees for administrative and maintenance work in places of internment and to detail such persons for work in the kitchens or for other domestic tasks, or to require such persons to undertake duties connected with the protection of internees against aerial bombardment or other war risks. No internee may, however, be required to perform tasks for which he is, in the opinion of a medical officer, physically unsuited. The Detaining Power shall take entire responsibility for all working conditions, for medical attention, for the payment of wages, and for ensuring that all employed internees receive compensation for occupational accidents and diseases. The standards prescribed for the said working conditions and for compensation shall be in accordance with the national laws and regulations, and with the existing practice; they shall in no case be inferior to those obtaining for work of the same nature in the same district. Wages for work done shall be determined on an equitable basis by special agreements between the internees, the Detaining Power, and, if the case arises, employers other than the Detaining Power, due regard being paid to the obligation of the Detaining Power to provide for free maintenance of internees and for the medical attention which their state of health may require. Internees permanently detailed for categories of work mentioned in the third paragraph of this Article shall be paid fair wages by the Detaining Power. The working conditions and the scale of compensation for occupational accidents and diseases to internees thus detailed shall not be inferior to those applicable to work of the same nature in the same district.

ARTICLE 96

All labour detachments shall remain part of and dependent upon a place of internment. The competent authorities of the Detaining Power and the commandant of a place of internment shall be responsible for the observance in a labour detachment of the provisions of the present Convention . . .

ARTICLE 135

The Detaining Power shall bear the expense of returning released internees to the places where they were residing when interned, or, if it took them into custody while they were in transit or on the high seas, the cost of completing their journey or of their return to their point of departure.

*Section V: Information Bureaux and Central Agency*

ARTICLE 136

Upon the outbreak of a conflict and in all cases of occupation, each of the Parties to the conflict shall establish an official Information Bureau responsible for receiving and transmitting information in respect of the protected persons who are in its power . . . It shall, furthermore, require its various departments concerned with such matters to provide the aforesaid Bureau promptly with information concerning all changes pertaining to these protected persons, as, for example, transfers, release, repatriations, escapes, admittances to hospitals, births and deaths.

ARTICLE 140

A Central Information Agency for protected persons, in particular for internees, shall be created in a neutral country . . . The function of the Agency shall be to collect all information of the type set forth in Article 136 which it may obtain through official or private channels and to transmit it as rapidly as possible to the countries of origin or of residence of the persons concerned, except in cases where such transmissions might be detrimental to the persons whom the said information concerns, or to their relatives . . .

## Part IV: Execution of the Convention

ARTICLE 144

Any civilian, military, police or other authorities, who in time of war assume responsibilities in respect of protected persons, must possess the text of the Convention and be specially instructed as to its provisions.

ARTICLE 146

The High Contracting Parties undertake to enact any legislation necessary to provide effective penal sanctions for persons committing, or ordering to be committed, any of the grave breaches of the present Convention defined in the following Article.

ARTICLE 147

Grave breaches to which the preceding Article relates shall be those involving any of the following acts, if committed against persons or property protected by the present Convention: wilful killing, torture or inhuman treatment, including biological experiments, wilfully causing great suffering or serious injury to body or health, unlawful deportation or transfer or unlawful confinement of a protected person, compelling a protected person to serve in the forces of a hostile Power, or wilfully depriving a protected person of the rights of fair and regular trial prescribed in the present Convention, taking of hostages and extensive destruction and appropriation of property, not justified by military necessity and carried out unlawfully and wantonly.

# 90. UN: Protocol Additional to the Geneva Conventions of 12 August 1949, and Relating to the Protection of Victims of International Armed Conflicts, 1977

**Commentary**: The First Additional Protocol (1125 *UNTS* 3, entry into force 1978) specifies further provisions applicable to international armed conflicts. Note that for the purposes of Protocol I, 'wounded', 'sick', 'shipwrecked' and 'medical' or 'religious' personnel mean persons 'whether military or civilian' and medical 'units' or 'transports' means establishments or means 'whether military or civilian' (Article 8). Thus the protections applicable to these categories (not reproduced below) also apply to civilian organisations. Annex I, Chapter 6, Article 16 identifies the international special sign for works and installations containing dangerous forces (a group of three bright orange circles of equal size placed on the same axis with the distance between each circle being one radius).

### Part I: General Provisions

*Article 1: General Principles and Scope of Application*

2. In cases not covered by this Protocol or by other international agreements, civilians and combatants remain under the protection and authority of the principles of international law derived from established custom, from the principles of humanity and from the dictates of public conscience.
3. This Protocol, which supplements the Geneva Conventions of 12 August 1949 for the protection of war victims, shall apply in the situations referred to in Article 2 common to those Conventions.

### Part III: Methods and Means of Warfare, Combatant and Prisoner of War Status

*Article 43: Armed Forces*

1. The armed forces of a Party to a conflict consist of all organized armed forces, groups and units which are under a command responsible to that Party for the conduct of its subordinates, even if that Party is represented by a government or an authority not recognized by an adverse Party . . .

*Article 47: Mercenaries*

1. A mercenary shall not have the right to be a combatant or a prisoner of war.
2. A mercenary is any person who:

(a) Is specially recruited locally or abroad in order to fight in an armed conflict;
(b) Does, in fact, take a direct part in the hostilities;
(c) Is motivated to take part in the hostilities essentially by the desire for private gain and, in fact, is promised, by or on behalf of a Party to the conflict, material compensation substantially in excess of that promised or paid to combatants of similar ranks and functions in the armed forces of that Party;
(d) Is neither a national of a Party to the conflict nor a resident of territory controlled by a Party to the conflict;
(e) Is not a member of the armed forces of a Party to the conflict; and
(f) Has not been sent by a State which is not a Party to the conflict on official duty as a member of its armed forces.

## Part IV: Civilian Population

*Article 48: Basic Rule*

In order to ensure respect for and protection of the civilian population and civilian objects, the Parties to the conflict shall at all times distinguish between the civilian population and combatants and between civilian objects and military objectives and accordingly shall direct their operations only against military objectives.

*Article 50: Definition of Civilians and Civilian Population*

1. A civilian is any person who does not belong to one of the categories of persons referred to in Article 4 A (1), (2), (3) and (6) of the Third Convention and in Article 43 of this Protocol. In case of doubt whether a person is a civilian, that person shall be considered to be a civilian . . .

*Article 51: Protection of the Civilian Population*

1. The civilian population and individual civilians shall enjoy general protection against dangers arising from military operations. To give effect to this protection, the following rules, which are additional to other applicable rules of international law, shall be observed in circumstances.
2. The civilian population as such, as well as individual civilians, shall not be the object of attack. Acts or threats of violence the primary purpose of which is to spread terror among the civilian population are prohibited.
3. Civilians shall enjoy the protection afforded by this Section, unless and for such time as they take a direct part in hostilities.
4. Indiscriminate attacks are prohibited. Indiscriminate attacks are:

   (a) Those which are not directed at a specific military objective;
   (b) Those which employ a method or means of combat which cannot be directed at a specific military objective; or
   (c) Those which employ a method or means of combat the effects of which cannot be limited as required by this Protocol;

   and consequently, in each such case, are of a nature to strike military objectives and civilians or civilian objects without distinction . . .

*Article 52: General Protection of Civilian Objects*

1. Civilian objects shall not be the object of attack or of reprisals. Civilian objects are all objects which are not military objectives as defined in paragraph 2.
2. Attacks shall be limited strictly to military objectives. In so far as objects are concerned, military objectives are limited to those objects which by their nature, location, purpose or use make an effective contribution to military action and whose total or partial destruction, capture or neutralization, in the circumstances ruling at the time, offers a definite military of advantage.
3. In case of doubt whether an object which is normally dedicated to civilian purposes, such as a place of worship, a house or other dwelling or a school, is being used to make an effective contribution to military action, it shall be presumed not to be so used.

*Article 54: Protection of Objects Indispensable to the Survival of the Civilian Population*

1. Starvation of civilians as a method of warfare is prohibited.
2. It is prohibited to attack, destroy, remove or render useless objects indispensable to the survival of the civilian population, such as foodstuffs, agricultural areas for the production of foodstuffs, crops, livestock, drinking water installations and supplies and irrigation works, for the specific purpose of denying them for their sustenance value to the civilian population or to the adverse Party, whatever the motive, whether in order to starve out civilians, to cause them to move away, or for any other motive.

*Article 56: Protection of Works and Installations Containing Dangerous Forces*

1. Works or installations containing dangerous forces, namely dams, dykes and nuclear electrical generating stations, shall not be made the object of attack, even where these objects are military objectives, if such attack may cause the release of dangerous forces and consequent severe losses among the civilian population. Other military objectives located at or in the vicinity of these works or installations shall not be made the object of attack if such attack may cause the release of dangerous forces from the works or installations and consequent severe losses among the civilian population.
2. The special protection against attack provided by paragraph 1 shall cease:

   (a) For a dam or a dyke only if it is used for other than its normal function and in regular, significant and direct support of military operations and if such attack is the only feasible way to terminate such support;
   (b) For a nuclear electrical generating station only if it provides electric power in regular, significant and direct support of military operations and if such attack is the only feasible way to terminate such support;
   (c) For other military objectives located at or in the vicinity of these works or installations only if they are used in regular, significant and direct support of military operations and if such attack is the only feasible way to terminate such support.

3. In all cases, the civilian population and individual civilians shall remain entitled to all the protection accorded them by international law, including the protection of the precautionary measures provided for in Article 57. If the protection ceases and any of the works, installations or military objectives mentioned in paragraph 1 is attacked, all practical precautions shall be taken to avoid the release of the dangerous forces.
4. It is prohibited to make any of the works, installations or military objectives mentioned in paragraph 1 the object of reprisals.

5. The Parties to the conflict shall endeavour to avoid locating any military objectives in the vicinity of the works or installations mentioned in paragraph 1. Nevertheless, installations erected for the sole purpose of defending the protected works or installations from attack are permissible and shall not themselves be made the object of attack . . .
7. In order to facilitate the identification of the objects protected by this article, the Parties to the conflict may mark them with a special sign consisting of a group of three bright orange circles placed on the same axis, as specified in Article 16 of Annex I to this Protocol. The absence of such marking in no way relieves any Party to the conflict of its obligations under this Article.

*Article 57: Precautions in Attack*

1. In the conduct of military operations, constant care shall be taken to spare the civilian population, civilians and civilian objects.
2. With respect to attacks, the following precautions shall be taken:

   (a) Those who plan or decide upon an attack shall:

      (i) Do everything feasible to verify that the objectives to be attacked are neither civilians nor civilian objects and are not subject to special protection but are military objectives within the meaning of paragraph 2 of Article 52 and that it is not prohibited by the provisions of this Protocol to attack them;
      (ii) Take all feasible precautions in the choice of means and methods of attack with a view to avoiding, and in any event to minimizing, incidental loss of civilian life, injury to civilians and damage to civilian objects;
      (iii) Refrain from deciding to launch any attack which may be expected to cause incidental loss of civilian life, injury to civilians, damage to civilian objects, or a combination thereof, which would be excessive in relation to the concrete and direct military advantage anticipated;

   (b) An attack shall be cancelled or suspended if it becomes apparent that the objective is not a military one or is subject to special protection or that the attack may be expected to cause incidental loss of civilian life, injury to civilians, damage to civilian objects, or a combination thereof, which would be excessive in relation to the concrete and direct military advantage anticipated . . .

3. When a choice is possible between several military objectives for obtaining a similar military advantage, the objective to be selected shall be that the attack on which may be expected to cause the least danger to civilian lives and to civilian objects.
4. In the conduct of military operations at sea or in the air, each Party to the conflict shall, in conformity with its rights and duties under the rules of international law applicable in armed conflict, take all reasonable precautions to avoid losses of civilian lives and damage to civilian objects.
5. No provision of this Article may be construed as authorizing any attacks against the civilian population, civilians or civilian objects.

*Article 67: Members of the Armed Forces and Military Units*

2. Military personnel serving within civil defence organizations shall, if they fall into the power of an adverse Party, be prisoners of war. In occupied territory they may, but only

in the interest of the civilian population of that territory, be employed on civil defence tasks in so far as the need arises, provided however that, if such work is dangerous, they volunteer for such tasks.

*Article 75: Fundamental Guarantees*

2. The following acts are and shall remain prohibited at any time and in any place whatsoever, whether committed by civilian or by military agents:

   (a) Violence to the life, health, or physical or mental well-being of persons, in particular:

      (i) Murder;
      (ii) Torture of all kinds, whether physical or mental;
      (iii) Corporal punishment; and
      (iv) Mutilation;

   (b) Outrages upon personal dignity, in particular humiliating and degrading treatment, enforced prostitution and any form of indecent assault;
   (c) The taking of hostages;
   (d) Collective punishments; and
   (e) Threats to commit any of the foregoing acts

*Article 79: Measures of Protection for Journalists*

1. Journalists engaged in dangerous professional missions in areas of armed conflict shall be considered as civilians within the meaning of Article 50, paragraph 1.
2. They shall be protected as such under the Conventions and this Protocol, provided that they take no action adversely affecting their status as civilians, and without prejudice to the right of war correspondents accredited to the armed forces to the status provided for in Article 4 A (4) of the Third Convention.
3. They may obtain an identity card similar to the model in Annex II of this Protocol. This card, which shall be issued by the government of the State of which the journalist is a national or in whose territory he resides or in which the news medium employing him is located, shall attest to his status as a journalist.

# 91. UN: Protocol Additional to the Geneva Conventions of 12 August 1949, and Relating to the Protection of Victims of Non-International Armed Conflicts, 1977

**Commentary**: The Second Additional Protocol (1125 *UNTS* 609, entry into force 1978) provides additional protections for non-international armed conflicts. Article 2 thereof provides that the Protocol applies without distinction to all affected persons.

## Part I: Scope of this Protocol

*Article 1: Material Field of Application*

1. This Protocol, which develops and supplements Article 3 common to the Geneva Conventions of 12 August 1949 without modifying its existing conditions of application, shall apply to all armed conflicts which are not covered by Article 1 of the Protocol Additional to the Geneva Conventions of 12 August 1949, and relating to the Protection of Victims of International Armed Conflicts (Protocol I) and which take place in the territory of a High Contracting Party between its armed forces and dissident armed forces or other organized armed groups which, under responsible command, exercise such control over a part of its territory as to enable them to carry out sustained and concerted military operations and to implement this Protocol.
2. This Protocol shall not apply to situations of internal disturbances and tensions, such as riots, isolated and sporadic acts of violence and other acts of a similar nature, as not being armed conflicts.

## Part II: Humane Treatment

*Article 4: Fundamental Guarantees*

1. All persons who do not take a direct part or who have ceased to take part in hostilities, whether or not their liberty has been restricted, are entitled to respect for their person, honour and convictions and religious practices. They shall in all circumstances be treated humanely, without any adverse distinction . . .
2. Without prejudice to the generality of the foregoing, the following acts against the persons referred to in paragraph I are and shall remain prohibited at any time and in any place whatsoever:

   (e) Outrages upon personal dignity, in particular humiliating and degrading treatment, rape, enforced prostitution and any form of indecent assault;

(f) Slavery and the slave trade in all their forms;
(g) Pillage;
(h) Threats to commit any of the foregoing acts.

3. Children shall be provided with the care and aid they require . . .

*Article 5: Persons Whose Liberty Has Been Restricted*

1. In addition to the provisions of Article 4, the following provisions shall be respected as a minimum with regard to persons deprived of their liberty for reasons related to the armed conflict, whether they are interned or detained:

   (e) They shall, if made to work, have the benefit of working conditions and safeguards similar to those enjoyed by the local civilian population.

## Part IV: Civilian Population

*Article 13: Protection of the Civilian Population*

1. The civilian population and individual civilians shall enjoy general protection against the dangers arising from military operations. To give effect to this protection, the following rules shall be observed in all circumstances.
2. The civilian population as such, as well as individual civilians, shall not be the object of attack. Acts or threats of violence the primary purpose of which is to spread terror among the civilian population are prohibited.
3. Civilians shall enjoy the protection afforded by this Part, unless and for such time as they take a direct part in hostilities.

*Article 14: Protection of Objects Indispensable to the Survival of the Civilian Population*

Starvation of civilians as a method of combat is prohibited. It is therefore prohibited to attack, destroy, remove or render useless, for that purpose, objects indispensable to the survival of the civilian population, such as foodstuffs, agricultural areas for the production of foodstuffs, crops, livestock, drinking water installations and supplies and irrigation works.

*Article 15: Protection of Works and Installations Containing Dangerous Forces*

Works or installations containing dangerous forces, namely dams, dykes and nuclear electrical generating stations, shall not be made the object of attack, even where these objects are military objectives, if such attack may cause the release of dangerous forces and consequent severe losses among the civilian population.

# 92. UK/USA: Voluntary Principles on Security and Human Rights, 2000

**Commentary**: The Voluntary Principles were released through the Bureau of Democracy, Human Rights and Labor of the US Department of State: see www.state.gov/www/global/human_rights/001220_fsdrl_principles.html. For academic commentary, see Freeman B., Pica M.B. and Camponovo C.N. (2001), 'A new approach to corporate responsibility: the Voluntary Principles on Security and Human Rights', *Hastings International and Comparative Law Review*, **24** (3), 423–49; Murphy S.D. (2001), 'Voluntary human rights principles for extractive and energy companies', *American Journal of International Law*, **95**, 636–7. See also, 'Defence Industry Initiative on Business Ethics and Conduct' (www.dii.org), established in 1986 by 32 defence contractors who pledged to implement ethical principles acknowledging their federal-procurement-related responsibilities to the US government, general public and each other.

**Preamble**

The Governments of the United States and the United Kingdom, companies in the extractive and energy sectors ('Companies') and NGOs, all with an interest in human rights and corporate social responsibility, have engaged in a dialogue on security and human rights.

The participants recognize the importance of the promotion and protection of human rights throughout the world and the constructive role business and civil society – including NGOs, labour/trade unions, and local communities – can play in advancing these goals. Through this dialogue, the participants have developed the following set of voluntary principles to guide Companies in maintaining the safety and security of their operations within an operating framework that ensures respect for human rights and fundamental freedoms. Mindful of these goals, the participants agree to the importance of continuing this dialogue and keeping under review these principles to ensure their continuing relevance and efficacy.

Acknowledging that security is a fundamental need, shared by individuals, communities, businesses, and governments alike, and acknowledging the difficult security issues faced by Companies operating globally, we recognize that security and respect for human rights can and should be consistent;

Understanding that governments have the primary responsibility to promote and protect human rights and that all parties to a conflict are obliged to observe applicable international humanitarian law, we recognize that we share the common goal of promoting respect for human rights, particularly those set forth in the Universal Declaration of Human Rights, and international humanitarian law;

Emphasizing the importance of safeguarding the integrity of company personnel and property, Companies recognize a commitment to act in a manner consistent with the laws of the countries within which they are present, to be mindful of the highest applicable international standards, and to promote the observance of applicable international law enforcement principles (e.g., the UN Code of Conduct for Law Enforcement Officials and the UN Basic Principles on the Use of Force and Firearms by Law Enforcement Officials), particularly with regard to the use of force;

Taking note of the effect that Companies' activities may have on local communities, we recognize the value of engaging with civil society and host and home governments to contribute to the welfare of the local community while mitigating any potential for conflict where possible;

Understanding that useful, credible information is a vital component of security and human rights, we recognize the importance of sharing and understanding our respective experiences regarding, *inter alia*, best security practices and procedures, country human rights situations, and public and private security, subject to confidentiality constraints;

Acknowledging that home governments and multilateral institutions may, on occasion, assist host governments with security sector reform, developing institutional capacities and strengthening the rule of law, we recognize the important role Companies and civil society can play in supporting these efforts;

We hereby express our support for the following voluntary principles regarding security and human rights in the extractive sector, which fall into three categories, risk assessment, relations with public security, and relations with private security:

**Risk Assessment**

The ability to assess accurately risks present in a Company's operating environment is critical to the security of personnel, local communities and assets; the success of the Company's short and long-term operations; and to the promotion and protection of human rights. In some circumstances, this is relatively simple; in others, it is important to obtain extensive background information from different sources; monitoring and adapting to changing, complex political, economic, law enforcement, military and social situations; and maintaining productive relations with local communities and government officials.

The quality of complicated risk assessments is largely dependent on the assembling of regularly updated, credible information from a broad range of perspectives – local and national governments, security firms, other companies, home governments, multilateral institutions, and civil society knowledgeable about local conditions. This information may be most effective when shared to the fullest extent possible (bearing in mind confidentiality considerations) between Companies, concerned civil society, and governments.

Bearing in mind these general principles, we recognize that accurate, effective risk assessments should consider the following factors:

(i) identification of security risks. Security risks can result from political, economic, civil or social factors. Moreover, certain personnel and assets may be at greater risk than others. Identification of security risks allows a Company to take measures to minimize risk and to assess whether Company actions may heighten risk.

(ii) potential for violence. Depending on the environment, violence can be widespread or limited to particular regions, and it can develop with little or no warning. Civil society, home and host government representatives, and other sources should be consulted to identify risks presented by the potential for violence. Risk assessments should examine patterns of violence in areas of Company operations for educational, predictive, and preventative purposes.

(iii) human rights records. Risk assessments should consider the available human rights records of public security forces, paramilitaries, local and national law enforcement, as well as the reputation of private security. Awareness of past abuses and allegations can help Companies to avoid recurrences as well as to promote accountability. Also, identification of the capability of the above entities to respond to situations of violence in a lawful manner (i.e., consistent with applicable international standards) allows Companies to develop appropriate measures in operating environments.

(iv) rule of law. Risk assessments should consider the local prosecuting authority and judiciary's capacity to hold accountable those responsible for human rights abuses and for those responsible for violations of international humanitarian law in a manner that respects the rights of the accused.

(v) conflict analysis. Identification of and understanding the root causes and nature of local conflicts, as well as the level of adherence to human rights and international humanitarian law standards by key actors, can be instructive for the development of strategies for managing relations between the Company, local communities, Company employees and their unions, and host governments. Risk assessments should also consider the potential for future conflicts.

(vi) equipment transfers. Where Companies provide equipment (including lethal and non-lethal equipment) to public or private security, they should consider the risk of such transfers, any relevant export licensing requirements, and the feasibility of measures to mitigate foreseeable negative consequences, including adequate controls to prevent misappropriation or diversion of equipment which may lead to human rights abuses. In making risk assessments, companies should consider any relevant past incidents involving previous equipment transfers.

**Interactions between Companies and Public security**

Although governments have the primary role of maintaining law and order, security and respect for human rights, Companies have an interest in ensuring that actions taken by governments, particularly the actions of public security providers, are consistent with the protection and promotion of human rights. In cases where there is a need to supplement security provided by host governments, Companies may be required or expected to contribute to, or otherwise reimburse, the costs of protecting Company facilities and personnel borne by public security. While public security is expected to act in a manner consistent with local and national laws as well as with human rights standards and international humanitarian law, within this context abuses may nevertheless occur.

In an effort to reduce the risk of such abuses and to promote respect for human rights generally, we have identified the following voluntary principles to guide relationships between Companies and public security regarding security provided to Companies:

*1. Security Arrangements*

(i) Companies should consult regularly with host governments and local communities about the impact of their security arrangements on those communities.

(ii) Companies should communicate their policies regarding ethical conduct and human rights to public security providers, and express their desire that security be provided in a manner consistent with those policies by personnel with adequate and effective training.

(iii) Companies should encourage host governments to permit making security arrangements transparent and accessible to the public, subject to any overriding safety and security concerns.

*2. Deployment and Conduct*

(i) The primary role of public security should be to maintain the rule of law, including safeguarding human rights and deterring acts that threaten Company personnel and facilities. The type and number of public security forces deployed should be competent, appropriate and proportional to the threat.

(ii) Equipment imports and exports should comply with all applicable law and regulations. Companies that provide equipment to public security should take all appropriate and lawful measures to mitigate any foreseeable negative consequences, including human rights abuses and violations of international humanitarian law.

(iii) Companies should use their influence to promote the following principles with public security:

(a) individuals credibly implicated in human rights abuses should not provide security services for Companies;

(b) force should be used only when strictly necessary and to an extent proportional to the threat; and

(c) the rights of individuals should not be violated while exercising the right to exercise freedom of association and peaceful assembly, the right to engage in collective bargaining, or other related rights of Company employees as recognized by the Universal Declaration of Human Rights and the ILO Declaration on Fundamental Principles and Rights at Work.

(iv) In cases where physical force is used by public security, such incidents should be reported to the appropriate authorities and to the Company. Where force is used, medical aid should be provided to injured persons, including to offenders.

*3. Consultation and Advice*

(i) Companies should hold structured meetings with public security on a regular basis to discuss security, human rights and related work-place safety issues. Companies should also consult regularly with other Companies, host and home governments, and civil society to discuss security and human rights. Where Companies operating in the same region have common concerns, they should consider collectively raising those concerns with the host and home governments.

(ii) In their consultations with host governments, Companies should take all appropriate measures to promote observance of applicable international law enforcement principles, particularly those reflected in the UN Code of Conduct for Law Enforcement Officials and the UN Basic Principles on the Use of Force and Firearms.

(iii) Companies should support efforts by governments, civil society and multilateral institutions to provide human rights training and education for public security as well as their efforts to strengthen state institutions to ensure accountability and respect for human rights.

4. *Responses to Human Rights Abuses*

(i) Companies should record and report any credible allegations of human rights abuses by public security in their areas of operation to appropriate host government authorities. Where appropriate, Companies should urge investigation and that action be taken to prevent any recurrence.

(ii) Companies should actively monitor the status of investigations and press for their proper resolution.

(iii) Companies should, to the extent reasonable, monitor the use of equipment provided by the Company and to investigate properly situations in which such equipment is used in an inappropriate manner.

(iv) Every effort should be made to ensure that information used as the basis for allegations of human rights abuses is credible and based on reliable evidence. The security and safety of sources should be protected. Additional or more accurate information that may alter previous allegations should be made available as appropriate to concerned parties.

**Interactions between Companies and Private Security**

Where host governments are unable or unwilling to provide adequate security to protect a Company's personnel or assets, it may be necessary to engage private security providers as a complement to public security. In this context, private security may have to coordinate with state forces, (law enforcement, in particular) to carry weapons and to consider the defensive local use of force. Given the risks associated with such activities, we recognize the following voluntary principles to guide private security conduct:

Private security should observe the policies of the contracting Company regarding ethical conduct and human rights; the law and professional standards of the country in which they operate; emerging best practices developed by industry, civil society, and governments; and promote the observance of international humanitarian law.

Private security should maintain high levels of technical and professional proficiency, particularly with regard to the local use of force and firearms.

Private security should act in a lawful manner. They should exercise restraint and caution in a manner consistent with applicable international guidelines regarding the local use of force, including the UN Principles on the Use of Force and Firearms by Law Enforcement Officials and the UN Code of Conduct for Law Enforcement Officials, as well as with emerging best practices developed by Companies, civil society, and governments.

Private security should have policies regarding appropriate conduct and the local use of force (e.g., rules of engagement). Practice under these policies should be capable of being monitored by Companies or, where appropriate, by independent third parties. Such monitoring should encompass detailed investigations into allegations of abusive or unlawful acts; the availability of disciplinary measures sufficient to prevent and deter; and procedures for reporting allegations to relevant local law enforcement authorities when appropriate.

All allegations of human rights abuses by private security should be recorded. Credible allegations should be properly investigated. In those cases where allegations against private security providers are forwarded to the relevant law enforcement authorities, Companies should actively monitor the status of investigations and press for their proper resolution.

Consistent with their function, private security should provide only preventative and defensive services and should not engage in activities exclusively the responsibility of state military or law enforcement authorities. Companies should designate services, technology and equipment capable of offensive and defensive purposes as being for defensive use only.

Private security should (a) not employ individuals credibly implicated in human rights abuses to provide security services; (b) use force only when strictly necessary and to an extent proportional to the threat; and (c) not violate the rights of individuals while exercising the right to exercise freedom of association and peaceful assembly, to engage in collective bargaining, or other related rights of Company employees as recognized by the Universal Declaration of Human Rights and the ILO Declaration on Fundamental Principles and Rights at Work.

In cases where physical force is used, private security should properly investigate and report the incident to the Company. Private security should refer the matter to local authorities and/or take disciplinary action where appropriate. Where force is used, medical aid should be provided to injured persons, including to offenders.

Private security should maintain the confidentiality of information obtained as a result of its position as security provider, except where to do so would jeopardize the principles contained herein.

To minimize the risk that private security exceed their authority as providers of security, and to promote respect for human rights generally, we have developed the following additional voluntary principles and guidelines:

Where appropriate, Companies should include the principles outlined above as contractual provisions in agreements with private security providers and ensure that private security personnel are adequately trained to respect the rights of employees and the local community. To the extent practicable, agreements between Companies and private security should require investigation of unlawful or abusive behaviour and appropriate disciplinary action. Agreements should also permit termination of the relationship by Companies where there is credible evidence of unlawful or abusive behaviour by private security personnel.

Companies should consult and monitor private security providers to ensure they fulfil their obligation to provide security in a manner consistent with the principles outlined above. Where appropriate, Companies should seek to employ private security providers that are representative of the local population.

Companies should review the background of private security they intend to employ, particularly with regard to the use of excessive force. Such reviews should include an assessment of previous services provided to the host government and whether these services raise concern about the private security firm's dual role as a private security provider and government contractor.

Companies should consult with other Companies, home country officials, host country officials, and civil society regarding experiences with private security. Where appropriate and lawful, Companies should facilitate the exchange of information about unlawful activity and abuses committed by private security providers.

# 93. UN: Protocol against the Illicit Manufacturing of and Trafficking in Firearms, Their Parts and Components and Ammunition, supplementing the UN Convention against Transnational Organized Crime, 2001

**Commentary**: In 2001 the UN held a conference on the illicit trade in small arms and light weapons in all its aspects and formulated an action programme: see Conference Report, UN Doc A/CONF.192/15. See further, UN (2001), 'Report of the Ad Hoc Committee on the Elaboration of a Convention against Transnational Organized Crime on the work of its twelfth session', UN Doc A/55/383/Add.2 and the interpretative notes for the official records (*travaux préparatoires*) for the Protocol's negotiation in UN Doc A/55/383/Add.3 (2001). See also, UN (1999), 'Report on the feasibility of restricting the manufacture and trade of small arms to manufacturers and dealers authorized by States', UN Doc A/54/160; UN Secretary-General (2000), 'Report on the Illicit Traffic in Small Arms', UN Doc A/55/323.

Negotiators considered existing initiatives, including the '1991 Guidelines for International Arms Transfers: UN Disarmament Commission' (1991), UN Doc A/51/42, Annex to Report. See further, UN Secretary-General (1991), A compilation of all texts of principles, guidelines or recommendations on subject items adopted unanimously by the Disarmament Commission, UN Doc A/51/182; UN Secretary-General (1991), 'Ways and means of promoting transparency in international transfer of conventional arms', UN Doc A/46/301. The Protocol extracted below was adopted by UNGA Resolution 55/255 (2001) and is not yet in force. Article 6 contemplates confiscation, seizure and disposal, Article 7 provides for record-keeping and Article 9 envisages deactivating firearms. The first biennial meeting to consider implementing the programme of action was conducted during 2003: see UN Doc A/CONF.192/BMS/2003/1. The Conventional Arms Branch of the UN Department for Disarmament Affairs (http://disarmament2.un.org/cab) supervises two transparency measures: the UN Register of Conventional Arms and the Standardized Instrument for Reporting Military Expenditures.

Additional international instruments include the 1980 Convention on Prohibitions or Restrictions on the Use of Certain Conventional Weapons Which May Be Deemed to Be Excessively Injurious or to Have Indiscriminate Effects (the Convention on Certain Conventional Weapons (CCW) or Inhumane Weapons Convention) 1342 *UNTS* 137 (entry into force 1983, reviewed 1996 and 2001) together with its four Protocols; the 1997 Convention on the Prohibition of the Use, Stockpiling, Production and Transfer of Anti-Personnel Mines and on Their

Destruction (the Mine-Ban Convention) 1999 *ATS* No 3 (entry into force 1999). For regional initiatives, see the EU Programme for Preventing and Combating Illicit Trafficking in Conventional Arms; OAS (1998), Inter-American Convention against the illicit manufacturing of and trafficking in firearms, ammunition, explosives and other related materials 37 *ILM* 143. On the chemical industry and chemical weapons, see CEFIC/CMA (1991), 'Position on Chemical Weapons Issues Affecting the Chemical Industry', Brussels.

**Article 2: Statement of Purpose**

The purpose of this Protocol is to promote, facilitate and strengthen cooperation among States Parties in order to prevent, combat and eradicate the illicit manufacturing of and trafficking in firearms, their parts and components and ammunition.

**Article 3: Use of Terms**

For the purposes of this Protocol:

(a) 'Firearm' shall mean any portable barrelled weapon that expels, is designed to expel or may be readily converted to expel a shot, bullet or projectile by the action of an explosive, excluding antique firearms or their replicas. Antique firearms and their replicas shall be defined in accordance with domestic law. In no case, however, shall antique firearms include firearms manufactured after 1899;

(b) 'Parts and components' shall mean any element or replacement element specifically designed for a firearm and essential to its operation, including a barrel, frame or receiver, slide or cylinder, bolt or breech block, and any device designed or adapted to diminish the sound caused by firing a firearm;

(c) 'Ammunition' shall mean the complete round or its components, including cartridge cases, primers, propellant powder, bullets or projectiles, that are used in a firearm, provided that those components are themselves subject to authorization in the respective State Party;

(d) 'Illicit manufacturing' shall mean the manufacturing or assembly of firearms, their parts and components or ammunition:

  (i) From parts and components illicitly trafficked;
  (ii) Without a licence or authorization from a competent authority of the State Party where the manufacture or assembly takes place; or
  (iii) Without marking the firearms at the time of manufacture, in accordance with article 8 of this Protocol;

  Licensing or authorization of the manufacture of parts and components shall be in accordance with domestic law;

(e) 'Illicit trafficking': the import, export, acquisition, sale, delivery, movement or transfer of firearms, their parts and components and ammunition from or across the territory of one State Party to that of another State Party if any one of the States Parties concerned does not authorize it in accordance with the terms of this Protocol or if the firearms are not marked in accordance with article 8 of this Protocol;

(f) 'Tracing' shall mean the systematic tracking of firearms and, where possible, their parts and components and ammunition from manufacturer to purchaser for the purpose of assisting the competent authorities of States Parties in detecting, investigating and analysing illicit manufacturing and illicit trafficking.

**Article 4: Scope of Application**

1. This Protocol shall apply, except as otherwise stated herein, to the prevention of illicit manufacturing of and trafficking in firearms, their parts and components and ammunition and to the investigation and prosecution of offences established in accordance with article 5 of this Protocol where those offences are transnational in nature and involve an organized criminal group . . .

**Article 5: Criminalization**

1. Each State Party shall adopt such legislative and other measures as may be necessary to establish as criminal offences the following conduct, when committed intentionally:

   (a) Illicit manufacturing of firearms, their parts and components and ammunition;
   (b) Illicit trafficking in firearms, their parts and components and ammunition;
   (c) Falsifying or illicitly obliterating, removing or altering the marking(s) on firearms required by article 8 of this Protocol.

2. Each State Party shall also adopt such legislative and other measures as may be necessary to establish as criminal offences the following conduct:

   (a) Subject to the basic concepts of its legal system, attempting to commit or participating as an accomplice in an offence established in accordance with paragraph 1 of this article; and
   (b) Organizing, directing, aiding, abetting, facilitating or counselling the commission of an offence established in accordance with paragraph 1 of this article.

**Article 8: Marking of Firearms**

1. For the purpose of identifying and tracing firearms, States Parties shall:

   (a) At the time of manufacture of each firearm, either require unique marking providing the name of the manufacturer, the country or place of manufacture and the serial number, or maintain any alternative unique user-friendly marking with simple geometric symbols in combination with a numeric and/or alphanumeric code, permitting ready identification by all States of the country of manufacture;
   (b) Require appropriate simple marking on each imported firearm, permitting identification of the country of import and, where possible, the year of import and enabling the competent authorities of that country to trace the firearm, and a unique marking, if the firearm does not bear such a marking. The requirements of this subparagraph need not be applied to temporary imports of firearms for verifiable lawful purposes; . . .

2. States Parties shall encourage the firearms manufacturing industry to develop measures against the removal or alteration of markings.

**Article 10: General Requirements for Export, Import and Transit Licensing or Authorization Systems**

1. Each State Party shall establish or maintain an effective system of export and import licensing or authorization, as well as of measures on international transit, for the transfer of firearms, their parts and components and ammunition.
2. Before issuing export licences or authorizations for shipments of firearms, their parts and components and ammunition, each State Party shall verify:

   (a) That the importing States have issued import licences or authorizations; and
   (b) That, without prejudice to bilateral or multilateral agreements or arrangements favouring landlocked States, the transit States have, at a minimum, given notice in writing, prior to shipment, that they have no objection to the transit.

3. The export and import licence or authorization and accompanying documentation together shall contain information that, at a minimum, shall include the place and the date of issuance, the date of expiration, the country of export, the country of import, the final recipient, a description and the quantity of the firearms, their parts and components and ammunition and, whenever there is transit, the countries of transit. The information contained in the import licence must be provided in advance to the transit States.
6. States Parties may adopt simplified procedures for the temporary import and export and the transit of firearms, their parts and components and ammunition for verifiable lawful purposes such as hunting, sport shooting, evaluation, exhibitions or repairs.

**Article 11: Security and Preventive Measures**

In an effort to detect, prevent and eliminate the theft, loss or diversion of, as well as the illicit manufacturing of and trafficking in, firearms, their parts and components and ammunition, each State Party shall take appropriate measures:

(a) To require the security of firearms, their parts and components and ammunition at the time of manufacture, import, export and transit through its territory . . .

**Article 12: Information**

1. Without prejudice to articles 27 and 28 of the Convention, States Parties shall exchange among themselves, consistent with their respective domestic legal and administrative systems, relevant case-specific information on matters such as authorized producers, dealers, importers, exporters and, whenever possible, carriers of firearms, their parts and components and ammunition.
2. Without prejudice to articles 27 and 28 of the Convention, States Parties shall exchange among themselves, consistent with their respective domestic legal and administrative systems, relevant information on matters such as:

(a) Organized criminal groups known to take part or suspected of taking part in the illicit manufacturing of or trafficking in firearms, their parts and components and ammunition . . .

5. Subject to the basic concepts of its legal system or any international agreements, each State Party shall guarantee the confidentiality of and comply with any restrictions on the use of information that it receives from another State Party pursuant to this article, including proprietary information pertaining to commercial transactions, if requested to do so by the State Party providing the information. If such confidentiality cannot be maintained, the State Party that provided the information shall be notified prior to its disclosure.

**Article 13: Cooperation**

1. States Parties shall cooperate at the bilateral, regional and international levels to prevent, combat and eradicate the illicit manufacturing of and trafficking in firearms, their parts and components and ammunition.
3. States Parties shall seek the support and cooperation of manufacturers, dealers, importers, exporters, brokers and commercial carriers of firearms, their parts and components and ammunition to prevent and detect the illicit activities referred to in paragraph 1 of this article.

**Article 15: Brokers and Brokering**

1. With a view to preventing and combating illicit manufacturing of and trafficking in firearms, their parts and components and ammunition, States Parties that have not yet done so shall consider establishing a system for regulating the activities of those who engage in brokering. Such a system could include one or more measures such as:

(a) Requiring registration of brokers operating within their territory;
(b) Requiring licensing or authorization of brokering; or
(c) Requiring disclosure on import and export licences or authorizations, or accompanying documents, of the names and locations of brokers involved in the transaction . . .

# 94. UN: International Convention against the Recruitment, Use, Financing and Training of Mercenaries, 1989

**Commentary**: The legal concepts of 'armed attack' and 'self-defence' apply to non-State actors: ICJ, Case concerning Military Activities in and Against Nicaragua (1986) *ICJ Rep* 14: paragraph 195; Legal Consequences of the Construction of a Wall in the Occupied Palestinian Territory (2004): paragraph 139 & Declaration of Judge Buergenthal, paragraph 6; Security Council Resolution 1368 (2001). In particular, mercenaries threaten the political independence and territorial integrity of States. Their military efficiency may derive from failure to observe the laws and customs of warfare and human rights obligations such as the right of self-determination: UNHRC (1999), 'Report made pursuant to Commission Resolution 1998/6', UN Doc E/CN.4/1999/11: paragraph 75. The Convention extracted below (29 *ILM* 91, not yet in force) prohibits resort to their use. See further, Organisation of African Unity (OAU) (1972), Convention for the Elimination of Mercenarism in Africa, OAU Doc CM/433/RevL Annex I (entry into force 1985). However, neither international law nor public policy precludes contractual enforcement simply by virtue of the subject matter: *In the Matter of an International Arbitration under the UNCITRAL Rules between Sandline International Inc and the Independent State of Papua New Guinea* (2000) 117 *ILR* 551: para 11.1.

The nature of mercenary activity has also evolved: see Zarate J.C. (1998), 'The emergence of a new dog of war: private international security companies, international law and the new world disorder', *Stanford Journal of International Law*, **34**, 75–162. Private military companies (PMCs) have governments, international organisations and corporations as clients: UNHRC (1998), 'Report on the question of the use of mercenaries as a means of violating human rights and impeding the exercise of the right of peoples to self-determination', UN Doc E/CN.4/1998/31. On prospective corporate liability for hiring mercenaries, see Forcese C. (2000), 'Deterring "militarized commerce": the prospect of liability for "privatized" human rights abuses', *Ottawa Law Review*, **31** (2), 171–211. PMCs could also be deployed for UN peace enforcement operations: UN (1998), 'Secretary-General Reflects on "Intervention"', Press Release SG/SM/6613. PMCs are entitled to diplomatic protection and it is not improper for governments to exchange strategic information or engage in informal technical cooperation: Legg T. and Ibbs R. (1998), *Report of the Sierra Leone Arms Investigation*, London: HMSO: paragraph 11.9. On national legislative measures including licensing, see Regulation of Foreign Military Assistance Act, 15 of 1998 (South Africa); UK House of Commons (2002), *PMCs: Options for Regulation*, HC 577, London: HMSO. The Human Rights Committee has also recommended greater regulation: UNHRC (2000), 'Report pursuant to Commission Resolution 1999/3', UN Doc E/CN.4/2000/14: paras 71–2. For NGO perspectives, see International Alert (2001), *The Privatisation of Security: Framing a Conflict Prevention and Peacebuilding Policy Agenda*, London.

**Article 1**
For the purposes of the present Convention,

1. A mercenary is any person who:

   (a) Is specially recruited locally or abroad in order to fight in an armed conflict;
   (b) Is motivated to take part in the hostilities essentially by the desire for private gain and, in fact, is promised, by or on behalf of a party to the conflict, material compensation substantially in excess of that promised or paid to combatants of similar rank and functions in the armed forces of that party;
   (c) Is neither a national of a party to the conflict nor a resident of territory controlled by a party to the conflict;
   (d) Is not a member of the armed forces of a party to the conflict; and
   (e) Has not been sent by a State which is not a party to the conflict on official duty as a member of its armed forces.

2. A mercenary is also any person who, in any other situation:

   (a) Is specially recruited locally or abroad for the purpose of participating in a concerted act of violence aimed at :

      (i) Overthrowing a Government or otherwise undermining the constitutional order of a State; or
      (ii) Undermining the territorial integrity of a State;

   (b) Is motivated to take part therein essentially by the desire for significant private gain and is prompted by the promise or payment of material compensation;
   (c) Is neither a national nor a resident of the State against which such an act is directed;
   (d) Has not been sent by a State on official duty; and
   (e) Is not a member of the armed forces of the State on whose territory the act is undertaken.

**Article 2**
Any person who recruits, uses, finances or trains mercenaries, as defined in article 1 of the present Convention, commits an offence for the purposes of the Convention.

**Article 3**
1. A mercenary, as defined in article 1 of the present Convention, who participates directly in hostilities or in a concerted act of violence, as the case may be, commits an offence for the purposes of the Convention . . .

**Article 4**
An offence is committed by any person who:

(a) Attempts to commit one of the offences set forth in the present Convention;
(b) Is the accomplice of a person who commits or attempts to commit any of the offences set forth in the present Convention.

**Article 5**

1. States Parties shall not recruit, use, finance or train mercenaries and shall prohibit such activities in accordance with the provisions of the present Convention.
2. States Parties shall not recruit, use, finance or train mercenaries for the purpose of opposing the legitimate exercise of the inalienable right of peoples to self-determination, as recognized by international law, and shall take, in conformity with international law, the appropriate measures to prevent the recruitment, use, financing or training of mercenaries for that purpose.
3. They shall make the offences set forth in the present Convention punishable by appropriate penalties which take into account the grave nature of those offences.

**Article 6**

States Parties shall co-operate in the prevention of the offences set forth in the present Convention, particularly by:

(a) Taking all practicable measures to prevent preparations in their respective territories for the commission of those offences within or outside their territories, including the prohibition of illegal activities of persons, groups and organizations that encourage, instigate, organize or engage in the perpetration of such offences . . .

# 95. UN: Code of Conduct for Law Enforcement Officials, 1979

**Commentary**: The Code of Conduct (extracted below) was approved through UNGA Resolution 34/169 (1979). The commentary to Article 1 defines 'law enforcement official' as including all officers of the law, whether appointed or elected, who exercise police powers, especially powers of arrest or detention. It also includes military officers, whether uniformed or not, where police powers are ordinarily exercised by military authorities. The commentary to Article 3 notes that the use of force should be exceptional, only as is reasonably necessary for preventing crime or effecting arrest and proportionate to the objective to be achieved. Although the commentary to Article 5 refers to UNGA Resolution 3452 (1975) on the Declaration against Torture, reference should also be made to the relevant Convention (see below) and jurisprudence arising thereunder. The commentary to Article 6 defines 'medical attention' as referring to services rendered by any medical personnel, including certified medical practitioners and paramedics. Although the definition of corruption is subject to national law, the commentary to Article 7 notes that it 'should be understood to encompass the commission or omission of an act in the performance of or in connection with one's duties, in response to gifts, promises or incentives demanded or accepted, or the wrongful receipt of these once the act has been committed or omitted'. An 'act of corruption' encompasses attempted corruption. The commentary to Article 8 contemplates law enforcement officials bringing violations to public attention through the mass media where justified as a last resort and consistent with national law. See also, UN Standard Minimum Rules for the Treatment of Prisoners, ECOSOC Resolutions 663 (1957) and 2076 (1977). Providing support and direction to police activities may be sufficient to establish joint action in a common mission such that corporations become liable for violating particular rights: *United Steelworkers of America v Phelps Dodge Corporation* 865 *F.2d* 1539 (9th Cir 1989).

**Article 1**
Law enforcement officials shall at all times fulfil the duty imposed upon them by law, by serving the community and by protecting all persons against illegal acts, consistent with the high degree of responsibility required by their profession.

**Article 2**
In the performance of their duty, law enforcement officials shall respect and protect human dignity and maintain and uphold the human rights of all persons.

**Article 3**
Law enforcement officials may use force only when strictly necessary and to the extent required for the performance of their duty.

**Article 4**
Matters of a confidential nature in the possession of law enforcement officials shall be kept confidential, unless the performance of duty or the needs of justice strictly require otherwise.

**Article 5**
No law enforcement official may inflict, instigate or tolerate any act of torture or other cruel, inhuman or degrading treatment or punishment, nor may any law enforcement official invoke superior orders or exceptional circumstances such as a state of war or a threat of war, a threat to national security, internal political instability or any other public emergency as a justification of torture or other cruel, inhuman or degrading treatment or punishment.

**Article 6**
Law enforcement officials shall ensure the full protection of the health of persons in their custody and, in particular, shall take immediate action to secure medical attention whenever required.

**Article 7**
Law enforcement officials shall not commit any act of corruption. They shall also rigorously oppose and combat all such acts.

**Article 8**
Law enforcement officials shall respect the law and the present Code. They shall also, to the best of their capability, prevent and rigorously oppose any violations of them.
Law enforcement officials who have reason to believe that a violation of the present Code has occurred or is about to occur shall report the matter to their superior authorities and, where necessary, to other appropriate authorities or organs vested with reviewing or remedial power.

# 96. UN: Basic Principles on the Use of Force and Firearms by Law Enforcement Officials, 1990

**Commentary**: Corporations have been called upon to have regard to these Basic Principles on the Use of Force emanating from the Eighth UN Congress on the Prevention of Crime and the Treatment of Offenders in Havana. The term 'law enforcement officials' is construed consistently with the commentary to Article 1 of the Code of Conduct for Law Enforcement Officials (above). Resolution 14 of the Seventh UN Congress held at Varenna, Italy emphasised that the use of force should be commensurate with due respect for human rights: see further, ECOSOC Resolution 1986/10 (1986) and UNGA Resolution 41/149 (1986).

**General Provisions**

1. Governments and law enforcement agencies shall adopt and implement rules and regulations on the use of force and firearms against persons by law enforcement officials . . .
2. Governments and law enforcement agencies should develop a range of means as broad as possible and equip law enforcement officials with various types of weapons and ammunition that would allow for a differentiated use of force and firearms. These should include the development of non-lethal incapacitating weapons for use in appropriate situations, with a view to increasingly restraining the application of means capable of causing death or injury to persons. For the same purpose, it should also be possible for law enforcement officials to be equipped with self-defensive equipment such as shields, helmets, bullet-proof vests and bullet-proof means of transportation, in order to decrease the need to use weapons of any kind.
3. The development and deployment of non-lethal incapacitating weapons should be carefully evaluated in order to minimize the risk of endangering uninvolved persons, and the use of such weapons should be carefully controlled.
4. Law enforcement officials, in carrying out their duty, shall, as far as possible, apply non-violent means before resorting to the use of force and firearms. They may use force and firearms only if other means remain ineffective or without any promise of achieving the intended result.
5. Whenever the lawful use of force and firearms is unavoidable, law enforcement officials shall:

    (a) Exercise restraint in such use and act in proportion to the seriousness of the offence and the legitimate objective to be achieved;
    (b) Minimize damage and injury, and respect and preserve human life;

(c) Ensure that assistance and medical aid are rendered to any injured or affected persons at the earliest possible moment;
(d) Ensure that relatives or close friends of the injured or affected person are notified at the earliest possible moment.

6. Where injury or death is caused by the use of force and firearms by law enforcement officials, they shall report the incident promptly to their superiors, in accordance with principle 22.
7. Governments shall ensure that arbitrary or abusive use of force and firearms by law enforcement officials is punished as a criminal offence under their law.
8. Exceptional circumstances such as internal political instability or any other public emergency may not be invoked to justify any departure from these basic principles.

**Special Provisions**

9. Law enforcement officials shall not use firearms against persons except in self defence or defence of others against the imminent threat of death or serious injury, to prevent the perpetration of a particularly serious crime involving grave threat to life, to arrest a person presenting such a danger and resisting their authority, or to prevent his or her escape, and only when less extreme means are insufficient to achieve these objectives. In any event, intentional lethal use of firearms may only be made when strictly unavoidable in order to protect life.
10. In the circumstances provided for under principle 9, law enforcement officials shall identify themselves as such and give a clear warning of their intent to use firearms, with sufficient time for the warning to be observed, unless to do so would unduly place the law enforcement officials at risk or would create a risk of death or serious harm to other persons, or would be clearly inappropriate or pointless in the circumstances of the incident.
11. Rules and regulations on the use of firearms by law enforcement officials should include guidelines that:

(a) Specify the circumstances under which law enforcement officials are authorized to carry firearms and prescribe the types of firearms and ammunition permitted;
(b) Ensure that firearms are used only in appropriate circumstances and in a manner likely to decrease the risk of unnecessary harm;
(c) Prohibit the use of those firearms and ammunition that cause unwarranted injury or present an unwarranted risk;
(d) Regulate the control, storage and issuing of firearms, including procedures for ensuring that law enforcement officials are accountable for the firearms and ammunition issued to them;
(e) Provide for warnings to be given, if appropriate, when firearms are to be discharged;
(f) Provide for a system of reporting whenever law enforcement officials use firearms in the performance of their duty.

**Policing Unlawful Assemblies**

12. As everyone is allowed to participate in lawful and peaceful assemblies, in accordance with the principles embodied in the Universal Declaration of Human Rights and the

International Covenant on Civil and Political Rights, Governments and law enforcement agencies and officials shall recognize that force and firearms may be used only in accordance with principles 13 and 14.

13. In the dispersal of assemblies that are unlawful but non-violent, law enforcement officials shall avoid the use of force or, where that is not practicable, shall restrict such force to the minimum extent necessary.
14. In the dispersal of violent assemblies, law enforcement officials may use firearms only when less dangerous means are not practicable and only to the minimum extent necessary. Law enforcement officials shall not use firearms in such cases, except under the conditions stipulated in principle 9.

**Policing Persons in Custody or Detention**

15. Law enforcement officials, in their relations with persons in custody or detention, shall not use force, except when strictly necessary for the maintenance of security and order within the institution, or when personal safety is threatened.
16. Law enforcement officials, in their relations with persons in custody or detention, shall not use firearms, except in self-defence or in the defence of others against the immediate threat of death or serious injury, or when strictly necessary to prevent the escape of a person in custody or detention presenting the danger referred to in principle 9 . . .

**Qualifications, Training and Counselling**

18. Governments and law enforcement agencies shall ensure that all law enforcement officials are selected by proper screening procedures, have appropriate moral, psychological and physical qualities for the effective exercise of their functions and receive continuous and thorough professional training . . .
19. Governments and law enforcement agencies shall ensure that all law enforcement officials are provided with training and are tested in accordance with appropriate proficiency standards in the use of force . . .
20. In the training of law enforcement officials, Governments and law enforcement agencies shall give special attention to issues of police ethics and human rights, especially in the investigative process, to alternatives to the use of force and firearms, including the peaceful settlement of conflicts, the understanding of crowd behaviour, and the methods of persuasion, negotiation and mediation, as well as to technical means, with a view to limiting the use of force and firearms . . .
21. Governments and law enforcement agencies shall make stress counselling available to law enforcement officials who are involved in situations where force and firearms are used.

**Reporting and Review Procedures**

22. Governments and law enforcement agencies shall establish effective reporting and review procedures for all incidents referred to in principles 6 and 11(f). For incidents reported pursuant to these principles, Governments and law enforcement agencies shall ensure that an effective review process is available and that independent administrative or prosecutorial authorities are in a position to exercise jurisdiction in appropriate circumstances . . .

23. Persons affected by the use of force and firearms or their legal representatives shall have access to an independent process, including a judicial process . . .
24. Governments and law enforcement agencies shall ensure that superior officers are held responsible if they know, or should have known, that law enforcement officials under their command are resorting, or have resorted, to the unlawful use of force and firearms, and they did not take all measures in their power to prevent, suppress or report such use.
25. Governments and law enforcement agencies shall ensure that no criminal or disciplinary sanction is imposed on law enforcement officials who, in compliance with the Code of Conduct for Law Enforcement Officials and these basic principles, refuse to carry out an order to use force and firearms, or who report such use by other officials.
26. Obedience to superior orders shall be no defence if law enforcement officials knew that an order to use force and firearms resulting in the death or serious injury of a person was manifestly unlawful and had a reasonable opportunity to refuse to follow it. In any case, responsibility also rests on the superiors who gave the unlawful orders.

# 97. Additional initiatives

## i. EU: Code of Conduct for Arms Exports, 1998

**Commentary**: The Code identifies eight considerations relevant to issuing export licences for military equipment. These include: respect for existing international legal commitments; the risk that exports may be used for internal repression or violating human rights; the likelihood of provoking or prolonging armed conflicts or aggravating existing tensions within States or regionally; national security interests; the importing country's policies with respect to terrorism, crime, international legal compliance and non-proliferation; the risk of equipment being diverted or re-exported; and whether sustainable development will be hampered. Furthermore: 'It is recognised that Member States, where appropriate, may also take into account the effect of proposed exports on their economic, social, commercial and industrial interests, but that these factors will not affect the application of the above criteria' (paragraph 10). The Code has recently been reviewed for the first time: see the Sixth Annual Report (2004) *OJEC* C316/47. See also, the European Council's Common position 2003/468/CFSP on the control of arms brokering.

# PART IX

# International Criminal Law

# 98. USA/UK/USSR/France: Charter of the International Military Tribunal, 1945

**Commentary**: The Charter is annexed to the Agreement for the Prosecution and Punishment of the Major War Criminals of the European Axis (the London Agreement) 82 *UNTS* 280. Although permitting declarations of criminality against organisations, the International Military Tribunal (IMT) applied the Charter provisions extracted below as analogous to conspiracy since criminal guilt was personal and with a view to avoiding mass punishment: IMT (1947), 'Judgment', *American Journal of International Law* **41** (1) 172: 249–72. Declarations applied to individuals who voluntarily became members of the corporate 'instrumentality of cohesion' with knowledge of its criminal purposes but were declined where individuals never consciously acted as an affiliated group or could be conveniently tried individually.

Corporations utilised concentration camp interns, prisoners of war and civilians for forced labour and manufactured gas for use within those camps. Several senior corporate individuals were prosecuted: see *In re Flick & Ors* 14 *ILR* 266; *In re Krupp & Ors* 15 *ILR* 620; *In re Krauch & Ors* (the IG Farben Trial) 15 *ILR* 668. Although acquitted of crimes against peace, labour practices amounted to crimes against humanity, war crimes and violations of the laws and customs of warfare. Acquiring assets cheaply using the threat of seizure by the occupying power violated the belligerent obligation to respect private property. The argument that actors lacking public positions could not be liable for violating government obligations was rejected since acts adjudged criminal when committed by officials were equally so when committed by private individuals. While rejecting the national emergency defence, the pleas of superior orders and necessity were potentially applicable to civilian structures provided that individual intent did not coincide with that from which the alleged compulsion emanated. The requisite intent was either direct knowledge or inferred from continued participation and profit levels within the firm: see *US v Oswald Pohl et al* V *Trials of War Criminals Before the Nuremberg Military Tribunals* 1055; *Mauthausen Concentration Camp Trial (Trial of Hans Alfuldisch and Six Others)* 11 *War Crimes Law Reports* 15; *Trial of Burn Tesch and Two Others (the Zyklon B Case)* 13 *ILR* 250 (1946). On IG Farben, see Borkin J. (1979), *The Crime and Punishment of IG Farben*, London: André Deutsch. Rather than extinguishing its juristic personality, the intervening Cold War resulted in a dispersal of ownership: Allied High Commission Law No 35 (1950) 'Dispersion of Assets of IG'.

Corporations have also settled compensation claims for forced labour through resolution panels established in Switzerland: see Swiss Federal Decree concerning the historical and legal investigation on the fate of assets deposited in Switzerland following the advent of the National-Socialist Regime and Decree related to the Special Fund in favour of Needy Victims of the Holocaust 36 *ILM* 1272 (1997); Swiss Federal Banking Commission/Independent Committee of Eminent Persons/Swiss Bankers Association (1997), Statement on Comprehensive Claims Resolution Process for Dormant Accounts in Swiss Banks dating from prior to the end of World War Two and Announcement of the Claims Resolution Process 36 *ILM* 1379. German and Austrian companies acknowledged their moral responsibility provided that these fora remained the exclusive remedy: US–Germany (2000), Agreement concerning the Foundation 'Remembrance, Responsibility and the Future' 39 *ILM* 1298; Austria–US (2001), Agreement concerning the Austrian Fund 'Reconciliation, Peace and Cooperation' 40 *ILM* 523. The Austrian model envisages commercial and governmental contributions to a compensation fund, claims committee and arbitration panel: US–Austria (2001), Joint Statement and Exchange of Notes concerning the establishment of the General Settlement Fund for Nazi-Era and World War Two Claims 40 *ILM* 565.

These developments followed the dismissal of US litigation where prior reparations agreements foreclosed individual claims and comparable procedures were adjudged fair and reasonable: *Iwanowa v Ford Motor Co* 67 *F. Supp 2d* 424 (DNJ 1999); *Burger-Fischer v Degussa AG* 65 *F. Supp 2d* 248 (DNJ 1999); Sec 354.6 *California Code of Civil Procedure relating to World War Two Slave and Forced Labour Victims* 39 *ILM* 231 (2000); *In re World War II Era Japanese Forced Labour Litigation* 164 *F. Supp 2d* 1153 & 1160 (ND Cal 2001) (US); *In re Austrian and German Bank Holocaust Litigation* 80 *F. Supp 2d* 164 (SDNY 2000) & 250 *F.3d* 156 (2d Cir 2001); *Watman v Deutsche Bank* (CA 2nd Cir 2001); *In re Holocaust Victim Assets Litigation: Polish American Defence Committee v Swiss Bankers Association* 96 *Civ* 4849 (Dist Ct NY 2000 & CA 2nd Cir 2000); *Hirsch v State of Israel and State of Germany* 962 *F. Supp* 377 (Dist Ct NY 1997).

## The London Agreement

*Article 1*

There shall be established after consultation with the Control Council for Germany an International Military Tribunal for the trial of war criminals whose offences have no particular geographical location whether they be accused individually or in their capacity as members of organizations or groups or in both capacities.

## The Charter for the Constitution of the International Military Tribunal

*Article 6*

The Tribunal established by the Agreement referred to in Article 1 hereof for the trial and punishment of the major war criminals of the European Axis countries shall have the power to try and punish persons who, acting in the interests of the European Axis countries, whether as individuals or as members of organizations, committed any of the following crimes. The following acts, or any of them, are crimes coming within the jurisdiction of the Tribunal for which there shall be individual responsibility:

(a) 'Crimes against peace': namely, planning, preparation, initiation or waging of a war of aggression, or a war in violation of international treaties, agreements or assurances, or participation in a common plan or conspiracy for the accomplishment of any of the foregoing;

(b) 'War crimes': namely, violations of the laws or customs of war. Such violations shall include, but not be limited to, murder, ill-treatment or deportation to slave labour or for any other purpose of civilian population of or in occupied territory, murder or ill-treatment of prisoners of war or persons on the seas, killing of hostages, plunder of public or private property, wanton destruction of cities, towns or villages, or devastation not justified by military necessity;

(c) 'Crimes against humanity': namely, murder, extermination, enslavement, deportation, and other inhumane acts committed against any civilian population, before or during the war, or persecutions on political, racial or religious grounds in execution of or in connection with any crime within the jurisdiction of the Tribunal, whether or not in violation of the domestic law of the country where perpetrated.

Leaders, organizers, instigators and accomplices participating in the formulation or execution of a common plan or conspiracy to commit any of the foregoing crimes are responsible for all acts performed by any persons in execution of such plan.

*Article 9*

At the trial of any individual member of any group or organization the Tribunal may declare (in connection with any act of which the individual may be convicted) that the group or organization of which the individual was a member was a criminal organization. After receipt of the Indictment the Tribunal shall give such notice as it thinks fit that the prosecution intends to ask the Tribunal to make such declaration and any member of the organization will be entitled to apply to the Tribunal for leave to be heard by the Tribunal upon the question of the criminal character of the organization. The Tribunal shall have power to allow or reject the application. If the application is allowed, the Tribunal may direct in what manner the applicants shall be represented and heard.

*Article 10*

In cases where a group or organization is declared criminal by the Tribunal, the competent national authority of any Signatory shall have the right to bring individuals to trial for membership therein before national, military or occupation courts. In any such case the criminal nature of the group or organization is considered proved and shall not be questioned.

*Article 11*

Any person convicted by the Tribunal may be charged before a national, military or occupation court, referred to in Article 10 of this Charter, with a crime other than of membership in a criminal group or organization and such court may, after convicting him, impose upon him punishment independent of and additional to the punishment imposed by the Tribunal for participation in the criminal activities of such group or organization.

# 99. International Law Commission: Principles of International Law Recognized in the Charter of the Nuremberg Tribunal and in the Judgment of the Tribunal, 1950

**Commentary**: The ILC was requested to 'formulate the principles of international law recognized in the Charter of the Nuremberg Tribunal and in the judgment of the Tribunal': UNGA Resolution 177 (II)(a). Since the Principles had previously been affirmed by UNGA Resolution 95(1)(1946), the ILC considered it unnecessary to ascertain whether they constituted international law. For commentary, see ILC (1950), *Yearbook*, 2, 374–8. For the work of the ILC, see www.un.org/law/ilc.

**Principle I**
Any person who commits an act which constitutes a crime under international law is responsible therefor and liable to punishment.

**Principle VI**
The crimes hereinafter set out are punishable as crimes under international law:

a) Crimes against peace:

i) Planning, preparation, initiation or waging of a war of aggression or a war in violation of international treaties, agreements or assurances;
ii) Participation in a common plan or conspiracy for the accomplishment of any of the acts mentioned under (i).

b) War crimes:
Violations of the laws or customs of war which include, but are not limited to, murder, ill-treatment or deportation to slave-labour or for any other purpose of civilian population of or in occupied territory, murder or ill-treatment of prisoners of war, of persons on the seas, killing of hostages, plunder of public or private property, wanton destruction of cities, towns, or villages, or devastation not justified by military necessity.

c) Crimes against humanity:
Murder, extermination, enslavement, deportation and other inhuman acts done against any civilian population, or persecutions on political, racial or religious grounds, when

such acts are done or such persecutions are carried on in execution of or in connection with any crime against peace or any war crime.

**Principle VII**
Complicity in the commission of a crime against peace, a war crime, or a crime against humanity as set forth in Principle VI is a crime under international law.

# 100. UN: The Rome Statute of the International Criminal Court, 1998

**Commentary**: The Rome Statute (UN Doc A/CONF.183/9 (1998), entry into force 2002) envisages individual criminal responsibility for aggression, war crimes, crimes against humanity and genocide where offences occur on the territory of State Parties or by nationals thereof. Proposals to include corporate criminal responsibility were rejected on account of national legal differences: see Article 23(5), Draft Statute of the International Criminal Court, UN Doc A/CONF.183/2/Add.1 (1998). 'Most delegations held the view that it would be more useful to focus attention on individual responsibility, noting, at the same time, that corporations were in fact controlled by individuals': Preparatory Committee on the Establishment of an International Criminal Court (1996), 'Proceedings during the Period 25 March–12 April 1996', Draft summary prepared by Rapporteur Yoshida, UN Doc A/AC.249/CRP.3/Add.I: paragraphs 5–6. However, corporate liability 'could be important in the context of restitution'. See generally, www.un.org/law/icc. The European Parliament has called for a 'legally binding framework with sanctions for companies which contribute to conflicts' in unstable regions: European Parliament, Resolution on the Commission Communication on Conflict Prevention, COM(2001)211.

A Nuremberg Military Tribunal observed that in certain circumstances action by companies and their representatives in circumstances of an armed conflict 'cannot be differentiated from acts of plunder or pillage committed by officers . . . or . . . officials of the Third Reich': *US v Krauch* (1952) 8 *Control Council Law No 10 Trials* 1081, 1140 (US Military Tribunal VI 1948). Individual criminal responsibility arises *inter alia* when offenders are aided and abetted by acts or words lending encouragement. Mere presence is insufficient if unwilling or ignorant but is otherwise with knowledge and where it contributes directly and substantially to committing offences: International Criminal Tribunal for the former Yugoslavia (ICTY), *Prosecutor v Tadic* Case IT-94-1-T (Trial Cham 2 Judgment 1997): paragraphs 661–92. The military doctrine of command responsibility applies to civilian superiors where they exercise authority over subordinates, including the material ability to prevent and punish: ICTY, *Prosecutor v Delalic & Ors (the 'Celebici' Case)* Case No IT-96-21-A (2001): paragraphs 197, 238, 251 & 266; *The Government Commissioner of the General Tribunal of the Military Government for the French Zone of Occupation in Germany v Directors of the Roechling Enterprises* XIV *Trials of War Criminals Before the Nuremberg Military Tribunals* 1061: 1092–3.

**Article 25: Individual Criminal Responsibility**

1. The Court shall have jurisdiction over natural persons pursuant to this Statute.
2. A person who commits a crime within the jurisdiction of the Court shall be individually responsible and liable for punishment in accordance with this Statute.

3. In accordance with this Statute, a person shall be criminally responsible and liable for punishment for a crime within the jurisdiction of the Court if that person:

   (a) Commits such a crime, whether as an individual, jointly with another or through another person, regardless of whether that other person is criminally responsible;
   (b) Orders, solicits or induces the commission of such a crime which in fact occurs or is attempted;
   (c) For the purpose of facilitating the commission of such a crime, aids, abets or otherwise assists in its commission or its attempted commission, including providing the means for its commission;
   (d) In any other way contributes to the commission or attempted commission of such a crime by a group of persons acting with a common purpose. Such contribution shall be intentional and shall either:

      (i) Be made with the aim of furthering the criminal activity or criminal purpose of the group, where such activity or purpose involves the commission of a crime within the jurisdiction of the Court; or
      (ii) Be made in the knowledge of the intention of the group to commit the crime;

   (e) In respect of the crime of genocide, directly and publicly incites others to commit genocide;
   (f) Attempts to commit such a crime by taking action that commences its execution by means of a substantial step, but the crime does not occur because of circumstances independent of the person's intentions. However, a person who abandons the effort to commit the crime or otherwise prevents the completion of the crime shall not be liable for punishment under this Statute for the attempt to commit that crime if that person completely and voluntarily gave up the criminal purpose.

4. No provision in this Statute relating to individual criminal responsibility shall affect the responsibility of States under international law.

# 101. UN: The Slavery Convention, 1926

**Commentary**: As the first human rights issue to arouse international concern, slavery is addressed by the Slavery Convention (60 *LNTS* 253, entry into force 1927). The Protocol amending the Slavery Convention (182 *UNTS* 51, entry into force 1953) invested the UN with the duties and functions formerly undertaken by the League of Nations. For corporate responsibility under customary international law for using slave labour, see *Burger-Fischer v Degussa AG* 65 *F. Supp* 2d 248 (DNJ 1999).

**Article 1**
For the purpose of the present Convention, the following definitions are agreed upon:

1. Slavery is the status or condition of a person over whom any or all of the powers attaching to the right of ownership are exercised.
2. The slave trade includes all acts involved in the capture, acquisition or disposal of a person with intent to reduce him to slavery; all acts involved in the acquisition of a slave with a view to selling or exchanging him; all acts of disposal by sale or exchange of a slave acquired with a view to being sold or exchanged, and, in general, every act of trade or transport in slaves.

**Article 2**
The High Contracting Parties undertake, each in respect of the territories placed under its sovereignty, jurisdiction, protection, suzerainty or tutelage, so far as they have not already taken the necessary steps:

(a) To prevent and suppress the slave trade;
(b) To bring about, progressively and as soon as possible, the complete abolition of slavery in all its forms.

**Article 3**
The High Contracting Parties undertake to adopt all appropriate measures with a view to preventing and suppressing the embarkation, disembarkation and transport of slaves in their territorial waters and upon all vessels flying their respective flags . . .

**Article 5**
The High Contracting Parties recognise that recourse to compulsory or forced labour may have grave consequences and undertake, each in respect of the territories placed under its

sovereignty, jurisdiction, protection, suzerainty or tutelage, to take all necessary measures to prevent compulsory or forced labour from developing into conditions analogous to slavery.

It is agreed that:

1. Subject to the transitional provisions laid down in paragraph (2) below, compulsory or forced labour may only be exacted for public purposes.
2. In territories in which compulsory or forced labour for other than public purposes still survives, the High Contracting Parties shall endeavour progressively and as soon as possible to put an end to the practice. So long as such forced or compulsory labour exists, this labour shall invariably be of an exceptional character, shall always receive adequate remuneration, and shall not involve the removal of the labourers from their usual place of residence.
3. In all cases, the responsibility for any recourse to compulsory or forced labour shall rest with the competent central authorities of the territory concerned.

# 102. UN: The Supplementary Convention on the Abolition of Slavery, the Slave Trade, and Institutions and Practices Similar to Slavery, 1956

**Commentary**: The Supplementary Convention (226 *UNTS* 3, entry into force 1957) broadened the 1926 Convention's definition of slavery to include debt bondage, servile forms of marriage and the exploitation of children and adolescents. The OHCHR Working Group on Contemporary Forms of Slavery considers information on government measures to implement the three slavery-related Conventions: www.ohchr.org/english/issues/slavery/group.htm. A Voluntary Trust Fund has been established to facilitate NGO contributions to its deliberations and provide humanitarian, legal and financial assistance to victims: UNGA Resolution 46/122 (1991). See also, Fact Sheet No.14 (1991) on Contemporary Forms of Slavery, Geneva.

## Section I: Institutions and Practices Similar to Slavery

*Article 1*

Each of the States Parties to this Convention shall take all practicable and necessary legislative and other measures to bring about progressively and as soon as possible the complete abolition or abandonment of the following institutions and practices, where they still exist and whether or not they are covered by the definition of slavery contained in article 1 of the Slavery Convention signed at Geneva on 25 September 1926:

(a) Debt bondage, that is to say, the status or condition arising from a pledge by a debtor of his personal services or of those of a person under his control as security for a debt, if the value of those services as reasonably assessed is not applied towards the liquidation of the debt or the length and nature of those services are not respectively limited and defined;

(b) Serfdom, that is to say, the condition or status of a tenant who is by law, custom or agreement bound to live and labour on land belonging to another person and to render some determinate service to such other person, whether for reward or not, and is not free to change his status;

(c) Any institution or practice whereby:

    (i) A woman, without the right to refuse, is promised or given in marriage on payment of a consideration in money or in kind to her parents, guardian, family or any other person or group; or

(ii) The husband of a woman, his family, or his clan, has the right to transfer her to another person for value received or otherwise; or
(iii) A woman on the death of her husband is liable to be inherited by another person;

(d) Any institution or practice whereby a child or young person under the age of 18 years, is delivered by either or both of his natural parents or by his guardian to another person, whether for reward or not, with a view to the exploitation of the child or young person or of his labour.

**Section II: The Slave Trade**

*Article 3*

1. The act of conveying or attempting to convey slaves from one country to another by whatever means of transport, or of being accessory thereto, shall be a criminal offence under the laws of the States Parties to this Convention and persons convicted thereof shall be liable to very severe penalties.
2. (a) The States Parties shall take all effective measures to prevent ships and aircraft authorized to fly their flags from conveying slaves and to punish persons guilty of such acts or of using national flags for that purpose.
   (b) The States Parties shall take all effective measures to ensure that their ports, airfields and coasts are not used for the conveyance of slaves.

3. The States Parties to this Convention shall exchange information in order to ensure the practical co-ordination of the measures taken by them in combating the slave trade and shall inform each other of every case of the slave trade, and of every attempt to commit this criminal offence, which comes to their notice.

**Section III: Slavery and Institutions and Practices Similar to Slavery**

*Article 5*

In a country where the abolition or abandonment of slavery, or of the institutions or practices mentioned in article 1 of this Convention, is not yet complete, the act of mutilating, branding or otherwise marking a slave or a person of servile status in order to indicate his status, or as a punishment, or for any other reason, or of being accessory thereto, shall be a criminal offence under the laws of the States Parties to this Convention and persons convicted thereof shall be liable to punishment.

*Article 6*

1. The act of enslaving another person or of inducing another person to give himself or a person dependent upon him into slavery, or of attempting these acts, or being accessory thereto, or being a party to a conspiracy to accomplish any such acts, shall be a criminal offence under the laws of the States Parties to this Convention and persons convicted thereof shall be liable to punishment.
2. Subject to the provisions of the introductory paragraph of article 1 of this Convention, the provisions of paragraph 1 of the present article shall also apply to the act of inducing another person to place himself or a person dependent upon him into the servile

status resulting from any of the institutions or practices mentioned in article 1, to any attempt to perform such acts, to being accessory thereto, and to being a party to a conspiracy to accomplish any such acts.

## Section IV – Definitions

*Article 7*

For the purposes of the present Convention:

(a) 'Slavery' means, as defined in the Slavery Convention of 1926, the status or condition of a person over whom any or all of the powers attaching to the right of ownership are exercised, and 'slave' means a person in such condition or status;

(b) 'A person of servile status' means a person in the condition or status resulting from any of the institutions or practices mentioned in article 1 of this Convention;

(c) 'Slave trade' means and includes all acts involved in the capture, acquisition or disposal of a person with intent to reduce him to slavery; all acts involved in the acquisition of a slave with a view to selling or exchanging him; all acts of disposal by sale or exchange of a person acquired with a view to being sold or exchanged; and, in general, every act of trade or transport in slaves by whatever means of conveyance.

# 103. UN: Convention for the Suppression of the Traffic in Persons and of the Exploitation of the Prostitution of Others, 1949

**Commentary**: The Convention (96 *UNTS* 271, entry into force 1951) consolidated earlier agreements dating back to 1904. It targets the procurer rather than the prostitute and requires governments to introduce measures of prevention and rehabilitation. See also, UNHCHR (2002), 'Principles and Guidelines on Human Rights and Trafficking', E/2002/68/Add.1; UNICEF (2003), 'Guidelines for the Protection of the Rights of Children Victims Trafficking in Southeastern Europe'; Inter-American Convention on International Traffic in Minors (1994) 79 *OASTS*.

**Article 1**

The Parties to the present Convention agree to punish any person who, to gratify the passions of another:

1. Procures, entices or leads away, for purposes of prostitution, another person, even with the consent of that person;
2. Exploits the prostitution of another person, even with the consent of that person.

**Article 2**

The Parties to the present Convention further agree to punish any person who:

1. Keeps or manages, or knowingly finances or takes part in the financing of a brothel;
2. Knowingly lets or rents a building or other place or any part thereof for the purpose of the prostitution of others.

**Article 3**

To the extent permitted by domestic law, attempts to commit any of the offences referred to in articles 1 and 2, and acts preparatory to the commission thereof, shall also be punished.

**Article 4**

To the extent permitted by domestic law, international participation in the acts referred to in articles 1 and 2 above shall also be punishable.

To the extent permitted by domestic law, acts of participation shall be treated as separate offences whenever this is necessary to prevent impunity.

# 104. UN: Protocol to Prevent, Suppress and Punish Trafficking in Persons, Especially Women and Children, supplementing the UN Convention against Transnational Organized Crime, 2000

**Commentary**: The Protocol (UN Doc A/55/383 (2000), entry into force 2003) seeks to prevent and combat trafficking, protect and assist victims and promote international cooperation. See further, UNGA Resolution 55/25 (2000). In addition to the provisions extracted below, Article 7 contemplates adopting measures permitting victims of trafficking to temporarily or permanently remain within State territory. Article 8 envisages repatriating victims of trafficking to their States of nationality without undue or unreasonable delay and where personal safety permits. The UN Global Programme against Trafficking in Human Beings (GPAT) is administered by the UN Office on Drugs and Crime (UNODC) and engages in data collection, assessment and technical cooperation: www.unodc.org/unodc/en/trafficking_human_beings.html.

## I. General Provisions

*Article 2: Statement of Purpose*
The purposes of this Protocol are:

(a) To prevent and combat trafficking in persons, paying particular attention to women and children;
(b) To protect and assist the victims of such trafficking, with full respect for their human rights; and
(c) To promote cooperation among States Parties in order to meet those objectives.

*Article 3: Use of Terms*
For the purposes of this Protocol:

(a) 'Trafficking in persons' shall mean the recruitment, transportation, transfer, harbouring or receipt of persons, by means of the threat or use of force or other forms of coercion, of abduction, of fraud, of deception, of the abuse of power or of a position of vulnerability or of the giving or receiving of payments or benefits to achieve the consent of a person having control over another person, for the purpose of exploitation. Exploitation shall include, at a minimum, the exploitation of the prostitution of others or other forms of sexual exploitation, forced labour or services, slavery or practices similar to slavery, servitude or the removal of organs;

(b) The consent of a victim of trafficking in persons to the intended exploitation set forth in subparagraph (a) of this article shall be irrelevant where any of the means set forth in subparagraph (a) have been used;

(c) The recruitment, transportation, transfer, harbouring or receipt of a child for the purpose of exploitation shall be considered 'trafficking in persons' even if this does not involve any of the means set forth in subparagraph (a) of this article;

(d) 'Child' shall mean any person under eighteen years of age.

*Article 5: Criminalization*

1. Each State Party shall adopt such legislative and other measures as may be necessary to establish as criminal offences the conduct set forth in article 3 of this Protocol, when committed intentionally.
2. Each State Party shall also adopt such legislative and other measures as may be necessary to establish as criminal offences:

   (a) Subject to the basic concepts of its legal system, attempting to commit an offence established in accordance with paragraph 1 of this article;
   (b) Participating as an accomplice in an offence established in accordance with paragraph 1 of this article; and
   (c) Organizing or directing other persons to commit an offence established in accordance with paragraph 1 of this article.

## II. Protection of Victims of Trafficking in Persons

*Article 6: Assistance to and Protection of Victims of Trafficking in Persons*

3. Each State Party shall consider implementing measures to provide for the physical, psychological and social recovery of victims of trafficking in persons, including, in appropriate cases, in cooperation with NGOs, other relevant organizations and other elements of civil society, and, in particular, the provision of:

   (a) Appropriate housing;
   (b) Counselling and information, in particular as regards their legal rights, in a language that the victims of trafficking in persons can understand;
   (c) Medical, psychological and material assistance; and
   (d) Employment, educational and training opportunities.

6. Each State Party shall ensure that its domestic legal system contains measures that offer victims of trafficking in persons the possibility of obtaining compensation for damage suffered.

## III. Prevention, Cooperation and other Measures

*Article 9: Prevention of Trafficking in Persons*

1. States Parties shall establish comprehensive policies, programmes and other measures:

(a) To prevent and combat trafficking in persons; and
(b) To protect victims of trafficking in persons, especially women and children, from revictimization.

2. States Parties shall endeavour to undertake measures such as research, information and mass media campaigns and social and economic initiatives to prevent and combat trafficking in persons.
3. Policies, programmes and other measures established in accordance with this article shall, as appropriate, include cooperation with NGOs, other relevant organizations and other elements of civil society . . .

*Article 10: Information Exchange and Training*

1. Law enforcement, immigration or other relevant authorities of States Parties shall, as appropriate, cooperate with one another by exchanging information, in accordance with their domestic law, to enable them to determine:

   (c) The means and methods used by organized criminal groups for the purpose of trafficking in persons, including the recruitment and transportation of victims, routes and links between and among individuals and groups engaged in such trafficking, and possible measures for detecting them.

2. States Parties shall provide or strengthen training for law enforcement, immigration and other relevant officials in the prevention of trafficking in persons . . . The training should also take into account the need to consider human rights and child- and gender-sensitive issues and it should encourage cooperation with non governmental organizations, other relevant organizations and other elements of civil society.

*Article 11: Border Measures*

2. Each State Party shall adopt legislative or other appropriate measures to prevent, to the extent possible, means of transport operated by commercial carriers from being used in the commission of offences established in accordance with article 5 of this Protocol.
3. Where appropriate, and without prejudice to applicable international conventions, such measures shall include establishing the obligation of commercial carriers, including any transportation company or the owner or operator of any means of transport, to ascertain that all passengers are in possession of the travel documents required for entry into the receiving State.
4. Each State Party shall take the necessary measures, in accordance with its domestic law, to provide for sanctions in cases of violation of the obligation set forth in paragraph 3 of this article . . .

# 105. UN: International Convention on the Prevention and Punishment of the Crime of Genocide, 1948

**Commentary**: The Genocide Convention (78 *UNTS* 277, entry into force 1951) defines the constituent elements of the offence. Businesspersons have been adjudged criminally liable for participating in genocidal acts alongside government officials and civilly liable for incitement to genocide: International Criminal Tribunal for Rwanda (ICTR), *The Prosecutor v Clement Kayishema & Obed Ruzindana Case* No ICTR-95-1-T (1999); *Mushikiwabo & Ors v Barayagwiza* 107 *ILR* 457 (Dist Ct NY 1996).

**Article 2**
In the present Convention, genocide means any of the following acts committed with intent to destroy, in whole or in part, a national, ethnical, racial or religious group, as such:

(a) Killing members of the group;
(b) Causing serious bodily or mental harm to members of the group;
(c) Deliberately inflicting on the group conditions of life calculated to bring about its physical destruction in whole or in part;
(d) Imposing measures intended to prevent births within the group;
(e) Forcibly transferring children of the group to another group.

**Article 3**
The following acts shall be punishable:

(a) Genocide;
(b) Conspiracy to commit genocide;
(c) Direct and public incitement to commit genocide;
(d) Attempt to commit genocide;
(e) Complicity in genocide.

**Article 4**
Persons committing genocide or any of the other acts enumerated in article 3 shall be punished, whether they are constitutionally responsible rulers, public officials or private individuals.

# 106. UN: International Convention on the Suppression and Punishment of the Crime of Apartheid, 1973

**Commentary**: The Apartheid Convention (1015 *UNTS* 243, entry into force 1976) defines the constituent elements of the offence. For the first UN hearings on commercial roles and responsibilities within South Africa, see UNCTC (1986), UN Doc ST/CTC/68: Reports of the Panel of Eminent Persons and of the Secretary-General (Vol 1); Verbatim Records (Vol 2); Statements and Submissions (Vol 3); and Policy Instruments and Statements (Vol 4). For the second hearings during 1989, see UNCTC (1990), UN Doc ST/CTC/102: Report of the Panel of Eminent Persons & Background Documentation (Vol 1); and Statements and Submissions (Vol 2). For the activities and operations of corporations within Namibia and their contribution to South Africa's illegal occupation, see UN Secretary-General (1985), Report, UN Doc E/C.10/AC.4/1985/6. For the responsibilities of their home governments, see UNCTC (1986), UN Doc ST/CTC/84. For intergovernmental responses (including invalidity and non-recognition of property titles and contractual non-enforcement), see UN Council for Namibia Decree No 1 (1974) for the Protection of the Natural Resources of Namibia, UN Doc A/35/24 (Vol 1, Annex 2) as affirmed by UNGA Resolution 3295 (1974), 35/277 (1981), 39/50A (1984) and Security Council Resolution 301 (1971); UN Commissioner for Namibia (1986), 'Report on the Implementation of Decree No 1 for the Protection of the Natural Resources: Study of the Possibility of Instituting Legal Proceedings in the Domestic Courts of States', *American Journal of International Law*, **80** (2), 442–91. For national legislative measures, see, for example, The Comprehensive Anti-Apartheid Act 22 *USC* s5001–5116 (1988). See also, *In re South African Apartheid Litigation* 238 *F. Supp* 2d 1379 (SDNY 2002).

**Article I**

1. The States Parties to the present Convention declare that apartheid is a crime against humanity and that inhuman acts resulting from the policies and practices of apartheid and similar policies and practices of racial segregation and discrimination, as defined in article II of the Convention, are crimes violating the principles of international law, in particular the purposes and principles of the Charter of the UN, and constituting a serious threat to international peace and security.
2. The States Parties to the present Convention declare criminal those organizations, institutions and individuals committing the crime of apartheid.

**Article II**

For the purpose of the present Convention, the term 'the crime of apartheid', which shall include similar policies and practices of racial segregation and discrimination as practised in southern Africa, shall apply to the following inhuman acts committed for the purpose of establishing and maintaining domination by one racial group of persons over any other racial group of persons and systematically oppressing them:

(a) Denial to a member or members of a racial group or groups of the right to life and liberty of person:

(i) By murder of members of a racial group or groups;
(ii) By the infliction upon the members of a racial group or groups of serious bodily or mental harm, by the infringement of their freedom or dignity, or by subjecting them to torture or to cruel, inhuman or degrading treatment or punishment;
(iii) By arbitrary arrest and illegal imprisonment of the members of a racial group or groups;

(b) Deliberate imposition on a racial group or groups of living conditions calculated to cause its or their physical destruction in whole or in part;
(c) Any legislative measures and other measures calculated to prevent a racial group or groups from participation in the political, social, economic and cultural life of the country and the deliberate creation of conditions preventing the full development of such a group or groups, in particular by denying to members of a racial group or groups basic human rights and freedoms, including the right to work, the right to form recognized trade unions, the right to education, the right to leave and to return to their country, the right to a nationality, the right to freedom of movement and residence, the right to freedom of opinion and expression, and the right to freedom of peaceful assembly and association;
(d) Any measures including legislative measures, designed to divide the population along racial lines by the creation of separate reserves and ghettos for the members of a racial group or groups, the prohibition of mixed marriages among members of various racial groups, the expropriation of landed property belonging to a racial group or groups or to members thereof;
(e) Exploitation of the labour of the members of a racial group or groups, in particular by submitting them to forced labour;
(f) Persecution of organizations and persons, by depriving them of fundamental rights and freedoms, because they oppose apartheid.

**Article III**

International criminal responsibility shall apply, irrespective of the motive involved, to individuals, members of organizations and institutions and representatives of the State, whether residing in the territory of the State in which the acts are perpetrated or in some other State, whenever they:

(a) Commit, participate in, directly incite or conspire in the commission of the acts mentioned in article II of the present Convention;
(b) Directly abet, encourage or co-operate in the commission of the crime of apartheid.

# 107. UN: Convention against Torture and Other Cruel, Inhuman or Degrading Treatment or Punishment, 1987

**Commentary**: The Convention (23 *ILM* 1027 (1984) & 24 *ILM* 535 (1985), entry into force 1987) is administered by the Committee against Torture (CAT), a body of independent experts which assesses national reports concerning implementation of the Convention, undertakes inquiries, issues general comments on thematic issues and considers inter-State complaints. CAT may also consider communications from or on behalf of individuals claiming to be victims of violations by State Parties. An Optional Protocol (not yet in force) will enable in-country inspections of places of detention in conjunction with national institutions. A Voluntary Fund for Victims of Torture was established to enable NGOs to provide humanitarian assistance to victims and their families: UNGA Resolution 36/151 (1981). See further, www.ohchr.org.

Corporations may be held liable where they aid, abet or conspire with government officials in acts of torture: *Carmichael v United Technologies Corp* 835 *F.2d* 109 (5th Cir 1988). They may also be liable where they employ coercive government power to unlawfully detain individuals and extract favourable contractual concessions: *Eastman Kodak Company v Kavlin* 978 *F. Supp* 1078 (SD Fla 1997).

**Article 1**

1. For the purposes of this Convention, the term 'torture' means any act by which severe pain or suffering, whether physical or mental, is intentionally inflicted on a person for such purposes as obtaining from him or a third person information or a confession, punishing him for an act he or a third person has committed or is suspected of having committed, or intimidating or coercing him or a third person, or for any reason based on discrimination of any kind, when such pain or suffering is inflicted by or at the instigation of or with the consent or acquiescence of a public official or other person acting in an official capacity. It does not include pain or suffering arising only from, inherent in or incidental to lawful sanctions.
2. This article is without prejudice to any international instrument or national legislation which does or may contain provisions of wider application.

**Article 4**

1. Each State Party shall ensure that all acts of torture are offences under its criminal law. The same shall apply to an attempt to commit torture and to an act by any person which constitutes complicity or participation in torture.

2. Each State Party shall make these offences punishable by appropriate penalties which take into account their grave nature.

**Article 10**

1. Each State Party shall ensure that education and information regarding the prohibition against torture are fully included in the training of law enforcement personnel, civil or military, medical personnel, public officials and other persons who may be involved in the custody, interrogation or treatment of any individual subjected to any form of arrest, detention or imprisonment.
2. Each State Party shall include this prohibition in the rules or instructions issued in regard to the duties and functions of any such person.

# 108. UN: Convention against Transnational Organized Crime, 2000

**Commentary**: The Convention (40 *ILM* 335 (2001), entry into force 2003) facilitates the investigation, prosecution and punishment of crimes committed by organised criminal groups where either the crime or the group has a transnational element. Article 12 allows the confiscation and seizure of criminal proceeds or property and Article 14 for its subsequent disposal. See further, Ad Hoc Committee on the Elaboration of a Convention against Transnational Organized Crime (2000), 'Report on the work of its first to eleventh sessions and the interpretative notes for the official records (*travaux préparatoires*) of the negotiation of the Convention against Transnational Organized Crime and the Protocols', UN Doc A/55/383/Add.1. Related supplementary instruments concluded under Article 37 include the Protocol to Prevent, Suppress and Punish Trafficking in Persons, Especially Women and Children (extracted above), the Protocol against the Smuggling of Migrants by Land, Air and Sea (UN Doc A/55/383 (2000), entry into force 2004) and the Protocol against the Illicit Manufacturing of and Trafficking in Firearms, Their Parts and Components and Ammunition (extracted above). See also, www.unodc.org.

**Article 1: Statement of purpose**
The purpose of this Convention is to promote cooperation to prevent and combat transnational organized crime more effectively.

**Article 2: Use of terms**
For the purposes of this Convention:

(a) 'Organized criminal group' shall mean a structured group of three or more persons, existing for a period of time and acting in concert with the aim of committing one or more serious crimes or offences established in accordance with this Convention, in order to obtain, directly or indirectly, a financial or other material benefit;
(b) 'Serious crime' shall mean conduct constituting an offence punishable by a maximum deprivation of liberty of at least four years or a more serious penalty;
(c) 'Structured group' shall mean a group that is not randomly formed for the immediate commission of an offence and that does not need to have formally defined roles for its members, continuity of its membership or a developed structure;
(d) 'Property' shall mean assets of every kind, whether corporeal or incorporeal, movable or immovable, tangible or intangible, and legal documents or instruments evidencing title to, or interest in, such assets;

(e) 'Proceeds of crime' shall mean any property derived from or obtained, directly or indirectly, through the commission of an offence;
(f) 'Freezing' or 'seizure' shall mean temporarily prohibiting the transfer, conversion, disposition or movement of property or temporarily assuming custody or control of property on the basis of an order issued by a court or other competent authority;
(g) 'Confiscation', which includes forfeiture where applicable, shall mean the permanent deprivation of property by order of a court or other competent authority;
(h) 'Predicate offence' shall mean any offence as a result of which proceeds have been generated that may become the subject of an offence as defined in article 6 of this Convention;
(i) 'Controlled delivery' shall mean the technique of allowing illicit or suspect consignments to pass out of, through or into the territory of one or more States, with the knowledge and under the supervision of their competent authorities, with a view to the investigation of an offence and the identification of persons involved in the commission of the offence;

**Article 3: Scope of Application**

1. This Convention shall apply, except as otherwise stated herein, to the prevention, investigation and prosecution of:

   (a) The offences established in accordance with articles 5, 6, 8 and 23 of this Convention; and
   (b) Serious crime as defined in article 2 of this Convention; where the offence is transnational in nature and involves an organized criminal group.

2. For the purpose of paragraph 1 of this article, an offence is transnational in nature if:

   (a) It is committed in more than one State;
   (b) It is committed in one State but a substantial part of its preparation, planning, direction or control takes place in another State;
   (c) It is committed in one State but involves an organized criminal group that engages in criminal activities in more than one State; or
   (d) It is committed in one State but has substantial effects in another State.

**Article 5: Criminalization of Participation in an Organized Criminal Group**

1. Each State Party shall adopt such legislative and other measures as may be necessary to establish as criminal offences, when committed intentionally:

   (a) Either or both of the following as criminal offences distinct from those involving the attempt or completion of the criminal activity:

      (i) Agreeing with one or more other persons to commit a serious crime for a purpose relating directly or indirectly to the obtaining of a financial or other material benefit and, where required by domestic law, involving an act undertaken by one of the participants in furtherance of the agreement or involving an organized criminal group;

(ii) Conduct by a person who, with knowledge of either the aim and general criminal activity of an organized criminal group or its intention to commit the crimes in question, takes an active part in:

a. Criminal activities of the organized criminal group;
b. Other activities of the organized criminal group in the knowledge that his or her participation will contribute to the achievement of the above-described criminal aim;

(b) Organizing, directing, aiding, abetting, facilitating or counselling the commission of serious crime involving an organized criminal group.

2. The knowledge, intent, aim, purpose or agreement referred to in paragraph 1 of this article may be inferred from objective factual circumstances.
3. States Parties whose domestic law requires involvement of an organized criminal group for purposes of the offences established in accordance with paragraph 1(a)(i) of this article shall ensure that their domestic law covers all serious crimes involving organized criminal groups. Such States Parties, as well as States Parties whose domestic law requires an act in furtherance of the agreement for purposes of the offences established in accordance with paragraph 1(a)(i) of this article, shall so inform the Secretary-General of the UN at the time of their signature or of deposit of their instrument of ratification, acceptance or approval of or accession to this Convention.

**Article 6: Criminalization of the Laundering of Proceeds of Crime**

1. Each State Party shall adopt, in accordance with fundamental principles of its domestic law, such legislative and other measures as may be necessary to establish as criminal offences, when committed intentionally:

(a) (i) The conversion or transfer of property, knowing that such property is the proceeds of crime, for the purpose of concealing or disguising the illicit origin of the property or of helping any person who is involved in the commission of the predicate offence to evade the legal consequences of his or her action;
(ii) The concealment or disguise of the true nature, source, location, disposition, movement or ownership of or rights with respect to property, knowing that such property is the proceeds of crime;

(b) Subject to the basic concepts of its legal system:

(i) The acquisition, possession or use of property, knowing, at the time of receipt, that such property is the proceeds of crime;
(ii) Participation in, association with or conspiracy to commit, attempts to commit and aiding, abetting, facilitating and counselling the commission of any of the offences established in accordance with this article.

2. For purposes of implementing or applying paragraph 1 of this article:

(a) Each State Party shall seek to apply paragraph 1 of this article to the widest range of predicate offences;

(b) Each State Party shall include as predicate offences all serious crime as defined in article 2 of this Convention and the offences established in accordance with articles 5, 8 and 23 of this Convention. In the case of States Parties whose legislation sets out a list of specific predicate offences, they shall, at a minimum, include in such list a comprehensive range of offences associated with organized criminal groups;
(c) For the purposes of subparagraph (b), predicate offences shall include offences committed both within and outside the jurisdiction of the State Party in question. However, offences committed outside the jurisdiction of a State Party shall constitute predicate offences only when the relevant conduct is a criminal offence under the domestic law of the State where it is committed and would be a criminal offence under the domestic law of the State Party implementing or applying this article had it been committed there;
(d) Each State Party shall furnish copies of its laws that give effect to this article and of any subsequent changes to such laws or a description thereof to the Secretary-General of the UN;
(e) If required by fundamental principles of the domestic law of a State Party, it may be provided that the offences set forth in paragraph 1 of this article do not apply to the persons who committed the predicate offence;
(f) Knowledge, intent or purpose required as an element of an offence set forth in paragraph 1 of this article may be inferred from objective factual circumstances.

**Article 7: Measures to Combat Money-Laundering**

1. Each State Party:

(a) Shall institute a comprehensive domestic regulatory and supervisory regime for banks and non-bank financial institutions and, where appropriate, other bodies particularly susceptible to money-laundering, within its competence, in order to deter and detect all forms of money-laundering, which regime shall emphasize requirements for customer identification, record-keeping and the reporting of suspicious transactions;
(b) Shall, without prejudice to articles 18 and 27 of this Convention, ensure that administrative, regulatory, law enforcement and other authorities dedicated to combating money-laundering (including, where appropriate under domestic law, judicial authorities) have the ability to cooperate and exchange information at the national and international levels within the conditions prescribed by its domestic law and, to that end, shall consider the establishment of a financial intelligence unit to serve as a national centre for the collection, analysis and dissemination of information regarding potential money-laundering.

2. States Parties shall consider implementing feasible measures to detect and monitor the movement of cash and appropriate negotiable instruments across their borders, subject to safeguards to ensure proper use of information and without impeding in any way the movement of legitimate capital. Such measures may include a requirement that individuals and businesses report the cross-border transfer of substantial quantities of cash and appropriate negotiable instruments.
3. In establishing a domestic regulatory and supervisory regime under the terms of this article, and without prejudice to any other article of this Convention, States Parties are

called upon to use as a guideline the relevant initiatives of regional, interregional and multilateral organizations against money-laundering.

4. States Parties shall endeavour to develop and promote global, regional, subregional and bilateral cooperation among judicial, law enforcement and financial regulatory authorities in order to combat money-laundering.

**Article 8: Criminalization of Corruption**

1. Each State Party shall adopt such legislative and other measures as may be necessary to establish as criminal offences, when committed intentionally:

   (a) The promise, offering or giving to a public official, directly or indirectly, of an undue advantage, for the official himself or herself or another person or entity, in order that the official act or refrain from acting in the exercise of his or her official duties;
   (b) The solicitation or acceptance by a public official, directly or indirectly, of an undue advantage, for the official himself or herself or another person or entity, in order that the official act or refrain from acting in the exercise of his or her official duties.

2. Each State Party shall consider adopting such legislative and other measures as may be necessary to establish as criminal offences conduct referred to in paragraph 1 of this article involving a foreign public official or international civil servant. Likewise, each State Party shall consider establishing as criminal offences other forms of corruption.
3. Each State Party shall also adopt such measures as may be necessary to establish as a criminal offence participation as an accomplice in an offence established in accordance with this article.
4. For the purposes of paragraph 1 of this article and article 9 of this Convention, 'public official' shall mean a public official or a person who provides a public service as defined in the domestic law and as applied in the criminal law of the State Party in which the person in question performs that function.

**Article 9: Measures Against Corruption**

1. In addition to the measures set forth in article 8 of this Convention, each State Party shall, to the extent appropriate and consistent with its legal system, adopt legislative, administrative or other effective measures to promote integrity and to prevent, detect and punish the corruption of public officials.
2. Each State Party shall take measures to ensure effective action by its authorities in the prevention, detection and punishment of the corruption of public officials, including providing such authorities with adequate independence to deter the exertion of inappropriate influence on their actions.

**Article 10: Liability of Legal Persons**

1. Each State Party shall adopt such measures as may be necessary, consistent with its legal principles, to establish the liability of legal persons for participation in serious crimes involving an organized criminal group and for the offences established in accordance with articles 5, 6, 8 and 23 of this Convention.

2. Subject to the legal principles of the State Party, the liability of legal persons may be criminal, civil or administrative.
3. Such liability shall be without prejudice to the criminal liability of the natural persons who have committed the offences.
4. Each State Party shall, in particular, ensure that legal persons held liable in accordance with this article are subject to effective, proportionate and dissuasive criminal or non-criminal sanctions, including monetary sanctions.

**Article 18: Mutual Legal Assistance**

1. States Parties shall afford one another the widest measure of mutual legal assistance in investigations, prosecutions and judicial proceedings in relation to the offences covered by this Convention as provided for in article 3 and shall reciprocally extend to one another similar assistance where the requesting State Party has reasonable grounds to suspect that the offence referred to in article 3, paragraph 1 (a) or (b), is transnational in nature, including that victims, witnesses, proceeds, instrumentalities or evidence of such offences are located in the requested State Party and that the offence involves an organized criminal group.
3. Mutual legal assistance to be afforded in accordance with this article may be requested for any of the following purposes:

   (a) Taking evidence or statements from persons;
   (b) Effecting service of judicial documents;
   (c) Executing searches and seizures, and freezing;
   (d) Examining objects and sites;
   (e) Providing information, evidentiary items and expert evolutions;
   (f) Providing originals or certified copies of relevant documents and records, including government, bank, financial, corporate or business records;
   (g) Identifying or tracing proceeds of crime, property, instrumentalities or other things for evidentiary purposes;
   (h) Facilitating the voluntary appearance of persons in the requesting State Party;
   (i) Any other type of assistance that is not contrary to the domestic law of the requested State Party.

4. Without prejudice to domestic law, the competent authorities of a State Party may, without prior request, transmit information relating to criminal matters to a competent authority in another State Party where they believe that such information could assist the authority in undertaking or successfully concluding inquiries and criminal proceedings or could result in a request formulated by the latter State Party pursuant to this Convention.
5. The transmission of information pursuant to paragraph 4 of this article shall be without prejudice to inquiries and criminal proceedings in the State of the competent authorities providing the information. The competent authorities receiving the information shall comply with a request that said information remain confidential, even temporarily, or with restrictions on its use . . .
8. States Parties shall not decline to render mutual legal assistance pursuant to this article on the ground of bank secrecy.
22. States Parties may not refuse a request for mutual legal assistance on the sole ground that the offence is also considered to involve fiscal matters.

**Article 23: Criminalization of Obstruction of Justice**

Each State Party shall adopt such legislative and other measures as may be necessary to establish as criminal offences, when committed intentionally:

(a) The use of physical force, threats or intimidation or the promise, offering or giving of an undue advantage to induce false testimony or to interfere in the giving of testimony or the production of evidence in a proceeding in relation to the commission of offences covered by this Convention;
(b) The use of physical force, threats or intimidation to interfere with the exercise of official duties by a justice or law enforcement official in relation to the commission of offences covered by this Convention . . .

**Article 27: Law Enforcement Cooperation**

1. States Parties shall cooperate closely with one another, consistent with their respective domestic legal and administrative systems, to enhance the effectiveness of law enforcement action to combat the offences covered by this Convention. Each State Party shall, in particular, adopt effective measures:

    (b) To cooperate with other States Parties in conducting inquiries with respect to offences covered by this Convention concerning:

        (i) The identity, whereabouts and activities of persons suspected of involvement in such offences or the location of other persons concerned;
        (ii) The movement of proceeds of crime or property derived from the commission of such offences;
        (iii) The movement of property, equipment or other instrumentalities used or intended for use in the commission of such offences . . .

**Article 28: Collection, Exchange and Analysis of Information on the Nature of Organized Crime**

1. Each State Party shall consider analysing, in consultation with the scientific and academic communities, trends in organized crime in its territory, the circumstances in which organized crime operates, as well as the professional groups and technologies involved . . .

# 109. UN: International Convention for the Suppression of the Financing of Terrorism, 1999

**Commentary**: The Financing of Terrorism Convention (39 *ILM* 270 (2000), entry into force 2002) was prepared by an Ad Hoc Committee and a Working Group of the Sixth Committee: UN Doc A/C.6/54/L.2, Annex I. Governments have condemned all terrorist acts, methods and practices as criminal and unjustifiable, wherever and by whomever committed: UNGA Resolution 49/60 (1994) on the Declaration on Measures to Eliminate International Terrorism. UNGA Resolution 51/210 (1996), paragraph (3)(f), called upon governments to prevent the financing of terrorists and terrorist organisations both directly or indirectly through organisations claiming to have charitable, social or cultural goals or who are engaged in unlawful activities (such as illicit arms trafficking, drug dealing, racketeering or the exploitation of persons). The Resolution also called for regulatory measures to counteract financial movements suspected to be intended for terrorist purposes without impeding the freedom of legitimate capital movements. See further, Security Council Resolution 1373 (2001). In addition to the provisions extracted below, Article 8 envisages the identification, detection and freezing or seizure of funds. The Annex lists treaties with respect to unlawfully seizing aircraft, crimes against internationally protected persons, hostages, protecting nuclear material, unlawful acts against maritime navigation or fixed platforms located on the continental shelf and terrorist bombings.

**Article 1**

For the purposes of this Convention:

1. 'Funds' means assets of every kind, whether tangible or intangible, movable or immovable, however acquired, and legal documents or instruments in any form, including electronic or digital, evidencing title to, or interest in, such assets, including, but not limited to, bank credits, travellers cheques, bank cheques, money orders, shares, securities, bonds, drafts and letters of credit.
3. 'Proceeds' means any funds derived from or obtained, directly or indirectly, through the commission of an offence set forth in article 2.

**Article 2**

1. Any person commits an offence within the meaning of this Convention if that person by any means, directly or indirectly, unlawfully and wilfully, provides or collects funds

with the intention that they should be used or in the knowledge that they are to be used, in full or in part, in order to carry out:

(a) An act which constitutes an offence within the scope of and as defined in one of the treaties listed in the annex; or
(b) Any other act intended to cause death or serious bodily injury to a civilian, or to any other person not taking an active part in the hostilities in a situation of armed conflict, when the purpose of such act, by its nature or context, is to intimidate a population, or to compel a Government or an international organization to do or to abstain from doing any act.

2. (a) On depositing its instrument of ratification, acceptance, approval or accession, a State Party which is not a party to a treaty listed in the annex may declare that, in the application of this Convention to the State Party, the treaty shall be deemed not to be included in the annex referred to in paragraph 1, subparagraph (a). The declaration shall cease to have effect as soon as the treaty enters into force for the State Party, which shall notify the depositary of this fact;
(b) When a State Party ceases to be a party to a treaty listed in the annex, it may make a declaration as provided for in this article, with respect to that treaty.

3. For an act to constitute an offence set forth in paragraph 1, it shall not be necessary that the funds were actually used to carry out an offence referred to in paragraph 1, subparagraph (a) or (b).
4. Any person also commits an offence if that person attempts to commit an offence as set forth in paragraph 1 of this article.
5. Any person also commits an offence if that person:

(a) Participates as an accomplice in an offence as set forth in paragraph 1 or 4 of this article;
(b) Organizes or directs others to commit an offence as set forth in paragraph 1 or 4 of this article;
(c) Contributes to the commission of one or more offences as set forth in paragraph 1 or 4 of this article by a group of persons acting with a common purpose. Such contribution shall be intentional and shall either:

(i) Be made with the aim of furthering the criminal activity or criminal purpose of the group, where such activity or purpose involves the commission of an offence as set forth in paragraph 1 of this article; or
(ii) Be made in the knowledge of the intention of the group to commit an offence as set forth in paragraph 1 of this article.

**Article 5**

1. Each State Party, in accordance with its domestic legal principles, shall take the necessary measures to enable a legal entity located in its territory or organized under its laws to be held liable when a person responsible for the management or control of that legal entity has, in that capacity, committed an offence as set forth in article 2. Such liability may be criminal, civil or administrative.

2. Such liability is incurred without prejudice to the criminal liability of individuals who have committed the offences.
3. Each State Party shall ensure, in particular, that legal entities liable in accordance with paragraph 1 above are subject to effective, proportionate and dissuasive criminal, civil or administrative sanctions. Such sanctions may include monetary sanctions.

**Article 18**

1. States Parties shall cooperate in the prevention of the offences set forth in article 2 by taking all practicable measures, *inter alia*, by adapting their domestic legislation, if necessary, to prevent and counter preparations in their respective territories for the commission of those offences within or outside their territories, including:

   (a) Measures to prohibit in their territories illegal activities of persons and organizations that knowingly encourage, instigate, organize or engage in the commission of offences set forth in article 2;
   (b) Measures requiring financial institutions and other professions involved in financial transactions to utilize the most efficient measures available for the identification of their usual or occasional customers, as well as customers in whose interest accounts are opened, and to pay special attention to unusual or suspicious transactions and report transactions suspected of stemming from a criminal activity. For this purpose, States Parties shall consider:

      (i) Adopting regulations prohibiting the opening of accounts, the holders or beneficiaries of which are unidentified or unidentifiable, and measures to ensure that such institutions verify the identity of the real owners of such transactions;
      (ii) With respect to the identification of legal entities, requiring financial institutions, when necessary, to take measures to verify the legal existence and the structure of the customer by obtaining, either from a public register or from the customer or both, proof of incorporation, including information concerning the customer's name, legal form, address, directors and provisions regulating the power to bind the entity;
      (iii) Adopting regulations imposing on financial institutions the obligation to report promptly to the competent authorities all complex, unusual large transactions and unusual patterns of transactions, which have no apparent economic or obviously lawful purpose, without fear of assuming criminal or civil liability for breach of any restriction on disclosure of information if they report their suspicions in good faith;
      (iv) Requiring financial institutions to maintain, for at least five years, all necessary records on transactions, both domestic and international.

2. States Parties shall further cooperate in the prevention of offences set forth in article 2 by considering:

   (a) Measures for the supervision, including, for example, the licensing, of all money transmission agencies;
   (b) Feasible measures to detect or monitor the physical cross-border transportation of cash and bearer negotiable instruments, subject to strict safeguards to ensure

proper use of information and without impeding in any way the freedom of capital movements.

3. States Parties shall further cooperate in the prevention of the offences set forth in article 2 by exchanging accurate and verified information in accordance with their domestic law and coordinating administrative and other measures taken, as appropriate, to prevent the commission of offences set forth in article 2, in particular by:

(a) Establishing and maintaining channels of communication between their competent agencies and services to facilitate the secure and rapid exchange of information concerning all aspects of offences set forth in article 2;
(b) Cooperating with one another in conducting inquiries, with respect to the offences set forth in article 2, concerning:

(i) The identity, whereabouts and activities of persons in respect of whom reasonable suspicion exists that they are involved in such offences;
(ii) The movement of funds relating to the commission of such offences.

4. States Parties may exchange information through the International Criminal Police Organization (Interpol).

# PART X

# Corruption, Bribery and Extortion

# 110. UN: Convention against Corruption, 2003

**Commentary**: Several prominent instances of bribery between US corporations and foreign government officials occurred in the 1970s. This led to criminalising illicit payments under US law: Foreign Corrupt Practices Act 1977 (US) 17 *ILM* 214 (1978) & 28 *ILM* 455 (1989). Bilateral intergovernmental agreements facilitated information exchange with a view to prosecuting corporations: for example, Japan–US (1976), Agreement on Procedures for Mutual Assistance in Administration of Justice in the Lockheed Matter, 15 *ILM* 278 & 1010. Corruption also began to be addressed at the international level: UNGA Resolution 3514 (1975). An Ad hoc Intergovernmental Working Group within ECOSOC formulated a draft Convention: ECOSOC (1977), 'Report on the Problem of Corrupt Practices in International Commercial Transactions, Part A, Provisions relevant to the Elaboration of an International Agreement to Eliminate and Prevent Illicit Payments in whatever form, in connection with International Commercial Transactions by Transnational and Other Corporations, their Intermediaries and Others Involved', UN Doc E/6006; ECOSOC Resolution 2041 (1976) on Corrupt Practices and Illicit Payments in International Commercial Transactions. See further, UNCTC (1991), Report on efforts by the UN to address the issue of corrupt practices, UN Doc E/1991/31/Add.1. The UNGA called upon companies and financial institutions to implement its resolutions, observe national law and pursue ethical practices: UNGA Resolution 51/59 (1996) on Action Against Corruption, paragraph 10 & International Code of Conduct for Public Officials; UNGA Resolution 51/191 (1996), paragraph 6 and UN Declaration against Corruption and Bribery in International Commercial Transactions; UNGA Resolution 51/210 (1997) paragraphs 3(d) & (f).

Considering an effective international legal instrument to be desirable, the UNGA established an ad hoc negotiating committee: UNGA Resolution 55/61 (2000). The Convention extracted below (UN Doc A/58/422 (2003), not yet in force) is the final outcome of that process. Article 10 contemplates measures enhancing transparency in public administration and Article 13 the active participation of civil society, NGOs and community-based organisations in addressing corruption. In addition to the offences extracted below, governments undertook to establish as criminal offences embezzlement, misappropriation or other property diversions by public officials (Article 17), trading in influence (18), abusing functions or positions (19), illicit enrichment (20), laundering criminal proceeds (23), concealing or retaining property (24) and obstructing justice (25). Governments additionally undertook to establish as criminal offences participation in any capacity (accomplice, assistant or instigator), attempt and preparation (Article 27). Knowledge, intent or purpose can be inferred from objective factual circumstances (Article 28). Governments must also establish a long statute of limitations period (Article 29). Article 42 identifies the grounds for exercising jurisdiction. Under Chapter V (Asset Recovery), governments are to permit other governments to initiate civil proceedings establishing title to or ownership of property (Article 53). Regard is given to the rights of bona fide third parties with respect to intergovernmental cooperation for the purposes of confiscation (Article 55)

See further, UN Secretary-General (2001), 'Report on the analysis of existing international instruments and recommendations against corruption', UN Doc E/CN.15/2001/3; Ad Hoc Committee for the Negotiation of a Convention against Corruption (2003), 'Report on the work of its first to seventh sessions', UN Doc A/58/422; Report of the High-level Political Conference for the Purpose of Signing the UN Convention against Corruption, UN Doc A/CONF.205/2 (2003). The Convention is administered by the UN Office for Drug Control and Crime: www.unodc.org. Relevant regional instruments include OAS (1996), Inter-American Convention against Corruption, UN Doc E/1996/99; EU (1997), Convention on the Fight against Corruption involving Officials of the European Communities or Officials of Member States of the European Union (1997) *OJEC* C195; Council of Europe (1999), Criminal and Civil Law Conventions on Corruption *ETS* Nos 173 & 174; African Union (2003), Convention on Preventing and Combating Corruption, Assembly Decision AY/Dec.22 (II). For national governmental initiatives, see the 2002 Extractive Industries Transparency Initiative (EITI, www.dfid.gov.uk/News/News/files/eiti_guide_a.htm) introduced by the UK government at the 2002 WSSD and seeking to enhance financial transparency between companies within the extractive industry and host governments.

## Chapter I: General Provisions

*Article 1: Statement of Purpose*
The purposes of this Convention are:

(a) To promote and strengthen measures to prevent and combat corruption more efficiently and effectively;
(b) To promote, facilitate and support international cooperation and technical assistance in the prevention of and fight against corruption, including in asset recovery;
(c) To promote integrity, accountability and proper management of public affairs and public property.

*Article 2: Use of Terms*
For the purposes of this Convention:

(a) 'Public official' shall mean: (i) any person holding a legislative, executive, administrative or judicial office of a State Party, whether appointed or elected, whether permanent or temporary, whether paid or unpaid, irrespective of that person's seniority; (ii) any other person who performs a public function, including for a public agency or public enterprise, or provides a public service, as defined in the domestic law of the State Party and as applied in the pertinent area of law of that State Party; (iii) any other person defined as a 'public official' in the domestic law of a State Party. However, for the purpose of some specific measures contained in chapter II of this Convention, 'public official' may mean any person who performs a public function or provides a public service as defined in the domestic law of the State Party and as applied in the pertinent area of law of that State Party;

(b) 'Foreign public official' shall mean any person holding a legislative, executive, administrative or judicial office of a foreign country, whether appointed or elected; and any person exercising a public function for a foreign country, including for a public agency or public enterprise;
(c) 'Official of a public international organization' shall mean an international civil servant or any person who is authorized by such an organization to act on behalf of that organization;
(d) 'Property' shall mean assets of every kind, whether corporeal or incorporeal, movable or immovable, tangible or intangible, and legal documents or instruments evidencing title to or interest in such assets;
(e) 'Proceeds of crime' shall mean any property derived from or obtained, directly or indirectly, through the commission of an offence;
(f) 'Freezing' or 'seizure' shall mean temporarily prohibiting the transfer, conversion, disposition or movement of property or temporarily assuming custody or control of property on the basis of an order issued by a court or other competent authority;
(g) 'Confiscation', which includes forfeiture where applicable, shall mean the permanent deprivation of property by order of a court or other competent authority;
(h) 'Predicate offence' shall mean any offence as a result of which proceeds have been generated that may become the subject of an offence as defined in article 23 of this Convention;
(i) 'Controlled delivery' shall mean the technique of allowing illicit or suspect consignments to pass out of, through or into the territory of one or more States, with the knowledge and under the supervision of their competent authorities, with a view to the investigation of an offence and the identification of persons involved in the commission of the offence.

*Article 3: Scope of Application*

1. This Convention shall apply, in accordance with its terms, to the prevention, investigation and prosecution of corruption and to the freezing, seizure, confiscation and return of the proceeds of offences established in accordance with this Convention.
2. For the purposes of implementing this Convention, it shall not be necessary, except as otherwise stated herein, for the offences set forth in it to result in damage or harm to state property.

## Chapter II: Preventive Measures

*Article 7: Public Sector*

3. Each State Party shall also consider taking appropriate legislative and administrative measures, consistent with the objectives of this Convention and in accordance with the fundamental principles of its domestic law, to enhance transparency in the funding of candidatures for elected public office and, where applicable, the funding of political parties.

*Article 8: Codes of Conduct for Public Officials*

5. Each State Party shall endeavour, where appropriate and in accordance with the fundamental principles of its domestic law, to establish measures and systems requiring public officials to make declarations to appropriate authorities regarding, *inter alia*, their

outside activities, employment, investments, assets and substantial gifts or benefits from which a conflict of interest may result with respect to their functions as public officials.

*Article 9: Public Procurement and Management of Public Finances*

1. Each State Party shall, in accordance with the fundamental principles of its legal system, take the necessary steps to establish appropriate systems of procurement, based on transparency, competition and objective criteria in decision-making, that are effective, *inter alia*, in preventing corruption. Such systems, which may take into account appropriate threshold values in their application, shall address, *inter alia*:

   (a) The public distribution of information relating to procurement procedures and contracts, including information on invitations to tender and relevant or pertinent information on the award of contracts, allowing potential tenderers sufficient time to prepare and submit their tenders;
   (b) The establishment, in advance, of conditions for participation, including selection and award criteria and tendering rules, and their publication;
   (c) The use of objective and predetermined criteria for public procurement decisions, in order to facilitate the subsequent verification of the correct application of the rules or procedures;
   (d) An effective system of domestic review, including an effective system of appeal, to ensure legal recourse and remedies in the event that the rules or procedures established pursuant to this paragraph are not followed;
   (e) Where appropriate, measures to regulate matters regarding personnel responsible for procurement, such as declaration of interest in particular public procurements, screening procedures and training requirements. . . .

*Article 12: Private Sector*

1. Each State Party shall take measures, in accordance with the fundamental principles of its domestic law, to prevent corruption involving the private sector, enhance accounting and auditing standards in the private sector and, where appropriate, provide effective, proportionate and dissuasive civil, administrative or criminal penalties for failure to comply with such measures.
2. Measures to achieve these ends may include, *inter alia*:

   (a) Promoting cooperation between law enforcement agencies and relevant private entities;
   (b) Promoting the development of standards and procedures designed to safeguard the integrity of relevant private entities, including codes of conduct for the correct, honourable and proper performance of the activities of business and all relevant prófessions and the prevention of conflicts of interest, and for the promotion of the use of good commercial practices among businesses and in the contractual relations of businesses with the State;
   (c) Promoting transparency among private entities, including, where appropriate, measures regarding the identity of legal and natural persons involved in the establishment and management of corporate entities;
   (d) Preventing the misuse of procedures regulating private entities, including procedures regarding subsidies and licences granted by public authorities for commercial activities;

(e) Preventing conflicts of interest by imposing restrictions, as appropriate and for a reasonable period of time, on the professional activities of former public officials or on the employment of public officials by the private sector after their resignation or retirement, where such activities or employment relate directly to the functions held or supervised by those public officials during their tenure;
(f) Ensuring that private enterprises, taking into account their structure and size, have sufficient internal auditing controls to assist in preventing and detecting acts of corruption and that the accounts and required financial statements of such private enterprises are subject to appropriate auditing and certification procedures.

3. In order to prevent corruption, each State Party shall take such measures as may be necessary, in accordance with its domestic laws and regulations regarding the maintenance of books and records, financial statement disclosures and accounting and auditing standards, to prohibit the following acts carried out for the purpose of committing any of the offences established in accordance with this Convention:

(a) The establishment of off-the-books accounts;
(b) The making of off-the-books or inadequately identified transactions;
(c) The recording of non-existent expenditure;
(d) The entry of liabilities with incorrect identification of their objects;
(e) The use of false documents; and
(f) The intentional destruction of bookkeeping documents earlier than foreseen by the law.

4. Each State Party shall disallow the tax deductibility of expenses that constitute bribes, the latter being one of the constituent elements of the offences established in accordance with articles 15 and 16 of this Convention and, where appropriate, other expenses incurred in furtherance of corrupt conduct.

*Article 14: Measures to Prevent Money-Laundering*
1. Each State Party shall:

(a) Institute a comprehensive domestic regulatory and supervisory regime for banks and non-bank financial institutions, including natural or legal persons that provide formal or informal services for the transmission of money or value and, where appropriate, other bodies particularly susceptible to money-laundering, within its competence, in order to deter and detect all forms of money-laundering, which regime shall emphasize requirements for customer and, where appropriate, beneficial owner identification, record-keeping and the reporting of suspicious transactions;
(b) Without prejudice to article 46 of this Convention, ensure that administrative, regulatory, law enforcement and other authorities dedicated to combating money laundering (including, where appropriate under domestic law, judicial authorities) have the ability to cooperate and exchange information at the national and international levels within the conditions prescribed by its domestic law and, to that end, shall consider the establishment of a financial intelligence unit to serve as a national centre for the collection, analysis and dissemination of information regarding potential money laundering.

2. States Parties shall consider implementing feasible measures to detect and monitor the movement of cash and appropriate negotiable instruments across their borders, subject to safeguards to ensure proper use of information and without impeding in any way the movement of legitimate capital. Such measures may include a requirement that individuals and businesses report the cross-border transfer of substantial quantities of cash and appropriate negotiable instruments.
3. States Parties shall consider implementing appropriate and feasible measures to require financial institutions, including money remitters:

   (a) To include on forms for the electronic transfer of funds and related messages accurate and meaningful information on the originator;
   (b) To maintain such information throughout the payment chain; and
   (c) To apply enhanced scrutiny to transfers of funds that do not contain complete information on the originator.

4. In establishing a domestic regulatory and supervisory regime under the terms of this article, and without prejudice to any other article of this Convention, States Parties are called upon to use as a guideline the relevant initiatives of regional, interregional and multilateral organizations against money-laundering.
5. States Parties shall endeavour to develop and promote global, regional, subregional and bilateral cooperation among judicial, law enforcement and financial regulatory authorities in order to combat money-laundering.

## Chapter III: Criminalization and Law Enforcement

*Article 15: Bribery of National Public Officials*

Each State Party shall adopt such legislative and other measures as may be necessary to establish as criminal offences, when committed intentionally:

(a) The promise, offering or giving, to a public official, directly or indirectly, of an undue advantage, for the official himself or herself or another person or entity, in order that the official act or refrain from acting in the exercise of his or her official duties;
(b) The solicitation or acceptance by a public official, directly or indirectly, of an undue advantage, for the official himself or herself or another person or entity, in order that the official act or refrain from acting in the exercise of his or her official duties.

*Article 16: Bribery of Foreign Public Officials and Officials of Public International Organizations*

1. Each State Party shall adopt such legislative and other measures as may be necessary to establish as a criminal offence, when committed intentionally, the promise, offering or giving to a foreign public official or an official of a public international organization, directly or indirectly, of an undue advantage, for the official himself or herself or another person or entity, in order that the official act or refrain from acting in the exercise of his or her official duties, in order to obtain or retain business or other undue advantage in relation to the conduct of international business.
2. Each State Party shall consider adopting such legislative and other measures as may be necessary to establish as a criminal offence, when committed intentionally, the

solicitation or acceptance by a foreign public official or an official of a public international organization, directly or indirectly, of an undue advantage, for the official himself or herself or another person or entity, in order that the official act or refrain from acting in the exercise of his or her official duties.

*Article 21: Bribery in the Private Sector*
Each State Party shall consider adopting such legislative and other measures as may be necessary to establish as criminal offences, when committed intentionally in the course of economic, financial or commercial activities:

(a) The promise, offering or giving, directly or indirectly, of an undue advantage to any person who directs or works, in any capacity, for a private sector entity, for the person himself or herself or for another person, in order that he or she, in breach of his or her duties, act or refrain from acting;
(b) The solicitation or acceptance, directly or indirectly, of an undue advantage by any person who directs or works, in any capacity, for a private sector entity, for the person himself or herself or for another person, in order that he or she, in breach of his or her duties, act or refrain from acting.

*Article 22: Embezzlement of Property in the Private Sector*
Each State Party shall consider adopting such legislative and other measures as may be necessary to establish as a criminal offence, when committed intentionally in the course of economic, financial or commercial activities, embezzlement by a person who directs or works, in any capacity, in a private sector entity of any property, private funds or securities or any other thing of value entrusted to him or her by virtue of his or her position.

*Article 26: Liability of Legal Persons*
1. Each State Party shall adopt such measures as may be necessary, consistent with its legal principles, to establish the liability of legal persons for participation in the offences established in accordance with this Convention.
2. Subject to the legal principles of the State Party, the liability of legal persons may be criminal, civil or administrative.
3. Such liability shall be without prejudice to the criminal liability of the natural persons who have committed the offences.
4. Each State Party shall, in particular, ensure that legal persons held liable in accordance with this article are subject to effective, proportionate and dissuasive criminal or non-criminal sanctions, including monetary sanctions.

*Article 31: Freezing, Seizure and Confiscation*
1. Each State Party shall take, to the greatest extent possible within its domestic legal system, such measures as may be necessary to enable confiscation of:

   (a) Proceeds of crime derived from offences established in accordance with this Convention or property the value of which corresponds to that of such proceeds;
   (b) Property, equipment or other instrumentalities used in or destined for use in offences established in accordance with this Convention.

5. If such proceeds of crime have been intermingled with property acquired from legitimate sources, such property shall, without prejudice to any powers relating to freezing or seizure, be liable to confiscation up to the assessed value of the intermingled proceeds.
6. Income or other benefits derived from such proceeds of crime, from property into which such proceeds of crime have been transformed or converted or from property with which such proceeds of crime have been intermingled shall also be liable to the measures referred to in this article, in the same manner and to the same extent as proceeds of crime.
7. For the purpose of this article and article 55 of this Convention, each State Party shall empower its courts or other competent authorities to order that bank, financial or commercial records be made available or seized. A State Party shall not decline to act under the provisions of this paragraph on the ground of bank secrecy.

*Article 34: Consequences of Acts of Corruption*
With due regard to the rights of third parties acquired in good faith, each State Party shall take measures, in accordance with the fundamental principles of its domestic law, to address consequences of corruption. In this context, States Parties may consider corruption a relevant factor in legal proceedings to annul or rescind a contract, withdraw a concession or other similar instrument or take any other remedial action.

*Article 35: Compensation for Damage*
Each State Party shall take such measures as may be necessary, in accordance with principles of its domestic law, to ensure that entities or persons who have suffered damage as a result of an act of corruption have the right to initiate legal proceedings against those responsible for that damage in order to obtain compensation.

*Article 39: Cooperation between National Authorities and the Private Sector*
1. Each State Party shall take such measures as may be necessary to encourage, in accordance with its domestic law, cooperation between national investigating and prosecuting authorities and entities of the private sector, in particular financial institutions, relating to matters involving the commission of offences established in accordance with this Convention . . .

*Article 40: Bank Secrecy*
Each State Party shall ensure that, in the case of domestic criminal investigations of offences established in accordance with this Convention, there are appropriate mechanisms available within its domestic legal system to overcome obstacles that may arise out of the application of bank secrecy laws.

*Article 46: Mutual Legal Assistance*
2. Mutual legal assistance shall be afforded to the fullest extent possible under relevant laws, treaties, agreements and arrangements of the requested State Party with respect to investigations, prosecutions and judicial proceedings in relation to the offences for which a legal person may be held liable in accordance with article 26 of this Convention in the requesting State Party.
3. Mutual legal assistance to be afforded in accordance with this article may be requested for any of the following purposes:

(f) Providing originals or certified copies of relevant documents and records, including government, bank, financial, corporate or business records . . .

4. Without prejudice to domestic law, the competent authorities of a State Party may, without prior request, transmit information relating to criminal matters to a competent authority in another State Party where they believe that such information could assist the authority in undertaking or successfully concluding inquiries and criminal proceedings or could result in a request formulated by the latter State Party pursuant to this Convention.
5. The transmission of information pursuant to paragraph 4 of this article shall be without prejudice to inquiries and criminal proceedings in the State of the competent authorities providing the information. The competent authorities receiving the information shall comply with a request that said information remain confidential, even temporarily, or with restrictions on its use. However, this shall not prevent the receiving State Party from disclosing in its proceedings information that is exculpatory to an accused person

. . .

8. States Parties shall not decline to render mutual legal assistance pursuant to this article on the ground of bank secrecy.

## Chapter V: Asset Recovery

*Article 52: Prevention and Detection of Transfers of Proceeds of Crime*

1. Without prejudice to article 14 of this Convention, each State Party shall take such measures as may be necessary, in accordance with its domestic law, to require financial institutions within its jurisdiction to verify the identity of customers, to take reasonable steps to determine the identity of beneficial owners of funds deposited into high-value accounts and to conduct enhanced scrutiny of accounts sought or maintained by or on behalf of individuals who are, or have been, entrusted with prominent public functions and their family members and close associates. Such enhanced scrutiny shall be reasonably designed to detect suspicious transactions for the purpose of reporting to competent authorities and should not be so construed as to discourage or prohibit financial institutions from doing business with any legitimate customer.
2. In order to facilitate implementation of the measures provided for in paragraph 1 of this article, each State Party, in accordance with its domestic law and inspired by relevant initiatives of regional, interregional and multilateral organizations against money-laundering, shall:

(a) Issue advisories regarding the types of natural or legal person to whose accounts financial institutions within its jurisdiction will be expected to apply enhanced scrutiny, the types of accounts and transactions to which to pay particular attention and appropriate account-opening, maintenance and record-keeping measures to take concerning such accounts; and

(b) Where appropriate, notify financial institutions within its jurisdiction, at the request of another State Party or on its own initiative, of the identity of particular natural or legal persons to whose accounts such institutions will be expected to apply enhanced scrutiny, in addition to those whom the financial institutions may otherwise identify.

3. In the context of paragraph 2(a) of this article, each State Party shall implement measures to ensure that its financial institutions maintain adequate records, over an appropriate period of time, of accounts and transactions involving the persons mentioned in paragraph 1 of this article, which should, as a minimum, contain information relating to the identity of the customer as well as, as far as possible, of the beneficial owner.
4. With the aim of preventing and detecting transfers of proceeds of offences established in accordance with this Convention, each State Party shall implement appropriate and effective measures to prevent, with the help of its regulatory and oversight bodies, the establishment of banks that have no physical presence and that are not affiliated with a regulated financial group. Moreover, States Parties may consider requiring their financial institutions to refuse to enter into or continue a correspondent banking relationship with such institutions and to guard against establishing relations with foreign financial institutions that permit their accounts to be used by banks that have no physical presence and that are not affiliated with a regulated financial group.

*Article 55: International Cooperation for Purposes of Confiscation*

1. A State Party that has received a request from another State Party having jurisdiction over an offence established in accordance with this Convention for confiscation of proceeds of crime, property, equipment or other instrumentalities referred to in article 31, paragraph 1, of this Convention situated in its territory shall, to the greatest extend possible within its domestic legal system:

   (a) Submit the request to its competent authorities for the purpose of obtaining an order of confiscation and, if such an order is granted, give effect to it; or
   (b) Submit to its competent authorities, with a view to giving effect to it to the extent requested, an order of confiscation issued by a court in the territory of the requesting State Party in accordance with articles 31, paragraph 1, and 54, paragraph 1 (a), of this Convention insofar as it relates to proceeds of crime, property, equipment or other instrumentalities referred to in article 31, paragraph 1, situated in the territory of the requested State Party.

9. The provision of this article shall not be construed as prejudicing the rights of bona fide third parties.

*Article 57: Return and Disposal of Assets*

1. Property confiscated by a State Party pursuant to article 31 or 55 of this Convention shall be disposed of, including by return to its prior legitimate owners, pursuant to paragraph 3 of this article, by that State Party in accordance with the provisions of this Convention and its domestic law.
2. Each State Party shall adopt such legislative and other measures, in accordance with the fundamental principles of its domestic law, as may be necessary to enable its competent authorities to return confiscated property, when acting on the request made by another State Party, in accordance with this Convention, taking into account the rights of bona fide third parties.
3. In accordance with articles 46 and 55 of this Convention and paragraphs 1 and 2 of this article, the requested State Party shall:

(c) In all other cases, give priority consideration to returning confiscated property to the requesting State Party, returning such property to its prior legitimate owners or compensating the victims of the crime.

## Chapter VI: Technical Assistance and Information Exchange

*Article 60: Training and Technical Assistance*

1. Each State Party shall, to the extent necessary, initiate, develop or improve specific training programmes for its personnel responsible for preventing and combating corruption. Such training programmes could deal, *inter alia*, with the following areas:

(d) Evaluation and strengthening of institutions, public service management and the management of public finances, including public procurement, and the private sector . . .

# 111. OECD: Convention on Combating Bribery of Foreign Public Officials in International Business Transactions, 1997

**Commentary**: The OECD Bribery Convention (OECD Doc DAFFE/IME/BR(97)20 (1997), entry into force 1999, www.oecd.org) was formulated by the Working Group on Bribery in International Business Transactions of the Committee on International Investment and Multinational Enterprises. It addresses 'active bribery', that is, offences are committed by individuals who promise or provide bribes as contrasted with 'passive bribery' where offences are committed by officials who receive them. The OECD Convention also focuses exclusively on the bribery of public officials and not corruption within the private sector. Article 4 provides for the territoriality and nationality bases of jurisdiction and under Article 5, enforcement 'shall not be influenced by considerations of national economic interest, the potential effect upon relations with another State or the identity of the natural or legal persons involved'. Article 6 envisages an adequate statute of limitations period and Article 7 provides for money laundering. Article 9 contemplates mutual legal assistance and extradition appears under Article 10. Under Article 12, responsibility for monitoring and follow-up rests with the OECD Working Group on Bribery in International Business Transactions. The Convention text is accompanied by a useful explanatory commentary (omitted from the extracts below) to which reference should be made.

The OECD Revised Recommendation of the Council on Combating Bribery in International Business Transactions (C(97)123/FINAL, adopted 23 May 1997), contains provisions with respect to criminalising the bribery of foreign public officials, tax deductibility, accounting requirements, public procurement, institutional arrangements and relations with intergovernmental and non-governmental organisations. The Annex thereto specifies agreed common elements for criminal legislation. The Recommendation of the Council on the Tax Deductibility of Bribes to Foreign Public Officials (C(96)27/FINAL, adopted 11 April 1996) recommends 'that those Member countries which do not disallow the deductibility of bribes to foreign public officials re-examine such treatment with the intention of denying this deductibility' (paragraph 1). See also, OECD (2000), *Bribery and Codes of Corporate Conduct: An Analysis*, Paris.

**Article 1: The Offence of Bribery of Foreign Public Officials**

1. Each Party shall take such measures as may be necessary to establish that it is a criminal offence under its law for any person intentionally to offer, promise or give any undue pecuniary or other advantage, whether directly or through intermediaries, to a foreign public official, for that official or for a third party, in order that the official act or refrain

from acting in relation to the performance of official duties, in order to obtain or retain business or other improper advantage in the conduct of international business.

2. Each Party shall take any measures necessary to establish that complicity in, including incitement, aiding and abetting, or authorisation of an act of bribery of a foreign public official shall be a criminal offence. Attempt and conspiracy to bribe a foreign public official shall be criminal offences to the same extent as attempt and conspiracy to bribe a public official of that Party.
3. The offences set out in paragraphs 1 and 2 above are hereinafter referred to as 'bribery of a foreign public official'.
4. For the purpose of this Convention:

   a. 'foreign public official' means any person holding a legislative, administrative or judicial office of a foreign country, whether appointed or elected; any person exercising a public function for a foreign country, including for a public agency or public enterprise; and any official or agent of a public international organisation;
   b. 'foreign country' includes all levels and subdivisions of government, from national to local;
   c. 'act or refrain from acting in relation to the performance of official duties' includes any use of the public official's position, whether or not within the official's authorised competence.

**Article 2: Responsibility of Legal Persons**

Each Party shall take such measures as may be necessary, in accordance with its legal principles, to establish the liability of legal persons for the bribery of a foreign public official.

**Article 3: Sanctions**

1. The bribery of a foreign public official shall be punishable by effective, proportionate and dissuasive criminal penalties. The range of penalties shall be comparable to that applicable to the bribery of the Party's own public officials and shall, in the case of natural persons, include deprivation of liberty sufficient to enable effective mutual legal assistance and extradition.
2. In the event that, under the legal system of a Party, criminal responsibility is not applicable to legal persons, that Party shall ensure that legal persons shall be subject to effective, proportionate and dissuasive non-criminal sanctions, including monetary sanctions, for bribery of foreign public officials.
3. Each Party shall take such measures as may be necessary to provide that the bribe and the proceeds of the bribery of a foreign public official, or property the value of which corresponds to that of such proceeds, are subject to seizure and confiscation or that monetary sanctions of comparable effect are applicable.
4. Each Party shall consider the imposition of additional civil or administrative sanctions upon a person subject to sanctions for the bribery of a foreign public official.

**Article 8: Accounting**

1. In order to combat bribery of foreign public officials effectively, each Party shall take such measures as may be necessary, within the framework of its laws and regulations

regarding the maintenance of books and records, financial statement disclosures, and accounting and auditing standards, to prohibit the establishment of off-the-books accounts, the making of off-the books or inadequately identified transactions, the recording of non-existent expenditures, the entry of liabilities with incorrect identification of their object, as well as the use of false documents, by companies subject to those laws and regulations, for the purpose of bribing foreign public officials or of hiding such bribery.

2. Each Party shall provide effective, proportionate and dissuasive civil, administrative or criminal penalties for such omissions and falsifications in respect of the books, records, accounts and financial statements of such companies.

# 112. International Chamber of Commerce: Rules of Conduct on Extortion and Bribery in International Business Transactions, 1999

**Commentary**: The ICC has long called for stringent local regulation supported by a multilateral treaty: ICC Commission on Ethical Practices (1977), 'Extortion and Bribery in Business Transactions', Report adopted by the 131st Session of the ICC Council, Paris: ICC Pub No 135, Pt 2, Recommendations to Governments. First formulated in 1978, the ICC Rules of Conduct envisage complementary and mutually supportive action by governments, intergovernmental organisations and the business community to enhance transparency. In 1994 the ICC reviewed its 1977 Report, with the Rules subsequently revised during 1996 (35 *ILM* 1306).

The Foreword to the 1999 edition observed that extortion and bribery can undermine democratic governments and market economies as well as hinder trade liberalisation through unfair competition: www.iccwbo.org/home/statements_rules/rules/1999/briberydoc99.asp. The 1999 Rules are more stringent than the 1977 version: the latter prohibited extortion and bribery only when obtaining or retaining business, whereas the 1999 version prohibits these activities for any purpose. Hence extortion and bribery in judicial or legislative proceedings, tax matters, environmental and other regulatory cases are now covered. Although major responsibility for implementation rests with governments, the international business community is also committed to voluntarily addressing these issues. Governments are urged to regulate and publicly record political contributions and companies are encouraged to implement enforcement mechanisms for individual codes of conduct. Consistent with the roles and responsibilities of an NGO, the principal purpose of the ICC Standing Committee (envisaged in Part III) is to stimulate self-regulatory action rather than act as an investigatory Panel as originally envisaged in 1977. The Preface to the 1999 edition also notes that greater attention should be devoted to the demand side of corruption (that is, extortion by foreign public officials) and bribery within the private sector. The ICC has twice (1996 and 1999) recommended that the WTO assume an active role. See further, ICC (1999), 'Fighting Corruption: A Corporate Practices Manual', Paris, ICC Pub No 652, which accompanies the Rules of Conduct and specifies best commercial practice within this field. Note that the ICC Rules are undergoing revision during 2005.

For comparable private initiatives, see World Economic Forum/Basel Institute on Governance/Transparency International (2004), 'Business Principles for Countering Bribery in the Engineering and Construction Industry'; International Federation of Consulting Engineers (2001), 'Guidelines for Business Integrity Management in the Consulting Industry' (www.fidic.org). See also from the Wolfsberg Group of 12 major private banks (www.wolfsberg-principles.com/index.html) the Anti-Money Laundering (AML) Principles for Correspondent Banking (2002), the AML Principles on Private

Banking (2002), the Statement on the Suppression of the Financing of Terrorism (2002) and the Statement on Monitoring, Screening and Searching (2003). A corporate consensus is emerging on defining appropriate business conduct when addressing corruption: The Conference Board (1999), 'Global Corporate Ethics Practices: A Developing Consensus', Report No 1243-99-RR, Washington, DC. For example, independent monitoring or auditing systems and enhanced reporting have been identified as appropriate practices: Caux Roundtable (2000), 'Anti-Corruption Measures', Caux Roundtable Global Dialogue, Singapore. NGOs are also working to enhance transparency in public procurement: for example, Transparency International (1996), *The TI Best Practice Documentation Source Book*; Transparency International/Social Accountability International (2002), 'Business Principles for Countering Bribery'.

## Part I: Recommendations to Governments and International Organisations

*Recommendations for International Cooperation*

Basic criminal statutes of virtually all countries clearly prohibit extortion and bribery. In the interest of developing consistent standards of criminal legislation in this field, each government should review its statutes to ensure that they effectively prohibit, in conformity with its jurisdictional and other basic legal principles, all aspects of both the giving and the taking of bribes including promises and solicitation of bribes. Where no such legislation exists, the governments concerned should introduce it; in those countries where extortion and bribery are already clearly prohibited, the relevant legislation should be perfected.

Each government should take concrete and meaningful steps to enforce vigorously its legislation in this area. ICC also notes with approval that the OECD has urged governments to re-examine their legislation against extortion and bribery; action relating to the tax deductibility of bribes is of particular urgency. The WTO should involve itself with these issues to support the OECD in the implementation of its Convention and Recommendation.

*National Measures*

In order to deal with the problem of extortion and bribery, governments should, in conformity with their jurisdictional and other basic legal principles, take the following measures, if they have not already done so.

*Preventive Measures*

I. DISCLOSURE PROCEDURES

For the sake of transparency, procedures should be established providing for periodic reports to an authorized government body of measures taken to supervise government officials involved directly or indirectly in commercial transactions. Such reports should be open to public scrutiny. For enterprises engaged in transactions with any government or with any enterprise owned or controlled by government, disclosure procedures should provide for access, upon specific request, by the appropriate government authorities to information as to agents dealing directly with public bodies or officials in connection with any particular transaction, and as to the payments to which such agents are entitled. Governments should ensure the confidentiality of any such information received from enterprises and safeguard the trade secrets incorporated therein.

II. ECONOMIC REGULATIONS

When laying down any economic regulations or legislation, governments should, as far as possible, minimize the use of systems under which the carrying out of business requires the issuance of individual authorizations, permits, etc. Experience shows that such systems offer scope for extortion and bribery. This is because decisions involving the issue of permits or authorizations are frequently taken in ways which make it almost impossible to ensure effective control and supervision. Where individual permits and authorizations remain in place, governments should take appropriate measures to prevent their abuse.

III. TRANSACTIONS WITH GOVERNMENTS AND INTERNATIONAL ORGANIZATIONS

Such transactions should be subject to special safeguards to minimize the opportunities for their being influenced by extortion and bribery. The system for awarding government contracts might include disclosure, to an appropriate government entity independent of the one directly concerned in the transaction, as well as increased public disclosure, whenever feasible, of the criteria and conclusions upon which the award is based. ICC supports the growing practice of making government contracts dependent on undertakings to refrain from bribery, and recommends that such contracts should include appropriate provisions to ensure compliance with international, national or enterprise codes against extortion and bribery.

IV. POLITICAL CONTRIBUTIONS

Undisclosed political contributions can be a source of abuse. Governments should regulate the conditions under which political contributions can be made. Where payments by enterprises to political parties, political committees or individual politicians are permitted by the applicable legislation, governments should enact legislation which ensures that such payments are publicly recorded by the payors and accounted for by the recipients.

*Enforcement Measures*

Governments, in conformity with their jurisdictional and other basic legal principles, should ensure:

(i) that adequate mechanisms exist for surveillance and investigation, and
(ii) that those who offer, demand, solicit or receive bribes in violation of their laws are subject to prosecution with appropriate penalties.

Governments should periodically publish statistical or other information in respect of such prosecutions.

*Auditing*

Governments, if they have not already done so, should enact appropriate legislation providing for auditing by independent professional auditors of the accounts of economically significant enterprises.

*International Cooperation and Judicial Assistance*

IMPLEMENTATION OF THE OECD CONVENTION AND RECOMMENDATION

ICC believes that the OECD Convention and Recommendation on Bribery in International Business Transactions provide a useful framework for government action. All governments, including non-OECD governments, should promptly take action to adhere to the Convention and implement the steps set forth in the Recommendation.

*Cooperation in Law Enforcement*
Governments should agree, under appropriate provisions for confidentiality, and in conformity with the OECD Convention, to exchange through law enforcement agencies relevant and material information for the purpose of criminal investigation and prosecution of cases of extortion and bribery. They should also continue to cooperate bilaterally on matters involving extortion and bribery, on the basis of treaties providing for assistance in judicial and penal prosecution matters.

*Role of International Financial Institutions*
International financial institutions, e.g., the World Bank, the European Bank for Reconstruction and Development, should aim to make a significant contribution to the reduction of extortion and bribery in international business transactions. They should take all reasonable steps to ensure that corrupt practices do not occur in connection with projects which they are financing. Similarly, in negotiating cooperation agreements with non-member countries, whether countries with economies in transition or developing nations, the governing or coordinating bodies of the European Union, NAFTA, ASEAN and other regional institutions, should seek to satisfy themselves that appropriate legislation and administrative machinery to combat extortion and bribery exists in the countries concerned.

## Part II: Rules of Conduct to Combat Extortion and Bribery

*Introduction*
These Rules of Conduct are intended as a method of self-regulation by international business, and they should also be supported by governments. Their voluntary acceptance by business enterprises will not only promote high standards of integrity in business transactions, whether between enterprises and public bodies or between enterprises themselves, but will also form a valuable defensive protection to those enterprises which are subjected to attempts at extortion.

These Rules of Conduct are of a general nature constituting what is considered good commercial practice in the matters to which they relate but are without direct legal effect. They do not derogate from applicable local laws, and since national legal systems are by no means uniform, they must be read *mutatis mutandis* subject to such systems.

The business community objects to all forms of extortion and bribery. It is recognized, however, that under current conditions in some parts of the world, an effective programme against extortion and bribery may have to be implemented in stages. The highest priority should be directed to ending large-scale extortion and bribery involving politicians and senior officials. These represent the greatest threat to democratic institutions and cause the gravest economic distortions. Small payments to low-level officials to expedite routine approvals are not condoned. However, they represent a lesser problem. When extortion and bribery at the top levels is curbed, government leaders can be expected to take steps to clean up petty corruption.

*Basic Principle*

All enterprises should conform to the relevant laws and regulations of the countries in which they are established and in which they operate, and should observe both the letter and the spirit of these Rules of Conduct.

For the purposes of these Rules of Conduct, the term 'enterprise' refers to any person or entity engaged in business, whether or not organized for profit, including any entity controlled by a State or a territorial subdivision thereof; it includes, where the context so indicates, a parent or a subsidiary.

*Basic Rules*

ARTICLE 1: EXTORTION

No one may, directly or indirectly, demand or accept a bribe.

ARTICLE 2: BRIBERY AND 'KICKBACKS'

a) No enterprise may, directly or indirectly, offer or give a bribe and any demands for such a bribe must be rejected.
b) Enterprises should not (i) kick back any portion of a contract payment to employees of the other contracting party, or (ii) utilize other techniques, such as subcontracts, purchase orders or consulting agreements, to channel payments to government officials, to employees of the other contracting party, their relatives or business associates.

ARTICLE 3: AGENTS

Enterprises should take measures reasonably within their power to ensure:

a) that any payment made to any agent represents no more than an appropriate remuneration for legitimate services rendered by such agent;
b) that no part of any such payment is passed on by the agent as a bribe or otherwise in contravention of these Rules of Conduct; and
c) that they maintain a record of the names and terms of employment of all agents who are retained by them in connection with transactions with public bodies or State enterprises. This record should be available for inspection by auditors and, upon specific request, by appropriate, duly authorized governmental authorities under conditions of confidentiality.

ARTICLE 4: FINANCIAL RECORDING AND AUDITING

a) All financial transactions must be properly and fairly recorded in appropriate books of account available for inspection by boards of directors, if applicable, or a corresponding body, as well as auditors.
b) There must be no 'off the books' or secret accounts, nor may any documents be issued which do not properly and fairly record the transactions to which they relate.
c) Enterprises should take all necessary measures to establish independent systems of auditing in order to bring to light any transactions which contravene the present Rules of Conduct. Appropriate corrective action must then be taken.

ARTICLE 5: RESPONSIBILITIES OF ENTERPRISES

The board of directors or other body with ultimate responsibility for the enterprise should:

a) take reasonable steps, including the establishment and maintenance of proper systems of control aimed at preventing any payments being made by or on behalf of the enterprise which contravene these Rules of Conduct;
b) periodically review compliance with these Rules of Conduct and establish procedures for obtaining appropriate reports for the purposes of such review; and
c) take appropriate action against any director or employee contravening these Rules of Conduct.

ARTICLE 6: POLITICAL CONTRIBUTIONS

Contributions to political parties or committees or to individual politicians may only be made in accordance with the applicable law, and all requirements for public disclosure of such contributions shall be fully complied with. All such contributions must be reported to senior corporate management.

ARTICLE 7: COMPANY CODES

These Rules of Conduct being of a general nature, enterprises should, where appropriate, draw up their own codes consistent with the ICC Rules and apply them to the particular circumstances in which their business is carried out. Such codes may usefully include examples and should enjoin employees or agents who find themselves subjected to any form of extortion or bribery immediately to report the same to senior corporate management. Companies should develop clear policies, guidelines, and training programmes for implementing and enforcing the provisions of their codes.

## Part III: ICC Follow-up and Promotion of the Rules

To promote the widest possible use of the Rules set forth in Part II and to stimulate cooperation between governments and world business, ICC is establishing a Standing Committee on Extortion and Bribery. The Chairman of that body shall be nominated by the President of the ICC and the Secretary General shall be responsible for ensuring, in conjunction with ICC National Committees, that members of the Committee are representative of both developed and developing countries and that businessmen are adequately represented in the membership.

Among its primary tasks, the Standing Committee shall:

(i) Urge ICC National Committees promptly to take all appropriate measures to ensure that enterprises and business organizations in their country – whether multi-disciplinary or sectoral – give strong support to these Rules of Conduct. In particular, international business groups shall be encouraged to ensure that their subsidiaries endorse the Rules, or other corporate rules having similar effect, and publicize them in their local environment;
(ii) Collect through National Committees a wide range of company codes of conduct on ethical issues, including extortion and bribery, and serve as an information clearing house for businesses seeking to develop their own codes and requiring advice on the problems involved;
(iii) Promote the organization, both by ICC International Headquarters and by National Committees, of seminars designed to stimulate interest in, and discussion of, the Rules among the business community;
(iv) Encourage National Committees to impress upon their governments the need to

include, from the initial stages, the business community – through its representative organizations – in discussions aimed at enacting or strengthening legislation against extortion and bribery;

(v) Ensure liaison with the OECD, the WTO and other international organizations to provide the ICC point of view concerning progress at the international level in combating extortion and bribery;

(vi) Conduct a study within two years on the most appropriate policies and procedures practiced by top management of companies to minimize risks of exposure to extortion of, and bribery by, personnel dealing with sensitive issues (participation in public tenders, privatizations, etc.);

(vii) Issue at least every two years a report to ICC's Executive Board and Council on results achieved concerning worldwide recognition of the Rules of Conduct and of progress otherwise made by business in combating extortion and bribery. Decisions concerning the dissemination of the Report shall rest with the Executive Board and the Council;

(viii) Review these Rules in the light of experience and recommend amendments, as necessary, to the Executive Board and the Council.

# PART XI

# General Business Principles

# 113. USA: Model Business Principles, 1996

**Commentary**: The Principles (available through www.itcilo.it/actrav/actrav-english/telearn/global/ilo/guide/usmodel.htm) were formulated by the US Department of Commerce in consultation with business and human rights groups. They encourage all international businesses to adopt and implement voluntary codes of conduct.

Recognizing the positive role of US business in upholding and promoting adherence to universal standards of human rights, the Administration encourages all businesses to adopt and implement voluntary codes of conduct for doing business around the world that cover at least the following areas:

1. Provision of a safe and healthy workplace;
2. Fair employment practices, including avoidance of child and forced labour and avoidance of discrimination based on race, gender, national origin, or religious beliefs; and respect for the right of association and the right to organize and bargain collectively;
3. Responsible environmental protection and environmental practices;
4. Compliance with US and local laws promoting good business practices, including laws prohibiting illicit payments and ensuring fair competition;
5. Maintenance, through leadership of all levels, of a corporate culture that respects free expression consistent with legitimate business concerns, and does not condone political coercion in the workplace; that encourages good corporate citizenship and makes a positive contribution to the communities in which the company operates; and where ethical conduct is recognized, valued, and exemplified by all employees.

In adopting voluntary codes of conduct that reflect these principles, US companies should serve as models and encourage similar behaviour by their partners, suppliers, and subcontractors.

Adoption of codes of conduct reflecting these principles is voluntary. Companies are encouraged to develop their own codes of conduct appropriate to their particular circumstances. Many companies already apply statements or codes that incorporate these principles. Companies should find appropriate means to inform their shareholders and the public of actions undertaken in connection with these principles. Nothing in the principles is intended to require a company to act in violation of host country or US law. This statement of principles is not intended for legislation.

# 114. The Asian Pacific Economic Cooperation (APEC) Forum: Business Code of Conduct, 1999

**Commentary**: APEC is 'the primary international organization for promoting open trade and economic cooperation among 21 member economies around the Pacific Rim'. The APEC Business Code (available through www.cauxroundtable.org/APECForumBusinessCodeofConduct.html) was initiated by business leaders from APEC States. It seeks greater transparency and predictability within both the public and private sectors. The Code articulates seven standards for corporate conduct intended to supplement existing codes of conduct and identifies specific issues for company action. It also recommends policy measures for APEC governments.

International and Local Communities: A company must recognize its responsibilities toward the international and local communities within which it operates and the individuals that make up those communities;

Respect for Laws: A company must respect international and domestic rules and recognize that some behaviour, although legal, may still have adverse consequences;

Stakeholder Responsibility: A company must recognize the rights of stakeholders as established by laws and encourage active co-operation between companies and stakeholders in creating wealth, jobs, and the sustainability of financially sound enterprises;

Responsibility for the Environment: A company must protect and, where possible, improve the environment within which it operates, promote sustainable development and prevent the wasteful use of natural resources;

Free and Fair Competition: A company must support free and fair competition in our industries and avoid anti-competitive actions;

Company Governance: A company should implement a company governance framework that ensures timely and accurate disclosure on all material matters regarding the company;

Illicit Actions: A company must not participate in or condone extortion, bribery, money laundering, or other corrupt practices.

# 115. US–Russia: Basic Guidelines for Codes of Business Conduct, 1992

**Commentary**: In 1992 the US Department of Commerce established a Business Information Service for the Newly Independent States (BISNIS) for US companies exploring business opportunities within Russia as well as the Newly Independent States. These Basic Guidelines (www.bisnis.doc.gov/bisnis/country/codebusen.htm) were formulated by the Russian Chamber of Commerce and Industry, the US–Russia Business Development Committee, Russian and American trade organisations and individual businesses. See also, Slepak Foundation (1987), 'Slepak Principles', which were designed to assist US corporations to conduct business within the former Soviet Union. For academic commentary, see Perez-Lopez J.F. (1993), 'Promoting respect for worker rights through business codes of conduct', *Fordham International Law Journal*, **17**, 1–35.

## Introduction

In today's interconnected and interdependent world, where borders between states are becoming increasingly transparent, principles in business conduct are becoming criteria for building a good reputation in the international business community; they are the basis on which first impressions are formed and ongoing relationships maintained. The purpose of this set of guidelines is to articulate general principles and standards that have been accepted in international business transactions. Although these principles apply generally, they are not intended to be an all encompassing set of business practices and corporate principles. They must be adopted and implemented on a sector-by-sector and enterprise-by-enterprise basis to take into account applicable laws, regulations, and other specific circumstances (such as the size of the enterprise).

## Principles in Personal and Professional Relations

No laws or contracts can anticipate the possible vicissitudes of life. Very often an entrepreneur must make a decision based on the prompting of common sense and conscience. The key is to embody ethical and moral principles into personal and professional relations, and remember to:

(i) always do business within one's means;
(ii) have respect for the partners and participants in a shared business venture;
(iii) refrain from violence or the threat of violence as methods of achieving business success;
(iv) resist crime and corruption, and do one's part to see that crime and corruption become unprofitable for everyone; and

(v) live up to the trust placed in you; trust is the foundation of entrepreneurship and a key to success.
(vi) endeavour to earn a reputation for integrity, competency, and excellence.

**Corporate Governance: Relationships with Shareholders**

A trusting relationship between management and shareholders is critical. Investors and lenders must be satisfied with the manner in which shareholders oversee the performance of management and participate in key decisions.

Sound principles of corporate governance include the following:

(i) delineating in the company charter the respective roles and responsibilities of both management and shareholders;
(ii) transparency of voting rules;
(iii) respect for the rights of minority shareholders;
(iv) open communications with shareholders through the provision of audited accounts, and information about the progress and operations of the company; and
(v) a well-functioning board of directors who have the skills, the time, and the access to information needed to discharge its responsibilities effectively. The board will act in a fiduciary capacity on behalf of all the shareholders.

**Relationship with Employees**

Enterprises have an important responsibility towards their employees. A number of basic principles typically guide the attitudes of successful enterprises toward their employees:

(i) due regard for labour laws;
(ii) commitment to adequate standards of worker health and safety;
(iii) non-discrimination in the recruitment, compensation, and promotion of employees;
(iv) respect for the rights of workers to engage in union activity;
(v) effective systems for consultation with employees on employment conditions and other issues that affect the employees;
(vi) clearly stated and transparent policies relating to compensation, benefits, promotions, and other employment conditions; and
(vii) commitments by the enterprise for contributions to pension plans; and strict protection of the integrity of company-sponsored pension plans.

These principles do not limit the right of an enterprise to enforce discipline on its labour force or to terminate workers in accordance with applicable law.

**Relationship with Other Enterprises**

A relationship of mutual trust in which all parties benefit is the most significant aspect of relations between partners in joint ventures, contractual arrangements or business relations with other enterprises. The reputation of a company is its most valuable asset. Once the reputation of an enterprise is tarnished, it is very difficult to gain trust with the same or other business relations. A number of basic principles that typically promote mutual trust in business relations include:

(i) commitment to excellence in products and services;
(ii) commitment to gain respect and trust in all business relations;
(iii) respect for the sanctity of contracts and business relations;
(iv) in case of a commercial dispute, a willingness to negotiate and compromise in order to reach an amicable solution; and
(v) respect for the sanctity of rule of law, including abiding in a timely manner with decisions of any court, arbitral panels, or other administrative bodies.

**Relationship with the Global Community**

As a company is an integral part of the community in which it operates, a sound relationship with the community is essential. Caring for the environment is a responsibility of the enterprise towards the immediate community, but it also extends to all communities and areas whose environment may be affected by the enterprise's activities. Enterprises must:

(i) be sensitive to concerns of the local population;
(ii) communicate with the local population;
(iii) abide by all applicable environmental laws and regulations; and
(iv) show tolerance for people of other cultures, races, beliefs, and countries.

**Relationship with Government Authorities**

Well-managed enterprises are law abiding enterprises. To maintain a sound relationship with governmental authorities, enterprises must:

(i) pay all taxes that are owed and due;
(ii) abide by all mandatory government and local regulations;
(iii) obtain all governmental permits, licenses, and approvals required to do business;
(iv) deal with government authorities on an arm's length basis, and make no attempts to improperly influence governmental decisions;
(v) establish transparent procedures regarding transactions engaged in by enterprises with any government agency or official or in dealings with any enterprise owned or controlled by a government agency or official; and
(vi) in transactions with any government agency or officials or with any enterprise owned or controlled by government or government official, include appropriate provisions to ensure compliance with international or national codes against extortion and bribery.

**Proper Checks and Balances**

A proper system of checks and balances is necessary to ensure the ongoing integrity of the enterprise and of its relationship with its constituencies. Such a system must be based on the general principles of full disclosure, management accountability, separation of responsibility, and sound internal controls.

An enterprise should have a full disclosure policy concerning:

(i) statements of the enterprise's strategic aims and policies, how these have been achieved in the past reporting period and how the enterprise will act in the future;

(ii) prompt reports to the enterprise's constituencies on events that could have a material effect on the enterprise; and
(iii) prompt disclosure of all important relationships between officials of the enterprise and other parties.

The key element of a system of checks and balances is that the shareholders are able to monitor management's performance and to condemn poor performance, including through the removal of management.

**Prevention of Extortion and Bribery**

Principles concerning prevention of extortion and bribery are intended as a method of self-regulation by businesses. The voluntary acceptance of these principles by enterprises will not only promote high standards of integrity in business transactions, whether between enterprises and public bodies or between enterprises themselves, but will also protect enterprises that are subject to attempts at extortion.

The business community objects to all forms of extortion and bribery. The highest priority should be directed to ending extortion and bribery involving politicians and senior officials. Bribery and extortion threaten democratic institutions and cause grave economic distortions.

All enterprises should observe both the letter and spirit of the following rules:

(i) no one may, directly or indirectly, demand or accept a bribe;
(ii) no enterprise may, directly or indirectly, offer or give a bribe, and any demands for such a bribe must be rejected;
(iii) enterprises should take measures reasonably within their power to ensure that any payment made to any agent represents no more than an appropriate remuneration for legitimate services rendered by the agent; that no part of any such payment is passed on by the agent as a bribe or otherwise in contravention of these principles;
(iv) all financial transactions must be properly, accurately and fairly recorded in appropriate books of account available for inspection by the board of directors as well as by auditors. Enterprises must take all necessary measures to establish independent systems of auditing in order to bring to light any transactions that contravene these principles. The enterprise must then take appropriate corrective action;
(v) the board of directors of the enterprise should periodically review compliance with these principles, and take appropriate action against any director or employee who acts in a manner inconsistent with these principles; and
(vi) contributions to political parties or to individual politicians may be made only in accordance with applicable law, and in accordance with all applicable requirements for public disclosure of such contributions.

**Creation of a Culture that Fosters Sound Business Standards and Corporate Practices**

Ultimately, for an enterprise to live by sound business standards and ethical practices it must develop a culture that fosters such standards of integrity. This effort must be led by management and key shareholders. Steps that management and key shareholders may take to promote this positive attitude throughout the company include:

(i) the preparation and dissemination within the company of a code of conduct for employees;
(ii) employee training;
(iii) encourage proper conduct and sanctions against misconduct; and
(iv) creation of an ethics office and ethics officers to advise and educate employees, and provide guarantees for confidential counselling.

**Recommendations for Implementation of these Guidelines**

All enterprises that wish to become part of the international business community are recommended to:

(i) draft their own codes of business conduct consistent with these principles and apply them to the particular circumstances in which their business is carried out; and
(ii) develop clear policies, guidelines, and training programs for implementing and enforcing the provisions of their codes.

The extent to which enterprises decide to incorporate the above listed guidelines may depend on the size, specific circumstances, and the business of the company.

# 116. Caux Round Table: Principles for Business, 1994

**Commentary**: Established in 1986, the Caux Round Table (CRT, www.cauxroundtable.org) consists of European, Japanese and American business leaders 'committed to energizing the role of business and industry as a vital force for innovative global change'. Corporate responsibility is considered to be an important mechanism for reducing social and economic threats to world peace and stability. Drawing upon the Minnesota Principles (a statement of business behaviour formulated by the Minnesota Center for Corporate Responsibility), the CRT Principles embody principled business leadership. They seek to measure corporate behaviour against two ethical principles: living and working together for the common good (*kyosei*) and human dignity.

**Introduction**

The Caux Round Table believes that the world business community should play an important role in improving economic and social conditions. As a statement of aspirations, this document aims to express a world standard against which business behaviour can be measured. We seek to begin a process that identifies shared values, reconciles differing values, and thereby develops a shared perspective on business behaviour acceptable to and honoured by all.

These principles are rooted in two basic ethical ideals: *kyosei* and human dignity. The Japanese concept of *kyosei* means living and working together for the common good enabling cooperation and mutual prosperity to coexist with healthy and fair competition. 'Human dignity' refers to the sacredness or value of each person as an end, not simply as a means to the fulfilment of others' purposes or even majority prescription. The General Principles in Section 2 seek to clarify the spirit of *kyosei* and 'human dignity', while the specific Stakeholder Principles in Section 3 are concerned with their practical application.

In its language and form, the document owes a substantial debt to The Minnesota Principles, a statement of business behaviour developed by the Minnesota Centre for Corporate Responsibility. The Centre hosted and chaired the drafting committee, which included Japanese, European, and US representatives.

Business behaviour can affect relationships among nations and the prosperity and well-being of us all. Business is often the first contact between nations and, by the way in which it causes social and economic changes, has a significant impact on the level of fear or confidence felt by people worldwide. Members of the Caux Round Table place their first emphasis on putting one's own house in order, and on seeking to establish what is right rather than who is right.

## Section 1: Preamble

The mobility of employment, capital, products and technology is making business increasingly global in its transactions and its effects.

Law and market forces are necessary but insufficient guides for conduct.

Responsibility for the policies and actions of business and respect for the dignity and interests of its stakeholders are fundamental.

Shared values, including a commitment to shared prosperity, are as important for a global community as for communities of smaller scale.

For these reasons, and because business can be a powerful agent of positive social change, we offer the following principles as a foundation for dialogue and action by business leaders in search of business responsibility. In so doing, we affirm the necessity for moral values in business decision making. Without them, stable business relationships and a sustainable world community are impossible.

## Section 2: General Principles

*Principle 1: The Responsibilities of Businesses: Beyond Shareholders toward Stakeholders*

The value of a business to society is the wealth and employment it creates and the marketable products and services it provides to consumers at a reasonable price commensurate with quality. To create such value, a business must maintain its own economic health and viability, but survival is not a sufficient goal. Businesses have a role to play in improving the lives of all their customers, employees, and shareholders by sharing with them the wealth they have created. Suppliers and competitors as well should expect businesses to honour their obligations in a spirit of honesty and fairness. As responsible citizens of the local, national, regional and global communities in which they operate, businesses share a part in shaping the future of those communities.

*Principle 2: The Economic and Social Impact of Business: Toward Innovation, Justice and World Community*

Businesses established in foreign countries to develop, produce or sell should also contribute to the social advancement of those countries by creating productive employment and helping to raise the purchasing power of their citizens. Businesses also should contribute to human rights, education, welfare, and vitalization of the countries in which they operate. Businesses should contribute to economic and social development not only in the countries in which they operate, but also in the world community at large, through effective and prudent use of resources, free and fair competition, and emphasis upon innovation in technology, production methods, marketing and communications.

*Principle 3: Business Behaviour: Beyond the Letter of Law Toward a Spirit of Trust*

While accepting the legitimacy of trade secrets, businesses should recognize that sincerity, candour, truthfulness, the keeping of promises, and transparency contribute not only to their own credibility and stability but also to the smoothness and efficiency of business transactions, particularly on the international level.

*Principle 4: Respect for Rules*
To avoid trade frictions and to promote freer trade, equal conditions for competition, and fair and equitable treatment for all participants, businesses should respect international and domestic rules. In addition, they should recognize that some behaviour, although legal, may still have adverse consequences.

*Principle 5: Support for Multilateral Trade*
Businesses should support the multilateral trade systems of the GATT/World Trade Organization and similar international agreements. They should cooperate in efforts to promote the progressive and judicious liberalization of trade and to relax those domestic measures that unreasonably hinder global commerce, while giving due respect to national policy objectives.

*Principle 6: Respect for the Environment*
A business should protect and, where possible, improve the environment, promote sustainable development, and prevent the wasteful use of natural resources.

*Principle 7: Avoidance of Illicit Operations*
A business should not participate in or condone bribery, money laundering, or other corrupt practices: indeed, it should seek cooperation with others to eliminate them. It should not trade in arms or other materials used for terrorist activities, drug traffic or other organized crime.

## Section 3: Stakeholder Principles

*Customers*
We believe in treating all customers with dignity, irrespective of whether they purchase our products and services directly from us or otherwise acquire them in the market. We therefore have a responsibility to:

(i) provide our customers with the highest quality products and services consistent with their requirements;
(ii) treat our customers fairly in all aspects of our business transactions, including a high level of service and remedies for their dissatisfaction;
(iii) make every effort to ensure that the health and safety of our customers, as well as the quality of their environment, will be sustained or enhanced by our products and services;
(iv) assure respect for human dignity in products offered, marketing, and advertising; and respect the integrity of the culture of our customers.

*Employees*
We believe in the dignity of every employee and in taking employee interests seriously. We therefore have a responsibility to:

(i) provide jobs and compensation that improve workers' living conditions;
(ii) provide working conditions that respect each employee's health and dignity;
(iii) be honest in communications with employees and open in sharing information, limited only by legal and competitive constraints;

(iv) listen to and, where possible, act on employee suggestions, ideas, requests and complaints;
(v) engage in good faith negotiations when conflict arises;
(vi) avoid discriminatory practices and guarantee equal treatment and opportunity in areas such as gender, age, race, and religion;
(vii) promote in the business itself the employment of differently abled people in places of work where they can be genuinely useful;
(viii) protect employees from avoidable injury and illness in the workplace;
(ix) encourage and assist employees in developing relevant and transferable skills and knowledge; and
(x) be sensitive to the serious unemployment problems frequently associated with business decisions, and work with governments, employee groups, other agencies and each other in addressing these dislocations.

*Owners/Investors*
We believe in honouring the trust our investors place in us. We therefore have a responsibility to:

(i) apply professional and diligent management in order to secure a fair and competitive return on our owners' investment;
(ii) disclose relevant information to owners/investors subject to legal requirements and competitive constraints;
(iii) conserve, protect, and increase the owners/investors' assets; and
(iv) respect owners/investors' requests, suggestions, complaints, and formal resolutions.

*Suppliers*
Our relationship with suppliers and subcontractors must be based on mutual respect. We therefore have a responsibility to:

(i) seek fairness and truthfulness in all our activities, including pricing, licensing, and rights to sell;
(ii) ensure that our business activities are free from coercion and unnecessary litigation;
(iii) foster long-term stability in the supplier relationship in return for value, quality, competitiveness and reliability;
(iv) share information with suppliers and integrate them into our planning processes;
(v) pay suppliers on time and in accordance with agreed terms of trade; and
(vi) seek, encourage and prefer suppliers and subcontractors whose employment practices respect human dignity.

*Competitors*
We believe that fair economic competition is one of the basic requirements for increasing the wealth of nations and ultimately for making possible the just distribution of goods and services. We therefore have a responsibility to:

(i) foster open markets for trade and investment;
(ii) promote competitive behaviour that is socially and environmentally beneficial and demonstrates mutual respect among competitors;
(iii) refrain from either seeking or participating in questionable payments or favours to secure competitive advantages;

(iv) respect both tangible and intellectual property rights; and
(v) refuse to acquire commercial information by dishonest or unethical means, such as industrial espionage.

*Communities*
We believe that as global corporate citizens we can contribute to such forces of reform and human rights as are at work in the communities in which we operate. We therefore have a responsibility in those communities to:

(i) respect human rights and democratic institutions, and promote them wherever practicable;
(ii) recognize government's legitimate obligation to the society at large and support public policies and practices that promote human development through harmonious relations between business and other segments of society;
(iii) collaborate with those forces in the community dedicated to raising standards of health, education, workplace safety and economic well-being;
(iv) promote and stimulate sustainable development and play a leading role in preserving and enhancing the physical environment and conserving the earth's resources;
(v) support peace, security, diversity and social integration;
(vi) respect the integrity of local cultures; and
(vii) be a good corporate citizen through charitable donations, educational and cultural contributions, and employee participation in community and civic affairs.

# 117. Additional initiatives

### i. Keidanren (Japan Federation of Economic Organisations): Charter of Corporate Behaviour, 2002

**Commentary**: The Charter was first introduced during 1991 and subsequently revised in 1996, 2002 and 2004: see www.keidanren.or.jp. The original Japanese language version is the official text used by Keidanren. The Charter includes ten principles with respect to legal compliance, consumer confidence, fair competition, information disclosure, positive environmental involvement, committing to good corporate citizenship, promoting economic development, providing safe and comfortable working environments, rejecting relationships with organisations engaged in illegal activities and management responsibility for implementation in consultation with stakeholders. In the event of violations, management is expected to investigate, develop reforms, make information publicly available and initiate disciplinary action.

### ii. Social Venture Network: Standards of Corporate Social Responsibility, 1999

**Commentary**: The Social Venture Network (www.svn.org) was established in 1987 to promote business roles in solving social problems. Developed over four years and intended to be a living document, the Standards are a compendium of strategies and techniques for improving organisational performance. They were the product of collaboration between several SVN members in recognition that companies have social obligations to operate in an ethically, socially and environmentally responsible manner. Each Standard consists of Principles (a brief value statement), Practices (practical illustrations), Measures (tangible performance indicators observable in qualitative, quantitative or monetary terms) and Resources (additional information sources, tools, and techniques for implementing customised approaches). The Principles consist of a commitment to ethical behaviour, stakeholder accountability, good corporate governance, providing attractive and competitive financial returns, fair employment practices, honest business relationships, the highest levels of product and service value, community engagement and environmental protection. The Standards are also accompanied by an extensive glossary of terms. They do not proscribe any particular manner of implementation, and individual companies are left to form their own statement of corporate values in the light of organisational considerations. That said, the SVN encourages ongoing stakeholder consultation and annual assessments through independent social audits.

### iii. Clarkson Centre for Business Ethics & Board Effectiveness: The Clarkson Principles of Stakeholder Management, 1998

**Commentary**: In 1988, Max Clarkson established the Centre for Corporate Social Performance and Ethics which subsequently became the Clarkson Centre for Business Ethics & Board Effectiveness (CC(BE)2; www.rotman.utoronto.ca/ccbe/index1215.htm). The Clarkson Principles emerged after four management conferences which evaluated stakeholder theory and corporate responsibilities to employees, customers, suppliers, society and the environment. As hortatory standards they do not call for formal management adoption. The Principles define stakeholders as constituencies favourably or adversely affected by commercial operations. They also clarify the relationship between shareowners and stakeholders as well as identify legal and moral management duties. The Principles call upon management to take stakeholder concerns into account, regularly communicate with them, adopt processes and behavioural conduct sensitive to their interests, attempt to fairly distribute the benefits and burdens of corporate activity, to work with public and private entities so as to minimise risks and harms (including compensation where necessary), avoiding activities which jeopardise inalienable human rights and to address conflicts through open communication, reporting, incentive systems and third party review. Each Principle is also accompanied by a useful commentary.

# PART XII

# Additional Instruments

# 118. UN: Guidelines on Cooperation between the UN and the Business Community, 2000

**Commentary**: Issued by the UN Secretary-General on 17 July 2000, the Guidelines extracted below (footnotes omitted) provide guidance for private sector relations with the UN. Annex 1 contains the Global Compact. Annex 2 contains an explanatory background note on the use of the UN name and emblem (under Section V) and illustrates the various modalities listed under Section VI. See further, UN Secretary-General (1997), 'Secretary-General, in address to World Economic Forum, stresses strengthened partnership between UN, Private Sector', Press Release SG/SM/6153; UN Secretary-General Report (2001), 'Co-operation between the UN and all relevant partners, in particular the private sector', UN Doc A/56/323. For intergovernmental perspectives, see UN Department of Public Information (UNDPI) (1998), 'The UN and Business: New Dimensions in Co-operation: Case Studies from the UN System', New York; UN Joint Inspection Unit (1999), 'Report on Private Sector Involvement and Cooperation with the UN System', Geneva, UN Doc JIU/REP/99/6. For commercial perspectives, see PWBLF (2002), 'Building Partnerships: Co-operation between the UN and the Business Community', London. See also, Nelson, J. (2002), 'Building partnerships: co-operation between the UN system and the private sector', UNDPI/IBLF: New York; www.un.org/partners/business/index.asp.

## I. Background

1. The business community has played an active role in the UN since its inception in 1945. A number of UN organizations have a successful history of cooperating with business. Recent political and economic changes have fostered and intensified the search for collaborative arrangements.
2. The efforts of the Secretary-General to renew and reform the UN provide the overall rationale for closer cooperation and partnership between the UN and non-state actors, including the business community. A broad policy framework for cooperation with the business community has been established, including through joint statements.
3. The relationship with the business community has become more important as the role of business in generating employment and wealth through trade, investment and finance has grown and as UN member states have increasingly stressed the importance of private investment in development.
4. The business community is increasingly appreciative of the role of the UN: promoting peace and security, providing norms and standards in such diverse areas as trade laws, shipping, aviation, telecommunication, postal services and statistics; addressing issues of vulnerability, poverty, environmental degradation and social conflict. All of this is seen as helping provide a stable and favourable framework for business and development.

## II. Purpose and Rationale

5. Efforts to work with the business community must be seen in the proper institutional context. The UN is a global institution accountable to its member states. Non-state actors play an important role in the pursuit of UN goals. Drawing on the expertise and capacities of the business community is increasingly necessary to achieve these goals.
6. The purpose of these guidelines is to facilitate the formulation and implementation of cooperation between the UN and the business community in a manner that ensures the integrity and independence of the Organization.
7. These guidelines define 'business' as for-profit enterprises.
8. These guidelines are intended to serve as a common framework for all organizations of the UN proper. It may also serve as a framework for the other Organizations of the UN system.
9. UN organizations are encouraged to develop more specific guidelines in accordance with their particular mandates and activities.
10. Cooperation with business can take many forms, such as advocacy, fund-raising, policy dialogue, humanitarian assistance and development cooperation. Guidelines for cooperation are particularly relevant in cases where new forms of partnership are being pursued that do not directly involve active government participation.
11. Cooperation is often situation-specific and must be considered on a case-by-case basis. It is essential that each UN organization develop in-house capacities and clear lines of responsibility to devise, implement and evaluate cooperative arrangements with business.

## III. Choosing a Partner

12. The Global Compact, launched by the Secretary-General in 1999, provides an overall value framework for cooperation with the business community. The principles of the compact (see Annex 1) are based on intergovernmental agreements and at the same time are relevant for business. UN organizations should use them as a point of reference when choosing a business partner.

    a) Business partners should demonstrate responsible citizenship by supporting UN causes and core values as reflected in the Charter and other relevant conventions and treaties.
    b) Within their sphere of influence, private enterprises should have demonstrated a commitment to meeting or exceeding the principles of the Compact by translating them into operational corporate practice.
    c) Business entities that are complicit in human rights abuses, tolerate forced or compulsory labour or the use of child labour, are involved in the sale or manufacture of anti-personnel mines or their components, or that otherwise do not meet relevant obligations or responsibilities by the UN, are not eligible for partnership.

13. UN organizations are encouraged to develop additional criteria appropriate to their specific mission and advocacy role.

## IV. General Principles

14. Irrespective of the situation-specific nature of cooperative arrangements, they should be guided by the following general principles:

a) Advance UN goals: The objective needs to be articulated clearly and must advance UN goals as laid out in the Charter.
b) Clear delineation of responsibilities and roles: The arrangement must be based on a clear understanding of respective roles and expectations, with accountability and a clear division of responsibilities.
c) Maintain integrity and independence: Arrangements should not diminish the UN's integrity, independence and impartiality.
d) No unfair advantage: Every member of the business community should have the opportunity to propose cooperative arrangements, within the parameters of these guidelines. Cooperation should not imply endorsement or preference of a particular business entity or its products or services.
e) Transparency: Cooperation with the business community sector must be transparent. Information on the nature and scope of cooperative arrangements should be available within the Organization and to the public at large. UN organizations should post relevant information on the UN/Business website www.un.org/partners/business.

**V. Use of the UN Name and Emblem**

15. Pursuant to UNGA Resolution 92 (I) of 7 December 1946, the use of the UN name and emblem is limited to official purposes. The Organization has consistently interpreted this resolution to apply also to the use of the name and emblem of the UN Funds and Programs whose names include the 'UN' or its acronym (see Annex 2 for illustrative examples).
16. Recognizing the evolving new relationship with the business community, the following sets out general principles on the use of the name and emblem of the UN and its Funds and Programmes ('Name and Emblem') by the business community in the context of partnership with the private sector.

a) In principle, and subject to the appropriate terms and conditions, a business entity may be authorized to use the name and emblem on a non-exclusive basis.
b) The use of the name and emblem must be expressly approved in advance in writing and upon such terms and conditions as may be specified.
c) The use of the name and emblem by a business entity may be authorized, even if it involves the making of profit, so long as the principal purpose of such use is to show support for the purposes and activities of the UN, including the raising of funds for the Organization, and the generation of profit by the business entity is only incidental.
d) The use of the name and emblem may be authorized for the following purposes:

(i) To support the purposes, policies and activities of the organization;
(ii) To assist in the raising of funds for the Organization;
(iii) To assist in the raising of funds for entities that are not part of the Organization, but which are established to achieve the purposes and policies of the Organization.

e) When authorized, the use of the name and/or emblem shall be in accordance with the written specifications provided by the organization concerned.

f) With appropriate written approval, and subject to appropriate conditions on the time, manner and scope of such use, the use of a modified UN emblem may be exclusively authorized to a limited number of business entities in connection with the promotion of a special event or initiative, including fund-raising for such event or initiative.

17. Currently, the Office of Legal Affairs grants authorization for the use of the name and emblem of the UN.

## VI. Modalities

18. Modalities for entering into partnerships with the business community, which are distinct from procurement activities, require flexibility in order to reflect the particular purposes and objectives of the partnerships.

a) Direct contribution by the business partner: The modality for direct contribution for specific purposes would be made under a trust fund or special account agreement with the partner. The agreement would be subject to the applicable Financial Regulations and Rules, i.e., the purposes of the contribution would have to be consistent with the policies, aims and activities of the UN and that generally, the contribution would not entail any financial liabilities to the UN.
b) Indirect contribution by the business partner through the establishment of a charitable organization or foundation: Under this modality, a relationship agreement would be established between the UN and the charitable organization or foundation, laying out the terms of the relationship, including the issues related to the use of the name and emblem, liability, settlement of disputes and the privileges and immunities of the UN.
c) Partnership in technical assistance projects: This modality would involve either two direct bilateral agreements with the business partner and with the government of the country in which the assistance would be carried out, or a tripartite agreement among the business partner, the UN and the government.
d) Partnership in promoting the purposes and activities of the UN: This modality, whereby the business partner provides a forum to disseminate information about the UN, would involve direct agreements with the business partner, setting out the terms and conditions of the arrangement, including the UN's control of the information to be disseminated, the issues related to the use of the name and emblem, liability, settlement of disputes and the privileges and immunities of the UN.
e) Partnership in cooperative projects: This modality, whereby the UN and a business partner jointly develop a product or service, consistent with and in furtherance of the aims, policies and activities of the UN, would involve agreements with the business partner, setting out the terms and conditions of the arrangement, including the contributions each party could make to the development of the product service, the use of the name and emblem, liability, settlement of disputes and the privileges and immunities of the UN.

## VII. Institutional Capacities

19. Cooperative arrangements with the business community have often evolved on an ad hoc basis. UN organizations should further develop the policy frameworks and institutional capacities needed to manage successfully such arrangements.

a) Building institutional competencies: UN organizations that engage business in their work should develop the necessary competencies to properly assess and guide the relationship. Within each organization, a focal point should be nominated to ensure transparency, learning and a better understanding of the role and objectives of business and to ascertain whether they are compatible with the goals of the UN.
b) Responsibilities of focal points: Focal points will be responsible for developing guidance on contacts with the business community based on rules, regulations and administrative issuances of the UN to ensure transparency in the establishment and maintenance of contacts with the business community. The focal points should post relevant information on the UN/business website
c) Exchange experience: Focal points should exchange learning experiences on a regular basis and aim at building shared data banks and problem-solving methodologies and guides.

**VIII. Future Reviews**

20. Cooperation with the business community is influenced by changes in the political and economic environment. To remain valid, these guidelines should be critically reviewed regularly and updated in due course.

# 119. UN: Guidelines for Consumer Protection, 1999

**Commentary**: In recognition that consumer protection influenced economic and social development, ECOSOC requested the UN Secretary-General to prepare a survey (1977) and comprehensive report (1979) for the purposes of formulating an international policy framework (1981). Draft guidelines were prepared in 1983 prior to their final adoption: UNGA Resolution 39/248 (1985). They were intended to assist governments to develop national law and policy with respect to consumer protection. The CSD called for an expanded version (UN Doc E/1995/32) in the light of changing consumption patterns: see Agenda 21, Chapter 4 and UN Secretary-General Reports, UN Docs E/CN.17/1995/13 & E/1995/70. ECOSOC made similar requests: ECOSOC Resolutions 1995/53 and 1997/53. Various proposals were made to incorporate the concept of sustainable consumption: see UN Secretary-General Report, UN Doc E/CN.17/1998/5 and the recommendations of the Interregional Expert Group Meeting on Consumer Protection and Sustainable Consumption, São Paulo, UN Doc E/CN.17/1998/5. The UNGA Resolution adopting the version of the Guidelines (UN Doc A/C.2/54/L.24 (1999)) encouraged relevant NGOs to support effective implementation. The extracts below are limited to corporate roles and responsibilities. The ICC has also formulated several consumer codes stating best marketing practice: see the International Code of Advertising Practice (1937 and revised 1949, 1955, 1966, 1973, 1987 and 1997); the Guidelines on Advertising and Marketing on the Internet (1998); and the International Code of Direct Selling (1999). Codes formulated by consumer organisations emphasise corporate adherence to national competition and advertising law: see, for example, Consumers International (1997), 'A Consumer Charter for Global Business', London; Consumers International (2000), 'Consumer Protection in the Global Marketplace – from a Consumer Perspective', Kyoto.

## I. Objectives

1. . . . these guidelines for consumer protection have the following objectives:

   (c) To encourage high levels of ethical conduct for those engaged in the production and distribution of goods and services to consumers;

   (d) To assist countries in curbing abusive business practices by all enterprises at the national and international levels which adversely affect consumers;

## II. General Principles

7. All enterprises should obey the relevant laws and regulations of the countries in which they do business. They should also conform to the appropriate provisions of international

standards for consumer protection to which the competent authorities of the country in question have agreed . . .

**III. Guidelines**

9. The following guidelines should apply both to home-produced goods and services and to imports.
10. In applying any procedures or regulations for consumer protection, due regard should be given to ensuring that they do not become barriers to international trade and that they are consistent with international trade obligations.

*A. Physical Safety*

11. Governments should adopt or encourage the adoption of appropriate measures, including legal systems, safety regulations, national or international standards, voluntary standards and the maintenance of safety records to ensure that products are safe for either intended or normally foreseeable use.
12. Appropriate policies should ensure that goods produced by manufacturers are safe for either intended or normally foreseeable use. Those responsible for bringing goods to the market, in particular suppliers, exporters, importers, retailers and the like (hereinafter referred to as 'distributors'), should ensure that while in their care these goods are not rendered unsafe through improper handling or storage and that while in their care they do not become hazardous through improper handling or storage. Consumers should be instructed in the proper use of goods and should be informed of the risks involved in intended or normally foreseeable use . . .
13. Appropriate policies should ensure that if manufacturers or distributors become aware of unforeseen hazards after products are placed on the market, they should notify the relevant authorities and, as appropriate, the public without delay . . .
14. Governments should, where appropriate, adopt policies under which, if a product is found to be seriously defective and/or to constitute a substantial and severe hazard even when properly used, manufacturers and/or distributors should recall it and replace or modify it, or substitute another product for it; if it is not possible to do this within a reasonable period of time, the consumer should be adequately compensated.

*B. Promotion and Protection of Consumers' Economic Interests*

15. Government policies should seek to enable consumers to obtain optimum benefit from their economic resources. They should also seek to achieve the goals of satisfactory production and performance standards, adequate distribution methods, fair business practices, informative marketing and effective protection against practices which could adversely affect the economic interests of consumers and the exercise of choice in the market place.
16. Governments should intensify their efforts to prevent practices which are damaging to the economic interests of consumers through ensuring that manufacturers, distributors and others involved in the provision of goods and services adhere to established laws and mandatory standards . . .
18. Governments should adopt or maintain policies that make clear the responsibility of the producer to ensure that goods meet reasonable demands of durability, utility and reliability, and are suited to the purpose for which they are intended, and that the seller

should see that these requirements are met. Similar policies should apply to the provision of services.

19. Governments should encourage fair and effective competition in order to provide consumers with the greatest range of choice among products and services at the lowest cost.
20. Governments should, where appropriate, see to it that manufacturers and/or retailers ensure adequate availability of reliable after-sales service and spare parts.
21. Consumers should be protected from such contractual abuses as one-sided standard contracts, exclusion of essential rights in contracts, and unconscionable conditions of credit by sellers.
22. Promotional marketing and sales practices should be guided by the principle of fair treatment of consumers and should meet legal requirements. This requires the provision of the information necessary to enable consumers to take informed and independent decisions, as well as measures to ensure that the information provided is accurate.
24. Consumer access to accurate information about the environmental impact of products and services should be encouraged through such means as product profiles, environmental reports by industry, information centres for consumers, voluntary and transparent eco-labelling programmes and product information hotlines.
25. Governments, in close collaboration with manufacturers, distributors and consumer organizations, should take measures regarding misleading environmental claims or information in advertising and other marketing activities. The development of appropriate advertising codes and standards for the regulation and verification of environmental claims should be encouraged.
26. Governments should, within their own national context, encourage the formulation and implementation by business, in cooperation with consumer organizations, of codes of marketing and other business practices to ensure adequate consumer protection. Voluntary agreements may also be established jointly by business, consumer organizations and other interested parties. These codes should receive adequate publicity.

*C. Standards for the Safety and Quality of Consumer Goods and Services*

28. Governments should, as appropriate, formulate or promote the elaboration and implementation of standards, voluntary and other, at the national and international levels for the safety and quality of goods and services and give them appropriate publicity . . .

*D. Distribution Facilities for Essential Consumer Goods and Services*

31. Governments should, where appropriate, consider:

    (a) Adopting or maintaining policies to ensure the efficient distribution of goods and services to consumers; where appropriate, specific policies should be considered to ensure the distribution of essential goods and services where this distribution is endangered, as could be the case particularly in rural areas . . .

*E. Measures Enabling Consumers to Obtain Redress*

33. Governments should encourage all enterprises to resolve consumer disputes in a fair, expeditious and informal manner, and to establish voluntary mechanisms, including advisory services and informal complaints procedures, which can provide assistance to consumers.

*F. Education and Information Programmes*

35. Governments should develop or encourage the development of general consumer education and information programmes, including information on the environmental impacts of consumer choices and behaviour and the possible implications, including benefits and costs, of changes in consumption, bearing in mind the cultural traditions of the people concerned . . . Consumer groups, business and other relevant organizations of civil society should be involved in these educational efforts.

39. Business should, where appropriate, undertake or participate in factual and relevant consumer education and information programmes.

*G. Promotion of Sustainable Consumption*

42. Sustainable consumption includes meeting the needs of present and future generations for goods and services in ways that are economically, socially and environmentally sustainable.

43. Responsibility for sustainable consumption is shared by all members and organizations of society, with informed consumers, Government, business, labour organizations, and consumer and environmental organizations playing particularly important roles . . . Government policymaking should be conducted in consultation with business, consumer and environmental organizations, and other concerned groups. Business has a responsibility for promoting sustainable consumption through the design, production and distribution of goods and services . . .

44. Governments, in partnership with business and relevant organizations of civil society, should develop and implement strategies that promote sustainable consumption through a mix of policies that could include regulations; economic and social instruments; sectoral policies in such areas as land use, transport, energy and housing; information programmes to raise awareness of the impact of consumption patterns; removal of subsidies that promote unsustainable patterns of consumption and production; and promotion of sector-specific environmental-management best practices.

50. Governments, in partnership with the private sector and other relevant organizations, should encourage the transformation of unsustainable consumption patterns through the development and use of new environmentally sound products and services and new technologies, including information and communication technologies, that can meet consumer needs while reducing pollution and depletion of natural resources.

53. Governments, in cooperation with business and other relevant groups, should develop indicators, methodologies and databases for measuring progress towards sustainable consumption at all levels. This information should be publicly available.

**IV. International Cooperation**

66. To promote sustainable consumption, Governments, international bodies and business should work together to develop, transfer and disseminate environmentally sound technologies, including through appropriate financial support from developed countries, and to devise new and innovative mechanisms for financing their transfer among all countries, in particular to and among developing countries and countries with economies in transition.

# 120. WHO: Ethical Criteria for Medicinal Drug Promotion, 1988

**Commentary**: The Ethical Criteria (WHA Resolution WHA41.17) identifies the roles and responsibilities of *inter alia* pharmaceutical manufacturers and distributors, employers of medical representatives and advertisers with respect to promoting medicinal drugs. The Appendix contains a sample drug information sheet: see further, WHO (1985), 'Second Report of the WHO Expert Committee: The Use of Essential Drugs', Technical Report Series No 722. Other tools include WHO (1999), 'Guidelines for Drug Donations', WHO Doc WHO/EDM/PAR/99.4 (2nd edn); WHO (2000), 'Operational Principles for Good Pharmaceutical Procurement Supply and Marketing', WHO Doc WHO/EDM/PAR/99.5. See also, the series of WHO Policy Perspectives on Medicines: No 2 on access to essential drugs (in preparation); No 3 concerning globalisation, TRIPS and access to pharmaceuticals, WHO Doc WHO/EDM/2001.2 (2001). See generally, WHO (2000), 'Medicines Strategy: Framework for action in essential drugs and medicines policy', 2000–2003, WHO Doc WHO/EDM/2000.1 which updated WHA Resolutions WHA39.27 (1986) and WHA21.41 (1968). See also, the Medical Lobby for Appropriate Marketing (MaLAM), the International Federation of Pharmaceutical Manufacturers' Association (IFPMA) and www.who.int.

**Objective**

2. The main objective of ethical criteria for medicinal drug promotion is to support and encourage the improvement of health care through the rational use of medicinal drugs.

**Applicability and Implementation of Criteria**

4. These criteria constitute general principles for ethical standards which could be adapted by governments to national circumstances as appropriate to their political, economic, cultural, social, educational, scientific and technical situation, laws and regulations, disease profile, therapeutic traditions and the level of development of their health system. They apply to prescription and non-prescription medicinal drugs ('over-the-counter drugs'). They also apply generally to traditional medicines as appropriate, and to any other product promoted as a medicine. The criteria could be used by people in all walks of life; by governments; the pharmaceutical industry (manufacturers and distributors); the promotion industry (advertising agencies, market research organizations and the like); health personnel involved in the prescription, dispensing, supply and distribution of drugs; universities and other teaching institutions; professional associations; patients' and consumer groups; and the professional and general media (including publishers and editors of medical journals and related publications). All

these are encouraged to use the criteria as appropriate to their spheres of competence, activity and responsibility. They are also encouraged to take the criteria into account in developing their own sets of ethical standards in their own field relating to medicinal drug promotion.

5. The criteria do not constitute legal obligations; governments may adopt legislation or other measures based on them as they deem fit. Similarly, other groups may adopt self regulatory measures based on them. All these bodies should monitor and enforce their standards.

**Promotion**

6. In this context, 'promotion' refers to all informational and persuasive activities by manufacturers and distributors, the effect of which is to induce the prescription, supply, purchase and/or use of medicinal drugs.
7. Active promotion within a country should take place only with respect to drugs legally available in the country. Promotion should be in keeping with national health policies and in compliance with national regulations, as well as with voluntary standards where they exist. All promotion-making claims concerning medicinal drugs should be reliable, accurate, truthful, informative, balanced, up-to-date, capable of substantiation and in good taste. They should not contain misleading or unverifiable statements or omissions likely to induce medically unjustifiable drug use or to give rise to undue risks. The word 'safe' should only be used if properly qualified. Comparison of products should be factual, fair and capable of substantiation. Promotional material should not be designed so as to disguise its real nature.
8. Scientific data in the public domain should be made available to prescribers and any other person entitled to receive it, on request, as appropriate to their requirements. Promotion in the form of financial or material benefits should not be offered to or sought by health care practitioners to influence them in the prescription of drugs.
9. Scientific and educational activities should not be deliberately used for promotional purposes.

**Advertising**

*(a) Advertisements in All Forms to Physicians and Health-related Professionals*

10. The wording and illustrations in advertisements to physicians and related health professionals should be fully consistent with the approved scientific data sheet for the drug concerned or other source of information with similar content . . .
12. The following list, based on the sample drug information sheet contained in the second report of the WHO Expert Committee on the Use of Essential Drugs and appended for ease of reference, can serve as an illustration of the type of information that such advertisements should usually contain, among others:

    (i) the name(s) of the active ingredient(s) using either international non-proprietary names (INN) or the approved generic name of the drug;
    (ii) the brand name;
    (iii) content of active ingredient(s) per dosage form or regimen;
    (iv) name of other ingredients known to cause problems;

(v) approved therapeutic uses;
(vi) dosage form or regimen;
(vii) side-effects and major adverse drug reactions;
(viii) precautions, contra-indications and warnings;
(ix) major interactions;
(x) name and address of manufacturer or distributor;
(xi) reference to scientific literature as appropriate.

13. Where advertisements are permitted without claims (reminder advertisements), they ought to include at least the brand name, the international non-proprietary name or approved generic name, the name of each active ingredient, and the name and address of the manufacturer or distributor for the purpose of receiving further information.

*(b) Advertisements in All Forms to the General Public*

14. Advertisements to the general public should help people to make rational decisions on the use of drugs determined to be legally available without a prescription. While they should take account of people's legitimate desire for information regarding their health, they should not take undue advantage of people's concern for their health . . . While health education aimed at children is highly desirable, drug advertisements should not be directed at children. Advertisements may claim that a drug can cure, prevent, or relieve an ailment only if this can be substantiated . . .

16. The following list serves as an illustration of the type of information advertisements to the general public should contain, taking into account the media employed:

(i) the name(s) of the active ingredients(s) using either international non-proprietary names (INN) or the approved generic name of the drug;
(ii) the brand name;
(iii) major indication(s) for use;
(iv) major precautions, contra-indications and warnings;
(v) name and address of manufacturer or distributor.

Information on price to the consumer should be accurately and honestly portrayed.

**Medical Representatives**

17. . . . Employers are responsible for the basic and continuing training of their representatives . . .

19. Employers should be responsible for the statements and activities of their medical representatives. Medical representatives should not offer inducements to prescribers and dispensers. Prescribers and dispensers should not solicit such inducements. In order to avoid over-promotion, the main part of the remuneration of medical representatives should not be directly related to the volume of sales they generate.

**Free Samples of Prescription Drugs for Promotional Purposes**

20. Free samples of legally available prescription drugs may be provided in modest quantities to prescribers, generally on request.

**Free Samples of Non-Prescription Drugs to the General Public for Promotional Purposes**

21. . . . The provision of free samples of non-prescription drugs to the general public for promotional purposes is difficult to justify from a health perspective. If this practice is legally permitted in any country, it should be handled with great restraint.

**Symposia and Other Scientific Meetings**

23. The fact of sponsorship by a pharmaceutical manufacturer or distributor should clearly be stated in advance, at the meeting and in any proceedings . . .
24. Any support to individual health practitioners to participate in any domestic or international symposia should not be conditional upon any obligation to promote any medicinal product.

**Post-marketing Scientific Studies, Surveillance and Dissemination of Information**

25. . . . Substantiated information on such studies should be reported to the appropriate national health authorities and disseminated as soon as possible.
26. Post-marketing scientific studies and surveillance should not be misused as a disguised form of promotion.
27. Substantiated information on hazards associated with medicinal drugs should be reported to the appropriate national health authority as a priority, and should be disseminated internationally as soon as possible.

**Packaging and Labelling**

28. Appropriate information being important to ensure the rational use of drugs, all packaging and labelling material should provide information consistent with that approved by the country's drug regulatory authority. Where one does not exist or is rudimentary, such material should provide information consistent with that approved by the drug regulatory authority of the country from which the drug is imported or other reliable sources of information with similar content. Any wording and illustration on the package and label should conform to the principles of ethical criteria enunciated in this document.

**Information for Patients: Package Inserts, Leaflets and Booklets**

29. . . . When package inserts or leaflets are required by governments, manufacturers or distributors should ensure that they reflect only the information that has been approved by the country's drug regulatory authority . . . The wording of the package inserts or leaflets, if prepared specifically for patients, should be in lay language on condition that the medical and scientific content is properly reflected.

**Promotion of Exported Drugs**

31. Ethical criteria for the promotion of exported drugs should be identical with those relating to drugs for domestic use. It is desirable that exporting and importing countries that have not already done so should use the WHO Certification Scheme on the Quality of Pharmaceutical Products Moving in International Commerce.

# 121. WHO: International Code of Marketing of Breast-milk Substitutes, 1981

**Commentary**: The International Code was prepared by the WHO and UNICEF following consultation with governments, industry, professional associations and NGOs: see further, Resolution WHA33.32 (1980). It was finally adopted through WHA Resolution WHA34.22 (1981). WHA resolutions 'carry moral or political weight, as they constitute the judgement on a health issue of the collective membership of the highest international body in the field of health': Shubber, S. (1985), 'The International Code', *Digest of Health Legislation*, **36** (4), 884. Several additional resolutions have since been adopted to clarify or revise the International Code: see Resolutions WHA35.26 (1982), 37.30 (1984), 39.28 (1986), 41.11 (1988), 43.3 (1990), 45.34 (1992), 47.5 (1994), 49.15 (1996), 54.2 (2001) and 55.25 (2002). Manufacturers and distributors of infant baby food are expected to comply and NGOs, professional groups, institutions and individuals may report violations. See further, WHO (1994), 'Infant Formula and Related Trade Issues', WHA Doc WHA47/1994/REC/1/, Annex 1; WHO (2001), ' "Follow-Up Formula" in Nutrition for Health and Development', Geneva. For commentary, see UNCTC (1982), 'The International Code of Marketing Breast-Milk Substitutes', *The CTC Reporter*, **11**, 29–32. For commercial perspectives, see the International Council of Infant Formula Industries (1981), 'Infant Formula Marketing in the Third World', *National Journal*, 854. See also FAO, Codex Alimentarius Commission, Code of Hygienic Practice for Foods for Infants and Children.

**Article 1. Aim of the Code**

The aim of this Code is to contribute to the provision of safe and adequate nutrition for infants, by the protection and promotion of breastfeeding, and by ensuring the proper use of breast-milk substitutes, when these are necessary, on the basis of adequate information and through appropriate marketing and distribution.

**Article 2. Scope of the Code**

The Code applies to the marketing, and practices related thereto, of the following products: breast-milk substitutes, including infant formula; other milk products, foods and beverages, including bottle-fed complementary foods, when marketed or otherwise represented to be suitable, with or without modification, for use as a partial or total replacement of breast-milk; feeding bottles and teats. It also applies to their quality and availability, and to information concerning their use.

**Article 3. Definitions**
For the purposes of this Code:

'Breast-milk substitute' means any food being marketed or otherwise represented as a partial or total replacement for breast milk, whether or not suitable for that purpose.

'Complementary food' means any food, whether manufactured or locally prepared, suitable as a complement to breast milk or to infant formula, when either becomes insufficient to satisfy the nutritional requirements of the infant. Such food is also commonly called 'weaning food' or 'breast-milk supplement'.

'Container' means any form of packaging of products for sale as a normal retail unit, including wrappers.

'Distributor' means a person, corporation or any other entity in the public or private sector engaged in the business (whether directly or indirectly) of marketing at the wholesale or retail level a product within the scope of this Code. A 'primary distributor' is a manufacturer's sales agent, representative, national distributor or broker.

'Health care system' means governmental, nongovernmental or private institutions or organisations engaged, directly or indirectly, in health care for mothers, infants and pregnant women; and nurseries or childcare institutions. It also includes health workers in private practice. For the purposes of this Code, the health care system does not include pharmacies or other established sales outlets.

'Health worker' means a person working in a component of such a health care system, whether professional or non-professional, including voluntary, unpaid workers.

'Infant formula' means a breast-milk substitute formulated industrially in accordance with applicable Codex Alimentarius standards, to satisfy the normal nutritional requirements of infants up to between four and six months of age, and adapted to their physiological characteristics. Infant formula may also be prepared at home, in which case it is described as 'home prepared'.

'Label' means any tag, brand, mark, pictorial or other descriptive matter, written, printed, stencilled, marked, embossed or impressed on, or attached to, a container (see above) of any products within the scope of this Code.

'Manufacturer' means a corporation or other entity in the public or private sector engaged in the business or function (whether directly or through an agent or through an entity controlled by or under contract with it) of manufacturing a product within the scope of this Code.

'Marketing' means product promotion, distribution, selling, advertising, product public relations, and information services.

'Marketing personnel' means any persons whose functions involve the marketing of a product or products coming within the scope of this Code.

'Samples' means single or small quantities of a product provided without cost.

'Supplies' means quantities of a product provided for use over an extended period, free or at a low price, for social purposes, including those provided to families in need.

### Article 4. Information and Education

4.2 Informational and educational materials, whether written, audio, or visual, dealing with the feeding of infants and intended to reach pregnant women and mothers of infants and young children, should include clear information on all the following points:

(i) the benefits and superiority of breastfeeding;
(ii) maternal nutrition, and the preparation for and maintenance of breastfeeding;
(iii) the negative effect on breastfeeding of introducing partial bottle feeding;
(iv) the difficulty of reversing the decision not to breastfeed; and
(v) where needed, the proper use of infant formula, whether manufactured industrially or home prepared.

When such materials contain information about the use of infant formula, they should include the social and financial implications of its use; the health hazards of inappropriate foods or feeding methods; and, in particular, the health hazards of unnecessary or improper use of infant formula and other breast-milk substitutes. Such materials should not use any pictures or text which may idealise the use of breast-milk substitutes.

4.3 Donations of informational or educational equipment or materials by manufacturers or distributors should be made only at the request and with the written approval of the appropriate government authority or within guidelines given by governments for this purpose. Such equipment or materials may bear the donating company's name or logo, but should not refer to a proprietary product that is within the scope of this Code, and should be distributed only through the health care system.

### Article 5. The General Public and Mothers

5.1 There should be no advertising or other form of promotion to the general public of products within the scope of this Code.

5.2 Manufacturers and distributors should not provide, directly or indirectly, to pregnant women, mothers or members of their families, samples of products within the scope of this Code.

5.3 In conformity with paragraphs 1 and 2 of this Article, there should be no point-of-sale advertising, giving of samples, or any other promotion device to induce sales directly to the consumer at the retail level, such as special displays, discount coupons, premiums, special sales, loss leaders and tie-in sales, for products within the scope of this Code. This provision should not restrict the establishment of pricing policies and practices intended to provide products at lower prices on a long-term basis.

5.4 Manufacturers and distributors should not distribute to pregnant women or mothers of infants and young children any gifts of articles or utensils which may promote the use of breast-milk substitutes or bottle feeding.

5.5 Marketing personnel, in their business capacity, should not seek direct or indirect contact of any kind with pregnant women or with mothers of infants and young children.

**Article 6. Health Care Systems**

6.3 Facilities of health care systems should not be used for the display of products within the scope of this Code, for placards or posters concerning such products, or for the distribution of material provided by a manufacturer or distributor other than that specified in Article 4.

6.4 The use by the health care system of 'professional service representatives', 'mothercraft nurses' or similar personnel, provided or paid for by manufacturers or distributors, should not be permitted.

6.6 Donations or low-price sales to institutions or organisations of supplies of infant formula or other products within the scope of this Code, whether for use in the institutions or for distribution outside them, may be made . . . Such donations or low-price sales should not be used by manufacturers or distributors as a sales inducement.

6.8 Equipment and materials, in addition to those referred to in Article 4.3, donated to a health care system may bear a company's name or logo, but should not refer to any proprietary product within the scope of this Code.

**Article 7. Health Workers**

7.2 Information provided by manufacturers and distributors to health professionals regarding products within the scope of this Code should be restricted to scientific and factual matters, and such information should not imply or create a belief that bottle feeding is equivalent or superior to breastfeeding . . .

7.3 No financial or material inducements to promote products within the scope of this Code should be offered by manufacturers or distributors to health workers or members of their families, nor should these be accepted by health workers or members of their families.

7.4 Samples of infant formula or other products within the scope of this Code, or of equipment or utensils for their preparation or use, should not be provided to health workers except when necessary for the purpose of professional evaluation or research at the institutional level . . .

7.5 Manufacturers and distributors of products within the scope of this Code should disclose to the institution to which a recipient health worker is affiliated any contribution made to him or on his behalf for fellowships, study tours, research grants, attendance at professional conferences, or the like . . .

**Article 8. Persons Employed by Manufacturers and Distributors**

8.1 In systems of sales incentives for marketing personnel, the volume of sales of products within the scope of this Code should not be included in the calculation of bonuses, nor should quotas be set specifically for sales of these products. This should not be understood to prevent the payment of bonuses based on the overall sales by a company of other products marketed by it.

8.2 Personnel employed in marketing products within the scope of this Code should not, as part of their job responsibilities, perform educational functions in relation to pregnant women or mothers of infants and young children . . .

**Article 9. Labelling**

9.1 Labels should be designed to provide the necessary information about the appropriate use of the product, and so as not to discourage breastfeeding.

9.2 Manufacturers and distributors of infant formula should ensure that each container has a clear, conspicuous, and easily readable and understandable message printed on it, or on a label which cannot readily become separated from it, in an appropriate language, which includes all the following points:

(i) the words 'Important Notice' or their equivalent;
(ii) a statement of the superiority of breastfeeding;
(iii) a statement that the product should be used only on the advice of a health worker as to the need for its use and the proper method of use;
(iv) instructions for appropriate preparation, and a warning against the health hazards of inappropriate preparation.

Neither the container nor the label should have pictures of infants, nor should they have other pictures or text which may idealise the use of infant formula. They may, however, have graphics for easy identification of the product as a breast-milk substitute and for illustrating methods of preparation. The terms 'humanised', 'maternalised' or similar terms should not be used. Inserts giving additional information about the product and its proper use, subject to the above conditions, may be included in the package or retail unit. When labels give instructions for modifying a product into infant formula, the above should apply.

9.3 Food products within the scope of this Code, marketed for infant feeding, which do not meet all the requirements of an infant formula, but which can be modified to do so, should carry on the label a warning that the unmodified product should not be the sole source of nourishment of an infant. Since sweetened condensed milk is not suitable for infant feeding, nor for use as a main ingredient of infant formula, its label should not contain purported instructions on how to modify it for that purpose.

9.4 The label of food products within the scope of this Code should also state all the following points:

(i) the ingredients used;
(ii) the composition/analysis of the product;
(iii) the storage conditions required; and
(iv) the batch number and the date before which the product is to be consumed, taking into account the climatic and storage conditions of the country concerned.

**Article 10. Quality**

10.1 The quality of products is an essential element for the protection of the health of infants and therefore should be of a high recognised standard . . .

**Article 11. Implementation and Monitoring**

11.2 Monitoring the application of this Code lies with governments acting individually, and collectively through the WHO as provided in paragraphs 6 and 7 of this Article.

The manufacturers and distributors of products within the scope of this Code, and appropriate nongovernmental organisations, professional groups, and consumer organisations should collaborate with governments to this end.

11.3 Independently of any other measures taken for implementation of this Code, manufacturers and distributors of products within the scope of this Code should regard themselves as responsible for monitoring their marketing practices according to the principles and aim of this Code, and for taking steps to ensure that their conduct at every level conforms to them.

11.4 Nongovernmental organisations, professional groups, institutions, and individuals concerned should have the responsibility of drawing the attention of manufacturers or distributors to activities which are incompatible with the principles and aim of this Code, so that appropriate action can be taken. The appropriate governmental authority should also be informed.

11.5 Manufacturers and primary distributors of products within the scope of this Code should apprise each member of their marketing personnel of the Code and of their responsibilities under it.

11.6 In accordance with Article 62 of the Constitution of the World Health Organization, Member States shall communicate annually to the Director-General information on action taken to give effect to the principles and aims of this Code.

11.7 The Director-General shall report in even years to the World Health Assembly on the status of implementation of the Code; and shall, on request, provide technical support to Member States preparing natural legislation or regulations, or taking other appropriate measures in implementation and furtherance of the principles and aim of this Code.

# 122. WHO: Framework Convention on Tobacco Control, 2003

**Commentary**: The Framework Convention on Tobacco Control (FCTC) (WHA Resolution WHA56.1 (2003), entry into force 2005) is the first treaty negotiated under WHO's auspices and addresses both demand reduction strategies and supply-side concerns. WHA Resolution WHA 48.11 (1995) requested the Director-General to consider the feasibility of a framework convention: see WHO (1997), 'The Feasibility of an International Instrument for Tobacco Control', WHO Doc EB97/INF.DOC.4; WHO Executive Board (EB) Resolution EB97.R8. WHA Resolution WHA49.17 then requested the Director-General to initiate an FCTC. WHA Resolution WHA52.18 (1999) established a technical working group and an intergovernmental negotiating body. After two sessions the former produced a provisional draft (WHO Document A53/12) which initiated intergovernmental negotiations: WHA Resolution WHA53.16. The first session of the intergovernmental negotiating body was preceded by a public hearing where the public health community, tobacco industry and farmers' groups made submissions. Two NGOs were subsequently admitted into official relations: see WHO Docs EB107/19 & A/FCTC/INB2/6 Add.1 as well as WHO Decision EB107(2). An international conference on the illicit tobacco products trade was held during 2002.

In addition to the provisions extracted below, Article 7 envisages non-price measures for reducing tobacco demand and complementing Article 6. Article 14 contemplates governments promoting the cessation of tobacco use and adequately treating tobacco dependence. Article 17 envisages governments supporting economically viable alternatives for tobacco workers, growers and sellers. Governments also agreed under Article 18 to consider environmental protection and human health in relation to tobacco cultivation and manufacture. Governments also intend to address criminal and civil liability, including compensation where appropriate (Article 19). Article 23(5) enables the COP to request the services of competent NGOs and to receive relevant information from them. WHA Resolution WHA 56.1 (2003) adopting the FCTC urges 'observers and other interested parties to support the preparatory activities referred to in this resolution and effectively to encourage prompt entry into force and implementation of the Convention' (paragraph 5). See also, WHO (2000), 'Tobacco industry strategies to undermine tobacco control activities at the WHO'; WHO (2001), 'Confronting the tobacco epidemic in an era of trade liberalization'; www.who.int/tobacco.

**Article 1: Use of Terms**

For the purposes of this Convention:

(a) 'illicit trade' means any practice or conduct prohibited by law and which relates to production, shipment, receipt, possession, distribution, sale or purchase including any practice or conduct intended to facilitate such activity;

(c) 'tobacco advertising and promotion' means any form of commercial communication, recommendation or action with the aim, effect or likely effect of promoting a tobacco product or tobacco use either directly or indirectly;

(d) 'tobacco control' means a range of supply, demand and harm reduction strategies that aim to improve the health of a population by eliminating or reducing their consumption of tobacco products and exposure to tobacco smoke;

(e) 'tobacco industry' means tobacco manufacturers, wholesale distributors and importers of tobacco products;

(f) 'tobacco products' means products entirely or partly made of the leaf tobacco as raw material which are manufactured to be used for smoking, sucking, chewing or snuffing;

(g) 'tobacco sponsorship' means any form of contribution to any event, activity or individual with the aim, effect or likely effect of promoting a tobacco product or tobacco use either directly or indirectly . . .

**Article 3: Objective**

The objective of this Convention and its protocols is to protect present and future generations from the devastating health, social, environmental and economic consequences of tobacco consumption and exposure to tobacco smoke by providing a framework for tobacco control measures to be implemented by the Parties at the national, regional and international levels in order to reduce continually and substantially the prevalence of tobacco use and exposure to tobacco smoke.

**Article 4: Guiding Principles**

To achieve the objective of this Convention and its protocols and to implement its provisions, the Parties shall be guided, *inter alia*, by the principles set out below:

1. Every person should be informed of the health consequences, addictive nature and mortal threat posed by tobacco consumption and exposure to tobacco smoke and effective legislative, executive, administrative or other measures should be contemplated at the appropriate governmental level to protect all persons from exposure to tobacco smoke.

7. The participation of civil society is essential in achieving the objective of the Convention and its protocols.

**Article 5: General Obligations**

2. Towards this end, each Party shall, in accordance with its capabilities:

   (b) adopt and implement effective legislative, executive, administrative and/or other measures and cooperate, as appropriate, with other Parties in developing appropriate policies for preventing and reducing tobacco consumption, nicotine addiction and exposure to tobacco smoke.

3. In setting and implementing their public health policies with respect to tobacco control, Parties shall act to protect these policies from commercial and other vested interests of the tobacco industry in accordance with national law.

**Article 6: Price and Tax Measures to Reduce the Demand for Tobacco**

1. The Parties recognize that price and tax measures are an effective and important means of reducing tobacco consumption by various segments of the population, in particular young persons.
2. Without prejudice to the sovereign right of the Parties to determine and establish their taxation policies, each Party should take account of its national health objectives concerning tobacco control and adopt or maintain, as appropriate, measures which may include:

   (a) implementing tax policies and, where appropriate, price policies, on tobacco products so as to contribute to the health objectives aimed at reducing tobacco consumption; and
   (b) prohibiting or restricting, as appropriate, sales to and/or importations by international travellers of tax- and duty-free tobacco products . . .

**Article 8: Protection from Exposure to Tobacco Smoke**

1. Parties recognize that scientific evidence has unequivocally established that exposure to tobacco smoke causes death, disease and disability.
2. Each Party shall adopt and implement in areas of existing national jurisdiction as determined by national law and actively promote at other jurisdictional levels the adoption and implementation of effective legislative, executive, administrative and/or other measures, providing for protection from exposure to tobacco smoke in indoor workplaces, public transport, indoor public places and, as appropriate, other public places.

**Article 9: Regulation of the Contents of Tobacco Products**

The Conference of the Parties, in consultation with competent international bodies, shall propose guidelines for testing and measuring the contents and emissions of tobacco products, and for the regulation of these contents and emissions . . .

**Article 10: Regulation of Tobacco Product Disclosures**

Each Party shall, in accordance with its national law, adopt and implement effective legislative, executive, administrative or other measures requiring manufacturers and importers of tobacco products to disclose to governmental authorities information about the contents and emissions of tobacco products. Each Party shall further adopt and implement effective measures for public disclosure of information about the toxic constituents of the tobacco products and the emissions that they may produce.

**Article 11: Packaging and Labelling of Tobacco Products**

1. Each Party shall, within a period of three years after entry into force of this Convention for that Party, adopt and implement, in accordance with its national law, effective measures to ensure that:

(a) tobacco product packaging and labelling do not promote a tobacco product by any means that are false, misleading, deceptive or likely to create an erroneous impression about its characteristics, health effects, hazards or emissions, including any term, descriptor, trademark, figurative or any other sign that directly or indirectly creates the false impression that a particular tobacco product is less harmful than other tobacco products. These may include terms such as 'low tar', 'light', 'ultra-light', or 'mild'; and
(b) each unit packet and package of tobacco products and any outside packaging and labelling of such products also carry health warnings describing the harmful effects of tobacco use, and may include other appropriate messages. These warnings and messages:

(i) shall be approved by the competent national authority,
(ii) shall be rotating,
(iii) shall be large, clear, visible and legible,
(iv) should be 50% or more of the principal display areas but shall be no less than 30% of the principal display areas,
(v) may be in the form of or include pictures or pictograms.

2. Each unit packet and package of tobacco products and any outside packaging and labelling of such products shall, in addition to the warnings specified in paragraph 1(b) of this Article, contain information on relevant constituents and emissions of tobacco products as defined by national authorities.
3. Each Party shall require that the warnings and other textual information specified in paragraphs 1(b) and paragraph 2 of this Article will appear on each unit packet and package of tobacco products and any outside packaging and labelling of such products in its principal language or languages.
4. For the purposes of this Article, the term 'outside packaging and labelling' in relation to tobacco products applies to any packaging and labelling used in the retail sale of the product.

**Article 12: Education, Communication, Training and Public Awareness**
Each Party shall promote and strengthen public awareness of tobacco control issues, using all available communication tools, as appropriate. Towards this end, each Party shall adopt and implement effective legislative, executive, administrative or other measures to promote:

(c) public access, in accordance with national law, to a wide range of information on the tobacco industry as relevant to the objective of this Convention;
(e) awareness and participation of public and private agencies and nongovernmental organizations not affiliated with the tobacco industry in developing and implementing intersectoral programmes and strategies for tobacco control . . .

**Article 13: Tobacco Advertising, Promotion and Sponsorship**
1. Parties recognize that a comprehensive ban on advertising, promotion and sponsorship would reduce the consumption of tobacco products.

2. Each Party shall, in accordance with its constitution or constitutional principles, undertake a comprehensive ban of all tobacco advertising, promotion and sponsorship. This shall include, subject to the legal environment and technical means available to that Party, a comprehensive ban on cross-border advertising, promotion and sponsorship originating from its territory. In this respect, within the period of five years after entry into force of this Convention for that Party, each Party shall undertake appropriate legislative, executive, administrative and/or other measures and report accordingly in conformity with Article 21.
3. A Party that is not in a position to undertake a comprehensive ban due to its constitution or constitutional principles shall apply restrictions on all tobacco advertising, promotion and sponsorship . . .
4. As a minimum, and in accordance with its constitution or constitutional principles, each Party shall:

   (a) prohibit all forms of tobacco advertising, promotion and sponsorship that promote a tobacco product by any means that are false, misleading or deceptive or likely to create an erroneous impression about its characteristics, health effects, hazards or emissions;
   (b) require that health or other appropriate warnings or messages accompany all tobacco advertising and, as appropriate, promotion and sponsorship;
   (c) restrict the use of direct or indirect incentives that encourage the purchase of tobacco products by the public;
   (d) require, if it does not have a comprehensive ban, the disclosure to relevant governmental authorities of expenditures by the tobacco industry on advertising, promotion and sponsorship not yet prohibited. Those authorities may decide to make those figures available, subject to national law, to the public and to the Conference of the Parties, pursuant to Article 21;
   (e) undertake a comprehensive ban or, in the case of a Party that is not in a position to undertake a comprehensive ban due to its constitution or constitutional principles, restrict tobacco advertising, promotion and sponsorship on radio, television, print media and, as appropriate, other media, such as the internet, within a period of five years; and
   (f) prohibit, or in the case of a Party that is not in a position to prohibit due to its constitution or constitutional principles restrict, tobacco sponsorship of international events, activities and/or participants therein.

**Article 15: Illicit Trade in Tobacco Products**

1. The Parties recognize that the elimination of all forms of illicit trade in tobacco products, including smuggling, illicit manufacturing and counterfeiting, and the development and implementation of related national law, in addition to subregional, regional and global agreements, are essential components of tobacco control.
2. Each Party shall adopt and implement effective legislative, executive, administrative or other measures to ensure that all unit packets and packages of tobacco products and any outside packaging of such products are marked to assist Parties in determining the origin of tobacco products, and in accordance with national law and relevant bilateral or multilateral agreements, assist Parties in determining the point of diversion and monitor, document and control the movement of tobacco products and their legal status. In addition, each Party shall:

(a) require that unit packets and packages of tobacco products for retail and wholesale use that are sold on its domestic market carry the statement: 'Sales only allowed in (insert name of the country, subnational, regional or federal unit)' or carry any other effective marking indicating the final destination or which would assist authorities in determining whether the product is legally for sale on the domestic market; and
(b) consider, as appropriate, developing a practical tracking and tracing regime that would further secure the distribution system and assist in the investigation of illicit trade.

3. Each Party shall require that the packaging information or marking specified in paragraph 2 of this Article shall be presented in legible form and/or appear in its principal language or languages.
4. With a view to eliminating illicit trade in tobacco products, each Party shall:

(a) monitor and collect data on cross-border trade in tobacco products, including illicit trade, and exchange information among customs, tax and other authorities, as appropriate, and in accordance with national law and relevant applicable bilateral or multilateral agreements;
(b) enact or strengthen legislation, with appropriate penalties and remedies, against illicit trade in tobacco products, including counterfeit and contraband cigarettes;
(c) take appropriate steps to ensure that all confiscated manufacturing equipment, counterfeit and contraband cigarettes and other tobacco products are destroyed, using environmentally-friendly methods where feasible, or disposed of in accordance with national law;
(d) adopt and implement measures to monitor, document and control the storage and distribution of tobacco products held or moving under suspension of taxes or duties within its jurisdiction; and
(e) adopt measures as appropriate to enable the confiscation of proceeds derived from the illicit trade in tobacco products.

7. Each Party shall endeavour to adopt and implement further measures including licensing, where appropriate, to control or regulate the production and distribution of tobacco products in order to prevent illicit trade.

**Article 16: Sales to and by Minors**

1. Each Party shall adopt and implement effective legislative, executive, administrative or other measures at the appropriate government level to prohibit the sales of tobacco products to persons under the age set by domestic law, national law or eighteen. These measures may include:

(a) requiring that all sellers of tobacco products place a clear and prominent indicator inside their point of sale about the prohibition of tobacco sales to minors and, in case of doubt, request that each tobacco purchaser provide appropriate evidence of having reached full legal age;
(b) banning the sale of tobacco products in any manner by which they are directly accessible, such as store shelves;

(c) prohibiting the manufacture and sale of sweets, snacks, toys or any other objects in the form of tobacco products which appeal to minors; and
(d) ensuring that tobacco vending machines under its jurisdiction are not accessible to minors and do not promote the sale of tobacco products to minors.

2. Each Party shall prohibit or promote the prohibition of the distribution of free tobacco products to the public and especially minors.
3. Each Party shall endeavour to prohibit the sale of cigarettes individually or in small packets which increase the affordability of such products to minors.
4. The Parties recognize that in order to increase their effectiveness, measures to prevent tobacco product sales to minors should, where appropriate, be implemented in conjunction with other provisions contained in this Convention.
5. When signing, ratifying, accepting, approving or acceding to the Convention or at any time thereafter, a Party may, by means of a binding written declaration, indicate its commitment to prohibit the introduction of tobacco vending machines within its jurisdiction or, as appropriate, to a total ban on tobacco vending machines . . .
6. Each Party shall adopt and implement effective legislative, executive, administrative or other measures, including penalties against sellers and distributors, in order to ensure compliance with the obligations contained in paragraphs 1–5 of this Article.

**Article 20: Research, Surveillance and Exchange of Information**

1. The Parties undertake to develop and promote national research and to coordinate research programmes at the regional and international levels in the field of tobacco control . . .
3. Parties recognize the importance of financial and technical assistance from international and regional intergovernmental organizations and other bodies. Each Party shall endeavour to:

(a) establish progressively a national system for the epidemiological surveillance of tobacco consumption and related social, economic and health indicators;
(b) cooperate with competent international and regional intergovernmental organizations and other bodies, including governmental and nongovernmental agencies, in regional and global tobacco surveillance and exchange of information on the indicators specified in paragraph 3(a) of this Article . . .

4. The Parties shall, subject to national law, promote and facilitate the exchange of publicly available scientific, technical, socioeconomic, commercial and legal information, as well as information regarding practices of the tobacco industry and the cultivation of tobacco, which is relevant to this Convention, and in so doing shall take into account and address the special needs of developing country Parties and Parties with economies in transition. Each Party shall endeavour to:

(c) cooperate with competent international organizations to progressively establish and maintain a global system to regularly collect and disseminate information on tobacco production, manufacture and the activities of the tobacco industry which have an impact on the Convention or national tobacco control activities . . .

**Article 21: Reporting and Exchange of Information**

4. The reporting and exchange of information under the Convention shall be subject to national law regarding confidentiality and privacy. The Parties shall protect, as mutually agreed, any confidential information that is exchanged.

**Article 22: Cooperation in the Scientific, Technical, and Legal Fields and Provision of Related Expertise**

1. The Parties shall cooperate directly or through competent international bodies to strengthen their capacity to fulfil the obligations arising from this Convention, taking into account the needs of developing country Parties and Parties with economies in transition. Such cooperation shall promote the transfer of technical, scientific and legal expertise and technology, as mutually agreed, to establish and strengthen national tobacco control strategies, plans and programmes aiming at, *inter alia*:

   (a) facilitation of the development, transfer and acquisition of technology, knowledge, skills, capacity and expertise related to tobacco control;
   (b) provision of technical, scientific, legal and other expertise to establish and strengthen national tobacco control strategies, plans and programmes, aiming at implementation of the Convention through, *inter alia*:

      (iii) assisting, as appropriate, tobacco growers in shifting agricultural production to alternative crops in an economically viable manner . . .

**Article 26: Financial Resources**

5. The Parties agree that:

   (a) to assist Parties in meeting their obligations under the Convention, all relevant potential and existing resources, financial, technical, or otherwise, both public and private that are available for tobacco control activities, should be mobilized and utilized for the benefit of all Parties, especially developing countries and countries with economies in transition . . .

# 123. UNCTAD: The Set of Multilaterally Agreed Equitable Principles and Rules for the Control of Restrictive Business Practices, 2000

**Commentary**: UNGA Resolutions 33/153 (1978) & 34/447 (1979) convened a UN Conference on Restrictive Business Practices under UNCTAD auspices during 1979 and 1980. The Conference adopted a set of multilaterally agreed equitable principles (Resolution of 22 April 1980, 7th plenary meeting) which were subsequently approved through UNGA Resolution 35/63 (1980). See further, UN Doc UNCTAD/RBP/CONF/10/Rev.2 (2000). In addition to the provisions of the Restrictive Business Practices Code extracted below, Section F contemplates intergovernmental collaboration, information exchange and consultation through UNCTAD or the UNCTC and arranging seminars for exchanging views 'among persons in the public and private sectors'. Four UN Conferences to Review All Aspects of the Set of Principles have since taken place (1985, 1990, 1995 and 2000). The Fourth Review reaffirmed their continuing validity, recommended the 'UN Set of Principles and Rules on Competition' as an appropriate subtitle and called for further implementation: see UNCTAD Doc TD/RBP/CONF.5/15 (2000) and the Fourth Conference Report, TD/RBP/CONF.5/16 (2000). See also, UNCTAD (2000), 'An Assessment of the Operation of the Set' TD/RBP/CONF.5/3; UNCTAD (1999), 'A Preliminary Assessment since the Third Review Conference', TD/B/COM.2/CLP/13; UNCTAD (1998), 'Continued Work on the Elaboration of a Model Law or Laws on Restrictive Business Practices', TD/B/RBP/81/Rev.5; UNCTAD (1996), 'Competition Policy and Restrictive Business Practices' TD/B/RBP/INF.36; UNCTAD (1997), 'Transnational Corporations, Market Structure and Competition Policy', UN Doc UNCTAD/ITE/IIT/5; www.unctad.org. See also, OECD (1995), 'Council Recommendation concerning co-operation between member countries on anti-competitive practices affecting international trade', OECD Doc C(95)130/FINAL. For bilateral initiatives, see, for example, US–EC (1998), Agreement on the Application of Positive Comity Principles in the Enforcement of their Competition Laws 37 *ILM* 1070. For commercial perspectives, see ICC (1996), 'Statement on International Cooperation Between Antitrust Authorities', ICC Pub No 225/450Rev 3, Paris; ICC (1998), 'Recommended Code of Practice for Competition Authorities on Searches and Subpoenas of Computer Records', ICC Pub No 225/507Rev, Paris.

**Section A: Objectives**

Taking into account the interests of all countries, particularly those of developing countries. the Set of Multilaterally Agreed Equitable Principles and Rules are framed in order to achieve the following objectives:

1. To ensure that restrictive business practices do not impede or negate the realization of benefits that should arise from the liberalization of tariff and non-tariff barriers affecting world trade, particularly those affecting the trade and development of developing countries;
2. To attain greater efficiency in international trade and development, particularly that of developing countries, in accordance with national aims of economic and social development and existing economic structures, such as through:

   a) The creation, encouragement and protection of competition;
   b) Control of the concentration of capital and/or economic power;
   c) Encouragement of innovation;

3. To protect and promote social welfare in general and, in particular, the interests of consumers in both developed and developing countries;
4. To eliminate the disadvantages to trade and development which may result from the restrictive business practices of TNCs or other enterprises, and thus help to maximize benefits to international trade and particularly the trade and development of developing countries . . .

**Section B: Definitions and Scope of Application**

For the purpose of this Set of Multilaterally Agreed Equitable Principles and Rules:

*i. Definitions*

1. 'Restrictive business practices' means acts or behaviour of enterprises which, through an abuse or acquisition and abuse of a dominant position of market power, limit access to markets or otherwise unduly restrain competition, having or being likely to have adverse effects on international trade, particularly that of developing countries, and on the economic development of these countries, or which through formal, informal, written or unwritten agreements or arrangements among enterprises, have the same impact.
2. 'Dominant position of market power' refers to a situation where an enterprise, either by itself or acting together with a few other enterprises, is in a position to control the relevant market for a particular good or service or group of goods or services.
3. 'Enterprises' means firms, partnerships, corporations, companies, other associations, natural or juridical persons, or any combination thereof, irrespective of the mode of creation or control or ownership, private or State, which are engaged in commercial activities, and includes their branches, subsidiaries, affiliates, or other entities directly or indirectly controlled by them.

*ii. Scope of Application*

4. The Set of Principles and Rules applies to restrictive business practices. including those of TNCs, adversely affecting international trade, particularly that of developing countries and the economic development of these countries. It applies irrespective of whether such practices involve enterprises in one or more countries.
5. The 'principles and rules for enterprises, including TNCs' apply to all transactions in good and services.
6. The 'principles and rules for enterprises including TNCs' are addressed to all enterprises.

7. The provisions of the Set of Principles and Rules shall be universally applicable to all countries and enterprises regardless of the parties involved in the transactions, acts or behaviour . . .

**Section C: Multilaterally-agreed Equitable Principles for the Control of Restrictive Business Practices**

In line with the objectives set forth, the following principles are to apply:

*i. General Principles*

1. Appropriate action should be taken in a mutually reinforcing manner at national, regional and international levels to eliminate, or effectively deal with, restrictive business practices, including those of TNCs, adversely affecting international trade, particularly that of developing countries and the economic development of these countries.
5. The provisions of the Set of Principles and Rules should not be construed as justifying conduct by enterprises which is unlawful under applicable national or regional legislation.

*ii. Relevant Factors in the Application of the Set of Principles and Rules*

6. In order to ensure the fair. and equitable application of the Set of Principles and Rules, States, while bearing in mind the need to ensure the comprehensive application of the Set of Principles and Rules, should take due account of the extent to which the conduct of enterprises, whether or not created or controlled by States, is accepted under applicable legislation or regulations, bearing in mind that such laws and regulations should be clearly defined and publicly and readily available, or is required by States.

*iii. Preferential or Differential Treatment for Developing Countries*

7. In order to ensure the equitable application of the Set of Principles and Rules, States, particularly developed countries, should take into account in their control of restrictive business practices the development, financial and trade needs of developing countries, in particular of the least developed countries, for the purposes especially of developing countries in:

    a) Promoting the establishment or development of domestic industries and the economic development of other sectors of the economy, and
    b) Encouraging their economic development through regional or global arrangements among developing countries.

**Section D: Principles and Rules for Enterprises, including Transnational Corporations**

1. Enterprises should conform to the restrictive business practices laws, and the provisions concerning restrictive business practices in other laws, of the countries in which they operate, and, in the event of proceedings under these laws, should be subject to the competence of the courts and relevant administrative bodies therein.
2. Enterprises should consult and co-operate with competent authorities of countries directly affected in controlling restrictive business practices adversely affecting the interests of those countries. In this regard, enterprises should also provide information,

in particular details of restrictive arrangements, required for this purpose, including that which may be located in foreign countries, to the extent that in the latter event such production or disclosure is not prevented by applicable law or established public policy. Whenever the provision of information is on a voluntary basis, its provisions should be in accordance with safeguards normally applicable in this field.

3. Enterprises, except when dealing with each other in the context of an economic entity wherein they are under common control, including though ownership, or otherwise not able to act independently of each other, engaged on the market in rival or potentially rival activities, should refrain from practices such as the following when, through formal, informal, written or unwritten agreements or arrangements, they limit access to markets or otherwise unduly restrain competition, having or being likely to have adverse effects on international trade, particularly that of developing countries, and on the economic development of these countries:

   a) Agreements fixing prices, including as to exports and imports;
   b) Collusive tendering;
   c) Market or customer allocation arrangements;
   d) Allocation by quota as to sales and production;
   e) Collective action to enforce arrangements, e.g. by concerted refusals to deal;
   f) Concerted refusal of supplies to potential importers;
   g) Collective denial of access to an arrangement, or association, which is crucial to competition.

4. Enterprises should refrain from the following acts or behaviour in a relevant market when, through an abuse[1] or acquisition and abuse of a dominant position of market power, they limit access to markets or otherwise unduly restrain competition, having or being likely to have adverse effects on international trade, particularly that of developing countries, and on the economic development of these countries:

   a) Predatory behaviour towards competitors, such as using below-cost pricing to eliminate competitors;
   b) Discriminatory (i.e. unjustifiably differentiated) pricing or terms or conditions in the supply or purchase of goods and services, including by means of the use of pricing policies in transactions between affiliated enterprises which overcharge or undercharge for goods or services purchased or supplied as compared with prices for similar or comparable transactions outside the affiliated enterprises;
   c) Mergers, takeovers, joint ventures or other acquisitions of control, whether of a horizontal, vertical or a conglomerate nature;
   d) Fixing the prices at which goods exported can be resold in importing countries;
   e) Restrictions on the importation of goods which have been legitimately marked abroad with a trademark identical with or similar to the trademark protected as to identical or similar goods in the importing country where the trademarks in question are of the same origin, i.e. belong to the same owner or are used by enterprises between which there is economic, organizational, managerial or legal interdependence and where the purpose of such restrictions is to maintain artificially high prices;
   f) When not for ensuring the achievement of legitimate business purposes, such as quality, safety, adequate distribution or service:

(i) Partial or complete refusals to deal on the enterprise's customary commercial terms;

(ii) Making the supply of particular goods or services dependent upon the acceptance of restrictions on the distribution or manufacture of competing or other goods;

(iii) Imposing restrictions concerning where, or to whom, or in what form or quantities, goods supplied or other goods may be resold or exported;

(iv) Making the supply of particular goods or services dependent upon the purchase of other goods or services from the supplier or his designee.

**Section E: Principles and Rules for States at National, Regional and Subregional Levels**

2. States should base their legislation primarily on the principle of eliminating or effectively dealing with acts or behaviour of enterprises which, through an abuse or acquisition and abuse of a dominant position of market power, limit access to markets or otherwise unduly restrain competition, having or being likely to have adverse effects on their trade or economic development, or which through formal, informal, written or unwritten agreements or arrangements among enterprises have the same impact.
3. States, in their control of restrictive business practices, should ensure treatment of enterprises which is fair, equitable, on the same basis to all enterprises, and in accordance with established procedures of law. The laws and regulations should be publicly and readily available.
5. Where, for the purpose of the control of restrictive business practices, a State obtains information from enterprises containing legitimate business secrets, it should accord such information reasonable safeguards normally applicable in this field, particularly to protect its confidentiality.
6. States should institute or improve procedures for obtaining information from enterprises including TNCs, necessary for their effective control or restrictive business practices, including in this respect details of restrictive agreements, understandings and other arrangements . . .

**Section G: International Institutional Machinery**

*i. Institutional Arrangements*

1. An Intergovernmental Group of Experts on Restrictive Business Practices operating within the framework of a Committee of UNCTAD will provide the institutional machinery.
4. In the performance of its functions, neither the Intergovernmental Group nor its subsidiary organs shall act like a tribunal or otherwise pass judgement on the activities or conduct of individual Governments or of individual enterprises in connection with a specific business transaction. The Intergovernmental Group or its subsidiary organs should avoid becoming involved when enterprises to a specific business transaction are in dispute.
5. The Intergovernmental Group shall establish such procedures as may be necessary to deal with issues related to confidentiality.

## Note

1. Whether acts or behaviour are abusive or not should be examined in terms of their purpose and effects in the actual situation, in particular with reference to whether they limit access to markets or otherwise unduly restrain competition, having or being likely to have adverse effects on international trade, particularly that of developing countries, and on the economic development of these countries, and to whether they are:

    (a) Appropriate in the light of the organizational, managerial and legal relationship among the enterprises concerned, such as in the context of relations within an economic entity and not having restrictive effects outside the related enterprises;
    (b) Appropriate in light of special conditions of economic circumstances in the relevant market such as exceptional conditions of supply and demand or the size of the market;
    (c) Of types which are usually treated as acceptable under pertinent national or regional laws and regulations for the control of restrictive business practices;
    (d) Consistent with the purposes and objectives of these principles and rules.

# 124. UNCTAD: Draft International Code of Conduct on the Transfer of Technology, 1985

**Commentary**: UNCTAD considered the feasibility of a transfer of technology (TOT) Code (TD/B/AC.11/22 (1974) & Corr.I) in the light of replies from governments: see UNCTAD Doc TD/B/C.6/AC.1/3 & Add.1–2 (1975). An intergovernmental expert group was appointed in 1975 to prepare an initial draft (TD/CODE TOT/1-TD/AC.1/18 (1978)) which was subsequently considered over six sessions by a UN Conference on an International Code of Conduct on the Transfer of Technology. Thereafter the Code went through several formulations: see TD/CODE TOT/14 (1979), TD/CODE TOT/20 (1979), TD/CODE TOT/25 & Corr.I (1980), TD/CODE TOT/33 (1981), TD/CODE TOT/41 (1983) and TD/CODE TOT/47 (1985) (extracted below). In view of the state of negotiations (TD/B/C.6/109 (1984)) and an expert report on outstanding issues (TD/CODE TOT/52 (1988)), the UNCTAD Secretary-General conducted further consultations in 1989 (TD/CODE TOT/54), 1990 (TD/CODE TOT/56) and 1992 (TD/CODE TOT/58). Recent technological developments relevant to the draft code were noted: see TD/CODE TOT/55 (1990). UNGA Resolution 40/184 (1985), paragraph 1, observed that 'progress has been made . . . but that there are still important problems outstanding'. UNGA Resolution 48/167 (1993), paragraph 1, similarly observed that 'conditions do not currently exist to reach full agreement on all outstanding issues'. The state of negotiations as at 1995 is described in TD/CODE TOT/60. In addition to the provisions extracted below, Article 3.4 identifies a range of measures with respect to the financial, technical, renegotiating and organisational aspects of technological transfer. Chapter 7 concerning intergovernmental collaboration contemplates information exchange and concluding international agreements. Several provisions (and many of their respective endnotes where text remains under consideration) have been omitted. For academic commentary, see Fikentscher W. (1980), *The Draft International Code of Conduct on the Transfer of Technology: A Study in Third World Development*, Weinheim: VCH Verlag. For commercial perspectives, see ICC (1972), 'The International Corporation and the Transfer of Technology', Paris. See also, UNEP Governing Council Decision 14/16 (1987) concerning promotion of the transfer of environmental protection technology.

**Chapter 1: Definitions and Scope of Application**

1.1. For the purposes of the present Code of Conduct:

(a) 'Party' means any person, either natural or juridical, of public or private law, either individual or collective, such as corporations, companies, firms, partnerships and other associations, or any combination thereof, whether created, owned or controlled by States, Government agencies, juridical persons, or individuals, wherever they operate, as well as States, Government agencies and international, regional and subregional organizations, when they engage in an international transfer of technology transaction which is usually considered to be of a commercial nature. The term 'party' includes, among the entities enumerated above, incorporated branches, subsidiaries and affiliates, joint ventures or other legal entities regardless of the economic and other relationships between and among them.

(b) 'Acquiring party' means the party which obtains a licence to use or to exploit, purchases or otherwise acquires technology of a proprietary or non-proprietary nature and/or rights related thereto in a transfer of technology.

(c) 'Supplying party' means the party which licenses, sells, assigns or otherwise provides technology of a proprietary or non-proprietary nature and/or rights related thereto in a transfer of technology.

1.2. Transfer of technology under this Code is the transfer of systematic knowledge for the manufacture of a product, for the application of a process or for the rendering of a service and does not extend to the transactions involving the mere sale or mere lease of goods.

1.3. Transfer of technology transactions are arrangements between parties involving transfer of technology, as defined in paragraph 1.2 above, particularly in each of the following cases:

(a) The assignment, sale and licensing of all forms of industrial property, except for trade marks, service marks and trade names when they are not part of transfer of technology transactions;

(b) The provision of know-how and technical expertise in the form of feasibility studies, plans, diagrams, models, instructions, guides, formulae, basic or detailed engineering designs, specifications and equipment for training, services involving technical advisory and managerial personnel, and personnel training;

(c) The provision of technological knowledge necessary for the installation, operation and functioning of plant and equipment, and turnkey projects;

(d) The provision of technological knowledge necessary to acquire, install and use machinery, equipment, intermediate goods and/or raw materials which have been acquired by purchase, lease or other means;

(e) The provision of technological contents of industrial and technical co-operation arrangements.

1.4. International transfer of technology transactions.

1.5. The Code of Conduct is universally applicable in scope and is addressed to all parties to transfer of technology transactions and to all countries and groups of countries, irrespective of their economic and political systems and their levels of development . . .

## Chapter 2: Objectives and Principles

*2.1. Objectives*

(i) To establish general and equitable standards on which to base the relationships among parties to transfer of technology transactions and governments concerned, taking into consideration their legitimate interests, and giving due recognition to special needs of developing countries for the fulfilment of their economic and social development objectives.

(ii) To promote mutual confidence between parties as well as their governments.

(iii) To encourage transfer of technology transactions, particularly those involving developing countries, under conditions where bargaining positions of the parties to the transactions are balanced in such a way as to avoid abuses of a stronger position and thereby to achieve mutually satisfactory agreements.

(iv) To facilitate and increase the international flow of technological information, particularly on the availability of alternative technologies, as a prerequisite for the assessment, selection, adaptation, development and use of technologies in all countries, particularly in developing countries.

(v) To facilitate and increase the international flow of proprietary and non-proprietary technology for strengthening the growth of the scientific and technological capabilities of all countries, in particular developing countries, so as to increase their participation in world production and trade.

(vi) To increase the contributions of technology to the identification and solution of social and economic problems of all countries, particularly the developing countries, including the development of basic sectors of their national economies.

(viii) To promote adequate arrangements as regards unpackaging in terms of information concerning the various elements of the technology to be transferred, such as that required for technical, institutional and financial evaluation of the transaction, thus avoiding undue or unnecessary packaging.

(ix) To specify restrictive [business] practices from which parties to technology transfer transactions [shall] [should] refrain.

(x) To set forth an appropriate set of responsibilities and obligations of parties to transfer of technology transactions, taking into consideration their legitimate interests as well as differences in their bargaining positions.

*2.2. Principles*

(i) The Code of Conduct is universally applicable in scope.

(ii) States have the right to adopt all appropriate measures for facilitating and regulating the transfer of technology, in a manner consistent with their international obligations, taking into consideration the legitimate interests of all parties concerned, and encouraging transfers of technology under mutually agreed, fair and reasonable terms and conditions.

(vi) Mutual benefits should accrue to technology supplying and recipient parties in order to maintain and increase the international flow of technology.

(vii) Facilitating and increasing the access to technology, particularly for developing countries, under mutually agreed fair and reasonable terms and conditions, are fundamental elements in the process of technology transfer and development.

(viii) Recognition of the protection of industrial property rights granted under national law.

(ix) Technology supplying parties when operating in an acquiring country should respect the sovereignty and the laws of that country, act with proper regard for that country's declared development policies and priorities and endeavour to contribute substantially to the development of the acquiring country. The freedom of parties to negotiate, conclude and perform agreements for the transfer of technology on mutually acceptable terms and conditions should be based on respect for the foregoing and other principles set forth in this Code.

## Chapter 3: National Regulation of Transfer of Technology Transactions

3.2. Measures adopted by States including decisions of competent administrative bodies should be applied fairly, equitably, and on the same basis to all parties in accordance with established procedures of law and the principles and objectives of the Code . . .

3.3. Each country adopting legislation on the protection of industrial property should have regard to its national needs of economic and social development, and should ensure an effective protection of industrial property rights granted under its national law and other related rights recognized by its national law.

## Chapter 4: [The Regulation of Practices and Arrangements Involving the Transfer of Technology] [Restrictive Business Practices]

*Section B: (List of Practices)*

1. [EXCLUSIVE] GRANT-BACK PROVISIONS

Requiring the acquiring party to transfer or grant back to the supplying party, or to any other enterprise designated by the supplying party, improvements arising from the acquired technology, on an exclusive basis [or] without offsetting consideration or reciprocal obligations from the supplying party, or when the practice will constitute an abuse of a dominant market position of the supplying party.

2. CHALLENGES TO VALIDITY

[Unreasonably] requiring the acquiring party to refrain from challenging the validity of patents and other types of protection for inventions involved in the transfer or the validity of other such grants claimed or obtained by the supplying party, recognizing that any issues concerning the mutual rights and obligations of the parties following such a challenge will be determined by the appropriate applicable law and the terms of the agreement to the extent consistent with that law.

3. EXCLUSIVE DEALING

Restrictions on the freedom of the acquiring party to enter into sales, representation or manufacturing agreements relating to similar or competing technologies or products or to obtain competing technology, when such restrictions are not needed for ensuring the achievement of legitimate interests, particularly including securing the confidentiality of the technology transferred or best effort distribution or promotional obligations.

4. RESTRICTIONS ON RESEARCH

[Unreasonably] restricting the acquiring party either in undertaking research and development directed to absorb and adapt the transferred technology to local conditions or in initiating research and development programmes in connection with new products, processes or equipment.

5. RESTRICTIONS ON USE OF PERSONNEL

[Unreasonably] requiring the acquiring party to use personnel designated by the supplying party, except to the extent necessary to ensure the efficient transmission phase for the transfer of technology and putting it to use or thereafter continuing such requirement beyond the time when adequately trained local personnel are available or have been trained; or prejudicing the use of personnel of the technology acquiring country.

6. PRICE FIXING

[Unjustifiably] imposing regulation of prices to be charged by acquiring parties in the relevant market to which the technology was transferred for products manufactured or services produced using the technology supplied.

7. RESTRICTIONS ON ADAPTATIONS

Restrictions which [unreasonably] prevent the acquiring party from adapting the imported technology to local conditions or introducing innovations in it, or which oblige the acquiring party to introduce unwanted or unnecessary design or specification changes, if the acquiring party makes adaptations on his own responsibility and without using the technology supplying party's name, trade or service marks or trade names, and except to the extent that this adaptation unsuitably affects those products, or the process for their manufacture, to be supplied to the supplying party, his designates, or his other licensees, or to be used as a component or spare part in a product to be supplied to his customers.

8. EXCLUSIVE SALES OR REPRESENTATION AGREEMENTS

Requiring the acquiring party to grant exclusive sales or representation rights to the supplying party or any person designated by the supplying party, except as to subcontracting or manufacturing arrangements wherein the parties have agreed that all or part of the production under the technology transfer arrangement will be distributed by the supplying party or any person designated by him.

9. TYING ARRANGEMENTS

[Unduly] imposing acceptance of additional technology, future inventions and improvements, goods or services not wanted by the acquiring party or [unduly] restricting sources of technology, goods or services, as a condition for obtaining the technology required when not required to maintain the quality of the product or service when the supplier's trade or service mark or other identifying item is used by the acquiring party, or to fulfil a specific performance obligation which has been guaranteed, provided further that adequate specification of the ingredients is not feasible or would involve the disclosure of additional technology not covered by the arrangement.

10. EXPORT RESTRICTIONS

11. PATENT POOL OR CROSS-LICENSING AGREEMENTS AND OTHER ARRANGEMENTS

Restrictions on territories, quantities, prices, customers or markets arising out of patent pool or cross-licensing agreements or other international transfer of technology interchange arrangements among technology suppliers which unduly limit access to new technological developments or which would result in an abusive domination of an industry or market with adverse effects on the transfer of technology, except for those restrictions appropriate and ancillary to co-operative arrangements such as co-operative research arrangements.

12. RESTRICTIONS ON PUBLICITY

Restrictions [unreasonably] regulating the advertising or publicity by the acquiring party except where restrictions of such publicity may be required to prevent injury to the supplying party's goodwill or reputation where the advertising or publicity makes reference to the supplying party's name, trade or service marks, trade names or other identifying items, or for legitimate reasons of avoiding product liability when the supplying party may be subject to such liability, or where appropriate for safety purposes or to protect consumers, or when needed to secure the confidentiality of the technology transferred.

13. PAYMENTS AND OTHER OBLIGATIONS AFTER EXPIRATION OF INDUSTRIAL PROPERTY RIGHTS
Requiring payments or imposing other obligations for continuing the use of industrial property rights which have been invalidated, cancelled or have expired recognizing that any other issue, including other payment obligations for technology, shall be dealt with by the appropriate applicable law and the terms of the agreement to the extent consistent with that law.

14. RESTRICTIONS AFTER EXPIRATION OF ARRANGEMENT

## Chapter 5: Responsibilities and Obligations of Parties

*Common Provision on Negotiating as well as Contractual Phase*

5.1. When negotiating and concluding a technology transfer agreement, the parties should, in accordance with this chapter, be responsive to the economic and social development objectives of the respective countries of the parties and particularly of the technology acquiring country, and when negotiating, concluding and performing a technology transfer agreement, the parties should observe fair and honest business practices and take into account the specific circumstances of the individual case and recognition should be given to certain circumstances, mainly the stage of development of technology, the economic and technical capabilities of the parties, the nature and type of the transaction such as any ongoing or continuous flow of technology between the parties.

*Negotiating Phase*

5.2. In being responsive to the economic and social development objectives mentioned in this chapter each party should take into account the other's request to include in the agreements, to the extent technically and commercially practicable and for adequate consideration, when appropriate, such as the case in which the supplying party incurs additional costs or efforts, items clearly related to the official economic and social development objectives of the country of the requesting party as enunciated by its government. Such items include, *inter alia*, where applicable:

(a) Use of locally available resources.

(i) specific provisions for the use for the tasks concerned of adequately trained or otherwise suitable local personnel to be designated and subsequently made available by the potential technology recipient including managerial personnel, as well as for the training of suitably skilled local personnel to be designated and subsequently made available by the potential technology recipient;

(ii) specific provisions for the use of locally available materials, technologies, technical skills, consultancy and engineering services and other resources to be indicated and subsequently made available by the potential technology recipient;

(b) Rendering of technical services.
Specific provisions for the rendering of technical services in the introduction and operation of the technology to be transferred;

(c) Unpackaging.
Upon request of the potential acquiring party, the potential supplying party should, to the extent practicable, make adequate arrangements as regards unpackaging in terms of information concerning the various elements of the technology to be transferred, such as that required for technical, institutional and financial evaluation of the potential supplying party's offer.

5.3. Business negotiating practices.
When negotiating a technology transfer agreement, the parties should observe fair and honest business practices and therefore:

(a) Both potential parties:

(i) Fair and reasonable terms and conditions.

(i) Should negotiate in good faith with the aim of reaching, in a timely manner, an agreement containing fair and reasonable commercial terms and conditions, including agreement on payments such as licence fees, royalties and other considerations;

(ii) The price or consideration to be charged should be fair and reasonable, it should be clearly indicated and, to the extent practicable, specified in such a manner that the acquiring party would be able to appreciate its reasonableness and fairness by comparing it to the price or consideration for other comparable technologies transferred under similar conditions, which may be known to him;

(ii) Relevant information.
Should consider requests to inform each other, to the extent appropriate, about their prior arrangements which may affect the contemplated technology transfer;

(iii) Confidential information.
Should keep secret, in accordance with any obligation, either legal or contractual, all confidential information received from the other party and make use of the confidential information received from a potential party only for the purpose of evaluating this party's offer or request for other purposes agreed upon by the parties;

(iv) Termination of negotiations.
May cease negotiations if, during the negotiations, either party determines that a satisfactory agreement cannot be reached;

(b) The potential acquiring party:
Relevant information.
Should provide the potential technology supplier in a timely manner with the available specific information concerning the technical conditions and official

economic and social development objectives as well as legislation of the acquiring country relevant to the particular transfer and use of the technology under negotiation as far as such information is needed for the supplying party's responsiveness under this chapter;

(c) The potential supplying party:
Relevant information.

(i) Should disclose, in a timely manner, to the potential technology acquiring party any reason actually known to him, on account of which the technology to be supplied, when used in accordance with the terms and conditions of the proposed agreement, would not meet particular health, safety and environmental requirements in the technology acquiring country, already known to him as being relevant in the specific case or which have been specifically drawn to his attention, as well as any serious health, safety and environmental risks known by the supplier associated with the use of the technology and of products to be produced by it;

(ii) Should disclose to the potential technology acquiring party, to the actual extent known to him, any limitation, including any pending official procedures or litigation which adversely concerns, in a direct manner, the existence or validity of the rights to be transferred, on his entitlement to grant the rights or render the assistance and services specified in the proposed agreement;

Provision of accessories, spare parts and components.

(iii) Should to the extent feasible, take into account the request of the acquiring party to provide it for a period to be specified with accessories, spare parts and components produced by the supplying party and necessary for using the technology to be transferred, particularly where alternative sources are unavailable.

*Contractual Phase – Chapeau*

5.4. The technology transfer agreement should, in accordance with 5.1., provide for mutually acceptable contractual obligations, including those relating to payments and, where appropriate, *inter alia*, the following:

(i) Access to improvements.
Access for a specified period or for the lifetime of the agreement to improvements to the technology transferred under the agreement;

(ii) Confidentiality.

(iii) Dispute settlement and applicable law.

(iv) Description of the technology.
The technology supplier's guarantee that the technology meets the description contained in the technology transfer agreement;

(v) Suitability for use.
The technology supplier's guarantee that the technology, if used in accordance with the supplier's specific instructions given pursuant to the agreement, is suitable for manufacturing of goods or production of services as agreed upon by the parties and stipulated in the agreement;

(vi) Rights to the technology transferred.
The technology supplier's representation that on the date of the signing of the agreement, it is, to the best of its knowledge, not aware of third parties' valid patent rights or similar protection for inventions which would be infringed by the use of the technology when used as specified in the agreement;

(vii) Quality levels and goodwill.
The technology recipient's commitment to observe quality levels agreed upon in cases where the agreement includes the use of the supplier's trade marks, trade names or similar identification of goodwill, and both parties' commitment to avoid taking actions primarily or deliberately intended to injure the other's goodwill or reputation;

(viii) Performance guarantees.
Specification to technical performance parameters which the supplying party has agreed to guarantee, including specification of requirements for the achievement of such parameters, details of the manner of determining whether the performance has been met and the consequences of failure to meet that performance;

(ix) Transmission of documentation.
The supplying party's commitment that relevant technical documentation and other data required from him for a particular purpose defined in terms directly specified in the agreement will be transferred in a timely manner and as correctly and completely for such purpose as agreed upon;

(x) Training of personnel and provision of accessories, spare parts and components.
Where negotiations under paragraphs 5.2(a)(i) and 5.3(c)(iii) have taken place, suitable provisions for training of personnel and supply of accessories, spare parts and components would be made, consistent with the results of the negotiations;

(xi) Liability.
Disposition concerning liability for the non-fulfilment by either party of its responsibilities under the technology transfer agreement including questions of loss, damage or injury.

## Chapter 6: Special Treatment for Developing Countries

6.1. Taking into consideration the needs and problems of developing countries, particularly of the least developed countries, governments of developed countries, directly or through appropriate international organizations, in order to facilitate and encourage the initiation and strengthening of the scientific and technological capabilities of developing countries so as to assist and co-operate with them in their efforts to fulfil their economic and social objectives, should take adequate specific measures, *inter alia*, to:

(i) facilitate access by developing countries to available information regarding the availabilities, description, location and, as far as possible, approximate cost of technologies which might help those countries to attain their economic and social development objectives;

(ii) give developing countries the freest and fullest possible access to technologies whose transfer is not subject to private decisions;[13]

(iii) facilitate access by developing countries, to the extent practicable, to technologies whose transfer is subject to private decisions;[13]
(iv) assist and co-operate with developing countries in the assessment and adaptation of existing technologies and in the development of national technologies by facilitating access, as far as possible, to available scientific and industrial research data;
(ix) co-operate in measures leading to greater utilization of the managerial, engineering, design and technical experience of the personnel and the institutions of developing countries in specific economic and other development projects undertaken at the bilateral and multilateral levels;

6.3. Governments of developed countries should take measures in accordance with national policies, laws and regulations to encourage and to endeavour to give incentive to enterprises and institutions in their countries, either individually or in collaboration with enterprises and institutions in developing countries, particularly those in the least developed countries, to make special efforts, *inter alia*, to:

(i) assist in the development of technological capabilities of the enterprises in developing countries, including special training as required by the recipients;
(ii) undertake the development of technology appropriate to the needs of developing countries;
(iii) undertake R and D activity in developing countries of interest to such countries, as well as to improve co-operation between enterprises and scientific and technological institutions of developed and developing countries;
(iv) assist in projects by enterprises and institutions in developing countries for the development and adaptation of new and existing technologies suitable to the particular needs and conditions of developing countries . . .

## Chapter 8: International Institutional Machinery

*8.2. Functions of the International Institutional Machinery*

8.2.2. In the performance of its functions, the International Institutional Machinery may not act like a tribunal or otherwise pass judgement on the activities or conduct of individual Governments or of individual parties in connection with a specific transfer of technology transaction. The International Institutional Machinery should avoid becoming involved when parties in a specific transfer of technology transaction are in dispute.

8.2.3. The International Institutional Machinery shall establish such procedures as may be necessary to deal with issues related to confidentiality.

### Notes (as they appear in the negotiated text)

13. The term 'private decision' in the particular context of this chapter should be officially interpreted in the light of the legal order of the respective country.

# 125. Additional initiatives

## i. An Interfaith Declaration: A Code of Ethics on International Business for Christians, Muslims and Jews, 1993

**Commentary**: A series of Interfaith consultations commenced in 1988 between theologians, academics, businesspersons and government officials to identify ethical business principles common to Christianity, Islam and Judaism. The process of formulating guidelines occupied five years and drew upon best commercial practice and the shared moral, ethical and spiritual values of the Abrahamic tradition. The Declaration (available through www.iit.edu/departments/csep/codes/coe/cmj_codes.html) is constructed around four key concepts: justice (fairness), mutual respect (love and consideration), stewardship (trusteeship) and honesty (truthfulness). It also recognises distinctions between the morality of different economic systems in which business activity occurs, the policies and strategies of particular organisations, relationships between shareholders and directors and finally, individual employee behaviour. Several ethical issues affect all commercial activities whereas others are unique to specific sectors. The primacy of national law is also acknowledged. The Declaration is expected to be endorsed by management, incorporated into company statements or codes of conduct and promoted during training. See further, Webley S. (1999), 'Values inherent in the Interfaith Declaration of International Business Ethics', in Georges Enderie (ed.), *International Business Ethics: Challenges and Approaches*, Notre Dame, IN: University of Notre Dame Press, pp. 356–75.

## ii. Taskforce on the Churches and Corporate Responsibility: Principles for Global Corporate Responsibility, 1998

**Commentary**: The Taskforce on the Churches and Corporate Responsibility (Canada), the Ecumenical Council for Corporate Responsibility (UK) and the Interfaith Centre on Corporate Responsibility (USA; www.iccr.org) first drafted ethical business standards in 1995. The Principles (www.web.net/%7Etccr/benchmarks/index.html) recognise stakeholders as the source of all economic activity. They also locate the business community within the context of local communities, indigenous communities, national communities and the wider community (including ecosystems). All employees, women, minority groups, the disabled, children, suppliers, shareholders, partners and consumers are to be treated in accordance with high ethical standards and financial integrity. Although the Principles do not contemplate a follow-up process, the Taskforce has since formulated benchmarks to measure business performance against a firm's own stated expectations.

# PART XIII

# Reporting and Accounting Initiatives

# 126. Reporting and Accounting Initiatives

**Commentary**: Beginning in 2005, EC Directive 2003/51/EC will require large and medium-sized enterprises to report on environmental and employee issues where such information is 'necessary for an understanding of the company's development, performance or position'. This part presents a brief overview of contemporary PVIs aiming to enhance corporate reporting on the 'triple bottom line' of economic, social and environmental performance. Since many of these initiatives institute management systems, they are not strictly classified as codes of conduct, principles or guidelines reflective of corporate policy: see, for example, UNEP/ICC/International Federation of Consulting Engineers (FIDIC), Environmental Management System Training Resource Kit. For environmental accounting procedures at the enterprise level, see the UN Intergovernmental Working Group of Experts on International Standards of Accounting and Reporting, Guide on Environmental Reporting, 1991 and its Position Paper on Accounting and Financial Reporting for Environmental Costs and Liabilities, 1998. See also, UNCTAD (2003), 'Disclosure of the Impact of Corporations on Society: Current Trends and Issues', UN Doc TD/B/COM.2/ISAR/20.

## i. UNEP Global Reporting Initiative (GRI): GRI Sustainability Reporting Guidelines, 2002

**Commentary**: The GRI is a permanent, international body with a multi-stakeholder governance structure involving companies, NGOs, international organisations, UN Agencies, consultants, accountancy organisations, business associations, universities and other stakeholders. First formulated in 2000, the GRI Guidelines (www.globalreporting.org) adapted the financial accounting tradition to facilitate reporting on economic, environmental and social performance. The 11 principles are designed to ensure that reports contain balanced and reasonable accounts concerning an organisation's long-term performance, identify contributions to sustainable development, facilitate comparisons over time and across organisations and credibly address stakeholder concerns. The Principles are grouped into four clusters: the reporting framework (transparency, inclusiveness, auditability), the reporting content (completeness, relevance, sustainability), measures ensuring quality and reliability (accuracy, neutrality, comparability) and reporting access (clarity and timeliness). Adhering organisations discuss the application or non-application of these principles in their reports and collectively 'define a compact' or common understanding between reporting organisations and report users. See further, the advisory assurance strategy paper produced by the GRI's Verification Working Group. See also, WBCSD, 'Sustainable Development Reporting Initiative' (www.wbcsd.org) which is partnered with the GRI.

The WBCSD Initiative intends to assist companies compile their sustainable development reports in a credible, transparent and accountable manner and to improve communication with the financial community. It offers 15 different methodologies and a comparative database.

## ii. Social Accountability International: Social Accountability 8000 (SA8000), 1998

**Commentary**: Social Accountability (www.sa-intl.org, formerly the Council on Economic Priorities Accreditation Agency, CEPAA) is a consumer organisation established during 1997. SA8000 became operational in 1998 and draws upon ILO Conventions and human rights standards with respect to child and forced labour, workplace health and safety, compensation, working hours, discrimination, employee discipline, freedom of association and collective bargaining. It is also derived from business strategies and quality assurance systems such as ISO 9000. SAI accredits firms to act as external auditors who certify compliance by manufacturers and issue publicly accessible reports. Companies additionally participating in the two-level Corporate Involvement Program (CIP) also release SAI-verified annual progress reports describing how decent working conditions are ensured by management systems and throughout the supply chain. SA8000 contemplates participation by and benefits accruing to workers and trade unions, companies, socially responsible investors, NGOs and governments. In addition to its accreditation and auditing programmes, SAI initiatives for advancing social accountability include research and development, training, technical assistance, outreach and alliance-building.

## iii. The Institute of Social and Ethical Accountability (AccountAbility): The AccountAbility 1000 (AA1000) Standard, 1999

**Commentary**: Established in 1995, AccountAbility is an international NGO dedicated to promoting accountable sustainable development with members and partners drawn from business, civil society and governments: see www.accountability.org.uk. AA1000 seeks to improve commercial accountability and operational performance by enhancing the quality of social and ethical accounting, auditing and reporting. It either underpins existing accountability standards or acts as a stand-alone instrument. AA1000 is process oriented: it contemplates a firm self-defining its governing values, ethical principles and social performance targets as well as establishing feedback loops directed at self-learning and continuous improvement. Implementation follows five stages: initial commitment and planning; accounting and collecting information; stakeholder reporting and external auditing; embedding structures and systems; and, finally, stakeholder engagement.

### iv. International Organization of Standardization (ISO): Proposed framework for an ISO standard on Corporate Social Responsibility, 2001

**Commentary**: Established in 1947, ISO is an NGO network of national standards institutes from 148 countries with a secretariat located in Geneva (www.iso.org). ISO 26000 on Guidelines for Social Responsibility is due for publication in 2008. Compliance with the proposed framework could reduce accidents, attract investment, satisfy consumer concerns, lower insurance premiums and improve relationships with business partners, suppliers, employees, local communities, governments and NGOs. The new framework would join existing ISO management systems such as the ISO 14000 and 9000 series with respect to environmental reporting. For initial comments, see Hamann R., Agbazue T., Kapelus, P. and Hein, A. (2005), 'Universalizing corporate social responsibility? South African challenges to the International Organization for Standardization's new social responsibility standard', *Business and Society Review*, **110** (1), 1–19.

# Index